C000019399

ISBN 978-0-260-53068-4
PIBN 10954344

REPORTS

OF

CASES ARGUED AND DETERMINED

IN THE

SUPREME COURT

OF THE

STATE OF IDAHO

By I. W. HART

(Ex-officio Reporter)

O

VOLUME 26

SAN FRANCISCO

BANCROFT-WHITNEY COMPANY

1915

SAN FRANCISCO
THE FILMER BROTHERS ELECTROTYPE COMPANY
TYPOGRAPHERS AND STEREOTYPERS

JUSTICES OF THE SUPREME COURT.

JAMES F. AILSHIE, Chief Justice[1].......Re-elected 1908

ISAAC N. SULLIVAN, Justice[2]...........Re-elected 1910

GEORGE H. STEWART, Justice[3].........Re-elected 1912

WARREN TRUITT, Justice[4].....Appointed Sept. 14, 1914

ALFRED BUDGE, Justice[5].......Appointed Nov. 28, 1914

WILLIAM M. MORGAN, Justice.............Elected 1914

District Judges.

W. W. WOODS, 1st District..............Re-elected 1914

E. C. STEELE, 2d District................Re-elected 1914

CARL A. DAVIS, 3d District.............Re-elected 1914

C. P. McCARTHY, 3d District...............Elected 1914

W. A. BABCOCK, 4th District..............Elected 1914

J. R. BOTHWELL, 4th District.............Elected 1914

J. J. GUHEEN,[6] 5th District......Appointed Nov. 28, 1914

F. J. COWEN, 6th District.................Elected 1914

ED. L. BRYAN, 7th District..............Re-elected 1914

R. N. DUNN, 8th District.................Re-elected 1914

J. M. FLYNN, 8th District.................Re-elected 1914

J. G. GWINN, 9th District................Re-elected 1914

OFFICERS OF THE COURT.

Clerk.

I. W. HART...................Appointed April 15, 1914

Attorney General.

J. H. PETERSON........................Re-elected 1914

---

1 Resigned July 20, 1914.

2 Became Chief Justice by resignation of Ailshie, C. J., July 20, 1914.

3 Died September 25, 1914.

4 To fill vacancy created by resignation of Ailshie, C. J.

5 To fill vacancy created by death of Justice Stewart.

6 To fill vacancy created by resignation of Judge Alfred Budge.

ATTORNEYS ADMITTED FROM MAY 12, 1914, TO MARCH 1, 1915.

ADAIR, RALPH W.............................June 13, 1914
ALBAUGH, RALPH L.........................Jan. 11, 1915
ANDERSON, REUBEN S.......................Feb. 25, 1915
ABNEY, J. WADE...........................Dec. 8, 1914

BENNETT, BASH L..........................Jan. 18, 1915
BOTTUM, FRANK ....Dec. 8, 1914

COUNTRYMAN, THOMAS F.....................Dec. 7, 1914
CROCKETT, GEORGE R.......................Jan. 18, 1915

DELONG, CARL L. ....Nov. 16, 1914

ECKHARDT, RALPH W........................Feb. 1, 1915

FELTHAM, KATE E. N.......................Sept. 22, 1914
FITZGERALD, JOHN L.......................Oct. 6, 1914

GRIFFIN, SAMUEL S........................Sept. 22, 1914
GRISWOLD, WILLARD R......................Jan. 18, 1915
GWINN, JAMES G...........................Nov. 9, 1914

HARVEY, JOS. E...........................Oct. 21, 1914
HASS, WM. C..............................Sept. 22, 1914
HEIGHTON, CHARLES H......................Oct. 6, 1914
HELMAN, JOHN H...........................Jan. 19, 1915
HILL, CLARENCE S.........................Sept. 23, 1914

JONES, JAMES L..........................Jan. 18, 1915
JONES, ROY WILLIAM......................May 25, 1914

LINGENFELTER, C. HOMER...................Jan. 19, 1915

MCFARLANE, GEORGE A......................Oct. 21, 1914
MORRISON, C. W..........................Jan. 16, 1915

NORTH, CHARLES A.........................June 16, 1914

REES, JOHN E............................Feb. 24, 1915
RYLAND, L. G............................June 29, 1914

SMITH, SIDNEY H.........................Oct. 5, 1914
STEPHAN, FRANK L........................Sept. 21, 1914
STEPHENS, EWING W.......................Oct. 6, 1914

TALBOTT, GEO. W.........................Jan. 11, 1915
THOMPSON, H. B..........................Sept. 21, 1914

WRIGHT, EDGAR M.........................Nov. 16, 1914

TABLE OF CASES REPORTED—VOL. 26.

	Page
American Falls, Village of, v. West	301
American Surety Company, State ex rel. Mills v.	652
Anderson, Coolin v.	47
Anixdale, Boise Butcher Co. v.	483
Application of Kessler	764
Aven v. Caldwell Commercial Bank	566
Aven, Wilkerson v.	559
Baldwin v. McFarland	85
Bank & Trust Company, Campbell v.	201
Bank of Orofino v. Wellman	425
Beaver River Power Company v. Blomquist	222
Bergstresser, Smith v.	322
Blaine County, School District No. 15 v.	285
Blomquist, Beaver River Power Company v.	222
Blomquist, Idaho Power & Light Company v.	222
Blucher v. Shaw	497
Board of County Commissioners of Nez Perce County, Davies v.	450
Bogris, State v.	587
Bohney, Richardson v.	85
Boise Association of Credit Men v. Ellis	438
Boise Butcher Co. v. Anixdale	483
Boise City, Boise City Development Company v.	347
Boise Development Company v. Boise City	347
Boise King Placers Company, Trask v.	290
Brown, Strong v.	1
Budge v. Gifford	521
Burley State Bank, Cauthorn v.	532
Caldwell Commercial Bank, Aven v.	566
Callahan v. Price	745
Cameron Lumber Co. v. Stack-Gibbs Lumber Co.	626
Cameron Lumber Co., Stack-Gibbs Lumber Co. v.	649
Campbell v. Bank & Trust Company	201
Cannon, State v.	182
Capital Lumber Co. v. Saunders	408
Cauthorn v. Burley State Bank	532
Cauthorn v. Lounsbury	550
Chandler v. Probate Court for Kootenai County	173
Cheney v. Minidoka County	471
Childs v. Neitzel	116, 133

                                                                    Page
City of Kellogg v. McRae..................................... 73
City of Lewiston, Thiessen v................................. 505
City of Payette, Coughanour v............................... 280
City of Payette, Pease v..................................... 793
Clearwater County, Northern Pacific Railway Co. v............ 455
Coolin v. Anderson.. 47
Coon v. Sommercamp... 776
Coughanour v. City of Payette............................... 280
County of Clearwater, Northern Pacific Railway Co. v.......... 455
Crescent Mining & Milling Company, Dickens-West Mining Co. v. 153

Davies v. Board of County Commissioners of Nez Perce County. 450
Dickens-West Mining Co. v. Crescent Mining & Milling Co..... 153
Drainage District No. 1 of Canyon County, In re.............. 311
Driskill, State v... 738

Elder v. Idaho-Washington Northern Railroad................. 209
Ellis, Boise Association of Credit Men v...................... 438
Exchange State Bank v. Taber............................... 723

Fales v. Weeter Lumber Company............................ 367
Federal Mining & Smelting Co. v. Public Utilities Commission.. 391
Fidelity & Deposit Co. of Maryland, State v.................. 332
Fife v. Village of Glenns Ferry.............................. 763
First National Bank of Ashton, Soule v....................... 66
First National Bank of Moscow v. Regents of the University of
    Idaho 15
Fix v. Gray... 19
Flaig, Stehle v. 271
Forch, State ex rel. Canyon County v........................ 755
Fox v. Spokane International Railway Company................ 60
Frazier v. Hastings... 623
Frost, Swanstrom v. 79

Gagnon v. St. Maries Light & Power Co...................... 87
Gifford, Budge v. 521
Glenns Ferry, Village of, Fife v............................. 763
Graham, Zilka v. 163
Grant, State v. 189
Gray, Fix v. 19
Gray, Montgomery v. 583, 585

Hare v. Young.......................................682, 691
Harrigfeld, McReynolds v. 26
Hartford Fire Ins. Co., Southern Idaho Conference Assn. of
    Seventh Day Adventists v. 712

Page

Hastings, Frazier v..................................... 623
Hodge, McConnon & Co. v.............................. 376
Holmes, Ward v....................................... 602
Hopkins, State v. 741

Idaho Hardware & Plumbing Co. v. Saunders.............. 424
Idaho Irrigation Company v. Pew...................... 272
Idaho Power & Light Company v. Blomquist.............. 222
Idaho Railway, Light & Power Company, Jennings v....... 703
Idaho-Washington Northern Railroad, Elder v. 209
In re Drainage District No. 1 of Canyon County........... 311

Janks, State v. 567
Jennings v. Idaho Railway, Light & Power Company......... 703
Johnson, State v. 203, 609

Kellogg, City of v. McRae............................. 73
Kennedy v. Tuttle................................... 495
Kessler, Application of............................... 764
Kissler v. Moss..................................... 516

Lewiston, City of, Thiessen v......................... 505
Lounsbury, Cauthorn v............................... 550
Lytle, Taylor v. 97

MacWilliams, Pettingill v............................. 344
Matter of Application of Kessler...................... 764
McCombs, Peavy v.................................... 143
McConnon & Co. v. Hodge............................. 376
McFarland, Baldwin v. 85
McRae, City of Kellogg v. 73
McReynolds v. Harrigfeld............................. 26
Merrill, Wright v.................................... 8
Miller v. Wallace.................................... 373
Minidoka County, Cheney v. 471
Montgomery v. Gray.............................583, 585
Moss, Kissler v. 516

Neitzel, Childs v. 116, 133
Northern Pacific Railway Company v. County of Clearwater.... 455

Oneida Irrigation District, Page v. 108

Page v. Oneida Irrigation District.................... 108
Payette, City of, Coughanour v....................... 280
Payette, City of, Pease v............................ 793

                                                                    Page
Pease v. City of Payette.................................... 793
Peavy v. McCombs.. 143
Pettingill v. MacWilliams.................................. 344
Pew, Idaho Irrigation Company v. 272
Pioneer Nurseries Co., State v. 332
Portneuf-Marsh Valley Irrigation Company, Woodland v....... 789
Price, Callahan v. 745
Probate Court for Kootenai County, Chandler v. 173
Public Utilities Commission, Federal Mining & Smelting Co. v... 391

Rasmussen v. Silk.. 341
Rawson-Works Lumber Co. v. Richardson...................37, 45
Regents of the University of Idaho, First National Bank of
    Moscow v. 15
Rice v. Rock.. 552
Richardson v. Bohney...................................... 35
Richardson, Rawson-Works Lumber Co. v....................37, 45
Rischar v. Shields.. 616
Rock, Rice v.. 552

Saunders, Capital Lumber Co. v............................. 408
Saunders, Idaho Hardware & Plumbing Co. v. 424
St. Maries Light & Power Co., Gagnon v..................... 87
School District No. 15 v. Blaine County.................... 285
Shaw, Blucher v... 497
Shields, Rischar v.. 616
Silk, Rasmussen v... 341
Smith v. Bergstresser..................................... 322
Sommercamp, Coon v.. 776
Soule v. First National Bank of Ashton.................... 66
Southern Idaho Conference Association of Seventh Day Adventists
    v. Hartford Fire Insurance Co......................... 712
Spokane International Railway Co., Fox v................... 60
Stack-Gibbs Lumber Co., Cameron Lumber Co. v.............. 626
Stack-Gibbs Lumber Co. v. Cameron Lumber Co............... 649
Stafford, State v... 381
State ex rel. Mills v. American Surety Company............ 652
State v. Bogris 587
State v. Cannon 182
State v. Driskill 738
State v. Fidelity & Deposit Co. of Maryland............... 332
State ex rel. Canyon County v. Forch...................... 755
State v. Grant.. 189
State v. Hopkins.. 741
State v. Janks......... 567
State v. Johnson.....................................203, 609
State v. Pioneer Nurseries Co............................. 332

Page

State v. Stafford.......... 381
Stehle v. Flaig... 271
Strong v. Brown... 1
Strong, Wycoff v... 502
Swanstrom v. Frost.. 79

Taber, Exchange State Bank v................................ 723
Taylor v. Lytle....................... '...................... 97
Thiessen v. City of Lewiston................................ 505
Trask v. Boise King Placers Company.......... 290
Tuttle, Kennedy v... 495

Village of American Falls v. West...................... 301
Village of Glenns Ferry, Fife v.............................. 763

Wallace, Miller v.. 373
Ward v. Holmes... 602
Washington County Land & Development Co. v. Weiser National
    Bank.......... 717
Weeter Lumber Company, Fales v............................ 367
Weiser National Bank, Washington County Land & Development
    Co. v. 717
Wellman, Bank of Orofino v................................. 425
West, Village of American Falls v........................... 301
Wilkerson v. Aven....... 559
Woodland v. Portneuf-Marsh Valley Irrigation Company....... 789
Wright v. Merrill... 8
Wycoff v. Strong... 502

Young, Hare v..682, 691

Zilka v. Graham.. 163

TABLE OF CASES CITED—VOL. 26.

                                                                    Page
A. B. Moss & Bro. v. Ramey, 14 Ida. 598........................ 753
A. B. Moss & Bro. v. Ramey, 25 Ida. 1...................753, 755
Achenbach v. Kincaid, 25 Ida. 768.......................768, 770
Ackerson v. People, 124 Ill. 563.............................. 600
Adams v. Bunker Hill etc. Min. Co., 12 Ida. 637....·.......... 84
Aerkfetz v. Humphreys, 145 U. S. 418......................... 219
Aldrich v. People, 101 Ill. 16................................ 573
Alexander v. State, 49 Tex. Cr. 93............................ 198
Amory v. Amory, 95 U. S. 186.............................. 667
Anderson v. Great Northern Ry. Co., 15 Ida. 513.............. 220
Andrews v. King County, 1 Wash. 46.......................... 463
Argenti v. City of San Francisco, 16 Cal. 277................. 632
Askew v. United States, 2 Okl. Cr. 155....................... 579
Atchison etc. R. Co. v. Sullivan, 173 Fed. 456................ 467
Atchison T. & S. F. Ry. Co. v. State, 40 L. R. A., N. S., 1, note.... 320
Atkinson v. Newcastle etc. Waterworks Co., 2 Ex. D. 441....... 672
Atlantic Coast Line R. Co. v. Miller, 53 Fla. 246.............. 221
Atlantic Coast Line Ry. Co. v. North Carolina Corp. Comm., 206
    U. S. 1... 255
Aurora v. United States, 7 Cranch (U. S.), 382................ 253

Baker v. First Nat. Bank, 25 Ida. 651........................ 586
Baker v. Haines, 6 Whart. (Pa.) 284......................... 596
Baldwin v. McFarland, 26 Ida. 85............................ 430
Baltimore Shipbuilding & Dry Dock Co. v. Baltimore, 195 U. S.
    375.................... 478
Bane v. Gwinn, 7 Ida. 439................................595, 596
Bank of Augusta v. Earle, 13 Pet. (U. S.) 519................ 710
Bannock County v. C. Bunting & Co., 4 Ida. 156...........152, 153
Barbour v. Paige Hotel Co., 2 App. Cas. (D. C.) 174........... 710
Barney v. Keokuk, 94 U. S. 324.............................. 754
Bartlett v. City of Bangor, 67 Me. 460....................... 511
Barton v. Schmershall, 21 Ida. 562..:....................... 254
Beech, In re Estate of, 63 Cal. 458........................... 13
Beinhorn v. Griswold, 27 Mont. 79............................ 6
Belding Land Co. v. City of Belding, 128 Mich. 79............. 150
Bellinger v. White, 5 Neb. 399............................... 479
Bergen v. Johnson, 21 Ida. 619.............................. 414
Bernhard v. Idaho Bank & Trust Co., 21 Ida. 598.............. 372
Bernhard v. Reeves, 6 Wash. 424............................. 737
Bird v. United States, 187 U. S. 118........................ 198

Page

Blackstone Mfg. Co. v. Blackstone, 13 Gray (Mass.), 488........ 710
Blair v. Territory, 15 Okl. 550................................. 580
Blalack v. Texas Traction Co. (Tex. Civ. App.), 149 S. W. 1086.. 93
Block v. Schwartz, 27 Utah, 387............................... 443
Blomquist v. Board of County Commrs., 25 Ida. 293............ 678
Board v. Bladen, 113 N. C. 379................................ 671
Board of Education v. Tafoya, 6 N. M. 292..................... 150
Board of Trustees v. City of Lexington, 112 Ky. 171........... 770
Boise City v. Hon, 14 Ida. 272................................ 511
Bonham Nat. Bank v. Grimes Pass Placer Min. Co., 18 Ida. 629.. 299
Bookman v. Seaboard Air Line Ry. Co., 152 Fed. 686........... 221
Booth v. Hoskins, 75 Cal. 271................................. 372
Bothwell v. Bingham County, 24 Ida. 125...................... 478
Bowman v. Bowman, 35 Or. 279................................ 33
Boyer v. Northern Pac. Ry. Co., 8 Ida. 74.................... 709
Brady v. Mattern, 125 Iowa, 158............................... 770
Brannock v. Elmore, 114 Mo. 55............................... 92
Brenham v. German-American Bank, 144 U. S. 173.............. 115
Brentnall v. Marshall, 10 Kan. App. 488...................... 621
Brigham v. Zaiss, 48 App. Div. 144........................... 401
Bright v. Barnett & Record Co., 88 Wis. 299.................. 93
Bright v. Barnett & Record Co., 26 L. R. A. 524, note.......... 94
Brown v. Bryan, 6 Ida. 1...................................... 414
Brown v. Nelson & Co., 43 Fed. 614........................... 668
Brunswick & W. R. Co. v. Wiggins, 113 Ga. 842................ 731
Buchanan v. Curtis, 25 Wash. 99.............................. 513
Burkhart v. Reed, 2 Ida. 503.................................. 150
Burlington etc. Ry. Co. v. Dunn, 122 U. S. 513............... 668
Bush v. Grant, 22 Ky. Law Rep. 1766.......................... 93

Cagwin v. Town of Hancock, 84 N. Y. 532·..................... 115
Calhoun County Bank v. Cain, 152 Fed. 983................... 71
Calkins v. Blackwell Lumber Co., 23 Ida. 128................. 84
Callan v. Pugh, 54 App. Div. 545.............................. 93
Cameron Lumber Co. v. Stack-Gibbs Lumber Co., 26 Ida. 626.... 651
Campbell v. Jones, 60 Wash. 265............................... 93
Campbell v. Kansas City etc. R. Co., 55 Kan. 536.............. 220
Carlton v. People, 150 Ill. 181................................ 600
Carrier v. Missouri Pac. Ry. Co., 175 Mo. 470................. 221
Carscallen v. Coeur d'Alene, etc. Transp. Co., 15 Ida. 444......... 84
Carson v. City of Genesee, 9 Ida. 244......................78, 364
Carter v. City of Portland, 4 Or. 339......................... 511
Cauthorn v. Burley State Bank, 26 Ida. 532................551, 552
Chandler v. Lee, 1 Ida. 349 761
Chandler v. State, 60 Tex. Cr. 329............................ 198

Page

Chemung Mining Co. v. Henley, 9 Ida. 786.................... 216
Chesapeake etc. Ry. Co. v. McCabe, 213 U. S. 207............. 668
Chicago etc. Co. v. Brazzell, 33 Okl. 122.................... 668
Chicago etc. R. Co. v. Scanlan, 170 Ill. 106.................. 216
Childs v. Neitzel, 26 Ida. 116.............................275, 278
Cincinnati etc. Ry. Co. v. Long, 112 Ind. 166................. 221
City of Allegheny v. People's Natural Gas Co., 172 Pa. 632...... 269
City of Atlanta v. Gate City Gas Light Co., 71 Ga. 106........ 269
City of Bellevue v. Daly, 14 Ida. 545.......................... 6
City of Genesee v. Latah County, 4 Ida. 141.................. 77
City of Racine v. Racine Gas Light Co., 6 W. R. C. R. 228...... 406
City Ry. Co. v. Citizens' St. R. R. Co., 166 U. S. 557........... 269
Clark v. St. Louis etc. R. Co., 234 Mo. 396.................... 92
Cleary v. Kincaid, 23 Ida. 789............................... 607
Clepper v. State, 4 Tex. 242 388
Clowers v. Wabash etc. Ry. Co., 21 Mo. App. 213.............. 299
Cohn v. Kingsley, 5 Ida. 416....................319, 320, 321, 386
Cole v. Louisiana Gas Co., 121 La. 771........................ 93
Collins v. Bryan, 40 Tex. Civ. App. 88....................... 433
Colorado Paving Co. v. Murphy, 78 Fed. 28.................... 671
Commonwealth v. Barney, 115 Ky. 475........................ 770
Commonwealth v. International Harvester Co., 131 Ky. 768...... 771
Consolidated Wagon & Mach. Co. v. Kent, 23 Ida. 690......... 160
Copp v. Maine Cent. R. Co., 100 Me. 568..................... 221
Cottam v. Oregon City, 98 Fed. 570.......................... 671
Coughanour v. City of Payette, 26 Ida. 280................... 797
Coughtry v. Globe Woolen Co., 56 N. Y. 124.................. 92
Coulter v. Stafford, 56 Fed. 564............................. 557
County of Dallas v. MacKenzie, 94 U. S. 660................. 115
Courtright v. Deeds, 37 Iowa, 503........................... 702
Cowardin v. Universal Life Ins. Co., 32 Gratt. (Va.) 445....710, 711
Crawford v. Winton, 102 Mich. 83.......................... 722
Crehore v. Ohio etc. Ry. Co., 131 U. S. 240.................. 668
Cruse v. State (Tex. Cr.), 77 S. W. 818...................... 198
Culbertson v. Blanchard, 79 Tex. 486....................... 104
Culver v. Kehl, 21 Ida. 595................................. 716
Curtis v. Whitney, 13 Wall. (U. S.) 68....................... 557

Daly v. Bernstein, 6 N. M. 380.............................. 34
Damon v. Wuldteufel, 99 Cal. 234........................... 737
Davis v. Winslow, 51 Me. 264............................... 644
Day v. Woodworth, 13 How. (U. S.) 363..................... 731
Debnam v. Southern Bell Tel. Co., 126 N. C. 831............. 668
Dewey v. City of Des Moines, 101 Iowa, 416................. 150
Diamond Bank v. Van Meter, 18 Ida. 243.................... 375
Dickson v. Kittitas County, 42 Wash. 429................... 469

Page

Divide Canal & Reservoir Co. v. Tenny (Colo.), 139 Pac. 1110.... 737
Doran v. Thomsen, 79 N. J. L. 99................................. 216
Drew v. Farnsworth, 186 Mass. 365............................... 299
Dunn v. Cavanaugh, 185 Fed. 451.................................. 93
Duryea v. Guthrie, 117 Wis. 399................................. 419

Eaton v. City of Weiser, 12 Ida. 544.........................78, 97
Edminson v. City of Abilene, 7 Kan. App. 305.................... 115
Ellis' Estate, In re, 55 Minn. 401.............................. 320
Erickson v. St. Paul etc. R. R. Co., 41 Minn. 500............... 221
Etheridge v. Sperry, 139 U. S. 266.............................. 547
Evans v. Blankenship, 4 Ariz. 307............................... 511
Everett v. Los Angeles etc. Ry. Co., 115 Cal. 105.............. 221

Farmers' Loan & Trust Co. v. City of Galesburg, 133 U. S. 156.... 115
Feeney v. Chester, 7 Ida. 324................................... 32
Fegtly v. Village Blacksmith Min. Co., 18 Ida. 536............. 301
Feil v. City of Coeur d'Alene, 23 Ida. 32..............360, 361, 366
Field v. Clark, 143 U. S. 649.................................. 253
Finney v. American Bonding Co., 13 Ida. 534.................... 670
First Nat. Bank Falls v. Shaw, 24 Ida. 134.................... 787
First Nat. Bank v. Holmes, 246 Ill. 362....................... 469
First Nat Bank v. Regents, 19 Ida. 440........................ 18
Fitch v. Applegate, 24 Wash. 25............................... 447
Flanagan v. People, 214 Ill. 170.............................. 600
Flint v. Comly, 95 Me. 251.................................... 722
Florence Oil & Ref. Co. v. Farrar, 109 Fed. 254.............. 731
Foore v. Simon Piano Co., 18 Ida. 167......................... 160
Francis v. Howard County, 50 Fed. 44.......................... 115

Gage v. Stewart, 127 Ill. 207................................. 556
Gale, In re, 14 Ida. 761...................................... 774
Gallus v. Elmer, 193 Mass. 106................................ 449
Garner v. Wright, 28 How. Pr. 92.............................. 106
Gerding v. Board of Commrs., 13 Ida. 444...................... 336
Gerrish v. Brown, 51 Me. 256.................................. 646
Gerst v. City of St. Louis, 185 Mo. 191....................... 171
Getts v. Jamesville Grocery Co., 163 Fed. 417................. 71
Golden v. Northern Pac. Ry. Co., 39 Mont. 435................. 668
Goldstein v. People, 82 N. Y. 231............................. 576
Goodpaster v. Voris, 8 Iowa, 334.............................. 731
Goodwin v. Garr, 8 Cal. 615................................... 702
Gorman v. Commissioners, 1 Ida. 655.....................671, 738
Gould v. Hammond, 10 Fed. Cas. No. 5636....................... 674
Grant v. First Nat. Bank, 97 U. S. 81......................... 545
Great Falls Water Works Co. v. Great Northern Ry. Co., 21 Mont.
    487.. 33

Page

Greathouse v. Heed, 1 Ida. 494............................ 761
Great Northern Ry. Co. v. St. Paul, 61 Minn. 1................. 511
Green v. Canaan, 29 Conn. 157............................. 513
Gregory v. Hartley, 113 U. S. 742......................... 667
Gresham v. Galveston County (Tex. Civ.), 36 S. W. 796......... 330
Guheen v. Curtis, 3 Ida. 443............................. 607

Hailey v. Huston, 25 Ida. 165............................. 336
Hale v. Henkle, 201 U. S. 43.............................. 404
Hall v. Weare, 92 U. S. 728............................... 731
Hanson v. Taylor, 23 Wis. 548............................ 513
Hare v. Young, 26 Ida. 682............................... 694
Harrington v. Harrington, 53 Vt. 649...................... 149
Hart v. Ogdensburg etc. R. Co., 69 Hun, 497................ 401
Hauser v. Hobart, 22 Ida. 749............................ 633
Heckman v. Espey, 12 Ida. 755 641
Heilig v. City Council of Puyallup, 7 Wash. 29.............. 150
Hendrick v. Maryland, 235 U. S. 610....................... 775
Henry Gold Min. Co. v. Henry, 25 Ida. 333................. 586
Herrick v. Sargent, 140 Iowa, 590........................ 479
Hickey v. City of Nampa, 22 Ida. 41.................363, 364, 366
High v. Bank of Commerce, 95 Cal. 386.................... 487
Hill v. Lowe, 6 Mackey (D. C.), 428....................... 492
Hirth-Krause Co. v. Cohen, 177 Ind. 1.................... 444
Hogan v. Chicago etc. R. Co., 59 Wis. 139................. 221
Hogue v. City of Albina, 20 Or. 182....................... 511
Holdane v. Cold Spring, 23 Barb. (N. Y.) 103.............. 513
Hollingsworth v. Thompson, 45 La. Ann. 222.............. 320
Holmes v. City of Mattoon, 111 Ill. 27 784
Hoppe v. City of Winona, 113 Minn. 252.................. 93
Horne v. Smith, 159 U. S. 40............................. 752
Howes v. Barmon, 11 Ida. 64..........................33, 34
Hufton v. Hufton, 25 Ida. 96............................. 586
Humbird Lumber Co. v. Thompson, 11 Ida. 614...........466, 468
Humphrey v. Spencer, 36 W. Va. 11....................... 435
Hurlbutt v. N. W. Spaulding Saw Co., 93 Cal. 55........... 106

Idaho Irr. Co. v. Dill, 25 Ida. 711......................273, 277
Illinois C. R. Co. v. Chicago, 176 U. S. 646............... 754
Illinois River R. Co. v. Zimmer, 20 Ill. 654................ 269
Indianapolis Water Co. v. American Strawboard Co., 57 Fed. 1000 306
Interstate Commerce Com. v. Baird, 194 U. S. 25........... 401
Interstate Commerce Com. v. Goodrich Transit Co., 224 U. S. 194. 253
Iowa R. R. Land Co. v. Fitchpatrick, 52 Iowa, 244.......... 479

Jenkins v. Waldron, 11 Johns. (N. Y.) 114................. 674
John P. Squire & Co. v. Tellier, 185 Mass. 18.............. 442

Page

Johnson v. Byler, 38 Tex. 606................................... 493
Johnson v. Hurst, 10 Ida. 308.................................. 755
Johnson v. Johnson, 14 Ida. 561...........................753, 755
Johnson v. Spear, 76 Mich. 139................................. 92
John Spry Lumber Co. v. Duggan, 182 Ill. 218................93, 94

Kane v. State, 81 N. J. L. 594................................. 775
Katalla Co. v. Johnson, 202 Fed. 353.......................... 93
Katz v. Herrick, 12 Ida. 1...............................151, 336
Katz v. Herrick, 12 Ida. 130.................................. 159
Keating v. Keating Min. Co., 18 Ida. 660...................... 160
Keith v. Maguire, 170 Mass. 210............................... 689
Kelly v. Leachman, 3 Ida. 392................................. 414
Kendall v. Stokes, 3 How. (U. S.) 87.......................... 674
Kentucky & Ind. Bridge Co. v. Louisville & N. R. Co., 34 Am. &
    Eng. R. R. Cas. (O. S.) 630............................... 257
Kessler v. Fritchman, 21 Ida. 30.........................336, 340
Kidd, Dater & Price Co. v. Musselman Grocer Co., 217 U. S. 461. 445
Kimmerle v. Far, 189 Fed. 295................................. 70
Kirby v. Bruns, 45 Mo. 234.................................... 434
Kleeb v. Bard, 12 Wash. 140................................... 732
Knapp v. Smith, 27 N. Y. 277.................................. 433
Kolander v. Dunn, 95 Minn. 422................................ 449

Lake Shore & Mich. S. R. R. Co. v. Ohio, 173 U. S. 285........ 248
Lamberson v. Jefferds, 116 Cal. 492........................... 782
Lancaster v. Collins, 115 U. S. 222........................... 731
Lane v. Pacific & I. N. Ry. Co., 8 Idaho, 230................. 65
Larson v. American Bridge Co., 40 Wash. 224................... 737
Lattig v. Scott, 17 Ida. 506.............................753, 755
Lee v. Gillen & Bonney, 90 Neb. 730........................... 449
Lee v. McLeod, 12 Nev. 280.................................... 32
Lemieux v. Young, 211 U. S. 489............................... 445
Lent v. Tillson, 72 Cal. 404.................................. 113
Levering v. Commonwealth, 132 Ky. 666....................197, 198
Lewis v. Wellard, 62 Wash. 590................................ 622
Lilly v. Menke, 143 Mo. 137................................... 215
Lincon & Kennebec Bank v. Richardson, 1 Greenl. (Me.) 79...... 269
Lorenzi v. Star Market Co., 19 Ida. 674....................... 308
Louisiana Nat. Life Assur. Soc. v. Segen, 28 Am. Bankr. Rep. 19. 539
Louisville etc. R. Co. v. Bosworth, 209 Fed. 380.............. 470
Louisville etc. R. Co. v. Cronbach, 12 Ind. App. 666.......... 221
Louisville Trust Co. v. Stone, 107 Fed. 305................... 465
Loving, Ex parte, 178 Mo. 194................................. 770
Lowe v. Board etc., 156 Ind. 163.............................. 771
Lowe v. Guthrie, 4 Okl. 287................................... 671

Page

Lewe v. Turner, 1 Ida. 107.................................... 723
Lynde v. McGregor, 13 Allen (Mass.), 182.................... 434

Maddox v. Summerlin, 92 Tex. 483....................431, 434
Male v. Leflang, 7 Ida. 348................................... 32
Maloney v. Winston Bros. Co., 18 Ida. 740.................... 84
Mannington v. Hocking Valley Ry. Co., 183 Fed. 133.......... 668
Mantle v. Dabney, 47 Wash. 394.............................. 216
Marchand v. Ronaghan, 9 Ida. 95............................. 696
Matthews v. Board of Corp. Commrs., 106 Fed. 7.............. 402
Maw v. Coast Lumber Co., 19 Ida. 396........................ 84
Mayor etc. of Baltimore v. Warren Mfg. Co., 59 Md. 96........ 306
Mayor of Nashville v. Ray, 19 Wall. (U. S.) 468............. 115
McBean v. City of Fresno, 112 Cal. 159...................... 361
McCallum v. Germantown Water Co., 54 Pa. 40................ 306
McClain v. Abshire, 72 Mo. App. 390......................... 437
McCormick v. West Duluth, 47 Minn. 272..................... 262
McDaniels v. J. J. Connelly Shoe Co., 30 Wash. 549.......... 446
McGhee v. Bell, 170 Mo. 121................................. 104
Means v. Dowd, 128 U. S. 273................................ 547
Melton v. State, 43 Ark. 367................................ 198
Mendilie v. Snell, 22 Ida. 663.............................. 330
Merrick v. Van Santvoord, 34 N. Y. 208...................... 710
Meservey v. Guillford, 14 Ida. 133.......................... 514
Miller v. Ouray E. L. & Power Co., 18 Colo. App. 131........ 671
Miller v. Wissert, 38 Okl. 808.............................. 104
Mills v. American Bonding Co., 13 Ida. 556.................. 670
Monroe v. Williamson, 81 Fed. 977 (984)..................... 668
Moore v. State, 4 Okl. Cr. 212.............................. 198
Morbeck v. Bradford-Kennedy Co., 19 Ida. 83.........666, 668, 670
Morgan v. Chicago etc. R. Co., 96 U. S. 716................. 512
Morrill v. Richey, 18 N. H. 295............................. 491
Moscow Hardware Co. v. Regents, 19 Ida. 420................. 18
Moss v. Cummings, 44 Mich. 359.......................671, 672
Munn v. Illinois, 94 U. S. 113.............................. 241
Murch Bros. Const. Co. v. Johnson, 203 Fed. 1............... 93
Murdock v. Clarke, 90 Cal. 427.............................. 737
Murphy v. Bartsch, 2 Ida. 636............................... 733
Murphy v. Chicago B. & Q. Ry. Co., 247 Ill. 614............. 363
Musselman Grocer Co. v. Kidd etc. Co., 151 Mich. 478........ 445
Mutual Nat. Bank of New Orleans v. Moore, 50 La. Ann. 1332... 721
Myers v. Edison Electric Illuminating Co., 225 Pa. 387...... 93

Neil v. Idaho & W. N. R. R. Co., 22 Ida. 74................. 212
Nelson v. Hudgel, 23 Ida. 335............................... 56
New York Edison Co. v. City of New York, 133 App. Div. 728,
    732..400, 406

Page

New York Life Ins. Co. v. Pike, 51 Colo. 238................... 709
Niles v. Cedar Point Club, 175 U. S. 300..................... 753
Nobach v. Scott, 20 Ida. 558...........................298, 301
Norfolk & Western R. Co. v. Dean, 107 Va. 505.............. 221
Norfolk & W. R. Co. v. Gesswine, 144 Fed. 56.............. 221
Northern National Bank v. Weed, 86 Wis. 212.............. 415
Northern Pac. Ry. Co. v. Gifford, 25 Ida. 196.............. 774
Northern Pac. Ry. Co. v. Myers, 172 U. S. 589.............. 479

Oliver v. Kootenai Co., 13 Ida. 281....................... 171
Oregon Ry. & Nav. Co. v. Taffe, 67 Or. 102................. 46
Otter Tail County v. Batchelder, 47 Minn. 512............. 469
Oxier v. United States, 1 Ind. Ter. 91.................... 580

Pacific Tel. & Tel. Co. v. Eshleman, 166 Cal. 640...........263, 264
Pacific Tel. & Tel. Co. v. Wright-Dickinson Hotel Co., 214 Fed.
  666.................. 264
Packer v. Bird, 71 Cal. 134.............................. 750
Palmer v. Pettingill, 6 Ida. 346......................... 673
Parsons v. Wrble, 21 Ida. 695............................ 24
Peck v. Brummagim, 31 Cal. 440........................... 435
Peery v. Quincy, O. & K. C. R. Co., 122 Mo. App. 177............ 216
Penick v. High Shoals Mfg. Co., 113 Ga. 592.............. 262
Penn. Mut. Life Ins. Co. v. City of Austin, 168 U. S. 685........ 114
Pennsylvania Co. v. Meyers, 136 Ind. 242................. 220
Pennsylvania Min. Co. v. Gallagher, 19 Ida. 101........... 160
People ex rel. Simon v. Bradley, 207 N. Y. 592............ 770
People v. Bunkers, 2 Cal. App. 197....................... 195
People v. Chambers, 18 Cal. 382.......................... 579
People v. Coffey, 161 Cal. 433........................... 195
People v. Creegan, 121 Cal. 554.......................... 195
People v. Fagan, 66 Cal. 534............................. 601
People v. Flagg, 16 Barb. (N. Y.) 503.................... 504
People v. Hoag, 54 Colo. 542............................. 671
People v. Kraker, 72 Cal. 459............................ 195
People v. Leddy, 53 Colo. 109............................ 320
People v. Morine, 61 Cal. 367............................ 575
People v. Rose, 203 Ill. 46.............................. 770
People v. Wilcox, 207 N. Y. 86........................... 260
People v. Yeager, 113 Mich. 228.......................... 612
Phoenix Ins. Co. v. Pechner, 95 U. S. 183................ 667
Pike v. State Land Board, 19 Ida. 268.................... 363
Pine v. Callahan, 8 Ida. 684............................. 641
Pioneer Irr. Dist. v. Bradley, 8 Ida. 310.................336, 340
Plano Mfg. Co. v. Murphy, 16 S. D. 380................... 669
Porter v. Title Guaranty & Surety Co., 21 Ida. 321.............. 299

Page

Portneuf-Marsh Valley Irr. Co. v. Portneuf Irr. Co., 19 Ida. 483.43, 46

Powell v. Springston Lumber Co., 12 Ida. 723................647, 669

Powers v. Elmendorf, 4 How. Pr. 60........................... 401

Proctor v. San Antonio St. Ry. Co., 26 Tex. Civ. App. 148....... 93

Protective Min. Co. v. Forest City Min. Co., 51 Wash. 643...... 161

Public Service Commission v. Northern Central Ry. Co. (Md.),
90 Atl. 105.. 255

Quarg v. Scher, 136 Cal. 406.................................. 104

Railroad Commission of Alabama v. Central of Georgia Ry. Co.,
170 Fed. 225.. 255

Randall v. Dailey, 66 Wis. 285................................ 25

Rash v. Allen, 1 Boyce (Del.), 444............................ 321

Raymond v. Chicago Union Traction Co., 207 U. S. 20........... 470

Rea v. Wilson, 112 Iowa, 517.................................. 696

Reagan v. United States, 202 Fed. 488......................... 612

Rector v. Hartt, 8 Mo. 448.................................... 512

Redford v. Spokane Street Ry. Co., 15 Wash. 419.............. 447

Reed v. Conway, 20 Mo. 43..................................... 674

Reese v. Westfield, 56 Wash. 415.............................. 622

Reisman v. Public Service Corp., 82 N. J. L. 464.............. 93

Reynolds v. Board of County Commissioners, 6 Ida. 787........ 254

Rice v. Gwinn, 5 Ida. 394..................................... 504

Ridgely v. Mayor, 119 Md. 567................................. 320

Riggs v. Palmer, 115 N. Y. 506................................ 761

Rima v. Rossie Iron Works, 120 N. Y. 433...................... 299

Robbins v. Porter, 12 Ida. 738................................ 641

Robichaux v. Morgan's L. & T. & S. S. Co., 131 La. 727........ 93

Robinson v. Elliott, 22 Wall. (U. S.) 513..................... 547

Rodgers v. Thomas, 193 Fed. 952............................... 113

Rosebloom v. State, 64 Neb. 343............................... 772

Rowley v. Stack-Gibbs Co., 19 Ida. 107........................ 301

Ryan v. Rogers, 14 Ida. 309...............................548, 549

Ryan v. St. Louis Transit Co., 190 Mo. 621.................93, 94

Ryus v. Gruble, 31 Kan. 767................................... 671

Sabin v. Burke, 4 Ida. 28..................................... 641

Salt Lake City v. Christensen Co., 34 Utah, 38............772, 774

Samuelson v. Cleveland etc. M. Co., 49 Mich. 164.............. 93

Schieble v. Hart, 11 Ky. Law Rep. 607......................... 171

School Dist. No. 80 v. Burress, 2 Neb. Unof. 554..........671, 672

Schuler, Ex parte, 167 Cal. 282...........................773, 774

Schultz v. Byers, 53 N. J. L. 442............................. 171

Scott v. Lattig, 227 U. S. 229............................752, 755

Setters, In re, 23 Idaho, 270................................. 198

                                                                    Page
Shaffer v. Des Moines Coal etc. Co., 122 Iowa, 233.............. 731
Shank v. Great Shoshone & Twin Falls Water Power Co., 205
    Fed. 833.................... 716
Shaw v. Ferguson, 78 Ind. 547................................. 331
Shaw v. Proffitt, 57 Or. 192..................................... 33
Shaw v. Quincy Min. Co., 145 U. S. 444....................... 710
Sheridan Gas, Oil & Coal Co. v. Pearson, 19 Ind. App. 252...... 106
Shiver v. United States, 159 U. S. 491........................ 480
Shoemaker v. Hatch, 13 Nev. 261.............................. 751
Sievers, In re, 91 Fed. 366.................................... 420
Simpson v. State, 111 Ala. 6.................................. 388
Slater v. United States, 1 Okl. Cr. 275....................579, 580
Sloggy v. Dilworth, 38 Minn. 179............................. 791
Small v. Harrington, 10 Ida. 499.........................644, 648
Smith v. Atlanta & C. R. Co., 130 N. C. 344.................. 220
Smith v. Davidson, 23 Ida. 555............................... 25
Smith v. Smith, 4 Ida. 1..................................... 57
South v. Maryland, 18 How. (U. S.) 396...................... 671
Spaulding v. Coeur d'Alene Ry. etc. Co., 6 Ida. 638............ 487
Springer v. Howes, 69 Fed. 850.............................. 668
Spurr v. Travis, 145 Mich. 721............................... 445
St. Clair County v. Lovingston, 23 Wall. 46................... 754
St. Joe Improvement Co. v. Laumierster, 19 Ida. 66............ 770
Staab v. Rocky Mt. Tel. Co., 23 Ida. 314.................84, 95, 97
Stack-Gibbs Lumber Co. v. Cameron Lumber Co., 26 Ida. 649... 638
State v. Barrett, 172 Ind. 169................................ 770
State v. Butterfield L. S. Co., 17 Ida. 441.................... 336
State v. Cochran, 55 Or. 157......................'........... 770
State v. Commercial Bank, 6 Sm. & M. (Miss.) 218.............. 171
State v. Corcoran, 1 Ida. 220.............................186, 187
State v. Dawson, 22 Ind. 272................................ 269
State v. Doherty, 3 Ida. 384....................336, 340, 774
State v. Dolan, 13 Ida. 693...........................336, 340
State v. Downing, 23 Ida. 540................................ 743
State v. Drew, 179 Mo. 315.................................. 601
State v. Driskill, 26 Ida. 738................................ 744
State v. Edwards, 136 Mo. 360............................... 149
State v. Erickson, 39 Mont. 280.............................. 320
State v. Harris, 89 Ind. 363...........................671, 672
State v. Hocker, 36 Fla. 358................................. 321
State v. Howell, 100 Mo. 628................................ 600
State v. Jones, 9 Ida. 693.........................336, 774
State v. Knudtson, 11 Ida. 524.............................. 194
State v. Krahmer, 105 Minn. 422............................ 557
State v. Marren, 17 Ida. 766................................ 575
State v. Paulsen, 21 Ida. 686............................... 761

Page

State v. Ridenbaugh, 5 Ida. 710 386
State v Sanford, 8 Ida. 187 ....581, 601
State v. Seymour, 7 Ida. 257 580
State v. Seymour, 10 Ida. 699 595
State v. Thompson, 144 Mo. 314 770
State v. Thornton, 10 S. D. 349 600
State v. Trask, 6 Vt. 355 513
State v. Tucker, 36 Iowa, 485 513
State v. Union Central Ins. Co., 8 Ida. 240 774
State v. Webb, 6 Ida. 428 600
Steed v. Petty, 65 Tex. 490 437
Steele v. City of Portland, 23 Or. 176 511
Steinbuchel v. Lane, 59 Kan. 7 750
Stevens v. United Gas & Electric Co., 73 N. H. 159 93
Stewart v. Weiser Lumber Co., 21 Ida. 340 ....86, 430
Stone v. State of South Carolina, 117 U. S. 430 668
Stowell v. Tucker, 7 Ida. 312 32
Strand v. Crooked River Min. & M. Co., 23 Ida. 577 787
Stuart v. Hauser, 9 Ida. 53 641
Swain v. Fritchman, 21 Ida. 783 320
Swarts v. Fourth Nat. Bank, 117 Fed. 1 543

Tarr v. Western Loan & Sav. Co., 15 Ida. 741 160
Tatum v. State, 66 Ala. 465 388
Taylor v. Louisville etc. R. Co., 88 Fed. 350 467
Territory v. Guthrie, 2 Ida. 432 187
Thomas v. Harrington, 72 N. H. 45 93
Thornton's Estate, In re (Wyo.), 133 Pac. 134 ....10, 14
Tilden v. Hubbard, 25 Ida. 677 586
Title Ins. & Trust Co. v. Ingersoll, 153 Cal. 1 564
Town of South Ottawa v. Perkins, 94 U. S. 260 115
Township of East Oakland v. Skinner, 94 U. S. 255 115
Tracy v. Wheeler, 15 N. D. 248 371
Trevorrow v. Trevorrow, 65 Mich. 234 702
Trueman v. Village of St. Maries, 21 Ida. 632 783
Truesdail v. Ward, 24 Mich. 117 737
Trustees of Saratoga Springs v. Saratoga Gas E. L. & P. Co., 191
    N. Y. 123 254
Turner v. Coffin, 9 Ida. 338 336

Ulbright v. Baslington, 20 Ida. 539, 542 ....49, 55, 58, 755
Union Bridge Co. v. United States, 204 U. S. 364 253
Union Traction Co. v. Fetters, 99 Fed. 214 92
United States v. Clark, 31 Fed. 710 674

Vanderhayden v. Young, 11 Johns. (N. Y.) 150 674
Vernor v. Secretary of State, 179 Mich. 157 773
Village of Pine City v. Munch, 42 Minn. 342 305

Page

Village of Sandpoint v. Doyle, 11 Ida. 642....................78, 305
Vinton v. Baldwin, 95 Ind. 433................................. 330
Voight v. Fidelity Inv. Co., 49 Wash. 612....................... 621
Voss v. Evans Marble Co., 101 Ill. App. 373.................... 711

Waechter v. Atchison T. & S. F. Ry. Co., 10 Cal. App. 70......... 710
Walker v. City of Spokane, 62 Wash. 312....................... 770
War Eagle Consol. Min. Co. v. Dickie, 14 Ida. 534................ 159
Warner v. Godfrey, 186 U. S. 365.............................. 215
Washburn v. Case, 1 Wash. Ter. 253............................ 106
Washington Water Power Co. v. Waters, 19 Ida. 595.............. 46
Watkins v. Lawton, 69 Ga. 671................................ 299
Weaver v. Devendorf, 3 Denio (N. Y.), 117.................... 674
Weeter Lumber Co. v. Fales, 20 Ida. 255....................369, 370
Weld v. Board of Gas & Electric Light Commissioners, 197 Mass.
  556 240
Wheeler v. Oregon R. & Nav. Co., 16 Ida. 375.................... 84
Wheeler v. Patterson, 1 N. H. 88.............................. 674
White v. Cotzhausen, 129 U. S. 329............................ 415
Wilkerson v. Aven, 26 Ida. 559............................... 566
Wilkes v. Dinsman, 7 How. (U. S.) 89......................... 674
Wilson v. Baker Clothing Co., 25 Ida. 378..................?..... 417
Wilson v. Boise City, 7 Ida. 69............................... 723
Wilson v. City Bank, 17 Wall. (U. S.) 473..................... 545
Wilson v. Hibbert, 194 Fed. 838.............................. 93
Wilson v. Mayor of New York, 1 Denio (N. Y.), 595.............. 674
Wilson v. United States, 221 U. S. 361........................ 404
Winston v. City of Spokane, 12 Wash. 524..................... 360
Wolford v. Oakley, 43 How. Pr. (N. Y.) 118................... 299
Worden v. Witt, 4 Ida. 404................................... 671
Wright v. Big Rapids Door & Blind Mfg. Co., 124 Mich. 91........ 93

Younie v. Blackfoot Light & Water Co., 15 Ida. 56..............96, 97
Young v. Waters-Pierce Oil Co., 185 Mo. 634.................... 93

CITATIONS—VOL. 26.

IDAHO.

		Page
CONSTITUTION.—Art.	1, sec. 13	611
Art.	1, sec. 17	404
Art.	3, sec. 13	314
Art.	3, sec. 15	314
Art.	3, sec. 16	336
Art.	3, sec. 22	149, 237
Art.	4, sec. 6	529, 530
Art.	4, sec. 10	237
Art.	5, sec. 2	241, 528
Art.	5, sec. 6	528
Art.	5, sec. 11	528
Art.	5, sec. 14	528
Art.	5, sec. 19	529, 530, 531
Art.	5, sec. 21	528
Art.	5, sec. 22	528
Art.	7, sec. 2	477, 768, 771, 774
Art.	7, sec. 3	477
Art.	7, sec. 5	477, 769, 773, 774
Art.	7, sec. 15	146, 147, 151, 152, 153
Art.	8, sec. 3	357, 360, 365
Art.	9, sec. 8	260
Art.	11, sec. 10	159
Art.	11, sec. 15	131
Art.	11, sec. 18	248, 258, 259, 260
Art.	15, sec. 1	131
Art.	15, sec. 2	131
Art.	18, sec. 6	605, 607

SESSION LAWS.

	Page
1895, p. 227	139, 279
1903, p. 347	335
1909, p. 335	121
1911, p. 30	310
1911, p. 158	76
1911, p. 162	77
1911, p. 163	77
1911, p. 268	282
1911, p. 340	177
1911, p. 345	606

SESSION LAWS—Continued.

	Page
1911, p. 375	787, 788
1911, p. 376	786, 788
1911, p. 377	171, 788
1911, p. 537	782, 783
1911, p. 664	198
1912, p. 8	77
1912, p. 43	555
1913, c. 33	147, 148, 149, 151, 153
1913, c. 58, sec. 99	146, 147, 148, 149, 151, 152, 153
1913, c. 58, secs. 127–144	482
1913, c. 61	395
1913, c. 179	767, 770, 771, 774, 776
1913, c. 179, sec. 12	767
1913, c. 179, sec. 16	768, 769
1913, p. 13	624
1913, p. 51	74
1913, p. 58	314
1913, p. 121	758
1913, p. 127	385, 389
1913, p. 132	625
1913, p. 160	708
1913, p. 173	477
1913, p. 206	783
1913, p. 221	606
1913, p. 247	232, 394
1913, p. 379	453
1913, p. 415	758
1913, p. 462	288
1913, p. 524	77
1913, p. 530	783

REVISED CODES.

SECTION	PAGE	SECTION	PAGE
3	151	896	77
149	606	900	77
150	606	901	77
169	606	1156	207
191	661, 680	1197	205, 206, 208
295	660, 674	1198	206
320	531	1199	208
324	531	1263	686, 688
329	531	1518	389
442	453, 454	1613	277
448	453, 454	1629	139, 277, 279
883a	76	1649	555
894	77	1755	24

REVISED CODES—Continued.

SECTION	PAGE	SECTION	PAGE
1762	556	4439	300
1763	555, 556, 558	4441	171
1770	556	4442	171
1960	148, 625	4443	171
2118	606	4479	563
2236	305	4510	487
2238	76, 282, 365	4552	480
2242	74, 75, 78	4554	480
2262	504	4808	375, 518, 780, 781, 782
2270	364, 365	4809	781, 788
2304	44	4818	787
2315	76	4824	37, 162
2676	86, 430, 562	4831	177
2679	562	4833	177
2680	563	4892	721, 722
2792	159, 160, 708	4935	781, 782, 783, 784
2970	676	5290	180
3001	671, 672, 673, 676, 679	5351	12, 14, 180
3004	676	5355	12, 13
3005	676, 677, 678, 680	5363	14
3092	171	5365	12, 13
3093	169	5466	178
3160	501	5467	178
3168	413, 422, 423	5468	178
3169	413, 422, 423, 433, 443	5593	178
3171	422	5598	178
3211	160	5599	178
3388	413	5600	178, 179
3391	413, 415	5602	178
3392	413	5611	178
3446	330	5628	180
3659	308	5650	180, 181
3666	310	5884	421
3818	737	5932	412, 413, 416, 418, 421
3820	633	5950	150
3890	721	6007	31, 34
4099	298	7008	198
4178	299	7057	570, 574
4229	177, 216, 298	7355	611
4231	36, 300	7509	388
4269	177	7795	186
4302	708	7855	601
4353	723	7871	194, 195
4360	722	8043	386, 388, 389
4372	186	8325	386
4383	731		

REVISED STATUTES.

SECTION   PAGE
403 674

ARIZONA.

Laws 1912, c. 90, sec. 50..................................... 238

CALIFORNIA.

Constitution, art. 12, sec. 22................................. 264
Code of Civil Procedure, sec. 1058............................. 782
Code of Civil Procedure, sec. 1369............................. 13
Code of Civil Procedure, sec. 1379............................. 13
Laws 1911, c. 14, sec. 50..................................... 238
Penal Code, sec. 1111....................................195, 196

CONNECTICUT.

Laws 1902, sec. 3846... 238

ILLINOIS.

Laws 1913, No. 907, sec. 55.................................. 239

INDIANA.

Acts 1909, c. 49, sec. 1...................................... 444

KANSAS.

Laws 1911, c. 238, sec. 31................................... 238

MAINE.

Rev. Stats. 1903, c. 51, sec. 3.............................. 238

MARYLAND.

Laws 1910, c. 180, secs. 26, 33............................... 238

MICHIGAN.

Constitution, art. 6, sec. 32................................. 445
Laws 1911, c. 138, sec. 7.................................... 238

MINNESOTA.

Laws 1899, c. 291, p. 357.................................... 449

MISSOURI.

Laws 1913, p. 557, sec. 53.................................. 239

NEBRASKA.

PAGE

Annotated Statutes of 1909, sec. 6048............................ 449

NEW HAMPSHIRE.

Laws 1911, c. 164, sec. 13.................................... 239

NEW YORK.

Laws 1910, c. 480, sec. 33................................... 239

OHIO.

Laws 1911, No. 325, sec. 54.................................. 239

PENNSYLVANIA.

Laws 1913, p. 1374, art. III, sec. 2........................... 240

SOUTH DAKOTA.

Sess. Laws 1907, c. 217, secs. 1, 2........................... 239

UNITED STATES.

Fourteenth Amendment, sec. 1................................ 445
29 Stats. 435.. 139
32 Stats. 388.. 477
32 Stats. 797.. 69
36 Stats. 592.. 477
36 Stats. 838.. 69
37 Stats. 265.. 478

WASHINGTON.

Constitution, art. 8, sec. 6................................. 360

WISCONSIN.

Laws 1909, sec. 74, p. 759.................................. 239

(April 15, 1914.)

ELISHA STRONG et al., Appellants, v. LUCIUS P. BROWN et al., Respondents.

[140 Pac. 773.]

MINING EXCAVATIONS—NEGLIGENCE—DAMAGES.

1. It is lawful for the miner to sink holes, pits and shafts on mineral lands, and to do so is not of itself an act of negligence, and an excavation, pit or shaft made by a miner in the prosecution of his work is not of itself a nuisance.

2. The owner of a mining claim is not liable to the owner of livestock for damages resulting from livestock running at large falling into a pit, prospect hole or mining shaft left open by the miner, and the locator or owner of mining claims is not bound by law to fence or inclose the same in order to protect livestock running at large on the public domain from being injured by falling into the same.

APPEAL from the District Court of the Fifth Judicial District, in and for Bear Lake County. Hon. Alfred Budge, Judge.

Action for damages. Judgment for defendant. Plaintiff appeals. *Affirmed.*

T. L. Glenn, for Appellants.

All persons have a common interest in the grass on the public lands of the United States except in so far as the grazing of sheep has been restricted by statute, and if the appellants in common with others had an interest in the grasses growing on the public domain and were entitled to graze their stock thereon, it was the duty of respondents to avoid creating any pitfalls on said public land and leaving them open or uninclosed, thus endangering both life and property. (*Sweet v. Ballentyne*, 8 Ida. 431, 69 Pac. 995; *Sifers v. Johnson*, 7 Ida. 798, 97 Am. St. 271, 65 Pac. 709, 54 L. R. A. 785; Cooley's Constitutional Lim., 6th ed., 704. *Commonwealth v. Alger*, 7 Cush. (Mass.) 53.) If the construction of a ditch is dangerous to travel, the digging of pits and leaving them uncovered or unfenced, whereby stock may fall therein and be killed or destroyed, constitutes a nuisance, especially on lands on which there is an implied right accorded by the United States to run or graze horses and cattle. (*City of Lewiston v. Booth*, 3 Ida. 692, 34 Pac. 809; Thomas on Negligence, p. 45.)

To create and maintain a nuisance dangerous to life or property is negligence *per se,* and such act is made punishable by our law; if one violates such law and injury results to either person or property of another, such wrongdoer is liable, criminally and civilly. (*Conway v. Monidah Trust Co.*, 47 Mont. 269, 132 Pac. 26.) "A mine owner is bound to so fence or guard the shaft openings as to prevent its being a source of danger to the cattle of the surface owner." (*Williams v. Groucott*, 4 Best & Sm. 149, 122 Eng. Reprint, 416; 15 Am. & Eng. Ency. Law, 589.)

"When one is engaged in an act which the circumstances indicate may be dangerous to others, and the event whose occurrence is necessary to make the act injurious can be readily seen as likely to occur under the circumstances, the defendant is liable if he does not take all the care which prudence may suggest to avoid the injury." (*McGrew v. Stone*, 53 Pa. 436; Webb's Pollock on Torts, p. 29; 1 Sedgwick on Damages, 8th ed., p. 28, sec. 29.)

Chas. E. Harris, for Respondents.

Idaho has no statute requiring the fencing or covering of excavations made by prospectors and miners on their own ground, and in the absence of statute the common law rules. (27 Cyc. 751; *Driscoll v. Clark*, 32 Mont. 172, 80 Pac. 1, 373; *Conway v. Monidah Trust Co.*, 47 Mont. 269, 132 Pac. 26; *Beinhorn v. Griswold*, 27 Mont. 79, 94 Am. St. 818, 69 Pac. 557, 59 L. R. A. 771; *Knight v. Abert*, 6 Pa. 472, 47 Am. Dec. 478, 49 Am. Dec. 261, notes.)

"The rightful use of one's own land may cause damage to another without any legal wrong." (*City of Bellevue v. Daly*, 14 Ida. 545, 125 Am. St. 179, 94 Pac. 1036, 14 Ann. Cas. 1136, 15 L. R. A., N. S., 992.)

Negligence cannot be predicated upon one's lawful and ordinary use of his own premises. (*Schimberg v. Cutler*, 142 Fed. 701, 74 C. C. A. 33; 15 Current Law, 147, and cases there cited; *King v. Oregon Short Line Ry.*, 6 Ida. 306, 55 Pac. 665, 59 L. R. A. 209; *West v. Shaw*, 61 Wash. 227, 112 Pac. 243; *Smalley v. Rio Grande Western R. Co.*, 34 Utah, 423, 98 Pac. 311.) And in connection with trespassing: *Holt v. Spokane etc. Ry. Co.*, 4 Ida. 443, 40 Pac. 56; 29 Cyc. 442, 444; 5 Current Law, 116, and cases cited; *Oakes Mfg. Co. v. New York*, 206 N. Y. 221, 99 N. E. 540, 42 L. R. A. 286.

"Plaintiff cannot recover where the allegations of the complaint show that his own negligence was the proximate cause of the injury." (*Goure v. Storey*, 17 Ida. 352, 105 Pac. 794.)

The duty of the defendants must be shown by a statement of facts from which the duty follows as a matter of law. And after showing that duty the complaint must allege a breach of such duty. (29 Cyc. 556; *Schmidt v. Bauer*, 80 Cal. 565, 22 Pac. 256, 5 L. R. A. 580.)

AILSHIE, C. J.—This action was commenced to recover damages for the loss of livestock that were running on the public range and strayed on to the premises of the defendants and fell into certain "pits" or excavations that had been made on the defendants' premises in the prosecution of work on their phosphate mines. A demurrer to the complaint was sustained and judgment of dismissal was entered and this appeal was thereupon prosecuted.

The only question arising, therefore, is as to the sufficiency of the complaint to state a cause of action. The material allegations thereof are as follows:

"2· That at all times herein mentioned the defendants were joint owners of and in possession of the following phosphate mining claims. (Here follows a description of the claims which are located in Bannock county.)

"3· That on the —— day of May, 1912, plaintiffs were and for some time prior thereto were the owners of, in possession of and entitled to the possession of the following described animals, to wit: (Here follows a description of the animals and allegations of the value thereof.) That in the month of April, 1912, the said mares and horses were turned upon the public range to graze, that so while on said range, the blue mare fell into a pit on said first claim and was killed thereby; that the gelding while so upon said range fell into a pit on said second claim and was killed thereby; that the said gray mare, while so upon said range, fell into a pit on said third claim, and was killed thereby; that the defendants in utter disregard of the rights of plaintiffs negligently, wrongfully and carelessly, after digging said pits, failed to inclose the same, so as to protect stock turned upon the range, and when said pits became filled with snow they were so hidden from view that the said horses walked into said pits and were thereby killed and destroyed to plaintiff's damage in the sum of five hundred and twenty-five dollars ($525.00)."

The important and material question in this case is whether a miner, prospector or land owner is guilty of negligence in leaving prospect holes, pits or shafts open and unfenced on the public domain or elsewhere upon mineral lands. In other words, must the miner and prospector fence and inclose prospect holes, pits and mining shafts and tunnels to protect livestock running at large from falling into them? In this case it stands admitted that the respondents were the owners and in possession of certain phosphate claims, and that they had opened "pits" on these claims and the horses belonging to the appellants strayed on to the claims, fell into the pits and died.

The statutes of the United States authorize the prospector and miner to go upon the public domain and prospect for precious metals and locate mining claims, and the statutes require that certain work must be done, which includes digging a pit or sinking a shaft in order to hold such location. It is clear, therefore, that to make such excavation, either on a man's own land or upon the public domain, is not of itself a wrongful act, and the thing done does not of itself constitute a nuisance. The miner has a right to do these things, and that right is not one of sufferance or tolerance, but it is authorized by positive statute. On the other hand, under the laws of this state a man may allow his horses to run at large, and they may roam and graze wherever their instinct may lead them upon unfenced and uninclosed lands. In other words, the owner of unfenced or uninclosed land cannot maintain an action for damages against the owner of such stock because they happen to feed and graze upon his lands.

Neither the government of the United States nor the state of Idaho has enacted any statute requiring the locator of a mining claim to fence the same or to in any way protect or inclose any pits, shafts or excavations on such claim against livestock. In order for one to be liable for damages he must be guilty of some act of negligence. Such negligence may consist of omission or commission. It seems to us that when a mining claim is left unfenced, as between the owner thereof and the owner of grazing livestock, there exists concurrent risks. The owner of the mining claim incurs the risk of having livestock herd and graze over his land and claim, and he takes the chances of any incidental damages which they may do his property by reason of having free ingress thereto. On the other hand, the owner of such livestock, while he has the privilege of permitting his livestock to run at large and graze over the uninclosed property, takes the concurrent risk of such stock getting into dangerous places, falling into pits or excavations or getting into buildings or works belonging to the land owner and getting maimed or killed.

While the owner of such trespassing livestock cannot be held
in damages by the owner of the real property unless the land
has been lawfully inclosed, on the other hand, the owner of
such realty should not be held liable for an injury which such
trespassing animals may receive under such circumstances.
The man who turns his livestock out on to the public range
takes innumerable risks of their being killed or injured. The
mountainous country is full of crags, canyons, pitfalls and
innumerable places where they may as easily become injured
as from falling into mining excavations. It would be a very
dangerous precedent to establish in a state like this, where
mining and prospecting are carried on by such a large number
of people, to say that every miner and prospector must fence
or in some way secure and protect every prospect hole, mining
shaft and pit against roaming livestock. We cannot believe
that the law imposes such an obligation.

This court, in considering the respective rights of property
owners to enjoy the free, unrestricted use of their several
properties, in the case of *City of Bellevue v. Daly*, 14 Ida.
545, 125 Am. St. 179, 94 Pac. 1036, 14 Ann. Cas. 1136,
15 L. R. A., N. S., 992, quoted with approval from Professor
Beach as follows:

"It may be stated as a general proposition that every man
has a right to the natural use and enjoyment of his property,
and if, while lawfully in such use and enjoyment without
negligence or malice on his part, an unavoidable loss occurs to
his neighbor, it is *damnum absque injuria*, for the rightful use
of one's own land may cause damage to another without any
legal wrong."

Our attention has been called to but one case which seems
to be in point on the facts under consideration in this case,
and that is the case of *Beinhorn v. Griswold*, 27 Mont. 79.
94 Am. St. 818, 69 Pac. 557, 59 L. R. A. 771. There the
defendant was the lessee of a mining claim and mill site. The
property was not inclosed by any legal fence. He had placed
upon the property a number of vats containing a solution of
certain poisonous chemicals and water, and the plaintiff's
cattle strayed on to the premises and drank of the solution and

died. The plaintiff thereupon commenced an action against the defendant to recover damages to the extent of the value of the cattle. The supreme court of Montana gave the matter a very thorough consideration, and reached the conclusion that the mine owner was not liable for damages, that he had committed no wrong or tort and was in no respect guilty of negligence, and should not be held for damages. In process of the court's discussion and consideration of this question it was said:

"This is his right, for the cattle are trespassing. The owners of domestic animals hold no servitude upon, or interest, temporary or permanent, in the open land of another, merely because it is open. If the land owner fails to 'fence out' cattle lawfully at large, he may not successfully complain of loss caused by such livestock straying upon his uninclosed land. For under these circumstances the trespass is condoned or excused—the law refuses to award damages. While the land owner, by omitting to fence, disables himself from invoking the remedy which is given to those who inclose their property with a legal fence, and while the cattle owner is thereby relieved from liability for casual trespasses, it is nevertheless true that the cattle owner has no right to pasture his cattle on the land of another, and that cattle thus wandering over such lands are not rightfully there. They are there merely by the forbearance, sufferance, or tolerance of the non-fencing land owner; there they may remain only by his tolerance. The cattle-owning plaintiff did not owe to the landowning defendant the duty to fence his cattle in. The latter did not owe to the former the duty to fence them out. Neither of them was under obligation to the other in that regard. The defendant is not liable in this action unless he was negligent. There cannot be negligence without breach of duty. Hence, manifestly, the defendant was not guilty of negligence in omitting to prevent the plaintiff's cattle from going upon his unfenced land."

The foregoing observations are peculiarly applicable to the facts of the case we have under consideration. We are satisfied that the trial court properly sustained the demurrer and dismissed the action, and that under the allegations of the complaint the defendants were not liable for damages.

The judgment should be affirmed, and it is so ordered, with costs in favor of respondent.

Sullivan, J., concurs.

Petition for rehearing denied.

(April 18, 1914.)

FRANK WRIGHT, Appellant, v. J. G. MERRILL, Respondent.

[140 Pac. 1101.]

ADMINISTRATOR—APPOINTMENT OF—RECOMMENDATION OF NONRESIDENT BROTHER—PRIORITY OF RIGHT—CREDITOR—ADMINISTRATOR—DELAY IN MAKING APPLICATION FOR APPOINTMENT OF.

1. The order of priority in right of administration on the estate of a person dying intestate is fixed by the provisions of sec. 5351, Rev. Codes.

2. Sec. 5365, Rev. Codes, which provides that administration may be granted to one or more competent persons although not other-wise entitled to the same, upon the written request of a person entitled, filed with the court, does not apply to nonresidents, since under the provisions of sec. 5355 a nonresident is not competent or entitled to appointment as an administrator.

3. Under the provisions of sec. 5363, Rev. Codes, letters of administration must be granted upon proper application, although it appears that other persons have better rights to the administration, when such persons fail to appear and claim the issuance of such letters to themselves within a reasonable time after the death of the intestate.

4. The provisions of this section require persons entitled or having better rights to administration to make application within a reasonable time for such appointment, and if they fail to make such application, letters should be granted to any qualified applicant who makes application therefor prior to the time that application is made by the one who may have had a better right.

APPEAL from the District Court of the Fifth Judicial District, in and for Bear Lake County. Hon. Alfred Budge, Judge.

Appeal from a judgment appointing an administrator of the estate of Rody Thornton, deceased. Judgment *reversed.*

Thos. L. Glenn, for Appellant, cites no authorities.

Gough & Kunz, for Respondent.

The sole question to be determined in the case at bar is whether or not a nonresident brother of the deceased, who is himself incompetent to administer by reason of his non-residence, can by request advance a person from the eleventh class to a priority over a person of the tenth class.

Sections 5351 and 5365 of our codes are identical with sections 1365 and 1379, Cal. Code Civ. Proc. And our contention is fully sustained by two decisions of the supreme court of that state, construing these sections with reference to this question. (*Estate of Beech,* 63 Cal. 458; *In re Meier's Estate,* 165 Cal. 456, 132 Pac. 764, 48 L. R. A., N. S., 858.)

As we understand the opinion of this court in *Estate of Daggett,* 15 Ida. 504, 98 Pac. 849, the reasoning there is to the same effect.

SULLIVAN, J.—This is an appeal from a judgment of the district court affirming the decision of a probate court in the appointment of J. G. Merrill as administrator of the estate of Rody Thornton, deceased.

It appears from the facts of the case that said deceased was at one time a resident of the state of Wyoming and died intestate in the county of Bear Lake, Idaho, while temporarily residing in Idaho. He left property in Bear Lake county of the estimated value of $3,525. He was unmarried at the time of his death and none of his heirs resided in this state. Said Thornton departed this life on the 4th day of May, 1912. At the time of his death he left in the state of Wyoming an estate consisting of personal and real property, the real estate being of the estimated value of $30,000 and the personal property of the value of $40,000. (See *In re Thornton's Estate* (Wyo.), 133 Pac. 134.) From that decision it appears that the said J. G. Merrill claimed to be heir to the entire estate under and by virtue of a nuncupative will alleged to have been made by said Thornton during his lifetime, which will was held invalid and void by said decision of the supreme court of Wyoming.

During the pendency of said case in the Wyoming courts nothing was done in the state of Idaho toward administering on that portion of said deceased's estate situated in this state, but after said decision was rendered by the supreme court of Wyoming holding said nuncupative will invalid, and on the 29th day of July, 1913, the appellant herein filed his petition in the probate court of Bear Lake county praying for letters of administration on said estate. Said petition was filed at the instance and written request of George Thornton, one of the brothers of said deceased, who acted therein for and on behalf of himself and the other heirs of said deceased, all of whom were nonresidents of the state. The next of kin surviving said deceased are as follows: George Thornton, Hugh Thornton and Peter Thornton, brothers of deceased; Anna J. Thornton McDonald, a sister, and the children and heirs of Perry Thornton, a brother of decedent, and the children of Mary Thornton Nolen, a sister of the decedent.

To said petition the respondent Merrill filed a protest and prayed that letters of administration on said estate be granted to him and that the application of said Frank Wright for letters be rejected. On the 13th day of August, 1913, said George Thornton filed his verified petition and affidavit in said cause, demanding and requesting that letters of administration be granted to the appellant Wright.

A hearing was had by the probate court in said matter and the probate court thereafter made an order denying the application or petition of Wright to be appointed administrator and granted the application or petition of Merrill, and thereupon issued letters of administration to the said Merrill,

from which order Wright appealed to the district court and
thereafter said matter was heard upon the records and files
of the case and the following stipulation of facts:

"It is hereby stipulated and agreed by and between the
parties herein, through their respective attorneys, as follows,
to wit:

"1st. That the applicant, Frank Wright, is a resident of
Bear Lake County, Idaho, and is a person competent to ad-
minister on the estate of the deceased, situate in said Bear
Lake County, Idaho.

"2nd. That the said deceased left no wife surviving him;
that his only heirs at law are his brothers and sisters and
nephews and nieces named in the petitions for letters herein;
and that all of his said brothers and sisters and nephews and
nieces are non-residents of the state of Idaho.

"3rd. That George Thornton, a brother of the deceased,
acting for himself and the other said heirs has requested in
writing filed in the Probate Court of Bear Lake County,
Idaho, the appointment of the said Frank Wright as administrator of the estate of said deceased, situate in said Bear
Lake County, Idaho.

"4th. That J. G. Merrill, the protestant and an applicant herein, is a resident of Bear Lake County, Idaho, and is
a competent person to act as administrator for the estate of
said deceased, situate in Bear Lake County, Idaho, and that
the said J. G. Merrill is a creditor of said estate.

"5th. That this matter may be heard in this court at this
time on the records and files herein and the facts stipulated
above."

The district court thereafter entered a judgment affirming
the decision of the probate court in the appointment of Merrill
as administrator of said estate.

Two errors are relied upon: 1st, that the court erred in
affirming the judgment of the probate court in its appointment of Merrill as administrator of said estate, for the reason that one of the brothers, on his own behalf and on behalf
of the other heirs, requested the appointment of said Wright
as administrator; 2d, that the court erred in appointing said

Merrill for the reason that Merrill had failed to apply within
a reasonable time for letters of administration, and not until
Wright had petitioned for such appointment. Merrill claims
to be a creditor of said estate and bases his application on
that ground.

Priority in rights of administration is provided by sec.
5351, Rev. Codes, and brothers are fourth in order, and creditors tenth in order under said section. Wright claims the
right of appointment under the application of a brother of
the deceased, which brother was a nonresident of the state.

It is admitted that both Wright and Merrill are competent
to act as such administrator, but it is contended by the appellant that since the brother and other heirs of said deceased
requested the appointment, he had the preference, because
the brothers of a deceased are fourth in the order entitled
to administration under the provisions of sec. 5351, Rev. Codes,
and a creditor is the tenth in order. It is also contended
that the brothers had a right to a preference over the creditor
under the provisions of sec. 5365, Rev. Codes, even though
they were nonresidents. Sec. 5365 is as follows:

"Administration may be granted to one or more competent
persons, although not otherwise entitled to the same, at the
written request of the person entitled, filed in the court.
When the person entitled is a nonresident of the state, affidavits taken *ex parte* before any officer authorized by the
laws of this state to take acknowledgments and administer
oaths out of the state, may be received as primary evidence
of the identity of the party, if free from suspicion, and the
fact is established to the satisfaction of the court."

It is contended by counsel for respondent, under the provisions of sec. 5355, that a nonresident brother is not competent to serve as an administrator and for that reason the
provisions of sec. 5365 are not applicable, and that the written
request of a brother who is not competent to act as an administrator because of his nonresidence does not come within
the provisions of said section; that such written request must
be made by one who is competent to act as an administrator
and a *bona fide* resident of the state. Counsel cites in support

of that contention *In re Estate of Beech,* 63 Cal. 458, which case was decided by the supreme court of California in June, 1883. In that case two applications were made for letters of administration, one by the public administrator and the other by a person who based his claim upon the written request of a son of the deceased residing in Great Britain, and the trial court decided in favor of the public administrator on the ground that no effect could be given the request of the son by reason of his nonresidence. The court here held, after reviewing certain other provisions of the statute, that the decision of the trial court was correct. In the decision of the supreme court, reference is made to sec. 1369 of the Code of Civil Procedure of California, which declares, among other things, that no person is competent or entitled to serve as an administrator who is not a *bona fide* resident of the state. That section corresponds to sec. 5355 of the Rev. Codes of this state. The court there also refers to sec. 1379 of the Code of Civil Procedure of California, which is substantially the same as sec. 5365 of the Rev. Codes of this state, and the question determined by that court was whether the two clauses of said sections were repugnant or irreconcilably inconsistent, and the court said:

"The former positively declares that no person is competent or *entitled* to serve as administrator who is not a *bona fide* resident of the state. The latter does not expressly declare that any person who is not a *bona fide* resident of the state shall be competent or entitled to serve. It says, '*When* the person so entitled is a nonresident' his identity may be proven in a certain way. But 'the person so entitled' never can be a nonresident so long as the clause which we have quoted from section 1369 stands unrepealed. So the legislature appears to have provided for a contingency which cannot arise under the law as it now stands, and until that contingency does arise the latter clause of section 1379 must remain practically inoperative."

The sections above referred to of the Idaho code were adopted from the California code, and were a part of the California code before the Revised Statutes of 1887 of this state were adopted, and that decision was rendered prior to 1887. We are therefore inclined to follow the California supreme court on the question under consideration and hold that the application of a nonresident brother and other heirs of the deceased does not give the person recommended by them a preference right over any others entitled to the appointment as administrator under the provisions of said sec. 5351.

It is next contended that since Merrill as a creditor of said estate neglected and failed to apply for letters of administration for more than a year after the death of said deceased and until after the application of Wright had been made, under the provisions of sec. 5363 the court erred in appointing Wright as administrator. Said section is as follows:

"Letters of administration must be granted to any applicant, though it appears that there are other persons having better rights to the administration, when such persons fail to appear and claim the issuing of letters to themselves."

It appears that the principal part of the estate of said deceased was situated in the state of Wyoming and that for about a year after the death of the deceased, Merrill was attempting to secure to himself said entire estate through a nuncupative will which the supreme court of Wyoming, in the case of *In re Thornton's Estate, supra,* held was not a valid will, and there is no doubt considerable feeling existing between the heirs of said deceased and the said Merrill. It also appears that the heirs claim there is considerably more property in Idaho belonging to said estate than Merrill admits belongs to the said estate, and under all of the facts of the case it certainly appears that Wright, who is conceded to be fully competent to act as administrator, ought to be more satisfactory to all concerned than one who has attempted, rightfully or otherwise, to procure said entire estate to himself.

Under the provisions of said last mentioned section, we think, on account of the long delay of Merrill in making his application for letters of administration and his not having made such application for some fourteen months after the death of the deceased and until after Wright had made application for such letters, that the court erred in appointing Merrill as such administrator.

The judgment of the trial court is therefore reversed and the cause is remanded, with instructions to the trial court to reverse its former judgment affirming the judgment of the probate court, and reverse the judgment or order of the probate court appointing Merrill as administrator, and to remand the cause to the probate court for further proceedings in accordance with the views expressed in this opinion.

Costs are awarded to appellant.

Ailshie, C. J., concurs.

(April 24, 1914.)

FIRST NATIONAL BANK OF MOSCOW, a Corporation, Respondent, v. THE REGENTS OF THE UNIVERSITY OF IDAHO, a Corporation, Appellant.

[140 Pac. 771.]

ACTION AGAINST BOARD OF UNIVERSITY REGENTS—JURISDICTION—POWER OF SUCCEEDING BOARD OF EDUCATION TO DEFEND—ELECTION OF REMEDIES.

1. The district court has jurisdiction to try an action against the Board of Regents of the State University to recover a balance for money advanced and material furnished in the construction of a building to be used by the university. *Moscow Hardware Co. v. Regents*, 19 Ida. 420, 113 Pac. 731, and *First Nat. Bank v. Regents*, 19 Ida. 440, 113 Pac. 735, approved and followed.

2. The act of March 6, 1913 (Sess. Laws 1913, p. 328), creating a State Board of Education, makes such board the successor to the old Board of Regents of the University of Idaho, and as such successor said State Board of Education has the power and authority to defend an action previously instituted against the old board for a pre-existing obligation.

3. *Held*, that the remedies sought by the plaintiff are not inconsistent remedies, and plaintiff could not be required to elect between them.

4. *Held*, that the lower court committed no error prejudicial to the rights of appellant.

APPEAL from the District Court of the Second Judicial District, in and for Latah County. Hon. Edgar C. Steele, Judge.

Action against the Board of Regents of the University of Idaho to recover for money advanced and material furnished in the construction of a university building. Judgment against the board in the sum of $6,506.35, and the State Board of Education, as successor to the former Board of Regents; appeals. *Affirmed.*

Forney & Moore, for Appellant.

An.action against the defendant arising out of its conduct in managing the affairs of the university is, in effect, an action against the state, and the district courts have no jurisdiction of either the subject matter of the action or the person of the defendant. (*Hollister v. State,* 9 Ida. 13, 71 Pac. 541; *Thomas v. State,* 16 Ida. 82, 100 Pac. 761; *Moody v. State's Prison,* 128 N. C. 12, 38 S. E. 131, 53 L. R. A. 855; *Marion County v. Wilson,* 105 Ky. 302, 49 S. W. 8, 799; *State v. Regents of University,* 55 Kan. 389, 40 Pac. 656, 29 L. R. A. 378; *Oklahoma Agricultural etc. College v. Willis,* 6 Okl. 593, 52 Pac. 921, 40 L. R. A. 677; *Lane v. Minnesota State Agricultural Soc.,* 62 Minn. 175, 64 N. W. 382, 29 L. R. A. 708; 23 Am. & Eng. Ency. of Law, 83; *Alabama Girls' Industrial School v. Reynolds,* 143 Ala. 579, 42 So. 114; *Memphis etc. R. R. Co. v. Tennessee,* 101 U. S. 337, 25 L. ed. 960; *South & North Alabama R. R. Co. v. Alabama,* 101 U. S. 832, 25 L. ed. 973; *Gibbons v. United States,* 8 Wall. (U. S.) 269, 19 L. ed. 453; *Clodfelter v. State,* 86 N. C. 51, 41 Am. Rep. 440; *Chapman v. State,* 104 Cal. 690, 43 Am. St. 158, 38 Pac. 457; *Green v. State,* 73 Cal. 29, 11 Pac. 602, 14 Pac. 610; *Melvin v. State,* 121 Cal. 22, 53 Pac. 416.)

All the issues raised upon the material allegations in plaintiff's complaint, by the first defense in the answer of the defendant, had been determined in this court, adversely to the plaintiff, and were *res adjudicata.* (*First Nat. Bank v. Regents etc.,* 19 Ida. 440, 113 Pac. 735; Rev. Codes, sec. 595, subd. 3; *Moscow Hardware Co. v. Regents etc.*, 19 Ida. 429, 113 Pac. 731.)

Where a contract is breached by one of the parties thereto, the adverse party may either sue upon the contract and recover on it in so far as it is performed, as well as the value of his bargain in so far as it is unperformed, on showing a loss of profits, or he may because of the breach waive the contract and sue on *quantum meruit*, and recover the value of his services, but he cannot pursue both remedies. (*Gabrielson v. Hague Box & Lumber Co.*, 55 Wash. 342, 133 Am. St. 1032, 104 Pac. 635; Pomeroy's Code Rem., 3d ed., sec. 576; Maxwell on Code Pldgs., p. 108.)

C. J. Orland, for Respondent.

This court has held in an action involving the same claim, as an original proceeding in this court, that it was without jurisdiction and that the action should have been brought in the district court. (*Moscow Hardware Co. v. Regents*, 19 Ida. 420, 113 Pac. 731; *First Nat. Bank v. Regents*, 19 Ida. 440, 113 Pac. 735.)

These decisions of this court, so far as its jurisdiction is concerned, should be final, and especially as to these parties, who are the same as in the original proceedings heretofore referred to.

It would be a new departure in judicial procedure for a court to hold that it was without jurisdiction, and then hold that the merits involved were *res adjudicata*, by reason of a finding, order or judgment, in such court. (*State v. Keller*, 8 Ida. 708, 70 Pac. 1051.)

If this court in the former case had no jurisdiction of the subject matter, its decision and act would be void and of no force, and may be the subject of attack collaterally. (*Risley v. Phenix Bank*, 83 N. Y. 320, 38 Am. Rep. 421; *Thompson v. Whitman*, 18 Wall. (U. S.) 457, 21 L. ed. 897; *Sache v. Wallace*, 101 Minn. 169, 118 Am. St. 612, 112 N. W. 387, 11 Ann. Cas. 348, 11 L. R. A., N. S., 803; *Spoors v. Coen*, 44 Ohio St. 497, 9 N. E. 132; *Waldron v. Harvey*, 54 W. Va. 608,

102 Am. St. 959, 46 S. E. 603; *Rhode Island v. Massachusetts,*
12 Pet. (U. S.) 657, 9 L. ed. 1233.)

There are no substantial or harmful errors in the admission
or rejection of evidence or the instructions of the court, and
if there were any errors, they affected no substantial right
of the appellant and should be disregarded. (*Smith v. Field,*
19 Ida. 565, Ann. Cas. 1912C, 354, 114 Pac. 668.)

PER CURIAM.—This action was commenced against the
Board of Regents of the University of Idaho to recover a
balance for money advanced and material furnished in the
construction of a building to be used by the university.
Judgment was obtained for the sum of $6,506.35, and the
State Board of Education and the Board of Regents of the
University of Idaho, as successor to the old Board of Regents,
prosecuted this appeal.

There is no merit in the contention that the district court
was without jurisdiction and that the only jurisdiction to
hear this case was in the supreme court. This court held to
the contrary in *Moscow Hardware Co. v. Regents,* 19 Ida. 420,
113 Pac. 731, and *First Nat. Bank v. Regents,* 19 Ida. 440,
113 Pac. 735. The doctrine there announced is sound and
consonant with the provisions of the constitution and statute,
and is affirmed in so far as it applies to the Board of Regents
of the State University.

It is unnecessary for us to deal with the question presented
by appellant as to the right to maintain such an action against
the State Board of Education, which is also made the Board
of Regents of the University, for the reason that this action
arose before the adoption of the act of March 6, 1913, which
created the Board of Education, which is also the Board of
Regents of the University of Idaho. The statute makes this
board the successor to the old Board of Regents, and whether
or not an action can be maintained against this board, they
have the power and authority to defend an action previously
instituted for a pre-existing obligation.

There is no merit in the contention that the court erred
in refusing to require the plaintiff to elect between two al-

leged remedies. The remedies sought by the plaintiff are not inconsistent remedies. There was no error in the ruling of the court refusing to require an election.

We discover no error in this case prejudicial to the rights of the appellant or that would call for a reversal of the judgment.

Considerable argument has been made by appellant in this case as to the manner of collection of the judgment herein in the event it should be affirmed. That is not a question which confronts us on this appeal. It is clear, however, that no execution can issue in the case and that this judgment is merely an adjudication and judicial determination of the amount justly due from the appellant to the respondent. If the board does not pay the judgment or is not supplied with funds out of which to pay the same, respondent will have to go before the legislature and seek its relief through that channel. This is a mere suggestion, however, and is in no way essential to the determination of this case.

The judgment is therefore affirmed, with costs in favor of respondent.

(April 25, 1914.)

JOHN M. FIX, Respondent, v. H. N. GRAY, Appellant.

[140 Pac. 771.]

DELINQUENT TAXES—DELINQUENT TAX SALE—DILIGENCE OF TAXPAYER
—FAILURE TO GIVE NOTICE TO TAXPAYER OF DELINQUENCY.

1. Where a land owner owns two separate tracts of real estate in the same county aggregating 760 acres and resides in another county, and had been in the habit for more than twenty years of writing to the assessor for statement of the amount of taxes due for the year, and upon receiving the statement of the amount sending his check in payment therefor, and in the year 1907 wrote a similar letter to the tax collector inquiring the amount of his taxes, but failed to give a description of the land he owned in the county, and the assessor replied giving a statement of the amount due, and

such statement omitted a tract of 320 acres, and the land owner paid the amount called for by the statement and received his receipt therefor, and failed and neglected to read the description contained in the receipt, and consequently failed to observe that he had not paid the taxes on all of his real estate in the county, but the amount so paid was approximately the same as he had paid the previous year upon his entire holdings in the county, and the 320 acres were thereafter advertised and sold for delinquent taxes, and the time for redemption expired and a tax deed was issued to the purchaser, and during the subsequent years the land owner had continued to pay the taxes on this tract of land as well as his other holdings in the county, and he had no notice of delinquency of taxes or sale of the property for 1907 until after the issuance of the deed, and he thereupon tendered the amount which had been paid together with interest and penalties, *held*, that the property owner upon payment of the taxes, together with interest, penalties and costs, will be entitled to a decree canceling and setting aside the tax deed and quieting his title to such property.

2. Where property was sold for taxes delinquent for the year 1907, and the red ink entry was entered upon the tax-roll as required by statute, and thereafter an entry was made opposite the description of the same land and on the same roll that the tax had been canceled by order of the board of commissioners, and the land owner never had any notice that there were any delinquent taxes held against the land nor that it had been sold for delinquent taxes, and paid his taxes from year to year thereafter on such land, and upon discovering that the land had been sold for delinquent taxes and immediately upon the issuance of a tax deed therefor tendered the amount of taxes so paid together with interest, penalties and costs to the purchaser, *held*, that the land owner was entitled to have the deed surrendered and canceled and that the tax sale was irregular and voidable.

APPEAL from the District Court of the Second Judicial District for Latah County. Hon. Edgar C. Steele, Judge.

Action to cancel tax deed and to quiet title. Judgment for plaintiff. Defendant appealed. *Affirmed.*

James E. Babb, for Appellant.

In the case at bar the party knew he was the owner of two entirely separate and distinct tracts located in different places and he had been paying on these for twenty or twenty-five years, prior to the date of the payment in question, and he further knew that the county officers had been "as a rule" making a mistake every time he asked them for his taxes and leaving off this very piece of property and furnishing him with the tax only on the other. The form of assessment in Idaho was such as to bring about this mistake since the property owner's name would be inserted at different places in the same or different assessment-rolls for the same year, and one inquiring without giving a list of his property, would doubtless get the taxes which the clerk first found under his name where the name was first discovered in the book. This plaintiff testifies that he did not furnish any description of his land in his inquiry made that year.

It is the owner's duty to furnish a description of his property and failing to do so he can have no relief; plaintiff is seeking relief on the ground of mistake. Equity does not grant such relief, especially where innocent third parties will be interfered with, except on a showing of freedom from negligence on the part of the plaintiff. (*Menasha Woodenware Co. v. Harmon,* 128 Wis. 177, 107 N. W. 299; *Easton v. Doolittle,* 100 Iowa, 374, 69 N. W. 672; 2 Cooley on Taxation, p. 1048; *Elliot v. District of Columbia,* 3 MacArthur (D. C.), 396; *Scroggin v. Ridling,* 92 Ark. 630, 121 S. W. 1053; *Browne v. Finlay,* 51 Neb. 465, 71 N. W. 34; *Philadelphia Mortgage etc. Co. v. Omaha,* 63 Neb. 280, 93 Am. St. 442, 88 N. W. 523, 57 L. R. A. 150; *Lamb v. Irwin,* 69 Pa. 436; *O'Connor v. Gottschalk,* 148 Mich. 450, 111 N. W. 1048; *Hickman v. Kempner,* 35 Ark. 505; *McGahen v. Carr,* 6 Iowa, 331, 71 Am. Dec. 421; *Conklin v. Cullen,* 29 Mont. 38, 74 Pac. 72; *Hoffman v. Silverthorn,* 137 Mich. 60, 100 N. W. 183; *Raley v. Guinn,* 76 Mo. 263; *Solenberger v. Strickler's Admr.,* 110 Va. 273, 65 S. E. 566.)

A court of equity will not relieve a party from a mistake which is the result of its own negligence, when the channels of information are open to him and no fraud or deception is practiced upon him. (*National Union Fire Ins. Co. v. John Spry Lumber Co.,* 235 Ill. 98, 85 N. E. 256; *Glenn v. Statler,* 42 Iowa, 107; *Miller v. Powers,* 119 Ind. 79, 21 N. E. 455;

4 L. R. A. 483; 19 Cent. Dig. (Equity) 16, and authorities cited.)

In *Smith v. Davidson*, 23 Ida. 555, 130 Pac. 1071, relied on by respondent, the property owner had been thrice told by the assessor that she was exempt and need not pay. Here there was no element of mistake or neglect on her part, even if the land had been taxable. The mistake was wholly on the part of the assessor's office, in showing the property subject to the tax and advertising and selling it, after due notice from the owner.

Miles S. Johnson, for Respondent.

"When a taxpayer calls upon the proper officer for a statement of all taxes due from him, and receives a statement and pays all the taxes included therein, and afterward the land is sold for the nonpayment of taxes in arrears at the time the statement was furnished, but which were omitted from the statement by the neglect of the officer or clerk, the title of the taxpayer is not divested by sale." (*People ex rel. Cooper v. Registrar of Arrears*, 114 N. Y. 19, 20 N. E. 611; *Corning Town Co. v. Davis*, 44 Iowa, 622.)

"A payment by the owner of all sums made known to him by the treasurer is equivalent to an actual payment of the whole, and will prevent a valid sale of the land for an unpaid balance not made known by the treasurer." (*Breisch v. Coxe*, 81 Pa. 336, 345; *Pottsville Lumber Co. v. Wells*, 157 Pa. 5, 27 Atl. 409; *Harness v. Cravens*, 126 Mo. 234, 28 S. W. 971; *Hintrager v. Mahoney*, 78 Iowa, 537, 43 N. W. 522, 6 L. R. A. 50.)

"It is the duty of a town treasurer to furnish taxpayers with information as to the amount of taxes payable upon their lands in the township; and, as they have a right to rely upon that information, they cannot be prejudiced by its incorrectness." (*Gould v. Sullivan*, 84 Wis. 659, 36 Am. St. 955, 54 N. W. 1013, 20 L. R. A. 487; *Hough v. Auditor General*, 116 Mich. 663, 74 N. W. 1045; *Bray & Choate Land Co. v. Newman*, 92 Wis. 271, 65 N. W. 494; *Edwards v. Upham*, 93 Wis. 455, 67 N. W. 728; *Nelson v. Churchill*, 117 Wis. 10,

93 N. W. 799; *Randall v. Dailey,* 66 Wis. 285, 28 N. W. 352;
Cooley on Taxation, 3d ed., 809.) If a taxpayer inquires of
an officer, authorized by law to collect taxes, as to the amount
that is due from him and pays the amount stated, he is in the
same position as though he had actually paid the entire
amount that was really due, and a tax deed issued thereafter
is absolutely void. (*Smith v. Davidson,* 23 Ida. 555, 130 Pac.
1071.)

AILSHIE, C. J.—This action was instituted by the plaintiff
to quiet his title to a certain tract of land to which the defendant held a tax deed. The cause was tried and findings
and judgment were made and entered in favor of the plaintiff, and defendant has appealed.

The action involved a tract of 320 acres of land situated
in Latah county. It appears that the respondent has owned
this land since 1884 and during all the time he has lived in
the city of Lewiston, Nez Perce county. The evidence discloses that respondent has some 760 acres of land in Latah
county and that he was in the habit each year of writing
over to the assessor of Latah county for statement of the
amount of taxes due on his holdings in that county, and on
receiving statement would return a check in payment therefor.

It seems that the assessor failed to send out the usual tax
notices for the year 1907, and so respondent wrote the assessor to know what his 1907 taxes were, but did not give
a description of any land he owned, merely inquiring as to
the amount of taxes due on his property. The assessor replied, stating that his taxes were $133. Thereupon and on
the 27th of December, 1907, respondent mailed a check to the
assessor for the sum of $133 in payment of what he supposed
to be his total taxes on all his lands in that county for the
year 1907. As a matter of fact, when the officer had written
respondent he had only sent him a statement of the amount
due on one tract comprising 440 acres and had overlooked
stating the amount due on another and separate tract of 320
acres. Respondent testifies that he supposed this covered
his entire holdings and that he did not read the description

in his tax receipt and did not notice or observe that his check
for $133 had not paid his taxes on his entire 760 acres. It
is also shown that the taxes on the entire 760 acres for the
year 1906 had amounted to $146.56, and respondent testifies
that the amounts were so nearly the same that he supposed
and understood that the $133 for 1907 covered his entire hold-
ings in Latah county for that year.

In this way the taxes on the 320 acres of land for 1907
became delinquent, the property was advertised and sold
for delinquent taxes, and the appellant herein bid in the
property and after the time for redemption expired secured
a tax deed. Respondent continued to pay the taxes on this
land for each subsequent year of 1908, 1909, 1910 and 1911,
and appears to have had no notice of the delinquency for
1907, and testifies that he knew nothing of the matter until
after the issuance of the tax deed.

It also appears that the assessor failed to enter in red ink
on the assessment-roll of 1907 the amount of delinquent taxes
that had previously accrued against this property, and that
on the assessment-roll of 1908 the red ink entry appeared
against the property of a delinquent tax for 1907 with a
further record that the same had been canceled by order of
the board of county commissioners, and it also appears that
the record of the board of county commissioners actually shows
an order canceling this delinquent tax.

The record finally stood, therefore, as if the red ink entry
required by sec. 1755, Rev. Codes, had never been made, and
in that respect brings this case within the rule announced in
Parsons v. Wrble, 21 Ida. 695, 123 Pac. 638. There was nothing in the record to give notice to the property owner that
this land had been sold for delinquent taxes.

Again, the record is quite clear that respondent was acting
in good faith, endeavoring to keep his taxes paid, and that
he did in fact pay all the taxes he had any notice were standing against his property or that had ever been assessed against
it. The taxpayer was evidently acting in good faith, and on
the other hand the assessor and tax collector seem also to

have acted in good faith and not with any purpose of deceiving, defrauding or misleading respondent.

While the facts and circumstances differ, the principle of law here involved is similar to that announced in *Smith v. Davidson,* 23 Ida. 555, 130 Pac. 1071, and for the same reason and on the same principle entitles the property owner to the same equitable relief which was granted in that case. (See, also, *Randall v. Dailey,* 66 Wis. 285, 28 N. W. 352; Cooley on Taxation, 3d ed., 809.)

A number of other reasons, some of which are valid, have been advanced in support of the judgment of the trial court and to the effect that the respondent herein was entitled to the relief which the judgment awarded him. In view of the fact that we have concluded that the judgment in this case should be affirmed, it is unnecessary to discuss these several questions. It is quite clear that the respondent, who is the owner of this land, has acted in good faith, and while perhaps not as diligent as he might have been, he ought not to lose his property under the circumstances where he is ready and willing to reimburse the purchaser at the tax sale for all his outlay, together with interest and penalties. On the other hand, the appellant, who was the purchaser at this delinquent sale, has been in no way prejudiced and will in no way be a loser, and he will receive his money back, together with a high rate of interest and such penalties as the statute prescribes.

We shall not further discuss the questions arising in this case. The judgment should be affirmed, and it is so ordered. The appellant will be taxed with the costs of this appeal.

The respondent, as a condition to clearing his title and canceling this tax deed, should pay to the appellant or to the clerk for his use and benefit, all sums paid out by appellant, together with interest and penalties allowed on redemption, and should also pay the costs of this action in the district court. The appellant was not in any way at fault or to blame for bidding in this property, and he took a tax deed in the manner authorized and provided by law. He should not now be required to pay the costs and expenses entailed in the district court in having this deed set aside. The whole costs incurred in the district court should be taxed up against the respondent. On the other hand, if the district court rightly decided the case, as we think it did, and that decision was against the appellant and he saw fit to prosecute this appeal, he should pay the costs incurred in bringing the case to this court.

The cause will therefore be remanded to the district court, with directions to enter a modified decree in accordance herewith, and as modified the judgment of the district court will be affirmed, and it is so ordered. Costs of this appeal awarded in favor of respondent.

Sullivan, J., concurs.

———

(May 5, 1914.)

A. L. McREYNOLDS et al., Appellants, v. GEORGE HARRIGFELD et al., Respondents.

[140 Pac. 1096.]

Right of Way for Irrigation Ditch—Parol License—Effect of—Section 6007, Revised Codes, Construed—Placing Parties in Statu Quo.

1. A parol license for a right of way for a ditch, if sought to be declared perpetual, would be an easement or interest in real property, which can only be created by operation of law, or a conveyance or other instrument in writing, subscribed by the party sought to be charged.

2. *Held*, that where the evidence fails to disclose that licensees have expended considerable money or made valuable improvements in reliance upon a parol license for a right of way for a ditch, and fails further to show that benefits or advantages have accrued to licensors thereunder, this court will not "by operation of law" declare such parol license an easement and not within the inhibition of sec. 6007, Rev. Codes.

3. If parties are placed in their original position and with their original rights, they are "*in statu quo.*"

4. Mere naked possession by the licensees of a right of way created by parol license is not sufficient to authorize such license to be declared irrevocable.

APPEAL from the District Court of the Ninth Judicial District for Fremont County.   Hon. James G. Gwinn, Judge.

Action to quiet title to ditch and right of way for same across lands and to obtain an injunction restraining defendants from interfering with plaintiffs' use of same. *Affirmed.*

Millsaps & Moon and C. H. Lingenfelter, for Appellants.

A parol license to enter and construct a ditch over lands by a gratuitous consent of the owner operates as an irrevocable grant after entry and construction of the ditch, its interrupted use for two years and expenditure of money to make the water available for the purpose of irrigation. (*De Graffenried v. Savage,* 9 Colo. App. 131, 47 Pac. 902; *Tynon v. Despain,* 22 Colo. 240, 43 Pac. 1039.)

The open and visible use of an easement consisting of an irrigating ditch for six years is notice of such easement to the grantee of the servient tenement. (*Croke v. American Nat. Bank,* 18 Colo. App. 3, 70 Pac. 229.)

Where the owner voluntarily consents to the construction of an irrigation ditch across his land, the right of the owner to maintain and use it is absolute. (*Arthur Irr. Co. v. Strayer,* 50 Colo. 371, 115 Pac. 724; *Jones v. Bondurant,* 21 Colo. App. 24, 120 Pac. 1047.)

"It is no objection to gaining an easement by prescription that the same was originally granted or bargained for by parol. That the use began by permission does not affect the prescriptive right, if it has been used and exercised for the requisite period under claim of right on the part of the owner of the dominant tenement." (Washburn's Easements and Servitudes, 4th ed., 89; *Huff v. McCauley,* 53 Pa. 206, 91 Am. Dec. 203; *Ashley v. Ashley,* 4 Gray (Mass.), 197; *Jewett v. Hussey,* 70 Me. 433; *Stearns v. Janes,* 12 Allen (Mass.), 582;

Clark v. Glidden, 60 Vt. 702, 15 Atl. 358; *Incorporated Town of Spencer v. Andrew*, 82 Iowa, 14, 47 N. W. 1007, 12 L. R. A. 115; *Messick v. Midland Ry. Co.*, 128 Ind. 81, 27 N. E. 419.)

"While a parol license to enter upon real estate is generally revocable at the pleasure of the licensor, it is settled that such license cannot be revoked when the licensee, on the faith of the license, with the knowledge of the licensor, has expended his money and labor in carrying out the object of the license. This is on the principle of estoppel." (*School Dist. v. Lindsay*, 47 Mo. App. 134; *Schilling v. Rominger*, 4 Colo. 100; *Tynon v. Despain*, 22 Colo. 240, 43 Pac. 1039; *Lee v. McLeod*, 12 Nev. 280, 284; *Rerick v. Kern*, 14 Serg. & R. (Pa.) 267, 16 Am. Dec. 497; *Summer v. Stevens*, 6 Met. (Mass.) 337; *Arbuckle v. Ward*, 29 Vt. 43; *Snowden v. Wilas*, 19 Ind. 1014, 81 Am. Dec. 370; *Talbott v. Thorn*, 91 Ky. 417, 16 S. W. 88; *Gyra v. Windler*, 40 Colo. 366, 91 Pac. 36, 13 Ann. Cas. 841; *Bowman v. Bowman*, 35 Or. 279, 57 Pac. 547.)

A parol license through some act on the servient estate is, when executed, irrevocable. (Washburn on Easements, sec. 560; *Morse v. Copeland*, 2 Gray (Mass.), 302; *Johnson v. Skillman*, 29 Minn. 95, 43 Am. Rep. 192, 12 N. W. 149; *North Powder Milling Co. v. Coughanour*, 34 Or. 9, 54 Pac. 223; *Wyatt v. Larimer etc. Irrigation Co.*, 18 Colo. 298, 36 Am. St. 280, 33 Pac. 144.)

The agreement with McIntosh, Green and McGavin amounted to something more than a license. (*Chicosa Irrigating Ditch Co. v. El Moro Ditch Co.*, 10 Colo. App. 276, 50 Pac. 731.)

N. D. Jackson, for Respondents.

The permission granted by the respondents being oral was a mere license and was revocable at the will of the licensors. It was a privilege to do certain acts upon the lands of the respondents but carried no estate therein. (*Howes v. Barmon*, 11 Ida. 64, 114 Am. St. 255, 81 Pac. 48, 69 L. R. A. 568.) McIntosh, Green and McGavin, who obtained the permission from the respondents, paid no consideration therefor. (*Great*

Falls Water Works Co. v. Great Northern Ry., 21 Mont. 487,
54 Pac. 963; 25 Cyc. 646, 647; *Yeager v. Woodruff*, 17 Utah,
361, 53 Pac. 1045.)

None of the original licensees are parties to this action
and none of them are interested in the result.   The privilege
granted to McIntosh, Green and McGavin was personal to
them and could not by them be assigned.   (*Howes v. Barmon,
supra; Fabian v. Collins*, 3 Mont. 215; *Fischer v. Johnson*,
106 Iowa, 181, 76 N. W. 658; *Ward v. Rapp*, 79 Mich. 469, 44
N. W. 934; *Johnson v. Skillman*, 29 Minn. 95, 43 Am. Rep.
192, 12 N. W. 149; *Polk v. Carney*, 17 S. D. 436, 97 N. W.
360.)

WALTERS, District Judge.—The appellants herein, who
were plaintiffs below, brought this action in the trial court
to obtain decree quieting in them title to a certain ditch and
right of way for the same, across the lands of the respondents, who were defendants below, and to obtain an injunction
perpetually restraining defendants from interfering with
plaintiff's use of the same.

After trial the lower court found that plaintiffs based
their claim of title to said ditch and right of way for the
same upon the fact that the predecessors in interest of plaintiffs had procured from the defendants a verbal license to
construct said ditch across defendant's lands, and found
further as a matter of law that said verbal license was
revocable at the will of the defendants; that prior to the
commencement of said action defendants, by certain acts,
had revoked said license, and that plaintiffs had no right, title
or interest in and to said ditch, or a right of way for same
over or across the lands of defendants.

The facts involved in this case do not seem to be in serious
dispute, and disclose that in the year 1901 John McIntosh
and Oscar Green went to the residence of the defendant,
George Harrigfeld, and represented to him that they wished
to build a ditch across a certain tract of raw, uncultivated
land then owned by defendants, and situated some several
miles from defendant's residence.

The defendant Harrigfeld testified that in the early part of the summer of 1901 McIntosh and Green drove up to his home on a Sunday afternoon and that McIntosh stated that he had a little hay on his place that he would like to save, and asked permission to make a ditch across the land in question, and promising that when Harrigfeld desired to cultivate the land, should the ditch be found to be situated not as Harrigfeld desired, he would change the same to such location as Harrigfeld should indicate, and that it was upon such an understanding that permission was given to McIntosh to construct the ditch across such land.

McIntosh and Green, who testified on behalf of plaintiffs, corroborated Harrigfeld in part, testifying, however, that they had no recollection that Harrigfeld required as a condition that the ditch should later be changed should he so desire when he put the land in cultivation, but that they did not desire to testify that Harrigfeld had not so required.

McIntosh, Green, and a third person named McGavin, neither of whom are parties to this action, constructed the ditch and used the same for four or five years, when they severally disposed of their lands. Green and McGavin abandoned such ditch and claim no interest therein, the plaintiffs herein basing their claim of title to said ditch and right of way for same on mesne conveyances from McIntosh.

The trial court further found the facts to be that the licensees (McIntosh, Green and McGavin) constructed said ditch in the summer of 1901 and that they, and the successors in interest to the lands of McIntosh, used the same · until the year 1910, at which time the tenants of the defendants plowed and cultivated the land covered by said ditch; that the tenants of defendants in the year 1911 again plowed and cultivated the land covered by said ditch, but that in the month of July of said year the plaintiffs opened the ditch and again used the same; that in the year 1912 the plaintiffs again undertook to use said ditch, when they were prevented from so doing by defendants, whereupon plaintiffs instituted this action; that the land formerly owned by the licensee McIntosh, for the irrigation of which the license for the construction of said ditch was obtained, is the same land now owned by the plaintiffs; that said ditch when constructed was constructed with reference to the natural surface of the ground and without reference to the lines or boundaries of the same, and that the seepage from the same renders some portion of defendants' land wet and useless for farming, and that it is necessary for defendants to construct flumes over said ditch in order to irrigate some portions of their own land.

It further appears that in the year 1911 the plaintiff Mc-Reynolds and the defendant George Harrigfeld had some conversation about the location of the ditch in question, when Harrigfeld informed McReynolds that if he must take water across defendants' land, that defendants would grant plaintiffs a full right of way for the same across defendants' land, to be, however, constructed along the fence line and of sufficient capacity to convey the forty inches of water owned by plaintiffs, where defendant asserted it could be easily constructed, would cause no damage, and be out of the way of everybody. To this offer the plaintiff McReynolds refused to accede, insisting that if the ditch was rebuilt elsewhere it should be done by defendants.

Based upon this record the trial court found, as conclusions of law, that the oral license obtained by the licensees (McIntosh and Green) from said defendants for the construction of said ditch, and upon which plaintiffs based title, was revocable at the will of the defendants; that the defendants, prior to the institution of this action, had revoked said license; that the plaintiffs have no right or other interest in or to said ditch or a right of way for the same, and decree was entered accordingly, from which plaintiffs prosecuted this appeal.

(1) It thus appears that the precise question here for inquiry is, when will a parol license for a right of way for a ditch over land be made perpetual, having in mind that such right of way is an easement or interest in real property, which sec. 6007 of the Rev. Codes declares can only be created by operation of law, or a conveyance or other instrument in

writing subscribed by the party granting such easement or right of way?

Inasmuch as it is not claimed that any consideration passed to, or benefit has been received by, the defendants for the license granted to construct the ditch across defendants' land, this case therefore does not fall within the rule announced by this court upholding oral agreements for such purposes in the following cases: *Stowell v. Tucker*, 7 Ida. 312, 62 Pac. 1033; *Feeney v. Chester*, 7 Ida. 324, 63 Pac. 192; *Male v. Leflang*, 7 Ida. 348, 63 Pac. 108.

(2) It should further be borne in mind that the record in this case is absolutely silent as to what amount of money the licensees or their successors in interest may have expended, if any, in reliance upon their license, or oral permission to construct said ditch; what additional acreage or improvements, if any, licensees, or their successors, may have developed or made. It is not shown that the defendants permitted said ditch to be constructed because of any benefit or advantage which may accrue to them, nor that any benefits or advantages have accrued to defendants by reason of the construction of said ditch. The testimony merely shows that defendants had granted licensees permission to build the ditch, and that they had so built it.

The question involved in this appeal has received some considerable attention by the courts, and it has been held, as the most liberal view, that when the licensee has acted under the authority conferred and has incurred expense in pursuance of it, by making valuable improvements on his own property or on the right of way, that equity will regard it as an executed contract and will not permit it to be revoked, regarding it substantially as an easement, the revocation of which would be a fraud on the licensee.

The supreme court of Nevada, in the case of *Lee v. McLeod*, 12 Nev. 280, has held: "A parol license to erect a dam upon another's land, or to convey water from a stream running through the land of another, for the purpose of erecting and conducting a flouring-mill, is, in our opinion, irrevocable after the party to whom the license was given has executed it by erecting the mill, or otherwise expended his money upon the faith of the license.''

In the case of *Bowman v. Bowman*, 35 Or. 279, 57 Pac. 546, it is said: ''For the rule is well settled in this state that a parol license cannot be revoked after the licensee has expended money or performed labor in making valuable and permanent improvements on real property upon the faith of such license.''

The question here mooted seems to have been exhaustively considered by the supreme court of Oregon in the recent case of *Shaw v. Proffitt*, 57 Or. 192, Ann. Cas. 1913A, 63, 109 Pac. 584, 110 Pac. 1092, wherein the following language is quoted with approval:

''The cases are practically agreed that on strict common-law principles a bare license is revocable at the will of the licensor, even though executed; but it is held by a very respectable line of authorities, as in the reported case, that on principles of equity the revocation of a license after the licensor has stood by and permitted the licensee to incur considerable expense on the faith of the license would amount to a constructive fraud, working an estoppel in the licensee's favor.'' To the same effect is *Great Falls Water Works Co. v. Great Northern Ry. Co.*, 21 Mont. 487, 54 Pac. 963. See, also, 25 Cyc. 646, and cases cited.

This court has heretofore recognized such principle of law in the case of *Howes v. Barmon*, 11 Ida. 64, 114 Am. St. 255, 81 Pac. 48, 69 L. R. A. 568, where it is held that a court of equity will not lend enforcement to a parol license for an easement in realty where the party invoking its aid has not parted with any consideration or property, and no irreparable damage is suffered and no fraud is inflicted upon him, and where he is *in statu quo* at the time of the commencement of his action.

So in the case at bar, it does not appear that the plaintiffs, nor their predecessors in interest, parted with any consideration or property for the permission given; neither does it appear that plaintiffs will suffer irreparable damage by a denial of the court to enforce the specific performance prayed; nor does it appear that, should the court refuse to grant plaintiffs the relief asked, they will not be left in their original position, nor defeated of their original rights. On the contrary, they will be absolutely *in statu quo,* and hence it clearly appears this is not a case authorizing or justifying the interference of a court of equity to make perpetual or permanent a parol license for an easement in realty.

(3) In the case of *Daly v. Bernstein,* 6 N. M. 380, 28 Pac. 764, the supreme court of New Mexico says: " '*In statu quo*' means being placed in the same position in which a party was at the time of the inception of the contract which is sought to be rescinded."

As was said in *Howes v. Barmon, supra:* "But courts of equity grant relief in such cases upon the principal theory that the parties cannot be placed in the position they originally occupied, and therefore equity will compel them to live up to their agreements."

(4) All that may be said in the case here considered is, that the plaintiffs, or licensees, have been let into possession of the property or right of way for ditch, and such fact alone is not sufficient for a court of equity to declare that "by operation of law" the provisions of sec. 6007, Rev. Codes, need not be observed. (*Howes v. Barmon, supra,* and cases there cited.)

We conclude that upon the evidence as contained in the record, and the law applicable thereto, the trial court was authorized to enter the judgment appealed from, and said judgment is *affirmed,* with costs awarded to respondents.

Ailshie, C. J., and Sullivan, J., concur.

(May 7, 1914.)

GEORGE A. RICHARDSON, Respondent, v. JOSEPH D. BOHNEY, Appellant.

[140 Pac. 1106.]

HARMLESS ERROR—SUFFICIENCY OF EVIDENCE.

1. No judgment will be reversed upon appeal by reason of errors or defects in the proceedings below which do not affect the substantial rights of the parties.

2. Evidence examined, and *held* that there is substantial evidence to support the verdict and findings of the jury.

APPEAL from the District Court of the Ninth Judicial District for Fremont County. Hon. James G. Gwinn, Judge.

Action to ascertain and determine the true boundary line between the homestead entries of plaintiff and defendant. Judgment for plaintiff. Defendant appeals. *Affirmed.*

Millsaps & Moon, for Appellant, cite no authorities on points decided.

Soule & Soule, for Respondent.

"The only question presented on this appeal is the sufficiency of the evidence, and there is evidence which supports the verdict. For these reasons the judgment must be affirmed." (*Meeker v. Trappett,* 24 Ida. 198, 133 Pac. 117.)

WALTERS, District Judge.—This action was commenced by the plaintiff for the purpose of ascertaining and determining the true boundary line between the homestead entries of the plaintiff and the defendant, Joseph D. Bohney. The plaintiff and defendant differed as to the location of said line as established by the original government survey. By answer the defendant put in issue the allegations of the complaint as to the location of said line, and such question was by trial presented to a jury who returned a general verdict in favor of the plaintiff, and made answers to interrogatories in each instance favorable to the contention of the plaintiff. The defendant brings this action here for review upon ten assignments of error, the first nine of which urge that the court erred in overruling the defendant's objection to some several questions on the ground that the same were incompetent, immaterial and irrelevant; were not proper rebuttal, or were not proper cross-examination.

(1) The record discloses that this action consumed five days for trial and that twenty-two witnesses were called and testified, the greater number of them being returned to the stand more than once, the transcript of the testimony being over six hundred pages in volume. From the length of time occupied in trying the case and the number of witnesses called, it may readily be seen that it would be quite extraordinary if erroneous rulings of the trial court upon some several questions on the ground that the same were incompetent, immaterial and irrelevant, or not proper rebuttal or proper cross-examination, would constitute reversible error, such as to authorize or justify the judgment being disturbed, where no controlling principle of law was involved. Counsel for appellant, however, concede that the law of the case as announced and invoked by the trial court was correct.

We can note no error in the particulars assigned sufficient to authorize or require a reversal of this judgment, for if there is any error in the rulings questioned it is but purely technical, and in no sense and no manner prejudicial, and at most can only be such harmless or technical error as abounds in every trial of some considerable length which is vigorously, and oftentimes blunderingly, contested. This court is admonished by sec. 4231 of the Revised Codes that no judgment shall be reversed or affected by reason of errors or defects which do not affect the substantial rights of the parties.

(2) It is further lastly urged by counsel for appellant in assignment of error No. 10 that the verdict and findings of the jury were not in accordance with the evidence. It may in short be said that there is very substantial evidence

to support the verdict and findings of the jury and the judgment duly entered herein, and that in accordance with the provisions of sec. 4824 of the Revised Codes requiring "that whenever there is substantial evidence to support a verdict the same shall not be set aside," the judgment entered herein should not be set aside and is hereby *affirmed.*

Costs are awarded to respondent.

Ailshie, C. J., and Sullivan, J., concur.

———

(May 8, 1914.)

RAWSON–WORKS LUMBER CO., a Corporation, Appellant, v. WALKER RICHARDSON et al., Respondents.

[141 Pac. 74.]

EMINENT DOMAIN—CONDEMNATION OF LAND—PUBLIC USE—MEASURE OF VALUE—COMPENSATION — EVIDENCE — INCOMPETENT — MEASURE OF DAMAGES—INSTRUCTIONS.

1. *Held,* that it was error for the court to admit evidence showing the value to the appellant of the land to be condemned, since such valuation is not based on the market value of the land but on the necessities of appellant.

2. Compensation for the land taken in such cases must be reckoned from the standpoint of what the land owner loses by having his property taken and not from the benefit the property may be to the party desiring to take it, and it is error to admit evidence of the necessities of the condemnor and the value of the property to him for the purpose to which he intends to apply it.

3. *Held,* that the court erred in giving certain instructions.

4. *Held,* that the court erred in refusing to give certain instructions requested by the plaintiff.

APPEAL from the District Court of the Second Judicial District, in and for Idaho County. Hon. Edgar C. Steele, Judge.

Action under the eminent domain statutes of the state for the condemnation of certain lands for public use. Judgment for the defendants. *Reversed.*

G. W. Tannahill, for Appellant.

Under the provisions of our statutes, the public acquired an easement over the land in question and embraced in the streets and alleys; the defendants did not own the fee-simple title thereto, but, notwithstanding this fact, the defendants were awarded the full price for the same, or a value equal to the lots and blocks. The instruction of the court and the evidence admitted relative to the value of the streets and alleys and the acreage therein was error. (*In re Lawrence Street,* 136 N. Y. Supp. 845; *In re Titus Street,* 152 App. Div. 752, 137 N. Y. Supp. 817.)

"Compensation must be reckoned from the standpoint of what the land owner loses by having his property taken, not by the benefit which the property may be to the other party to the proceedings." (15 Cyc. 757; 2 Lewis on Eminent Domain, 3d ed., p. 1231; *Black River etc. R. R. Co. v. Barnard,* 9 Hun (N. Y.), 104; *In re Boston Hoosac Tunnel etc. Ry. Co.,* 22 Hun (N. Y.), 176; *In re New York, Lackawanna & W. Ry. Co.,* 27 Hun (N. Y.), 116; *Sullivan v. Board of Supervisors of Lafayette Co.,* 61 Miss. 271; *Five Tracts of Land v. United States,* 101 Fed. 661, 41 C. C. A. 580; *San Antonio & A. P. Ry. Co. v. Southwestern Tel. etc. Co.* (Tex. Civ. App.), 56 S. W. 201; *Virginia & Truckee R. Co. v. Elliott,* 5 Nev. 358; *Providence etc. R. R. Co. v. City,* 155 Mass. 35, 29 N. E. 56; *Union Depot etc. Co. v. Brunswick,* 31 Minn. 297, 47 Am. Rep. 789, 17 N. W. 626; *St. Louis etc. Ry. Co. v. Knapp, Stout & Co.,* 160 Mo. 396, 61 S. W. 300; *Ligare v. Chicago etc. Ry. Co.,* 166 Ill. 249, 46 N. E. 803; *West Virginia etc. Ry. Co. v. Gibson,* 94 Ky. 234, 21 S. W. 1055; *Chicago B. & Q. Ry. Co. v. Chicago,* 166 U. S. 226, 17 Sup. Ct. 581, 41 L. ed. 979; *San Pedro etc. Ry. Co. v. Board of Education,* 35 Utah, 13, 99 Pac. 263; *Selma, Rome & D. R. R. Co. v. Keith,* 53 Ga. 178; *Oregon R. & Navigation Co.*

v. Taffe, 67 Or. 102, 134 Pac. 1024; *Portneuf-Marsh Valley Irr. Co. v. Portneuf Irr. Co.,* 19 Ida. 483, 114 Pac. 19.)

W. N. Scales and McNamee & Harn, for Respondent Richardson.

It was not error for respondents to be allowed to show by either direct or cross-examination of witnesses that the lands sought to be condemned were more valuable for mill sites or terminal grounds than for any other purpose, or to show special value of the property for the purposes for which it is taken. This rule is permissible in aiding the jury to arrive at its market value. (*Spring Valley Waterworks v. Drinkhouse,* 92 Cal. 528, 28 Pac. 681; *San Diego Land & Town Co. v. Neale,* 78 Cal. 63, 20 Pac. 372, 3 L. R. A. 83; *Mississippi & R. River Boom Co. v. Patterson,* 98 U. S. 403, 25 L. ed. 206; *Sargent v. Inhabitants of Merrimac,* 196 Mass. 171, 124 Am. St. 528, 81 N. E. 970, 11 L. R. A., N. S., 996, and note; *McGovern v. City of New York,* 229 U. S. 363, 33 Sup. Ct. 876, 57 L. ed. 1228, 46 L. R. A., N. S., 391; *Oregon R. & Nav. Co. v. Taffe,* 67 Or. 102, 134 Pac. 1024; *Sacramento Southern R. Co. v. Heilbron,* 156 Cal. 408, 104 Pac. 979; *United States v. Chandler-Dunbar Water Power Co.,* 229 U. S. 53, 33 Sup. Ct. 667, 57 L. ed. 1063; *Columbia etc. Rafting Co. v. Hutchinson,* 56 Wash. 323, 105 Pac. 636.)

Upon the lawful vacation of a street, the abutting land owner holds the fee presumably to the center line, discharged from all easements, either in favor of the public or other abutting owners. (*Lamm v. Chicago St. P. M. & O. Ry. Co.,* 45 Minn. 71, 47 N. W. 455, 10 L. R. A. 268.)

For exhaustive discussion of abutter's right in streets, see notes to *Rasch v. Nassau Electric R. Co.,* 36 L. R. A., N. S., 673, 838.

A. S. Hardy, for Respondent Wagner.

"The general rule is that if evidence erroneously admitted during the progress of a trial be distinctly withdrawn by the court, the error is cured." (38 Cyc. 1440, 1630; *McDannald*

v. Washington etc. R. R. Co., 31 Wash. 585, 72 Pac. 481;
Pennsylvania Co. v. Roy, 102 U. S. 451, 26 L. ed. 141.)

Any adaptability of lands for any purpose, whether previously used for such purpose or not, is to be taken into consideration in fixing the market value. (Portneuf-Marsh
Valley Irr. Co. v. Portneuf Irr. Co., 19 Ida. 483, 114 Pac. 19;
15 Cyc. 757; San Diego Land etc. Co. v. Neale, 78 Cal. 63,
20 Pac. 372, 3 L. R. A. 83; Mississippi & R. R. Boom Co. v.
Patterson, 98 U. S. 403, 25 L. ed. 206; Little Rock Junction
Ry. Co. v. Woodruff, 49 Ark. 381, 4 Am. St. 51, 5 S. W. 792;
Oregon R. & Nav. Co. v. Taffe, 67 Or. 102, 134 Pac. 1024; In
re New York L. etc. Ry. Co., 27 Hun (N. Y.), 116; Currie v.
Waverly etc. R. R. Co., 52 N. J. L. 381, 19 Am. St. 452, 20
Atl. 56; Brown v. Forest Water Co., 213 Pa. 440, 62 Atl. 1078;
In re Daly, 72 App. Div. 394, 76 N. Y. Supp. 28; Hartshorn
v. Illinois Valley Ry. Co., 216 Ill. 392, 75 N. E. 122; Cox v.
Philadelphia etc. R. Co., 215 Pa. 506, 114 Am. St. 979, 64
Atl. 729; In re New York W. & B. Ry. Co., 151 App. Div.
50, 135 N. Y. Supp. 234.)

SULLIVAN, J.—This is an action under the eminent domain law of the state. The plaintiff is a lumber manufacturing corporation and has considerable timber land in this state.
The entire acreage involved in this proceeding, including the
interest owned by the appellant corporation, is 48.53 acres,
of which appellant is the owner of 33.01 acres and the defendants of about 15.52 acres.

On the trial the jury awarded the defendants the sum of
$6,352, and the court entered judgment for that amount in
favor of the respective defendants in accordance with their
respective interests in and to said 15.52 acres of land. The
appeal is from the judgment.

Counsel for appellant contends that the value of the land
fixed by the jury is excessive and that the court erred in
the admission of evidence as to the value of the land; in
giving certain instructions to the jury and refusing to give
certain instructions requested, and in assessing the damages

to a portion of the land owned by respondent A. C. Richardson not condemned under this proceeding. Some forty-three errors are specified.

(1) Assigned errors 1 to 32, inclusive, are argued by appellant in his brief as one assignment of error. Those assigned errors relate to the admission of certain evidence and the refusal of the court to strike out certain evidence.

The case was tried upon the theory that the proper measure of damages to be awarded was the value of this particular tract of land to the appellant corporation. Nearly all of the opinion evidence given by the witnesses as to the value of said land was based upon the benefits that the appellant would derive from obtaining said land and not upon the damages suffered by the respondents or the actual market value of the land, and the trial proceeded upon the theory that the land owner was to be compensated, not in the amount he is damaged, but in the amount the party seeking to condemn is benefited; and the compensation was not reckoned from the standpoint of what the land owner loses by having his property taken, but by the benefit which the property may be to the condemning party.

The following are samples of question after question that were propounded to witnesses, which the witnesses were permitted to answer over the objection of counsel for appellant:

"Q. Mr. Nichols, if this tract of land sought to be condemned is the only available tract of land that the Rawson-Works Lumber Company could condemn for the purpose for which they seek to condemn, and if they had approximately a million dollars invested in timber and in their flume and in their sawmills and in their planing plant and power-house, and they owned one-half of this tract of land, what would you say the other half of the tract of land would be worth to them per acre for the purpose for which they seek to condemn?"

"Q. If this land sought to be condemned, this flat, is the only practical and available ground for the terminus of the flume for the planing-mill plant and piling yards, and if this Rawson-Works Lumber Company desires it for the outlet to something like $700,000 or a million dollars' worth of lumber, wouldn't that enhance its value, the fact it is the only available ground for that purpose?"

"Q. From your knowledge of the works which have been constructed by the Rawson-Works Lumber Company, and from the proposed erection of their planing plant, power-house, and western terminus of this flume, and considering that they have approximately one million dollars invested in their timber holdings, and in their flume and mills, and that this particular tract of land is suitable and available for this purpose, what would you say this land is worth per acre as a terminus of this flume, or for a planing plant or for the purpose to which the plaintiff seeks to put it?"

"A. Taking into consideration, as they state, having all of this vast amount of timber, and no other place for a mill site, I wouldn't let it go—I would have it if it cost me a thousand dollars an acre if I were in their place; that is the straight of it."

Much evidence along the line indicated by the above questions and answer was introduced over the objection of counsel for the defendant. This evidence clearly shows that the witnesses based their opinions almost wholly upon the fact that said land would be very valuable to the appellant company. The admission of all of this class of evidence was highly prejudicial to the appellant and placed a false value upon the land in question, for the reason that such valuation was not based on the real market value of the land but on the necessities of the appellant and the importance of its acquiring this particular tract of land for the conduct of its business. The court recognized that this was not proper evidence, but still permitted it to go in over the objection of the defendant, and undertook by an instruction to the jury to prevent their considering it at all, which instruction the jury clearly did not follow in its verdict, but gave more attention to this prejudicial evidence than to the instruction of the court. Why a court will permit highly prejudicial evidence to be repeated time and again in a case and permit its introduction on the trial over the objection of the defendant, is beyond our comprehension. It is a well-recognized fact that a court by an instruction cannot eradicate from the minds of a jury prejudicial evidence that has been testified to many times by different witnesses and admitted over the strenuous objection of counsel.

Compensation in condemnation cases must not be based on the benefits to be derived by the appellant, but upon the damages suffered by the respondent or the owner of the land— in other words, its market value. The numerous comments made by the court in regard to the matter on objection being made by counsel for appellant were clearly prejudicial. The rule that the land owner is to be compensated, not in the amount he is damaged, but in the amount the party seeking to condemn is benefited, is an erroneous rule.

It is stated in the text in 15 Cyc. 757, that compensation in such cases must be reckoned from the standpoint of what the land owner loses by having his property taken, and not by the benefit the property may be to the other party to the proceedings, and that authority holds that the particular purpose for which the condemnor seeks the land cannot be considered as an element of damages to the land owner.

In 2 Lewis on Eminent Domain, 3d ed., p. 1229, the author says:

"It is not a question of the value of the property to the owner. Nor can the damages be enhanced by his unwillingness to sell or because of any sentiment which he has for the property. On the other hand, the damages cannot be measured by the value of the property to the party condemning it, nor by its needs of the particular property."

This doctrine is fully sustained by the numerous authorities cited by said authors, and is also fully sustained by this court in *Portneuf-Marsh Valley Irr. Co. v. Portneuf Irr. Co.*, 19 Ida. 483, 114 Pac. 19.

(2) The 33d error assigned goes to the court's instruction directing the jury to compute the amount of interest to each of the defendants in the land sought to be condemned, and to include the streets and alleys in such computation. It appears from the record that said tract had been platted and

on said plat were represented certain streets and alleys. The plat was properly acknowledged and recorded as required by law and some of the defendants acquired title to the land by lots and blocks, and counsel contends that under the provisions of sec. 2304, Rev. Codes, that the acknowledgment and recording of such plat is equivalent to a deed in fee simple to the public of such portion of the premises platted, for streets and alleys; that such plat has never been vacated, and for those reasons the court erred in permitting said defendants to recover for the portion of said land included in such streets and alleys.

There world be merit in this contention provided the lots bordering on such streets had been sold to people who used such streets and alleys, but in the case at bar, all of the parties who purchased lots and blocks, aside from the defendants, have sold their interests to the appellant corporation and have no further use for the streets and alleys, and that will be the condition of the defendants provided their title is acquired by this condemnation suit. The company will get in this proceeding the entire interest of the defendants, including all their right, title and interest in and to the streets and alleys, and the court did not err in instructing the jury as above stated.

(3) It is next contended that the court allowed $50 damages to A. C. Richardson for land not taken and not condemned. A. C. Richardson testified on the trial as follows: "Q. And you did not see why it should damage it, either, did you?" (Referring to said land.) "A. No, it did not damage it." Under that evidence it was error to award $50 damages when the owner, or reputed owner of the land, testified that it had not been damaged.

(4) The refusal of the court to give instructions Nos. 1, 2, 3 and 5 requested by the appellant is assigned as error. Those instructions state the correct principles of law as applied to the facts of this case. Since the record is so full of prejudicial evidence admitted over the objection of appellant relating to the benefit this land would be to the appellant company, the court ought to have given said instructions.

Many of the witnesses testified that they based their evidence of value wholly upon the benefit said tract would be to the appellant company and not on the market value of the land. It appears that the respondent A. C. Richardson, less than two years prior to the commencement of this action, paid only $140 for the land for which the jury awarded him $2,220.00. In such cases the rule of law is well established that compensation must be reckoned from the standpoint of what the land owner loses by having his property taken and not by the benefit which the property may be to the other party to the proceedings. The court erred in refusing to give said instructions.

For the reasons above given, the judgment must be reversed and a new trial granted, unless within thirty days from the sending down of the *remittitur* in this case the defendants file with the clerk of the district court an acceptance of $300 per acre for the number of acres of land each claims to own and that is sought to be condemned in this action.

Costs awarded to the appellant.

Ailshie, C. J., concurs.

ON PETITION FOR REHEARING AND TO TAX COSTS.

(June 1, 1914.)

COSTS IN CONDEMNATION SUIT.

    1. In a suit in condemnation, under the constitution and statutes of this state, the costs of the proceeding and cost of appeal should be taxed against the condemnor where the appeal has been prosecuted by the party seeking condemnation.

McNamee & Harn and W. N. Scales, for Respondent Richardson.   A. S. Hardy, for Respondent Wagner.

The matter of costs was not especially presented to the court and the decision was made without argument thereon and contrary to the rule of this court heretofore adopted in cases for condemnation of property under the laws of eminent domain. (*Portneuf-Marsh Valley Irr. Co. v. Portneuf Irr. Co.*, 19 Ida. 492, 114 Pac. 19; approved in *Oregon R. & Navigation Co. v. Taffe*, 67 Or. 102, 135 Pac. 515; see, also, cases cited therein.)

AILSHIE, C. J.—A petition for rehearing on the question of taxation of costs has been filed, and the appellant has filed a cost bill and respondents have moved to strike the cost bill from the files. When the original opinion was filed in this case, the court in awarding costs overlooked the fact that this was a suit in *condemnation*, and that under such circumstances the condemnor should be required to pay all costs of the proceeding. It has been established by the decisions of this court and is well supported by the principles of justice and the constitution that the condemnor must pay just compensation for the property taken and must pay all costs necessarily incurred in the condemnation proceedings. (*Portneuf-Marsh Valley Irr. Co. v. Portneuf Irr. Co.*, 19 Ida. 483, 114 Pac. 19, and *Washington Water Power Co. v. Waters*, 19 Ida. 595, 115 Pac. 682. See, also, *Oregon R. & Navigation Co. v. Taffe* 67 Or. 102, 135 Pac. 515.)

The original opinion filed herein will therefore be modified so as to require the appellant to pay all costs both in the trial court and the cost of appeal. Appellant's cost bill will be stricken from the files.

Sullivan, J., concurs.

(May 8, 1914.)

ANDREW COOLIN, Respondent, v. W. A. ANDERSON, Appellant.

[140 Pac. 969.]

CONTRACT FOR CONVEYANCE OF FRACTIONAL SECTION ABUTTING ON LAKE —UNPLATTED AREA BETWEEN MEANDER LINE AND WATER LINE— MISTAKE OF LAW NOT BASIS FOR EQUITABLE RELIEF — ATTORNEY FEE IN FORECLOSURE SUIT.

1. Where the original government survey of a fractional section of land, abutting on a lake, left a tract of nearly 40 acres between the meander line of said section and the water line of the lake, which tract remained unsurveyed, and was not shown on the government plat, and thereafter a dispute arose between land owners and land claimants, as to whether such unplatted land belonged to the fractional section, such dispute involved a question of law which could not be determined by the parties without adjudication in the proper court.

2. The mistake of a purchaser, as to what was included within the bounds of a legal subdivision of land, cannot be the basis for equitable relief in his favor as against an action for the recovery of the purchase price, when it is not shown that any material misrepresentations were made by the vendor, and it appears that complainant himself was negligent.

3. *Held*, that the trial court committed no error in the admission or exclusion of evidence.

4. *Held*, that an attorney fee of $1,000, under the circumstances of this case, where the amount of $10,181.64 was recovered against defendant in a suit for foreclosure of a mortgage, defendant having gone to trial on an answer and cross-complaint, was properly allowed by the trial court.

APPEAL from the District Court of the Eighth Judicial District for Kootenai County. Hon. R. N. Dunn, Judge.

Action for foreclosure of mortgage and counterclaim on part of defendant. Judgment for plaintiff.   *Affirmed.*

E. N. LaVeine, for Appellant.

The court was not warranted in allowing an attorneys' fee of $1,000, for the reason that no contract was shown to have been entered into between the respondent and his attorneys. (*Porter v. Title Guaranty & Surety Co.,* 17 Ida. 364, 106 Pac. 299, 27 L. R. A., N. S., 111.)

The rule is that a purchaser may be entitled to an abatement of his purchase price for a defect in his title, a partial failure of title, a deficiency in quantity of land purchased or on account of other facts which make it inequitable that the vendor should receive the full purchase price. (*Dykes v. Bottoms,* 101 Ala. 390, 13 So. 582; *Archer v. Turrell,* 66 Ark. 171, 49 S. W. 568; *Ladd v. Chaires,* 5 Fla. 395; *Satterfield v. Spier,* 114 Ga. 127, 39 S. E. 930; *Scheible v. Slagle,* 89 Ind. 323; *Carlton v. Smith,* 33 Ky. Law, 647, 110 S. W. 873; *Rockwell v. Wells,* 104 Mich. 57, 62 N. W. 165; *Ransom v. Shuler,* 43 N. C. 304; *Sutton v. Kautsman,* 6 Ohio Dec. 910, 8 Am. Law Rec. 657; *Tyson v. Eyrick,* 141 Pa. 296, 23 Am. St. 287, 21 Atl. 635; *Rich v. Scales,* 116 Tenn. 57, 91 S. W. 50; *Holden v. Reed,* 45 Tex. Civ. App. 465, 101 S. W. 288; *Clarke v. Hardgrove,* 7 Gratt. (Va.) 399; *Baldwin v. Brown,* 48 Wash. 303, 93 Pac. 413; *Smith v. Ward,* 66 W. Va. 190, 66 S. E. 234, 33 L. R. A., N. S., 1030; *Turner v. Pierce,* 31 Wis. 342.)

McNaughton & Berg, for Respondent.

It cannot be said in the case at bar that Anderson had the same means of knowing whether or not the disputed meadow lands belonged to section 7 that Mr. Ulbright had. (*Murray v. Paquin,* 173 Fed. 319.)

This court has passed upon questions very similar to those raised in this case, concerning alleged fraud or misrepresentation in the making of a contract. (*Tipton v. Ellsworth,* 18 Ida. 207, 109 Pac. 134; *Smith v. Smith,* 4 Ida. 1, 35 Pac. 697.)

"A misrepresentation in order to affect the validity of a contract must relate to some matter of inducement to the making of the contract where the purchaser relies on the superior knowledge and information of the seller, not where the purchaser has equal means of information and may rely upon his own judgment." (*Hill v. Bush,* 19 Ark. 522; *Bennett v. Hickey,* 112 Mich. 379, 70 N. W. 900.)

"The law will not aid or help either of the parties on the ground that he himself has not used diligence and common sense, if the means of information is equally open to both and there has been a mistake without fraud or falsehood." (*Nelson v. Hudgel*, 23 Ida. 327, 130 Pac. 85; *Breshears v. Callender*, 23 Ida. 348, 131 Pac. 15.)

The $1,000 allowed by the lower court for attorneys' fees was a reasonable amount. Attorneys must necessarily exercise considerable care and painstaking in the preparation of the case under an answer as broad and indefinite as the answer filed in this case. (*Warren v. Stoddard*, 6 Ida. 692, 59 Pac. 540.)

AILSHIE, C. J.—Fractional sec. 7, Tp. 51 N., R. 5 W., B. M., in Kootenai county, is a strip of land containing somewhat over 200 acres, bordered on the west by the irregular meander line of Mud (or Sucker) lake. At the north end of this section the shore line of the lake, curving sharply to the west, diverges abruptly from the meander line, leaving a tract of nearly 40 acres between the meander line and the water line, immediately south of the north line of sec. 7 extended. In other words, the government surveyor fixed his meander line so far inland at this point that the tract of land referred to was left outside of any legal subdivision of his survey, and therefore had no official existence on the government plat.

The nondescript status of this tract of land gave rise to the controversy adjudicated in the case of *Ulbright v. Baslington,* 20 Ida. 542, 119 Pac. 294; and is also the moving cause of litigation in the present case.

On July 6, 1909, A. Ulbright and Mary H. Ulbright, husband and wife, entered into a contract with W. A. Anderson of Spokane, Wash., appellant herein. By this contract the Ulbrights agreed to convey to Anderson certain real and personal property situated in Kootenai county, including most of sec. 7, above referred to, in exchange for certain lands owned by Anderson in the state of Washington. The Ul-

brights were also to receive the further consideration of
$10,000 to be evidenced by two promissory notes in their favor,
secured by a mortgage on the Idaho lands conveyed to Anderson. One of these notes was to be for $2,000, due Aug. 25,
1909, the other for $8,000, to be due in five years. The notes
and mortgages were to be executed and deeds exchanged as
soon as certain conditions, specified in the contract, had been
complied with, such as surveying the land to be conveyed
by the Ulbrights, and furnishing abstract of title. The Ulbrights agreed to give possession of the property they were
transferring upon the payment of the $2,000 note.

On July 26, 1909, the parties executed the papers called
for by their contract of July 6th, although the Ulbrights
had not yet complied with the terms of the contract which
required them to have their land surveyed. It appears that
the appellant Anderson was already negotiating for a sale
of the Ulbright property and desired to acquire title to it
without further delay. He was therefore willing to waive
compliance with certain preliminary requirements called for
by the contract. On this date, therefore, at the solicitation
of Anderson, the deeds were executed by the parties, the notes
and mortgage were signed by Anderson and the papers placed
in escrow, to be delivered upon Anderson taking up the
$2,000 note.

The original contract of July 6th excepted from the transfer
of fractional sec. 7 about twenty acres at the south end of
the section, and it contained the following provision: "First
parties agree to pay second party $40 in cash for each acre
that the land in sec. 7, herein transferred, falls short of 200
acres above the waters of Sucker Lake; said payment of cash
to be made upon the termination of this contract." On
Aug. 19, 1909, the same parties made a supplemental contract,
wherein is recited the conveyance to Anderson of July 26th,
and continuing as follows:

"WHEREAS, it was understood and agreed by and between
the parties hereto that the said Anderson was to have possession of said lands on or before August 25, 1909; and

"Whereas, certain controversies have arisen between the parties of the first part and pretended owners of a portion of the lands above described; and

"Whereas, the said parties of the first part are unable to give possession of the lands in controversy and are also unable to give possession to the party of the second part of the crop of hay on the lands in controversy, at the time as agreed upon;

"Now, Therefore, as a consideration for the extending of the time to the parties of the first part to obtain possession of the lands in controversy for and on behalf of the party of the second part, and as a waiver of the rights of the said W. A. Anderson as to the crop of hay now standing and growing upon said lands in controversy, the parties of the first part do hereby agree to convey to the party of the second part the following described lands, situate in Kootenai County, State of Idaho, to wit":

Then follows a description of the twenty acres remaining in section 7 which had been excepted by the Ulbrights in their deed of July 26th, after which the agreement concludes with the following paragraph:

"It being understood, however, that this agreement does not in any way release the parties of the first part from the terms of the warranty deed first above mentioned, and from using all diligence in obtaining possession of the disputed lands for the party of the second part herein and that said title is to be obtained by said parties of the first part for the party of the second part within a reasonable time from date hereof."

On the same day, Aug. 19th, Anderson paid the $2,000 note specified in the contract, though by the terms of the contract it was not due until the 25th, and the papers evidencing the entire transaction were delivered to the parties entitled to them, including a deed for the remaining twenty acres in sec. 7 not included in the original contract of July 6th.

By the terms of the mortgage given the Ulbrights to secure Anderson's $8,000 note, the mortgagees had the option of declaring the note and mortgage due on default of any interest payment. No payments of interest were ever made. On

Jan. 9, 1912, the Ulbrights assigned the note and mortgage to
one Perry Krebs, and on Oct. 30, 1912, Krebs assigned to
Andrew Coolin, the respondent in this case. Soon after obtaining this assignment Coolin began foreclosure proceedings,
upon the termination of which he secured judgment in the
lower court for $10,181.64, and the further sum of $1,000
as attorney fees, and costs, from which judgment this appeal
was taken.

During the whole period of these transactions between the
Ulbrights and Anderson, a dispute had been in progress between the Ulbrights and certain land owners or claimants
adjoining them on the north,—Baslington and Wright,—as
to the ownership of the unsurveyed and unplatted tract of
land referred to in the beginning of this opinion. The contention of appellant is that the Ulbrights concealed this dispute from him at the time he contracted for the purchase of
sec. 7, and that Mr. Ulbright positively represented to him,
at the time he showed him over the land, that the unsurveyed
and unplatted tract referred to was a part of sec. 7, thereby
inducing him to make the purchase.

In his answer the defendant admitted the execution of
the note and mortgage and the nonpayment of interest, but
denied that the plaintiff was the lawful holder. In his affirmative defense he recites the conditions of the contract of
July 6th, and makes the following allegation:

"That at the time of said purchase of said section seven
(7) hereinabove set forth, in order to induce the defendant
herein to make said purchase and to execute said mortgage and
said notes as a part of the purchase price thereof, said above
mentioned A. Ulbright and Mary H. Ulbright, his wife, did
show to this defendant said section seven (7) hereinabove set
forth and included in said mortgage, and did, at the time of
showing said lands take this defendant upon said section
seven and show him the north line of said section seven and
show him all of the land lying south of said north line of said
section seven between said north line of said section seven
and the water line of what is known as Sucker lake, and did,
at said time represent to this defendant, that they were the

owners of and possessed of all of said section seven, and did represent to this defendant, that all of the land lying south of the north line of said section seven, and particularly the land lying between said north line of said section seven and the water line of said Sucker lake, bounded on the west by the north and south line of said section seven, which said line is the same as the west line of Township Fifty-one (51), Range Five (5) W., B. M., when extended into the waters of Sucker lake, was owned by said A. Ulbright and Mary H. Ulbright, his wife, and was a part of said section seven, and did sell the same to this defendant as a part of said purchase and sale.

"That said land so shown and represented to be owned and possessed by said A. Ulbright and Mary H. Ulbright, his wife, in said section seven, as above set forth, between the north line thereof, and the said water line of Sucker lake, was very valuable land, and this defendant, relying on the value thereof and the representations made by said A. Ulbright and Mary H. Ulbright his wife, that they were the owners thereof, was thereby induced to purchase said lands as above set forth, and to execute said notes and mortgage set forth in the complaint."

In a succeeding paragraph he alleges his damage in the sum of $10,000 on account of not being placed in possession of said land.

Defendant's allegations of misrepresentation on the part of the Ulbrights, as to the land embraced in sec. 7, were not proved on the trial; in fact, the preponderance of the testimony was the other way. Against the testimony of Anderson that these representations were made is the testimony of Ulbright, to the effect that Anderson was informed, before the contract of July 6th was entered into, of the dispute in regard to the unsurveyed land. Ulbright is corroborated in this by the witness Mauser, who went with Ulbright and Anderson at the time Ulbright showed Anderson the boundaries of the land he proposed to sell to appellant. Mauser testified that Ulbright said at that time in the presence of Anderson: "He figured about fifteen or sixteen acres in that meadow, but that he was not positive that that belonged to section 7."

By referring to the recitals in the agreement of Aug. 19, 1909, above quoted, it is apparent that Anderson was at that time certainly aware of the controversy over the land in dispute, since one of the considerations for the deeding of the additional twenty acres by the Ulbrights was, "Whereas, certain controversies have arisen between the parties of the first part (Ulbrights) and pretended owners of a portion of the lands above described; and

"Whereas, the said parties of the first part are unable to give possession of the lands in controversy."

Nevertheless, at this time Anderson proceeded to make the first payment of $2,000 on the contract and the purchase was consummated by delivery of the deeds to the property.

It is contended by counsel for appellant that language in the contract of Aug. 19th amounts to an unconditional guaranty of title from Ulbright to the land in controversy. A reading of the contract, the material parts of which we have set forth above, will show that it does not bear out such construction. As already stated, the contract begins by reciting the conveyance made to Anderson by Ulbrights on June 26th, and it then describes exactly, *by legal subdivisions*, the lands conveyed by Ulbrights at that time. It specifies "and all of section seven (7) except a strip of ground," followed by the reservation already mentioned. When, therefore, the contract goes on to say: "Whereas, certain controversies have arisen between the parties of the first part and pretended owners of a portion of the *lands above described*," the assumption is plainly made that the lands in dispute are a part of sec. 7, and it is evident that only upon that assumption did Ulbright contract to use "all diligence in obtaining possession of the disputed lands for the party of the second part herein, and that said title is to be obtained by said parties of the first part for the party of the second part within a reasonable time from date hereof." The conclusion follows that when the "disputed lands" were adjudicated not to belong to sec. 7, Ulbright's obligation to secure title for them to his grantee ceased.

Soon after the deal was closed between Anderson and the Ulbrights for the transfer of sec. 7, the Ulbrights, in accordance with their agreement of Aug. 19th, began a suit in the district court against Baslington for possession of the disputed area. This suit was decided in Ulbright's favor in the district court and appealed to this court, in which the judgment of the lower court was reversed. (*Ulbright v. Baslington*, 20 Ida. 542, 119 Pac. 294.) By this decision it was held that "the appellant (Wright, intervenor), is entitled to take the upland between his meander line and the lake within side or boundary lines drawn from the end of the meander line at each side of his tract of land to the center of the lake," and Wright accordingly secured the disputed land. That controversy was thus finally settled adversely to the contention of Ulbright and his grantee Anderson.

In our opinion the vital and controlling question in this case is: Can the mistake of a purchaser, as to what is included within the bounds of a legal subdivision of land, be the basis for equitable relief in his favor as against an action for the recovery of the purchase price?

As above stated, the appellant entirely failed to prove at the trial that any deceit or imposition was practiced upon him by the vendor Ulbright. The evidence shows that the bargain was of appellant's seeking; his own testimony discloses that the original contract for the transfer of this property was drawn from memoranda made by appellant himself. This contract is carefully drawn, with the evident design of protecting appellant in every possible way. However, appellant did not wait for certain preliminary requirements or conditions of the contract to be performed by the Ulbrights before making the first payment and receiving his deed. Again, he was the active or moving party, and, as the evidence shows, induced the Ulbrights against their inclination to accelerate the transaction and close the deal, in advance of the time specified in the contract, in order that he might acquire title and be in a position to make another deal which he had in view. All this time he had knowledge, according to the preponderance of the testimony, of the uncertainty existing as to the actual area of fractional sec. 7. Moreover, according to the abstract of title to the property, which is an exhibit in the case, he had constructive notice that a claim to the disputed area was of record in the county recorder's office at the time he signed the original contract on July 6th. When the deeds were exchanged and the transaction consummated on Aug. 19th, he voluntarily waived the contractual requirement for the establishment of lines and corners, and it is apparent that at least a part of the consideration for the deeding of the additional twenty acres which he received from the Ulbrights on that date was the relinquishment on his part of any claim to rebate on the purchase price, should sec. 7 eventually prove to contain less than 200 acres.

Counsel for respondent have cited in their brief a number of cases on the question of mistake in contract, most of which relate to the question of equitable relief for mistakes of fact. As held by this court in a recent case:

"Where parties are mutually cognizant of the facts acted upon, or stand upon the same footing with relation to them, and there exists no fiduciary relation between them, the law will not lend its aid to help the injured party for the simple reason that he has not himself used diligence and common sense, if the means of information is equally open to both parties, and there has been a mistake without fraud or falsehood." (*Nelson v. Hudgel,* 23 Ida. 335, 130 Pac. 85.)

A somewhat different question is raised in the present case. The controversy as to the legal area of fractional sec. 7 involves not a question of fact, but a question of law. By no known method of investigation for the ascertainment of facts could it be determined how this question might be resolved in the courts.

Suppose, for instance, Anderson had insisted that Ulbright comply with that provision of the original contract which required of Ulbright that "All lines and corners are to be properly extended and marked according to official survey," and an expensive and elaborate survey had accordingly been made. It is apparent that the legal question as to whether the unsurveyed and unplatted tract of land in controversy belonged to sec. 7 would not have been affected in the least by such survey. The only means of settling that question was by judicial procedure. Ulbright appears in good faith to have promptly resorted to that mode of determination. Almost immediately after the contract of July 6th was made he began suit in the district court to have this matter adjudicated.

It is obvious that neither he nor anyone else could know in advance what would be the result of that suit. In other words, Anderson took his chance on the issue of this litigation. Even if the Ulbrights made the misrepresentations to Anderson in reference to this land being a part of sec. 7, which Anderson avers, such misrepresentations would have been statements of a proposition of law.

"A statement of a proposition of law which the defendant had just as good an opportunity to ascertain the correctness of as had the plaintiff, whether true or false, could not be used as a defense in an action upon the note." (*Smith v. Smith,* 4 Ida. 1, 35 Pac. 697.)

It may indeed be admitted that the rule, that a mistake of law does not excuse, would not apply where the mistake of one party to the contract was induced by misrepresentations of the other. But, as we have seen, no such misrepresentations have been proved in this case.

It may also be conceded that where ignorance of the law on the part of both parties to a contract has conferred on one of them an unconscionable advantage, and where there has been neither misrepresentation on one side nor negligence on the other, the rule will be relaxed in a court of equity. But here again we are confronted with the circumstance that appellant in this case was not an innocent purchaser. His own contract of Aug. 19th discloses his knowledge of the doubt which clouded the title to the land in controversy; nevertheless he hastened to make his first payment and conclude the transaction.

Considerable documentary evidence was introduced at the trial of this case, including the papers which evidence the transactions between the parties, and in particular a number of letters written by the appellant subsequent to the consummation of the negotiations. The latter are of slight evidentiary value, as we view the question at issue. These letters disclose an excusable endeavor on the part of Anderson to commit his grantor, Ulbright, to a guaranty of title to the land in dispute, and to hold him responsible in damages for failure to give possession. There are also appended to the deposition of the witness Golden in the transcript copies of papers entitled Defendant's Exhibits "A" and "B" for identification, the contents of which appear to be identical, purporting to be signed by Ulbright and "to agree to settle in full with said Anderson for all losses which shall or may result from not having peaceable possession of, said crops properly harvested and possession of said lands and buildings, for the year 1910, and as long thereafter as quiet and peaceable possession of said lands and crops is disputed or denied by any person or claimant of ownership thereto." It is not clear, however, that the originals were admitted in evidence, and their authenticity was disputed on the stand by Mr. Ulbright.

In the view which the court takes of the underlying equities of this case, it is unnecessary to discuss whether respondent was a holder in due course, or whether the successive transfers of the note were properly alleged and proved. Appellant's contention that respondent took the note subject to all defenses may be conceded, but it cannot aid defendant when his defenses fail. The trial judge was liberal in his admission of evidence which might for any reason be material or relevant to the points at issue. We have carefully gone over the evidence, and we do not find any error in that regard. Neither do we find any prejudicial error in the rulings of the court below excluding certain offered evidence on behalf of defendant. Counsel particularly assigns as error the court's refusal to admit the files in the case of *Ulbright v. Baslington,* already referred to. The court committed no error in that respect, as the matter offered was not shown to be material to the issues, and its admission would not have aided appellant. Exception is also taken to the allowance of an attorney fee of $1,000. Plaintiff in his complaint prayed for a fee of $1,500, which the lower court reduced to $1,000, and under the circumstances of this case we are not inclined to disturb the amount fixed by the trial court.

The judgment of the lower court is affirmed. Costs awarded in favor of respondent.

Sullivan, J., concurs.

ON PETITION FOR REHEARING.

(June 16, 1914.)

AILSHIE, C. J.—A petition for rehearing has been filed on behalf of appellants, from which it would appear that counsel do not clearly apprehend the grounds upon which the decision of the court was based or its legal effect. It is true, as urged by counsel, that a court of equity may properly, under certain circumstances, grant relief from the consequences of a mistake of law, but not when the party seeking the relief has himself been negligent in safeguarding his interests, and is charged with notice of doubtful title as regards the property he is bargaining for, before consummating the transaction of which he complains.

Counsel calls our attention to the following language in the opinion: "Soon after the deal was closed between Anderson and the Ulbrights for the transfer of section 7, the Ulbrights, in accordance with their agreement of August 19th, began a suit in the district court against Baslington for possession of the disputed area," and it is pointed out that this suit was started on July 22d, nearly a month previous to the contract of Aug. 19th, and could not, therefore, have been in pursuance of that contract. The closing of the deal referred to in the sentence above quoted was evidenced by the original contract of July 6th, to which the contract of Aug.

19th was ancillary. In any event it is immaterial whether the Ulbrights began this suit in pursuance of the contract of July 6th, or in accordance with a later understanding which was evidenced by the contract of Aug. 19th, or independent entirely of any express agreement so to do. The record shows that soon after the negotiations for the property were substantially closed by the contract of July 6th, they did in apparent good faith begin and prosecute a suit for the purpose of acquiring title to the land in dispute on behalf of their grantee.

The petition for rehearing is denied.

Sullivan, J., concurs.

(May 9, 1914.)

AUGUST FOX, Respondent, v. SPOKANE INTERNATIONAL RAILWAY COMPANY, Appellant.

[140 Pac. 1103.]

SPECIFIC PERFORMANCE—PART CONSIDERATION FOR RAILROAD RIGHT OF WAY—CONSTRUCTION OF CROSSING.

1. Where a railroad company purchased a right of way across the lands of F. and paid certain cash consideration and entered into an agreement to construct a crossing over its right of way and track for the convenience, use and benefit of F., and for such consideration and upon the execution of such a contract F. conveyed to the railroad company such right of way, and the company constructed its road thereon, it will not be sufficient excuse to constitute a defense to an action for specific performance of the contract that the roads by and over F.'s land have been changed and that the railroad track at the place where the crossing was to be constructed runs through a deep cut instead of on the surface, and that it will be necessary to build an overhead crossing instead of a grade crossing, and that the expense of constructing and maintaining the same will be heavier than was anticipated by the company at the time the contract was made.

2. Where the knowledge or means of knowledge of the future condition or changes that may take place are peculiarly within the

possession of the railroad company which is about to construct a railroad and has agreed to maintain a crossing over its right of way and track, and it enters into a contract to maintain a crossing, it will not thereafter be heard to complain on the ground that the contract was unfair and became more onerous than was anticipated at the time the contract was entered into by reason of the track having to be laid through a cut instead of on the surface of the ground, and that other conditions have changed since the contract was entered into.

3. Facts of this case examined and considered and *held* that it is a proper case for the specific performance of the contract and that no just defense is presented which would excuse or relieve the company from specific performance.

APPEAL from the District Court of the Eighth Judicial District for Bonner County. Hon. John M. Flynn, Judge.

Action for specific performance. Judgment for plaintiff. Defendant appealed. *Affirmed.*

Allen & Allen and H. H. Taylor, for Appellant.

The changed conditions existing now to what they existed at the time the contract was made has made it very inequitable and unjust to compel a specific performance of the contract. (Pomeroy on Contracts (Specific Performance), sec. 185, and authorities cited.)

G. H. Martin, for Respondent.

The rule for the specific enforcement of a contract for the construction and maintenance of an improvement has most often been applied to railroad companies which acquire the right of way from the land owner on the faith of its contract to construct for the convenience of the owner a passage beneath or over its track; to fence its right of way; to construct a station; to put in a sidetrack for owner's convenience; to bridge its tracks or to build a road, or wharf, or a drain. (36 Cyc. 584; *Baltimore etc. R. Co. v. Brubaker*, 217 Ill. 462, 75 N. E. 523; *Owens v. Carthage etc. Ry. Co.*, 110 Mo. App. 320, 85 S. W. 987; *Gloe v. Chicago etc. R. Co.*, 65 Neb. 680, 91 N. W. 547; *Johnson v. Ohio River R. Co.*, 61 W. Va. 141,

56 S. E. 200; *Post v. West Shore R. Co.*, 123 N. Y. 580, 26
N. E. 7; *Cincinnati etc. R. R. v. Wall*, 48 Ind. App. 605, 96
N. E. 389; *Taylor v. Florida East Coast R. Co.*, 54 Fla. 635,
127 Am. St. 155, 45 So. 574, 14 Ann. Cas. 472, 16 L. R. A.,
N. S., 307.)

The defense of hardship and expense in maintaining farm
crossings does not avail the company when such crossings are
necessary for the convenient use of the plaintiff's farm.
(*Baltimore etc. R. Co. v. Brubaker, supra.*)

We have no statutory provision in Idaho for the construction by railway companies of a private crossing. The case
of *Lane v. Pacific & I. N. Ry. Co.*, 8 Ida. 230, 67 Pac. 656, is
decisive of the case at bar.

AILSHIE, C. J.—This action was brought to compel the
appellant railway company to construct an open crossing over
its track where it runs through the respondent's land, and
to recover damages for the failure and neglect so to do. It is
alleged and admitted that on or about the 8th of November,
1905, respondent and appellant entered into an agreement,
by the terms of which respondent agreed to convey to the
railway company a strip of land one hundred feet wide, being
fifty feet on each side of the center line of its railroad track,
across the S. E. ¼ of the N. W. ¼ and the N. W. ¼ of the
N. E. ¼ of sec. 32, and thereafter the railway company constructed its road across this land. The company agreed to
pay the respondent $125 in cash, and to construct and main-
tain an open crossing over its right of way and track near
by the respondent's residence. The right of way granted
runs through respondent's land, dividing it into two tracts,
one on each side of the railroad track. Pursuant to this
agreement the respondent executed and delivered to appellant
a deed for the right of way across the land, and appellant paid
therefor $125, and at the same time executed and delivered
to respondent a written agreement for the construction of the
crossing, which agreement is as follows:

"Laclede, Idaho, Nov. 8, 1905.

"Pursuant to a deed executed this date for a right of way granted by August Fox to the Spokane International Railway Company across NW. ¼ of NE. ¼ and SE. ¼ NW. ¼, Sec. 32, Twp. 56 N., R. 3 W., Boise Meridian, the said railway agrees to construct and maintain an open crossing across said right of way on the road used by said Fox leading east from his residence.

> "(Signed)   SPOKANE INTERNATIONAL RAIL-
> .WAY COMPANY,
>> "By ARTHUR J. SHAW,
>>> "Right of Way Agent."

After the road was constructed the matter ran along from time to time without any crossing being made, and in the meanwhile it appears that some change was made in the public road or thoroughfare across and by respondent's land. In the summer of 1912 the railroad company fenced its right of way without making provision for the construction of the crossing as provided for in its agreement. Thereafter, on the 5th day of August, 1912, respondent, through his attorney, made written demand upon appellant for the construction of the crossing, and thereafter, on the 6th day of August, 1912, the president of the appellant company, D. C. Corbin, wrote to the attorney for respondent in reply to the demand for the construction of the crossing as follows:

"Spokane International Railway Co.

> "Spokane, Washington, August 6, 1912.

"Mr. G. H. Martin, Attorney, Sandpoint, Idaho.

"Dear Sir—I have your letter of the 5th inst. You may inform your client that we will comply with our agreement with him very shortly.

> "Yours truly,
>> "(Signed)   D. C. CORBIN, President."

The controversy arose over the fact that the railroad company had made a deep cut through respondent's land in the place where it was agreed this crossing should be maintained, and it became impracticable to construct and maintain a grade crossing, but, on the contrary, would be necessary to construct and maintain an overhead crossing in the event any crossing is maintained there at all.

The chief contention made by appellant is that to construct and maintain an overhead crossing over appellant's road will be a continuing and perpetual expense and charge on the railroad company, and that the failure to construct such crossing can be adequately compensated in damages and that under such circumstances specific performance should not be ordered. In justification and support of this contention appellant quotes at length from Pomeroy on Contracts, at sec. 185, where the author discusses the subject of specific performance as follows:

"Not only must the agreement be fair and reasonable in its terms and its surrounding circumstances, it is also a well-settled doctrine that its specific execution must not be oppressive—that is, the performance must not be a great hardship to the parties. This rule includes the one treated of in the last section—since every unfair contract is essentially unconscionable and hard—but it is more extensive—since the oppressive nature of the performance may result from the situation or relations of the parties exterior to and unconnected with the terms of the contract itself or the circumstances of its conclusion. The oppression and hardship, therefore, which fall within the scope of the doctrine may result from the unequal, unconscionable provisions of the contract itself, or from external facts, events or circumstances which control or affect the situation and relations of the defendant with respect to the performance."

In our opinion, the present case is not one presenting such facts as will bring it within the rule which Mr. Pomeroy suggests. Here the contract was fairly made and the facts were equally known to both parties. The promise to construct and maintain the crossing was part of the consideration for the right of way, and while its maintenance will be a continuing and permanent charge on the railroad company, that was necessarily included in the terms of the contract and must have been foreseen and contemplated at the time of the execution of the contract.   While it may not have been anticipated that a grade crossing could not be maintained, that knowledge was peculiar to the railroad company and not to the land owner, and respondent cannot be charged with such knowledge or with in any way overreaching appellant in securing a contract for a more expensive crossing than it could foresee or anticipate.   The company had charge of establishing its grades and in so laying its road as to make a cut at the place where this crossing was to be built and maintained.   On the other hand, if the court should refuse to decree a specific performance of this contract, it would result in perpetually lessening the value of respondent's land and impairing its use to the owner, and if he should want to sell it to someone else, he would not be able to realize as much from such sale without this crossing as he would be able to get with it.

This case seems to fall within the rule adopted in *Lane v. Pacific & I. N. Ry. Co.*, 8 Ida. 230, 67 Pac. 656, and the discussion contained in the opinion of that case is well applicable here.

The judgment should be affirmed, and it is so ordered. Costs awarded in favor of respondent.

Sullivan, J., concurs.

(May 9, 1914.)

H. W. SOULE, Trustee for the ASHTON HARDWARE & IMPLEMENT COMPANY, a Corporation, Bankrupt, Respondent, v. FIRST NATIONAL BANK OF ASHTON, a Corporation, Appellant.

[140 Pac. 1098.]

ERRONEOUS INSTRUCTIONS — REQUISITE PROOF — INTENT — BURDEN OF PROOF—STATUTE REPEALED—ADMISSION.

1. Instructions examined and found erroneous.

2. In an action by a trustee of a bankrupt estate to set aside a transfer on the ground that a preference has, by such transfer, been created within the inhibition of the act of Congress, and the several acts amendatory thereof, to establish a uniform act of bankruptcy in the United States, said trustee must prove by sufficient evidence that the bankrupt (1) while insolvent, (2) within four months of the bankruptcy, (3) made the transfer in question, (4) that the creditor receiving the transfer will be thereby entitled to obtain a greater percentage of his debts than other creditors of the same class, and (5) that the creditor had reasonable cause to believe that the enforcement of such transfer would effect a preference.

3. In an action of this character an inquiry as to the intent of the bankrupt to effect a preference is not necessary.

4. The burden of proof that the creditor had reasonable cause to believe that the enforcement of a transfer would effect a preference is upon the trustee.

5. An instruction based upon a legislative enactment which had theretofore been repealed, and which was not then in force, is error.

6. Instruction based upon lack of denial, and admission thereby made, examined and found sufficient.

APPEAL from the District Court of the Ninth Judicial District for Fremont County. Hon. James G. Gwinn, Judge.

Action to recover the value of notes and money, and to set aside the transfer of the same as a preference prohibited by the bankruptcy act. Judgment for plaintiff. Defendant appealed. *Reversed.*

N. D. Jackson, for Appellant.

The right of the trustee in bankruptcy to avoid a preference is made to depend not upon the fact that the preference was given, but upon the knowledge of the person receiving. (*Coder v. Arts*, 213 U. S. 223, 29 Sup. Ct. 437, 53 L. ed. 772, 16 Ann. Cas. 1008.)

Soule & Soule, for Respondent.

In a case where a fact is alleged in the complaint and not denied in the answer, the jury should be instructed that the fact is admitted in the pleadings (where the pleadings are verified as they are in this case). (*Tevis v. Hicks*, 41 Cal. 123; *Irwin v. Buffalo-Pitts Co.*, 39 Wash. 346, 81 Pac. 849; *Landers v. Bolton*, 26 Cal. 393; *Baker v. Baker*, 13 Cal. 87, 98.)

"The rules of pleading, under our system, are intended to prevent evasion, and to require a denial of every specific averment in a sworn complaint, in substance and in spirit, and not merely a denial of its literal truth, and whenever the defendant fails to make such denial, he admits the averment." (*Higgins v. Wortell*, 18 Cal. 333; *Woodworth v. Knowlton*, 22 Cal. 164, 169; *Landers v. Bolton*, 26 Cal. 417; *Camden v. Mullen*, 29 Cal. 564; *Blood v. Light*, 31 Cal. 115; *Marsters v. Lash*, 61 Cal. 622.)

WALTERS, District Judge.—This action was brought in the trial court by H. W. Soule as trustee for the Ashton Hardware and Implement Company, a bankrupt, as plaintiff, against the First National Bank of Ashton, as defendant.

The complaint charges that certain notes and moneys of the property of the hardware and implement company were placed in the hands of defendant bank for safekeeping pending settlement and payment of the claims of the creditors of the hardware and implement company, and that within four months prior to the institution of the bankruptcy proceedings, the defendant bank conspired with the hardware and implement company and converted the notes and money to its

own use, and refused, upon demand, to deliver the same to the
trustee; that said act of conversion thus created the defendant
bank a preferred creditor in violation of the act of Congress
of the United States to establish a uniform act of bankruptcy.
Plaintiff asks for judgment against defendant for the value
of the notes and money and that the transfer of the same be
set aside as a preference prohibited under said bankruptcy
act.

(1) After answer the cause was tried to a jury and judgment rendered in favor of the plaintiff as prayed for. The
defendant appeals and assigns as error the giving of certain
instructions by the court.

Instructions Nos. 3 and 6 were in part, and as objected to,
as follows:

"3. You are therefore instructed that if you find that the
notes in question in this case were not transferred and assigned by the bankrupt company to defendant in good faith
and four months prior to the date of filing the petition in
bankruptcy and that defendant refuses to account for them to
plaintiff, then the plaintiff is entitled to recover their value
in this action, and if you find that the money in question was
not placed in defendant bank in the regular course of business
as hereinafter defined, but was placed therein for the benefit
of all creditors, then the title to the same is also in the plaintiff and he is entitled to recover the same in this action."

"6. You are further instructed that where a preference,
as defined in the last instruction, is given by a bankrupt to
one creditor over other creditors, that it is the duty of the
trustee of the bankrupt to take such proceedings as may be
necessary to set such preference aside, and any property that
is taken by one creditor from the bankrupt which creates or
will operate as a preference as defined in the last instruction,
takes the same subject to the title of the trustee to recover
the property or its value to be taken back into the estate of
the bankrupt and distributed as provided under the bankrupt
act. And, if you find from the evidence that within four
months before the filing of the petition in the bankruptcy
proceedings the bankrupt made a transfer of the notes in

question to the defendant and the effect and force of such
transfer would be to enable the bank to obtain a greater
percentage of the debt due the bank than any other such
creditor of the same class, then you are instructed that such
transfer is void, and that the plaintiff is entitled to recover
the said property, or its value from said defendants in this
proceeding.''

It is objected by the appellant that said two instructions
are at fault in that they do not take into consideration the
provisions of subdiv. "b" of sec. 13 of chap. 487 of the Laws
of the 57th Congress, approved February 5, 1903 (32 U. S.
Stats. at L. 797), amending sec. 60 of the old act and defining
the conditions under which a preference shall be voidable by
the trustee, said subdiv. "b" being in part as follows:

"b. If a bankrupt shall have given a preference, and the
person receiving it, or to be benefited thereby, or his agent
acting therein, shall have had reasonable cause to believe
that it was intended thereby to give a preference, it shall be
voidable by the trustee, and he may recover the property or
its value from such person. . . . . "

Appellant urges that instructions 3 and 6, *supra*, should,
because of the provision last quoted, be qualified by requiring,
before the trustee can recover, proof that the defendant bank
"had reasonable cause to believe that it was intended thereby
to give a preference," and that such omission constitutes a
fatal defect.

It is asserted by counsel for appellant, and conceded by
counsel for respondent, that subdiv. "b" of sec. 13, *supra*,
was the law at the time this action was instituted, but our
investigation has led to the discovery that such was not the
law, inasmuch as said subdiv. "b," upon which counsel rely,
was further amended by chap. 412 of the Laws of the 61st
Congress, approved June 25, 1910 (36 U. S. Stats. at L.
838), which amendment was in force a year prior to the institution of the bankruptcy proceedings involved herein, and
almost three years prior to the trial of this action, and was
a part of the law to be followed by the trial court in this
action.

Said subdiv. "b," as amended by sec. 11 of chap. 412 of the Laws of the 61st Congress, approved June 25, 1910, in so far as the same is pertinent to this inquiry, is in language as follows:

"If a bankrupt shall have procured or suffered a judgment to be entered against him in favor of any person or have made a transfer of any of his property, and if, at the time of the transfer, or of the entry of the judgment, or of the recording or registering of the transfer if by law recording or registering thereof is required, and being within four months before the filing of the petition in bankruptcy or after the filing thereof and before the adjudication, the bankrupt be insolvent and the judgment or transfer then operate as a preference, *and the person receiving it or to be benefited thereby, or his agent acting therein, shall then have reasonable cause to believe that the enforcement of such judgment or transfer would effect a preference,* it shall be voidable by the trustee and he may recover the property or its value from such person. . . . . "

It will be noted that while the trial court in instructions 3 and 6 advised the jury under what circumstances the transfer in question would be void and the plaintiff entitled to recover, the statement is entirely omitted that before such transfer would be void and the plaintiff entitled to recover, that it must also be proven by plaintiff that the defendant bank "had reasonable cause to believe that the enforcement of such judgment or transfer would effect a preference."

(2) In other words, the plaintiff in this case, before a right of recovery can be had must prove by sufficient evidence not only that the bankrupt (1) while insolvent, (2) within four months of the bankruptcy (3) made the transfer in question, and (4) that the creditor receiving the transfer will be thereby entitled to obtain a greater percentage of his debt than other creditors of the same class (*Kimmerle v. Far,* 189 Fed. 295, 111 C. C. A. 27), but must also in addition prove (5) that the creditor "had reasonable cause to believe that the enforcement of such judgment or transfer would effect a preference."

The jury was not advised that the plaintiff's right of recovery was predicated also upon this last requirement, and they were thus permitted to find a verdict against defendant upon an insufficient and an incorrect statement of required proof.

(3) It will be noted that prior to the amendment of 1910, in an action of this character, the intent of the bankrupt to effect a preference must be shown, but that by said amendment such proof is not now required. This statement finds expression in 1 Loveland on Bankruptcy, 978, in the following language:

"Prior to the amendment of 1910 the intent of the bankrupt to prefer was essential to a preference.

"The act as originally passed, and as amended in 1903, included as an element of voidable preference that the creditor 'had reasonable cause to believe that it was intended thereby to give a preference.' This language was held to imply that the debtor must intend the transfer to be a preference at the time it was made. The intent of the bankrupt might be presumed from the necessary result of the transaction.

"This language of section 60 of the act was changed by the amendment of 1910 to 'had reasonable cause to believe the enforcement of such judgment or transfer would effect a preference.' This makes the intent of the debtor immaterial. The test is clearly the effect of the transaction without regard to the intent of the debtor."

(4) In reference to the burden of proof as to the reasonable cause of belief that the enforcement of a contested transfer would effect a preference, it is stated in 3 Remington on Bankruptcy, 419, that "the burden of proof of the existence of the reasonable cause of belief is on the trustee"; citing *Getts v. Janesville Grocery Co.*, 163 Fed. 417; *Calhoun County Bank v. Cain*, 152 Fed. 983, 82 C. C. A. 114.

(5) It is urged by counsel for plaintiff, respondent here, that the error complained of in instructions 3 and 6 is cured by instruction 16 given by the court to the jury, which is as follows:

"The mere giving of a preference to a creditor of the bankrupt within four months of the filing of a petition in bankruptcy, or after the filing of a petition in bankruptcy, does not make the preference void, and it is not even voidable unless the creditor or his agent acting therein had reason to believe that it was intended thereby to give a preference."

Counsel for respondent urge that this instruction is drawn in conformity with the amendment of 1903, *supra*, and read with instructions 3 and 6 makes a sufficient statement of the law.

A sufficient answer to such contention is that instruction No. 16 did not contain a correct statement of the law for the control of this case, by reason of the amendment of said subdivision "b" made in 1910 and hereinbefore discussed.

(6) The plaintiff alleges the value of the notes, by the collection of which, by defendant, it is charged a voidable preference was created, is the sum of $1,800. For the failure on the part of the defendant to deny the value of said notes as laid in the complaint, the court charged that the value of the same was by defendant admitted.

Appellant assigns the giving of this instruction as error, maintaining that the answer sufficiently denied the value of said notes.

We have examined the pleadings and the instruction in question and find no error in the giving of the same.

Inasmuch as counsel for the parties hereto were each in error as to the law applicable to a case of this nature at the time of trial, it quite naturally followed that the trial court erred in the instructions given, and it appearing that such error is prejudicial to the rights of the appellant, this judgment must be reversed and the cause remanded for a new trial. Costs will be awarded to appellant.

Ailshie, C. J., and Sullivan, J., concur.

(May 9, 1914.)

CITY OF KELLOGG, Appellant, v. A. P. McRAE et al., as County Commissioners of Shoshone County, Respondents.

[141 Pac. 86.]

COMPLAINT—GENERAL DEMURRER—COUNTY COMMISSIONERS—ROAD DISTRICTS — HIGHWAYS — JURISDICTION OVER WITHIN CITY LIMITS—BRIDGES—CONSTRUCTION OF—STATUTORY CONSTRUCTION.

1. *Held*, under the statutes of this state that the city council or village trustees of incorporated cities and villages have the exclusive control of the streets and highways within such corporate limits, and have full power to construct bridges and repair and maintain the same within such corporate limits.

2. *Held*, that the board of county commissioners have not the control of the roads and bridges within the corporate limits of a city or village, and that they are not required, under the law, to construct and maintain bridges exceeding sixty feet in length at the expense of the county, over streams crossing highways within such corporate limits.

APPEAL from the District Court of the First Judicial District, in and for Shoshone County. Hon. W. W. Woods, Judge.

Application for a writ of mandate to compel the board of county commissioners to construct a bridge over the south fork of the Coeur d'Alene river where it runs through the corporate limits of the town of Kellogg. Writ denied. *Affirmed.*

Z. F. Pattison, for Appellant, cites no authorities.

Carlton Fox, for Respondents.

Sec. 2230, subd. 16, Rev. Stat. of 1887, giving towns and villages the right "to keep in repair, and unobstructed from rubbish, filth, or other deleterious substance, all highways, streets and alleys within such town or village," conferred exclusive jurisdiction upon such town or village over such highways, streets and alleys, and therefore the board of county commissioners could not authorize its road overseer, or any road overseer, to go within the limits of any organized town or village to repair or in any way interfere with its streets and alleys.

The reasoning of this case is peculiarly applicable to the case at bar, for the reason that our present laws defining the jurisdiction of incorporated towns and villages over their highways, streets and alleys are much broader than was the law construed in this decision.

In construing sec. 81, act of 1899 (Sess. Laws 1899, p. 208), which is identical with sec. 2242, Rev. Codes (being the section relied on by appellant), together with sec. 887, Rev. Stat. of 1887, which is substantially the same as sec. 893, Rev. Codes (*supra*), the supreme court of this state held that thereby all control over roads within incorporated cities or villages was taken away from the board of county commissioners. To the same effect is the *Village of Sandpoint v. Doyle,* 11 Ida. 642, 83 Pac. 598, 4 L. R. A., N. S., 810.

SULLIVAN, J.—This action was brought in the district court for a writ of mandate commanding the board of county commissioners of Shoshone county to remove a bridge which is situated across the south fork of Coeur d'Alene river within the limits of the city of Kellogg, and to compel them to build or construct a new bridge across said stream. A general demurrer was interposed to the amended complaint and sustained by the court, whereupon the plaintiff refused to plead further and judgment of dismissal was entered. This appeal is from said judgment.

The action of the court in sustaining the demurrer is assigned as error, and the question is directly presented whether the county under the law is required to construct and keep in repair said bridge, which it is alleged is more than sixty feet in length, and the contention is based on the provisions of sec. 2242, Rev. Codes, as amended by the twelfth session of the legislature (see Sess. Laws 1913, p. 51). Said section provides, among other things, that "All public bridges exceeding sixty feet in length over any stream crossing a state or county highway shall be constructed and kept in repair by the county."

The bridge in question is essential to, and the only means of travel from, that portion of the county lying on one side of the city of Kellogg to that portion of the city lying on the other side thereof. It is contended by counsel for appellant that the section of the statute from which the excerpt above quoted is taken must be construed as a whole and *in pari materia* with other sections of the statute relating to roads and bridges as well as the respective powers and duties of the board of commissioners, on the one hand, and councils or trustees of incorporated cities and villages, on the other.

Said sec. 2242 as amended is as follows:

"The city councils of cities of the second class and board of trustees of villages shall have the care, supervision and control of all public highways, bridges, streets, alleys, public squares and commons within such city or village, and shall cause the same to be kept open and in repair and free from nuisances.

"All public bridges exceeding sixty feet in length over any stream crossing a state or county highway shall be constructed and be kept in repair by the county: Provided, that when any city or village has constructed a bridge over a sixty foot span on any county or state highway within its corporate limits and has incurred a debt for the same, then the treasurer of the county in which said bridge is located shall pay to the treasurer of such city or village seventy-five per cent of all bridge taxes collected in said city or village until said debt and interest upon the same is fully paid: Provided, further, that the city council or board of trustees may appropriate in the manner hereinafter provided, a sum not exceeding five dollars per linear foot to aid in the construction of any county bridge within the limits of such city or village on a highway leading to the same, or any bridge across any unnavigable river which divides the county in which said

city or village is located, from another state, and that no
street or alley which shall hereafter be dedicated to the public
use by the proprietor of ground in any city or village, shall
be deemed a public street or alley, or be under the use or
control of the city council or board of trustees, unless the
dedication shall be accepted and confirmed by an ordinance
especially passed for such purpose."

Each incorporated city, town or village of this state constitutes a separate road district, and the city council of each
city and the board of trustees of each town or village, as far
as relates to their city, town or village, have the powers conferred, and the duties imposed by law, upon the board of
county commissioners in respect to roads and bridges within
their respective corporate limits, and must appoint a road
overseer on whom is imposed all of the duties of road overseer under the provisions of the statute. Such council or
trustees must regulate the length, grade and size of the
bridges, causeways and culverts, and are given full power
over streets and alleys within their respective corporations.

Under the provisions of sec. 2238, Rev. Codes, a city or
village is empowered by ordinance or by-law to establish,
lay out, alter or open any street or alleys and establish grades
and construct bridges and repair and maintain the same.

Under the provisions of said sections of the statute, a city
council or board of trustees of a city, town or village is given
the care, supervision and control of all public highways,
bridges, streets and alleys within the limits of such city or
village, and by the provisions of sec. 2315 they are given
authority to issue municipal bonds not exceeding fifteen per
cent of the real estate value within such corporation, according to the assessment of the preceding year, and to provide,
among other things, for the construction of bridges, across
streams within such corporate limits or contiguous to, or
within one mile of, the exterior limits of such city or village.
By sec. 883a (Sess. Laws 1911, p. 158) the board of county
commissioners is given power to appoint road supervisors
within their county, which road supervisors shall have con-

trol of all highways within the county "except those within the limits of any incorporated city, town or village or of a good roads district or highway district."

By the provisions of sec. 894, as amended by laws of 1912, p. 8, the levy of an annual road poll tax is provided for, and it is also provided that when such tax is collected within the limits of any incorporated city, town or village seventy-five per cent of any sum so collected shall be paid over to the city, town or village for the benefit of its road fund. Sec. 896, as amended by Laws of 1911, p. 162, provides for a general property road tax, and by the provisions of sec. 900, as amended by Laws of 1913, p. 524, twenty-five per cent of that portion of such general property road tax which shall have been assessed and collected within the limits of any incorporated city must be paid to such city or village for its road fund; and sec. 901, as amended by Laws of 1911, p. 163, excepts all property within the limits of any incorporated city, town or village from the levy of a special highway tax by the county.

It will therefore be observed under the provisions of such sections of the statute, so far as finances are concerned, incorporated cities and villages receive seventy-five per cent of all road poll taxes collected within their limits, and twenty-five per cent of all property tax. In addition to this, they may raise further revenue for bridge purposes by special levies and bond issues and are exempt from the burdens of special levies for county, road and bridge purposes.

It follows that since the road and bridge finances of cities and villages are thus provided for by statute, it is clear that the legislature intended that such municipalities may construct the highways and bridges within their corporate limits. However, if the county or state is willing to assist the municipality in constructing bridges or highways within the municipality, the proper officers of such municipality may permit the county or state to do so.

This court held in the *City of Genesee v. Latah County,* 4 Ida. 141, 36 Pac. 701, that boards of county commissioners could not authorize county road overseers to build, repair or in any way interfere with the highways of an incorporated town or village. Cities and villages are given exclusive jurisdiction over the highways within their corporate limits, and that provision of sec. 2242 above quoted, requiring the county to construct and keep in repair all public bridges exceeding sixty feet in length over any stream within the county, was not intended to give the county commissioners jurisdiction within the corporate limits of a city or village over the roads and bridges within such corporate limits; hence that provision was intended to apply only to public bridges over sixty feet in length built over streams within that part of the county over which the board of county commissioners had jurisdiction of the highways and bridges.

This court held in *Carson v. City of Genesee*, 9 Ida. 244, 108 Am. St. 127, 74 Pac. 862, that incorporated cities and villages under the general laws of the state had exclusive control over the streets and alleys and were liable in damages for the negligent discharge of the duty of keeping such streets and alleys in a reasonably safe condition for use by travelers in the usual mode of travel. (See, also, *Village of Sandpoint v. Doyle*, 11 Ida. 642, 83 Pac. 598, 4 L. R. A., N. S., 810, and *Eaton v. City of Weiser*, 12 Ida. 544, 118 Am. St. 225, 86 Pac. 541.)

We therefore conclude that the court did not err in sustaining said demurrer and entering the judgment of dismissal. The judgment must therefore be affirmed, and it is so ordered. Each party to pay its own costs of this appeal.

AILSHIE, C. J., Concurring Specially.—I concur in affirming the judgment of the lower court. The board of commissioners cannot be compelled by *mandamus* to construct a bridge. Neither can the city be so compelled. The building of bridges is within the discretion of the county or city authorities.

I also agree to the proposition that incorporated cities and villages have exclusive control of the streets and alleys within their corporate limits. The expression, however, of "exclusive control" should be considered with special reference to the streets and alleys laid out and constructed by or under the direction or authority of the municipality, as distinguished from those thoroughfares laid out and constructed by the county or state which may pass through the municipality. While it is the duty of the city to keep up and in repair its streets, alleys and any bridges which may form a part of those streets and alleys, still I do not think the county or state can be excluded by the municipality from entering upon a county or state highway within the limits of the municipality and repairing and improving the same or in constructing or repairing a bridge on a public highway which has been laid out and constructed either by the county or state through such municipality.

While I agree that the county cannot be compelled by *mandamus* to repair or construct the bridge here in question, I have no doubt, on the other hand, but that it has the authority and power to enter within the municipal limits of the city of Kellogg and repair or construct the bridge in question if it so desires or the county authorities think it just and equitable to do so.

(May 12, 1914.)

OTTO SWANSTROM, Respondent, v. W. E. FROST, Doing Business as the FROST–COPE LUMBER CO., Appellant.

[140 Pac. 1105.]

PERSONAL INJURY—NEGLIGENCE—CONTRIBUTORY NEGLIGENCE—ASSUMPTION OF RISK.

1. Facts of this case examined, and *held* sufficient to support a verdict that the defendant was guilty of negligence and to warrant a verdict and judgment for damages.

2. Where a log decker was injured by being knocked off the deck by a "gunning" log and sues his employer for damages and charges that the master was negligent in that he furnished a deaf teamster to drive the team that was doing the cross hauling, and

that he did not furnish a reasonably safe place for the team, and that, on the contrary, the place where the team had to walk was so muddy, swampy and unsafe that it irritated and excited the team so that they could not be stopped upon signal, and that his injuries resulted from either a failure of the driver to hear the signal or the inability of the driver to stop the team upon receiving the signal, and there is some evidence in the record which would sustain either one or both of the contentions, the verdict and judgment in favor of the party injured will not be disturbed, even though the preponderance of the evidence is against his contention.

APPEAL from the District Court of the Eighth Judicial District for the County of Bonner. Hon. John M. Flynn, Judge.

Action for damages. Judgment for plaintiff. Defendant appeals. *Affirmed.*

G. H. Martin, for Appellant.

Negligence cannot be based on problematical causes. The plaintiff must show that his injuries resulted from some cause, which was not one of the hazards incident to the business. (*Minty v. Union Pac. Ry. Co.,* 2 Ida. 471, 21 Pac. 660, 4 L. R. A. 409.)

A master is not required to furnish the servant with a safe place to work as against a danger, which is temporary and arises from the risks and hazards of the work itself and which is known to the servant. In such a case the servant assumes the risk. (*Rippetoe v. Feely,* 20 Ida. 619, 637, 119 Pac. 465; *Davis v. Trade Dollar Consol. Min. Co.,* 117 Fed. 122, 54 C. C. A. 636; *Armour v. Hahn,* 111 U. S. 313, 4 Sup. Ct. 433, 28 L. ed. 440; *Koontz v. Chicago etc. R. R. Co.,* 65 Iowa, 224, 54 Am. Rep. 5, 21 N. W. 577; *McKee v. Chicago etc. Ry. Co.,* 83 Iowa, 616, 50 N. W. 209, 13 L. R. A. 817; *Lowe v. Oak Point etc. Lumber Co.,* 75 Wash. 518, 135 Pac. 219; Labatt, Master and Servant, sec. 269.)

A recovery on the part of the servant is denied where it appears that the servant himself selected the course of action which led to the injury complained of. (Labatt, Master and

Servant, sec. 258; *Hanson v. Shipley,* 71 Wash. 632, 129 Pac. 377.)

The act of the plaintiff in deliberately stepping toward the log and then stepping upon it was the cause of his injuries. No ordinarily prudent man familiar with that kind of work, as the plaintiff was, would have done what the plaintiff did under the circumstances, and this is the test of contributory negligence. (*Rippetoe v. Feely,* 20 Ida. 637, 119 Pac. 465; *Goure v. Storey,* 17 Ida. 352, 105 Pac. 794; *Lowe v. Oak Point etc. Lumber Co., supra.*)

O. J. Bandelin and Geo. M. Ferris, for Respondent.

"When a given state of facts is such that reasonable men may fairly differ upon the question as to whether there was negligence or not, the determination of the matter is for the jury. It is only where the facts are such that all reasonable men must draw the same conclusion from them, that the question of negligence is ever considered as one of law for the court." (*Calkins v. Blackwell Lumber Co.,* 23 Ida. 141, 129 Pac. 435; *Texas etc. R. Co. v. Gentry,* 163 U. S. 353, 16 Sup. Ct. 1104, 41 L. ed. 186; *Staab v. Rocky Mt. Bell Tel. Co.,* 23 Ida. 314, 129 Pac. 1078.)

It is a positive duty which the master owes to an employee not only to provide him with a reasonably safe place in which to work—so far as the nature of the work undertaken and the exigencies of the case will permit the same to be made reasonably safe—but also to observe such care as will not expose the employee to perils and dangers which may be guarded against by reasonble care and diligence. (*Myrberg v. Baltimore etc. Min. Co.,* 25 Wash. 364, 65 Pac. 539.)

As to whether the negligence charged was the proximate cause of the injury was clearly a question for the jury. (*Pilmer v. Boise Traction Co.,* 14 Ida. 341, 125 Am. St. 161, 94 Pac. 432, 15 L. R. A., N. S., 254.)

Where the injury would not have happened but for unknown defects, the servant is not held to have been guilty of contributory negligence. (*Missouri Pac. Ry. Co. v. Somers,*

78 Tex. 439, 14 S. W. 779; *Maloney v. Winston Bros. Co.*, 18 Ida. 748, 111 Pac. 1080, 47 L. R. A., N. S., 634; *Westerlund v. Rothschild*, 53 Wash. 626, 102 Pac. 765.)

Defects in the instrumentality are not among the risks assumed, and employee was not guilty of contributory negligence in failing to make an inspection. (*De Maries v. Jameson*, 98 Minn. 453, 108 N. W. 830.)

A servant is not necessarily chargeable with negligence because he failed to select the best means of security in that emergency. (*Carscallen v. Coeur D'Alene etc. Transp. Co.*, 15 Ida. 444, 98 Pac. 622, 16 Ann. Cas. 544; *Wheeler v. Oregon R. & Nav. Co.*, 16 Ida. 375, 102 Pac. 347; *Maw v. Coast Lumber Co.*, 19 Ida. 396, 114 Pac. 9; 1 Labatt on Master and Servant, p. 929, sec. 358.)

When the question of contributory negligence is presented, and there is a conflict in the evidence, the jury are the exclusive judges of the weight and preponderance of the evidence and may determine for themselves as to whether the defense of contributory negligence has been made out. (*Staab v. Rocky Mt. Tel. Co., supra; Rippetoe v. Feely*, 20 Ida. 635, 119 Pac. 465.)

AILSHIE, C. J.—This action was instituted by the plaintiff in the lower court for the recovery of damages for personal injuries resulting from the alleged negligence of the defendant. The plaintiff received his injuries while "decking" logs. It appears that the plaintiff, who is respondent in this court, was a log decker, and was set to work by appellant decking sawlogs while the logs were being hauled upon the deck by means of a team attached to a long chain, and the logs were thus being elevated to the deck by a method called "cross-hauling." The team was driven by another employee of the appellant. While the logs were being hauled up the skidway to the deck, it was the duty of respondent to signal the teamster whenever he desired the team to stop, and it was the duty of the teamster to stop on the signal from the man

The grounds of negligence charged are, (1st), that the
teamster employed by appellant was deaf, and could not,
and did not, hear the signal to stop; and, (2d), that the ground
over which the team had to travel in hauling the logs on to
the deck was so muddy, swampy and in such a dangerous condition as not to afford the team sure or safe footing, which
resulted in irritating the team and rendering them unmanage-
able, and making it impossible to stop them promptly on
giving the signal.

In hauling a log on to the deck, after the deck had been
built to a height of about sixteen feet, one end of the log
moved up the skidway faster than the other, pointing cross-
wise of the deck, which is called by lumbermen "gunning."
The respondent claims that he gave two or three signals to
the driver to stop, but that the driver either failed to hear
the signal, or neglected or was unable to stop the team, and
so they kept going, and respondent, in his effort to get out
of the way of the log, was thrown off the deck, receiving severe
injuries, for which this action has been prosecuted.

The case was tried to a jury and a verdict rendered in
favor of the respondent, and this appeal was thereupon
prosecuted. It is contended that the evidence fails to disclose any negligence on the part of the appellant and that,
on the contrary, the respondent both assumed the risk and
was guilty of contributory negligence.

If we were adjudging this case in the capacity of jurors
for the purpose of weighing the evidence and determining
the preponderance of the evidence, we are inclined to the
opinion that upon the record as it comes to us on appeal we
should conclude that the respondent both assumed the risk
and so contributed in negligent acts as to bar a recovery.
We are mindful, however, of the fact that in this case there
must have been some circumstances and conditions which confronted the jury and trial court which we cannot see or learn
from a record. There is also some evidence in the record
which may be considered material and substantial that would
support such a verdict. In our opinion, there is sufficient
in this case to bring it within the rule this court has announced

in *Adams v. Bunker Hill etc. Min. Co.*, 12 Ida. 637, 89 Pac. 624, 11 L. R. A., N. S., 844, *Carscallen v. Coeur d'Alene etc. Transp. Co.*, 15 Ida. 444, 98 Pac. 622, 16 Ann. Cas. 544, *Wheeler v. Oregon R. & Nav. Co.*, 16 Ida. 375, 102 Pac. 347, *Maloney v. Winston Bros. Co.*, 18 Ida. 740, 111 Pac. 1080, 47 L. R. A., N. S., 634, *Maw v. Coast Lumber Co.*, 19 Ida. 396, 114 Pac. 9, *Staab v. Rocky Mt. Tel. Co.*, 23 Ida. 314, 129 Pac. 1078, and *Calkins v. Blackwell Lumber Co.*, 23 Ida. 128, 129 Pac. 435.

The question argued by appellant that respondent was at fault in that he received the injury while attempting to "square" the log by throwing his weight on it when it was "gunning" is not a controlling question here. This question went to the jury, and they evidently thought the respondent did not act negligently or recklessly. The jury may have concluded that the team used on the "cross-haul" was not a safe team or that the driver was deaf and that the employer was negligent in furnishing such a team or such a driver, or in both respects. These reasons were advanced by respondent as grounds of negligence on the part of the employer.

We find no error in the giving or refusing to give instructions.

The judgment is affirmed. Costs awarded in favor of respondent.

Sullivan, J., concurs.

(May 15, 1914.)

ALICE E. BALDWIN, Respondent, v. W. B. McFARLAND, Sheriff, et al., Appellants.

[141 Pac. 76.]

COMMUNITY PROPERTY—SEPARATE PROPERTY OF WIFE—SUFFICIENCY OF EVIDENCE.

1. Evidence in this case examined, and *held* sufficient to support the finding and judgment that the property levied upon was the separate property of the wife and not the community property of the husband and wife.

2. Evidence examined and *held* sufficient to support the judgment.

APPEAL from the District Court of the Eighth Judicial District for the County of Kootenai. Hon. R. N. Dunn, Judge.

Action to restrain and enjoin the sale of certain real estate on execution issued against the plaintiff's husband. Judgment for the plaintiff. Defendants appeal. *Affirmed.*

Ezra R. Whitla, for Appellants.

"Real estate conveyed to the wife during coverture is presumed to be community property. . . . . " (*Stowell v. Tucker,* 7 Ida. 312, 62 Pac. 1033.)

When this presumption has passed it then follows that it is incumbent upon the plaintiff or anyone attempting to show property to be separate property to make this appear by clear and convincing proof.

McNaughton & Berg, for Respondent.

The judgment debtor having put nothing into the property, his creditors can take nothing out of it. (*Gladstone Lumber Co. v. Kelly,* 64 Or. 163, 129 Pac. 763; *Heinrich v. Heinrich,* 2 Cal. App. 479, 84 Pac. 326; *Oldershaw v. Matteson & Will-*

iamson Mfg. Co., 19 Cal. App. 179, 125 Pac. 263; *Flournoy v. Flournoy,* 86 Cal. 286, 21 Am. St. 39, 24 Pac. 1012; *Stewart v. Weiser Lumber Co.,* 21 Ida. 340, 121 Pac. 775.)

AILSHIE, C. J.—This action was brought by the plaintiff, Alice E. Baldwin, against W. B. McFarland, as sheriff of Kootenai county, and against the other defendants to enjoin and restrain the sale of certain real estate which the sheriff had levied upon under an execution issued in the case of W. H. Ferrell against J. B. Baldwin. J. B. Baldwin is the husband of the respondent, Alice E. Baldwin. The property had been levied upon for the collection of a judgment against the husband. The wife commenced this action to enjoin the sale of the property, alleging that the property levied upon was her separate estate.

The complaint alleges, and the evidence discloses, a detailed history of the acquisition of this property. It would be entirely useless to reiterate the history of these several transactions and of the acquisition of this property in a written opinion. The important and decisive question to be determined in the case is as to whether this was the separate property of the wife, or community property of both husband and wife. The appellant has the same understanding of the question involved, and states in his brief as follows: ·

"The whole issue in this case resolves itself down to a question as to whether or not the plaintiff has the title to the property in controversy, and whether or not it was secured so as to make it her separate property within the meaning of sec. 2676, Rev. Codes."

Our examination and consideration of the record and briefs in the case, and the law applicable thereto, satisfies us that the trial judge reached the correct conclusion, and that this property is the separate property of the wife, and was not subject to execution for the collection of the husband's debt. To our minds this case falls within the rule announced in *Stewart v. Weiser Lumber Co.,* 21 Ida. 340, 121 Pac. 775, and the long line of cases from this court followed in the Stewart-Weiser Lumber Company case.

The judgment should be affirmed, and it is so ordered. Costs awarded in favor of the respondent.

Sullivan, J., concurs.

(May 16, 1914.)

LOUIS GAGNON, Appellant, v. ST. MARIES LIGHT & POWER CO., LTD., a Corporation, Respondent.

[141 Pac. 88.]

PLEADING—DEMURRER ON GROUND OF CONTRIBUTORY NEGLIGENCE—ON GROUND OF DEFECT OF PARTIES—PERSONAL INJURY—EMPLOYEE OF INDEPENDENT CONTRACTOR—ELECTRICAL APPLIANCES—DEGREE OF PROTECTION TO INVITEE.

1. *Held*, that the complaint in this case states a cause of action.

2. Under the rule in force in this state requiring a liberal construction of pleadings, a demurrer to the complaint in a personal injury case should not be sustained on the ground that it disclosed contributory negligence on its face, when all the allegations of the complaint taken together, and considered in the sense in which the pleader has evidently used and employed the language therein contained, charge negligence of the defendant and care and diligence on the part of plaintiff.

3. Where an electric light and power company made a contract for the painting of its transformer station, and an employee of the contractor, not familiar with the premises or the appliances, was injured by coming in contact with uninsulated and unprotected loose wires which were not obviously dangerous, and in regard to which he had received no warning, an action for damages may properly be prosecuted by the employee of the contractor against such corporation.

4. The employee of an independent contractor doing work on the premises of another is an invitee by special agreement, and the proprietor of such premises is under obligation to see that he have a reasonably safe place to work and that he have reasonable protection against the consequences of hidden dangers known to the proprietor.

5. Those who deal in electricity as a business are held to the highest degree of care with reference to all persons not themselves wrongdoers who in any capacity may accidentally or otherwise come in contact with their electrical appliances.

APPEAL from the District Court of the Eighth Judicial District for Kootenai County. Hon. R. N. Dunn, Judge.

Action for damages for personal injury received by plaintiff while in the employ of an independent contractor. Demurrer to complaint sustained. *Reversed.*

E. N. LaVeine, W. D. Keeton and W. F. Morrison, Jr., for Appellant.

John P. Gray and Frank M. McCarthy, for Respondent.

The authorities cited by counsel are mentioned in the opinion *infra.*

AILSHIE, C. J.—The complaint in this action, after setting forth the corporate capacity of the defendant, alleges that at the times mentioned it was operating an electric lighting and power plant and engaged in furnishing electric light and power in the vicinity of the city of St. Maries; that for such purpose it maintained a frame building in said city which it used for a transformer station and office, with which were connected transmission wires carrying a load of about 2,200 volts of electricity; that these wires entered the building about three feet below the eaves; "that at the point where said wires were connected to said building, the defendant carelessly and negligently allowed and permitted two short, separate wires connected with said transmission wires which were bare and uninsulated and unprotected at the ends, which wires were *unused,* to hang down and dangle loosely near the side of said building, and carelessly and negligently allowed and permitted a strong current of electricity to pass into and be in said loose ends of said wires so hanging down from said connection as aforesaid."

Then follow allegations of carelessness and negligence in that the defendant permitted such loose wires, so charged with electric current, to hang uninsulated and unprotected, and an averment of its duty "to see that persons employed to work upon said building were afforded a reasonably safe protection from the said dangerous agency." The fifth and seventh paragraphs we quote in full:

"V. That some time prior to the 16th day of April, 1913, defendant engaged one R. B. Ward, a contracting painter, to paint the aforesaid station and office building; that said R. B. Ward hired, among others, the plaintiff to paint said building; that, shortly after commencing to work in the employment aforesaid, on the afternoon of the 16th day of April, 1913, plaintiff let himself down below said charged wires and connections; that in painting he carefully avoided contact with said charged wires which entered said building and which evidently were or might have been carrying electricity; that while engaged in painting and while exercising due care in so avoiding said wires, and inadvertently, but without negligence or lack of care on his part, plaintiff's left forearm came in contact with the uninsulated and unprotected ends of the said two unused wires which were separately and loosely hanging down the side of said building as aforesaid, and that by reason of said contact with the ends of said wires plaintiff was severely burned, and shocked by reason of said injury, suffered great bodily pain and mental anguish, and was compelled to expend large sums of money for medical attendance and care and is still required to be attended by a physician."

"VII. That plaintiff had no knowledge of the danger lurking in said two unused and unprotected wires, and had no reason to apprehend any danger from contact with them; that plaintiff had a right to rely, and did rely, upon the defendant furnishing a reasonably safe place for him to work, and if said wires were dangerous to have had them joined, protected or insulated, or a warning given him of their dangerous character, or to have them removed; that the said loose ends were by reason of the carelessness and negligence of the

said defendant, its officers, servants or employees, not removed, nor connected and insulated, nor was plaintiff warned
by defendant nor by any person by or on behalf of the defendant, of the dangerous character of said loose wires; that
defendant remained and was at all of the said times in possession of said building and in control of said wires and
said electric current and that all of the hidden danger due
to or arising out of the carelessness, negligence and improper
care of said wires, was solely within the knowledge of the
said defendant or should by the exercise of reasonable care
have been within its said knowledge."

The remaining paragraphs of the complaint set forth the
permanent injury to plaintiff's left hand and arm and allege
his earning capacity. To this complaint defendant demurred
on the following grounds:

"1· That said complaint does not state facts sufficient to
constitute a cause of action against the defendant.

"2· That there is a defect of parties defendant as appears
upon the face of said complaint in this: That it is alleged in
paragraph five of said complaint that the plaintiff at the time
of the alleged injury was working for R. E. Ward, a contracting painter, and upon the face of the complaint it shows
that plaintiff's cause of action, if any he has, is against said
Ward, his master, and not against the defendant named."

A third ground is that of uncertainty with reference to the
allegations of earning capacity, but which counsel do not urge
in this court.

The trial court sustained the demurrer specifically on the
first ground, viz., that the complaint fails to state facts sufficient to constitute a cause of action, and gave plaintiff leave
to amend. Plaintiff elected to stand on his pleading and
appeals from the order of the trial court dismissing the
action.

Respondent contends that the complaint itself shows appellant to have known and appreciated the danger of his
employment on respondent's premises, and that he therefore
assumed the risk.· He particularly calls attention to the language used in paragraph 5, where after stating that plaintiff

"carefully avoided contact" with the main transmission wires which entered the building, the pleader goes on to say: "and inadvertently, but without negligence or lack of care on his part, plaintiff's left forearm came in contact with the uninsulated and unprotected ends of the said two unused wires." From this language, and especially the use of the word "inadvertently," it is urged that both knowledge of the danger and negligence in the avoidance of it is imputable to plaintiff, and that for this reason alone he could not recover.

We think, however, that the meaning of the pleader may be fairly gathered from a succeeding allegation in paragraph 7, where he avers that plaintiff "had no knowledge of the danger lurking in said wires, and had no reason to apprehend any danger from contact with them." We are not disposed to commend the allegations of paragraph 5 as affording a model of good pleading in a personal injury case, but taking the complaint as a whole, and viewing the allegations of paragraph 5 together with those of paragraph 7, at the same time bearing in mind the rule for liberal construction of pleadings which has been so often applied by this court, we are inclined to think that so far as this contention is concerned, the demurrer should have been overruled.

A more important question is raised by the second ground of defendant's demurrer, and although the lower court did not sustain the demurrer specifically on this ground, yet as the same question must arise in proceeding further under the complaint, it seems advisable to dispose of it in this opinion. It is also true that if the demurrer was good on any ground stated, it would be the duty of this court to sustain the trial court, even though he sustained the demurrer on an erroneous ground.

Respondent's contention is, that since the complaint shows the appellant to have been the employee of an independent contractor, the respondent corporation was not liable for any injury received by him under the facts stated. It is pointed out that respondent exercised no supervision or control over and had no contractual relation whatever with the appellant,

and it is therefore urged that respondent was under no obligation, such as ordinarily devolves on the master toward the
servant, to furnish the contractor's employee a safe place to
work, or to warn him in regard to dangers on the premises.
which might not be obvious to a stranger; that if any such
obligation existed, it was on the part of the contractor toward
his employee.

Counsel for both appellant and respondent cite and comment upon a number of cases involving the question of liability
for injury to the servant of an independent contractor upon
a property owner's premises. From an analysis of these
cases, it is apparent that they constitute a class by themselves
where the questions of fact are peculiarly diverse on account
of the various elements that enter into consideration. In the
first place, there is an infinite diversity of manner and capacity in which one may be injured on the premises of another.
Confining the class of persons who may be so injured to employees of independent contractors, we are confronted with
varying conditions of relationship between the employee and
the contractor on the one hand and both of them with the
proprietor on the other. Then, again, there are the various
gradations in degree of care required on the part of the
proprietor for the protection of those who have a right to
be on his premises, corresponding both to the nature of his
own business and the business of the invitee. If it is a dangerous business, of course a higher degree of care is required.
On the other hand, if the invitee is familiar with the premises or particular conditions thereof, he assumes propor-
tionately more risk. Possibly, therefore, there is not so much
a conflict of authority running through the cases as a remarkable diversity of facts and conditions.

Appellant cites, as sustaining his contention on this point,
Clark v. St. Louis etc. R. Co., 234 Mo. 396, 137 S. W. 583;
1 Thompson on Negligence, secs. 680–979; *Coughtry v. Globe
Woolen Co.,* 56 N. Y. 124, 15 Am. Rep. 387; *Johnson v. Spear,*
76 Mich. 139, 15 Am. St. 298, 42 N. W. 1092; *Brannock v.
Elmore,* 114 Mo. 55, 21 S. W. 451; *Union Traction Co. v.
Fetters,* 99 Fed. 214, 39 C. C. A. 474; *Samuelson v. Cleveland*

etc. M. Co., 49 Mich. 164, 43 Am. Rep. 456, 13 N. W. 499;
John Spry Lumber Co. v. Duggan, 182 Ill. 218, 54 N. E.
1002; 29 Cyc. 456, note 12, and cases cited; *Ryan v. St. Louis
Transit Co.*, 190 Mo. 621, 89 S. W. 865, 2 L. R. A., N. S., 777;
Stevens v. United Gas & Electric Co., 73 N. H. 159, 60 Atl.
848, 70 L. R. A. 119; *Thomas v. Harrington*, 72 N. H. 45, 54
Atl. 285, 65 L. R. A. 742; *Young v. Waters–Pierce Oil Co.*,
185 Mo. 634, 84 S. W. 929; *Wilson v. Hibbert*, 194 Fed. 838,
114 C. C. A. 542; *Katalla Co. v. Johnson*, 202 Fed. 353, 120
C. C. A. 481; *Murch Bros. Const. Co. v. Johnson*, 203 Fed. 1;
121 C. C. A. 353; *Bright v. Barnett & Record Co.*, 88 Wis.
299, 60 N. W. 418, 26 L. R. A. 524; *Dunn v. Cavanaugh*, 185
Fed. 451, 107 C. C. A. 521; *Hoppe v. City of Winona*, 113
Minn. 252, Ann. Cas. 1912A, 247, 129 N. W. 577, 33 L. R. A.,
N. S., 449.

Respondent cites the following authorities on this question:
Myers v. Edison Electric Illuminating Co., 225 Pa. 387, 74
Atl. 223; *Callan v. Pugh*, 54 App. Div. 545, 66 N. Y. Supp.
1118; *Proctor v. San Antonio St. Ry. Co.*, 26 Tex. Civ. App.
148, 62 S. W. 939; *Bush v. Grant*, 22 Ky. Law Rep. 1766, 61
S. W. 363; *Reisman v. Public Service Corp.*, 82 N. J. L. 464,
81 Atl. 838, 38 L. R. A., N. S., 922; *Campbell v. Jones*, 60
Wash. 265, 110 Pac. 1083; *Wright v. Big Rapids Door &
Blind Mfg. Co.*, 124 Mich. 91, 82 N. W. 829, 50 L. R. A. 495;
Cole v. Louisiana Gas Co., 121 La. 771, 46 So. 801; *Blalack
v. Texas Traction Co.* (Tex. Civ. App.), 149 S. W. 1086;
Robichaux v. Morgan's L. & T. & S. S. Co., 131 La. 727,
60 So. 206.

In the first place, it must be conceded that appellant in
this case was at least an invitee upon the premises of the
respondent corporation.

Judge Thompson in his work on "Negligence," vol. 1, sec.
680, says: "The servant of the contractor must be deemed
to be upon the premises of the proprietor by his invitation,
express or implied; and therefore he owes him the same duty
of guarding him against the consequences of hidden dangers
on the premises, that a proprietor would in any case owe to

a guest, a customer, or other person coming by invitation upon his premises.''

In some of the cases it is pointed out that the employee of a contractor is more than an invitee,—in the sense that the term "invitee" may mean anyone belonging to the general public,—since the proprietor voluntarily contracted for his presence on the premises, knew that he or some other employee of the individual with whom he had contracted would come on his place to carry out his contract; and knew what he would have to do and where he would have to be to do the work required under the contract, so that the proprietor thereby became obligated to exercise more care for his safety while upon his premises than in the case of a mere invitee, to the extent that he was affected with more particular notice. (*John Spry Lumber Co. v. Duggan*, 182 Ill. 218, 54 N. E. 1002.)

The general trend of authority on this question appears to be correctly stated by the author of the case note in 26 L. R. A. 524 (*Bright v. Barnett & Record Co.*), wherein it is said:

"With few exceptions the cases agree in holding that premises upon which an independent contractor is required to labor for the benefit of the owner must be reasonably safe for the purposes of such labor so far as freedom from concealed dangers is concerned.''

And in a later case (*Ryan v. St. Louis Transit Co.*, 190 Mo. 621, 89 S. W. 865, 2 L. R. A., N. S., 777), the author of the note in the latter series says:

"The duty charged on one who is engaged in the generation of electricity to keep the wires within and about his building safe for the servants of another, who has contracted to perform certain work in or about the former's building, is imposed by the well established and familiar doctrine that every man who, expressly or by implication, invites others to come upon his premises, assumes, to all who accept the invitation, the duty to protect them from any danger incurred by coming, which he knows of or ought to know of, and of which they are not aware.''

And this duty extends to places on the premises not accessible to the general public, but which a stranger might have occasion to visit in the performance of some work of necessity, as this court has recently held in a personal injury case resulting from coming in contact with electric appliances.

"Where an electric light and power company maintains its poles within a foot of the poles of a telephone company, and carries and maintains live wires charged with electrical current, it is chargeable with notice that laborers and linemen working on the telephone company's poles and wires may and will come in close contact with the electric light wires, and such company is chargeable with the duty of protecting them from injury." (*Staab v. Rocky Mountain Bell Telephone Co.*, 23 Ida. 314, 129 Pac. 1078.) In the latter case, it was contended that the telephone employee who lost his life was not only not an invitee but was a trespasser, and his relationship, contractual or otherwise, with the electric light company was more remote than that of appellant in the present case.

We do not believe that the principle upon which these cases should be adjudicated is encompassed within the limitations of the master and servant rule. If it be once conceded that this rule applies, the conclusion of course follows that there is no contractual obligation on the part of the owner to furnish the employee of the contractor with a safe place to work. An examination of the cases convinces us that the courts generally have very properly declined to apply that rule in its strictness to this class of cases, but have recognized the expediency and justice of applying the broader and more humane rule of holding the property owner responsible for the safety of any person rightfully on the premises and not an actual wrongdoer, who may be innocently injured upon his premises by the existence of hidden dangers known to the owner or which he should be presumed to know.

In the case at bar, the facts are few and uncontroverted. The plaintiff Gagnon, the employee of the independent contractor, Ward, was upon defendant's premises by agreement.

The agents and servants of the defendant corporation knew
that he or some other person was going to visit their premises to do the work contracted for. They must have known
that such person would perform labor near the precise spot
where the danger existed and the injury occurred. The fact
that the unused wires in question were uninsulated and unprotected was peculiarly within their own knowledge. They
had complete control of the premises. Unlike some of the
cases cited, the independent contractor was not in possession
of these premises, even temporarily. Unlike other cases cited,
neither the contractor nor his employees are shown to have
had any familiarity with these premises, or with the dangers
of the business or appliances. Plaintiff came to the transformer station of the defendant corporation to do his work
as a painter. He received no warning from defendant
against hidden dangers in his place of work. The statement
in the complaint of how he came to be injured, while not a
masterpiece of the art of pleading, is a natural account of
how such an injury might occur. The plaintiff noticed the
main transmission wires which entered the building. He
knew that they were likely to be dangerous and carefully
avoided coming in contact with them. He also saw the unused
ends of wires dangling down, without apparent connection
or purpose so far as being a working part of the operating
plant. He did not know what they were for and was not
chargeable with apprehending any danger from them. He
did not mean to touch them, but "inadvertently" came in
contact with them and was injured. It could not be said that
he assumed the risk, for the danger that he encountered was
certainly one not ordinarily incident to the business.

This court has repeatedly declared that "electric companies
are held to the highest degree of care practicable to avoid
injuries to persons who may accidentally or otherwise come
in contact with their wires. Electricity is recognized as one
of the most destructive agencies we have, and the highest
degree of care and diligence is required by those who are
operating electrical plants in order to avoid injury to person
and property." (*Younie v. Blackfoot Light & Water Co.*,

15 Ida. 56, 96 Pac. 193; *Eaton v. City of Weiser*, 12 Ida. 544, 118 Am. St. 225, 86 Pac. 541; *Staab v. Rocky Mountain Bell Tel. Co., supra.*)

The complaint states a cause of action. The lower court should have overruled the demurrer and required the .defendant to answer. The judgment is reversed and the cause is remanded, with direction to overrule the demurrer and allow the defendant to answer. Costs awarded in favor of appellant.

Sullivan, J., concurs.

(May 18, 1914.)

H. C. TAYLOR, Appellant, v. CLARENCE L. LYTLE, Respondent.

[141 Pac. 92.]

COMPLAINT—DEMURRER TO—DEFECT OF PARTIES PLAINTIFF—NECESSARY PARTY.

1. *Held*, that the court erred in holding that there was a defect of parties plaintiff and that the Springston Lumber Company was a necessary party plaintiff to the action.

APPEAL from the District Court of the Eighth Judicial District, in and for Kootenai County. Hon. John M. Flynn, Judge.

Action to recover damages on account of misrepresentation and fraud as to the boundary of certain land on which the plaintiff purchased the timber. A demurrer to the complaint was sustained on the ground that there was a defect of parties plaintiff, and the plaintiff having refused to amend, judgment of dismissal was entered. *Reversed.*

E. R. Whitla, for Appellant.

Where one sells property and makes representations as to the quantity of land sold, he is liable in an action for damages in case his representations—whether believed by him to be true or not—are in fact false, and the boundary pointed out by him is not the true boundary and the vendee suffers any loss by reason thereof. (*Miller v. Wissert*, 38 Okl. 808, 134 Pac. 62; *McGhee v. Bell*, 170 Mo. 121, 70 S. W. 493, 59 L. R. A. 761; *Hoock v. Bowman*, 42 Neb. 80, 47 Am. St. 691, 60 N. W. 389; *Castenholz v. Heller*, 82 Wis. 30, 51 N. W. 432; *Porter v. Beattie*, 88 Wis. 22, 59 N. W. 499; *Davis v. Nuzum*, 72 Wis. 439, 40 N. W. 497, 1 L. R. A. 774; *Pringle v. Samuel*, 1 Litt. (Ky.) 43, 13 Am. Dec. 214; *Trenchard v. Kell*, 127 Fed. 596.)

Even honesty in making a mistake is no defense, as it is incumbent upon the vendor to know the facts. (*Culbertson v. Blanchard*, 79 Tex. 486, 15 S. W. 700.)

Nonjoinder of a proper, as distinguished from a necessary, party is not ground for demurrer. (31 Cyc. 293.)

"In general, in an action founded upon tort the person who suffers the injury must bring the action, for he is the party in interest." (Bliss on Code Pleading, 521.)

"It is not necessary to join as plaintiff persons who do not appear by the complaint to be united in interest with the plaintiff in all the relief sought thereby." (*Garner v. Wright*, 28 How. Pr. 92; *Washburn v. Case*, 1 Wash. Ter. 253; *Sheridan Gas, Oil & Coal Co. v. Pearson*, 19 Ind App. 252, 65 Am. St. 402, 49 N. E. 357; *Moore v. Harmon*, 142 Ind. 555, 41 N. E. 599.)

"Where a suit is brought on a contract, a person who is not a party to the contract and has no interest therein is not a necessary or proper party to the suit." (*Hurlbutt v. N. W. Spaulding Saw Co.*, 93 Cal. 55, 28 Pac. 795.)

C. H. Potts, for Respondent.

The cause of action in this case is based on alleged fraudulent representations which resulted in the conveyance to the Springston Lumber Company of the standing timber described in the complaint. The lumber company is the grantee in the conveyance of the timber; the legal title was taken by it; it paid the cash consideration therefor, and executed the promissory note sought to be canceled by this action. It is therefore the real party in interest. Any private arrangement between the plaintiff and the lumber company as to how the title shall be held, or otherwise, could not affect the defendant. It is not alleged in the complaint that the defendant had knowledge of any arrangement between the plaintiff and the lumber company.

"The person having the legal interest in a contract can alone maintain an action thereon." (*Wolverton v. Geo. H. Taylor & Co.*, 157 Ill. 485, 42 N. E. 49; *Gardner v. Armstrong*, 31 Mo. 535; *Frankem v. Trimble's Heirs*, 5 Pa. 520; *Forrest v. O'Donnell*, 42 Mich. 556, 4 N. W. 259.)

The allegation in the complaint that the Springston Lumber Company was an accommodation maker of the note in question does not change the situation in any particular. Under the provisions of the negotiable instruments law an accommodation maker of a promissory note is the real party in interest in any action based on such note and is primarily liable thereon. (*Union Trust Co. v. McGinty*, 212 Mass. 205, Ann. Cas. 1913C, 525, 98 N. E. 679; *Vanderford v. Farmers' etc. Nat. Bank*, 105 Md. 164, 66 Atl. 47, 10 L. R. A., N. S., 129; *Cellers v. Meachem*, 49 Or. 186, 89 Pac. 426, 10 L. R. A., N. S., 133, 13 Ann. Cas. 997; *Wolstenholme v. Smith*, 34 Utah, 300, 97 Pac. 329; *Bradley etc. Mfg. Co. v. Heyburn*, 56 Wash. 628, 134 Am. St. 1127, 106 Pac. 170; *National Citizens' Bank v. Toplitz*, 81 App. Div. 593, 81 N. Y. Supp. 422; *Richards v. Market Exchange Bank Co.*, 81 Ohio St. 348, 90 N. E. 1000, 26 L. R. A., N. S., 99; *Lane v. Hyder*, 163 Mo. App. 688, 147 S. W. 514; *Lumbermen's National Bank v. Campbell*, 61 Or. 123, 121 Pac. 427.)

"In all actions those between whom there is a unity of legal interest must be joined as plaintiffs." (*Burkett v. Lehmen-Higginson Grocery Co.*, 8 Okl. 84, 56 Pac. 856; *Culver v. Smith*, 82 Mo. App. 390.)

SULLIVAN, J.—This action was brought to recover damages in the sum of $3,250 with interest, on account of alleged fraud and misrepresentation by the vendor to the plaintiff

as to the location and boundary of a certain piece of timber
land, the timber on which the plaintiff purchased from the
respondent. A demurrer was filed to the second amended
complaint, based on two grounds: (1) That said amended
complaint did not state facts sufficient to constitute a cause
of action; and (2) that there was a defect of parties plaintiff in that the Springston Lumber Company, a corporation,
was not made a party plaintiff and was a necessary party.
After hearing said demurrer, the court sustained it on the
second ground, to wit, that there was a defect of parties
plaintiff in that the Springston Lumber Company was not
made a party to the action. The plaintiff thereupon refused to plead further and judgment of dismissal was
entered.

The only question then presented for determination is
whether the court erred in holding that said corporation was
a necessary party plaintiff.

It is alleged in the complaint that on or about October,
1911, the defendant offered to sell to the plaintiff certain
timber growing upon the south half of the northwest quarter, and the northwest quarter of the southwest quarter of
section 34, and the southeast quarter of the northeast quarter of section 33, township 49, north of range 2, west of Boise
meridian, in Kootenai county; that the plaintiff was desirous
of purchasing said timber and especially the white pine
timber growing on said land, and thereafter, at the instance
and request of said defendant, went with him to the locality
of said land; that plaintiff was not familiar with that locality
and did not know the lines or boundaries of said land; that
defendant pointed out to him what he claimed was the correct boundaries of the land in order that plaintiff might get
an estimate of the timber standing thereon; that the defendant, with intent of deceiving and defrauding plaintiff
and inducing him to purchase said timber, pointed out to him
a certain blazed line which he stated was the southern line
of the south half of the northwest quarter of said section
34, and the southeast quarter of the northeast quarter of
section 33, and stated that said blazed line was the northern

boundary line of said land; that said blazed line was not
the northern boundary line, but was about 260 feet north
and parallel to the true and correct boundary line of said
land, and that defendant knew that it was not the correct
boundary of said land at the time he pointed the same out to
the plaintiff, but fraudulently made said representation to
the plaintiff because there was standing on said strip of
land, about 260 feet in width between the true and false
boundary line, a large amount of valuable white pine timber
consisting of 250,000 feet of the stumpage value of $1,500, and
600,000 feet of mixed timber of the stumpage value of $1,500,
and 100 cedar poles of the value of $75; that because of the
quantity and quality of the timber on said strip of land and
because it was lying so that it could be conveniently logged
at a small cost, the value of the timber on the entire tract of
land was increased; that plaintiff believed the representations and statements of the defendant as to said boundary
line, and because of such false representations and statements
the plaintiff was induced to purchase the timber upon the
legal subdivisions before set forth, and that without such rep-
sentations having been made plaintiff would not have purchased such timber; that because of such representations
plaintiff purchased said timber from the defendant for the
sum of $12,000; that after so purchasing said timber, plain-
tiff built roads upon said strip of land for the purpose of
logging the timber upon the same, and that at least $150
was expended for the sole and only purpose of removing the
timber upon said strip of land lying between the correct
boundary line and the false and untrue boundary line so
pointed out to plaintiff by defendant; that plaintiff, relying
upon the false representations of defendant as to the location of said boundary line and believing them to be true,
went upon said strip of land and cut down 33,000 feet of
white pine timber, and thereafter learned that said strip of
land lying between the alleged boundary line pointed out by
the defendant and the true boundary line belonged to one
W. J. Johnson and the United States government; that plaintiff, because of said representations, cut $175 worth of timber

upon said Johnson's land and $75 worth of timber growing upon government land; that plaintiff first discovered that the statements and representations made by defendant as to the location of said north boundary line were false and untrue on or about the 21st day of September, 1912, and that prior to said date plaintiff had thought said boundary lines pointed out to him by the defendant were true and correct; that had it not been for these false representations plaintiff would not have purchased said timber; that the representations of the defendant as to these boundaries were made for the purpose of inducing plaintiff to purchase the timber, and did induce plaintiff to purchase the same, and by reason thereof he has been damaged in the sum of $3,250.

It is also alleged that at the time said timber was purchased, plaintiff was unable to secure the money with which to make the payment therefor, and "at said time arranged with the Springston Lumber Company for a loan to him, said plaintiff, of the sum of $6,000 in cash, and agreed with defendant to accept the notes of said Springston Lumber Company for an additional six thousand dollars in payment of the balance of said purchase price, and at said time for the purpose of securing said Springston Lumber Co. for the money so secured and borrowed from it and the notes executed by it for plaintiff and on his behalf, plaintiff did cause deed to said timber to be taken in the name of the Springston Lumber Co., but said deed was held by the Springston Lumber Co. only as security for the sum so borrowed from it by plaintiff; that by reason thereof plaintiff paid to the defendant the sum of six thousand dollars in cash and the balance of said purchase price in notes, all of which said notes were signed by the Springston Lumber Co. and all thereof have been paid with the exception of one note for the sum of $2,000 with interest at the rate of 8% per annum from on or about the —— day of December, 1911, and which plaintiff is informed and believes, and therefore alleges the fact to be, is now owned and held by the defendant; that said property was purchased by plaintiff and said deed so taken by the Springston Lumber Co. was to secure it for the loan to plaintiff and for no other purpose whatever, and the Springston Lumber Co. holds title to said property only as security for the indebtedness due it by plaintiff; that said Springston Lumber Co. is a corporation duly authorized to do business in the state of Idaho and is now engaged in doing business in the state of Idaho; that said notes so executed by the Springston Lumber Co. to said defendant were executed for and on behalf of plaintiff and plaintiff promised and agreed to and with the Springston Lumber Co. to make payment of said notes and is personally bound to said company for the full sum thereof, and said notes were and are in fact accommodation notes made by the Springston Lumber Co. and for and on behalf of this plaintiff; that no other person, company or corporation whatsoever has any interest in or to this controversy other than the plaintiff herein, and that the damages caused by reason of the acts of said defendant were caused to the plaintiff and plaintiff has lost thereby the sums herein mentioned.''

It was upon the above-quoted allegations that the trial court must have come to the conclusion that the Springston Lumber Company. was a necessary party to said action.

Counsel for appellant contends that the above-quoted allegations were made in order that there might be no misunderstanding or claim on the trial of the case that the defendant was surprised and in order that the complaint might fully set forth the facts upon which the plaintiff's cause of action was based. It is therein alleged that the Springston Lumber Company was simply the surety or became the security for the plaintiff in the payment of said purchase price, and that in order to secure the Springston Lumber Company for becoming such surety, the deed to said timber was taken in the name of the Springston Lumber Company. The complaint also alleges that all of the notes signed by the Springston Lumber Company had been paid with the exception of one for $2,000; that said notes are in fact accommodation notes signed by the Springston Lumber Company for 'and on behalf of the plaintiff; that no other person, company, or corporation whatever has any interest in or to the controversy other than the plaintiff, and that the damage done and the acts complained of were suffered by the plaintiff, and that plaintiff has lost the sums mentioned and prays for judgment for $3,250, and also prays that if it appears that the defendant is still the owner of the said $2,000 note, that said note be set off and canceled as against any judgment recovered by plaintiff.

Then the question presented for determination is whether said complaint on its face shows that the Springston Lumber Company is a necessary party plaintiff to this action. Counsel for appellant first contends that the authorities are uniform in holding that where one sells real estate and makes representations as to the quantity of land sold, that he is liable in an action for damages in case his representations, whether believed by him to be true or not, are in fact false, and the boundary lines pointed out by him are not the true boundary lines and the purchaser suffers any loss by reason thereof.

It was said in *Miller v. Wissert*, 38 Okl. 808, 134 Pac. 62, that "False representations of a vendor as to the quantity of a tract of land he offers for sale are not mere matters of opinion, but are material, and he cannot avoid their consequences merely because the vendee might have ascertained their falsity by a survey of the land or by reference to official plats and records."

In *Quarg v. Scher*, 136 Cal. 406, 69 Pac. 96, the court held that where the vendor represents that a tract of land contains a certain number of acres, the vendee can rely on the statement, and may rescind the sale, or have the purchase price decreased, if there is less land than vendor states. (*McGhee v. Bell*, 170 Mo. 121, 70 S. W. 493, 59 L. R. A. 761.)

It was held in *Culbertson v. Blanchard*, 79 Tex. 486, 15 S. W. 700, that even honesty in making a mistake is no defense, as it is incumbent upon the vendor to know the facts.

It is not necessary for us to pursue this point further. As we understand the record, the learned district judge held that the complaint stated a cause of action, but sustained the demurrer solely on the ground of nonjoinder, and held that the Springston Lumber Company was a necessary party plaintiff.

It will be observed from the allegations of the complaint above set forth that this is not an action for the cancelation of the $2,000 note, but is an action for damages by one claiming to be the vendee against the vendor. The contract alleged in the complaint is based upon the fact that the plaintiff and the defendant were the only parties to the contract for the purchase and sale of said timber; they are the real parties. The defendant by the demurrer admitted the material allegations of the complaint. He admitted that the timber was purchased by the plaintiff from him and admitted the pointing out of said boundary lines and that said boundary lines were not correct, and that the deed to the timber was made to the Springston Lumber Company for the purpose of security only. Then the only question remaining is as to whether, under all of those admitted facts, the Springston Lumber Company is a necessary party plaintiff to the action.

Under our practice act, if another person is a necessary party to an action, then the demurrer for nonjoinder will lie; but if such person is only a *proper* party, as distinguished from a *necessary* party, the demurrer for defective parties or nonjoinder will not lie.

It is stated in 31 Cyc. 293, as follows: "Under the codes and practice acts, a 'defect of parties' is expressly enumerated as a ground of demurrer, and such provisions apply equally well to a defect of parties plaintiff, as well as a defect of parties defendant. But nonjoinder of a proper, as distinguished from necessary, party is not ground for demurrer."

A "necessary" party is universally held to be one without whom the cause cannot proceed to final determination, whereas a "proper" party is one without whom the cause might have proceeded, but whose presence will allow a decree or judgment to more clearly settle the controversy between all of the parties.

It is stated in Bliss on Code Pleading, 21, that "In general, in an action founded upon tort, the person who suffered the injury must bring the action, for he is the party in interest."

The allegations of the complaint clearly show that the plaintiff is the one who suffered the alleged injury, and since it is alleged that the Springston Lumber Company was only security for the payment of the purchase price for said timber, it has not suffered any injury, as it has the title to said timber which it took as security, and such title is not sought to be affected in any way by this action. Injury is alleged to the plaintiff; no injury is alleged to the Springston company; no intimation is made in the complaint that the Springston company has a legal interest in this cause of action and that it could enforce it, notwithstanding a full and complete recovery were had by the plaintiff. It is not necessary to join as plaintiffs persons who do not appear by the allegations of the complaint to be united in interest with the plaintiff in the relief sought. (*Garner v. Wright*, 28 How. Pr. 92; *Washburn v. Case*, 1 Wash. Ter. 253; *Sheridan Gas, Oil & Coal Co. v. Pearson*, 19 Ind. App. 252, 65 Am. St. 402, 49 N. E. 357.)

According to the allegations of the complaint, the Springston Lumber Company was not a party to the contract for the purchase of said timber. The representations alleged to have been made to the plaintiff to induce him to buy the timber could not be relied upon by the Springston company, since it was not a party to the contract and had no interest therein, and it is a well-recognized rule of law that one who is not a party to a contract and has no interest in the contract is neither a necessary nor a proper party to an action because of a breach of the contract. (*Hurlbutt v. N. W. Spaulding Saw Co.*, 93 Cal. 55, 28 Pac. 795.) If the defendant can show by allegations in his answer that a complete determination of this controversy cannot be had without the Springston Lumber Company being made a party, it would then become the duty of the court to direct it to be brought in.

We therefore conclude that the court erred in holding that

there was a defect of parties plaintiff, in that the Springston Lumber Company was not made a party.

The judgment of dismissal must therefore be reversed, and it is so ordered, with directions to the trial court to overrule the demurrer and to permit the defendant to answer. Costs are awarded to the appellant.

AILSHIE, C. J., Concurring Specially.—In concurring in a reversal of the judgment in this case, I want to state the reasons which lead me to do so. I do not think upon the face of the complaint the question could be fairly presented to the court by demurrer that the Springston Lumber Company was a necessary party to the adjudication of any cause of action alleged as existing between plaintiff and defendant. On the other hand, I do not see where there would be any protection to either plaintiff or defendant under any judgment on this contract as against the Springston Lumber Company. A determination that the Springston Lumber Company had no real interest in the contract and only appeared as a nominal party thereto would be binding as between the parties to this action, but it would be in no sense binding upon the Springston Lumber Company and would in no way bar the company from prosecuting its action on the contract, or any action against either party involving any right under the contract. For that reason, I have no doubt but that the Springston Lumber Company is a "proper party," if not a "necessary party," and it would have been entirely proper, and I think wise, for the trial judge to have ordered the plaintiff to bring in the Springston Lumber Company and make it either a defendant or a plaintiff in the action.

While I agree that so far as the complaint shows, it cannot be said that the Springston Lumber Company was a necessary party, I am fully persuaded that it was a proper party, and that it should have been brought into this action and required to set up any interest it may have in the matter, so that justice may be done all the parties under the contract in the one action.

(May 23, 1914.)

JAMES PAGE, Appellant, v. ONEIDA IRRIGATION DISTRICT, a Corporation, Respondent.

[141 Pac. 238.]

TAXPAYER ESTOPPED—IRREGULARITY IN BOND ISSUE—VOID BOND ISSUE.

1. Where it is shown that a land owner within an irrigation district seeks to avoid the payment of assessments levied against his land by the district because of alleged irregularities or infirmities in the issue of bonds, and who, with full knowledge of such alleged defects or infirmities, has, by his silence, acquiesced in the expenditure of the fund derived from the sale of said bonds, and who has had knowledge that said bonds were passing into the hands of *bona fide* purchasers, *held*, that he will be estopped by his laches from being heard to object to the payment of such assessments.

2. A taxpayer may, by his conduct, be estopped from questioning the validity of municipal bonds because of alleged irregularities or infirmities in their issue.

APPEAL from the District Court of the Fifth Judicial District for the County of Franklin. Hon. Alfred Budge, Judge.

Action to have declared void certain liens and encumbrances created by assessments levied by an irrigation district, and to have determined the nature and amount of such liens as were legally created, and for the purpose of enjoining respondent from creating or attempting to create other or additional liens or encumbrances by levying future assessments. Judgment for defendant. *Affirmed.*

W. A. Lee and W. H. Wilkins, for Appellant, cite no authorities on points decided.

Richards & Haga, for Respondent.

"A taxpayer is barred by laches from enjoining the collection of a tax where he has stood by and permitted large numbers of taxpayers to pay such taxes." (*Kennedy v. Montgomery County*, 98 Tenn. 165, 38 S. W. 1075; Abbot, Public

Securities, sec. 62; *Schnell v. City of Rock Island,* 232 Ill. 89, 83 N. E. 462, 14 L. R. A., N. S., 874.)

"There is estoppel where the validity of bonds has been recognized by duly authorized public officials whereby the corporation has evidenced by its course of conduct that existing outstanding securities are valid obligations." (*Amey v. Mayor of Allegheny,* 24 How. (U. S.) 364, 16 L. ed. 614; Abbot, Public Securities, sec. 330.)

"The requirement of diligence and the loss of the right to invoke the arm of a court of equity in cases of laches is particularly applicable where the subject matter of the controversy is a public work." (*Penn Mutual Life Ins. Co. v. City of Austin,* 168 U. S. 685, 18 Sup. Ct. 223, 42 L. ed. 626.)

We call the court's attention to the case of *Rogers v. Thomas,* 193 Fed. 952, 113 C. C. A. 580, which is quite similar to the case at bar.

Ordinarily, the want of power to issue bonds for a given purpose may be raised as a defense to the enforcement of the bonds, but once the power to issue securities is conceded, it is not competent to defend against their collection upon the ground of fraud in their execution, or any irregularities in their delivery. (*Baxter v. Vineland Irr. Dist.,* 136 Cal. 185, 68 Pac. 601; *Leeman v. Perris Irr. Dist.,* 140 Cal. 540, 74 Pac. 24.)

WALTERS, District Judge.—The appellant, who was the plaintiff below, is a land owner within the bounds of the respondent irrigation district, said lands being subject to certain liens and encumbrances created by said irrigation district.

This action was brought by appellant for the purpose of having declared void said liens and encumbrances which had been created by assessments made by respondent irrigation district and which appellant had failed to pay; that the court determine the nature and amount of the liens, if any, which had been legally created by defendant; and for the further purpose of enjoining respondent from creating or attempting to create other or additional liens or encumbrances by levying future assessments.

The relief asked for by plaintiff was by the trial court refused, from which judgment and the denial of a motion for new trial the plaintiff has prosecuted this appeal.

The record discloses that the defendant irrigation district was organized under and pursuant to the laws of the state of Idaho on the 3d day of May, 1902, after which it caused surveys and plans to be made and formulated for the construction of an irrigation canal system; that to defray the expenses of the construction of said canal system said district authorized and caused four separate bond issues to be executed and disposed of in the years 1902, 1905, 1906 and 1910.

It further appears that certain assessments have been levied against the land of plaintiff for the payment of interest on said bonds and for maintenance of the canal system.

The court found that in addition to the bonded debt a certain other debt was outstanding and unpaid, but that no levies of assessments or taxes have been made for the payment of the same, nor interest thereon.

The plaintiff charges (1) that a portion of said bonds was disposed of by said defendant for less than par with accrued interest; (2) that a portion of said bonds was delivered to various persons for work and labor performed for defendant district; (3) that a portion of said bonds was delivered to a certain person for which the defendant district received no consideration, and (4) that a portion of said bonds was not legally executed, in that they were not signed by the president of the defendant district.

In relation thereto the court found, and the evidence authorizes the court in so finding, (1) that a portion of said bonds was sold for their full cash value and accrued interest, but that after repeated efforts upon the part of the district to sell the bonds, they employed a broker to sell the same, paying him a commission therefor; (2) that a portion of said bonds had been delivered to contractors or others for work or labor in lieu of cash and in payment for work and labor performed and materials furnished, and that said bonds so delivered were accepted at their full face or par value with accrued interest; (3) that certain of said bonds given to certain contractors in payment of work and labor performed and material furnished were by said contractors placed as collateral security with a certain bank for loans made and moneys advanced to said contractors; that for default in the payment of said loans said bank now claims to hold said bonds as a *bona fide* purchaser; (4) and that certain of said bonds were signed by the president of said defendant district after his term of office had expired, inasmuch as the bonds had been dated and prepared for signature at a time when said person was president aforesaid; that said signature had been affixed to said bonds at the request of the board of directors and the then president of said defendant district, and with the full knowledge, acquiescence and consent of the same.

The court found that practically all of said bonds had passed from the original purchaser directly or by means of sales through bond brokers into the hands of many and divers persons not parties to this suit, who had purchased the same in good faith for value, and without any notice or knowledge of the facts which plaintiff claims created defects and infirmities in said bonds as hereinbefore set forth.

.1. From our view of the case it will be unnecessary to discuss or determine the merit or lack of merit in the objections made by plaintiff to the payment of assessments for the purpose of meeting interest on the bonds in question and maintenance charges for the operation of the canal system, inasmuch as it appears that the plaintiff in this action was a holder of land within the bounds of the irrigation district at the time of its organization in 1902 until the present time, and has ever since the completion of the defendant's canal in the year 1907 used water from the same for the irrigation of his said land and has accepted the benefits conferred by the construction of said canal system; that during all of said period of time since the issuance of the first series of bonds the plaintiff knew that all of said bonds were treated as valid obligations of the district except a small portion of said bonds held by a local banking concern, upon which interest has not been paid by said district; that plaintiff acquiesced in the validity of said bonds and in the validity of the assessments levied to pay interest on the same, and that said plaintiff paid assessments levied upon his said lands from the year 1904 to 1908 inclusive; that plaintiff knew that a portion of said bonds, and to which he now raises objection, was being delivered to contractors for work and labor and to material men. It appears that a portion of said bonds at said time was delivered to plaintiff himself in payment of work and labor; that appellant has not paid assessments for the years 1909 to 1912, inclusive, and neither does he make tender of any sum for said purpose, although he has accepted the full benefit of the water delivered by said irrigation district. It appears that the plaintiff has stood silently by and permitted the canal system to be constructed, bonds issued and sold and assessments collected and interest paid, and has accepted all the benefit to be derived, and has never raised the objections which he now proposes until the filing of this suit in the fall of 1912, when it is plainly shown by the record that he has had full knowledge for many years past of the facts upon which he now predicates his objections.

In the light of these facts it to our mind appears that the plaintiff should be estopped from being heard in a court of equity to urge the matters by him now proposed. The appellant has been a member of the defendant irrigation dis- trict since its inception, and he has known of the efforts of the district to sell the bonds in question that it might procure funds with which to construct the canals, and has for a number of years stood by and acknowledged the validity of the bonds by accepting them for collateral and by paying interest on them for several years, and now when the system has been practically completed, and he has received the full benefit of this expenditure, he for the first time makes objection to what has been done years ago.

2. The principle of estoppel has been recognized in cases akin to this by text-writers and by many courts. In Abbot, Public Securities, sec. 162, it is said: "The taxpayer may be

estopped from contesting the validity of a tax levy by his laches, acquiescence or other conduct which will bring him within the operation of the general principles under which the doctrine of estoppel is applied. . . . . ''

And again, at sec. 320, this same author says: ''It is a fundamental rule of equity that the courts will not permit one to sit idly by while rights are being asserted adverse to his interests without promptly acting for his protection. This doctrine is applied in favor of the *bona fide* holder of public securities and the courts have repeatedly held that where a public corporation fails to raise defenses which are open to it within a reasonable length of time, that it will thereafter be estopped by laches to question the validity of securities in the hands of *bona fide* holders in respect to irregularities and infirmities in their issue.''

In applying the doctrine of estoppel in the case of *Lent v. Tillson*, 72 Cal. 404, 14 Pac. 71, the following language is used: ''Under such circumstances, they could not remain silent, and permit the money obtained of the bondholders to be expended in the improvement of their property, and then escape liability on the plea that the officers charged with the work, who were in a sense their agents, were guilty of misconduct and fraud, which they by proper diligence could have prevented.''

It is held in *Rodgers v. Thomas*, 193 Fed. 952, 113 C. C. A. 580, that a land owner within an irrigation district was estopped from questioning the validity of the bonds of said district when it appeared that the contractor's right to maintain an action at law, to recover for his work, was barred by limitation; such holding being indicated in the following language:

''So in the present case, if the irrigation district sold the bonds in a manner unauthorized by statute, the contractor could, if the validity of the bonds had been questioned in time, have recovered on his contract, in the event the bonds were held invalid because of the manner in which they were sold. But, instead of raising the question of the validity of the bonds promptly, as the district or any taxpayer therein had the right to do, both the corporation and all of the taxpayers, with full knowledge of the facts, recognized these bonds as valid obligations of the district and accepted the benefits to their lands derived from the construction of the irrigation works until several years after the rights of the contractor to sue upon the contract or to bring an action based on a *quantum meruit* was barred by the statute of limitations, and his right to recover at law forever lost. Furthermore, the suit to cancel the bonds was not brought for about eight years after the bonds were delivered. Therefore the cause of action, if any, arising out of the matters set out in the bill of complaint, did not accrue within four years before the bill was filed, and, if the case was at law, would be barred by the statute of limitations of Nebraska. For eight years the district and the taxpayers accepted the benefits of the contract for which the bonds were given in payment, and there is not a single allegation in the bill nor a particle of proof introduced in their behalf tending to show that there were any impediments to an earlier prosecution of a suit to test the validity of the bonds."

To like effect is the case of *Penn Mut. Life Ins. Co. v. City of Austin*, 168 U. S. 685, 695, 18 Sup. Ct. 223, 42 L. ed. 626, wherein it is stated: "The requirement of diligence, and the loss of the right to invoke the arm of a court of equity in case of laches, is particularly applicable where the subject matter of the controversy is a public work. In a case of this nature, where a public expenditure has been made, or a public work undertaken, and where one having full opportunity to prevent its accomplishment has stood by and seen the public work proceed, a court of equity will more readily consider laches."

3. It should be noted that plaintiff does not question the power of the irrigation district to issue the bonds in question, nor charge that it exceeded its authority in so doing, but rests his objection to certain asserted irregularities in the manner of disposing of said bonds by the district, or irregularities in the clerical work of issuing the same; therefore, the doctrine of this case should not be confused with

that line of cases which hold that estoppel cannot be invoked against an interested party who seeks to have declared void, bonds which have been issued without warrant of law, or in excess of the power conferred upon the issuing body.

This principle last mentioned was affirmed by the supreme court of the United States in the case of *Township of East Oakland v. Skinner,* 94 U. S. 255, 24 L. ed. 125, in the following language:

"We have held that there can be no *bona fide* holding where the statute did not in law authorize the issue of the bonds. The objection in such case goes to the point of power. There is an entire want of jurisdiction over the subject. It is not the case of an informality, an irregularity, fraud or excess of authority, in an authorized agent. Where there is a total want of authority to issue the bonds, there can be no such thing as a *bona fide* holding."

The authorities are unanimous in holding that negotiable bonds issued by a public or municipal corporation without legislative or constitutional authority are void, even in the hands of *bona fide* purchasers, as is evidenced by the following cases: *Mayor of Nashville v. Ray,* 19 Wall. (U. S.) 468, 22 L. ed. 164; *Town of South Ottawa v. Perkins,* 94 U. S. 260, 24 L. ed. 154; *County of Dallas v. MacKenzie,* 94 U. S. 660, 24 L. ed. 182; *Farmers' Loan & Trust Co. v. City of Galesburg,* 133 U. S. 156, 10 Sup. Ct. 316, 33 L. ed. 573; *Brenham v. German-American Bank,* 144 U. S. 173, 12 Sup. Ct. 559, 36 L. ed. 390; *Francis v. Howard County,* 50 Fed. 44; *Edminson v. City of Abilene,* 7 Kan. App. 305, 54 Pac. 568; *Cagwin v. Town of Hancock,* 84 N. Y. 532.

For the foregoing reasons we conclude that the judgment of the district court must be affirmed, and it is so ordered. Costs are awarded to respondent.

Ailshie, C. J., and Sullivan, J., concur.

(January 21, 1914.)

C. C. CHILDS et al., Respondents, v. N. J. NEITZEL et al., Appellants.

[141 Pac. 77.]

IRRIGATION PROJECT — PROMOTION OF — CONSTRUCTION OF SYSTEM — WATER CONTRACTS—CONSTRUCTION OF—ASSIGNMENT OF—RIGHTS OF PARTIES—COMPLETION OF SYSTEM—MORTGAGEE—ASSIGNEE— RIGHTS OF—CONSTITUTIONAL LAW.

1. Where a company is incorporated for the promotion of an irrigation scheme and to construct an irrigation system, consisting of reservoirs, dams and ditches, and such corporation enters into contracts with persons having land within such project to furnish them water at an agreed price per acre, divided into annual payments with interest on deferred payments, and agrees to complete such system within a certain time and furnish the purchasers of water rights with water, and agrees to turn such system over to such purchasers of water rights after its completion, and thereafter mortgages its interest in such system and water right and also assigns such water right contracts as security for borrowed money, which money is used in the construction of such system, *held*, that the person loaning the money only acquires such rights and interest as the irrigation company has in such project and such water right contracts, and cannot collect the payments that become due after the time has expired for the completion of such irrigation system and the delivery of water until the said system is completed and the water delivered in accordance with the terms of the water right contracts.

2. Under the provisions of said water right contracts, the Murphy Land & Irrigation Company agreed to complete said irrigation system and turn the same over to the purchasers of water rights within a specified time, and the Murphy company was not the trustee or agent of the water right purchasers for the construction of said system.

3. Neitzel, who loaned the money to said Murphy Land & Irrigation Company and took a mortgage and an assignment of said water contracts as security for the payment of the money so loaned, did not become an insurer for the Murphy company to the water right claimants that said system would be completed and the water furnished as provided by said contracts, but acquired no other right than that which the Murphy Irrigation Company had in the collec-

tion of deferred payments provided for by said contracts, and cannot enforce the collection of such payments and apply the same on his mortgage debt until said system has been completed and turned over to the water right purchasers as provided by such contracts.

4.   The fact that the purchasers of such water rights authorized the Murphy company to assign them does not estop them from setting up as a defense against the payment thereof that said system has not been completed as required by said contracts.

5.   Mortgagees or assigns of irrigation project corporations can acquire no greater interest in such project or water right contracts connected therewith than such corporations have.

6.   Sec. 15 of art. 11 of the state constitution prohibits the legislature from passing any law which would permit the leasing or alienation of any franchise so as to release or relieve such franchise or property held thereunder from any liabilities of the lessor or grantor or lessee or grantee, contracted or incurred in the operation, use or enjoyment of such franchise or any of its privileges.

7.   Under the provisions of sec. 2 of art. 15 of the constitution, the right to collect rates or compensation for the use of water is a franchise and cannot be exercised except by authority of and in the manner prescribed by law.

8.   Sec. 1 of art. 15 provides that the use of all water now appropriated or that may hereafter be appropriated for sale, rental or distribution is a public use, subject to the regulation and control of the state in the manner prescribed by law.

9.   The Murphy Land & Irrigation Company is a public service corporation.

APPEAL from the District Court of the Third Judicial District, in and for Ada County. Hon. Carl A. Davis, Judge.

Action to determine the rights of the several parties under certain water right contracts.   Judgment for the intervenors. *Affirmed.*

Davidson & Davidson and Richards & Haga, for Appellants.

The record conclusively shows that the land owners had full knowledge that the only assets of the defendant company consisted of the proceeds to be derived from the payment of the amounts due on water contracts, that such payments were to be made from year to year until December, 1916, and that such company having no other assets, it was a matter of absolute necessity to use these contracts to borrow money with which to commence construction, and it was necessary and the respondents did consent to the use of such contracts as collateral security for the money so to be borrowed by the defendant company as the owner thereof, and the defendant company and the defendant Neitzel having advanced the money for this purpose on the faith of these contracts as collateral security, the respondents will not be permitted to repudiate such ownership by the defendant company for the purpose intended. (*Hill v. Wand*, 47 Kan. 340, 27 Am. St. 288, 27 Pac. 988; *First Nat. Bank v. Kissare*, 22 Okl. 545, 132 Am. St. 644, 98 Pac. 433.)

This is an equitable action, and he who induces another to his injury to act on a given state of facts will not be permitted to repudiate such facts. (2 Pom. Eq. Jur., sec. 804; *Illinois Trust & Savings Bank v. City of Arkansas*, 76 Fed. 271, 293, 22 C. C. A. 171, 34 L. R. A. 518.)

One who by act intended to influence the conduct of another and thereby lead him into a line of conduct prejudicial to his interests is estopped from a retraction of such act. (*Leland v. Isenbeck*, 1 Ida. 469; *Lane v. Pacific & I. N. R. Co.*, 8 Ida. 230, 67 Pac. 656; *Marysville Mercantile Co. v. Home Fire Ins. Co.*, 21 Ida. 377, 121 Pac. 1026; *Lick v. Munro*, 8 Ida. 510, 69 Pac. 285; *Brigham Young Trust Co. v. Wagener*, 12 Utah, 1, 40 Pac. 764; *Branson v. Wirth*, 17 Wall. (U. S.) 32, 21 L. ed. 566; *Dickerson v. Colgrove*, 100 U. S. 578, 25 L. ed. 618; *The Ottumwa Belle*, 78 Fed. 643.)

Hawley, Puckett & Hawley, for Respondents, file no brief.

Karl Paine and C. E. Winstead, for Intervenors, cite no authorities.

SULLIVAN, J.—This action was brought by C. C. Childs against N. J., R. E. and H. R. Neitzel, W. D. McReynolds and H. A. Toole, directors of the Murphy Land & Irrigation Co., and the Murphy Land & Irrigation Company, for the purpose of ousting said Neitzels, McReynolds and Toole from the office of directors of said company and to have the offices of president, vice-president, secretary and treasurer declared vacant, and to have a certain mortgage executed by said corporation in favor of H. R. Neitzel declared void and for other relief, and for the appointment of a receiver to take charge of the property of said corporation.

The answer put in issue many of the material allegations of the complaint. This action was based upon the ownership of 2,000 shares of the capital stock of the defendant corporation by said Childs and not upon a contract for a water right.

Upon the trial of the case the lower court granted Childs certain relief prayed for by him and an accounting, but before the findings in the case were filed, Childs waived an accounting, owing to the insolvency of the corporation and the refusal of certain intervenors to assume the major part of the expense of an accounting before a referee. Childs did not appeal from the judgment entered and is only a nominal party in this court, and it appears from the record that the rights of appellant H. R. Neitzel are alone before this court for consideration, so far as appellants are concerned.

A complaint and an amended complaint in intervention were filed in said action, and it is alleged in the amended complaint that the intervenors are holders of certain contracts for water rights under the said Murphy Land & Irrigation Company project, and are the owners and in the possession of more than 3,500 acres of land under said project, which lands intervenors have settled upon and improved at great expense and labor and upon which they and their families are dependent for support. A copy of said water contracts is attached to said complaint in intervention and made a part thereof. The contracts, so far as the covenants and agreements contained therein are concerned, are all the same.

The defendant corporation entered into such agreements with the intervenors and divers other persons, wherein it contracted to construct a certain irrigation system in Owyhee county known as the Murphy project, and to sell to said intervenors and such other persons shares of water appropriated and impounded by it, also certain rights in and to the irrigation system itself. Among other things said contracts contain the following stipulation:

"Each of such shares [of water] shall represent a carrying capacity in said canal sufficient to deliver water at the rate of one-eightieth of one cubic foot of water, per acre, per second of time, or in lieu thereof, in event the company shall hereafter elect to distribute the waters flowing and to flow in its canals by a system of rotation, then the company agrees to deliver to second party under such rotation system a quantity of water equivalent thereto in service."

The contract also provides that all dams, reservoirs, headgates, conduits, canals, laterals and other works for the diversion of water shall, at the discretion of the defendant corporation, be and remain its sole property until such time as the said irrigation system shall have been fully completed, and all waters to be diverted and beneficially applied under the said system shall have been sold by it. The corporation also agreed that within one year after the final completion of the whole project and within five years from December 31, 1906, it would turn over the entire project to its water users under its water contracts. The contract also contains the following provision:

"The water to be furnished under this contract may not be available to the purchaser prior to May 15, 1908, and if for any reason the canal shall not be completed so as to enable the company to furnish water through the same by said date, the date of maturity of each and every deferred payment shall be advanced one year, with a waiver of interest upon all such payments for a like period of one year."

The contract also provides that the purchase price of water rights is $35 per acre except in certain cases, and that the purchase price should be paid in ten annual instalments, the first in cash and the second on December 1, 1908, and the remaining eight instalments on December 1st of each succeeding year. Deferred payments were to draw interest at the rate of 6% per annum. The corporation was authorized to collect annually from its water users a maintenance of sixty cents an acre on the entire tract covered by their contracts whether water was used on the whole of said land or not. The last provision of said contract is as follows: "It is agreed that the stipulations, covenants and agreements in this contract shall be mutually binding upon the parties hereto, their and each of their heirs, executors, administrators, successors and assigns." The contracts had the following indorsement printed thereon: "I hereby consent to the assignment of the within contract," which consent was signed by the intervenors and all other purchasers of water rights.

This contract is the basis of the intervenors' cause of action. The intervenors allege in their amended complaint, among other things, substantially as follows:

That the defendant corporation had never completed said irrigation project and had refused and neglected to do so, and had never delivered and was unable to deliver to the intervenors and the holders of contracts for water rights the amount of water which it had agreed to deliver to them, and that it would be unable to deliver the same until the said irrigation system was fully completed; that the lands included in the contracts were arid in character and required the amount of water bargained for in said contracts in order to grow crops thereon, and that water was not available from any other source for the irrigation of said lands; that the defendant corporation had never turned over said project to its water users; that the defendant had made contracts for the irrigation of about 6,000 acres of land; that there were about $100,000 remaining unpaid on the purchase price of said water rights, all of which would have to be expended in order to complete said system and deliver to the water users the amount of water sold to them; that the defendant threatened to sell other water rights although it had failed to comply with the laws of 1909 (Sess. Laws, p. 335), providing for the regulation and control of the sale of water rights, etc.; that. said contracts for water rights had been assigned by the defendant corporation to the defendant H. R. Neitzel to secure an alleged indebtedness of $150,000 for money advanced by the defendant H. R. Neitzel to the Murphy company for the purpose of constructing said system, together with interest thereon at the rate of 12% per annum, interest payable semi-annually; that said corporation was unable to pay its debts or meet its current obligations as they accrued and was insolvent in law and in fact; that the intervenors had failed and refused to pay the 1912 instalment of principal and interest due on their said water contracts because of the said default of the defendant corporation in the completion of said system and in the delivery of water and its insolvency, and because of the mortgage given to the appellant Neitzel on the irrigation system and the said assignment of said contracts to the defendant H. R. Neitzel, and the intention of appellants to apply the payments made on the unpaid purchase price of water rights to the payment of said alleged indebtedness to H. R. Neitzel with interest thereon at the rate of 12% per annum; that the intervenors were jointly interested in, and were joint owners with, the other water users of said irrigation system, and that they and the other water users were entitled to have the proceeds received by the defendant corporation from said contracts as principal, interest and maintenance applied to the completion, maintenance and repair of said irrigation system, and to have all other terms and conditions of said contracts kept and performed by the defendant corporation.

The defendant corporation admitted that the form of the contract attached to the complaint in intervention was a copy of those issued to all purchasers of water rights; denied that the system had never been completed or that it was unable to deliver to the water users the amount of water contracted to be delivered to them; denied that it threatened to sell other water rights or that it was insolvent or in default, or that it never offered to turn over said irrigation project to the water users.

Upon the issues thus presented, after a trial the court made findings of fact to the following effect: That the contracts of the form attached to the complaint in intervention had been issued for water for the irrigation of about 6,000 acres of land and that said contracts were in full force and

effect; that the defendant corporation had not completed the
said irrigation project, and that it had never delivered and
was unable to deliver the amount of water sold to the water
users under said contracts, and would not be able to keep
its contracts in that respect until the irrigation system had
been completed; that the lands covered by said contract were
arid in character and required the amount of water for their
irrigation that the appellant corporation had agreed to deliver for that purpose, and that water was not available from
any other source for the irrigation of said lands; that on the
1st day of December, 1912, there became due from the intervenors, with the exception of two of them who held paid-up
contracts, one instalment of principal and interest; that the
defendant corporation had never turned over the project to
its water users or offered to turn it over to them; that the
interest on the $150,000 loaned to said corporation by the said
H. R. Neitzel at the rate of 12% per annum, if collected,
would have the effect of exhausting the proceeds of principal,
interest and maintenance fund due and unpaid on the said
contracts, and that appellants threatened to collect interest
thereon at said rate and to compel the water users to pay
the sum of $150,000 with interest thereon at said rate before
turning over said system to them; that the said holders of
contracts had paid the defendant corporation the sum of
about $122,000, exclusive of maintenance dues, on the pur-
chase of said water rights; that the defendant corporation
threatened to issue other contracts for water rights although
it had failed to comply with the laws of 1909 providing for
the regulation and control of the sale of water rights, etc.;
that the holders of water contracts had refused to pay the
defendant corporation and the defendant H. R. Neitzel the
instalment of principal and interest on deferred payments
which became payable by the terms of said contracts on the
1st day of December, 1912; that otherwise they had fully
performed their contract in all things to be kept and performed by them; that said intervenors based such refusal
on the insolvency of the defendant corporation and its default and the threat of appellants to apply all payments on

the purchase price of said contract to the payment of the alleged indebtedness owing to the defendant Neitzel, including interest thereon at the rate of 12% per annum; that the defendant corporation was unable to pay its debts or meet its current obligations as they accrued, as it was insolvent and without means to maintain the said system or to pay the said indebtedness to the defendant H. R. Neitzel.

From said findings of fact proper conclusions of law were made by the court and judgment entered in favor of the intervenors. Among other conclusions of law were the following: "That there is now unpaid on the contracts for water rights issued by the defendant corporation the sum of about $100,000.00, which money the holders of said contracts are entitled to have expended in the completion, operation and repair of said irrigation system so far as may be necessary to comply with said contracts; that the use of the waters now held or appropriated by the defendant corporation is a public use and the right of the defendant corporation to collect rates or compensation from the holders of said contracts for the use of water supplied or to be supplied to them ·is a franchise, and the money remaining unpaid on said contracts for water rights is a trust fund, of which the defendant corporation or the defendant H. R. Neitzel, as assignee, is the trustee; that the holders of said contracts are jointly interested in the said irrigation system, including the water appropriated by the defendant corporation to be used in the irrigation of the lands lying under said project, and are the equitable owners of the said irrigation system to the extent necessary to supply water as provided in said contracts, and that the defendant corporation holds the legal title to said irrigation system, subject to said claim and said contracts; that the defendant corporation, or the defendant H. R. Neitzel, as assignee, is entitled to any surplus remaining unpaid on the purchase price of said water rights after the said contracts for water rights have been fully kept and performed by the defendant corporation; that by reason of the failure and neglect of the defendant corporation to complete said system and of its inability to deliver to the holders of said contracts for water rights the amount of water to which they are entitled for the irrigation of their lands, and because of its insolvency, the holders of said contracts for water rights have failed and refused to make the payments due under their contracts in December, 1911 (1912), and still refuse to make said payments, as they have a right to do; that the probable cost of completing the said irrigation system and making it possible to deliver the required amount of water for the irrigation of the lands owned by the holders of said contracts for water rights is, approximately, $100,000.00, and that there are no assets available for the completion of the said system except the amount remaining unpaid on said contracts."

After entering judgment for the intervenors, a receiver was appointed and was authorized to collect the unpaid part on the purchase price of said water rights with the accrued interest thereon and the maintenance fees, and was directed to manage and operate and complete the construction of said irrigation system, subject, however, to the right of the appellant corporation to co-operate with the receiver in the completion thereof.

The rights of appellant H. R. Neitzel and the rights of the intervenors under said contracts for water are involved in this appeal, and so far as the intervenors are concerned, their claim is based on the breach of the provisions of said contracts by the defendant corporation. The object and purpose of the action on behalf of the intervenors is the enforcement of such contracts through the instrumentality of a receiver and to restrain the appellant H. R. Neitzel from collecting the money due on said water contracts and applying it to the payment of his said mortgage indebtedness, and for general relief.

It is contended by counsel for appellant that the facts as found by the court clearly show that the appellant corporation was organized solely to provide a system of irrigation for certain lands, the cost of which was to be paid by the owners of such lands, and that to provide funds for the construction of such system $150,000 was borrowed by said corporation, and to secure the payment of the same a mortgage was given by said corporation covering its interest in such system, and also by an assignment of said water contracts. The mortgage was given to said H. R. Neitzel and the said water contracts were assigned to him. The sum so borrowed was used in the construction, maintenance and operation of said system but was insufficient to complete the same. The court found that there had been paid on said water contracts about $122,000 to the appellant corporation. Upon that state of facts, counsel for appellant propounds the following question: In the light of these facts, the question presented for determination is, Can such land owners apply the balance due on such written obligations to the completion, operation and maintenance and repair of such system instead of applying the same to the payment of the money so borrowed? Counsel contends that the defendant company was the mere instrument or legal means for providing the lands with water, the cost thereof to be paid by such land owners or purchasers of water under said contracts.

We cannot agree with counsel in that contention. The Murphy company agreed to complete said irrigation system with its dams, reservoirs and canals and turn the same over to the purchasers of water rights within a specified time, the price per acre for such water rights being stipulated in most of the contracts at $35 per acre. The Murphy company no doubt contemplated making a considerable profit for itself in the construction of said system. It was not an eleemosynary corporation or the trustee or agent of the water right purchaser for the construction of said irrigation system, but was a corporation organized for the purpose of making a profit to its stockholders from the construction of said system. If any profits had arisen to the company from the construction of said system, the purchasers of said water rights could not, under said contracts, share in them with the Murphy company. The Murphy company had employed engineers and experts to examine said irrigation project as to its feasibility, the quantity of water that could be obtained for the irrigation of said land and the cost of the construction of said system to make the water available to the land to be irrigated, and after that was done, an estimate was made of the amount to be charged for each acre water right that would be necessary and sufficient to construct said system and pay a good profit to the Murphy company. Under said water contracts it was not expected, contemplated or necessary for the purchasers of water rights to employ engineers and other experts to make a proper estimate of the amount of water obtainable and the cost of the construction of the system, and to ascertain whether the company could place the water at feasible points near the land to be irrigated. That had been done by the Murphy company, and it sold water rights upon the representations that it had water sufficient to furnish each purchaser with the amount called for in his water contract, and also was able to construct said system and complete it. Hence the purchasers of water rights under such system had a legal right to depend upon the estimates made by the irrigation company and upon their contracts with it to the effect that the company would finish and complete the system and furnish the water according to the terms of the contract. They did not purchase under the rule *caveat emptor.*

Said contracts show their exact terms on their face and include mutual covenants, and since H. R. Neitzel received said contracts by assignment, he had notice of all the covenants contained therein. Those contracts were made by the purchasers of water rights with the Murphy company, and that company could not have enforced the collection of the deferred payments and interest thereon without complying with the terms thereof as to the construction of said system and the delivery of water, and neither the mortgagee nor the assignee could acquire any greater rights in that regard than the Murphy company itself had under said water contracts. H. R. Neitzel, by loaning said money to the Murphy company and taking as security for the payment of the same a mortgage on said company's interest in said system and water rights and an assignment of said water right contracts, did not become an insurer for the Murphy company to the water right claimants that said system would be completed and the water furnished, but he stands in the shoes of the Murphy company so far as the collection of the deferred payments is concerned and cannot enforce their collection until said system is completed and the water furnished in accordance with the terms of said water right contracts.

The purchasers of water rights depended upon their contracts as to what their water rights and said system would cost them, and had they considered that their water rights would cost them more than $35 per acre, they might not have entered into said contracts. It would have been an easy matter to have worded said contracts so as to have required such purchasers to pay the entire cost of said system had that been the intention of the parties. That was clearly not the intention, as the agreement was to pay $35 per acre for the right, and no more. The Murphy company had agreed to turn over to the purchasers of said water rights certain amounts of water with a canal system completed in such a manner as to make it feasible to irrigate said lands, and until that was done neither the Murphy company nor its assigns could enforce the payment of the amounts that were to become due upon said contracts.

When H. R. Neitzel loaned the said Murphy company $150,000 he knew that only a part of the money due on the contracts was payable prior to the time the Murphy company had agreed to complete the system and turn it over to said purchasers. He certainly knew that if his assignor, the Murphy company, made default and failed to complete said system, it would be necessary for him to complete the project or lose his security, at least to the extent of the cost of completing the system.

The fact that the purchasers of said water rights authorized the Murphy company to assign said contracts does not estop them from setting up as a defense to the payment thereof the fact that the Murphy company has not complied with its contract in the construction and completion of said canal system. The purchasers of water rights were not the stockholders in the appellant corporation; they had no voice whatever in directing its affairs, and, as before stated, they could not share in the profits of the enterprise had there been any profits realized, nor can they be required to stand the loss incurred in case there is a loss on the part of the Murphy company in completing said system in accordance with the terms of the contract. The purchasers of water rights ought not to be penalized because they were so unfortunate as to purchase a water right from an irresponsible and unreliable company. The obligation rests upon the person who loans money to such a corporation to investigate the financial condition of the corporation and its ability to perform its covenants with the purchasers of water rights, and if he does so investigate, he has full notice that the deferred payments for such water rights cannot be collected until the system is completed and the water delivered. The purchasers of the water rights, as shown by the record, have neglected no duty they owed to the appellant H. R. Neitzel; they have been guilty of no fraud, have made no false representations, and, so far as the record shows, have committed no wrong, legal or equitable.

It is a part of the irrigation history of the state that under the representations made by many such irrigation companies, persons have sold their holdings elsewhere and been induced to settle upon lands under such projects with the understanding and agreement that they should receive water at a certain price per acre, and were thus induced to take up land and settle upon it under such projects. If a corporation thus inducing people to purchase and settle upon such lands is permitted to violate its contract and increase the price per acre for a water right without the purchasers' consent, it would be most unjust to the settler.

The last provision of said water contract is to the effect that the covenants and agreements in said contract shall be mutually binding upon the parties thereto, their and each of their heirs, executors, administrators, successors and assigns.

Counsel for appellants contend that in lending the money to the Murphy company, Neitzel relied upon said water contracts as security, and for that reason the water users are estopped to deprive him of the benefit of such security. From the admissions in the answer of appellants, it appears that Neitzel's chief reliance for the payment of said money was not entirely on the security which he received but in his faith in his judgment as to what it would cost to complete the project and in his ability to carry out the contracts.

It is alleged in appellants' answer as follows: "That on the 15th day of January, 1910, the defendant H. R. Neitzel, acting for himself entered into a contract with the plaintiff C. C. Childs and the defendant R. E. Neitzel, by the terms of which said defendant H. R. Neitzel agreed to finance to completion the project of the Murphy Land & Irrigation Company in Owyhee County," etc. Neitzel's object in entering into that contract no doubt was to protect and preserve his security, but since the system is going to cost much more than was anticipated to complete it, he is seeking to avoid the natural consequences of his own mistaken judgment. It is not claimed that the water users made any inducements or representations to him as to the cost of the completion of said system. It was the Murphy company which promoted this scheme; it prepared the printed form of contracts for the water users to sign and made and held out all the inducements that were offered by anyone connected with the enterprise. The Murphy company was the one that had carefully gone into all of the facts relative to the cost of said system and the amount of water that could be conserved thereby. It represented to the purchasers that it had the ability to deliver to them a completed system so that each of the purchasers of water rights should have water for his land delivered within a short distance thereof at a point feasible for him to take it upon his land. Under such contracts the water users were empowered to enforce them against the company or its assignee, and the company upon complying with the terms of the contract required to be performed by it could enforce the payment of the purchase price from the original purchaser of a water right or his assign.

Construction companies of this kind will not be permitted to do indirectly what they are prohibited from doing directly. They will not be permitted to make contracts with third parties in regard to the construction or completion of an irrigation system whereby the land owners or purchasers of water rights can be deprived of the rights acquired under their water right contracts. For instance, if a company, such as the Murphy company, fails to complete its system and furnish the water as provided in the water right contracts, or if such company should sublet the construction of its system and fail and neglect to pay such subcontractor, the subcontractor could not acquire greater rights as against the water right purchasers than the irrigation company itself had under its contract with the purchasers of water rights, and could not deprive the purchasers of water rights under such system of their rights or acquire a right by foreclosure of a lien or mortgage for such construction work as would deprive the water right purchasers of their rights under their contracts.

Sec. 15 of art. 11 of the constitution provides that the legislature shall not pass any law permitting the leasing or alienation of any franchise so as to release or relieve the franchise or property held thereunder from any of the liabilities of the lessor or grantor, or lessee or grantee, contracted or incurred in the operation, use, or enjoyment of such franchise, or any of its privileges.

Sec. 2 of art. 15 is as follows: "The right to collect rates or compensation for the use of water supplied to any county, city, or town, or water district, or the inhabitants thereof, is a franchise, and cannot be exercised except by authority of and in the manner prescribed by law."

Sec. 1 of art. 15 provides that the use of all waters now appropriated or that may hereafter be appropriated for sale, rental or distribution, is declared to be a public use subject to the regulation and control of the state in the manner prescribed by law.

The Murphy company was a public service or a *quasi* public corporation, and the use it was making of its irrigation system and of the waters appropriated by it was a public use, and the right it was exercising in selling water shares and rights in the irrigation system and issuing contracts therefor and collecting rates and compensation was a franchise, and such franchise could not be granted to it in any manner so as to relieve it of its duty to the public or release its franchise and the property acquired thereunder of any liability for a failure to complete its system. In loaning money to such a corporation, the one loaning must rely primarily on the borrower to carry out the contracts with the water right purchasers. The mere consent of the water right users to the assignment of said contracts was not a waiver of their right to have the system completed; but the assignment was given subject to the obligation of the Murphy company, or its assigns, to carry out and complete said irrigation system and deliver the water.

It is contended by counsel for appellants that the court erred in decreeing that the amounts remaining due and unpaid on said water contracts, or so much thereof as may be necessary, be expended in the completion, operation, maintenance and repair of said irrigation system by the receiver, and that this decree places no limitation as to the time or conditions in which this money can be so used in maintaining, operating and repairing such system, and that said water contracts provide that such land owners must pay sixty cents an acre annually as an operating and maintenance fee. Under the terms of said contract, the Murphy company was to maintain and operate said canal until the system was completed, and turned over to the water users. Now, this matter has been placed in the hands of a receiver whereby the Murphy company is permitted to co-operate with the receiver in the work of completing and maintaining said system, and the receiver is authorized to collect the maintenance fee of sixty cents per acre as well as the deferred payments, which moneys are to be applied in the maintenance and completion of said system. Counsel intimates that there is no time limit to which such moneys may be used for the operation and maintenance of said system. Counsel is there mistaken, for the Murphy company or its assigns may complete the system as quickly as possible, and when completed may turn it over to the water users and thus avoid any further expenses in connection with it. There is nothing in this contention. The receiver has full authority to proceed and expend the deferred payments on said contracts in the completion of said canal.

He has authority also to collect sixty cents an acre maintenance fee, which must be applied as provided by said contracts.

The judgment must therefore be affirmed, and it is so ordered, with costs of this appeal in favor of the respondent intervenors.

Ailshie, C. J., and Budge, District Judge, concur.

(May 28, 1914.)

ON REHEARING.

[141 Pac. 83.]

DEFERRED PAYMENTS—PAYMENT OF TO RECEIVER.

1. *Held*, under the water right contracts involved in this case, the deferred payments for such water rights do not become due until water is made available for the reclamation and irrigation of the lands as provided by the terms of such contract; and when the water is made so available, the deferred payments become a lien on the land and the water right.

2. *Held*, that where a water contract holder pays any part or the whole of the deferred payments to the receiver, under the order of the court, he is entitled to a credit on such contract for the, amount paid.

REHEARING on appeal from the District Court of the Third Judicial District, in and for Ada County. Hon. Carl A. Davis, Judge.

Action to determine the rights of the several parties under certain water right contracts. Judgment for the intervenors. *Affirmed.*

Davidson & Davison and Richards & Haga, for Appellants.

The appointment of a receiver does not have the effect of changing contractual relations between parties. (High on Receivers, secs. 201, 204, 318.)

The specific performance of such a contract would require constant supervision of the court for years unless the receiver should succeed in immediately enforcing payment from all settlers, and unless the funds so collected should prove sufficient to complete the project. (6 Pomeroy, Eq. Jur., sec. 760; Fry, Specific Performance, sec. 48; *Ross v. Union Pac. Ry. Co.*, Fed. Cas. No. 12,080, Woolw. 26; *Texas & Pac. Ry. Co. v. City of Marshall*, 136 U. S. 393, 10 Sup. Ct. 846, 34 L. ed. 385; *Beck v. Allison*, 56 N. Y. 366, 15 Am. Rep. 430; *Alabama Western R. Co. v. State ex rel. Garber*, 155 Ala. 491, 46 So. 468, 16 Ann. Cas. 485, 19 L. R. A., N. S., 1173; *Farmers' Loan & Trust Co. v. Burbank Power & Water Co.* (D. C.), 196 Fed. 539.)

Karl Paine and C. E. Winstead, for Intervenors, cite no authorities on rehearing.

Ira E. Barber, as *Amicus Curiae.*

The rule that specific performance will not be decreed in building and construction contracts on account of the inconvenience of enforcing such decree is subject to important exceptions. (*Wilson v. Furness Ry. Co.*, L. R. 9 Eq. 28, 38, 39 L. J. Ch. 19, 21 L. T., N. S., 416, 553; *Gregory v. Ingwersen*, 32 N. J. Eq. 199; *Stuyvesant v. Mayor etc. of New York*, 11 Paige Ch. (N. Y.) 414; *Grubb v. Starkey*, 90 Va. 831, 20 S. E. 784; *Birchett v. Bolling*, 5 Munf. (Va.) 442; *Wolverhampton v. Emmons*, 1 K. B. (1901) 515; *Storer v. Great Western R. Co.*, 12 L. J. Ch. 65; 36 Cyc. 583, and cases cited, note 54.)

Equity will not refuse specific performance because a contract has several years to run. (*Prospect Park & Coney Island R. Co. v. Coney Island & Brooklyn R. Co.*, 144 N. Y. 152, 39 N. E. 17, 26 L. R. A. 610.)

SULLIVAN, J.—A rehearing was granted in this case upon the petition of appellant Neitzel, and additional briefs and oral arguments were presented on such rehearing. Ira E.

Barber, Esq., and N. M. Ruick, Esq., appeared as friends of the court and filed briefs.

In limine, C. C. Childs brought this action to oust the board of directors of the Murphy Land & Irrigation Co. and to have a certain mortgage, executed by said corporation to the appellant, H. R. Neitzel, canceled and held for naught, and for an accounting and for the appointment of a receiver to take charge of the property of said defendant corporation, for the purpose of conserving the same for the benefit of said corporation and its creditors and all other persons having any interest therein, and that such receiver have full management of the business of such company under the order and direction of the court.

Thereafter many of those holding contracts for water from said corporation intervened in said action and took full charge of said case. Said intervenors filed their complaint in intervention on their own behalf and on the behalf of all others holding water contracts issued by said corporation. The intervenors named as plaintiffs represented about 3,500 acres of land within said project out of a total of about 6,000 acres. Extracts from the said water contract are set forth in the original opinion in this case. Under the terms of said contract, said corporation was to complete said system and turn it over to the water contract holders on or before December 31, 1911. Said system was partially completed and some of the purchasers of water rights received water therefrom. The corporation became insolvent and was unable to complete the system.

The record shows that H. R. Neitzel was the controlling spirit of said corporation, as early, at least, as 1910. He was president of the corporation; his nephew was secretary and he and his wife and nephew were members of the board of directors of said corporation. The appellant Neitzel had full knowledge of the financial condition of said corporation, of its insolvency, and of its inability to complete said irrigation system in accordance with the terms of said water contract. It was conceded on the argument that the correct rule was laid down by this court in its original opinion in this case, to the effect that the person loaning money to such a corporation, to be used in constructing its irrigation system, acquires only such rights and interests as the irrigation company has in such project and such water right contracts, and cannot collect payments on such contracts until the water has been made permanently available to the user under the terms of said contracts, not only for one season, but for all seasons. In other words, the corporation is required to make provision for a sufficient permanent supply of water and a reasonably permanent system of reservoirs, dams and ditches of sufficient capacity to hold and convey such water to the users as per the terms of said water contracts, before the water user is required to make the deferred annual payments provided for in said contracts.

The main contention of counsel for appellant Neitzel on oral argument was in substance that the receiver could not proceed and complete the system under the direction of the court, first, because there were no plans and specifications by which the receiver could be guided in the completion of said system; and, second, that the receiver had no funds with which to complete the system and had no authority under the water contracts to collect the annual payments agreed to be paid until the water had been delivered to the owners.

There is nothing in the first contention of counsel, for the reason that the record shows the plans and specifications for the construction of said system is a part of the public records and files of the state in the state engineer's office, which plans and specifications have been approved by the state engineer. It is alleged in the fifth paragraph of the complaint that the plans and specifications for the reservoirs, ditches, dams, etc., of said Murphy project are on file with the state engineer of the state of Idaho, and that allegation is admitted by the answer of the defendants.

As to the second contention, this court in its former opinion did not intend to hold that the receiver could proceed and collect the annual instalments agreed to be paid by the owners of such water contracts until such instalments became due. The court did not intend to make a new contract in regard to the payment of said instalments, but since the intervenors named in the complaint in intervention owning over half of the land within said project appéared for themselves and on behalf of all others having similar con-* tracts and asked for the appointment of a receiver to take charge of said system and complete it and turn it over to the water users, as per the terms of said water contracts, this court took it for granted that they were all anxious to have the system completed, and that if a receiver could be appointed to take charge of said matter and could find a contractor who would be willing to go on and complete said system for the balance, or a part of the balance, owing and to become due from the water right contract holders when water was made permanently available for the irrigation of their lands, they would pay said instalments.

The trial court, as a court of equity, had the power to appoint such receiver and under its supervision complete said system. The trial court, as well as this court, recognizes the rights of appellant Neitzel and the irrigation company, and supposed they were both interested in the completion of said system in accordance with the intention of the parties, and if anything could be saved to the mortgagee or the irrigation company after the completion of said system, that would be done, and that the trial court, through its receiver, would protect the interests of all concerned under all of the facts and circumstances of the case. It was not the intention of the trial court to authorize the receiver to collect the future instalments on said water contracts before such instalments matured. But it was the intention to empower him to enforce said contracts according to their terms and conditions.

The fifth conclusion of law by the trial court is as follows: "That the receiver should be appointed by the court to take possession of the irrigation system of the defendant corporation and to manage, operate, maintain, repair and complete said irrigation system, according to the requirements of the contracts for water rights, and that such receiver should be authorized to collect from the holders of said water contracts the amounts due and owing thereon and to become due and owing thereon, from time to time, and all maintenance fees to be paid by said water contract holders, as in said water contracts provided."

. The conclusion and judgment of the trial court was founded upon the fact that the irrigation company is insolvent and unable to complete the system. The judgment of the district court and the decision of this court authorize the receiver to proceed and collect the instalments as they become due from the water users who have already received water and are receiving water for the irrigation of their lands in the quantity required by the terms of said contract, and do not relieve the water users from their obligations to pay the purchase price for their water rights when water is available for them. The decision is intended to protect all parties interested in their rights, and to have said system completed, if possible, in accordance with the terms of said contracts, and it is placed in the hands of a receiver on account of the inability of the irrigation company to complete it and the unwillingness of appellant Neitzel to do so. The water right purchasers are entitled to have said system completed, if that can be done, with the funds that would become due from the water users upon making the water permanently available for the reclamation and irrigation of their lands as provided by the terms of said contracts.

We did not mean to hold in the original opinion that the annual instalments provided for by said water contracts did not become due and payable until the entire system was completed; but when the system was so far completed as to make water permanently available for any particular user for all seasons, the instalments agreed to be paid by the user would become due and payable in accordance with the terms of the contract. Then he has no reason to complain of lack of water for other land owners because he has water available for the irrigation of his land. However, if water has not been made available to others holding water contracts, in case the construction company is insolvent, such water right owners might be injured by the noncompletion of the system, and upon proper application a court of equity might require the payments due and to become due from the water users to whom water had been made available to be paid to a receiver to be used in the completion of such system.

While the Murphy project is not a Carey Act project, the contracts entered into with the purchasers of water rights are similar in many respects to those entered into by the purchasers of water rights under the Carey Act.

The amendment by Congress to the Carey Act, approved June 11, 1896 (29 Stats. at L., p. 435), clearly authorizes a lien to be created by the state upon such lands as are granted to the state under said act, and when created shall be valid on and against the separate legal subdivisions of the land reclaimed for the actual cost and necessary expense of reclamation, and a reasonable interest thereon from the date of reclamation until disposed of to the actual settler, and provides as follows: "And when an ample supply of water is actually furnished in a substantial ditch or canal, or by artesian wells or reservoirs, to reclaim a particular tract or tracts of such lands, then patents shall issue for the same to such state, without regard to settlement or cultivation." That provision for a lien contemplates an ample supply of water shall have been actually furnished in a substantial ditch or canal or by artesian wells or reservoirs to reclaim such land in order to create a lien. That is making water permanently available to the user. Prior to that amendment by Congress to the Carey Act, the legislature of Idaho had enacted a law authorizing and granting a lien on lands and water rights for the cost of reclamation. (See Laws 1895, p. 227; sec. 1629, Rev. Codes.) Said section provides, among other things, that "Any person, company or association, furnishing water for any tract of land, shall have a first and prior lien on said water right and land upon which said water is used, for all deferred payments for said water right; said lien to be in all respects prior to any and all other liens created or attempted to be created by the owner or possessor of said land," etc. The law clearly contemplates that after water has been made permanently available for the irrigation of the land of a water right owner, all deferred payments for such water right shall become a lien on the land and the water right, and such deferred payments may be collected by the owner of such water right contracts in case a court of equity has not directed that such payments must be applied to the completion of the system, and in such a case the court may direct all such payments to be made to a receiver appointed by the court to collect the same and complete the system. In case the water contract holders pay the balance due on such contracts, or any part thereof, to the receiver, under the order of the trial court, they would be entitled to a credit on their contracts for the amount paid.

The water contracts in the case at bar make the deferred payments a lien upon the water rights and land; but such liens do not attach until the water has been made permanently available for the reclamation of the land.

It is suggested by counsel for appellant that should the receiver in this case undertake to ·enforce the collections provided for by said water right contracts, he would not be able to procure the evidence of the amount due or to get possession of the original contract on which to sue, in case suit for the collection thereof was necessary. It is sufficient to say that appellant Neitzel is a party to this suit and the court has jurisdiction of him, and it further appears that said contracts were assigned to him, and the trial court no doubt could find a means to compel him to turn over said contracts to a receiver, if that were needed. And no doubt said contracts are all of record in the proper county recorder's office, and it would not be difficult to establish the amount remaining unpaid thereon.

It is also suggested by counsel for appellant that the trial court has prescribed no time limit in which the receiver shall complete the system, or that there is no assurance that the system can be completed with the money remaining unpaid on the contracts for the water rights. It is sufficient to say that a court of equity has full power and control of this matter and will see to it that if the system can be completed, that it will be done as soon as practicable. The court will certainly see to it, upon proper application, that the receiver acts as promptly in this matter as is consistent with the best interests of all concerned, and will not permit him to fritter away his time and the money of the settlers in the completion of said system. The record shows that the system can be completed for about one hundred thousand dollars, the amount remaining unpaid on the contracts for water rights. When the instalments become due on such contracts, if the parties owing the same refuse to pay, the trial court may authorize the receiver to bring proper actions for the collection of the same.

Counsel for appellant contend that the court erred in directing the specific performance of the contract for the completion of said system. This objection is predicated upon the general rule that contracts for erecting buildings or doing construction work will not be enforced specifically by a court of equity. The reason for that general rule is that the enforcement of such contracts would cause the courts great inconvenience, but there is no question but that courts of equity have jurisdiction to require the specific performance of such contracts if they conclude it is necessary to do so in order to protect the rights of the parties. If a court of equity is without authority to specifically enforce the contracts in question, the water users would have no remedy whatever by which they could protect their rights. There would exist a wrong without a remedy, and that is contrary to the well-recognized maxim that equity will not suffer wrong to be without a remedy. It would be a grievous wrong to the owners of contracts for water rights to be compelled to pay for such rights and have no remedy whatever to compel the contracting party to furnish them water.

There is nothing in the record to show that the water contracts, which by their terms require the completion of said system, are not susceptible of specific performance. The record before this court shows that it will cost about one hundred thousand dollars to complete the system, but there is nothing in the record to show that the court, through its receiver, may not complete said system in accordance with the terms of the contract and thus protect the rights of all the parties. In case a contract can be let for the completion of said system in accordance with the plans and specifications for less than the amount to become due on said contracts, there certainly would be no difficulty in having the system completed; but in case the amount to become due on such contracts is not quite sufficient to complete the system, the court through its receiver may complete the system so far as it may be done with such funds, and the settlers may then be able to devise ways and means for the entire completion of the system. But there certainly will be no serious difficulty in having said system completed so far as the instalments to become due on said water contracts will pay for the same, and if the system cannot be completed so as to give some of the contract holders water, then such holders cannot be required to pay for something they do not get. The district court, as a court of equity, has full power and authority in said matter to proceed as indicated by its findings and judgment already entered in this case and protect the rights of all the parties as far as can be done under the facts of this case.

It must be remembered that this action was prosecuted by the intervenors on their own behalf and on behalf of all holders of water contracts. These holders not named in the complaint in intervention may become parties and be permitted to share in the fruits of this action upon complying with such reasonable conditions as the lower court may impose, and they alone can object to the right of the receiver to collect from them. They, of course, have a right to their day in court, and if they do not come in or are not brought in, and required to comply with the orders of the court, the court will not require the receiver to complete the system so as to furnish them water, as originally contemplated.

We therefore adhere to the rules of law laid down in the original opinion as amplified in this opinion on rehearing. The judgment of the trial court is affirmed and the cause remanded for further proceedings in accordance with the views expressed in said opinions of this court. Costs are awarded to the respondent intervenors.

Ailshie, C. J., and Walters, District Judge, concur.

————

(May 29, 1914.)

O. L. PEAVY, Respondent, v. GEORGE McCOMBS et al., Appellants.

[140 Pac. 965.]

ISSUANCE OF COUNTY BONDS TO REDEEM WARRANTS—STATUTES IN PARI
  MATERIA PASSED AT SAME SESSION — CONSTRUCTION OF — RETRO-
  ACTIVE STATUTE—PARTICULAR APPLICATION OF TO SECTION 99, CHAP.
  58, SESSION LAWS 1913.

1. · The rule that statutes *in pari materia* should be construed together applies with peculiar force to statutes passed at the same session of the legislature; they are to be construed together, and should be so construed, if possible, as to harmonize and give force and effect to the provisions of each.

2. Where two statutes passed at the same session of the legislature are necessarily inconsistent, that one which deals with the common subject matter in a more minute and particular way will prevail over one of a more general character.

3. Where two conflicting acts upon the same subject matter are passed at the same session of the legislature, and their conflict is such that they cannot be harmonized, and one of them contains an emergency clause and the other does not, and the one containing the emergency clause was passed by both Houses of the legislature and approved by the governor later than the other, *held*, under the circumstances, the act containing the emergency clause repeals the other to the extent of the inconsistency between them.

4. No act of the legislature shall be construed to be retroactive or retrospective unless the intention on the part of the legislature is clearly expressed. The word "retroactive" need not be used in the statute, but the intent of the legislature may be gleaned from any language which appropriately expresses such purpose.

5. Sec. 99 of chap. 58 of Sess. Laws 1913 was passed in obedience to the mandate of sec. 15 of art. 7 of the constitution. By

said provision the legislature declared its purpose to place the counties of the state upon a cash basis.

6. By sec. 99 of chap. 58 of Sess. Laws 1913, the power of the board of county commissioners to issue bonds for the payment or redemption of outstanding county warrants is abrogated. This applies to warrants which were issued before said law went into effect, as well as to warrants which were issued after it went into effect.

7. Sec. 99 of chap. 58 of Sess. Laws 1913 repeals sec. 1960 of the Rev. Codes as amended by chap. 33 of the Laws of 1913, so far as said sec. 1960 empowers the county commissioners to issue county bonds to pay or redeem outstanding warrant indebtedness.

APPEAL from the District Court of the Eighth Judicial District for Bonner County. Hon. John M. Flynn, Judge.

Action to enjoin the defendants from issuing, signing and delivering certain county bonds of Bonner county to pay and redeem certain outstanding warrant indebtedness. *Affirmed.*

William J. Costello, for Appellants, filed no brief.

H. H. Taylor, for Respondent.

With the exception of the case of *Bannock County v. C. Bunting & Co.*, 4 Ida. 156, 37 Pac. 277, the points here raised have not been directly passed upon by this court. There was no occasion for controversy until sec. 15, art. 7 of the constitution was made effective by the laws of 1913.

The enactment of the revenue law of 1913 calls for this construction, and it cannot be construed otherwise, for having been enacted subsequent to the enactment of sec. 1960, Rev. Codes, it plainly prohibits the issuance of bonds to take up outstanding warrants.

McCARTHY, District Judge.—The following are the material facts of this case as they appear from the allegations of the complaint: The plaintiff is a resident and taxpayer of Bonner county, Idaho, and the defendants, George McCombs, John C. Nagel and Don. C. McColl, are now and were at all

times concerned in this action the county commissioners of
Bonner county, Idaho. The defendant Andrew Christensen
is and was at all times concerned in the action the clerk of
said board of county commissioners.

In April, 1912, the board of county commissioners of
Bonner county, in accordance with the provisions of the
revenue law in force at that time, appropriated by resolution
for the current expenses of said county for the fiscal year
beginning on the second Monday in April, 1912, the net sum
of $76,967. To raise the money required by this appropria-
tion the board levied a tax of three mills, which would produce
only $30,913.38, or less than one-half of the amount required
by the appropriation. As a consequence there were outstanding and unpaid in July, 1913, warrants drawn on the current
expense fund for the fiscal year 1912–13 in the amount of
$43,759.04. In addition to these warrants there were other
warrants of the county outstanding and unpaid which brought
the total amount of warrant indebtedness up to the amount
of $100,000.

On July 18, 1913, at an adjourned regular session, the
board of county commissioners resolved to issue negotiable
coupon funding bonds of the county in an amount sufficient
to redeem or pay the outstanding warrant indebtedness, and
at a later session ordered the clerk of the board to cause to be
published according to law a notice of their intention. The
notice has been published and the bonds have been awarded
and the defendants, unless restrained, will make, execute and
deliver the negotiable coupon bonds of the county in an
amount in excess of $100,000 for the purpose of redeeming or
paying the warrant indebtedness.

The defendants demurred generally to the plaintiff's complaint upon the ground that the facts set forth in it and outlined above are not sufficient to constitute a cause of action.
This demurrer was overruled by the trial court and the defendants elected to stand upon their demurrer. The trial
court then rendered judgment in favor of the plaintiff and
against the defendants, permanently enjoining and restraining the latter from proceeding further in the matter of the

execution of negotiable coupon funding bonds of Bonner county, for the purpose of redeeming or paying outstanding warrants of the county, or from signing, executing or delivering bonds of the county to pay or redeem outstanding warrants. From this judgment of the trial court the defendants appeal to this court.

An examination of this case involves the consideration and construction of certain provisions of the state constitution and of the statutes. Sec. 15 of art. 7 of the constitution of the state of Idaho reads as follows:

"The legislature shall provide by law, such a system of county finance, as shall cause the business of the several counties to be conducted on a cash basis. It shall also provide that whenever any county shall have any warrants outstanding and unpaid, for the payment of which there are no funds in the county treasury, the county commissioners, in addition to other taxes provided by law, shall levy a special tax, not to exceed ten (10) mills on the dollar, of taxable property, as shown by the last preceding assessment, for the creation of a special fund for the redemption of said warrants; and after the levy of such special tax, all warrants issued before such levy, shall be paid exclusively out of said fund. All moneys in the county treasury at the end of the fiscal year, not needed for current expenses, shall be transferred to said redemption fund."

Sec. 99 of chap. 58 of the Sess. Laws of 1913 provides that upon all taxable property of the county the board of county commissioners must each year levy a tax for the redemption of outstanding county warrants issued prior to the second Monday of April in said year, to be collected and paid into the county treasury and apportioned to the county redemption fund, which levy must be sufficient for the redemption of all such outstanding county warrants before the second Monday of April in the succeeding year, unless the amount of such outstanding warrants exceeds the amount that would be raised by a levy of one hundred cents on each one hundred dollars of such assessed valuation, in which case the board must annually levy a tax of one hundred cents on each one hundred dollars of such assessed valuation for the redemption of such outstanding warrants.

Sec. 101 of said chap. 58 provides that the county auditor must furnish the board with a statement of the amount of outstanding county warrants for the current year and for the prior years.

Sec. 212 provides that "all acts and parts of acts in conflict with this act are hereby repealed."

Chap. 33, Sess. Laws 1913, provides as follows: "The board of county commissioners of any county in this state, may issue negotiable coupon bonds of their county for the purpose of paying, redeeming, funding or refunding the outstanding indebtedness of the county, as hereinafter provided, whether the indebtedness exists as warrant indebtedness, or bonded indebtedness. Said bonds shall be issued as near as practicable in denominations of one thousand dollars each, but bonds of the denominations of five hundred and one hundred dollars may be issued when necessary. Said bonds must bear interest at a rate of not to exceed six per cent per annum, the interest to be paid on the first day of January and the first day of July in each year, at the office of the county treasurer, or at such bank in the city of New York as may be designated by the board of county commissioners; such bonds to be redeemed by the county in the following manner: Ten per cent of the total amount issued to be paid in ten years from the date of issue; and ten per cent annually thereafter until all of said bonds are paid. But said bonds or any part thereof may, at the option of the county issuing the same, be redeemed at any time after five years from the date of their issue, provided such time and option be stated upon the face of each bond, and each bond must be redeemed in the order it is numbered."

In this opinion chapters 33 and 58 of Sess. Laws 1913 will be referred to simply as chapter 33 and chapter 58.

It is apparent that sec. 99 of chap. 58 was enacted and approved for the purpose of carrying out the provisions and directions of sec. 15, art. 7 of the constitution. Chap. 58 carries an emergency clause, and was approved March 13,

1913. Chap. 33 does not carry an emergency clause and was approved February 25, 1913. The twelfth session of the legislature, which enacted both these statutes, adjourned on March 8, 1913, and chap. 33 did not go into effect until sixty days from said date, since it did not carry an emergency clause.

Chap. 33 is amendatory of sec. 1960 of the Civil Code of Idaho and makes no change in that section except to provide that the bonds may be redeemed at any time after five years from the date of their issuance, whereas sec. 1960 provides that they may be redeemed after ten years from the date of their issuance. The provision empowering the board of county commissioners to issue negotiable coupon bonds for the purpose of paying outstanding warrant or bonded indebtedness was not amended or changed in the least, and in this respect chap. 33 reads just like the original section 1960 of the codes.

The precise question involved in this action is, whether or not, since the passage and approval of chap. 58, the board of county commissioners has the right to issue bonds of the county to pay or redeem outstanding warrants of the county issued prior to the time when said chap. 58 went into effect. It is a fact that the warrants, for the purpose of paying and redeeming which the county bonds in question were issued, were issued prior to such time.

The appellants concede that chap. 58 removes the power of the county commissioners to issue county bonds for the payment of warrant indebtedness which may be issued subsequent to the time when chap. 58 went into effect. They contend, however, that it was not the intention of the legislature to make sec: 99 of chap. 58 relate to warrants issued before the statute went into effect, and that the legislature intended when enacting chap. 33 to keep in effect the provisions of sec. 1960, Rev. Codes, which permitted the county commissioners to issue bonds to pay warrant indebtedness, so far as warrants issued before chap. 58 went into effect are concerned.

Since it is necessary to construe several statutes passed at the same session of the legislature, certain fundamental rules of statutory construction should be borne in mind. Chap. 33 and chap. 58 relate to revenue and the power of the commissioners in relation to it. The rule that statutes *in pari materia* should be construed together applies with peculiar force to statutes passed at the same session of the legislature; they are to be construed together, and should be so construed, if possible, as to harmonize and give force and effect to the provisions of each. If, however, they are necessarily inconsistent, the statute which deals with the common subject matter in a more minute and particular way will prevail over a statute of a more general nature. These rules are so well established as to neither require nor justify any citations of authorities in support of them.

Since chap. 58 contains an emergency clause, and chap. 33 does not, chap. 58 went into effect before chap. 33.

The general rule at common law seems to have been that of two inconsistent statutes enacted at the same session of the legislature, the one which went into effect at the later date would prevail. (*Harrington v. Harrington*, 53 Vt. 649; *State v. Edwards*, 136 Mo. 360, 38 S. W. 73; Sutherland on Statutory Construction, 2d ed., p. 541, sec. 280, note 45.)

At common law this was a sensible rule, because the general rule was that a statute went into effect from the date of its passage, that is, from the date of the last act necessary to complete the process of legislation and give the bill the force of law. (Sutherland on Statutory Construction, 2d ed., p. 308, sec. 172.) Under our constitution no act takes effect until sixty days from the end of the session at which the same shall have been passed, except in case of emergency, which emergency shall be declared in the law. (Const., art. 3, sec. 22.) Thus, except in the case of emergency acts, all acts of the legislature go. into effect at the same time. Therefore, in thé great majority of cases, the common-law rule would not be an effective guide. While it is not necessary for the purposes of this case to lay down a general rule for all cases, we will say in passing that we are inclined to the opinion that, in case of an irreconcilable conflict between two acts passed at the same session of the legislature, the one should prevail which was last approved by the governor, the approval of the governor being the last act in the process of legislation under our constitution and statutes.

It has been held that where two conflicting acts upon the same subject matter are passed at the same session of the legislature, and their conflict is such that they cannot be harmonized and stand together, where one of them contains an emergency clause and the other does not and the one containing the emergency clause was passed by both houses of the legislature after the other, under such circumstances the act containing the emergency clause should prevail over the other. (*Heilig v. City Council of Puyallup*, 7 Wash. 29, 34 Pac. 164.)   The supreme court of Washington says in the last-mentioned case: "The simple fact of there being an emergency clause would tend to show that the subject matter of the act was more clearly and pointedly before the legislature than the subject matter of the other act."   Another reason for the decision is that the act which is passed later is the later expression of the legislative will.   To the same effect see *Belding Land etc. Co. v. City of Belding*, 128 Mich. 79, 87 N. W. 113; *Dewey v. City of Des Moines*, 101 Iowa, 416, 70 N. W. 605; *Board of Education v. Tafoya*, 6 N. M. 292, 27 Pac. 616.

This court takes judicial notice of the journals of the House of Representatives and Senate of this state in passing upon legislation. (Sec. 5950, subd. 3, Rev. Codes; *Burkhart v. Reed*, 2 Ida. 503, 22 Pac. 1.)   Chap. 33 passed the House and was transmitted to the Senate on February 5, 1913, and passed the Senate and was returned to the House on February 20, 1913; it was presented to the governor on February 24th. (House Journal, pp. 183 and 360; Senate Journal, p. 212, printed copies.)   It was approved by the governor on February 25th.   Chap. 58 passed the House and was transmitted to the Senate on March 4th, was passed by the Senate and returned to the House on March 8th, and was presented to the governor on March 8th.   (House Journal, pp. 503 and 615; Senate Journal, p. 393, printed copies.)   It was approved by the governor on March 13, 1913.

It thus appears that chap. 58 passed both Houses and was approved by the governor later than chap. 33, and therefore was a later expression of the legislative will than chap. 33. The fact that chap. 58 carries an emergency clause signifies that it was considered more' urgent and more important by the legislature than chap. 33, which does not carry an emergency clause.

For these reasons we think that in case of an irreconcilable inconsistency it should be held that chap. 58 repeals chap. 33 to the extent of such inconsistency.

The defendants contend that to make chap. 58 apply to warrants issued before it went into effect would be to render it a retroactive or retrospective law. It is the rule that all statutes are to be considered as having only a prospective operation unless the purpose and intention of the legislature to give them a retrospective effect is clear. (36 Cyc. 1205, "c," and cases cited; *Katz* v. *Herrick,* 12 Ida. 1, 86 Pac. 873.) This rule is embodied in sec. 3, Rev. Codes, which provides that "No part of these Revised Codes is retroactive, unless expressly so declared." We do not think, however, that this section means that the statute must use the words "this statute is to be deemed retroactive." We think it is sufficient if the enacting words are such that the intention to make the law retroactive is clear. In other words, if the language clearly refers to the past as well as to the future, then the intent to make the law retroactive is expressly declared within the meaning of sec. 3, Rev. Codes.

Bearing in mind the rules of statutory construction which are outlined above, the question is, What was the intention of the legislature in enacting chap. 33 and chap. 58 so far as the precise point which we are considering is concerned? Sec. 15, art. 7 of the constitution made it the duty of the legislature to enact chap. 58, and it should have been enacted long before it was,—in fact, at the first session of the legislature. After directing that such a law should be passed, it says: "And after the levy of such special tax, all warrants issued before such levy, shall be paid exclusively out of such fund." Of course the legislature had this language in mind when it passed and enacted chap. 58.

This court held, in *Bannock County v. C. Bunting & Co.,* 4 Ida. 156, 37 Pac. 277, that sec. 15, art. 7 of the constitution was not self-executing, for the reason that it did not provide necessary machinery for its execution. However, when such machinery was provided by chap. 58, sec. 99, we think that the language of said section just above quoted is self-executing, and that all warrants issued before the levy of the tax for the purpose of paying warrant indebtedness must be paid out of that fund to the exclusion of any other method.

Sec. 99 of chap. 58 says that the board must levy a tax for the redemption of outstanding county warrants issued prior to the second Monday of April in the year in which the tax is levied. Reading this language in the light of the constitutional provision, it seems to us that it clearly refers to all warrants issued before the levy of the tax. Sec. 15, art. 7 of the constitution makes it the duty of the legislature to pass such laws as shall place and maintain the counties of the state upon a cash basis. We do not think that a law passed in obedience to such a mandate should be given a construction which would defeat in part the mandate itself.

It should be borne in mind that chap. 58 is a remedial statute, or one relating to procedure. It does not impair any existing right or indebtedness, but simply relates to the method of procedure which shall be followed in paying an indebtedness. The provision of sec. 101 of chap. 58 that the county auditor shall furnish the board with a statement of the amount of outstanding warrants for the current year and for prior years also enforces the conclusion that the legislature did not mean to confine the operation of the law to warrants issued after the law went into effect. We conclude that the legislature, when enacting sec. 99 of chap. 58, intended to make it apply to all warrant indebtedness irrespective of whether the warrants were issued before or after that chapter went into effect, that there is no rule of law which prevents or inhibits such construction, and that such construction should be placed upon the statute. It follows, then, that

chap. 58 repeals the provision of chap. 33, which empowers
the commissioners to issue funding bonds for the purpose of
paying any warrant indebtedness.   Chap. 33 is not, however,
entirely repealed, but is still in effect so far as bonded indebtedness is concerned. ·

Counsel for both plaintiff and defendants have referred to
the decision in the case of *Bannock County v. C. Bunting &
Co.*, 4 Ida. 156, 37 Pac. 277.   We cannot see that this decision
is directly in point.   It of course holds by implication that
sec. 15 of art. 7 of the constitution is not self-operative.   Sec.
99 of chap. 58 makes that provision of the constitution operative.   In that case the court upholds the old law granting
the commissioners power to bond not only for refunding
bonded indebtedness but also for warrant indebtedness.   The
court, however, had no such provision before it as the provision of sec. 99 of chap. 58, which, as we hold in this opinion,
abrogates such power.

The judgment of the lower court should be affirmed, and
it is so ordered.   Costs awarded to respondent.

Ailshie, C. J., and Sullivan, J., concur.

(June 2, 1914.)

DICKENS–WEST MINING CO., a Corporation, Respondent, v. CRESCENT MINING & MILLING CO., a Corporation, Appellant.

[141 Pac. 566.]

MINING CLAIMS—SUIT TO QUIET TITLE—FOREIGN CORPORATIONS—COM-
PLIANCE WITH STATE LAW — STATUTORY CONSTRUCTION — VOID
CONVEYANCE—ANNUAL LABOR—AFFIDAVIT OF—PRIMA FACIE EVI-
DENCE—SUBSTANTIAL CONFLICT.

1. Where a foreign corporation fails to comply with the laws of
this state in filing its articles of incorporation and designating an
agent upon whom service of process may be made with the Secretary of State and with the clerk of the district court of the county

in which its principal place of business is located, it has no authority to do business in the state.

2. Under the provisions of sec. 2792, Rev. Codes, a foreign corporation cannot take or hold title to any realty within this state prior to making the proper filings of its articles of incorporation and designation of agent, and any deed or conveyance of real property to such corporation prior to such filings shall be absolutely void.

3. *Held*, that the evidence fails to show that the annual assessment work was performed upon the mining claim, the title to which is involved in this action.

APPEAL from the District Court of the First Judicial District, in and for Shoshone County. Hon. W. W. Woods, Judge.

Action to quiet title to a mining claim. Judgment for plaintiff. *Reversed.*

W. H. Hanson and Therrett Towles, for Appellant.

When a foreign corporation attempts to allege its compliance with the foreign corporation laws of this state by reciting the things the corporation has done, failure to set forth the performance of all the things required by the constitution and statute leaves the complaint open to demurrer on the ground of failure to show capacity to sue. (*Valley Lumber etc. Co. v. Driessel,* 13 Ida. 662, 93 Pac. 765, 15 L. R. A., N. S., 299, 13 Ann. Cas. 63; *Valley Lumber etc. Co. v. Nickerson,* 13 Ida. 682, 93 Pac. 24; *Consolidated Wagon & Machine Co. v. Kent,* 23 Ida. 690, 132 Pac. 305.) Sec. 10, art. 11 of our constitution was held in the case of *Katz v. Herrick,* 12 Ida. 1, 86 Pac. 873, to be self-acting, but for the purpose of eliminating all question or doubt, the legislature of this state passed sec. 2792, Rev. Codes.

The constitutional and statutory provisions with reference to the qualifications of a foreign corporation to do business in this state are mandatory, and must be complied with in order to enable such corporation to maintain an action in the courts of this state to enforce its contracts. (*Tarr v. Western Loan & Savings Co.,* 15 Ida. 741, 99 Pac. 1049, 21 L. R. A., N. S.,

707; *Cincinnati Mut. Health Assurance Co. v. Rosenthal*, 55 Ill. 85, 8 Am. Rep. 626.)

The U. S. supreme court held by inference at least that the legislature could declare an absolute forfeiture if it desired to incorporate the same in the statute. (*Fritts v. Palmer*, 132 U. S. 282, 10 Sup. Ct. 93, 33 L. ed. 317.)

Conveyances of real estate to a foreign corporation in violation of such a statutory or charter prohibition are void and do not transfer titles. (Thompson on Corporations, sec. 6688, and cases there cited.)

Mere proof of the expenditure of $100 for assessment work is not of itself sufficient. The test as to the reasonable value of any work or improvements is not what was paid for it, or what was supposed to be paid for it, or what the contract price was, but it depends entirely upon whether or not the work or improvements were reasonably worth the sum of $100. (*Mattingly v. Lewisohn*, 13 Mont. 508, 35 Pac. 111; 2 Lindley on Mines, sec. 635; *McCulloch v. Murphy*, 125 Fed. 147.)

Although the burden of proof of forfeiture is conceded in this instance to be upon the party claiming it, if this presumption has been rebutted by concrete evidence of the failure to perform the assessment work, the burden is thrown back upon the owner of the claim to prove that the work was done. (Elliott on Evidence, secs. 86, 91; Wigmore on Evidence, sec. 2487.)

It thus became the duty of the respondent to show by actual evidence, and not by presumptions, where the work had been done and what it was. (*Sherlock v. Leighton*, 9 Wyo. 297, 63 Pac. 580, 934; *Hausner v. Leebrick*, 51 Kan. 591, 33 Pac. 375; *Copper Mountain Mining etc. Co. v. Butte & Corbin Consol. Copper etc. Min. Co.*, 39 Mont. 487, 133 Am. St. 595, 104 Pac. 540; *Little Dorrit Gold Min. Co. v. Arapahoe Gold Min. Co.*, 30 Colo. 431, 71 Pac. 389; *Fredricks v. Klauser*, 52 Or. 110, 96 Pac. 679.)

A. G. Kerns and Featherstone & Fox, for Respondent.

The appellant corporation does not occupy a position where it has either a legal or equitable right to ask a forfeiture of the property of the respondent in its favor. (*Fritts v. Palmer*, 132 U. S. 282, 10 Sup. Ct. 93, 33 L. ed. 317.)

"It has never been held, however, so far as we know, that the single act of taking title to a tract of real estate, as appears in this case, constituted 'doing business' within the meaning of such a constitutional or statutory provision." (*War Eagle Consol. Min. Co. v. Dickie*, 14 Ida. 534, 94 Pac. 1034; *Foore v. Simon Piano Co.*, 18 Ida. 167, 108 Pac. 1038.)

It was not the intention of the legislature in enacting sec. 2792, Rev. Codes, to open a way for adventurers to exploit and confiscate the property of foreign corporations that had in good faith complied or attempted to comply with the laws of the state. And this court has in a number of decisions held that it would not in a collateral proceeding allow a litigant to take advantage of a technical noncompliance with that law. (*Keating v. Keating Min. Co.*, 18 Ida. 660, 672, 112 Pac. 206; *Pennsylvania-Coeur D'Alene Min. Co. v. Gallagher*, 19 Ida. 101, 112 Pac. 1044.)

SULLIVAN, J.—This is a suit to quiet title to a certain mining claim located and known as the Montana lode mining claim in Yreka mining district, Shoshone county.

Upon the issues made by the pleadings, findings of fact and judgment were made and entered, quieting the title to said mining claim in the plaintiff as prayed for in the complaint. This appeal is from the judgment.

It is alleged in the complaint that the respondent corporation was duly organized and existing under the laws of the state of Washington and that it complied with the laws of the state of Idaho in relation to foreign corporations by filing its articles of incorporation, designating an agent upon whom process might be served, and paying the license fee; that the appellant was a corporation organized and existing under the laws of the state of Idaho; that the respondent corporation was the owner and in the possession and entitled to the possession of said Montana lode mining claim, which claim had been located March 29, 1897, by one Amelia H. Cameron, and upon which respondent or its predecessors in interest had done the annual assessment work during each and every year since last mentioned date up to the year 1912, and that it was prevented from doing such work that year through means of force used by the appellant company, and that unless the respondent is aided by the equitable intervention of the court, the said mining claim would be subject to forfeiture and the respondent's rights imperiled.

A demurrer was interposed to said complaint and overruled by the court. The appellant answered, admitting the incorporation of the respondent, but denied that it had complied with all or any of the laws of the state of Idaho, and affirmatively alleged that respondent had never complied with the laws of the state of Idaho relating to foreign corporations, and denied the performance of the assessment work claimed to have been done by the respondent during the years mentioned in the complaint, and denied the allegation that the respondent was prevented by force from performing the assessment work on said claim in 1912.

The appellant corporation also set up as an affirmative defense by way of cross-complaint that on the 29th of January, 1912, said mining claim was duly located by one Inghram and named by him the "Halfmoon" mining claim, and that long prior to the commencement of this action the appellant became the owner thereof by purchase and ever since has been and now is the owner thereof; that at the time of the location of said Halfmoon lode the area embraced within its boundaries was vacant, unoccupied public land and subject to location, and that on October 7, 1912, the appellant, being in possession of said claim, the agents of the respondent corporation, during the absence of the agents of appellant, entered into possession of said property, and that thereafter the appellant instituted an action in the probate court of Shoshone county for the purpose of securing restitution of said premises and for damages, but before service of process could be secured on the agent of respondent this action was instituted.

The appellant by its cross-complaint prayed for judgment that its title in the said Halfmoon lode claim be quieted and confirmed, and that a perpetual injunction issue in said action against respondents and its agents. Service of said answer and cross-complaint was made upon the attorneys for respondent on April 3, 1913. On May 19, 1913, the default of the plaintiff corporation for not answering the cross-complaint or appearing therein was entered by the clerk of the trial court. The cause was thereafter tried by the court and judgment entered in favor of the plaintiff, as above stated. The court, however, failed to make any findings as to the allegations of the cross-complaint.

The respondent on the trial, to prove that it had complied with the laws of the state of Idaho in regard to foreign corporations, introduced in evidence a certificate which showed the filing of a certified copy of its articles of incorporation with the Secretary of State of the state of Idaho on July 18, 1907, and its designation of an agent on August 9, 1907, in the said office of the Secretary of State, and also proved the filing of a certified copy of its articles of incorporation in the office of the recorder of Shoshone county on July 9, 1907. Its designation of agent was not filed in Shoshone county until December 7, 1912, which was after the commencement of this action. The respondent also introduced in evidence a certificate of location covering the said Montana lode mining claim, and also a deed from one Amelia H. Cameron, purporting to convey said claim to the respondent corporation, dated June 5, 1907, and recorded December 7, 1912.

The only evidence offered by the respondent as to the performance of the annual assessment or representation work on said claim for the year 1911, consisted of the affidavit or proof of labor made by T. V. Lowney, and the testimony of one J. L. Whitney, who was the assistant secretary of the respondent corporation, and D. R. Cameron, the president of said corporation, to the effect that $100 had been paid for doing the assessment work for the year 1911.

In order to show that the assessment work for 1911 had not been performed, the appellant corporation introduced several witnesses who testified that they had examined said claim and that not more than four or five dollars' worth of work had been performed upon said mining claim in the year 1911, by the respondent corporation. Inghram, the locator, of the Halfmoon claim, testified that the only work done there by respondent corporation was a small cut about four or five feet long on the sidehill in loose rock and dirt; that the cost of making such excavation would not be more than a day's work for one man, or about four dollars, and that there was no other work done on said claim in the year 1911; that he examined said claim carefully and that that was all the work that was done. Two or three other witnesses testified substantially to the same effect. It appears that there were some tunnels and other work that had been done in previous years, and appellant showed by its evidence that there was no work whatever done in said tunnels or openings during the year 1911; that no work except the small cut above referred to was done on said claim in 1911.

The first contention made by counsel for appellant is that the deed executed by Mrs. Cameron purporting to convey said Montana lode claim to the respondent corporation, dated June 5, 1907, and not filed for record until December 7, 1912, was absolutely void for the reason that said foreign corporation had not complied with the laws of this state in regard to filing its designation of an agent in the office of the clerk of the district court of Shoshone county, as such designation was not filed until 1912, some five years after said conveyance was executed, and said contention is based on the provisions of sec. 2792, Rev. Codes. That section provides for the filing by foreign corporations of their articles of incorporation and the designation of an agent, and provides, among other things, as follows: "Such corporation cannot take or hold title to any realty within this state prior to making such filings, and any pretended deed or conveyance of real estate to such corporation prior to such filings shall be absolutely null and void." That section of the statute is mandatory, and any conveyance made to a corporation that has failed to comply with said law is, as there declared, null and void. As bearing upon this question see sec. 10, art. 11, Const. of Idaho; *War Eagle Consolidated Min. Co. v. Dickie*, 14 Ida. 534, 94 Pac. 1034; *Katz v. Herrick*, 12 Ida. 130, 86 Pac. 873;

Tarr v. Western Loan & Savings Co., 15 Ida. 741, 99 Pac. 1049, 21 L. R. A., N. S., 707; *Foore v. Simon Piano Co.,* 18 Ida. 167, 108 Pac. 1038; *Keating v. Keating Min. Co.,* 18 Ida. 660, 112 Pac. 206; *Pennsylvania Min. Co. v. Gallagher,* 19 Ida. 101, 112 Pac. 1044; *Consolidated Wagon & Machine Co. v. Kent,* 23 Ida. 690, 132 Pac. 305.

The evidence clearly shows that said foreign corporation, the respondent, neglected and failed to file its designation of an agent upon whom service of process might be made until about five years after Mrs. Cameron had attempted to convey said mining claim to it. Therefore, the respondent had no title to said Montana lode mining claim and never has had any title thereto, as said conveyance was absolutely void under the provisions of said sec. 2792.

The next contention of counsel is that the annual assessment work for the year 1911 was not performed upon said Montana lode mining claim, and that the ground included therein was open to location on the 1st day of January, 1912, and was so open at the time it was located by said Inghram.

Under the provisions of sec. 3211, Rev. Codes, the affidavit of annual labor referred to therein is made *prima facie* evidence of the performance of such labor, but when that *prima facie* evidence is met and overcome by positive evidence that the labor had not been performed, it then devolves upon the respondent to show by evidence of a positive and affirmative nature other than the affidavit that the work had actually been performed. The mere fact that the respondent in rebuttal showed that it had actually paid the $100 for the performance of such assessment work was not sufficient evidence that the work was actually done, in view of the fact that several witnesses had testified that only about four or five dollars' worth of work had been performed upon said mining claim during the year 1911. While the evidence of the payment of the $100 would tend to show good faith on the part of the respondent, *good faith* is not sufficient; the law requires the *actual performance* of the work. In such a case the principal question is not whether the money was paid for the work, or whether the owner honestly believed the work was done, but whether the work was *actually performed*. The statute is mandatory requiring such work to be done and must be substantially complied with.

Mr. Lindley, in his work on Mines, 3d ed., sec. 635, says: "Owners of mining claims are sometimes imposed upon by those who are paid for doing the work, but the obligation rests on the owner to see that the work is actually done."

Upon the same point see *Protective Min. Co. v. Forest City Min. Co.*, 51 Wash. 643, 99 Pac. 1033, where the court said: "It is true it [the mining company] paid the sum of $500 to parties whom it had no doubt employed in good faith, but who did no more than go upon the ground and make pretense of doing the work. This is not a compliance with the law. The work must be done as required in the federal statutes or a forfeiture results."

The evidence of the appellant shows that not more than five dollars' worth of work was done upon said claim during the year 1911. If any other work had been done or performed by the respondent, or any other person in its behalf, it was the duty of the respondent, after the introduction of said testimony on the part of the appellant, to show that the work was actually done; but instead of doing that, all the respondent offered in rebuttal was the evidence that it had paid the $100. (See 2 Lindley on Mines, sec. 624.) The record shows that the appellant might have procured the testimony of Lowney, who made the affidavit of annual labor and who the respondent claimed performed said work, but it failed to do so. This is a significant fact in itself, and it was incumbent upon the respondent, after the *prima facie* case made by it was so overwhelmingly overcome by evidence on behalf of appellant, to produce the evidence of the witness who did the work, or the evidence of other parties who knew it was done. The affidavit of annual labor should be taken by the courts for what it is worth, and where it concerns the annual labor for a recent year, and the owner has it within his power to produce the testimony of the person who actually did the work, in a case where the *prima facie* evidence provided for by the statute is flatly contradicted by positive proof, such affidavits do not make the substantial conflict in the evidence contemplated by the decisions of this court wherein it is held that where there is a substantial conflict in the evidence, the findings of the court or the verdict of the jury will not be set aside, and as contemplated by sec. 4824, Rev. Codes.

Thus it appears that the respondent is not entitled to recover in this action for two reasons: First, that it failed to comply with the law in regard to foreign corporations and that it received no title whatever to said mining claim through the conveyance of Mrs. Cameron; and, second, there was a failure to perform the annual labor for the year 1911.

The judgment must be reversed and a new trial granted. Costs awarded to the appellant.

Ailshie, C. J., concurs.

DUNN, District Judge, Dissenting.—The deed made in 1907 by Amelia H. Cameron to the Dickens-West Mining Company, being void, did not pass the legal title of the Montana lode claim to that company, consequently that title must have remained in the grantor, but the corporation, having paid the grantor the full consideration agreed upon, became the equitable owner and entitled to a valid conveyance upon completing its compliance with the laws of this state governing foreign corporations.

As to the performance of the annual labor for the year 1911, it seems clear to me that the record shows a substantial conflict in the evidence, which requires this court to sustain the judgment of the trial court. A careful examination of evidence convinces me that the trial judge, with the witnesses before him, might easily and not unreasonably take the view that the *ex parte* affidavit, together with the evidence that the company actually paid $100.00 for the work, would outweigh the testimony of the two witnesses who swore that the work was not done. And certainly the trial judge is the only one who can fairly determine the value and weight of the testimony of the witnesses and whether or not the affidavit, which the statute makes *prima facie* evidence that the work was done, has been overcome. I think the judgment of the district court ought to be affirmed.

(June 13, 1914.)

JOSEPH ZILKA, Respondent, v. TERESA M. GRAHAM, Appellant, and MAX ENGLAND, Respondent.

[141 Pac. 639.]

JOINT TORT-FEASORS—INSTRUCTIONS—VERDICT—MOTION FOR JUDGMENT —EVIDENCE—SUFFICIENCY OF—TAXING COSTS.

1. Where two persons are sued as joint tort-feasors and the evidence clearly shows that only one of them is liable for the tort, judgment may be rendered against the one who is liable for the trespass.

2. *Held*, that the court did not err in overruling the demurrer to the amended complaint.

3. *Held*, that the court did not err in the admission of certain evidence.

4. *Held*, that the court did not err in giving a certain instruction to the jury.

5. A motion to set aside a verdict and judgment and for a judgment *non obstante veredicto* comes too late if made after judgment has been entered. Such motion must be made after the verdict and before the judgment is rendered.

6. Under the provisions of sec. 3092, Rev. Codes, it is made the duty of a coterminous owner of real estate to give previous reasonable notice to another coterminous owner of his intention to make excavations on his adjoining land.

7. Excavation by an owner on his own land, causing damage to a building on an adjoining owner's land, without the knowledge of, or previous notice to, such adjoining owner, is evidence of want of care in doing the work.

8. *Held*, that there is substantial evidence to sustain the verdict of the jury.

9. *Held*, that the court did not err in taxing the costs.

APPEAL from the District Court of the Eighth Judicial District, in and for the County of Kootenai. Hon. John M. Flynn, Judge.

Action to recover damages for alleged carelessness and negligent acts in the excavation of a certain lot adjoining the lot of plaintiff. Judgment for plaintiff. *Affirmed.*

McFarland & McFarland, for Appellant Graham.

The defendant was entitled to a charge to the jury that she was not liable if the damages were produced by the act of an independent contractor, or his servant. (*Aston v. Nolan*, 63 Cal. 269; *Sullivan v. Zeiner*, 98 Cal. 346, 33 Pac. 209, 20 L. R. A. 730; *Ulrick v. Dakota Loan & Trust Co.*, 2 S. D. 285, 49 N. W. 1054; *Hannicker v. Lepper*, 20 S. D. 371, 129 Am. St. 938, 107 N. W. 202, 6 L. R. A., N. S., 243.)

One who has contracted with a competent and fit person exercising an independent employment to do a piece of work not in itself unlawful or attended with danger to others, according to the contractor's own methods, and without his being subject to control, except as to the results of his work, will not be answerable for the wrongs of such contractor, his subcontractors or servants, committed in the prosecution of such work. (2 Thompson on Negligence, p. 899, sec. 22; *Crenshaw v. Ullman*, 113 Mo. 633, 20 S. W. 1077; *McGrath v. City of St. Louis*, 215 Mo. 191, 114 S. W. 611; *Harrison v. Kiser*, 79 Ga. 588, 4 S. E. 320; *Myer v. Hobbs*, 57 Ala. 175, 29 Am. Rep. 719; *Laycock v. Parker*, 103 Wis. 161, 79 N. W. 327.)

Where the master and servant are sued jointly as in this case, the master is joined and held only under the doctrine of *respondeat superior* for the acts of the servant. A verdict acquitting the servant acquits also his respondent. (*McGinnis v. Chicago R. I. & Pac. R. Co.*, 200 Mo. 347, 118 Am. St. 661, 98 S. W. 590, 9 L. R. A., N. S., 880, 9 Ann. Cas. 656; *Doremus v. Root*, 23 Wash. 710, 63 Pac. 572, 54 L. R. A. 649, and notes; *Stevick v. Northern Pac. R. Co.*, 39 Wash. 501, 81 Pac. 999; *Indiana etc. Torpedo Co. v. Lippincott Glass Co.*,

165 Ind. 361, 75 N. E. 649; *City of Anderson v. Fleming*, 160 Ind. 597, 67 N. E. 443, 66 L. R. A. 119; *Portland Gold Min. Co. v. Stratton's Independence*, 158 Fed. 63, 85 C. C. A. 393, 16 L. R. A., N. S., 677-680; *Chicago etc. R. Co. v. McManigal*, 73 Neb. 580, 103 N. W. 305, 107 N. W. 243; *Hayes v. Chicago Tel. Co.*, 218 Ill. 414, 75 N. E. 1003, 2 L. R. A., N. S., 764; *New Orleans & N. E. R. Co. v. Jopes*, 142 U. S. 18, 12 Sup. Ct. 109, 35 L. ed. 919.)

Elder & Elder and E. R. Whitla, for Respondent Zilka.

An application for a judgment notwithstanding verdict must be made at the time the verdict is received and before judgment is entered thereon. (*Schieble v. Hart*, 11 Ky. Law Rep. 607, 12 S. W. 628; *State v. Commercial Bank*, 6 Smedes & M. (Miss.)˙ 218, 45 Am. Dec. 280; Freeman on Judgments, par. 7.)

A special order made after final judgment has been entered must be appealed from within the time provided by sec. 4807, Rev. Codes, as amended 1911 Sess. Laws, p. 367, and if such appeal is not taken within that time, this court obtains no jurisdiction to pass upon the question. (*Oliver v. Kootenai County*, 13 Ida. 281, 90 Pac. 107; *Coey v. Cleghorn*, 10 Ida. 162, 77 Pac. 331; *Campbell v. First Nat. Bank of Rexburg*, 13 Ida. 95, 88 Pac. 639; *Balfour v. Eves*, 4 Ida. 488, 42 Pac. 508; *Marshalltown Stone Co. v. Des Moines Brick Mfg. Co.* (Iowa), 101 N. W. 1124; *Marshal v. Davis*, 122 Ky. 413, 91 S. W. 714; 23 Cyc. 871.)

If, in excavating, a land owner failed to prosecute the work skilfully or without proper care to avoid injury to the structures on the adjoining land and damages are sustained by the adjoining land owner, the person making the excavation will be liable for all damages resulting from his wrongful or negligent conduct. (1 Cyc. 782; *Gilmore v. Driscoll*, 122 Mass. 199; 23 Am. Rep. 312; *Gerst v. St. Louis*, 185 Mo. 191, 105 Am. St. 580, 84 S. W. 34; 1 Thompson on Negligence, p. 1006, sec. 1115.)

A person employing a contractor to do an act, the doing of which casts upon him a duty, cannot, by delegating it to

the contractor, escape from the responsibility attaching to him
to see that duty performed. (*Cabot v. Kingman*, 166 Mass.
403, 44 N. E. 344, 33 L. R. A. 45; *Bonaparte v. Wiseman*, 89
Md. 12, 42 Atl. 918, 44 L. R. A. 482; *Green v. Berge*, 105 Cal.
52, 45 Am. St. 25, 38 Pac. 539; *Barnes v. City of Waterbury*,
82 Conn. 518, 74 Atl. 902; *Samuel v. Novak*, 99 Md. 558, 58
Atl. 19; *Davis v. Summerfield*, 133 N. C. 325, 45 S. E. 654,
63 L. R. A. 492.)

"The excavating by an owner on his own land adjoining
another's building causing damage, without his knowledge
or previous notice to him, is evidence of want of care in doing
the work." (*Schultz v. Byers*, 53 N. J. L. 442, 26 Am. St.
435, 22 Atl. 514, 13 L. R. A. 569; *Krish v. Ford*, 19 Ky. Law
Rep. 1167, 43 S. W. 237; *Davis v. Summerfield*, 133 N. C.
325, 45 S. E. 654, 63 L. R. A. 492; *Gildersleeve v. Hammond*,
109 Mich. 431, 67 N. W. 519, 33 L. R. A. 46.)

The adjacent owner of land has no right to deprive his
neighbor of the natural support afforded by his soil; and his
right, whatever that may be, to excavate must be exercised
with due care and skill at his peril to prevent injury to his
neighbor. (*Ulrick v. Dakota Loan & Trust Co.*, 2 S. D. 285,
49 N. W. 1054; *Hannicker v. Lepper*, 20 S. D. 371, 129 Am. St.
938, 107 N. W. 202, 6 L. R. A., N. S., 243; *City of Covington
v. Geyler*, 12 Ky. Law Rep. 466; *Serio v. Murphy*, 99 Md. 545,
105 Am. St. 316, 58 Atl. 435; *Riley v. Continuous Rail Joint
Co.*, 110 App. Div. 787, 97 N. Y. Supp. 283; *Green v. Berge*,
105 Cal. 52, 45 Am. St. 25, 38 Pac. 539.)

It is only where the servant's acts are the sole cause of action that the doctrine of *respondeat superior* applies, and it
does not apply where any act or omission of the master enters
into or contributes to the injury complained of. (*Doremus
v. Root*, 23 Wash. 710, 63 Pac. 572, 54 L. R. A. 649.)

This question has often been passed upon on the question
of a separable cause of action. (*Southern Ry. Co. v. Edwards*, 115 Ga. 1022, 42 S. E. 375; 26 Cyc. 1644.)

Where several defendants are joined in an action for tort,
a verdict may be rendered against any number thereof, and
the other acquitted. (*Kinkler v. Junica*, 84 Tex. 116, 19

S. W. 359.) The rule is also statutory in this state. (Rev. Codes, 4351, 4352; *Bingham v. Lipman*, 40 Or. 363, 67 Pac. 98; *Moore v. Fitchburg Railroad Corp.*, 4 Gray (Mass.), 465, 64 Am. Dec. 83; *Gulf C. & S. F. Ry. Co. v. James*, 73 Tex. 12, 15 Am. St. 743, 10 S. W. 744; *Westerfield Gas & Milling Co. v. Abernathy*, 8 Ind. App. 73, 35 N. E. 399; *Groot v. Oregon Short Line Ry. Co.*, 34 Utah, 152, 96 Pac. 1019; *Muller v. Hale*, 138 Cal. 163, 71 Pac. 81; 29 Cyc. 487.)

"The successful party should be allowed witness fees for attendance during the time the trial was delayed, and additional traveling expenses resulting from a continuance, when caused by the fault of his opponent." (11 Cyc. 119.)

The *per diem* of a witness who attends in obedience to a subpoena is properly computed according to the time during which he is in actual attendance, and not limited to the time when he is actually testifying, or to the days on which the trial actually takes place. (40 Cyc. 2184b; *Hunter v. Russell*, 59 Fed. 964; *Farmer v. Stillwater Water Co.*, 86 Minn. 59, 90 N. W. 10.)

C. H. Potts, for Respondent Max England.

Where the servant does the work which he is employed to do, under the direction of the employer, or his agents, relying upon them as to the method in which such work should be done or performed, and performing such work without negligence on his part, he is not liable for injury sustained by a third person, caused by the manner in which such work was performed, unless he knew or had reason to believe that the manner in which he was performing such work was hazardous and liable to occasion injury. (*Gustafson v. Chicago etc. R. R. Co.*, 128 Fed. 85–90.)

The respondent England could be held liable only for actual negligence in the performance of his work, while Mrs. Graham, as the owner of the property, would become liable to the plaintiff for her failure to perform the obligations imposed upon her by statute as the owner of the land.

The liability of master and servant for the negligence of the servant while acting for the master within the scope of his employment is both joint and several. (*Gardner v. Southern R. R. Co.,* 65 S. C. 341, 43 S. E. 816.)

SULLIVAN, J.—This action was brought to recover from the defendants damages in the sum of $9,500, alleged to have occurred by the carelessness and negligent acts of the defendants in the excavation of a certain lot belonging to the appellant Graham and adjoining the lot of the plaintiff, whereby a certain brick building standing on the lot of the plaintiff collapsed and fell because of such excavation.

The complaint contains a statement of three causes of action. The first involves the destruction of said building, the second involves the rents and revenues of said building, and the third, the cost of removing the wreck of said building.

The defendants appeared by separate attorneys and answered separately and put in issue the material allegations of the complaint. As an affirmative defense the defendant Graham alleged that she employed the defendant England to excavate the said premises, and that if any damages were caused to plaintiff's building on account of such excavation, England alone was responsible therefor.

The issues as made by the pleadings were tried by the court with a jury and verdict rendered against the defendant Graham in favor of Zilka for the sum of $3,000. A motion for a new trial was denied and the appeal of Graham is from the order denying the new trial. Zilka, the plaintiff, also appeals from the judgment rendered in favor of England, and also from the order of the trial court in taxing costs in the judgment against Graham.

The defendants were sued as *joint tort-feasors* and counsel for appellant first contends that the judgment must be reversed, for the reason that it is manifest from the record that all of the negligence and trespass charged against the defendants Graham and England as joint *tort-feasors* was tied to Graham exclusively by the jury under the charge of the court in disregard of the evidence in the record and the law applicable thereto.

It appears from the record that the defendant Graham desired to erect on said lot owned by her a building to be used as a postoffice building, in the city of Coeur d'Alene, and that she arranged with the defendant England to excavate said lot for the purpose of erecting said building; that he was to do the work for thirty cents per cubic yard; that she did not inform the plaintiff Zilka that she intended to make said excavation nor give him the notice required by the provisions of sec. 3093, Rev. Codes, of her intention to make such excavation; that Williams, who was the architect of the defendant Graham, superintended the work of making said excavation; that England talked with the architect about shoring and bracing up the Zilka wall; that England had had no experience in doing that kind of work and he so informed the defendant Graham.

Under the evidence the jury no doubt found that architect Williams superintended said excavation and was informed of the way that England intended to shore or brace the walls of the Zilka building. It also appears that the manner in which plaintiff's building was shored and protected was not the ordinary and customary method of protecting brick walls and was not the method used by prudent and careful workmen.

It appears from the evidence that it was the intention of England to put in concrete piers in place of the wooden ones; that he had put in only a part of the wooden posts when the building collapsed. Plaintiff's building next to defendant's lot was sixty feet in length and constructed of brick, and at the time it collapsed there were six posts under it, two at the corners and four at equal distances through the center, and the evidence shows that that method of protecting the wall was not a proper method, or at least there was substantial evidence supporting that view, and the jury must have taken that view. The evidence on the part of respondent England shows that he was performing said work under the direction of appellant Graham and her architect and that he did the work in accordance with the instructions or advice of the architect; that he was simply a servant working for Mrs. Graham, and the jury must have taken that view of the evidence and found that he was not a joint tort-feasor and not responsible for the falling of the wall, and there is evidence in the record that would justify the jury in so finding.

The action of the court in overruling the demurrer to the amended complaint is assigned as error. Upon an examination of the demurrer and complaint, we are satisfied that the court did not err in overruling said demurrer.

Assignments of error Nos. 2 to 37, inclusive, relate to the admission of evidence. Upon an examination of those assignments, we are fully satisfied that there is no reversible error in the action of the court involved in said assignments.

Assignments Nos. 38 to 41, inclusive, go to the action of the court in giving certain instructions, but the only instruction the appellant argues in her brief is instruction No. 15, which instruction is as follows: "The court instructs the jury that in such cases as this the defense that the work was done by an independent contractor is not maintainable, as the party doing the excavating cannot escape responsibility by contracting with someone else to do the work for him. And if you find in this case that Max England was doing the work for the defendant, Teresa M. Graham, then Teresa M. Graham would be just as responsible as if she did the work herself."

Had the evidence showed that England was an independent contractor and did not do the work under the direction of Mrs. Graham and her architect, said instruction would be objectionable, but since the evidence shows that he did the work under the direction of the appellant's architect, we do not think the giving of said instruction was reversible error.

Assignment of error No. 46 refers to the action of the court in denying plaintiff's motion to set aside the judgment and verdict and enter a judgment in favor of appellant Graham. It appears from the record that the judgment was entered on the 14th of October, 1913, that said motion was made on the 12th of November, 1913, and the order denying the same was made on the 21st of November, 1913. The order denying said motion, therefore, was made after the judgment was entered and was an appealable order. No appeal was taken therefrom. It is a well-established rule that a motion to set aside a judgment and for a judgment *non obstante veredicto* comes too late if made after judgment is entered. Such motion must be made immediately after the verdict and before the judgment is entered. (*Oliver v. Kootenai Co.*, 13 Ida. 281, 90 Pac. 107; *Schieble v. Hart*, 11 Ky. Law Rep. 607, 12 S. W. 628; *State v. Commercial Bank*, 6 Smedes & M. (Miss.) 218, 45 Am. Dec. 280; Freeman on Judgments, sec. 7; 23 Cyc. 871.) Said motion cannot be considered as a part of this appeal as no appeal was taken from said order, and the alleged error claimed by the motion was not presented to the court on the motion for a new trial and is therefore not reviewable under the provisions of secs. 4441–4443, Rev. Codes, as amended by Laws of 1911, p. 377.

Under the provisions of sec. 3092, Rev. Codes, it was the duty of the appellant to notify the respondent that she was about to make excavations on her said lot, which she failed to do. That section imposes the duty of giving notice upon the coterminous owner and not upon any servant, and any servant engaged on behalf of the master has the right to presume that the property owner who has employed him to do the work has done that which the statute requires. In *Schultz v. Byers*, 53 N. J. L. 442, 26 Am. St. 435, 22 Atl. 514, 13 L. R. A. 569, it is held that the excavating by an owner on his own land adjoining another's building causing damage, without his knowledge, or previous notice to him, is evidence of want of care in doing the work.

Under the law it is clear that if in making an excavation the land owner fails to prosecute the work skilfully or with proper care, the owner making such excavation is liable for damages resulting to adjacent land owners. As touching upon this point, see *Gerst v. City of St. Louis*, 185 Mo. 191, 105 Am. St. 580, 84 S. W. 34.

In 1 Thompson on Negligence, sec. 1115, the author states: "If an excavation results in a *trespass* upon adjacent property, in consequence of the work being done in conformity with plans furnished by the proprietor, he will be responsible, although the work was done by an independent contractor."

There is substantial evidence to sustain the verdict of the jury and we find no reversible error in the record.

The respondent Zilka appeals from an order of the court taxing costs. He filed his cost bill showing witnesses' fees paid by him to his witnesses, and appellant Graham filed a motion to retax. The motion was based on the ground that the plaintiff's witnesses ought not to be allowed for but one day's attendance as their entire testimony was given on one day. The court taxed the costs allowing some of the witnesses for five days' attendance and others for less.

The record shows that this case was set for trial on the 3d of October, 1913. Another case had been set for October 2d, and the trial of that case was commenced and occupied the attention of the court until the 7th of October, on which day the case at bar was called for trial, and continued until October 11th. It appears that some of the witnesses of respondent were residents of Coeur d'Alene City, the place where the court was being held. The trial court on the motion to tax costs allowed some of such witnesses *per diem* for five days, and this court, on the facts as presented by the record, is not inclined to reverse said order of the court. The trial court was conversant with all of the facts in the case, and we are satisfied was justified in taxing the costs as it did. The judgment is affirmed, with costs of the main appeal awarded in favor of plaintiff Zilka, and the costs of the appeal from the order taxing costs in favor of defendant Graham.

Ailshie, C. J., concurs.

(June 13, 1914.)

L. W. CHANDLER and LETTIE LEE CHANDLER, Plaintiffs, v. THE PROBATE COURT FOR KOOTENAI COUNTY, State of Idaho, and Hon. BERT A. REED, Judge of the Said Court, Defendants.

[141 Pac. 635.]

SETTLEMENT OF ESTATE—POWER OF PROBATE COURT TO RELIEVE FOR EXCUSABLE NEGLECT—JURISDICTION OF PROPERTY IN DIFFERENT STATES—WHERE PROPERLY ADMINISTERED—SUBSEQUENTLY DISCOVERED PROPERTY.

1. Under sec. 4229, Rev. Codes, a probate court has jurisdiction and power to relieve a party from a judgment, order or other proceeding taken against him through his mistake, inadvertence, surprise or excusable neglect.

2. Application for such relief must be made within a reasonable time, not later than six months from the rendering of the decree, or the making of the order, or the occurrence of the proceeding sought to be set aside.

3. It is not the duty of an administrator of the estate of a deceased person to file with the probate court claims against the estate which have been rejected by him.

4. Under sec. 5600, Rev. Codes, it is the duty as well as the right of anyone opposed to the final settlement of an administrator's account and final distribution of the estate, in a case where the proper statutory notice is given, to appear in the probate court, file his exceptions in writing, and contest the same. If an interested party neglects to do this, he is not entitled to have the order settling the account and the decree of final distribution set aside under sec. 4229, Rev. Codes.

5. If a creditor whose claim is rejected by the administrator of an estate neglects to file his exceptions to the final account of the administrator and the petition for final distribution and to contest the same, and the court, after giving the proper statutory notice, settles said account and renders a decree of final distribution, such creditor, upon later bringing his action against the estate, is not entitled to have said order and decree set aside under sec. 4229, Rev. Codes, on the ground that no money has been paid into the probate court to cover his claim.

6. Where promissory notes owned by a deceased resident of a California county and secured by mortgage on real estate in an

Idaho county are duly administered in probate proceedings in the California county, and proceedings are later instituted in the probate court of an Idaho county to administer certain real estate situated in said county which the deceased owned at the time of his death, and the account of the Idaho administrator is settled and a final distribution of said real estate made by the Idaho court, the fact that the promissory notes were administered in the California court and were not included in the inventory or administered in the Idaho court is not ground for the Idaho court, upon petition of a creditor, to set aside the order settling the account and the final decree of distribution.

7. Where certain property belonging to the deceased is not administered in probate proceedings, and the fact is not discovered until a final decree of distribution has been entered, the final decree should not for this reason be set aside on application of a creditor or party interested. The proper remedy is furnished by sec. 5650, Rev. Codes, which provides for the subsequent issuance of letters testamentary whenever other property of the deceased is discovered.

Application for writ of *mandamus* to compel the judge of the probate court of Kootenai county to set aside an order settling the final account of an administrator and a decree of final distribution. Alternative writ quashed.

Jas. H. Frazier, for Plaintiffs.

Probate courts have equity powers to set aside final settlements on the ground of fraud, mistake or accident. (*Sellew's Appeal*, 36 Conn. 186; *Ayer v. Messer*, 59 N. H. 279; *Pew v. Hastings*, 1 Barb. Ch. (N. Y.) 452; *Smith v. Rix*, 9 Vt. 240; *Adams v. Adams*, 21 Vt. 162.) The power is conferred by statute in the following cases: *Williams v. Price*, 11 Cal. 212; *Estate of Cahalan*, 70 Cal. 604, 12 Pac. 427; *Dillman v. Barber*, 114 Ind. 403, 16 N. E. 825; *Smith v. Dutton*, 16 Me. 308; *Stetson v. Bass*, 9 Pick. (Mass.) 27; *McCollom v. Box*, 8 Smedes & M. (Miss.) 619; *Engle v. Crombie*, 21 N. J. L. 614; *Matter of Tilden*, 98 N. Y. 434; *Meckel's Appeal*, 112 Pa. 554, 4 Atl. 447.

Bert A. Reed and C. H. Potts, for Defendants, file no brief.

McCARTHY, District Judge.—On February 2, 1914, the defendant, as probate judge of Kootenai county, rendered a final decree of distribution and made an order of discharge of the administrator in the matter of the estate of Frederick J. Johnson, deceased. On March 24, 1914, the petitioners in this case filed a petition in said probate court for the purpose of setting aside said order and decree. The material facts set forth in said petition are as follows:

1. That Frederick J. Johnson, deceased, died on or about February 23, 1913, at Santa Cruz, California, leaving an estate within Kootenai county, Idaho; that he left a will which was admitted to probate in Kootenai county, and P. W. Johnson was appointed administrator.

2. That final decree of distribution in said estate was made by the probate court of Kootenai county on February 2, 1914, at which time the estate was closed and the administrator released.

3. That said estate was illegally and fraudulently closed in that the following property owned by the deceased was not included in the inventory nor probated in said proceedings, to wit: A note for $1,000 given to deceased by Leonard and Ida McCrea, secured by mortgage on real estate in Kootenai county; a note for $1,500 given by the same parties to deceased, secured in the same way; and an unsecured note for $250 given by one Herman Hansen to deceased; that the first two named notes were fraudulently included in the inventory filed in certain proceedings (presumably probate proceedings) in Santa Cruz county, state of California; that the $250 note was paid during the administration of the estate in Kootenai county to Edward G. Johnson, the sole heir; that said $250 note was not included in said probate proceedings in California or in Idaho.

4. That said deceased was at the time of his death, and still is, indebted to the petitioners in the sum of $2,860.53, with legal interest thereon from March 12, 1911; that said claim was duly presented to the administrator; that said administrator failed and refused to approve or reject said claim and that said claim was deemed rejected on December 25, 1913; that within three months from said date petitioners

filed suit in the district court of the eighth judicial district for Kootenai county on said claim.

5. That the administrator and one Edward G. Johnson, the sole heir under said will, knew that the property of the deceased was worth more than the sum of $700, and that they caused and allowed to be included in the inventory of the deceased's property filed in the probate court of Kootenai county, property to the value of only $700, excluding the promissory notes mentioned, and caused the first two promissory notes mentioned to be included in the property of the estate in California; that they did this fraudulently for the purpose of closing the estate in Kootenai county out of due course and to prevent the petitioners from the recovery of their claim.

6. It inferentially appears from the petition that no money was reserved by the probate court to cover the petitioners' claim.

The petition filed in this court, and upon which the alternative writ of mandate was issued, contains practically the same allegations as those contained in the petition filed in the probate court and outlined above; it expressly alleges that no money was reserved by the probate court to cover the petitioners' claim; that the petitioners did not know that said estate had been probated in California and did not know of the payment or existence of the $250 note at the time the estate was closed, and did not receive actual notice of the intention to close said estate.

The petition then goes on to allege that the petition, which is outlined above, was filed in said probate court, that the probate judge refuses to issue any citations for the purpose of having a hearing on said petition, and refuses to reopen said estate or set aside said order and decree.

Upon this petition an alternative writ of mandate issued out of this court. To the petition, and in response to the writ, defendant filed a demurrer and answer. No evidence was taken; the only question now before this court is whether the demurrer should be overruled or sustained.

If a very narrow view were taken of this matter, it might be considered that the only question before the court is whether or not the defendant should be compelled by mandate to make an order in response to the petition filed by the petitioners. We are not disposed to take such a narrow view of the case for the following reasons: First, the question as to whether or not the petition sets up a meritorious case was argued before us on the merits, the petitioners themselves asking this court to command the said probate judge to set aside said decree and order; second, if the probate judge were ordered to make an order of record, he would undoubtedly make an order denying the petition. It seems that such order would not be appealable. (Sec. 4831, Rev. Codes.) There is no provision for an appeal from an order of the probate court made subsequent to the closing of the estate. The matter being squarely before us on the merits, it might as well be squarely passed upon at this time.

The petitioners claim that the probate court has jurisdiction and power, under sec. 4229, Rev. Codes, to relieve a party from a judgment, order, or other proceeding taken against him through his mistake, inadvertence, surprise or excusable neglect. We think that under this statute the probate court has such jurisdiction and power. The statute provides that this power cannot be exercised after the expiration of six months from the adjournment of the term at which the judgment was rendered. Terms of the probate court have been abolished in this state. (Sec. 4833, Rev. Codes, as amended by chap. 96, Sess. Laws 1911, p. 340.) The statute says, however, that the application must be made within a reasonable time. We think the maximum reasonable time would be six months from the rendering of the decree or the making of the order sought to be set aside.

While generally basing their right to relief upon the provision of sec. 4269, Rev. Codes, the petitioners set up three specific grounds for relief: 1st, because their claim was a disputed one, and no property or money was reserved in court for the payment of the same; 2d, because the $1,000 and

$1,500 promissory notes were fraudulently probated in Santa Cruz county, California, instead of being probated in Kootenai county; 3d, because the $250 note was not included either in the probate proceedings in Kootenai county or California.

We will take up these matters in the order just above named.

Sec. 5611, Rev. Codes, provides that if there is any contingent or disputed claim against the estate, the amount thereof, or such part of the same as the holder would be entitled to if the claim were due, established or absolute, must be paid into the court and there remain to be paid over to the party when he becomes entitled thereto. A claim which has been rejected by the administrator need not be reported by him to or filed by him in the probate court. (Secs. 5466, 5467 and 5593, Rev. Codes.) It is only claims which have been allowed which must be filed in the probate court.

Sec. 5468, Rev. Codes, provides that when a claim is rejected either by the executor, administrator or probate judge, the holder must bring suit in the proper court within three months after the date of the rejection, if it be then due. Secs. 5598 and 5599, Rev. Codes, provide for the notice which must be given of a hearing upon a petition for settlement of the administrator's account and for decree of final settlement and distribution. Such notice was duly given in this case. Sec. 5600 provides that on the day appointed any person interested in the estate may appear and file his exceptions in writing to the account and contest the same. Sec. 5602 provides that the settlement of the account and the allowance thereof by the court is conclusive against all persons in any way interested in the estate. The petitioners' claim was rejected by operation of law on December 25, 1913, the notice of petition for final distribution was given on January 21, 1914, and the petitioners failed to except to or object to the petition for final distribution.

Since there is no provision of law which makes it the duty of the administrator to file with the probate court claims rejected by him, since the probate judge cannot be supposed to act upon matters which are not presented to him in his judicial capacity, since he cannot be expected to hold in court money for the payment of any claim when he has no knowledge that it is disputed, since under the provisions of sec. 5600, Rev. Codes, any parties interested in the estate may object to the final settlement, for these reasons we think that it was incumbent upon the petitioners, who, in common with everybody else, had the only notice of the hearing on the petition for final settlement which was required by law and which was furnished by the probate judge, to appear in the probate court and file their exceptions or make their objections. We think this is the intent of the statutes which we have just reviewed. Since the petitioners neglected to do this, how can they contend that this proceeding was taken against them through their excusable neglect? They knew whether or not they were going to dispute the action of the administrator in failing to allow their claim; they knew that the settlement of the estate was pending in the probate court; they had statutory notice of the petition for final settlement. Under these circumstances their failure to keep track of the proceedings and file their exceptions was such a failure to protect themselves in the way provided by law as constitutes laches, and prevents them from now pleading that the proceedings were taken against them through excusable neglect.

The second ground relied upon is the failure to include the $1,000 and $1,500 notes in the probate proceedings in Idaho and the including of them in the probate proceedings in California. The promissory notes are personal property, even though they happen to be secured by mortgage on real estate.

Petitioners' case inevitably involves an attack upon the proceedings in California. Aside from the grave question as to whether or not an attack may be made upon the decree of the probate court in California by means of a petition to set aside a decree in the probate court in Idaho, we cannot see that any valid ground of attack upon the decree or proceedings of the California court would be stated in this petition, even if the method selected were a proper one. While the brief contains several statements to the effect that the deceased was a resident of Kootenai county for several years and up to within a few months of his death, there is no allegation in the petition that the deceased was a resident of Kootenai county at the time of his death. On the other hand, the petition alleges that the deceased died at Santa Cruz, California, leaving an estate in the county of Kootenai. (Par. 2 of the petition filed in the probate court and par. 5 of petition filed in this court.) Said allegations are consistent with the supposition that he was a resident of Santa Cruz at the time of his death. If he were, the proceedings had there were entirely legal and valid against any attack of the sort attempted to be made here.

Under such circumstances it would be only the fact that the deceased owned real estate in Kootenai county which would make it necessary to administer said estate in the probate court of said county, and such administration would have to be had only to the extent of such real estate, which was just what was done in this case. (Secs. 5290, 5351 and 5628, Rev. Codes.)

So far as the allegations of the petition show, the proceedings in California were entirely lawful. The administrator and heir had a right to do just what they did, and this second ground of attack is without foundation. This being so, the plaintiffs cannot base their claim for relief on said ground. Admitting that they did not know about the proceedings in California or the existence of the notes up to the time that the estate was closed in Idaho, such fact is immaterial, because even if they had known these facts, they would not have availed to prevent the closing of the estate.

The third point raised is that there was property which was not probated in Kootenai county or in California. Reference is undoubtedly made to the $250 note. Sec. 5650 provides for the subsequent issuance of letters testamentary whenever other property of the estate is discovered, or whenever it becomes necessary or proper, for any cause, that letters should be again issued. If the existence of this note and the fact that it was not included in the probate proceedings in either jurisdiction give the petitioners the right to any relief so far as the proceedings in Idaho are concerned, then it is this section which gives them the relief, and it is not the relief sought in this action. The existence of the $250 note would be no ground for setting aside the decree of distribution in the face of sec. 5650.

Our conclusion is that the defendant's demurrer to plaintiffs' petition should be sustained, for the reason that the facts set forth in the petition and admitted by the demurrer are not sufficient to justify the court in making the alternative writ peremptory.

It came out on the trial that on April 1, 1914, within the sixty days allowed by law, the petitioners attempted to file in the probate court a notice of appeal from the order of settlement of account and decree of final distribution, and that the defendant refused to file it, fearing that he might be in contempt of the order to show cause and alternative writ which had been issued by this court. The same holds true of an undertaking on appeal which petitioners attempted to file within the sixty days. We think that the probate judge was not justified in his fear that the filing of the notice and undertaking would have been in violation of the order of this court, and that it would have been proper for him to have filed them. As this is not an action to compel him to do so, we make no order in the matter; nor do we express any opinion as to whether or not the appeal would lie, nor, if so, what conclusion should be reached upon such appeal. If the probate judge files said notice of appeal and undertaking *nunc pro tunc,* which he doubtless will do, such questions will be considered and decided, when, if ever, they are properly presented to this court for decision.

Defendants' demurrer to plaintiffs' petition is sustained and the alternative writ is hereby quashed. Costs awarded to defendants.

Ailshie, C. J., and Sullivan, J., concur.

(June 17, 1914.)

STATE, Respondent, v. DWIGHT E. CANNON and FERDINAND SCHUSTER, Appellants.

[140 Pac. 963.]

CRIMINAL LAW—CONTINUANCE—POSTPONEMENT.

1. Where an affidavit for the postponement of the trial of a criminal action is based on the absence of a material witness and of a document in the possession of such witness, even though the testimony of such witness and the document itself are of impeaching character, and the affidavit shows that after being served with a subpoena in the case such witness has left the state to answer to a charge of felony in another state, refusing to surrender such document because he deems it material in his own trial, but there is reasonable probability that he will return with the document and testify if the present trial is postponed as requested, for a period of ten days or two weeks, and it does not appear that either the court or the state will be incommoded by such postponement, it is an abuse of discretion on the part of the trial court to refuse such postponement.

APPEAL from the District Court of the Fourth Judicial District, in and for the County of Twin Falls. Hon. Edward A. Walters, Judge.

Defendants were convicted of selling intoxicating liquor in violation of the local option law, and sentenced to terms of imprisonment and to pay a fine of $500 each. Judgment *reversed*.

W. P. Guthrie and A. M. Bowen, for Appellants.

"A defendant in a criminal action is undoubtedly entitled to the personal attendance of his witnesses at the trial, if the same can be obtained without unreasonable delay." (*Cremeans v. Commonwealth,* 104 Va. 860, 52 S. E. 362, 2 L. R. A., N. S., 721; *People v. Dodge,* 28 Cal. 445, 448.)

"It is improper to compel a defendant to go to trial upon the admission only of part of a showing, if material and proper, as the accused is entitled to have it considered in its entirety." (9 Cyc. 186.)

If a defendant has relied on the promise of a material witness, residing beyond the jurisdiction of the court, to attend the trial, and so has omitted to take his deposition, and the witness fails to appear, a continuance should be granted. (*People v. Brown*, 46 Cal. 102.)

J. H. Peterson, Atty. Genl., J. J. Guheen, E. G. Davis and T. C. Coffin, Assistants, for Respondent.

The courts have been uniform in holding that a continuance should not be granted upon a showing of this nature, wherein the testimony to be adduced is only of an impeaching nature. (*Gerstenkorn v. State*, 38 Tex. Cr. App. 621, 44 S. W. 503; *Gipson v. State*, 58 Tex. Cr. App. 403, 126 S. W. 267; *Giles v. State* (Tex. Cr. App.), 157 S. W. 943; 4 Ency. Pl. & Pr. 853; Dec. Digest, Criminal Law, sec. 596, subd. 3.)

FLYNN, District Judge.—Defendants were convicted of violating the local option law, under an information containing two counts: The first charging the defendants with an illegal sale of whisky on April 5, 1913, and the second, charging a like sale on the following day. From a judgment of fine and imprisonment against each defendant on each count, and from an order overruling their motion for a new trial, defendants appeal.

The first assignment of error is that the trial court abused its discretion in refusing to grant a postponement of the trial for a period of ten days or two weeks. The information was filed on April 30, 1913, and defendants on the following day pleaded not guilty. Before the case was set for trial, affidavits for continuance were filed and the case continued for the term. On October 10, 1913, the case was set for trial on October 21st. The record does not show that the case was called or reached until October 31st, on which day it was again set for trial on November 6th, 1913. At the opening of court on November 5th, defendants moved for a postponement of the trial for a period of ten days or two weeks and filed in support of said motion the affidavit of defendant Cannon. The motion was denied and a recess was taken by the court until 1:30 P. M. of that day, at which time defendants filed a supplementary affidavit of Cannon in support of their motion for postponement, and the motion was again denied, whereupon the trial proceeded with the result above stated.

Without desiring to countenance a practice which might permit or encourage attorneys to fire one charge of legal ammunition at a trial court and await results before firing again, we think that these two affidavits should be considered as a whole in determining whether there was error in denying the postponement prayed for. The first of these two affidavits recites that on October 11, 1913, affiant caused a subpoena to issue, which was served on one Hutto, a necessary and material witness for defendant; that Hutto agreed to be present and testify, but that through no fault of affiant or of his own Hutto is compelled to be absent from the state, for the reason that Hutto is under bail to appear before the district court of Elko county, Nevada, on an indictment for a felony therein pending, the trial of which has been set for November 10th, 1913; that said Hutto has been compelled to go to Nevada to answer to said indictment and to properly defend himself to the charge therein; that without affiant's knowledge and notwithstanding the service of said subpoena, Hutto left the state of Idaho and refuses to return until after his own trial in Nevada; that Hutto agrees to be present and will be present and testify on behalf of defendant if this cause is postponed to another day of the present term. The affidavit states that Hutto will testify that on and prior to May 10, 1913, T. F. McConvill, the prosecuting witness against this defendant on the charge herein, stated to Hutto that he, McConvill, had never purchased or been given any liquor by this defendant and that he had no relations with this defendant in regard to any matters which might constitute a violation of the liquor laws of this state; that McConvill stated that any testimony given by him against this defendant would be false, and that he considered it best to leave the state of

Idaho so that he might not be compelled to take the stand; that
he requested Hutto to procure a conveyance for him so that
he might leave the state and go to Mexico; that he did leave
the state May 10, 1913; that in the presence of said Hutto, he
signed the following written statement:

"State of Nevada,   ⎫
  County of ———,   ⎬ ss.
                    ⎭

"T. F. McConvill, being by me first duly sworn, upon his
oath, says: I am the prosecuting witness in the criminal actions, wherein the State of Idaho is prosecuting S. W. Harris,
James T. Nelson, Fred Estes, Dwight E. Cannon and Ferdi-
nand Schuster for illegal sale of intoxicating liquors, now
pending in the District Court of the Fourth Judicial District
of the State of Idaho, in and for the county of Twin Falls, and
I am a witness for the state in each and all of said cases.

"I make the statement freely and voluntarily that I have
never at any time bought of said parties above named, or
either of them, any intoxicating liquors, and neither of said
parties has at any time given me any intoxicating liquors.
                              "T. F. McCONVILL."

Cannon's second affidavit is in substance as follows: A re-
iteration and adoption of the statements and allegations of
his first affidavit; that Hutto has the original statement alleged
to have been signed by McConvill, and refuses to surrender
the same, because he deems it material evidence in his own
behalf at his forthcoming trial in Nevada; that if this trial is
postponed until a later date of the present term, or until on
or about November 17, 1913, affiant will be able to procure the
said original statement from Hutto and show by an inspection thereof and comparison with other documents signed by
McConvill and also by handwriting experts and others
familiar with McConvill's signature that said statement was
in fact signed by McConvill; that affiant is informed that
McConvill intends to deny his signature thereto and that affiant cannot corroborate Hutto's testimony except by production of the original document.

The prosecuting attorney objected to the postponement, but
gave no reasons therefor, and admitted that if Hutto were

present in court he would testify to the facts set forth in
the first of the foregoing affidavits, whereupon the application
for postponement was denied.

Defendant's bill of exceptions, certified to by the trial
judge, recites "that it appeared to the court that said postponement would not require the cause to go over for the term
of court but that the said term would and did continue until
after the 20th day of December of said year, during which
time a jury would be and actually was in attendance upon the
said court for the trial of any and all causes coming before the
same."

Section 7795, Rev. Codes, provides that "When an indictment is called for trial, or at any time previous thereto, the
court may, upon sufficient cause, direct the trial to be postponed to another day of the same or of the next term." What
is "sufficient cause" is a matter to be determined by the trial
court, and its action in respect of the postponement or continuance can be disturbed only where the record shows an
abuse of judicial discretion. This court has heretofore held
that "To entitle the defendant to a postponement of the trial
on the ground of the absence of a witness, he must show what
he expects to and will prove by such witness; that such evidence is material to his defense; that such evidence is true;
that the witness is not absent by his procurement or with his
consent; that he has used due diligence to procure the presence of said witness at the trial, and failed to do so; and that
there is a reasonable probability that he can and will procure
the attendance of said witness at the next term of the court."
(*State v. Corcoran*, 7 Ida. 220, 61 Pac. 1034.)

It has also been decided that the provisions of sec. 4372,
Rev. Codes, are applicable to the trial of criminal actions.
That statute provides: "A motion to postpone a trial on the
ground of the absence of evidence can only be made upon affidavit showing the materiality of the evidence expected to be
obtained, and that due diligence has been used to procure it.
The court may also require the moving party to state, upon
affidavit, the evidence which he expects to obtain; and if the
adverse party thereupon admit that such evidence would be

given, and that it be considered as actually given on the trial, or offered and overruled as improper, the trial must not be postponed.'' (*Territory v. Guthrie*, 2 Ida. 432, 17 Pac. 39.)

Under the rules prescribed by the foregoing statutory provisions, as construed in the above decisions, did the trial court err in refusing to postpone the trial? In determining this question, we are of the opinion that the period of the postponement asked for is a very material element to be considered. Though there might be no abuse of discretion in refusing to permit a continuance which would cause the trial to go over the term, it may easily happen that under the same showing it would be error to deny a postponement of the trial until a later day in the same term. Trial courts are usually fully justified in refusing not only continuances, but even temporary postponements, where such postponements would so disarrange their calendars as to leave the court and jury without cases to hear or necessitate an unreasonable retention of trial juries and the consequent expense to the county, or the prolonged detention of the state's witnesses with the added expense and possible loss of their testimony; but none of these reasons appear here, and the record fails to show the grounds of the prosecuting attorney's objection to postponement.

The affidavits for a postponement in this case are in conformity with the rule stated in *State v. Corcoran, supra,* except that they fail to state ''that such evidence is true,'' but inasmuch as the affidavits state explicitly that the written statement of McConvill was signed by him, that Hutto saw him sign it and would so testify and would present the statement in court for inspection, we think that the affidavits should not be held insufficient in this regard.

While we recognize and approve the rule that continuances should not be granted to secure testimony for the purpose of impeachment, we feel that the interests of justice and the right of defendant to have all the material evidence available in his behalf presented to the jury would have been better preserved by granting the postponement in this case. It does not appear that the postponement would have incommoded the court or the prosecution; and it is shown that defendants were diligent in their efforts to obtain the absent evidence; that the evidence was material; that there was a reasonable probability of securing it within ten days or two weeks. Keeping in mind the fact that there is a difference between an application for a continuance over the term and a short postponement within the term, we feel that where an affidavit for the postponement of the trial of a criminal action is based upon the absence of a material witness and of a document in the possession of such witness, even though the testimony of such witness and the document itself are of impeaching character, and after being served with a subpoena in the case such witness has left the state to answer to a charge of felony in another state, refusing to surrender such document because he deems it material in his own trial, but there is reasonable probability that he will return with the document and testify if the present trial is postponed as requested for a period of ten days or two weeks, and it does not appear that either the court or the state will be incommoded by such postponement, it is an abuse of discretion on the part of the trial court to refuse such postponement.

This determination renders it unnecessary to pass on the other assignments of error. It is therefore ordered that the judgment of the trial court be reversed and that a new trial be granted to defendants.

No oral argument has been made in this case and the foregoing conclusion has been reached solely from an examination of the record and briefs on file in this court.

Ailshie, C. J., and Sullivan, J., concur.

(June 18, 1914.)

STATE, Respondent, v. WALTER A. GRANT, Appellant.

[140 Pac. 959.]

ARSON—CORROBORATION OF EVIDENCE OF ACCOMPLICE—SEC. 7871 CONSTRUED—INSTRUCTIONS—QUESTION OF ACCOMPLICE FOR JURY—WHAT NECESSARY TO CONSTITUTE ACCOMPLICE—INDETERMINATE SENTENCE ACT—DISCRETION OF TRIAL COURT IN DENYING MOTION FOR NEW TRIAL.

1. Under the provisions of sec. 7871, Rev. Codes, the corroborating evidence required to substantiate the testimony of an accomplice must be upon some material fact or circumstance which, standing alone and independent of the testimony of the accomplice, tends to connect the defendant with the commission of the offense. (*State v. Knudston,* 11 Ida. 524, 83 Pac. 226, approved.)

2. When the question, as to whether a witness is an accomplice, arises in a criminal case under sec. 7871, Rev. Codes, it is the duty of the trial court to instruct the jury on the law of accomplices, and leave the question as to whether or not any witness is an accomplice in the commission of the offense charged, for the decision of the jury as a matter of fact, unless it appear without substantial conflict in the testimony that such witness was an accomplice.

3. In order to make a person an accomplice in the commission of a crime, some aiding, abetting or actual encouragement, by such person must be shown. Mere presence at the plotting of a crime or silent acquiescence in its commission is not, in the absence of a legal duty to act, sufficient to constitute one an accomplice.

4. The failure to disclose known facts regarding the commission of a crime does not render one having such knowledge an accomplice of the person who committed the crime.

5. *Held,* that under the provisions of sec. 1, chap. 200, of the laws of 1911 (Sess. Laws. 1911, p. 664), amending sec. 1 of the indeterminate sentence act of 1909, taken together with sec. 7008, Rev. Codes, fixing the penalty for the crime of arson in the first degree at a minimum sentence of two years and maximum for life, the defendant was legally sentenced to serve a maximum term of fifty years in the state penitentiary, with a minimum of twenty-five years.

6. A wide discretion is vested in the trial court in determining the weight to be given to the statements contained in affidavits on motion for a new trial on the ground of newly discovered evidence, and the action of the trial court in denying such motion will not be disturbed where the discretion reposed is not shown to have been abused.

7. The action of the trial court refusing to strike from the files counter-affidavits submitted by the state on defendant's showing on motion for a new trial, on the ground that such counter-affidavits are immaterial and irrelevant, is not a ground for reversal of a judgment of conviction, where it does not appear that the defendant has been prejudiced by allowing such counter-affidavits to remain in the record.

APPEAL from the District Court of the Fifth Judicial District, in and for Bannock County. Hon. J. M. Stevens, Judge.

The defendant was convicted of the crime of arson in the first degree and appealed. Judgment *affirmed.*

Clark & Budge and Carl Barnard, for Appellant.

"The corroborating evidence required by sec. 7871, Rev. Codes, must be upon some material fact or circumstance which, standing alone and independent of the evidence of the accomplice, tends to connect the defendant with the commission of the offense." (*State v. Knudtson,* 11 Ida. 524, 83 Pac. 226; *State v. Bond,* 12 Ida. 424, 86 Pac. 43.)

"Where the facts are not in dispute, where the acts and conduct of the witness are admitted, it becomes a question of law for the court to say whether or not those acts and facts make the witness an accomplice." (*People v. Coffey,* 161 Cal. 433, 119 Pac. 901, 39 L. R. A., N. S., 704; *People v. Bunkers,* 2 Cal. App. 197, 84 Pac. 364, 370.)

This court held in the *Matter of Setters,* 23 Ida. 270, 128 Pac. 1111, that under the provisions of the indeterminate sentence act of March 11, 1909, where the minimum sentence is fixed by law, the court has no power to fix a different minimum.

The affidavits of George Charles Edwards and Barney Horgan set forth facts sufficient to have justified and required the trial court to grant appellant's application for a new trial. (*Bates v. State* (Miss.), 32 So. 915; *Stewart v. State,* 52 Tex. Cr. 100, 105 S. W. 809; *Piper v. State,* 57 Tex. Cr. 605, 124 S. W. 661.)

J. H. Peterson, Atty. Genl., J. J. Guheen and T. C. Coffin, Assistants, and D. C. McDougall, for Respondent.

As to whether or not a witness is an accomplice is a question for the jury, even though the testimony is not in conflict, for it is almost always necessary to construe the language used by the witnesses for the purpose of determining the precise connection of a witness with the one who committed the crime. (*People v. Creegan,* 121 Cal. 554, 53 Pac. 1082; *People v. Coffey,* 161 Cal. 433, 119 Pac. 901, 39 L. R. A., N. S., 704; *People v. Bunkers,* 2 Cal. App. 197, 84 Pac. 364, 370.)

Consenting and acquiescing in the commission of a crime does not render one an accomplice within the meaning of sec. 7871, or a principal within the meaning of sec. 6342, Rev. Codes. (*Moore v. State,* 4 Okl. Cr. 212, 111 Pac. 822.)

The witness Truman, alias Edwards, was not an accomplice in the commission of the crime in the case at bar. (*Levering v. Commonwealth,* 132 Ky. 666, 136 Am. St. 192, 117 S. W. 253, 19 Ann. Cas. 140.)

The corroboration in the case at bar, independent of the testimony of Edwards, is sufficient under sec. 7871, Rev. Codes. (*Chandler v. State,* 60 Tex. Cr. 329, 131 S. W. 598.)

When a new trial is asked upon the ground of newly discovered evidence, the truth of the affidavits and their materiality are essential elements. (*Arnold v. Skaggs,* 35 Cal. 684; *People v. Weber,* 149 Cal. 325, 86 Pac. 671.)

"Mere concealment of a crime, or falsifying about knowledge thereof, does not render a witness an accessory or accomplice." (*Alexander v. State,* 49 Tex. Cr. 93, 90 S. W. 1112; *Schackey v. State,* 41 Tex. Cr. 255, 53 S. W. 877; *Alford v. State,* 31 Tex. Cr. 299, 20 S. W. 553.)

AILSHIE, C. J.—In the month of July, 1913, the appellant, Walter A. Grant, and one W. M. Truman, generally known as Billie Edwards, were engaged in conducting in the city of Pocatello the Horseshoe Pool Hall, which contained in addition to pool tables a stock of tobacco and cigars. An important part of the business was an illegal traffic in intoxicating liquors, the county being at that time prohibition territory. Edwards was a partner of appellant in this illegal traffic, but had no interest in the legitimate part of the business. Associated with these two men about this time, as an assistant in their clandestine operations and as a hanger-on about the place, was a negro by the name of John L. Thomas, commonly known as "Frisco"; also another man by the name of McIlvaine. All these men, with the possible exception of Edwards, who had recently arrived in town, were already at that time in ill favor with the authorities. The appellant himself had been indicted at the March term of the district court for Bannock county upon two charges, one for maintaining a common nuisance in a prohibition district, the other for a violation of the anti-gambling law. To the first charge he plead guilty and was fined $500, which he paid. The second charge was still pending at the time of the occurrence of the events herein referred to. McIlvaine had been repeatedly arrested for bootlegging, and Thomas, according to his own testimony, was being constantly hounded by the police.

On July 21, 1913, according to the testimony of Edwards and Thomas, appellant sent a message to Thomas by Edwards that he would like to see him at the pool hall about midnight of that day. In the interview between appellant and Thomas at that hour in the back room of the pool hall, Edwards was present part of the time, passing back and forth, drinking with Grant and Thomas, and listening to much of their conversation. In this conversation Grant offered Thomas $100 if he would burn the residence of the prosecuting attorney, C. D. Smith, stating as a reason that he wanted to teach him a lesson for interfering too zealously with the bootlegging business. After some parley, Thomas agreed to commit the crime for that sum, and it was agreed that on the following day appellant should show Thomas where Smith lived. On the afternoon of July 22d Thomas met Edwards and Grant at the pool hall and started with them to go to Smith's house, which was in another part of the city. On their way, however, they saw a policeman at a distance and the members of the party separated. Later on in the afternoon Thomas again joined appellant, and the two proceeded to the locality of Smith's house, which was pointed out to Thomas by appellant. During the evening of that day Grant, Edwards, Thomas and McIlvaine met in the back part of the pool hall, and arrangements were completed, not only for the burning of Smith's house by Thomas, but for the burning of a policeman's house on the other side of the city by McIlvaine, with the avowed purpose of having the fires occur at the same time so as to embarrass the fire department in controlling them. At this interview also the parties partook freely of liquor to brace their nerves and make bigger fools of themselves than they usually were.

At about 2:30 on the morning of the 23d, Thomas made two attempts to carry out his part of the program. The first time the fire went out before getting well started. On returning to the pool hall he met Grant and Edwards there. Grant accused him of not having made a good job of it because no alarm had sounded. In about half an hour he started out again and made a second attempt, after which he returned to the pool hall finding Grant and Edwards still there. On this occasion the fire got quite a start, an alarm was given, and the conflagration was extinguished by the fire department. No alarm was heard at the pool hall and Grant again accused Thomas of having made a bad job of the undertaking. Shortly after the parties separated. Later on in the same day and toward evening they met again in Edward's lodgings. Thomas demanded pay for his services. Edwards said that he ought to receive something, and Grant thereupon gave him $5.

Other evidence was introduced by the state, mostly in the way of corroboration of the statements made by Thomas and Edwards. Concerning this evidence, it is sufficient to observe that although Thomas and Edwards are corroborated in minor details by credible witnesses for the state as to circumstances attending the commission of the crime, the circumstances testified to can hardly be deemed to connect the defendant with the crime. (*State v. Knudtson,* 11 Ida. 524, 83 Pac. 226.)

It was shown, among other things, that he had a motive for ill-will against the prosecuting attorney, and it was testified that he had made a threat against him several months before. But on the whole such corroboration was not sufficient, and his conviction must be considered to depend upon the evidence of the witnesses Thomas and Edwards, the first of whom is a self-confessed accomplice. Sec. 7871, Rev. Codes is as follows:

"A conviction cannot be had on the testimony of an accomplice, unless he is corroborated by other evidence, which in itself, and without the aid of the testimony of the accomplice, tends to connect the defendant with the commission of the offense; and the corroboration is not sufficient, if it merely shows the commission of the offense, or the circumstances thereof."

The trial judge instructed the jury as follows: "You are instructed that an 'accomplice' is one who is concerned in the commission of a crime or connected with the crime committed, either as principal offender or as one who advises, aids or assists in the commission of the unlawful act.

"If you find from the evidence that on or about the 23d day of July, 1913, the place of residence of C. D. Smith of Pocatello, was burned and that the witnesses, W. M. Edwards and John L. Thomas, were concerned in the burning of said building, that is to say, that said Edwards and Thomas were accomplices in the commission of said crime; and if you further find that the evidence connecting the defendant, Grant, with the commission of said crime, is the testimony of said Edwards and Thomas, uncorroborated by other evidence, which in itself, and without the aid of the testimony of said Edwards and Thomas, tends to connect said defendant with said crime, then you are instructed that you must find the defendant not guilty."

Inasmuch as the jury found the defendant guilty with this instruction before them, they must have concluded, either that there was corroborating evidence connecting Grant with the commission of the crime, independent of the evidence of Edwards and Thomas, or that the witness Edwards was not an accomplice.

Our statute, sec. 7871, requiring the evidence of an accomplice to be corroborated, is taken *verbatim* from the California Penal Code, sec. 1111, and has been repeatedly construed by the California court.

In *People v. Creegan*, 121 Cal. 554, 53 Pac. 1082, that court says: "It must be assumed from the verdict that, upon the evidence before them, the jury found that he was not an accomplice, and if this evidence was properly received their verdict must be accepted as conclusive of the fact."

And in the case of *People v. Coffey*, 161 Cal. 433, 119 Pac. 901, 39 L. R. A., N. S., 704, the same court observes:

"When the question of an accomplice arises in the trial of a case, the general and accepted rule is for the court to instruct the jury touching the law of accomplices, and leave the question whether or not the witness be an accomplice for the decision of the jury as a matter of fact. (*People v. Kraker*, 72 Cal. 459, 1 Am. St. 65, 14 Pac. 196.)"

The court continues further: "Whenever the facts themselves are in dispute, that is to say, wherever the question is whether the witness did or did not do certain things, which, admittedly, if he did do them, make him an accomplice, the jury's finding, upon familiar principles, is not disturbed. But where the facts are not in dispute, where the acts and conduct of the witness are admitted, it becomes a question of law for the court to say whether or not those acts and facts make the witness an accomplice."

And in *People v. Bunkers*, 2 Cal. App. 197, 84 Pac. 364, 370, it is stated in the syllabus as follows: "Before a conviction for crime can be set aside for want of testimony corroborating the evidence of an accomplice, as required by Penal

Code, sec. 1111, it must appear without substantial conflict in the evidence that the witnesses who gave corroborative evidence were also accomplices, and where there is a conflict on that question, it will be presumed in aid of the verdict that the jury found that such witnesses were not accomplices." We believe that this correctly states the law.

In the first place, it will be noted that Edwards is not alleged to have participated in the actual commission of the crime by the man Thomas, but to have aided, abetted and encouraged its commission in association with the appellant Grant. It is admitted that he had a complete knowledge of what was going on; he was familiar with every step of the conspiracy; he was present at the successive interviews at which the crime was planned. Counsel for appellant have set forth in their brief at length those passages from the testimony which they claim show his criminal participation. But taking all this at its face value, none of the evidence cited shows active participation on the part of Edwards. He was present at these interviews, but he had a right to be on the premises in the pool hall where they occurred, being a partner in business with Grant.

It is charged that his actions indicate he kept watch on customers or others entering the premises, in order that appellant and Thomas might not be disturbed or overheard by others in the discussion of their nefarious undertaking. But this is not conclusive; the testimony shows that liquor was constantly in evidence at all these interviews in the back room of the pool hall, a condition of itself to be guarded from prying eyes in prohibition territory and on behalf of men who were already known violators of the law. On the other hand, it was brought out in the cross-examination of Thomas that Edwards at a certain stage of the conspiracy expressed strong disapproval of this plot, which circumstance Edwards also states in his own testimony. Asked upon cross-examination why he did not interfere to prevent it, or notify anyone, he replied: "I didn't think that he would do it; I thought that it was whisky talk."

But granting counsel's contention to the extent that the attitude of Edwards was on the whole an attitude of acquiescence, that he was quite willing the crime should be committed, that he knew all that was going on and still concealed his knowledge from the officers of the law and the party against whom the crime was concocted, does that attitude make him an accomplice?

As we have seen, the trial court defined the meaning of the term "accomplice" in his instruction to the jury in this case, as "one who is concerned in the commission of a crime or connected with the crime committed, either as principal offender, or as one who advises, aids or assists in the commission of the unlawful act." While this definition might perhaps have been made more explicit, it properly advises the jury that an accomplice must at least be "one who advises, aids or assists." The evidence does not show that Edwards was anything more than an interested listener at these interviews, not present at all the conversation, taking little part in it himself, not encouraging in any way the commission of the crime. The most overt act of which he can be accused, so far as disclosed by the record before us, was accompanying the appellant and Thomas on the occasion when appellant proposed to show Thomas where Smith's house was.

Now, a mere mental state of uncommunicated consent or acquiescence on the part of a bystander, where a crime is being instigated, is not sufficient to make him an accomplice in its commission. Some aiding, abetting or actual encouragement on his part is essential. (12 Cyc. 186.) As said in the leading case of *Levering v. Commonwealth*, 132 Ky. 666, 136 Am. St. 192, 117 S. W. 253, 19 Ann. Cas. 140; "To constitute one either a principal, an accessory, an aider and abettor, or an accomplice, he must do something; must take some part; must perform some act or owe some duty to the person in danger that makes it incumbent on him to prevent the commission of the crime. Mere presence or acquiescence in, or silent consent to, is not, in absence of duty to act, legally sufficient, however reprehensible it may be, to constitute one a principal or an accessory, or an aider or abettor, or an accomplice." See, also, on this point, *Moore v. State*, 4 Okl. Cr. 212, 111 Pac. 822; *Chandler v. State*, 60 Tex. Cr. 329, 131 S. W. 598; 1 Am. & Eng. Ency. of Law, 391.

Edwards held toward Smith, the prosecuting attorney, no such relation as would make the failure on Edwards' part to endeavor to prevent the execution of a plot to burn Smith's house evidence of Edwards' guilty agency in the perpetration of the crime. (Wharton on Criminal Law, 11th ed., sec. 171; *Levering v. Commonwealth, supra.*)

Nor does the failure to disclose facts regarding the commission of a crime render a person having knowledge of such facts an accomplice of the one who committed the crime, (*Bird v. United States*, 187 U. S. 118, 23 Sup. Ct. 42, 47 L. ed. 100; *Melton v. State*, 43 Ark. 367; *Cruse v. State* (Tex. Cr.), 77 S. W. 818; *Alexander v. State*, 49 Tex. Cr. 93, 90 S. W. 1112.)

It is further contended by counsel for appellant that the judgment of conviction in this case is illegal, in that appellant was given a sentence of not less than 25 nor more than 50 years. The penalty provided by our statute for the crime of arson in the first degree is a minimum of two years, which may be extended to life. (Sec. 7008, Rev. Codes.) This court held in the case of *In re Setters*, 23 Ida. 270, 128 Pac. 1111, that under sec. 1 of the indeterminate sentence act of 1909, where the minimum sentence is fixed by law, the court is not authorized to fix a different minimum. In the case at bar, however, the defendant was sentenced under the provisions of sec. 1, chap. 200 of the Laws of 1911 (Sess. Laws 1911, p. 664), amending sec. 1 of the indeterminate sentence act of 1909, in which amendment the following language occurs: "The court imposing sentence shall not fix a definite term of imprisonment, but shall fix a minimum term of imprisonment which shall be not less than the minimum prescribed by law, nor less than six months in any case . . . . and the minimum term of imprisonment fixed by the court shall not exceed one-half of the maximum term of imprisonment fixed by statute; provided further: that in all cases when the maximum sentence, in the discretion of the court, may be for life or any number of years, the court imposing the sentence shall fix a maximum sentence.''

Under this provision of the amended statute the appellant was lawfully sentenced.

Appellant also assigns as error the overruling of his motion for a new trial, and the overruling of his motion to strike the counter-affidavits filed by the state. The affidavits submitted by defendant upon this motion purport to make a showing of newly discovered evidence. The two principal affidavits are made by George Charles Edwards and Barney Horgan, both inmates of the county jail and convicted bootleggers. The first sets forth various conversations overheard by affiant between Billy Edwards and the negro Thomas, who were at the same time confined in the county jail, from which it is made to appear that the conviction of appellant was the result of a conspiracy between Edwards and Thomas to give perjured testimony against appellant at his trial. Horgan's affidavit alleges admissions made by the witness Edwards as to appellant's innocence.

The state filed a number of counter-affidavits, and among others, two by other inmates of the county jail, stating that they were offered $50 by the affiant Horgan, if they would make affidavits on behalf of appellant. The state also filed an affidavit by R. W. Jones, court reporter, setting forth a conversation between Thomas and Edwards long subsequent to the commission of the crime. It is difficult to see the materiality of this last affidavit as a part of the state's counter-showing, and the trial court might properly have stricken it from the files, but it is not shown how its being allowed to remain there has prejudiced appellant.

The trial court, in denying the motion for new trial on the ground of newly discovered evidence, doubtless viewed with some suspicion the source of the showing made, and under the circumstances would have been justified in distrusting the credibility and disinterestedness of the affiants, George Charles Edwards and Barney Horgan. A wide discretion is vested in the trial court in determining the weight to be given to the statements contained in affidavits upon motion for a new trial, and we do not think that discretion was abused by the trial judge in this instance.

Counsel for appellant in his argument before this court made certain statements of fact *dehors* the record, accompanied by the explanation of peculiar exigencies, which in his opinion made it his duty to do so, and at the same time informally presented to the court an unauthenticated report of the testimony of the witness Thomas upon the later trial of the witness Edwards for the same offense of which appellant was convicted; such testimony having been given at a date subsequent to the filing of the transcript in the case at bar in this court. We sympathize with the zeal displayed by counsel on behalf of his client, and may here properly observe that the client is in no respect going to suffer from any lack of diligence on the part of his counsel. We have, however, examined this purported testimony of Thomas at the trial of Edwards, from which it appears that Thomas avers his testimony upon the trial of appellant Grant, with regard to the noncomplicity of Edwards, to have been false and perjured, and that in giving that testimony he purposed to shield Edwards, whom he now charges to have been equally culpable with appellant in the commission of this crime. But his testimony on the later trial in no way tends to relieve the appellant Grant from the stigma of guilt. Furthermore, the jury may as well have believed the original testimony given by the witness, as that upon the second trial wherein he testified that his first story was false.

The matters thus presented might possibly afford ground for the exercise of executive clemency, but this court in determining any case submitted to it upon appeal is necessarily confined to a consideration of such facts as are made to appear from the record.

Under the well-known rule, the jury who heard the witnesses in this case and observed their demeanor on the stand were the exclusive judges of the weight to be attached to their evidence. They listened to the narrative of Thomas, who committed the crime at the instigation of appellant and confessed to them in detail the manner of its instigation and

perpetration. They heard the corroborating testimony of
Edwards, and under the instruction of the court were the
proper arbiters of the question as to whether his participation
in the instigation of this felony was such as to make him an
accomplice in the commission of it. They listened to the witnesses for the defense, each one of whom, including the defendant, is shown by the record to have been a convicted
violator of the law. It was for the jury to say whom among
these witnesses they believed and whom they disbelieved, and
we are not inclined to disturb their verdict.

The judgment of the lower court is *affirmed.*

Sullivan, J., concurs.

––––––––––––––

(June 23, 1914.)

W. E. CAMPBELL, Appellant, v. THE BANK & TRUST
CO., a Corporation, and W. H. RALPH, Respondents.

[141 Pac. 1102.]

EVIDENCE—SUFFICIENCY OF.

1. *Held,* that the evidence is sufficient to support the findings.

APPEAL from the District Court of the Second Judicial
District, in and for Nez Perce County. Hon. E. C. Steele,
Judge.

Action to have certain conveyances of real estate and certain transfers of personal property canceled and held for
naught. Judgment for defendants. *Affirmed.*

C. T. McDonald and J. S. McDonald, for Appellant, cite no
authorities on point decided.

James E. Babb, for Respondents.

If the court should find even that there is only a substantial
controversy in the evidence as to whether the findings made

by the court below are true, it would be necessary to affirm the judgment, since an appellate court will not reverse findings of fact of the lower court where there is a substantial controversy in the evidence, even though the appellate court may believe the court below was wrong. (*Dearing v. Hockersmith,* 25 Ida. 140, 136 Pac. 994, syllabus No. 5, and cases cited.)

SULLIVAN, J.—This action was brought to have certain deeds to real property and transfers of personal property which were executed by the appellant to the defendant bank set aside and canceled, and the ground relied upon for such relief was duress in the execution of said deeds and the transfer of said personal property.

The issues being joined by the answer, the cause was tried by the court and findings of fact made and judgment entered in favor of the defendants.

Several errors are assigned, but the main error is the insufficiency of the evidence to support the findings.

Upon an examination of the evidence, we are satisfied that it is amply sufficient to sustain the findings and that no prejudicial errors at law were committed by the court in the trial of the case.

The judgment must therefore be affirmed, and it is so ordered, with costs of this appeal in favor of the respondents.

Ailshie, C. J., concurs.

(June 24, 1914.)

STATE, Appellant, v. J. C. JOHNSON, G. F. HARTLEY and JOSEPH IRVIN, Respondents.

[141 Pac. 565.]

EXTERMINATION OF PREDATORY ANIMALS—SECS. 1197 AND 1198, REV. CODES, CONSTRUED—POWERS OF STATE SANITARY BOARD AND STATE VETERINARIAN UNDER—PAYMENT OF BOUNTIES NOT AUTHORIZED BY.

1. Secs. 1197 and 1198, Rev. Codes, provide for the extermination of predatory animals through the employment by the livestock sanitary board of "experienced, competent and skilful hunters and trappers" at a *per diem* compensation. Such method having been specified by the statute, the board and the state veterinarian acting with it are precluded from resorting to other methods of extermination not authorized by law, such as the payment of bounties for the destruction of such aminals by persons not in the employ of the sanitary board.

2. If a statute is found by experience to be unwise or impracticable, relief must be sought through the legislature. Neither a state board in executing such statute, nor a court in construing it, has any authority to alter or amend it.

3. *Held*, that the trial court properly advised the jury to acquit the defendants.

APPEAL from the District Court of the Third Judicial District, in and for the County of Ada. Hon. Carl A. Davis, Judge.

Defendants were prosecuted on information for conspiracy in attempting to collect predatory animal bounty on spurious and fraudulent claims. Defendants acquitted. State appeals. *Affirmed.*

J. H. Peterson, Atty. Gen., T. C. Coffin, J. J. Guheen and E. G. Davis, Assts., for Appellant.

"Conflict and repugnance in statutes should always be avoided by construction, if possible. Indeed, a statute ought, upon the whole, to be so construed that, if it can be prevented, no clause, sentence or word should be superfluous, void or insignificant." (*Jackson v. Kittle*, 34 W. Va. 207, 12 S. E. 484.)

The narrow construction placed on this statute by the district court, has the effect of making the expression, "to devise and put into operation," equivalent to the expression, "exercise no independent judgment whatever, nor put into operation any method save what is hereafter set forth."

"A contemporaneous construction, after a lapse of time, without change of that construction by legislation or judicial decision, has been declared to be generally the best construction." (Sutherland, Stat. Const., sec. 472; *Smith v. Bryan*, 100 Va. 199, 40 S. E. 652.)

An extreme case of where courts followed the contemporaneous construction of officers charged with the enforcement of a statute is the case of *Pennoyer v. McConnaughy*, 140 U. S. 1, 11 Sup. Ct. 699, 35 L. ed. 363.

Karl Paine and Solon Orr, for Respondents.

A perusal of secs. 1197–1204, Rev. Codes, shows that in the enactment of this act, the legislature purposed that the destruction of predatory animals should be prosecuted systematically; and that the predatory animal fund is appropriated to bear the expenses of such destruction and not as a bounty fund. The intention is to be ascertained by considering the entire statute. (Sutherland, Stat. Const., sec. 239.)

Sec. 1199 imposes upon the hunters and trappers employed by the board the duty of exercising the greatest care in putting out poison. The section makes a violation of any of its provisions by any of the hunters or trappers employed by the board a misdemeanor. A bounty claimant who so baited out poison would not be guilty of a misdemeanor under this section, because he is not employed by the board. Thus sec. 1199 would remain without operation or effect, and out of harmony with the remainder of the statute.

Statutes must be so construed as to give effect to all their provisions, so that no part will be inoperative, and so that one part will not destroy another. (Sec. 380, Lewis' Sutherland, Stat. Const.)

Secs. 1200, 1204, and indeed the major portions of section 1197 and all of sec. 1198, are in like manner rendered inoperative under appellant's construction, though they are serially related in subject matter.

"Where there are in an act specific provisions relating to a particular subject, they must govern in respect to that subject, as against general provisions in other parts of the statute, although the latter, standing alone, would be broad enough to include the subject to which the more particular provisions relate." (*Ihmsen v. Monongahela Nav. Co.*, 32 Pa. 153; *King v. Armstrong*, 9 Cal. App. 368, 99 Pac. 527; *Frandzen v. San Diego County*, 101 Cal. 317, 35 Pac. 897; *Nance v. Southern Ry.*, 149 N. C. 366, 63 S. E. 116.)

While section after section of this act teems with provisions governing the work of the hunters and trappers, not a syllable is expressed with respect to bounty claimants, nor the allowance of a bounty.

There can be no intent of a statute not expressed in its words. (Sec. 388, Lewis' Sutherland, Stat. Const.)

AILSHIE, C. J.—The defendants were jointly informed against and charged with the crime of conspiracy.

It was alleged that the defendants presented to the state veterinarian for allowance certain claims on the bounty fund, claiming a bounty for the killing and destruction of certain animals, and that these claims were fictitious, fraudulent and false. Proofs were submitted in support of the allegations of the information, but upon request of counsel for the de-fendants the trial court advised the jury to return a verdict in favor of the defendants, on the ground that the state livestock sanitary board and veterinary surgeon had no power or authority to allow claims for bounties for killing predatory animals, and that the only authority they had to pay for the killing of such animals was by employing hunters and trappers as authorized by sec. 1197 of the Rev. Codes. Defendants were acquitted and the state has appealed.

The only question presented for our consideration is "as to whether or not under the provisions of secs. 1197 and 1198 of the Rev. Codes, the livestock sanitary board and state veterinarian have the authority to provide for the allowance of bounties for the killing of predatory animals." It is quite clear to us that the board has no such authority. Secs. 1197 and 1198 of the Rev. Codes, known as the predatory animal act or livestock sanitary act, provide as follows:

Sec. 1197. "It is hereby made the duty of the sanitary board to exercise a general supervision over the subject of the killing and destruction of wolves, coyotes, wildcats and such other wild animals as are in the habit of preying upon and destroying sheep, calves, colts, pigs, poultry and other domestic animals and fowls and wild game, and to devise and put into operation such methods and means as will best secure and attain the object of exterminating such wild, destructive and pestiferous animals, and to this end they are hereby authorized and empowered to employ one or more experienced, competent and skilful hunters and trappers, as they may deem necessary, in each or any inspection district of the state; whose duty it shall be to work constantly and diligently with guns, traps, poison and any and every practicable means and methods, to procure and bring about the destruction of as many of such predatory animals as possible."

Sec. 1198. "The hunters employed in accordance with the preceding section shall each receive such compensation as may be agreed upon beforehand, not exceeding three dollars and fifty cents per day, and their employment shall always be liable to be discontinued at any time, at the pleasure of the board, and it shall be the duty of each and all of them, at all times, to work at such localities and along such plans of operation as the board may, from time to time, direct, and the board is hereby empowered and authorized to purchase old or undersized and cheap horses and other animals to be killed and used as bait for the purpose of poisoning the pestiferous animals hereinbefore mentioned, as well as all necessary poisons to be used in connection therewith, and also such traps and ammunition as shall be necessary or useful for the purposes aforesaid: *Provided*, that the said trappers and hunters must use their own guns; and *provided, further*, that the board shall never expend a greater sum of money in any one year than thirty-five thousand dollars, and whenever that amount has been expended in the year, then and thereafter any and all further expenditures for the purposes of this article shall terminate and cease."

Sec. 1156 authorizes the state veterinarian to act in conjunction with the livestock sanitary board in the enforcement of the act.

It will be seen from an examination of the foregoing provisions of the statute that it is made "the duty of the sanitary board to exercise a general supervision over the subject of the killing and destruction of wolves, coyotes, wildcats and such other wild animals as are in the habit of preying upon and destroying sheep . . . . and to devise and put into operation such methods and means as will best secure and attain the object of exterminating such wild animals . . . . and to this end they are hereby authorized and empowered to employ one or more experienced, competent and skilful hunters and trappers, as they may deem necessary, in each or any inspection district of the state."

Now, while the statute vests the general *supervision* of the subject in the board and authorizes them to *devise means* and point out methods of carrying on the work, the statute specifically designates the *agency* through which the work shall be accomplished, namely, through hunters and trappers to be employed by the board. If it had been the intention of the legislature to authorize the payment of bounties, they would undoubtedly have so provided in the statute, as had been prescribed in previous statutes in force in both territorial times and during statehood. Evidently the legislature did not intend to authorize the payment of bounties. Previous experiences under such law had proven unsatisfactory and had opened the way to a great deal of fraud which had been practiced upon the several counties. The legislature, therefore, created a livestock sanitary board and vested it with the power and authority to employ hunters, and gave them absolute control and supervision over such employees and the power to direct and prescribe the means and methods such employees should use in carrying on the work. Not only this, but by sec. 1199 of the statute certain restrictions are laid upon hunters and trappers who may be employed by the board, and for a violation thereof or a failure to observe such restrictions such employees may be deemed guilty of a misdemeanor and punished accordingly. The restrictions of sec. 1199 would evidently not apply to mere bounty claimants and those who are not working in the employ of the state board acting under the authority of sec. 1197. Again, the moment the board converts this statute into a bounty statute and begins paying bounties, it opens the doors to the perpetration of the very frauds which are charged in this action and which the legislature evidently intended to guard against.

It is suggested that the board cannot accomplish anything by employing hunters and trappers, for the reason that they spend their time in their own work or do nothing and still claim their pay and that no results will be accomplished. That may be true, but it would seem that the board might be able to employ honest men for this kind of work as well as at anything else. However that may be, if the statute is unwise or impracticable, relief must be sought through the legislature. Neither the board, nor the courts, have any right to alter or amend the statute.

The trial court properly advised the jury to acquit the defendants, and the judgment should be affirmed, and it is so ordered.

Sullivan, J., and Walters, District Judge, concur.

(June 24, 1914.)

J. T. ELDER, Administrator, Appellant, v. IDAHO-WASHINGTON NORTHERN RAILROAD, a Corporation, Respondent.

[141 Pac. 982.]

AMENDMENT—REFUSAL OF—NONSUIT—JUDGMENT OF.

1. It is not an abuse of discretion upon the part of the trial court to refuse permission to amend a pleading where upon appeal a case has been remanded for a new trial, and where the amendments sought were directly contradictory to the original allegations, and where the amendments were sought for the apparent purpose of avoiding matters formerly alleged and proven in the case, and upon which issue had been joined, where no showing is made of excusable inadvertence or mistake, or of fraud upon the part of the other party contributing thereto.

2. Evidence examined and *held* that upon close of plaintiff's case a nonsuit was properly granted.

APPEAL from the District Court of the Eighth Judicial District for Kootenai County. Hon. John M. Flynn, Judge.

Action to recover damages for personal injuries. Judgment of nonsuit entered at close of plaintiff's case. Motion for a new trial denied. Plaintiff appeals from judgment of nonsuit and from order denying new trial. *Affirmed.*

Elder & Elder and Stiles & Devaney, for Appellant.

The court should have permitted the amended complaint to be filed and served, and in failing to do so it did not make reasonable use of a sound discretion in the premises, and its action should therefore be reversed and the amendments permitted. (*Flaherty v. Butte Electric Ry. Co.*, 43 Mont. 141, 115 Pac. 40.)

Where the defendant has discovered or should have discovered the peril of a person to which his own negligence may have exposed him in the first instance, and it is apparent that he cannot escape therefrom or for any reason does not make the effort to do so, or is apparently oblivious to or unaware of his exposed condition and danger, the duty at once becomes imperative for the defendant to use all reasonable care under the circumstances with the means and facilities at hand to avoid injuring him, and if this is not done the defendant becomes liable in damages notwithstanding the negligence of the injured party. (*Pilmer v. Boise Traction Co.*, 14 Ida. 327, 125 Am. St. 161, 94 Pac. 432, 15 L. R. A., N. S., 254; *Anderson v. Great Northern Ry. Co.*, 15 Ida. 513, 99 Pac. 91; 2 Bailey on Personal Injuries, 2d ed., sec. 504; *Havel v. Minneapolis etc. R. Co.*, 120 Minn. 195, 139 N. W. 137; *Neary v. Northern Pac. R. Co.*, 37 Mont. 461, 97 Pac. 944, 19 L. R. A., N. S., 446.)

The question of negligence should have been submitted to the jury. (*Schulz v. Chicago M. & St. Paul Ry. Co.*, 57 Minn. 271, 59 N. W. 192; *Chamberlain v. Missouri Pac. Ry. Co.*, 133 Mo. 587, 33 S. W. 437, 34 S. W. 842; *Anderson v. Great Northern Ry. Co.*, 15 Ida. 513, 99 Pac. 91.)

"Where the appearance indicates that a person upon the track is in such condition as to be either insensible of his danger or unable to avoid it, those in charge of the train must use all available means consistent with the safety of those on the train to stop." (*Campbell v. Kansas City etc. R. Co.*, 55 Kan. 536, 40 Pac. 997; *Cincinnati etc. Ry. Co. v. Long*, 112 Ind. 166, 13 N. E. 659; *Carrier v. Missouri Pac. R. Co.*, 175 Mo. 470, 74 S. W. 1002; *Isbell v. New York etc. R. Co.*, 27 Conn. 393, 71 Am. Dec. 78.)

Chas. L. Heitman, for Respondent.

Said amendments change the nature of the cause of action, as set forth in the original complaint. The court committed no error in refusing to allow the proposed amended complaints to be filed. (*Chemung Mining Co. v. Hanley*, 9 Ida. 786, 77 Pac. 226; *Warner v. Godfrey*, 186 U. S. 365, 376, 22 Sup. Ct. 852, 46 L. ed. 1203; *Union Pac. R. Co. v. Wyler*, 158 U. S. 285, 15 Sup. Ct. 877, 39 L. ed. 983.)

On a second trial, a party will not be permitted to amend his pleading, made with knowledge of all the facts, so as to deny facts which he had previously alleged, and upon which an opinion on appeal had been based. (*Lilly v. Menke,* 143 Mo. 137, 44 S. W. 730; *Box v. Chicago, R. I. & P. Ry. Co.,* 107 Iowa, 660, 78 N. W. 694.)

"In actions *ex delicto,* the wrongful act complained of is the cause of action, and an amendment of the petition should not be permitted where the effect would be either to substitute as a cause of action a wrongful act different from that alleged in the original petition, or to inject such wrong into the case as an additional cause." (*Peery v. Quincy etc. R. Co.,* 122 Mo. App. 177, 99 S. W. 14; *Chicago & A. R. Co. v. Scanlan,* 170 Ill. 106, 48 N. E. 826; *Illinois Cent. R. Co. v. Campbell,* 170 Ill. 163, 49 N. E. 314; *Crosby v. Seaboard Air Line Ry.,* 83 S. C. 575, 65 S. E. 827; *Peterson v. Pennsylvania R. Co.,* 195 Pa. 494, 46 Atl. 112; *Doran v. Thomsen,* 79 N. J. L. 99, 74 Atl. 267; *Mantle v. Dabney,* 47 Wash. 394, 92 Pac. 134; *Coker v. Monaghan Mills,* 119 Fed. 706; *Brown v. Edmonds,* 9 S. D. 273, 68 N. W. 734; *Ingold v. Symonds,* 134 Iowa, 206, 111 N. W. 802.)

The employees of respondent, in charge of switch engine 22, moving slowly, its bell ringing, the engine laboring and making a loud noise, were not bound to presume or to assume that an employee, familiar as Neil was with the manner of operating there, would ignore the going and coming of cars, and that they had a right to act upon the belief that Neil in the yards would take reasonable precaution for his own safety against the approach of switch engines, and had a right to assume that he would step off the track before engine No. 22 reached him. (*Aerkfetz v. Humphreys,* 145 U. S. 418, 12 Sup. Ct. 835, 36 L. ed. 758; *Anderson v. Great Northern Ry. Co.,* 15 Ida. 513, 99 Pac. 91; *Smith v. Atlanta & C. R. Co.,* 130 N. C. 344, 42 S. E. 139; *Pennsylvania Co. v. Meyers,* 136 Ind. 242, 36 N. E. 32; *Louisville & N. R. Co. v. Cronbach,* 12 Ind. App. 666, 41 N. E. 15; *Campbell v. Kansas City etc. R. Co.,* 55 Kan. 536, 40 Pac. 997; *Cincinnati etc. Ry. Co. v. Long,* 112 Ind. 166, 13 N. E. 659, 663; *Carrier v. Missouri Pac. Ry. Co.,* 175 Mo. 470, 74 S. W. 1002.)

The railroad company owed to Neil or to any other of its employees who might be upon its track in its switching yards the duty only to exercise ordinary care. The requirements of ordinary care and diligence are fully complied with when the usual signals are given and the train is being operated and the business conducted when the accident happens in the usual manner. (*Hogan v. Chicago etc. R. Co.*, 59 Wis. 139, 17 N. W. 632; *Norfolk & W. R. Co. v. Gesswine*, 144 Fed. 56, 75 C. C. A. 214.)

Engineers running locomotives are not bound to stop, or even decrease the speed of the locomotive, merely because they see persons walking upon the track. They may ordinarily assume that such persons have made themselves aware of the approach of the locomotive and will seasonably leave the track for its free passage. (*Copp v. Maine Cent. R. Co.*, 100 Me. 568, 62 Atl. 735; *Everett v. Los Angeles etc. Ry. Co.*, 115 Cal. 105, 43 Pac. 207, 46 Pac. 889, 34 L. R. A. 350; *Bookman v. Seaboard Air Line Ry.*, 152 Fed. 686, 81 C. C. A. 612; *Erickson v. St. Paul etc. R. Co.*, 41 Minn. 500, 43 N. W. 332, 5 L. R. A. 786; *Norfolk & Western R. Co. v. Dean*, 107 Va. 505, 59 S. E. 389; *Teel v. Ohio River R. Co.*, 49 W. Va. 85, 38 S. E. 518; *Raines v. Chesapeake & O. Ry. Co.*, 39 W. Va. 50, 19 S. E. 565, 24 L. R. A. 226; *Norwood v. Raleigh etc. R. Co.*, 111 N. C. 236, 16 S. E. 4; *Louisville & N. R. Co. v. Black*, 89 Ala. 313, 8 So. 246; *Nichols v. Louisville & N. R. Co.*, 9 Ky. Law Rep. 702, 6 S. W. 339; *Exum v. Atlantic Coast Line R. Co.*, 154 N. C. 408, 70 S. E. 845, 33 L. R. A., N. S., 169; *Hebert v. Louisiana etc. R. R.*, 104 La. 483, 29 So. 239; *Smalley v. Southern Ry. Co.*, 57 S. C. 243, 35 S. E. 489; *Waldron v. Boston etc. R. R.*, 71 N. H. 362, 52 Atl. 443; *Atlantic Coast Line R. Co. v. Miller*, 53 Fla. 246, 44 So. 247; Ray on Negligence of Imposed Duties, p. 134; Elliott on Railroads, sec. 1258; 33 Cyc. 800.)

WALTERS, District Judge.—This action has been before this court heretofore on appeal and is reported in *Neil v. Idaho & W. N. R. R. Co.*, 22 Ida. 74, 125 Pac. 331. The cause upon such former appeal was remanded for a new trial, and during which, upon the close of plaintiff's testimony, the defendant moved that plaintiff be nonsuited, which motion was by the trial court granted and judgment of such import duly entered.

Motion for new trial was made by the plaintiff and by the court denied, and thereupon plaintiff has prosecuted an appeal from the judgment of nonsuit and dismissal and from said order denying the motion for a new trial. The original plaintiff, Joseph Neil, died after the second trial and prior to this appeal, and J. T. Elder, administrator, was substituted as party plaintiff.

1. After the cause was by this court remanded for a new trial, and prior to the same, plaintiff sought permission, by motion upon two separate occasions to file an amended complaint, and at the time of trial sought permission by motion to file an amendment to the original complaint, which each of said motions for amendment was by the trial court refused, and the rulings of the trial court in such regard are urged by the appellant as error.

The original complaint alleged, and upon which the action was first tried, that on the morning of October 4, 1910, the plaintiff was employed by defendant as a freight train conductor; that upon said morning said plaintiff was walking upon a track running parallel with the track upon which the freight train of which he had charge was standing, and at said time was inspecting the brakes, rods and other appliances on his said train; that while plaintiff was so engaged a switch engine in charge of certain of defendant's employees was run and propelled over and upon said track upon which plaintiff was walking, and over and upon plaintiff whereby he was injured; that the employees of defendant upon said switch engine *saw* plaintiff walking upon said track so engrossed in his work at a point 500 feet from said engine, and *saw* and *knew* that plaintiff remained upon said track from the time he was first seen by defendant's employees upon said switch engine down to the time he was struck and run over by said switch engine; that plaintiff did not see said switch engine, but that, on the contrary, during all of said time the employees on said switch engine *did see* plaintiff upon said track and *knew* that plaintiff was in a position of imminent peril and *knew* that plaintiff did not know of the approach of said locomotive.

By the several amendments which plaintiff sought to make, after this case was by the court remanded for new trial, and prior to a retrial of the same, it was sought to withdraw the allegations of knowledge upon the part of defendant's employees upon said switch engine of the presence of plaintiff upon the track, or that they had seen plaintiff upon the track prior to his injury.

It was sought to insert in lieu thereof allegations charging that the reason plaintiff had been run down by the switch engine was because defendant failed to station a "pilot" or "lookout" upon the rear of said engine so that those in charge of said engine might give suitable warning to any person in danger; that it had been the custom prior thereto for defendant to maintain such "lookout" upon switch engines when in motion, and further, that the same custom was observed by other steam railway companies; that those in charge of said engine failed and neglected to keep or maintain constantly or otherwise, or at all, a lookout or watch over or upon said railway track, but that had said defendant's employees done so, they would have observed plaintiff to be in a position of peril.

In short, it appears that the plaintiff sought to amend his original complaint from an allegation that defendant's employees had seen him prior to the injury, to an allegation that they had not seen him; had sought by amendment to deny what he had prior thereto affirmed; had quite clearly sought to change his form of action. Plaintiff sought to so do after his original action had been tried and upon appeal returned for retrial. The statute of limitations had run prior to the time two of said proposed amendments were applied for. The rule permitting amendments should not be so liberal as to permit litigants to speculate with the courts as to both the law and the facts, and if it should be ascertained after trial that the court views the law more favorable as to certain facts than to those pleaded, then by amendment to shift sail and assert the direct contrary as to facts in order to catch the more favorable law.   To permit the amendments to be made here sought would make possible such procedure.

In *Warner v. Godfrey*, 186 U. S. 365, 22 Sup. Ct. 852, 46 L. ed. 1203, the plaintiff brought suit to set aside a conveyance for actual fraud.   After the case had been carried to an appellate court and decided there, they sought leave to amend their bill by asserting constructive fraud.   The court held such amendment could not be made and spoke as follows:

"It would be highly inequitable to permit a litigant to press with the greatest pertinacity for years unfounded demands for specific and general relief, however much confidence he may have had in such charges, necessitating large expenditures by the defendants to make a proper defense thereto, after the submission of the cause, when the grounds of relief actually asserted were found to be wholly without merit, to allow averments to be made by way of amendment, constituting a new and substantive ground of relief."

In *Lilly v. Menke*, 143 Mo. 137, 44 S. W. 730, the court held that on a second trial, a party will not be permitted to amend his pleading, made with knowledge of all the facts, so as to deny facts which he had previously alleged, and upon which an opinion on appeal had been based, and said:

"It is intolerable to allow a party to assert a fact and maintain it at every step in a cause, until the court draws some unfavorable conclusion from the fact thus conclusively established, and then permit the same party, without any showing of inadvertence or mistake upon his part or any fraud on the part of his adversary contributing thereto, to deny his own assertion.   To countenance this practice would be to encourage deceit and negligence. . . . . The rule requiring consistency of action is not an arbitrary one, but is grounded upon the nature of courts of justice.   'If,' says Bigelow in his work on Estoppel, 'parties in court were permitted to assume inconsistent positions in the trial of their causes, the usefulness of courts of justice would in most cases be paralyzed.'   Certainly there can never be an end of litigation if, every time a suitor is cast upon the grounds assumed by himself, he may avoid all the consequences thereof by flatly contradicting, without so much as an excuse for his conduct, all that he had alleged.''

In *Peery v. Quincy, O. & K. C. R. Co.,* 122 Mo. App. 177, 99 S. W. 14, the circuit court of appeals of Missouri held that:

"In actions *ex delicto,* the wrongful act complained of is the cause of action, and an amendment of the petition should not be permitted where the effect would be either to substitute as a cause of action a wrongful act different from that alleged in the original petition, or to inject such wrong into the case as an additional cause.''

The supreme court of Illinois in *Chicago & A. R. Co. v. Scanlan,* 170 Ill. 106, 48 N. E. 826, held:

"In an action for injuries caused by the falling of a scaffold, the original declaration averred that the scaffold fell owing to its faulty construction. An amended declaration, filed after the statute of limitations had run, charged negligence in overloading the scaffold. *Held,* that as this stated a new cause of action, the statute was a bar.''

It is held in *Doran v. Thomsen,* 79 N. J. L. 99, 74 Atl. 267, as follows:

"Where, in an action to recover damages for personal injuries resulting from negligence, a judgment for the plaintiff has been reversed and a new trial awarded, an amendment of the plaintiff's declaration will not be allowed which would operate to institute a new and different suit between the parties and presenting other questions.''

In *Mantle v. Dabney,* 47 Wash. 394, 92 Pac. 134, the supreme court of Washington laid down the following rule:

"Refusal to allow a defendant, after reversal of a judgment in his favor, to amend his answer by an allegation inconsistent with it and with the evidence and the theory of the case on the first trial, is not error.''

In *Chemung Mining Co. v. Hanley,* 9 Ida. 786, 77 Pac. 226, this court has held as follows:

"Section 4229 was enacted for the protection of the diligent and those who have acted in good faith, and not for those guilty of inexcusable laches and who have neglected to preserve their rights when they have had abundant opportunity accorded them for that purpose.''

It appearing that two of the three applications to amend were made after the statute of limitations had run; that all of the amendments were requested after this case had been returned for a new trial; that they were sought for the apparent purpose of avoiding proof of facts, which had been an obstacle to plaintiff on the appeal, and that the amendments sought were directly contradictory to the original allegation, we conclude that the trial judge did not abuse his discretion in refusing to permit appellant to amend his complaint in the respect requested. What is herein said, it must be understood, would not of necessity be the rule if applications to amend were made prior to answer, or possibly prior to trial or during the trial; nor where a satisfactory showing is made by the moving party of excusable inadvertence or mistake, or of fraud upon the part of his opponent, contributing thereto.

2. At the conclusion of the plaintiff's testimony a motion for a nonsuit was made by the defendant and was by the court sustained. The evidence introduced by plaintiff, as shown by the record upon this appeal, was practically the same as the testimony introduced by plaintiff at the former trial. Such facts are set out at some length in the former decision of this case, hereinbefore cited, and will not be referred to herein at length.

This action was brought under the act of Congress relative to injuries received by employees of interstate railroads, and the defendant in urging its motion for nonsuit relied upon the fact that the testimony introduced on behalf of plaintiff failed to disclose any negligence whatever on the part of the defendant, which view was adopted by the trial court and accordingly a judgment of nonsuit entered.

This phase of this appeal presents the question of whether or not an employee of long experience in railroading, of mature years, in the possession of his faculties, who for a long time prior had been in the employ of the defendant, and had had long experience in its yard where the injury occurred, and who was thoroughly familiar with the yards and tracks

and their uses, can go upon a track which he knows to be a
switching track, and upon which he knows cars are about to
be moved at any time, and regardless of consequences, pay no
attention to the movement of trains upon the track, and upon
injury charge the defendant with negligence under any and
all circumstances. It appears that the plaintiff was injured
by a switch engine hauling four loaded cars of coal and back-
ing up a switch track on a one per cent grade; that the engine
was traveling eight or ten miles per hour; that the bell was
constantly ringing and the engine was laboring hard in blow-
ing off steam and making a noise which could be heard a considerable distance; that one of the employees of the defendant
upon said switching engine saw Neil about five hundred feet
distant from said engine, but did not observe him again;
that another of said employees on said switch engine saw Neil
from about the same distance on the track down to about one
car's length from the engine; that said employee recognized
Neil as a freight conductor in the employ of defendant and
knew that he was in the possession of all his faculties and was
a man of long experience in the railroad business; it further
appears that each and all of said employees of defendant believed, and had good reason for believing, that Neil knew of
the approach of said engine and believed, and had good reason
for believing, that he would step off from the track before
he was injured. Under this state of facts as proved by the
defendant, and under what appears to be the well-settled law,
we conclude that the motion for nonsuit was by the trial court
properly granted.

Before the plaintiff could have recovered in this case under
any circumstances whatever, it must be shown that those in
charge of the railroad train knew, or had reasonable cause for
knowing, that Neil did not hear the warnings or did not heed
them, and that they then negligently continued to run their
train, and as a result thereof injured him. They had the right
to presume that he would step off the track in time to avoid
injury up to the last moment before he was struck, and at
the speed this engine was traveling, but a very few feet dis-

tance between Neil and the engine would suffice for Neil to step off the track in ample time to avoid being run down.

There is no testimony in the record whatever which proves or tends to prove that the defendant's employees on the engine failed to make every possible effort to stop the locomotive after they or any of them had reason to believe that Neil was not aware of the approach of the locomotive. Neil testified that he was told immediately after the accident by the brakeman of the defendant company, who was riding on the engine, that he had noticed Neil on the track and noticed him there until the engine was about a car's length, but it further appears that the brakeman thought that Neil would step off the track, and it would appear that there was ample opportunity for him to do so.

The former opinion of this court discloses that this class and character of cases has received the attention of a great many of the courts, both federal and state, and the holding has quite uniformly been that trainmen in a switch yard, noting another railroad employee on the track, have a right to presume, when the engine is not traveling at an excessive speed, and when they are giving due and sufficient warning of the approach of the engine, that the employee on the track will step aside and avoid injury, and that they are authorized in so presuming until they are in some manner made aware· that such person on the track is not aware of the approach of the engine, or is laboring under some disability which prevents him from protecting himself, and if such appears a fact, then they are chargeable with using every effort at their command to immediately stop their engine and avoid the impending injury.

A case very similar to the one here under consideration is *Aerkfetz v. Humphreys*, 145 U. S. 418, 12 Sup. Ct. 835, 36 L. ed. 758, wherein it is said:

"The engine was moving slowly, so slowly that any ordinary attention on the part of the plaintiff to that which he knew was a part of the constant business of the yard would have made him aware of the approach of the cars, and enabled him to step one side as they moved along the track. It cannot be that, under these circumstances, the defendants were compelled to send some man in front of the cars for the mere sake of giving notice to employees who had all the time knowledge of what was to be expected."

This court has heretofore held in *Anderson v. Great Northern Ry. Co.*, 15 Ida. 513, 99 Pac. 91, that "when an engineer sees an adult on the track ahead of him, he ordinarily has a right to presume that he will get off the track before the train reaches him."

In *Campbell v. Kansas City etc. R. Co.*, 55 Kan. 536, 40 Pac. 997, it is said:

"It was contended that Campbell was seen 500 feet ahead of the engine, and therefore the engineer should have stopped the train before reaching him. An engineer, however, is not bound to stop a train whenever he sees a person ahead upon the railroad, but has a right to assume that an adult person, apparently in the possession of his faculties, will exercise his senses, and step out of the way of danger before the engine reaches him. The engineer is required to keep a reasonable lookout for trespassers upon the track, and to exercise such care as the circumstances require to prevent injury to them. Campbell was undoubtedly seen by the engineer several hundred feet away; but he was awake and moving and appeared to be in the full possession of all his senses and faculties. Although there were some piles of ballast along the track, he could have stepped aside without difficulty; and, as there was no apparent disability, the engineer had a right to presume until the last moment that he would heed the warning which had been given, and leave the track in time to avoid injury. . . . . . Campbell was a man of mature years, who had the use of his faculties; and, as he was moving and apparently capable of taking care of himself, the engineer had a right to presume until the last moment that he would leave the track, and not be run over."

Other cases wherein it has been held that plaintiff could not recover under facts similar to those disclosed by this record are as follows: *Smith v. Atlanta & C. R. Co.*, 130 N. C. 344, 42 S. E. 139; *Pennsylvania Co. v. Meyers*, 136 Ind. 242,

36 N. E. 32; *Louisville & N. R. Co. v. Cronbach*, 12 Ind. App. 666, 41 N. E. 15; *Cincinnati etc. Ry. Co. v. Long*, 112 Ind. 166, 13 N. E. 659; *Carrier v. Missouri Pac. Ry. Co.*, 175 Mo. 470, 74 S. W. 1002; *Hogan v. Chicago etc. R. Co.*, 59 Wis. 139, 17 N. W. 632; *Norfolk & W. R. Co. v. Gesswine*, 144 Fed. 56, 75 C. C. A. 214; *Copp v. Maine Central R. Co.*, 100 Me. 568, 62 Atl. 735; *Everett v. Los Angeles etc. Ry. Co.*, 115 Cal. 105, 43 Pac. 207, 46 Pac. 889, 34 L. R. A. 350; *Bookman v. Seaboard Air Line Ry.*, 152 Fed. 686, 81 C. C. A. 612; *Erickson v. St. Paul etc. R. R. Co.*, 41 Minn. 500, 43 N. W. 332, 5 L. R. A. 786; *Norfolk & Western R. Co. v. Dean's Admr.*, 107 Va. 505, 59 S. E. 389; *Atlantic Coast Line R. Co. v. Miller*, 53 Fla. 246, 44 So. 247.

We conclude that the motion for a nonsuit made by the defendant at the close of plaintiff's testimony was by the court properly granted, and the judgment of dismissal and denial of motion for new trial should be, and is, hereby affirmed. Costs awarded to respondent.

Ailshie, C. J., and Sullivan, J., concur.

(June 27, 1914.)

IDAHO POWER & LIGHT COMPANY, a Corporation, Plaintiff, v. J. A. BLOMQUIST, A. P. RAMSTEDT and D. W. STANDROD, as the Public Utilities Commission of the State of Idaho, Defendants, and THE BEAVER RIVER POWER COMPANY, a Corporation, Plaintiff, v. J. A. BLOMQUIST, A. P. RAMSTEDT and D. W. STANDROD, as the Public Utilities Commission of the State of Idaho, Defendants.

[141 Pac. 1083.]

PUBLIC UTILITIES ACT — PUBLIC UTILITIES COMMISSION — CONSTITU-
TIONAL LAW — STATUTORY CONSTRUCTION — LEGISLATIVE POWER—
DELEGATION OF—CITY ORDINANCE—CONTRACTS AND VESTED RIGHTS—
ORDERS OF COMMISSION—REVIEW OF BY COURTS—CERTIORARI.

1. The act known as the "Public Utilities Act" was passed at the twelfth session of the Idaho legislature, which session was adjourned on the 8th day of March, 1913, and said act was approved by the governor on March 13, 1913, and went into effect sixty days after the adjournment of said session of the legislature, to wit, on the 8th day of May, 1913. (Sess. Laws 1913, p. 247.) Said act provided for the organization of a public utilities commission and defined its powers and duties, and also the rights, remedies, powers and duties of public utilities, their officers, agents and employees, and the rights and remedies of patrons of public utilities.

2. Under the provisions of sec. 10 of art. 4 of the constitution, every bill passed by the legislature becomes a law upon the approval and signing of the same by the governor.

3. All property devoted to public use is held subject to the power of the state to regulate or control its use in order to secure the general safety, health and public welfare of the people, and when a corporation is clothed with rights, powers and franchises to serve the public, it becomes in law subject to governmental regulation and control.

4. The legislature has plenary power in all matters of legislation except as limited by the constitution.

5. There is nothing in the constitution that prohibits the legislature from enacting laws to regulate and control public utility corporations.

6. The police power of the state is sufficiently broad and comprehensive to enable the legislature to regulate by law public utili-

ties in order to promote the health, comfort, safety and welfare of the people, and thus regulate the manner in which public utility corporations shall construct their systems and carry on their business within the state.

7. Under the state's police power, the legislature has authority to authorize said utility commission to determine whether a duplication of an electrical plant is required in a town or city for the convenience and necessity of the inhabitants.

8. Under the provisions of said act, the commission has power absolutely to fix the rates, and it is unlawful for the utility to charge more or less than the rates so fixed.

9. Formerly competition was supposed to be the proper means of protecting the public and promoting the general welfare in respect to service of public utility corporations, but experience has demonstrated that public convenience and public needs do not require the construction and maintenance of numerous instrumentalities in the same locality, but, rather, the construction and maintenance only of those necessary to meet the public necessities, when such utilities are properly regulated by law.

10. Said public utilities act provides that competition between public utility corporations of the classes specified shall be allowed only where public convenience and necessity demand or require it.

11. Sec. 18, art. 11, of the state constitution prohibits combinations for the purpose of fixing prices or regulating production, and requires the legislature to pass appropriate laws to enforce the provisions of that section, and said public utilities act is justified by the provisions of said section, since its ultimate effect will be to prevent unreasonable rates and combinations by public utilities.

12. Unregulated competition is the tool of unregulated monopoly.

13. Under the provisions of said act, unregulated competition is not needed to protect the public against unreasonable rates or unsatisfactory service; and there can now be no justification for unregulated competition or a duplication of utility plants under the pretense of preventing monopoly.

14. Experience and history clearly show that public utility corporations cannot be safely intrusted to properly serve the public until they are regulated and placed under public control.

15. The legislature has ample power to give the public utilities commission authority to refuse to give a certificate of convenience and necessity to a public utility where it seeks to duplicate a plant or system that is amply sufficient to serve properly the inhabitants of a community.

16. The legislature may not delegate its purely legislative power to a commission, but having laid down by law the general rules of action under which a commission may proceed, it may require of that commission the application of such rules to particular situations and conditions and authorize an investigation of facts by the commission with a view to making orders in a particular matter within the rules laid down by such law.

17. Power to regulate public utilities presupposes an intelligent regulation and necessarily carries with it the power to employ the means necessary and proper for such intelligent regulation.

18. Under the law the standard by which rates, services, etc., must be fixed clearly contemplates reasonable rates, services, etc., which is a legislative matter and cannot be delegated; but the authority to determine what is a reasonable rate is purely administrative and can be delegated and was delegated to the commission in our public utilities act, and the several acts authorized to be performed by the commission may be reviewed by this court on a writ of *certiorari* or review, as provided by sec. 63a of said act, and under the provisions of that section all orders made by the commission may be reviewed by this court, and this court has the authority to determine whether such orders are unlawful.

19. The contract right given to a public utility corporation by ordinance of a city does not come within the contract clause of the constitution of the United States, in that it can in no manner be affected by the police power of the state, and when a corporation acquires a franchise for the purpose of carrying on a corporate business within a city, it is accepted subject to the police power.

20. It is provided by sec. 48a of said act that no electrical corporation shall "henceforth" begin the construction of an electrical plant, etc., without having first obtained a certificate of convenience and necessity from the commission; and a public utility corporation cannot slip in between the passage and approval of such act and its going into effect and procure an ordinance that would deprive the state of its right to regulate it in its operations under the police power of the state, especially where such corporation had not begun actual construction work and was not prosecuting such work in good faith and uninterruptedly and with reasonable diligence in proportion to the magnitude of the undertaking, as provided by sec. 48b of said act; for under the facts of this case the plaintiffs had not begun actual construction work on their system in either of said cities.

21. The last proviso of sec. 48a provides that power companies may, without such certificate, increase the capacity of existing plants or develop new generating plants and market the product thereof. That proviso must not be so construed as to nullify the

clear object and purpose of said act. If construed to give such corporations the power to establish new plants and lines and enter into new fields for the sale of their products, then the main object and purpose of said act would be nullified and defeated; and if that proviso be construed in that way, it must be held as nugatory and be disregarded.

22. It was not the intention of the legislature under the provisions of sec. 48b to permit such corporations to extend their lines into territory already occupied by a similar utility corporation, without first securing a certificate of convenience and necessity from said commission.

23. *Held,* that the power of regulation as provided by said act is not required to be specifically conferred by the provisions of the state constitution, and that there is no inhibition in the constitution upon the legislature prohibiting the enactment of such law.

Original proceeding in this court for a writ of review to determine the validity of the order of the public utilities commission, requiring the plaintiffs to refrain from constructing their proposed plants in either the city of Twin Falls or Pocatello, on the ground that such companies have not obtained a certificate of public convenience and necessity requiring such service. *The order and action of the commission affirmed.*

Hawley, Puckett & Hawley and H. R. Waldo, for Plaintiffs.

The provision requiring a written acceptance of a city franchise is merely one of the conditions subsequent which may be waived and the acceptance may be evidenced by acts. (4 McQuillin on Mun. Corp., sec. 1650; *Postal Tel. Cable Co. v. Newport,* 25 Ky. Law Rep. 635, 76 S. W. 159; *City of Allegheny v. People's Natural Gas etc. Co.,* 172 Pa. 632, 33 Atl. 704, 705; *City Railway Co. v. Citizens' Street R. R. Co.,* 166 U. S. 557, 17 Sup. Ct. 653, 41 L. ed. 1114; *Lincoln & Kennebec Bank v. Richardson,* 1 Greenl. (Me.) 79, 10 Am. Dec. 34; *Illinois River R. Co. v. Zimmer,* 20 Ill. 654.)

And it has ever been held that an acceptance will be presumed from the fact that the franchise was granted on the application of the grantee. (*City of Atlanta v. Gate City Gas*

Light Co., 71 Ga. 106; *State v. Dawson,* 22 Ind. 272; *Perkins v. Sanders,* 56 Miss. 733.)

The effect of a franchise granted on conditions subsequent is to vest the estate in the grantee subject to be defeated by the omission to perform the conditions. (*Hook v. Bowden,* 144 Mo. App. 331, 128 S. W. 261; *Brooklyn Cent. R. Co. v. Brooklyn City R. Co.,* 32 Barb. (N. Y.) 358, 364.)

"The court has frequently determined that except with reference to local affairs, a legislature may not delegate its powers of deciding questions of public policy." (Reeder, Validity of Rate Regulations, p. 62.)

"The power conferred upon the legislature to make laws cannot be delegated by that department to any other body or authority." (Cooley, Const. Limitations, 2d ed., p. 163; *Board of Harbor Commrs. v. Excelsior Redwood Co.,* 88 Cal. 491, 22 Am. St. 321, 26 Pac. 375; *O'Neil v. American Fire Ins. Co.,* 166 Pa. 72, 45 Am. St. 650, 30 Atl. 943, 26 L. R. A. 715; *Schaezlein v. Cabaniss,* 135 Cal. 466, 87 Am. St. 122, 67 Pac. 755, 56 L. R. A. 733; *Noel v. People,* 187 Ill. 587, 79 Am. St. 238, 58 N. E. 616, 52 L. R. A. 287; *Barto v. Himrod,* 8 N. Y. 483, 59 Am. Dec. 506.)

The scope of the writ of review cannot be enlarged now beyond the scope of the writ as it was at the time the constitution was adopted. (*Camron v. Kenfield,* 57 Cal. 550; *Pacific Telephone etc. Co. v. Eshleman,* 166 Cal. 640, 137 Pac. 1119, 50 L. R. A., N. S., 652.)

The writ of *certiorari* and review has in this state only common-law powers. (*Stein v. Morrison,* 9 Ida. 426, 75 Pac. 246.)

J. H. Peterson, Atty. Gen., J. J. Guheen and E. G. Davis, Assts., for Defendants.

The whole question of the delegation of power by the legislature has recently been before the U. S. supreme court in the case of *Union Bridge Co. v. United States,* 204 U. S. 364, 27 Sup. Ct. 367, 51 L. ed. 523. The opinion in that case reviews the authorities. (See, also, *Stone v. Farmers' Loan & Trust Co.,* 116 U. S. 307, 6 Sup. Ct. 334, 388, 1191, 29 *ine R. o v North Carolina*

Corp. Commission, 206 U. S. 1, 27 Sup. Ct. 585, 51 L. ed.
933, 11 Ann. Cas. 398; *Kansas City v. Union Pac. Ry. Co.*,
59 Kan. 427, 53 Pac. 468, 52 L. R. A. 321; *Minneapolis etc.
R. Co. v. Railroad Commission*, 136 Wis. 146, 116 N. W. 905,
17 L. R. A., N. S., 821; *Oregon R. & Nav. Co. v. Campbell*,
173 Fed. 957; *Chicago B. & Q. R. R. Co. v. Jones*, 149 Ill. 361,
41 Am. St. 278, 37 N. E. 247, 24 L. R. A. 141.)

Just as it cannot be contended that the legislature itself
has not the power to prescribe rates, it is no longer open to
question that this power may be delegated, within certain
clearly defined limits, to a rate-making body. (Reeder,
Validity of Rate Regulations, p. 67.)

The question of the economic policy of attempting to substitute the regulation of public utilities by a commission for
the old style method of regulation by competition is one for
the legislature to determine. (*Des Moines Water Co. v. Des
Moines*, 192 Fed. 193; *La Crosse v. La Crosse Gas & Electric
Co.*, 145 Wis. 408, 130 N. W. 530; *Calumet Service Co. v. City
of Chilton*, 148 Wis. 334, 135 N. W. 131; *State v. Kenosha
Electric R. Co.*, 145 Wis. 337, 129 N. W. 600; *Weld v. Board
of Gas & Electric Light Commrs.*, 197 Mass. 556, 84 N. E.
101; *Attorney General v. Walworth Light etc. Co.*, 157 Mass.
86, 31 N. E. 482, 16 L. R. A. 398; *State ex rel. Webster v.
Superior Court*, 67 Wash. 37, Ann. Cas. 1913D, 78, 120 Pac.
861.)

"If the legislature had no power to alter its police laws
when contracts would be affected, then the most important
and valuable reforms might be precluded by the simple device
of entering into contracts for the purpose. No doctrine to
that effect would be even plausible, much less sound and
tenable." (*Kentucky & Indiana Bridge Co. v. Louisville &
N. R. Co.*, 34 Am. & Eng. R. R. Cas., O. S., 630; Parsons on
Contracts, 6th ed., 675; Jones, Tel. & Tel. Companies, art.
214; *City of Dawson v. Dawson Tel. Co.*, 137 Ga. 62, 72
S. E. 508; *Chicago B. & Q. R. R. Co. v. State*, 170 U. S. 57,
18 Sup. Ct. 513, 42 L. ed. 948; *Louisville & N. R. R. Co. v.
Mottley*, 219 U. S. 467, 31 Sup. Ct. 265, 55 L. ed. 297, 34

L. R. A., N. S., 671; *Chicago I. & L. Ry. Co. v. United States,*
219 U. S. 486, 31 Sup. Ct. 272, 55 L. ed. 305.)

"When the first clause of a section conforms to the obvious
policy and intention of the legislature, it is not rendered inoperative by later inserted clauses which do not conform to
this policy and intention. In such cases the latter clause is
nugatory and must be disregarded." (*McCormick v. Village
of West Duluth,* 47 Minn. 272, 50 N. W. 128; 2 Lewis, Sutherland, Stat. Const., secs. 350, 352; *State v. Williams,* 8 Ind.
191; *Savings Inst. v. Makin,* 23 Me. 360, 1 Kent's Com. 462;
Folmer's Appeal, 87 Pa. 133; *Kansas Pac. Ry. Co. v. Wyan-
dotte County Commrs.,* 16 Kan. 587; *Renner v. Bennett,* 21
Ohio St. 431, 445.)

"A proviso in a statute is to be strictly construed. Its
province is not to enlarge or change the purpose of the enacting clause and its terms may be limited by the general scope
of the enacting clause to avoid repugnancy." (*Greathouse
v. Heed,* 1 Ida. 494.)

S. H. Hays, for Great Shoshone & Twin Falls Water Power
Co.

"So far as the municipality is concerned, the granting of
a franchise to use the streets is not binding on it until the
grant has been accepted." (McQuillin's Mun. Corp., sec.
1670.)

A grant of a franchise "does not become a contract or a
vested right so as to be protected by the constitution of the
state or of the United States until the company has, to say
the least, begun to do the thing required by the charter as the
consideration for the grant of such privilege." (*Capital City
Light & Fuel Co. v. Tallahassee,* 186 U. S. 401, 22 Sup. Ct.
866, 46 L. ed. 1219; *Pearsall v. Great Northern R. R. Co.,* 161
U. S. 646, 16 Sup. Ct. 705, 40 L. ed. 838; *Atchison St. Ry. Co.
v. Nave,* 38 Kan. 744, 5 Am. St. 800, 17 Pac. 587.)

Subject to such limitations as are expressly or impliedly
imposed by the federal and state constitutions, a state has
plenary power to legislate on all subjects. (*St. Joe Imp. Co.*

v. Laumierster, 19 Ida. 66, 112 Pac. 683; Joyce on Franchises, sec. 137.)

The utility act is administrative and does not give to the commission either legislative or judicial power in the constitutional sense. (*Speer v. Stephenson,* 16 Ida. 707, 102 Pac. 365; *Barton v. Schmershall,* 21 Ida. 562, 122 Pac. 385; *Jeffries v. Bacastow,* 90 Kan. 495, 135 Pac. 582.)

Whether or not it is wise to enact a public utilities law is a matter for the legislature and not for the court. (*Seattle Electric Co. v. City of Seattle* (Wash.), 138 Pac. 892.)

The legislature, in the absence of a constitutional prohibition, may directly or through a subordinate board grant an exclusive franchise. (*New Orleans Gas-Light Co. v. Louisiana Light & Heat P. & Mfg. Co.,* 115 U. S. 650, 6 Sup. Ct. 252, 29 L. ed. 516; 20 Am. & Eng. Ency. of Law, 863; 27 Cyc. 892, 896; *State v. Milwaukee Gas-Light Co.,* 29 Wis. 454, 9 Am. Rep. 598.)

Sec. 1023, Rev. Codes of Idaho, relating to ferries, is not unconstitutional on the ground that it grants a special privilege or monopoly. (*Fortain v. Smith,* 114 Cal. 494, 46 Pac. 381.)

The trend of present day thought upon the subject is set forth in 2 Wilcox on Mun. Franchises, p. 99, and the remarks there are specially directed toward street railway franchises but apply to all public utilities. See, also, vol. 1, p. 186, as showing the results of competition. (Floy, Valuation of Public Utility Properties, p. 36.)

The right of the state to control public utility corporations is too well settled to call for an extended citation of authorities. (*Lake Shore & Michigan Southern R. R. Co. v. Ohio,* 173 U. S. 285, 19 Sup. Ct. 465, 43 L. ed. 702; *Atlantic Coast Line Ry. Co. v. North Carolina Corp. Com.,* 206 U. S. 1, 27 Sup. Ct. 585, 51 L. ed. 933, 11 Ann. Cas. 398.)

On the proposition of plaintiff that the statute vests either legislative or judicial power in the commission, see the following additional cases: *Village of Saratoga Springs v. Saratoga Springs Gas etc. Co.,* 191 N. Y. 123, 83 N. E. 693, 14 Ann. Cas. 606, 18 L. R. A., N. S., 713; *United States v. Grimaud,*

220 U. S. 506, 31 Sup. Ct. 480, 55 L. ed. 563; *President etc. of Monongahela Bridge Co. v. United States,* 216 U. S. 177, 30 Sup. Ct. 356, 54 L. ed. 435; *Zakonaite v. Wolf,* 226 U. S. 272, 33 Sup. Ct. 31, 57 L. ed. 218; *Louisville & Nashville R. R. Co. v. Garrett,* 231 U. S. 298, 34 Sup. Ct. 48, 58 L. ed. 000. See, also, Ivins & Mason, Control of Public Utilities, p. 51.

Richards & Haga and McKeen F. Morrow, *Amici Curiae.*

The power of the legislature, so long as it observes the restrictions imposed by the state and the federal constitution to regulate the relative rights and equities of all persons and corporations within its jurisdiction, in order to conserve, not merely the health, safety and morals of the people of the state, but also the general welfare, undoubtedly exists, whether it is called police power or merely governmental or legislative power. (*Lake Shore & Michigan Southern R. R. Co. v. Ohio,* 173 U. S. 285, 19 Sup. Ct. 465, 43 L. ed. 702.)

Competition is now recognized as a needless economic waste, and regulation by commissions supplants competition and furnishes a regulation which competition cannot give, thereby avoiding the expense of duplication in the investment, maintenance and operation of public utilities. (*Des Moines Water Co. v. Des Moines,* 192 Fed. 193; *Des Moines Gas Co. v. Des Moines,* 199 Fed. 204; *State v. Tucson Gas Electric etc. Co.* (Ariz.), 138 Pac. 781; *People ex rel. New York Edison Co. v. Wilcox,* 207 N. Y. 86, 100 N. E. 705, 45 L. R. A., N. S., 629.)

It is urged that because the commission is authorized to determine whether, in a given case, public convenience and necessity requires the construction of additional power lines or plants, or the exercise of rights, privileges and franchises in municipalities, legislative power is delegated, and petitioners insist that these matters are left entirely to the arbitrary determination of the commission. Similar contentions have been made in regard to almost every such commission created in this country, and in many other cases of powers conferred upon administrative officers or boards, and these contentions have been overruled with substantial unanimity.

The question has been definitely laid to rest by a long series

of decisions in the United States supreme court, beginning
with the case of *The Aurora v. United States,* 7 Cranch
(U. S.), 382, 3 L. ed. 378, decided in 1813, and ending with
Interstate Commerce Commission v. Goodrich Transit Co., 224
U. S. 194, 32 Sup. Ct. 436, 56 L. ed. 729.

T. C. Coffin, *Amicus Curiae.*

The elementary proposition that railways, from the public
nature of the business by them carried on, and the interest
which the public have in their operation, are subject, as to
their state business, to state regulations which may be asserted
either directly or by the legislative authority or by administrative bodies endowed with power to that end, is not and could
not be successfuly questioned, in view of the long line of authorities sustaining that doctrine. (*Atlantic Coast Line Ry.
Co. v. North Carolina Corp. Com.,* 206 U. S. 1, 27 Sup. Ct.
585, 51 L. ed. 933, 11 Ann. Cas. 398. See, also, *Saratoga
Springs v. Saratoga Springs Gas etc. Co.,* 191 N. Y. 123, 83
N. E. 693, 18 L. R. A., N. S., 713, 14 Ann. Cas. 606; *Railroad
Commission of Alabama v. Central of Georgia R. Co.,* 170
Fed. 225, 95 C. C. A. 117.)

A late case wherein these principles were considered as settled is *Public Service Commission v. Northern Central Ry.
Co.* (Md.), 90 Atl. 105, 111.

Sec. 53 of the public utilities act of New York (formerly
sec. 59), sec. 74 of the Wisconsin act, sec. 54 of the Ohio act,
and sec. 50 of the California act, all require certificates of
necessity practically the same as sec. 48 of the Idaho act, and
so far as I have been able to find their constitutionality in this
regard has never even been questioned. In New York the
section was under consideration in the case of *People ex rel.
Steward v. Board of Railroad Commrs.,* 160 N. Y. 202, 54
N. E. 697.

It was clearly intended by the legislature in the enactment
of sec. 63 of the public utilities act to grant a much broader
field of review than the mere inquiry into the jurisdiction of
the commission when acting, and to allow a review on questions of law. The reasonableness of the orders of the com-

mission is a question of law. (*Detroit & M. R. Co. v. Michigan Railroad Commission*, 203 Fed. 864.)

The cases of *People ex rel. Steward v. Railroad Commission, supra, People ex rel. Babylon R. R. Co. v. Board of Railroad Commissioners*, 32 App. Div. 179, 52 N. Y. Supp. 908 (affirmed in 158 N. Y. 711, 53 N. E. 1129), and *People ex rel. Loughran v. Board of Railroad Commissioners*, 158 N. Y. 421, 53 N. E. 163, establish the proposition that in such cases the court on review can inquire into the reasonableness of the order of the commission.

SULLIVAN, J.—On this hearing two separate and distinct applications for writs of review under sec. 63a of the act known as the public utilities act (Laws 1913, p. 247), are involved. One case is entitled the *Idaho Power & Light Co., a Corporation, v. J. A. Blomquist, A. P. Ramstedt and D. W. Standrod, as the Public Utilities Commission of the State of Idaho* (which is known as the Twin Falls case); and the other is entitled, *The Beaver River Power Co., a Corporation, v. J. A. Blomquist, A. P. Ramstedt and D. W. Standrod, as the Public Utilities Commission of the State of Idaho* (known as the Pocatello case).

In the application in each case for a writ of review, the plaintiff complains of the order made by the public utilities commission requiring the plaintiff to refrain from constructing its proposed plants in either the city of Twin Falls or Pocatello, for the purpose of furnishing such cities and inhabitants with electrical energy, on the ground that such company has not obtained a certificate of public convenience and necessity requiring such service, in compliance with secs. 48a, 48b and 48c of said act.

It is provided by sec. 63a that the applicant may apply to this court for a writ of review for the purpose of having the lawfulness of any order of the utilities commission inquired into and determined, and that such review shall not extend further than to determine whether the commission has regularly pursued its authority, including a determination of whether the order or decision under review violates any right of the petitioner under the constitution of the United States or of the state of Idaho, and whether the evidence is sufficient to sustain the findings and conclusions of the commission.

A complaint was filed with the public utilities commission on the 22d day of November, 1913, by the Great Shoshone & Twin Falls Water Power Co., a public utility corporation, which was then supplying the city of Twin Falls with electrical energy, and by J. H. Seaver, a resident and citizen of the said city of Twin Falls; in which complaint it was set up that the Idaho Power & Light Co., the plaintiff herein, and its predecessors in interest, had not procured the certificate of necessity and convenience required to be procured by the provisions of said act before any public utility is permitted or authorized to construct power lines into a territory already served by some other public utility of like character.

After various proceedings were had in said matter, an answer was filed with the public utilities commission and the decision of the commission was rendered on the 18th of February, 1914, to the effect that it was necessary, under the provisions of said act, for the plaintiff to secure a certificate of convenience and necessity before constructing its lines and works in the city of Twin Falls. A rehearing was applied for and denied and the matter now comes before this court for hearing on a writ of review.

The point in issue in this proceeding is as to the constitutionality of said act, and if constitutional, whether or not the Idaho Power & Light Company, the plaintiff, must obtain a certificate of convenience and necessity before constructing its lines into the said cities. It is admitted that said public utilities act was approved by the governor and went into effect on the 8th day of May, 1913, if constitutional. The facts are stipulated in these cases, and it appears therefrom that the Great Shoshone & Twin Falls Water Power Company has for more than three years last past been supplying the city of Twin Falls and its inhabitants with electricity for light and power purposes; that on April 29, 1913, the city council of Twin Falls passed ordinance No. 134, granting to the Beaver River Power Company, the predecessor of the plaintiff, the right, authority, privilege and franchise to distribute electricity and electrical current for the purpose of furnishing the same for light, heat, power and all other purposes, to the city of Twin Falls and to the inhabitants thereof, and granting it the right to use the streets and alleys, etc., of said city for said purpose. By section 7 of said ordinance certain rates were provided. Said ordinance further provides that the franchise and rights granted thereunder are voluntarily transferable only by ordinance duly and regularly passed. Section 12 of said ordinance provides that the Beaver River Company, or its successors, or assigns shall file with the city of Twin Falls a good and sufficient bond in the sum of $2,500, conditioned upon its compliance with the provisions of section 11 of said ordinance, and section 14 provides that said corporation or its assigns shall within sixty days from the passage of said ordinance file an unconditional acceptance thereof in writing with the clerk of said city, and that "any rights and privileges granted shall be null and void unless such acceptance is so filed." On the 28th of June, 1913, nearly two months after said public utilities act went into effect, the Beaver River Company filed an acceptance of said ordinance, and on October 3, 1913, a bond in the sum of $2,500 was filed with the city clerk.

On the 6th of October, 1913, ordinance No. 141 was passed by the city council of said city, authorizing the Beaver River Power Company to transfer to the Idaho Power & Light Company all of its rights, privileges and franchises granted under the provisions of said ordinance No. 134.

Up to that time nothing whatever had been done by the Beaver River Power Company under ordinance No. 134 toward constructing its plant or lines within the corporate limits of said city. In the month of October, 1913, the plaintiff commenced the construction of a distribution system within the corporate limits of said city. Such construction work was not commenced until after the Beaver River Company had transferred its rights and interests thereunder in October, 1913, to the Idaho Light & Power Company. The proceedings in the Twin Falls case were begun before said commission, as above stated, in November, 1913.

It appears from the record that the Beaver River Company had commenced the construction of a power plant on the Malad river in Lincoln county, about thirty miles distant from the city of Twin Falls, and that at the time said act went into effect had done nothing toward extending its lines from its said plant to the city of Twin Falls. It thus appears that sometime after the passage of said public utilities act, and only a few days before it went into effect, the Beaver River Company procured from the city of Twin Falls the passage of said ordinance granting it the right to supply electricity to the inhabitants of said city, and, as above stated, said ordinance provided that it was void unless a written acceptance was filed within sixty days after its passage. Said acceptance and bond were not filed until after said act went into effect. Thus at the time the law went into effect, said ordinance was an unaccepted offer to the Beaver River Company, and it was within the power of that company to accept or refuse it for sometime after said law went into effect. It certainly was not a franchise contract until said written acceptance was made.

In the Pocatello case the following facts, among others, are stipulated: That the city of Pocatello passed ordinance No. 281 on May 5, 1913, granting said Beaver River Power Company the right to construct its plant and lines within the corporate limits of said city; that prior to the passage of said ordinance the Beaver River Company expended considerable money investigating the electrical market of Pocatello and in securing the passage of said ordinance, and also paid for the publication of said ordinance; that after making certain investigations in regard to the feasibility of establishing a plant in said city and in about the month of August, 1913, a contract was entered into by the Beaver River Company for a 500 horse-power Diesel engine, to cost approximately $25,000, to be used solely for the purpose of generating electrical energy for said city, and work on the distribution system within the corporate limits of said city was begun in the month of November, 1913, and has been continued diligently and uninterruptedly, and about $2,500 has been expended in an underground and overhead distribution system; that the power system contemplated to be used in said city calls for the instalation of four engines of similar design to the one purchased; that prior to November, 1913, no work of any character under said franchise had been done within the city limits of Pocatello, and that said Diesel engine was constructed outside of the city of Pocatello. It was not the intention of plaintiff to supply the inhabitants of Pocatello with electrical energy from its Malad plant, but to erect a new plant in said city and use Diesel engines in manufacturing electrical energy.

The proceedings in the Pocatello case were brought before the public utilities commission by the Southern Idaho Water Power Company, a corporation, which company had been supplying the city of Pocatello and its inhabitants with electric power long prior to the passage of said ordinance No. 281.

The proceedings were brought in each case to have the commission determine whether the convenience and necessity of the inhabitants of said cities required the construction and instalation of another electrical plant or system, or whether under the provisions of sec. 48a of said public utility act the plaintiff company had the right, without such certificate, to proceed as it did in attempting to furnish said cities with electrical power.

On the facts stipulated, it is claimed by the plaintiff corporation that it is authorized by law to construct and operate its electrical power system without securing any certificate of public convenience and necessity from the public utilities commission, for the following reasons:

(1) Because plaintiffs' right under the franchises granted by said ordinances (which ordinances were passed prior to the date when the public utilities law became effective) became contract rights within the protection of the constitutional provision.

(2) Because the plaintiffs come within the terms of the proviso of sec. 48a of said act, which declares "that power companies may, without such certificate, increase the capacity

of existing generating plants or develop new generating plants and market the products thereof.''

(3) Because the plaintiffs come within the terms of the proviso of sec. 48b of said act which declares that ''this section shall not be construed to . . . . impair any vested right in any franchise or permit heretofore granted.''

(4) Because plaintiffs come within the proviso in sec. 48b of said act which declares, ''That when the commission shall find, after hearing that a public utility has heretofore begun actual construction work and is prosecuting such work in good faith, uninterruptedly and with reasonable diligence in proportion to the magnitude of the undertaking, under any franchise or permit heretofore granted but not heretofore actually exercised, such public utility may proceed to the completion of such work and may, after such completion exercise such right or privilege.''

It will be observed that plaintiffs' real contention is based upon the proposition that they had procured franchises from each of said cities subsequent to the passage by the legislature of said public utilities act and shortly prior to its going into effect, and therefore under said ordinances they had secured vested rights under and by which they were authorized to construct their lines into said cities and furnish the inhabitants electrical power.

In order to determine the questions presented in this case, it will require a review and construction of many of the provisions of said public utilities act and application of some provisions of the constitution thereto.

Said act is a very comprehensive one and was passed at the twelfth session of the legislature and was approved by the governor on the 13th of March, 1913. It contained no emergency clause, and under the provisions of sec. 22, art. 3, of the constitution did not take effect until sixty days after the end of the session at which it was passed, which session adjourned on the 8th day of March, 1913; hence the act did not take effect until the 8th day of May, 1913. By the provisions of sec. 10 of art. 4 of the constitution, every bill passed by the legislature shall before it becomes a law be presented to the governor, and "If he approve, he shall sign it and thereupon *it shall become a law.*" Under that provision of the constitution, said act became a law on the 13th day of March, 1913, but did not go into effect until the 8th day of May.

Many of the states of this Union have passed similar public utility laws, a compilation of which may be found in the publication known as "Commission Regulation of Public Utilities," published by the National Civic Federation (1913), and the provisions in such laws regarding "Certificates of Convenience and Necessity" may be found at page 800 et seq. of that work.

In Arizona a public utility must first obtain a certificate before beginning the construction of its works. (Laws 1912, chap. 90, sec. 50.) The California law is to the same effect. (Laws 1911, chap. 14, sec. 50.) Much of our public utilities law was copied from the California act. In Connecticut no steam railway or interurban road shall be parallel to any other unless it appears that public convenience and necessity require it. Application in that state must be made to the superior court or judge for a certificate. (Laws 1902, sec. 3846.) In Kansas no public utility can transact business until it has obtained a certificate that public convenience would be promoted by the transaction of such utility business. (Laws 1911, chap. 238, sec. 31.) In Maine the directors of a railroad must present to the commission a petition, and if after a hearing it appears that the public convenience requires the construction of the road, a certificate must be granted. (Rev. Stats. 1903, chap. 51, sec. 3.) In Maryland the public utilities act provides that no common carrier shall begin construction without a certificate, and no gas or electrical corporation shall begin construction or exercise any right or privilege without first having obtained the permission and approval of the commission. (Laws 1910, chap. 180, secs. 26, 33.) In Michigan it is necessary for a telephone company to apply to the railroad commission for a certificate. (Laws 1911, chap. 138, sec. 7.) In New Hampshire no public utility shall commence business without first having obtained the permission and approval of the commission. (Laws 1911, chap. 164, sec. 13.) In New York no gas or electrical corporation shall begin construction of a plant without the approval of the commission, and no such corporation shall exercise any right or privilege under any franchise granted without having first obtained the consent of the commission. (Laws 1910, chap. 480, sec. 33.) In Ohio no telephone company can exercise any franchise in a place where there is already in operation a telephone company, unless such company first secures from the commission, after public hearing, a certificate that the exercise of such franchise is proper and necessary for the public convenience. (Laws 1911, No. 325, sec. 54.) In South Dakota no railroad hereafter constructed shall parallel another line within eight miles of the same for a greater distance than ten miles in every 100 miles, and permits to build railroads must be obtained from the commission. (Sess. Laws 1907, chap. 217, secs. 1 and 2.) In Wisconsin the law provides that no franchise shall be granted in any municipality where there is in operation a public utility engaged in similar service without first securing from the commission a declaration, after a public hearing, that there is a reasonable necessity therefor. (Laws 1909, sec. 74, p. 759.) In Illinois it is provided that no public utility shall begin the construction of any plant until it shall have obtained from the commission a certificate of necessity. (Laws 1913, House Bill No. 907, sec. 55.) In Missouri the law provides that no common carrier shall begin the construction of any railroad or any extension thereof without having first obtained from the commission a certification that the present or future public convenience and necessity require or will require such construction. The Missouri law contains provisions similar to the Idaho law in regard to franchises theretofore granted but not theretofore actually exercised. (Laws 1913, p. 557, sec. 53.) The Colorado law provides that public utilities shall not henceforth begin construction without first having obtained from the commission a certificate that the future public convenience and necessity require such construction, and it also contains the same provisions as the

Idaho law in regard to franchises not heretofore actually exercised. The laws of Pennsylvania provide that a certificate of public convenience must first be had and obtained before any public utility begins to exercise any right, power, franchise or privilege under any ordinance, municipal contract or otherwise. (Laws 1913, p. 1374, art. III, sec. 2.)

Thus it appears that public utility acts similar to the Idaho act have been passed by many states and are in full operation therein. Massachusetts was the first state to adopt a public utility act. That act was intended as a substitution for the control of public utilities by competition. Pond, in his work on Public Utilities, sec. 610, quotes from *Weld v. Board of Gas & Electric Light Commrs.*, 197 Mass. 556, 84 N. E. 101, as follows:

"In the first place, in reference to this department of public service, we have adopted, in this state, legislative regulation and control as our reliance against the evil effects of monopoly, rather than competitive action between two or more corporations, where such competition will greatly increase the aggregate cost of supplying the needs of the public, and perhaps cause other serious inconveniences. . . . . The state, through the regularly constituted authorities, has taken complete control of these corporations so far as is necessary to prevent the abuses of monopoly. Our statutes are founded on the assumption that, to have two or more competing companies running lines of gas-pipe and conduits for electric wires through the same streets would often greatly increase the necessary cost of furnishing light, as well as cause great inconvenience to the public and to individuals from the unnecessary digging up of the streets from time to time, and the interference with pavements, street railway tracks, water-pipes and other structures. . . . . In reference to some kinds of public service, and under some conditions, it is thought by many that regulation by the state is better than competition."

The courts of last resort of several of the above-named states have already passed upon the public utilities acts of their respective states and held them constitutional and valid.

However, the public utilities act is attacked by counsel for the plaintiffs on three grounds: (1) That the legislature had no power to grant to the public utilities commission power to restrict competition; (2) That legislative authority is delegated to said commission in an unconstitutional manner; (3) That said commission is a judicial body established in contravention of sec. 2, art. 5, of the Idaho constitution.

First, has the legislature power to restrict competition of public utilities through the public utilities commission?

The doctrine that private property devoted to public use is subject to public regulation is too well settled to require the citation of many authorities. We have not only a long line of decisions by the supreme court of the United States, commencing as early, at least, as the decision of *Munn v. Illinois*, 94 U. S. 113, 24 L. ed. 77, but a long line of state decisions, and the law is well settled that all property is held subject to the power of the state to regulate or control its use in order to secure the general safety, health and the public welfare of the people, and that when a corporation is clothed with the rights, powers and franchises to serve the public, it becomes in law subject to governmental regulation and supervision.

The constitution of the state of Idaho is a limitation upon the legislative power in all matters of legislation, and is not a grant of power. The legislature has plenary power in all matters of legislation except as limited by the constitution. There is nothing in the constitution that prohibits the legislature from enacting laws prohibiting competition between public utility corporations, and the legislature of this state no doubt concluded that a business like that of transmitting electricity through the streets of the city and furnishing light and power to the people must be transacted by a regulated monopoly, and that free competition between as many companies or as many persons as might desire to put up wires in the streets is impracticable and not for the best interests of the people. The police power in regard thereto is sufficiently broad and comprehensive to enable the legislature to regulate public utilities in order to promote the health, comfort, safety and welfare of society. One of the fundamental principles upon which our government is founded is the police power, and the exercise of that power is absolutely essential to its general welfare. Upon that power rests the peace and tranquillity of society and the enjoyment of health and property; and when any corporation acquires a franchise for the purpose of carrying on a corporate business within a state, it is accepted subject to the police power. By granting a franchise to a public utility corporation, the state does not abrogate its rights to exercise the police power of the state over it. It therefore follows, under the state's inherent power of police regulation, that it may regulate the manner in which public utility corporations shall construct their lines and carry on their business within the state. (Jones on Telegraph & Telephone Lines, sec. 214.)

In the 41st Report of the Georgia Railroad Commission, it is said by that commission as follows:

"We do not believe competition can ever be a consistent and economical regulator of rates and other conditions, in a local public utility field.

"In such a field it means a duplication of investments, organization and operating expenses, which is unnecessary to the service, and burdensome upon the public. It is rarely maintained permanently.

"The commission is strongly convinced that it would be wise if the General Assembly should enact legislation prohibiting the grant by municipal authorities of franchises to local utilities, where there is an established utility rendering safe, adequate and proper service at reasonable rates, already occupying the field, prior to application to and issuance by this commission of a certificate of public convenience and necessity.

"In our opinion, the government which properly assumes to prescribe reasonable rates and compel adequate service by public utilities, should also protect such utilities and the public from unwise and useless competition, and the wasteful investment of capital in the unnecessary duplication of plants."

As touching upon this question, see Public Service Regulation, p. 247; Floy on Valuation of Public Utility Property, p. 36.

The regulating of rates and compelling proper service is for the purpose of obtaining rates and service as nearly equitable as possible to both the consumer and the utility corporation, and competition can have no other effect than to destroy the very groundwork of regulation, and therefore competition may be regulated by a commission under laws enacted by the legislature.

By the public utility laws of the several states, attempts have been made on the part of their legislatures to correct existing difficulties between public service corporations and the communities which they serve. The first general steps taken by the legislatures were to provide for rate regulation in order that the consumer might be protected in cases where there was no competition. Competition at that time was looked upon as a regulator and rate regulation was accepted as a protection to the public. Competition between public utility corporations led to rate wars in which each company tried to get the advantage of or destroy the other, and usually resulted in the destruction of one of the competing corporations, or in a division of the territory between them, or in the consolidation of such corporations. Statutes to prevent such consolidation and to prevent the division of the territory have been enacted. Those regulating laws were differently viewed by different classes of people. Those who furnishd the money for the construction of the utility system, represented by stockholders, bondholders or mortgagees, was one class; the consumer, another; promoters, another. The latter desired no regulation whatever, since it hampered their ability to sell prospective utilities. On the other hand, the people who furnished the money desired stability for their investment. It was the desire of the stockholder, bondholder or mortgagee not to have his investment jeopardized and it was the desire of the consumer to receive the services at a reasonable rate or compensation. Rate wars affected such investments and either one company or the other finally had to go out of busiuess, and experience shows that there can never be any *permanent* competition in matters of this kind.

Under these various utility acts, the commission is generally given power to regulate rates and fix a specific rate, instead of a mere maximum, and that took away the opportunity for rate-cutting, one of the principal instruments of warfare between such corporations. Under the act in question, the commission is given power to fix the rate absolutely and neither of the competing companies can charge more or less than the rate fixed. Under those conditions competition can amount to nothing, and the only reason for having two corporations covering the same field is to secure satisfactory service. But under our utilities act, the commission is the arbitrator in regard to all matters of service. If the utility corporation is not giving satisfactory service, the commission has absolute power to compel it to do so. If its facilities are such that the cost of operation is unnecessarily high, the commission can enforce the instalation of proper machinery and facilities and a correspondingly proper charge for the commodity furnished. The commission may force the public utility to keep abreast of the times in the employment of proper machinery and appliances in their plants and in the economic conduct of its business. If wasteful methods are indulged in, the public utility must bear the loss and not the consumer. Thus the reason for competition is entirely taken away. The rate to be determined by the commission in each case is a reasonable rate—a rate fair to both the consumer and the supplier. If there are other methods or machinery that might be used in a plant that would materially reduce the cost of production, the commission may direct the utility to install such machinery or appliances, and in case it refuses to do so, upon proper application, may issue a certificate of convenience and necessity to a utility corporation that will do so.

A power company already occupying a field may be giving service to many localities where it cannot charge sufficient to obtain a profitable return. Another corporation might thereafter construct its plant and lines into the profitable markets of such company and thus compete for the most desirable business. In this way it might take the cream of the business at the very least expense, and cripple the company that was furnishing the commodity to the more extensive field.

There is another question that affects the general public in such cases: An existing utility has already expended, say, a million dollars in the power plant and transmission lines and distribution system in a town. Another utility coming in must also provide a power plant and transmission lines and a distributing system. If there is to be unrestricted competition, then the later distribution system must cover the same area as that of the older one. If it costs the same money, then there is an additional million dollars expended in a town where a one million dollar system would be amply sufficient. There would be two sets of poles and transmission wires in the streets, the construction and keeping in repair of which would necessarily interfere with and obstruct the free use of the streets by the people more than one set of poles and wires; and two sets of electrical wires in a city would necessarily increase the danger to the lives and limbs of the people, and thus interfere with the peace, health and welfare of the community. In such a case, when a commission comes to fix rates, it will be confronted with this situation: It finds the town provided with duplicate plants; each company is entitled to have a rate fixed so as to give a return upon its *bona fide* investment, therefore the rates paid by the people must be upon two million dollars instead of upon one million dollars, and the amount of money collected by the utilities, if they are to be given a fair return on their investments, must be much more on the two investments than it would be upon the one. And the total amount paid by the consumers must be more than it need be if there were only one investment and one system. It is for the benefit of the public that the highest efficiency be obtained from a public utility and that it serve the public at the lowest cost, and such an end cannot be reached if the community is served by duplicate plants. Where a one million dollar plant is amply sufficient, a duplication of such plant is a waste of resources and an extra tax on the people.

If rates are absolutely fixed by the commission with no permission to the utilities corporations to charge more or less, the public can receive no advantage from competition. Experience shows that while the people, or some of the people, may receive a temporary advantage from cut-throat competition, the general public can receive no substantial advantage therefrom. Then the question is presented from the standpoint of public policy, Shall plants be duplicated in order to give efficiency of service? The law has fully answered this by putting the supervision of the service in the hands of a commission so that there can be no duplication without a necessity for it. The commission has the power to compel the utility company to give good service for reasonable compensation. What need is there of a competitive plant where the commission has absolute control so far as service and rates to be charged are concerned, and rates must be fixed so as to give the company a reasonable interest on its investment and a sufficient sum to keep up the system and operate it?

The city of Twin Falls has one company already serving it, and if another company is permitted to enter, there will be two sets of poles and lines erected in said city, and it does not seem possible that anyone would contend that where one company is amply able to serve the wants of the people, so far as electrical power is concerned, that the interests of the public would require another system to cover the same ground, when there can be no cut-throat competition under the law.

The only practical difference between systems operated under the utilities act and municipal ownership is that under the former system the money or means is provided by a bond issue or mortgage by a private corporation and the employees are named by the corporation furnishing the money, while under the latter, the money is furnished and the employees named by the municipality. The control of a city council over municipal works is perhaps a little more complete than that of the commission over the utility under the present law. The state having taken away the rights of such corporations to fix their own rates, and having assumed supervisory power over the service in every material particular, it ought to provide some sort of a safeguard for those who furnish the money to construct the system, and the state has attempted to meet this situation by providing that the utility already in the field shall have that field unless public necessity and convenience require an additional utility, and as to whether the public convenience and necessity require an additional utility is an administrative matter left .with the commission to ascertain and determine under supervisory power of the court.   Any erroneous action on the part of the commission in that regard may be corrected by the court.

The law relating to public service should be based on the public needs, rather than on the desire of any corporation to serve the public.   The purpose of such laws should be to promote the common welfare and equally to protect the parties who furnish the money for the erection of the plant and those who use its product.

The general impression has been that competition was supposed to be a legitimate and proper means of protecting the interests of the public and promoting the general welfare of the people in respect to service by public utility corporations; but history and experience has clearly demonstrated that public convenience and the necessities of the community do not require the construction and maintenance of several plants or systems of the same character to supply a city or the same locality, but that public convenience and necessity require only the maintenance of a sufficient number of such instrumentalities to meet the public demands.   If more than one instrumentality is to be sustained when one is amply sufficient, the actual cost to the public served is not only necessarily greater than it would be under one system, but also less convenient.   If public convenience and necessity do not demand a duplication of power systems, why should the public be burdened with the expense of maintaining such duplicate systems, and the annoyance of perpetual solicitation to make or break contracts for service, and the inconvenience to the people of the occupation of the streets and alleys of a town or city by such corporations in constructing and keeping in repair the two systems?

The public utilities act merely declares the will of the people as expressed through the legislature, to the effect that competition between public utility corporations of the classes specified shall be allowed only where public convenience and necessity demand it, and in any case the commission is thereby given power to fix the rates to be charged, which cannot be varied by such corporations. The legislature has concluded by the passage of said act that it is not for the best interests of the people or the public welfare to permit public utility corporations to compete with each other where public convenience and necessity do not require such competition.

Sec. 18 of art. 11 of the constitution prohibits combinations for the purpose of fixing prices or regulating production, and requires the legislature to pass appropriate laws to enforce the section. The public utilities act is justified by that provision of the constitution, for it is largely concerned with preventing unreasonable rates and combinations by public utilities. Those provisions were intended to prevent monopoly and cut-throat competition which can only result in monopoly. Past history shows that unregulated competition is a tool of unregulated monopoly, as the word "monopoly" is usually understood.

The power of the legislature, so long as it observes the restrictions imposed by the state and federal constitutions, to regulate the relative rights and equities of all persons and corporations within its jurisdiction, in order to conserve, not merely the health, safety and morals of the people of the state, but also the general welfare, undoubtedly exists, whether it is called police power or merely governmental or legislative power. (*Lake Shore & Michigan S. R. R. Co. v. Ohio*, 173 U. S. 285, 19 Sup. Ct. 465, 43 L. ed. 702.)

Said act substitutes reasonable rates to be determined by the commission for those that would otherwise be fixed by competition, in the one case, or the rule of charging what the traffic will bear, in the absence of competition. Under this law it must therefore be conceded that competition with its disastrous effects is no longer needed to protect the public against unreasonable rates, hence there is no longer any justification whatever for competition or the duplication of utility plants under the pretense of preventing monopoly.

In vol. 1 of Wilcox on Municipal Franchises, sec. 41, p. 29, the author discusses the establishment of monopolies by franchises and says:

"In spite of the practically uniform experience of cities, the authorities still cling to competition, as if it were a fetich, for the regulation of public service utilities. Year after year and decade after decade, the same old story is repeated, of franchises granted to new street railway companies, gas companies, electric companies, telephone companies, which in a few years, by the inevitable logic of events, either absorb their predecessors or are absorbed by them."

The author quotes the following from the report of the National Civic Federation Commission on Public Ownership and Operation, found in part 1, vol. 1, p. 26, of Municipal and Private Operation of Public Utilities, as follows: "Public utilities, whether in public or in private hands, are best conducted under a system of legalized and regulated monopoly." The author then says: "The reasons for this statement are not far to seek. The available space in the streets for the use of permanent fixtures is strictly limited. Furthermore, the construction and maintenance of any particular outfit of fixtures entails upon the public great inconvenience and loss through the tearing up of the streets, the obstruction of traffic, and the resulting dangers and inconveniences. . . . . From the standpoint of the companies supplying public services, the advantages of monopoly are obvious. Street railway tracks, gas and water pipes, electrical conduits, poles and wires, all require the investment of very large amounts of capital in providing the facilities for the distribution of the commodity or service. If one of these distributing systems is duplicated in the same streets or in the same territory, there is involved a duplication of investment which, with competitive rates, is ruinous to the enterprise. After capital has once been invested in unnecessary fixtures, the pressure of competing rates leads the owners of the different fixtures to combine in order to maintain prices and avoid insolvency.''

In referring to said report of the Civic Federation Commission, the author states that the conclusion reached by that commission is in line with reason and experience, and says: ''In each center of population every public utility should be controlled and operated as a monopoly.'' The author there has in mind regulated monopoly—not monopoly that may charge all a business will bear. He then refers to the past oppression of monopolies and says: ''It is the experience or the fear of such oppression as the outgrowth of private monopoly, that keeps alive the dream of competition in franchise grants.'' And in section 42 the author says: ''It is evident, however, that no monopoly of a necessary and universal service can be safely intrusted to private operation unless it is kept under strict public control.''

As touching on this question see *In re Petition of Schuylkill L. H. & Power Co.*, a decision rendered by the Public Service Commission of Pennsylvania (not yet reported but published in pamphlet form).

A volume entitled ''Commission Regulation of Public Utilities,'' by the National Civic Federation, N. Y., contains a compilation and analysis of the laws of forty-three states and of the federal government for the regulation by central commissions of railroads and other utilities. It is stated in the preface to that work, page 6, that the material contained in said volume represents forty-four different jurisdictions, to wit, the federal act to regulate commerce with its amendments and supplements, and the laws of forty-three states, which in 1912 had central commissions for the regulation of public utilities. The states of Delaware, Idaho, Utah, West Virginia and Wyoming are not represented in said volume because they had at that time no public utilities law providing for a commission. That volume contains much valuable information.

Bruce Wyman, Esq., was counsel for said commission and is author of the two volume work of Wyman on Public Service Corporations. The author states in his preface to vol. 1 of said work, at page 5, as follows:

"Free competition, the very basis of the modern social organization, superseded almost completely the medieval restrictions, but it has just come to be recognized that the process of free competition fails in some cases to secure the public good, and it has been at last admitted that some control is necessary over such lines of industry as are affected with a public interest."

In section 36 the author says: "In all of the businesses to be discussed in these chapters, competition, although from a legal point of view possible, is from the economic point of view improbable. So far as one can see, virtual competition is at an end in these industries, and virtual monopoly will henceforth prevail."

Some will no doubt become incensed by the action of the public utilities commission when it refuses to permit a utility corporation to duplicate an amply sufficient plant to supply the needs of the community, because they think they may receive service at a little less rate; but they overlook the fact that under said public utilities act the commission may fix rates and neither company can furnish light and power at a less rate. The public utilities commission has ample authority to fix just and equitable rates, both to the people and to the corporation; that is made a part of its duty, and the consumer cannot insist on a less rate than would realize to the corporation a fair return on its legitimate investment and sufficient to pay for the up-keep of the plant or system, and the legitimate expense necessarily connected with the operation of such system.

The cry "monopoly" by promoters and agitators will not be given much weight by thinking people when they come to study the question of public utilities carefully and to thoroughly consider from various view points the welfare and financial interests of those who furnish the money for the construction of utility plants and those who are in need of and demand the products or services of such plants for their comfort and prosperity. Those who furnish the money should be given a reasonable interest thereon; the corporation should be allowed sufficient to keep the plant in good repair so as to give the patrons good service; the people who do the work should be paid a reasonable wage; the consumer should receive the product or service at a reasonable compensation or rate. The interests of these four classes are entitled to fair and just consideration. It is conceded at the present time by the leading thinkers of the country upon this subject that the best method of arriving at a reasonable rate to be charged for such services can be better established by a public utility commission than by competition, especially that competition which must culminate in unregulated monopoly. If monopoly is to be regulated, it ought to be regulated in a way that equal justice may be done to all. The consensus of opinion at the present time clearly is that that object or purpose can be best achieved by public utilities laws similar to the one under consideration.

The public mind has been so long impregnated with the idea that competition is the only relief against oppressive monopoly, it is difficult for the people to understand, without some thought and study, that such oppressive monopoly may be removed by fair and just regulation, and where a utility corporation has had no competition in a city or town and a duplicate plant is proposed for serving the same city or town and by its promoters better rates are offered, it is but natural for the people to want the reduced rates, and to encourage the erection of a duplicate plant. But experience shows that such duplication must be paid for by the community. But if a public utilities commission can establish reasonable rates, both for the corporation and the users of its product, it will in the end be better for all concerned than cut-throat competition.

It is suggested by counsel for plaintiffs that legislative authority has been delegated to the commission in an unconstitutional manner. It is contended that because the utilities commission is authorized to determine whether in a given case public convenience and necessity require the construction of an additional power line or plant or the exercise of rights, privileges and franchises in municipalities, legislative power is delegated, and counsel insist that these matters are left entirely to the arbitrary determination of the commission.

There is nothing in that contention. That question has been settled definitely against the contention of plaintiff by the decision of many courts.) We have a long series of decisions contrary to contention of counsel from the supreme court of the United States, beginning with *The Aurora v. United States,* 7 Cranch (U. S.), 382, 3 L. ed. 378, decided in 1813, and ending with(the *Interstate Commerce Commission v. Goodrich Transit Co.,* 224 U. S. 194, 32 Sup. Ct. 436, 56 L. ed. 729, decided in 1912. In the latter case the court said: "Furthermore, it is said that such construction of sec. 20 makes it an unlawful delegation of legislative power to the commission. We cannot agree to this contention. The Congress may not delegate its purely legislative power to a commission, but, having laid down the general rules of action under which a commission shall proceed, it may require of that commission the application of such rules to particular situations and the investigation of facts, with a view to making orders in a particular matter within the rules laid down by the Congress. This rule has been frequently stated and illustrated in recent cases in this court, and needs no amplification here."

In *Field v. Clark,* 143 U. S. 649, 12 Sup. Ct. 495, 36 L. ed. 294, the court says:

" 'The true distinction,' as Judge Ranney, speaking for the supreme court of Ohio, has well said, 'is between the delegation of power to make the law, which necessarily involves a discretion as to what it shall be, and conferring authority or discretion as to its execution, to be exercised under and in pursuance of the law. The first cannot be done; to the latter no valid objection can be made.' "

Many of the authorities on this question are reviewed in the case of *Union Bridge Co. v. United States,* 204 U. S. 364, 27 Sup. Ct. 367, 51 L. ed. 523, where a statute giving the Secretary of War power to determine whether bridges over navigable rivers were unreasonable obstructions to navigation and to order their removal, was upheld. As touching on this question, see *Reynolds v. Board of County Commrs.*, 6 Ida. 787, 59 Pac. 7⊂0; *Barton v. Schmershall*, 21 Ida. 562, 122 Pac. 385.

It is too late to question the power of the legislature to regulate public utilities respecting rates, service, etc. That power presupposes an intelligent regulation and necessarily carries with it the power to employ the means necessary and proper for such intelligent regulation. It would be almost impossible for the legislature of this state to undertake intelligent regulation of utility corporations by the legislature itself. Under the constitution there is a regular session of the legislature every two years, and such sessions are usually sixty days in length. It would not be possible for the legislature in the length of time it sits to regulate intelligently the rates, service and other matters which need regulation in connection, with utility corporations. The necessity of regulating such corporations and the inability of the legislature to administer such regulation is at least a strong argument in favor of the delegation of that power to a commission under laws established by the legislature. The delegation of power to a commission to fix rates and service clearly contemplates reasonable rates and service. That is the standard by which service and rates must be fixed. The common law prescribes the same standard, and in the absence of the provisions of sec. 12 of the public utility law, the delegation of the power to the commission to fix rates and determine service would necessarily be limited by that standard. It was suggested by counsel for plaintiffs on oral argument that where the legislature fixed only a standard of "reasonableness," it was not fixing such a standard as would entitle the commission to exercise its delegated power.) That question has been thoroughly considered by the New York court of appeals in the case of the *Trustees of Village of Saratoga Springs v. Saratoga Gas E. L. & P. Co.*, 191 N. Y. 123, 83 N. E. 693, 18 L. R. A., N. S., 713, 14 Ann. Cas. 606. In that case the court held a contrary view to that expressed by counsel, and, among other things, said:

"But it is said that, granting this, 'reasonable' is really no standard, but a mere generality. Again we are of a different opinion. Indeed, if the statute assumed to fix any other standard for rates than that they should be reasonable, I think it would be much more open to attack than its present form. A lawmaker may exhaust reflection and ingenuity in the attempt to settle on the elements which affect the reasonableness of a rate, only to find that in a particular case he had omitted the factor which controlled the disposition of that case."

There is still another consideration which leads inevitably to the conclusion that while the power of establishing uniform rates is legislative, the exercise of the power, a standard having been prescribed, is administrative purely. Practically every state in the Union has a constitutional inhibition against special legislation in the nature of rate-making. No one would contend that the legislature had the power to say that passenger rates on a certain railroad should be three cents a mile and on another five cents a mile, but the legislature would have the power to say that all railroad fares should be "reasonble," and after having so enacted to declare what was reasonable in one case and what in another, when acting upon proper information. However, (if the legislature declares that all rates must be reasonable by a general law, that declaration is purely legislative and cannot be delegated, but the authority to determine what is reasonable is purely administrative and can be delegated, and was delegated in our public utilities act to the commission.) As touching upon this question, see *Atlantic Coast Line Ry. Co. v. North Carolina Corporation Commission*, 206 U. S. 1, 27 Sup. Ct. 585, 51 L. ed. 933, 11 Ann. Cas. 398; *Railroad Commission of Alabama v. Central of Georgia Ry. Co.*, 170 Fed. 225, 95 C. C. A. 117; *Public Service Commission v. Northern Central Ry. Co.* (Md.), 90 Atl. 105.

If the public utilities commission may prescribe rates and regulate service and issue certificates of convenience and necessity, which rates and service must conform to the standard of "reasonableness," the commission must act intelligently and upon evidence, and must consider many facts, and must determine those questions in fairness to the public as well as to the public utility, and if after fixing rates and regulating service, another utility may come in and compete for the business, the regulation of the commission would amount to nothing.

(Sec. 63a of said act provides that the action of the commission may be reviewed in the supreme court on a writ of *certiorari* or review, and that "No new or additional evidence may be introduced in the supreme court, but the cause shall be heard on the record of the commission as certified by it. The review shall not be extended further than to determine whether the commission has regularly pursued its authority, including a determination of whether the order or decision under review violates any right of the petitioner under the constitution of the United States or of the state of Idaho and whether the evidence is sufficient to sustain the findings and conclusions of the commission. The findings and conclusions of the commission on questions of fact shall be regarded as *prima facie* just, reasonable and correct; such questions of fact shall include ultimate facts and the findings and conclusions of the commission on reasonableness and discrimination." This court is there given substantially the same authority in reviewing such orders as on appeal. It has the same record before it that the commission had and may determine whether the evidence is sufficient to sustain the findings and conclusions of the commission, and in so doing must weigh the evidence. It may decide whether the orders of the board are unlawful or whether they violate a right of the petitioner under the constitution of the United States or the state of Idaho, and whether the evidence is sufficient to sustain the findings and conclusions of the commission. It will thus be seen that this court is given ample power to review the orders of the commission and to correct any mistakes that may have been made.)

It is next contended by counsel for the plaintiffs that its franchise rights under said ordinances had, prior to the time the utilities law went into effect, become contract rights within the protection of the contract clause of the constitution of the United States and cannot be affected by the utilities act.

The question then is directly presented whether the state of Idaho grants to its towns and cities power to make contracts in the form of franchises which cannot be reached or affected even by the state under its police power. The contract right given to a public utility corporation by an ordinance of the city does not come within the contract clause of the constitution of the United States. In the case of *Kentucky & Indiana Bridge Co. v. Louisville & N. R. Co.*, 34 Am. & Eng. R. R. Cases, O. S., 630, the court said:

"If the legislature had no power to alter its police laws when contracts would be affected, then the most important and valuable reforms might be precluded by the simple device of entering into contracts for the purpose. No doctrine to that effect would be even plausible, much less sound and tenable."

It is stated in Jones on Telegraph & Telephone Companies, sec. 214, as follows:

"No government can advance in civilization, in wealth, and in influence without an enforcement of these [police] powers. When any corporation acquires a franchise for the purpose of carrying on a corporate business within a state, it is accepted subject to the police power. By giving the franchise [we may say, permitting it to be exercised] the state did not abrogate its power over the public highways; nor in any way curtail its power to be exercised for the general welfare of the people."

It is well settled by the decisions that the making of contracts between individuals or between individuals and corporations or municipalities and corporations, as in the case at bar, can never be held to abrogate or prevent the exercise by the state of its police power in any manner that it may consider just and proper. If it were conceded that such contracts could be entered into, every substantial power granted to the commission by the legislature in the public utilities act could easily have been nullified and set at naught by the simple act of making contracts prior to the time the act

became effective, as was, in fact, done in this case, the act
having been approved by the governor on March 13th and
gone into effect on May 8th, and the franchise contracts referred to passed on the 29th of April and the 5th of May,
respectively, just prior to the time the act went into effect.
Any future exercise by the state of its police power cannot
thus be thwarted and prevented by the mere procuring by a
utility corporation of the passage of an ordinance by a city
or town granting it certain rights. Such contracts must be
held not to be protected by any provision of the state or
federal constitution against the proper exercise by the state
of its police power. Said act became a law when approved
by the governor, but did not go into effect until May 8th,
there being sixty days between the adjournment of the session
when said act was passed and its going into effect. And it
was not intended that a public utility corporation should
thwart the purpose of said act simply by procuring the passage of an ordinance granting it certain rights that could not
be granted after the law went into effect.

It is provided in sec. 48a that no electrical corporation,
etc., shall "henceforth" begin the construction of an electrical plant, etc. It was not intended that a public utility
corporation should slip in between the passage and approval
of said act and its going into effect and procure rights that
would deprive the state of the right to regulate it in its operations and in making it amenable to the police regulation of
the state, especially where it had not begun "actual construction work and is prosecuting such work in good faith and
uninterruptedly and with reasonable diligence in proportion
to the magnitude of the undertaking," as provided by sec.
48b of said act. Under the facts of this case it clearly appears that the plaintiff had not begun actual construction
work on its systems within either of said cities.

It is next contended by counsel for plaintiff that the provisions of sec. 18, art. 11, of the constitution, prohibit the
legislature from passing a law that would create a monopoly;
that the provisions of said section prohibit combinations to
regulate either production or prices of commodities used by

the people; also that the provisions of said section by implication recognize freedom of competition. Counsel then propounds the following question: "Can the legislature delegate its power, if power it has, to restrict the business of carrying on and generating electricity?"

In reply we would say that the legislature has not delegated its legislative power to restrict the carrying on of any business. The public utilities act was passed by the legislature and the administration of it was placed in the hands of said commission and the courts. The legislature could not go into the facts of each individual case and determine whether the various public utility corporations should be permitted to carry on business within the state, but committed that administrative power to said commission and declared the public policy of the state to be that it was not for the best interests and welfare of the people to have a duplication of public utility plants in the same community where one was amply sufficient to serve the necessities and convenience of the people, unless authorized by said commission. The policy of said act is not to permit a duplication of plants where it is not for the welfare, convenience and necessity of the people, and under said act the body first to determine that question is the public utilities commission. It is clearly apparent that the questions required to be determined under said law may be best determined by a commission in the first instance. If such questions were first to be determined by the courts, the courts of the state would have to be increased in order to perform the additional duties which now devolve upon the commission. The legislature no doubt in the enactment of said law considered said matter and concluded that it would be better to establish the commission to hear and determine such cases first than to impose that duty on the courts.

While said sec. 18 of the constitution prohibits combinations to regulate either production or prices of articles of commerce, etc., it does not either directly or indirectly prohibit the legislature from enacting a law whereby rates to be charged by public utility corporations for their services and product may be made or established.

The legislature has determined by the adoption of said act that as a matter of public policy it is for the best interest and welfare of the people of the state to direct the operation of utility corporations by a commission and thus prevent what may be denominated cut-throat competition, which invariably results in private monopoly. We find nothing in the constitution prohibiting the legislature from doing so.

This matter involves the police powers of the state, and it is declared in sec. 8, art. 9, of the constitution that the police powers of the state shall never be abridged or so construed as to permit corporations to conduct their business in such manner as to infringe the equal rights of individuals or the general well-being of the state. Now, the state, through the legislature, has concluded that where a city or community is amply served by one utility corporation, it may not be for the best interests of such city or community to permit a duplication of the plant that is serving it, and that question is left to said commission. The monopoly that counsel contend is so created is clearly not such a monopoly as is referred to in said sec. 18 of the constitution. Said act provides for such a regulation and control of utility corporations as would prevent, on the one hand, the evils of unrestricted rights of competition, and, on the other hand, the abuse of unregulated monopoly. (*People ex rel. New York Edison Co. v. Wilcox,* 207 N. Y. 86, 100 N. E. 705, 45 L. R. A., N. S., 629.) Unrestricted competition, as experience has shown, generally results in the very worst kind of monopoly.

Monopoly may be created by combination, by dividing the territory to be supplied, or by driving out the weaker corporation by the stronger, and thereafter taxing the business all it will stand. That is the kind of monopoly and combination that the framers of the constitution had in mind. They did not have in mind a public utility corporation governed and controlled by law, as the legislature has sought to govern and regulate such corporations by the provisions of the act in question. In other words, they had in mind unrestricted monopoly and not a monopoly that is governed and controlled by law and not permitted to charge more than just and fair rates for serving the people. So far as public utilities are concerned, in order to secure for the people the largest degree of satisfactory service, efficiency and economy, the state must regulate them, and if such regulation results in a regulated monopoly, it will be far better for the people than competition which results in a duplication of plants, combinations, bankruptcies or receiverships. No honest man or community would ask for such services as the public utilities give without being willing to pay a fair and just compensation therefor.

At the present time it must be conceded that the legislatures of nearly all of the states of the Union have concluded that the best method for regulating public utility corporations is by a commission under laws similar to the act in question. There is nothing in the contention of counsel for plaintiffs to the effect that under said law said commission is permitted to establish such a monopoly or such a combination as was intended to be prohibited by any of the provisions of our state constitution.

It is contended that the last proviso to sec. 48a authorizes public utility corporations, without a certificate of public convenience and necessity from the commission, to increase the capacity of existing generating plants or to develop new generating plants and market the products thereof. Said proviso is as follows: "*Provided:* That power companies may, without such certificate, increase the capacity of existing generating plants or develop new generating plants and market the products thereof."

It is conceded that said proviso was attached to said section by one or both of the attorneys for the utility corporations involved in this case, or was suggested by them, and in all probability was not carefully considered by the legislature, or, at least, the legislature did not give it the interpretation or meaning now contended for by counsel for the plaintiff. If that proviso is given the meaning contended for by counsel, it would nullify the main intention and purpose of said 80-section public utilities act. If under that proviso existing utility corporations in the state may increase the capacity of or develop new generating plants and construct lines for marketing the products thereof into any of the cities or towns of the state without the certificate of public convenience and necessity, it gives the existing corporations an absolute monopoly of furnishing electricity or electrical power to every city or town or community in the state without procuring a certificate, and thus sets at naught one of the main objects and purposes of said act. Provisos must not be so construed as to nullify the clear object and purpose of the act.

It is stated in 2 Lewis' Sutherland, Statutory Construction, sec. 347, that "General words may be cut down when a certain application of them would antagonize a settled policy of the state."

In *McCormick v. West Duluth*, 47 Minn. 272, 50 N. W. 128, the court held that when the first clause of a section conforms to the obvious policy and intention of the legislature, it is not rendered inoperative by a later inconsistent clause which does not conform to this policy and intent. In such cases the later clause is nugatory and must be disregarded.

The decisions hold that laws must be interpreted according to what on the whole must have been the intention of the lawmakers, and if the principal object of the act cannot be accomplished and stand under the restrictions of the proviso, the proviso must be held void for repugnancy. It is held in vol. 2, sec. 352, Lewis' Sutherland, Statutory Construction, that if a proviso is repugnant to the body of the act, it should be rejected. (See *Penick v. High Shoals Mfg. Co.*, 113 Ga. 592, 38 S. E. 973.) If said last proviso to said section is construed to mean that such corporations may increase the capacity of their existing plants or build new ones and market the products thereof over existing lines or those which may be constructed in accordance with the clear legislative intent as expressed in said act, then the act and proviso can be construed together and both be permitted to stand. If the proviso can be construed as being not repugnant to the main object and purpose of the act, it ought to be so construed.

Under that proviso no certificate is required to increase the capacity of an existing plant, or even perhaps to build a new plant and market the product thereof, over any lines already constructed by the utility corporation in accordance with the law, or to supply an increasing demand in a city or town or place already occupied and supplied by such utility, and it may extend its instrumentalities for conducting such power to the place of intended use.   That clause of said section, to wit, "and market the products thereof," does not grant permission to build new lines into the territory occupied by other utility corporations, since the clear intention of the legislature was to prohibit the duplication of such plants unless a certificate of convenience and necessity was first obtained, and as before stated, the plaintiff corporation had not commenced "construction" operation in either of said cities prior to the time said act went into effect.   They had simply procured the passage of ordinances granting them the right.   The first proviso of said sec. 48a is that said section shall not be construed to require any such corporation to secure such certificate for an extension within any city, county or town within which it shall have theretofore lawfully commenced operation, or for an extension into territory either within or without a city, county or town, contiguous to its street railroad, or line, plant or system, *and not theretofore served by a public utility of like character*, or for an extension within or to territory already served by it, necessary in the ordinary course of its business.   From those and other provisions, the clear intention of the legislature was not to permit such corporation to extend its lines into territory already occupied by a similar utility corporation without first procuring a certificate of convenience and necessity from said commission.

Counsel for plaintiffs lay considerable stress upon the decision of the supreme court of California in the case of *Pacific Telephone & Telegraph Co. v. Eshleman*, 166 Cal. 640, 137 Pac. 1119, 50 L. R. A., N. S., 652, wherein it was held that the public utilities act of California would have been held void and unconstitutional but for that provision of the constitution embodied in art. 12, sec. 22, wherein it is declared that no provision of the constitution shall be construed as a limitation upon the authority of the legislature to confer upon the railroad commission additional powers of the same kind, or different from those conferred therein, not inconsistent with those conferred upon the commission by the constitution. That case involved an order of the railroad commission requiring a telephone company, having both long distance and local lines, to permit a physical connection to be made between its long distance lines and the local lines of another company competing with it locally.

A decision or order by the district court of the United States for the district of Oregon, in the case of *Pacific Telephone & Telegraph Co., a Corporation, v. Wright-Dickinson Hotel Co., a Corporation, et al.*, 214 Fed. 666, was filed May 4, 1914, in which substantially the same question was raised as that in the California case. Said decision has not been published in the Federal Reporter, but has been printed in circular form by the Home Telephone & Telegraph Company of Portland, Oregon, a copy of which decision is before me. After a statement of the case and a reference to the provisions of the public utilities act of Oregon, the court, speaking through District Judge Wolverton, said:

"In other words, the power to regulate within the purpose and spirit of the act includes the power to require physical connection; otherwise regulation would prove largely ineffectual in practical application. We are not impressed with the suggestion that this power of regulation must be specifically conferred by constitutional authority. . . . . The opposite view is entertained in an exhaustive and ably considered case from California—*Pacific Telephone & Telegraph Co. v. Eshleman*, 166 Cal. 640, 137 Pac. 1119, 50 L. R. A., N. S., 652—but we are unable to give assent thereto."

We are in accord with the views of the U. S. district court for the district of Oregon, and hold that the power of regulation provided for by the public utilities act of this state is not repugnant to the provisions of the constitution of the state of Idaho or the constitution of the United States, and that it is not necessary that the power of regulation as provided by said act must be specifically conferred by constitutional authority.

We therefore conclude that the legislature had the power to authorize said commission to restrict competition between public utilities; that said act is not repugnant to the provisions of the commerce clause of the constitution of the United States, or repugnant to the provisions of the constitution of this state; that the plaintiffs have no legal right to construct their lines into either of said cities without first obtaining a certificate of convenience and necessity; that no vested rights of the plaintiffs have been in any manner interfered with by the orders complained of, and that the orders made in the above-entitled cases by the commission are not unreasonable or unlawful, and must be affirmed, and it is so ordered.   Costs awarded in favor of the defendants.

Walters, District Judge, concurs.

AILSHIE, C. J., Dissenting.—It seems to me that the construction placed on the statute by the opinion of my associate thwarts and sets at naught the intention of the legislature and renders meaningless the plain language of the statute.

Two things are made perfectly plain by secs. 48a and 48b of the act.   First, that a power company that was engaged in business in the state when the act went into effect should not be required to secure permission from the commission to continue in business or to *"increase the capacity"* of an *existing plant "and market the products thereof"*; and, second, that the commission could not prevent a company going ahead and completing its plant and works and serving customers where it had secured a permit or franchise from the proper authorities prior to the utilities act going into effect and had commenced actual construction and prosecuted the same with reasonable diligence thereafter.

It is worthy of note that the statute, sec. 48a, closes with the following proviso: *"Provided that power companies may, without such certificate, increase the capacity of existing generating plants or develop new generating plants and market*

the products thereof.'' And there is immediately added the
following proviso in section 48b, ''Provided, that when the
commission shall find, after hearing that a public utility has
heretofore *begun actual construction work and is prosecuting
such work in good faith,* uninterruptedly and with reasonable
diligence in proportion to the magnitude of the undertaking,
under any franchise or permit heretofore granted but not
heretofore actually exercised, such public utility may proceed
to the completion of such work, and may, after such completion, exercise such right or privilege.''

The foregoing scarcely admits of construction; the layman
can understand that as well as the lawyer. The majority
opinion, however, seems to hold these provisos to the statute
as ''nugatory'' and that they should be ''disregarded.''

The commission itself originally took the same view of the
statute I have above expressed, in a case designated as
''*Ashton & St. Anthony Case.* No. F–5.'' There the company secured a franchise from Ashton on March 18, 1913, and
from Marysville April 7, 1913, which was only a short time
before the utilities act went into effect. The company did
some trivial work on its power site a couple of miles outside
of the city prior to the going into effect of the utilities act.
The commission held that, ''Under this clause of the statute
and under the facts so found, it would seem that the Ashton
& St. Anthony Power Company, Limited, may proceed to the
completion of its work and may after such completion exercise the rights and privileges granted to it by these franchises. It would appear from the statute and from such
findings *that no certificate of public convenience and necessity is required* from the commission in order that the applicant company may proceed to the completion of its works, and
after such completion may exercise the rights and privileges
granted by the franchises aforesaid.'' The commission appears to have receded from the view there expressed in the
present case.

Let us now see what the facts are in the case under consideration. In 1908 the predecessor of the plaintiff secured
from the state engineer a permit for the diversion of 1,000

second-feet of water from the Malad river in what is now Gooding county. That work has been prosecuted diligently ever since and diversion works have been constructed and power plants erected so that about 7,500 horse-power has been developed and utilized, and approximately 20,000 horse-power can be developed under this permit and diversion; that in the construction of diversion works and power and generating plants, $600,000 has been expended, and the total expenditure made by the company in constructing diverting works, power and generating plants and transmission and distribution lines aggregates about $1,500,000. It is claimed that more than one million of this investment had been made when the utilities act was passed. Prior to the time the utilities commission was created by act of the legislature, plaintiff's predecessor, the Beaver River Light & Power Company, had constructed a transmission line from the power plant on the Malad river by way of Glenns Ferry and Mountainhome to Boise, a distance of something like 86 miles, and was then furnishing light and power in Boise City and towns along the course of the transmission line. The stipulation shows that even all these points did not consume all the electricity that plaintiff was then prepared to generate, and it had not yet developed more than about one-third of its water-power possibilities under its permit from the state and the diversion made thereunder. In the meanwhile, many other towns were much closer to its power and generating plant than Boise and other towns already supplied, Twin Falls being only thirty miles away. It is also stipulated that the plan of development and purpose of plaintiff and its predecessor is and has been to develop the entire available power of the Malad river as rapidly as possible and as fast as the terms of their water permit would require, and to seek a market for the product of the plants.

The utilities act went into effect on May 8, 1913, and prior to that date the plaintiff's predecessor, the Beaver River Power Company, secured a franchise from the city of Twin Falls to construct transmission lines through the city and to deliver light and power to the city and its inhabitants, but

had not commenced any actual construction work within the
city limits.

It is admitted, however, that it was already equipped with
a sufficient plant to supply all the electricity that would be
needed or could be used at this place.   In the meanwhile, the
Great Shoshone and Twin Falls Water Power Company was
supplying electricity to Twin Falls and neighboring towns.

Now, the question arises: *Did the legislature, when writing
and enacting into law the above-quoted sections of the statute,
intend to permit the utilities commission to exclude either one
of these companies, or any company already in the field, from
continuing to operate and seek a market for its products?*
To my mind, it is clear that the legislature intended to allow
them to continue to operate and seek every available market
for the products of their plants to the extent of the full
capacity of their power and generating possibilities and to
confer on the commission plenary power to regulate the service and fix rates.   *The chief thing the legislature had in
mind was to confer the power to regulate public service corporations and fix rates to be charged consumers.   They had
no idea of discriminating between public service companies
already in the field with their money invested and plants in
operation; neither did they intend to make a pet monopoly
out of one and wreck another that already had hundreds of
thousands in cash invested in the state.*   I cannot conceive
that lawmakers attempting to legislate for the people of the
state could have meant any such thing, and it seems to me
that they made it very plain by the above-quoted provisos
that they did not intend such a thing.

It is said that because the plaintiff company had not commenced work within the corporate limits of Twin Falls, it
had not done any work under its franchise.   That is like say-
ing that the man who shoves his hand through the window
and takes your coat off the hook didn't steal the coat from
your dwelling-house because the motive and will power were
outside the house.

We don't generally have great water-power sites in the city.
We rather have to go out and build power and generating

plants where the streams flow and then convey the current long distances over transmission lines to places of consumption, and we find the bulk of consumers in the town and cities. The diversion of the water and construction of plants at the power site is as much a part of the work of supplying a city and its inhabitants with light and power as is the building of distributing lines. Again, it would seem to me that a plant large enough to generate current for transmission 86 miles to supply a city of twenty-five or thirty thousand people is certainly within the 'same "field" of operation comprising a city of nine or ten thousand that is only thirty miles distant.

Again, it would be the height of folly to say they can enlarge or increase existing plants and generate more electricity and still they cannot build more transmission or distributing lines but must carry the additional load and distribute it over existing lines or not at all. The mere statement of such a proposition refutes the claim. New and additional consumers must be served over other and different lines.

The fact that the plaintiff, Idaho Light & Power Company, had not filed an acceptance of the terms of the ordinance granting it a franchise prior to the time the utilities act took effect is without shadow of merit. That the franchise was granted on the company's application was itself an acceptance and would bind it to the terms of the ordinance granting the same so long as the ordinance provided the exact terms proposed by the company soliciting the franchise. *It is well settled that doing work under the terms of a franchise is an acceptance of its terms and conditions.* (*City of Allegheny v. People's Natural Gas Co.*, 172 Pa. 632, 33 Atl. 704, 705; *City Railway Co. v. Citizens' Street R. R. Co.*, 166 U. S. 557, 17 Sup. Ct. 653, 41 L. ed. 1114, 1118; *Lincoln & Kennebec Bank v. Richardson,* 1 Greenl. (Me.) 79, 10 Am. Dec. 34; *Illinois River R. Co. v. Zimmer,* 20 Ill. 654; *City of Atlanta v. Gate City Gas Light Co.,* 71 Ga. 106, 117; *State v. Dawson,* 22 Ind. 272, 274.)

If the utilities act is valid and constitutional, then there can be no question about *the right of the commission to regulate the service of the plaintiff and all other like concerns and to fix the rates it may charge, but it has no right to exclude it from the field and grant its competitor an exclusive monopoly of the business.*

Entertaining, as I do, the opinion of this case just expressed, it would be useless for me to enter into any discussion as to the constitutional questions presented, and I accordingly refrain from any consideration of that phase of the case, or the expression of any opinion thereon.

It has been iterated and reiterated by counsel for the state and counsel for the utilities commission, and also by counsel for both corporations here represented, that the public utilities act of this state does away with competition in Idaho so far as all public service corporations are concerned, and that it provides for the creation of monopolies in all public utilities regulated by a commission. The opinion by Mr. Justice Sullivan adopts the same view and asserts that this statute provides for regulated monopolies. I cannot concur in all the views advanced on this phase of the question, but I think it well that the construction to be placed on this law is made plain so the people may know and understand the scope and purpose of the law as viewed by the court and the utilities commission.

What I have said with reference to the Twin Falls case is equally applicable to the Pocatello case. There it was proposed to generate electricity by means of a Diesel Internal Combustion oil engine, and a franchise was procured from the city prior to the utilities act going into effect, and plans and specifications were made and the company paid for publication of the ordinance and did some preliminary work in the way of investigations and survey of the field. Thereafter, and prior to commencement of proceedings before the commission, the company ordered and had constructed a 500 horse-power engine, which it installed in the city of Pocatello, and all together incurred an expense of about $50,000, and still *in the face of this state of facts, the utilities com-*

mission contend that they have the power to exclude this company from supplying light or power to the people of Pocatello. I repeat that the commission has the undoubted power to fix the rates to be charged by this company and to regulate the service by it, but the legislature never dreamed of vesting the commission with the power to exclude the company from serving the people of Pocatello under these conditions and to confer a monopoly on the company already there.

The order of the commission is clearly erroneous and ought to be vacated and set aside.

(June 30, 1914.)

AUGUSTA STEHLE, Executrix, Appellant, v. B. FLAIG, Ex-Guardian, Respondent.

[141 Pac. 1196.]

ADMINISTRATION OF ESTATE—EXCEPTIONS TO FINAL ACCOUNT OF EX-GUARDIAN.

APPEAL from the District Court of the First Judicial District for Shoshone County. Hon. W. W. Woods, Judge.

Action by executrix on exceptions to final account of ex-guardian of the estate of an incompetent person. Plaintiff appeals. *Affirmed.*

James Hopkins and W. W. Bixby, for Appellant.

A. G. Kerns, for Respondent.

DUNN, District Judge.—In this case, while the record shows some irregularities in the acts of the respondent as guardian of the incompetent, Joseph Stehle, there is a total lack of evidence to sustain the charges of the appellant.

The judgment of the district court should be affirmed. Costs awarded in favor of respondent.

Ailshie, C. J., and Sullivan, J., concur.

(July 3, 1914.)

IDAHO IRRIGATION COMPANY, LTD., a Corporation, Respondent, v. ADOLPH PEW and H. E. CORNELL, Appellants.

[141 Pac. 1099.]

FORECLOSURE OF CAREY ACT LIEN—GROUNDS OF DEMURRER TO COM-
PLAINT—SEC. 1629, REV. CODES, AND FEDERAL CAREY ACT CON-
STRUED—CONTRACTS BETWEEN STATE AND IRRIGATION COMPANY AND
COMPANY AND SETTLER—WAIVER—ESTOPPEL.

1. In an action to foreclose a Carey Act lien under the provisions of sec. 1629, Rev. Codes, it is not necessary to allege in the complaint that the entire irrigation system has been completed, if it appears from the allegations of the complaint that an ample supply of water has been made permanently available for the tract of land upon which the lien is sought to be foreclosed, to the extent that the contract of the irrigation company to furnish such supply to the land in question has been fulfilled.

2. Sec. 1629, Rev. Codes, conferring a lien on land and water for water furnished to land, and the amendment to the federal Carey Act (29 U. S. Stats. at L., p. 435), authorizing the state to create a lien on the land, must be construed together, and the lien cannot attach until the provisions of both acts have been complied with.

3. The amendment to the federal Carey Act in fixing the amount of the lien upon the land to be created by the state at "the actual cost of reclamation and reasonable interest thereon from the date of reclamation until disposed of to actual settlers," contemplates the determination of such cost by the state, and that in a contract between the state and a corporation for the construction of irrigation works, such cost must be estimated or determined in advance as a basis for the contract between them.

4. In a contract between a Carey Act irrigation company and a settler, in which, by reference, the terms and conditions of the contract between the state and the irrigation company are assented to, and the price of water rights is fixed upon the basis of the estimated cost of the works contained in the state contract, both the company and the settler are estopped from afterward raising the question as to whether such estimated cost is the actual cost of the works.

5. In a suit to foreclose a Carey Act lien the cause of action arises under the state statute, and it is not necessary to allege in the complaint that a requirement of the federal statute, not contained in the state statute, has been complied with.

6. *Held,* that the complaint in this case is not demurrable on the ground of being ambiguous, unintelligible or uncertain.

APPEAL from the District Court of the Third Judicial District, in and for Ada County. Hon. Carl A. Davis, Judge.

Action to foreclose a Carey Act lien for default in payment by defendants of deferred payments upon a water right, purchased by defendant Pew under contract from the plaintiff corporation. Demurrer to complaint overruled, and from the order overruling the demurrer defendant Cornell appeals. *Affirmed.*

B. W. Oppenheim, for Appellants, cites no authorities.

N. M. Ruick, for Respondent.

The reclamation project need not be completed before the construction company is entitled to foreclose its lien on a particular tract. (*Childs v. Neitzel, ante,* p. 116, 141 Pac. 77.)

Under the provisions of sec. 1629, Rev. Codes, upon the default of any deferred payments, the lienholders may foreclose the same in accordance with the terms and conditions of the contract for the purchase of the water right. (*Idaho Irr. Co. v. Dill,* 25 Ida. 711, 139 Pac. 714.)

AILSHIE, C. J.—The complaint in this case is almost identical with the one in *Idaho Irr. Co. v. Dill,* recently decided by this court (25 Ida. 711, 139 Pac. 714), and the action is of the same nature. In that case the question presented was whether the lower court erred in sustaining a demurrer to the complaint upon the ground that the United States was a necessary party to the action, and upon that question this court reversed the court below.

By stipulation of counsel it was agreed that the contract which the plaintiff corporation made with the defendant in

this case was the same as in the Dill case, the only difference
being in the date, name of purchaser, description of the land,
etc., which minor differences were admitted to be immaterial,
and the contracts introduced in evidence in the Dill case,
including the contract and supplemental contract between
the company and the state, were stipulated to be considered
part of the record in this case.

The defendant Pew, the original purchaser, had assigned
all his interest under the contract to the defendant Cornell,
who alone appeared and demurred to the complaint. The
lower court overruled the demurrer. Defendant elected to
stand thereon and declined to plead further. The demurrer
alleged that the complaint did not state facts sufficient to
constitute a cause of action, and particularly in (1) that the
plaintiff has not alleged that the irrigation system, which by
the terms of the contracts set up in the complaint it agreed
to construct, has been completed; (2) that the plaintiff has
not alleged that the amounts sued upon and for which a lien
is claimed are "the actual cost of reclamation (of the land
described in the complaint) and reasonable interest thereon
from the date of reclamation until disposed of to (an) actual
settler(s)"; (3) "that no valid lien can be created under existing law against either land or water, as is attempted to be
done under the allegations of the complaint herein."

1. We do not think it necessary for the plaintiff to allege
that the entire reclamation system has been completed, in an
action to foreclose a lien against a single purchaser of a water
right under the Carey Act. The essential thing that concerns
the particular land owner and purchaser of the water right
is whether or not the reservoir and main canal have been so
far completed as to enable the company to regularly and permanently supply him with water for the irrigation of his land,
and that the company has commenced and continues to do
so. The amendment to the Carey Act (29 U. S. Stats. at L.,
p. 435), after authorizing the state to create the lien against
the land for the cost of reclamation, continues as follows:
"And when an amply supply of water is actually furnished
in a substantial ditch or canal, or by artesian wells or reser-

voirs, to reclaim a particular tract or tracts of such lands, then patents shall issue for the same to such state without regard to settlement or cultivation." This language explicitly refers to a "particular tract," implying that the issuance of patent for any one tract is not dependent on the completion of the whole reclamation system, but on the actual furnishing of a permanent supply of water to that "particular tract." The government then considers that the contract has been executed on the side of the state so far as that tract is concerned, and parts with its title accordingly, and it would certainly seem that the settler is assured of a permanent water supply when the "particular tract" has been so far reclaimed in the view of the government of the United States as to entitle the state and himself to a patent therefor. The fact that some other land owner and purchaser of a water right is not yet receiving water, or that the system has not been so far completed as to furnish another with water, does not justify one who has and is receiving a permanent and continuous supply of water for the irrigation of his land in refusing to pay for it. We find no provision in the Carey Act, nor in the laws of this state, nor in the contracts in evidence, which requires that the reclamation works shall be entirely completed before any of the deferred payments shall mature. If, as a matter of fact, a company that is seeking to foreclose such a lien has not made water permanently available to the land in question, and available in sufficient quantities and seasons to comply with the provisions of the contract, such defense will always be open to the settler.

A similar question arose on rehearing in the recent case of *Childs v. Neitzel, ante,* p. 116, 141 Pac. 77, in which the contract with the settler also contemplated the payment for water rights by annual instalments, and the court said:

"We did not mean to hold in the original opinion that the annual instalments provided for by said water contracts did not become due and payable until the entire system was completed; but when the system was so far completed as to make water permanently available for any particular user for all

seasons, the instalments· agreed to be paid by the user would
become due and payable in accordance with the terms of the
contract.   Then he has no reason to complain of lack of water
for other land owners, because he has water available for the
irrigation of his land."

There are practical reasons which Congress doubtless had
under consideration when by the 1896 amendment to the
Carey Act it specified the character of completion necessary
in order to obtain patent, with reference to "a particular
tract or tracts of such lands," instead of making it apply to
all the lands embraced in the project.   For instance, a Carey
Act project may include several distinct segregations or units
of land to be reclaimed, but all of which are covered by the
one contract with the state.   The entire completion of such
a system may extend over a comparatively long period.   An
ample supply of water may be permanently furnished to one
or more of these units for years before other portions of
the system are finished.   It would manifestly be a great financial burden upon the enterprise to exact from its promoters
the condition that no deferred payments should be collected
nor liens securing them attach until all lands on all the tracts
embraced in the project were permanently supplied with
water.   Such a requirement, besides being unnecessary to
protect a settler who was already in possession of what he
had contracted for, would obviously increase the cost of the
enterprise to the settler by making the investment less attrac-
tive to the capitalist, who would require a higher rate of
interest, or its equivalent, to compensate him for the increased
risk.

2. The next question raised by defendant's demurrer is
that the complaint does not allege that the amounts sued for,
and for which a lien is sought to be foreclosed, are the actual
cost of reclamation of the land described in the complaint
and reasonable interest thereon.   The language of the 1896
amendment to the Carey Act on this point is as follows: "A
lien or liens is hereby authorized to be created by the state
. . . . against the separate legal subdivisions of land reclaimed, for the actual cost and necessary expenses of reclama-

tion and reasonable interest thereon from the date of reclamation until disposed of to actual settlers.'' This "actual cost of reclamation'' in any given case was evidently intended by the act to be determined by the state, and that determination would at least constitute *prima facie* proof that the amount the state allowed the company to charge and collect for a water right was the "actual cost'' within the purview of the act of Congress. The Carey Act authorizes the state itself to reclaim the land or to contract with a corporation to do so. The presumption must be that the state will act fairly and justly, and that the price it permits to be charged and collected is clearly within the direction and authority of the congressional act.

This court has already held in *Idaho Irr. Co. v. Dill, supra*, that "Under the provisions of section 1629, Rev. Codes, any company or association furnishing water for any tract of land is given a first and prior lien on the water right and the land upon which said water is used for all deferred payments for the water right, and upon default of any deferred payments the lienholder may foreclose the same in accordance with the terms and conditions of the contract for the purchase of the water right.''

Counsel for appellant contends in his brief that "so far as the state lien is broader than the lien allowed by the national law it is invalid, for by sec. 1613 Rev. Codes, our legislature accepts the conditions of the Carey Act. The national law is paramount. The state is not authorized to create any lien against either land or water except for 'the actual and necessary expenses of reclamation and reasonable interest thereon.' '' This contention may be conceded in the main, but subject to an important qualification. The national Carey Act authorizes a lien only against the land. It apparently recognizes the right of the state to control the disposition of its public waters. The state statute authorizes a lien against both the land and water, as it has a right to do, and to this extent is broader in its lien conferring provisions. But so far as the land itself is concerned, the lien of course must be subject to the limitations of the congressional act.

Before the state and the constructing company can enter
into any contract for the reclamation of a tract of land, they
must have agreed upon the estimated cost of construction and
the corresponding price to be charged for water rights, in
order to defray such cost. That agreement as to cost is the
basis of the contract between the company and the state.
Again, when the company first comes into relation with the
settler, it must have contractual assurance from him that he
will reimburse it for his share of this estimated cost, and the
settler on the other hand must be safeguarded by a fixed contract price for the water right if he enters upon the land.
This arrangement impresses us as not only unavoidable in the
very nature of the conditions existing, but as eminently fair
and just to all parties. If the prospective settler considers
the estimated cost of construction excessive he need not contract for the purchase of water rights under that project.
He is under no compulsion to contract with the company at
all. He is not dependent on the company when he makes his
contract with it, for the law does not permit him to enter
the land before he makes the water right contract. If he does
enter into a contract for the purchase of water rights to be
paid for in instalments, subject to foreclosure if the deferred
payments are not made, it must be assumed that he does so
with his eyes open, with the knowledge that the contract is
one specifically authorized by statute, and at the same time
receiving the assurance that he is protected by the provisions
of the national Carey Act amendment, the effect of which
is, that the lien cannot attach until the company has fully
executed its part of the contract. (*Childs v. Neitzel, supra.*)

After the recitals of the settlers' contract with the company the first article of the agreement begins as follows:
"This agreement is made in accordance with the provisions
of said contract between the state of Idaho and the company,
which, together with the laws of the state of Idaho, under
which this agreement is made, shall be regarded as defining
the rights of the respective parties."

In making that contract the settler assents to the estimate
authorized by the state as to the cost of reclamation. Can

he then be deemed to reserve any right to have another or later estimate made of the cost of constructing the works? We think not. He has contracted to make these payments with full knowledge of all these facts and circumstances, and in an action to foreclose the lien is estopped and precluded from questioning or denying that the price fixed by the contract represents the actual cost of reclamation and reasonable interest thereon, as contemplated by the Carey Act.

Suppose, on the other hand, that the estimated cost is largely exceeded by the actual cost of construction, as is said to often be the case.   Could it for a moment be maintained that the construction company would be entitled, under authority of the national act, to a lien sufficient to cover that increased "actual cost," in the face of the contract which it had made?

In concluding our consideration of this part of the case, it may be pointed out that the amendment of 1896 to the federal Carey Act does not create the lien.   It in effect ratifies the previous creation of the lien by the state statute (Act of 1895, Sess. Laws 1895, p. 227; sec. 1629, Rev. Codes), but contains a condition not contained in the provisions of our statute. However, since the cause of action arises under our statute we do not think it strictly necessary for the complaint to allege that the requirement of the federal statute has been complied with, that is to say, that the amount of the lien claimed represents "the actual cost and necessary expenses of reclamation," etc.   But it occurs to us that it would certainly be good practice to, insert such an allegation in any complaint for the foreclosure of a Carey Act lien.

3. In the light of the foregoing considerations there can be no doubt, after construing together the federal and state statutory provisions on the subject, that the purchaser of a water right under a Carey Act project may so contract as to eventually result in a lien being created upon all the property rights which he acquires.

4. Defendant demurred specially to paragraph 8 of the complaint, on the ground "that the same is ambiguous, unintelligible and uncertain, in this, that plaintiff alleges 'that

plaintiff has performed all the conditions of the said contract required to be performed to entitle it to the relief sought in this action,' and that from said allegation it cannot be determined what conditions, if any, have been performed by plaintiff, sufficient to enable this defendant to answer said complaint.'' It appears by an examination of the complaint that this general allegation is preceded by specific allegations which recite certain acts of plaintiff company purported to have been done in compliance with the conditions specified in the contract. The complaint is not demurrable on this ground.

The judgment of the lower court is *affirmed.* Costs awarded in favor of respondent.

Sullivan, J., concurs.

(July 9, 1914.)

W. A. COUGHANOUR, Appellant, v. CITY OF PAYETTE, a Municipal Corporation, Respondent.

[142 Pac. 1076.]

MUNICIPAL LAW—IMPROVEMENT DISTRICT—INJUNCTION—ORDINANCE OF INTENTION—DESCRIPTION.

1. Under the provisions of sec. 2338, Rev. Codes, as amended by Sess. Laws 1911, p. 268, where the resolution or ordinance of intention describes the exterior boundaries of an improvement district proposed to be established, and also contains the number of the lots and blocks within such district that will be affected by such improvement, it is a sufficient compliance with the statute, since the streets and alleys can be readily ascertained and determined from said description.

2. The test as to whether the ordinance of intention complies with the law is whether it affords a proper opportunity to be heard by anyone who desires to protest against the establishment of an improvement district, and give reasonable notice of the intention of the city council to establish such district and make improvements therein.

3. Where the plaintiff as a property owner protests against the creation of a proposed improvement district, he thereby admits that he received notice of the intention to create said district.

4. *Held,* that Ordinance No. 246 substantially complies with the law in regard to what such an ordinance must contain.

5. *Held,* that the court did not err in dissolving the temporary injunction.

APPEAL from the District Court of the Seventh Judicial District for Canyon County. Hon. Ed. L. Bryan, Judge.

Action to restrain the city of Payette from proceeding to create an improvement district and the construction of sidewalks and curbing therein, in which a temporary restraining order was granted, and upon motion of the city was thereafter dissolved. Action of ·the court in dissolving such injunction *affirmed.*

Varian & Norris, for Appellant.

If there is any ambiguity in the terms of a notice, rendering its meaning doubtful, the construction must be most strongly against the party giving the notice. (*Carpentier v. Thurston,* 30 Cal. 123.)

A requirement that an ordinance shall specify the nature, character, locality and description of an improvement is mandatory. Particularity in this regard may be furnished by reference to plans and specifications upon file, or reference may be made to some specific object or thing. (See 28 Cyc. 998 (11); *McChesney v. City of Chicago,* 171 Ill. 253, 49 N. E. 548; *Hays v. City of Vincennes,* 82 Ind. 178; *Browne v. City of Boston,* 166 Mass. 229, 44 N. E. 127.)

Failure to give notice as provided by charter or statute will invalidate proceedings for improvements and assessments to pay for the same. (28 Cyc. 979, 980; *Barber Asphalt Paving Co. v. Edgerton,* 125 Ind. 455, 25 N. E. 436; *Kiphart v. Pittsburgh etc. Ry. Co.,* 7 Ind. App. 122, 34 N. E. 375; *Mills v. Detroit,* 95 Mich. 422, 54 N. W. 897; *Eddy v. Omaha,* 72 Neb. 550, 101 N. W. 25, 102 N. W. 70, 103 N. W. 692; *Ackerman v. Nutley,* 70 N. J. L. 438, 57 Atl. 150; *In re Anderson,*

60 N. Y. 457; *Joyce v. Barron,* 67 Ohio St. 264, 65 N. E. 1001; *Bank of Columbia v. Portland,* 41 Or. 1, 67 Pac. 1112.)

A. H. Bowen and Scatterday & Van Duyn, for Respondent.

The test as to whether the notice of intention complies with the law is whether it furnishes an effective opportunity to be heard and gives reasonable notice thereof. (Page & Jones, Taxation by Assessment, sec. 730; *In re Common Council of City of Amsterdam,* 126 N. Y. 158, 27 N. E. 272; *Williams v. Eggleston,* 170 U. S. 304, 18 Sup. Ct. 617, 42 L. ed. 1047.)

SULLIVAN, J.—This action was brought to restrain the city of Payette, its officers and agents, from constructing sidewalks and curbs as proposed in Ordinances Nos. 240 and 246, passed by said city. On filing the complaint the court granted a temporary restraining order and thereafter the city moved to have said order set aside, and after a hearing the motion was granted and the temporary injunction dissolved. This appeal is from the order dissolving said injunction.

The main contention of appellant is that the ordinance of intention did not state the names of the streets and alleys to be improved, and counsel contend that under sec. 2238, as amended by chap. 81, Sess. Laws 1911, p. 268, it was necessary to state in the ordinance of intention the names of the streets, alleys, etc., that were intended to be improved. Said section provides, among other things, as follows:

"4· The City Council or Trustees shall, before or during the grading, paving, or other improvement of any street or alley, the cost of which is to be levied and assessed upon the property benefited, first pass at a regular or special meeting, a resolution or ordinance declaring its intention to make such improvement, and stating in such resolution or ordinance the name of the street or alley to be improved, the points between which said improvement is to be made, the general character of the proposed improvement, and the estimate of the cost of the same, and that the cost of the same is to be assessed against the property abutting, fronting, contiguous or tributary (and included in the assessment district herein provided) on such street proposed to be improved, and shall fix the time, not less than ten (10) days in which protests against said proposed improvement may be filed in the office of the City clerk.''

Said ordinance of intention is in part as follows:

"Be it ordained by the Mayor and Council of the City of Payette, Idaho:

"Section 1. That notice is hereby given that it is the intention of the City of Payette, Idaho, by its Mayor and Council to create a local improvement district to be known as Local Sidewalk and Curbing Improvement District No. 1, of the City of Payette, for the purpose of building sidewalks and placing curbing within the territory embraced within said District, to wit:

"Beginning at the intersection of 3rd Ave. A and Sixth St., thence east along the center line of 3rd Ave. S. 1250 feet,'' etc.

The ordinance then prescribes the exterior boundaries of said improvement district and thereafter proceeds to give the number of blocks and all lots within said improvement district to be affected by said improvements.

The question then directly presented is whether the ordinance is a substantial compliance with that provision of the statute above quoted which declares that the resolution or ordinance shall give the names of the streets and alleys to be improved.

The ordinance in question gave the exterior boundaries of the district by metes and bounds along certain streets and alleys and in addition thereto gave the numbers of each block and lot to be affected by said improvement. The lot owner certainly could not be misled by not having the streets and alleys named, as the same thing was substantially accomplished by giving the exterior boundaries of the district, and the numbers of the lots and blocks within the district. Said Ordinance No. 240 conforms to the law in regard to the beginning of sidewalking and curbing and the ending of the same upon each street, since it asserts that the sidewalk and

curbing is to be laid on every street included within said
exterior boundaries. The beginning of the work on each
street would be at a point where it is intersected by one
boundary line and the termination, and ending of each would
be at the boundary line where the street is intersected at
the other end of the tract. The general character of the
improvement is stated to be "sidewalk and curb," and the
cost of the same is stated as ten cents per square foot, and
the assessment is to be made against the property abutting,
fronting, contiguous and tributary to such improvement.

We think the ordinance is a substantial compliance with
the law. The test as to whether the notice of intention complies with the law is whether it furnishes an effective opportunity to be heard and gives reasonable notice thereof to
those interested; in other words, gives to all a fair opportunity
to protest and be heard.

It is apparent from the allegations of the complaint that
the people understood what streets and alleys were to be
improved and that they had an opportunity to present a
protest, which they were authorized to do under the law.
It is alleged in the complaint that 102 other property owners,
aside from the plaintiff, protested, and said protests were
overruled and Ordinance No. 246 was passed by a vote of
the required number of councilmen. The petitioner has certainly had his opportunity to protest against the establishment
of said improvement district, since he admits that he received notice and filed his protest. He certainly has not
been damaged by any defect in said ordinance of intention.

Ordinance No. 246 substantially complies with the law in
regard to the creation of improvement districts. This ordinance properly names the district, provides the kind and
nature of the improvements, that the cost and expense thereof
shall be assessed and taxed upon all property in said improvement district and the proportion of its assessment to be
borne by the property. It names every street and says exactly where the sidewalking and curbing are to be laid, and
specifies the material of which same is to be composed. Said
ordinance provides that the council shall make the assess-

ments in proportion to the benefits to be derived, and if they fail to do that, the party injured has his remedy.

We therefore conclude that said ordinances are in substantial compliance with the provisions of the law.

After a careful consideration of other questions raised on this appeal, we are satisfied that the court did not err in the dissolution of said restraining order. The action of the court in that regard must therefore be affirmed and it is so ordered, with costs in favor of respondent.

Ailshie, C. J., concurs.

Petition for rehearing denied.

(July 9, 1914.)

SCHOOL DISTRICT No. 15, in Blaine County, Appellant, v. BLAINE COUNTY, a Municipal Corporation, Respondent.

[142 Pac. 41.]

SCHOOL DISTRICTS — ORGANIZATION OF — COUNTY SUPERINTENDENT — POWERS OF—COUNTY COMMISSIONERS—POWERS OF—APPORTIONMENT OF EXISTING INDEBTEDNESS.

1. The duty of the county superintendent to apportion the indebtedness of an organized school district between a new district formed out of the old district and the remaining area thereof should be exercised only after the necessary legal steps leading to the creation of such new district have been taken, and such apportionment is not a necessary prerequisite or jurisdictional act in the formation of such district.

2. Where all proceedings for the purpose of dividing a school district and establishing a new district out of portions of an old one are regular and favorable to such creation up to and including the action of the county commissioners, the failure of the county superintendent thereafter to apportion the bonded indebtedness of the old district between the remaining portion thereof and the new district would not defeat or invalidate the creation of such new district, even though it were the duty of the county superintendent to take such action, which latter question is not decided.

APPEAL from the District Court of the Fourth Judicial District for the County of Blaine. Hon. C. O. Stockslager, Judge.

Proceedings to reverse the judgment of the district court affirming the order of the board of county commissioners creating School District No. 61. *Affirmed.*

J. W. Edgerton and Sullivan, Sullivan & Baker, for Appellant.

Sec. 51, chap. 159, 1911 Sess. Laws, the act of the board of county commissioners, the act of the district court in affirming the action of the board, and the refusal of the county superintendent of public instruction under the provisions of said section to apportion the bonded indebtedness, impair the obligation of the contract of the bond, and bring it within the prohibition of sec. 10, of art. 1 of the constitution of the United States. It reduces the amount of land solemnly pledged for the payment of the bonds, and exempts from taxation, for the purpose of paying interest and principal, eight sections of land, which, under the law in force at the time the bonds were issued, were liable for their proportion of the bonded indebtedness. (Black on Constitutional Law, 723; 8 Cyc. 951; 35 Cyc. 973; *Callaway v. Denver & R. G. R. Co.,* 6 Colo. App. 284, 40 Pac. 573.)

McFadden & Brodhead, for Respondent.

There is nothing whatever in the law as it existed at the time of the bond issue or at this time showing that the apportionment of the debt was a "condition precedent to the creation of a new district." The county superintendent had nothing whatever to do with the apportionment until after the board had acted.

The duties imposed upon officers to be performed after the election or creation of the district were directory and ministerial, and a failure on the part of the officers to perform such a duty did not affect the validity of the school district. (*Pickett v. Board of Commissioners*, 24 Ida. 200, 133 Pac. 112.)

DAVIS, District Judge.—In this action School District No. 15, in Blaine county, has appealed from an order of the district court of the fourth judicial district confirming the action of the county commissioners of Blaine county, in creating a new district designated as District No. 61 out of the area of said former District No. 15, without first requiring the bonded indebtedness of such old district to be apportioned by the county superintendent between the remaining area of such old district and the new district.

It is stipulated that the old organized District No. 15 had created a bonded indebtedness of $4,500, and that at the time the commissioners ordered the creation of District No. 61 there was only $700 available for the payment of said bonded indebtedness, and that the commissioners did not require the county superintendent to apportion said debt as a condition precedent to the creation of said new district, and that she did not do so at any time.

The appellant claims that the county superintendent should have been required to apportion said indebtedness before the order creating said new district had been entered by the commissioners or affirmed by the court as a part of the necessary proceedings leading up to the creation of such district, and that in case she failed to make such apportionment before said order was entered or confirmed, that she should have done so immediately afterward, and that her failure to make such apportionment would render invalid and void the attempt to create such district, and that therefore the judgment of the district court should be reversed and the order of the commissioners of Blaine county creating said new District No. 61 should be set aside and declared of no effect.

The appellant has cited authorities and has argued earnestly that the law should be interpreted so as to require the county superintendent to apportion the bonded indebtedness between such districts, and that by reason of her failure to do so, the attempt to create said new district was invalid and void.

But the first question that should be considered is as to what acts are necessary to the creation of a new school district out of portions of an old one, and whether or not the apportionment of indebtedness is one of them.

The law relative to the creation of new school districts in force at the time the order appealed from was entered reads as follows (Sess. L. 1913, p. 462):

"Sec. 47 (a). The Board of County Commissioners may, at any regular meeting of said board, create new districts, or change the boundaries of existing districts, or attach to one or more districts the territory of any district which shall have lapsed for any reason. All proceedings under this section shall be commenced by petition, which must be filed in the office of the County Superintendent at least twenty (20) days preceding the meeting of the Board of Commissioners at which it is to be presented. All petitions, either for the formation of a new district or any other change of boundaries, shall set forth in general terms the proposed changes and shall be accompanied by, and refer to, a map showing all existing boundaries of districts affected and all proposed new boundaries which will be established by the granting of such petition.

"(b) A petition for a new district, whether to be created from unorganized territory or in part from territory embraced within the boundaries of one (1) or more school districts or independent school districts shall be sufficient if signed by the parents or guardians of fifteen (15) or more children of school age who are residents of the proposed new district, and no further signers shall be required. In all other cases, excepting a proposed union of contiguous districts,—proposing a change of boundaries of any district, the petition therefor must be signed by at least two thirds (⅔) of those who are heads of families and residents of each of the districts whose boundaries will be affected by the change. No such change of boundaries or organization of a new district shall take effect until the opening of the next school year."

It is evident that the law referred to does not require apportionment of a debt as a condition or preliminary to the creation of such a new district, and it is difficult to understand how the old indebtedness could effectively be apportioned before the new district has been formed. It is more reasonable to hold that the power and duty to create new school districts is vested in the county commissioners after certain preliminary steps required by law have been taken, and that the duty of the county superintendent to apportion the indebtedness of an organized school district between the remaining area thereof and a new district formed out of the old district should be exercised only after the creation of such new district by the county commissioners, and that such apportionment is not a necessary preliminary or jurisdictional act in the formation of such new district.

And where a district is thus created and all proceedings are regular, the failure of the county superintendent thereafter to apportion the bonded indebtedness of the old district between such new districts would not defeat or invalidate the creation of such districts, even though it be assumed that the superintendent should take such action. But since the nature of this proceeding is to test the legality of the creation of School District No. 61, it is not necessary in this opinion to interpret the law governing the duty of the school superintendent relative to the apportionment of bonded indebtedness after the creation of such new district.

It appears that the order appealed from was a legal exercise of authority, and is valid in every way, and the judgment of the district court is therefore affirmed. Costs awarded in favor of respondent.

Ailshie, C. J., concurs.

Sullivan, J., sat at the hearing but took no part in the decision.

(July 13, 1914.)

INA M. TRASK, Respondent, v. THE BOISE KING PLACERS COMPANY, Appellant.

[142 Pac. 1073.]

PLEADINGS—AMENDMENTS TO—INVITED ERROR—FAILURE TO DEMUR AT
PROPER TIME — APPOINTMENT OF GUARDIAN AD LITEM AFTER
TRIAL—INFORMALITY OF VERDICT—APPORTIONMENT BY COURT OF
AMOUNT OF JUDGMENT.

1. Where an action for injuries to a minor child was commenced
by the mother on the theory that the mother, as the natural guardian
of such child, could recover for such injuries, both on her own
behalf and on behalf of the minor, and the allegations of the complaint showed that to be plaintiff's theory of the case, and defendant answered on the same theory of the case, and evidence was
introduced without objection sustaining the allegations of the complaint, and at the close of the introduction of evidence and by
consent of counsel for defendant the complaint was amended by
inserting in the title of the action the additional words, "For herself and on behalf of her minor son, W. E. Trask," and other
amendments were allowed at the same time, additional instructions
covering the amendments being given by the court to the jury, and
such amendments did not involve the introduction of any further evidence or any new state of facts, and it appeared that defendant was
in no way misled or prejudiced by the making of such amendments,
the allowance thereof did not constitute a new cause of action, and
was properly granted by the court under sec. 4229, Rev. Codes.

2. A judgment will not be reversed on account of alleged errors
that have been consented to or invited, especially where it appears
that appellant has not been prejudiced thereby.

3. Under the provisions of sec. 4178, Rev. Codes, failure on the
part of defendant to seasonably raise by demurrer questions involving lack of capacity on the part of the plaintiff to sue, or
defect or misjoinder of parties, must be deemed to be a waiver of
the right to thereafter raise such questions.

4. The appointment of a guardian *ad litem* after the trial of a
case and on the hearing of a motion for new trial, by an order of
the trial court *nunc pro tunc*, is not a jurisdictional defect, but at
most an irregularity which does not of itself vitiate the proceedings.

5. Where the title of the cause as inserted in the verdict of the
jury designates the plaintiff as "Mrs. Ina M. Trask," whereas in

accordance with an amendment to the complaint previously made
by consent the words "for herself and on behalf of her minor son
W. E. Trask" should have been added, but were omitted through
inadvertence, such informality will not vitiate or render uncertain
the verdict, which is to be read with the aid of the pleadings and in
the light of the instructions of the court.

6. Indefiniteness of a verdict is not a ground for granting a new
trial under the provisions of sec. 4439, Rev. Codes.

7. Where, in an action to recover for injuries to a minor child,
the jury rendered a verdict of $8,000 in favor of the mother and
minor child, and on motion for new trial the court reduced the
judgment to $5,000, and apportioned that sum, $1,000 to the mother
and $4,000 to the minor child, on condition that the mother and
the minor, through his guardian *ad litem*, should file disclaimers of
any greater sums, and such disclaimers were filed with the court,
both the mother and the minor are bound by the judgment, and the
defendant cannot be heard to complain in the absence of any showing that it is prejudiced by the action of the court in so apportioning the judgment.

8. A minor is bound by a judgment in a case wherein he is a
party and represented by a guardian *ad litem* regularly appointed,
when such guardian accepts the judgment of the court on behalf
of his ward.

9. *Held,* that it does not appear from the record in this case
that any substantial rights of appellant have been materially affected
by any error or defect that may have occurred during the trial or
proceedings.

APPEAL from the District Court of the Third Judicial
District for Ada County. Hon. Carl A. Davis, Judge.

Action to recover for personal injury to a minor child
by the mother on behalf of herself and child. Verdict of.
$8,000 for plaintiffs, which on motion for new trial was re-
duced by the lower court to $5,000 and apportioned between
plaintiffs. From this judgment and order overruling motion,
defendant appealed. *Affirmed.*

C. H. Hartson, P. E. Cavaney and A. A. Fraser, for
Appellant.

The court erred in permitting, at the close of the trial,
the plaintiff to amend her complaint by alleging that she

brought the action for herself and on behalf of her minor
son, W. E. Trask, for the reason that such an amendment constituted an entirely new cause of action; second that no
general guardian or guardian *ad litem* had been appointed
for the minor; third, for the reason that the action was not
prosecuted in the name of W. E. Trask. (Sec. 4095, Rev.
Codes; *McCloskey v. Sweeney,* 66 Cal. 53, 4 Pac. 943; *Johnston v. San Francisco Sav. Union,* 63 Cal. 554.)

The action must be brought in the name of the minor and
not in the name of the guardian on behalf of the minor.
(*Fox v. Minor,* 32 Cal. 111; 91 Am. Dec. 566; *Wilson v.
Wilson,* 36 Cal. 447, 451, 95 Am. Dec. 194.)

If a new cause of action is injected into the suit by an
amendment or otherwise, the attorneys in the original action
have no authority to bind their client in the new proceeding
by accepting process of any kind. (*Ashcraft v. Powers,* 22
Wash. 440, 61 Pac. 161; *Erskine v. McIlrath,* 60 Minn. 485,
62 N. W. 1130.)

An order can be entered *nunc pro tunc* to make a record
of what was previously done by the court, although not then
entered, but where the court has wholly omitted to make an
order which it might or ought to have made, it cannot afterward be entitled *nunc pro tunc.* (25 Cyc. 1516; *State ex
rel. Gordon Hardware Co. v. Langley,* 13 Wash. 636, 43 Pac.
875; *Southern Pac. Co. v. Pender* (Ariz.), 134 Pac. 289;
Clark v. Bank of Hennessey, 14 Okl. 572, 79 Pac. 217, 2 Ann.
Cas. 219; *Clark v. Strouse,* 11 Nev. 76; *Lombard v. Wade,*
37 Or. 426, 61 Pac. 856; 1 Black on Judgments, sec. 132.)

. Such orders are issued to make the record conform to the
truth   (*State v. Bush,* 136 Mo. App. 608, 118 S. W. 670;
Gormley v. St. Louis Transit Co., 126 Mo. App. 405, 103
S. W. 1147); and supply only the record not the order.
(*Finch v. Finch,* 111 Ill. App. 481; *Klein v. Southern Pac.
Co.,* 140 Fed. 213.)

When a case is tried by a jury, one verdict settles the
whole issue, and unless set aside, furnishes the complete basis
of a judgment, which cannot in anything depart from it;
and there is and can be no issue which the jury do not dis-

pose of. (*Brown v. Kalamazoo Circuit Judge*, 75 Mich. 274, 13 Am. St. 438, 42 N. W. 827, 5 L. R. A. 226; *First Nat. Bank v. Vander Stucken* (Tex. Civ. App.), 37 S. W. 170.) "The verdict forms the basis of the judgment and hence the judgment must conform thereto." (*Clark v. Clark*, 21 Tex. Civ. App. 371, 51 S. W. 337; *Letot v. Peacock* (Tex. Civ. App.), 94 S. W. 1121.)

A judgment must conform to the verdict not only as to the amount, but as to the parties against whom the finding is made. (*Morsch v. Besack*, 52 Neb. 502, 72 N. W. 953; *Dysart v.' Terrell* (Tex. Civ. App.), 70 S. W. 986; *Galveston H. & S. A. Ry. Co. v. Johnson*, 24 Tex Civ. App. 180, 58 S. W. 622; *Smith v. Eagle Mfg. Co.*, 25 Okl. 404, 108 Pac. 626.)

Where there are two plaintiffs or two defendants, and the judgment is against only one, and fails to designate which one, the judgment is void for uncertainty. It must state for which one it is given. (*Holt v. Gridley*, 7 Ida. 416, 63 Pac. 188; *Richards v. Scott*, 7 Ida. 726, 65 Pac. 433.)

A several judgment cannot be entered on a joint verdict. (23 Cyc. 823; *Eastman v. Jennings-McRae Logging Co.* (Or.), 138 Pac. 216.)

In actions *ex delicto* the cause of action alleged in the original pleading must be adhered to and its identity preserved, and hence a change by way of amendment, pleadin : a different liability on the part of the defendant, is an attempt to introduce a new and distinct cause of action and the amendment will not be allowed. (31 Cyc. 416; *Central of Georgia Ry. Co. v. Williams*, 105 Ga. 70, 31 S. E. 134.)

Earl C. Miller and E. G. Davis, for Respondents.

The court may, in the furtherance of justice, allow a party to amend any pleading or proceeding by adding or striking out the name of any party. (Sec. 4229, Rev. Codes; *Perine v. Grand Lodge A. O. U. W.*, 48 Minn. 82, 50 N. W. 1022.)

The appellants, being clearly apprised of the complaint, were authorized, under sec. 4174, Rev. Codes, to demur. Their failure to do so must be regarded, under sec. 4178, as a waiver. (*Bonham Nat. Bank v. Grimes Pass Placer Min. Co.*, 18 Ida. 629, 633, 111 Pac. 1078; *Porter v. Title Guaranty & Surety Co.*, 21 Ida. 312, 121 Pac. 548; *Smith v. Carney*, 127 Mass. 179.)

The omission of the name of the minor in an action by his guardian is not a jurisdictional defect and is one which may be remedied by amendment. (*Love v. Southern Ry. Co.*, 108 Tenn. 104, 65 S. W. 475, 55 L. R. A. 471; 31 Cyc. 738; *Lombard v. Morse*, 155 Mass. 136, 29 N. E. 205, 14 L. R. A. 273; *Delisle v. Bourriague*, 105 La. 77, 29 So. 731; 54 L. R. A. 420; *Deming v. Darling*, 148 Mass. 504,' 20 N. E. 107, 2 L. R. A. 743; *St. Louis A. T. Ry. Co. v. Triplett*, 54 Ark. 289, 15 S. W. 831, 11 L. R. A. 773; *Chicago etc. R. Co. v. Shaw*, 63 Neb. 380, 88 N. W. 508, 56 L. R. A. 341.)

The omission to appoint a guardian *ad litem* of an infant plaintiff before the bringing of an action is not a jurisdictional defect, but is an irregularity merely. (*Rima v. Rossie Iron Works*, 120 N. Y. 433, 24 N. E. 940; *Jones v. Steele*, 36 Mo. 324; *Chudleigh v. Chicago etc. P. Ry. Co.*, 51 Ill. App. 491; *Evans v. Collier*, 79 Ga. 319, 4 S. E. 266.)

Courts have authority to appoint guardians *ad litem* by orders issued *nunc pro tunc*. (*Guild v. Cranston*, 8 Cush. (62 Mass.) 506; *West Chicago St. R. Co. v. Johnson*, 77 Ill. App. 142; *Hamilton v. Foster*, 1 Brev. (S. C.) 464; *Rima v. Rossie Iron Works, supra.*)

The power to allow amendments at any time before final judgment is ample. It may well be exercised where some error has been made in bringing a suit for a minor. (*Drew v. Farnsworth*, 186 Mass. 365; 71 N. E. 783; *Smith v. Carney*, 127 Mass, 179; *Wolford v. Oakley*, 43 How. Pr. (N. Y.) 118.)

A caption to a verdict naming the parties is surplusage, and an error therein should be disregarded. (*Rogers v. Overton*, 87 Ind. 410.)

On the question of whether or not the minor is bound by the verdict, see *Watkins v. Lawton*, 69 Ga. 671; *Evans v. Collier*, 79 Ga. 319, 322; 4 S. E. 266; *Taylor v. Pullen*, 152 Mo. 434, 53 S. W. 1086; *Rima v. Rossie Iron Works, supra.*

A verdict should receive a reasonable construction, aided by the petition and in the light of the instructions. (14 Current Law, 2340, 2341, and authorities cited.)

A verdict is sufficient if it is intelligible and can be rendered certain by reference to the pleadings. (*James v. Wilson*, 7 Tex. 230; *Smith v. Johnson*, 8 Tex. 418; *Westphal v. Sipc*, 62 Ill. App. 111; *Texas & P. Ry. Co. v. Watkins* (Tex. Civ. App.), 26 S. W. 760; *Shannon v. Jones*, 76 Tex. 141, 13 S. W. 477.)

A judgment should not be reversed where the appellant does not show that he has been prejudiced by an erroneous ruling of the court below. (*Fegtly v. Village Blacksmith Min. Co.*, 18 Ida. 536, 111 Pac. 129; *Rowley v. Stack-Gibbs Lumber Co.*, 19 Ida. 107, 12 Pac. 1041; *Nobach v. Scott*, 20 Ida. 558; 119 Pac. 295; *Jones v. Parrish*, 1 Pinn. (Wis.), 494; *Green v. Gilbert*, 21 Wis. 395, 401; *Corcoran v. Harran*, 55 Wis 121, 12 N. W. 468; *Dawson v. Wisner*, 11 Iowa, 6.)

The district court may impose conditions upon the successful party to avoid the granting of a new trial in actions of either contracts or torts (*Brockman v. Berryhill*, 16 Iowa 183), and "upon condition that plaintiff will remit such sum as will, in the judgment of the court, leave the recovery not excessive." (*Pratt v. Pioneer Press Co.*, 35 Minn. 251, 28 N. W. 708.)

"When the assent of the party is obtained whom alone the correction will prejudice, the other party has nothing of which to complain; such order of the court being in his favor." (*Broquet v. Tripp*, 36 Kan. 700, 14 Pac. 227.)

A court may make a division of a judgment where the verdict of the jury has been for a lump sum. (*Galveston H. & S. A. Ry. Co. v. Johnson*, 24 Tex. Civ. App. 180, 58 S. W. 622.)

AILSHIE, C. J.—This action was instituted by the plaintiff Mrs. Ina M. Trask, on her own behalf and on behalf of her minor son, W. E. Trask, to recover damages alleged to have occurred through the negligence of the defendant company. The defendant answered and the case was thereafter tried by the court with a jury and a verdict returned in favor of the plaintiff in the sum of $8,000, and this appeal is from the judgment made and entered therein and also from an order denying a new trial.

Appellant urges that the court erred in permitting the plaintiff at the close of the trial to amend her complaint by alleging that she brought the action for herself and on behalf of her minor son, W. E. Trask. This objection is based upon the contention that the amendment constituted an entirely new cause of action, and that no general guardian or guardian *ad litem* had been appointed for the minor, and for the further reason that the action was not prosecuted in the name of W. E. Trask.

It is clearly shown by the complaint, and indeed is admitted on all sides, that the action was commenced on the theory that the mother, *as the natural guardian of her minor son*, could, under the law, recover for the injuries sustained both by herself and her minor son through the negligence of the defendant.

A general demurrer to the complaint was filed but was overruled.

It appears from the answer that the defendant proceeded on the same theory as to the rights of the plaintiff to litigate the cause of action both in her favor and that of her minor son. The court seems to have accepted this theory of the case, and the evidence was admitted without objection tending to support and establish the allegations of the complaint upon this theory, and in a written order made by the court after the trial it is stated as follows:

"And while this case was undoubtedly tried by all parties on the theory that W. E. Trask was an interested party, and there is uncertainty as to the law applicable on some points involved, it appears proper to endeavor to correct the record so as not to prejudice the defendants' rights and to permit the judgment to stand," etc.

The case proceeded throughout the trial upon the theory above stated. The court prepared its instructions and had read them to the jury and the case was ready for argument when the hour for the noon recess arrived. At the opening of the afternoon session, counsel for defendants came into court and requested an additional instruction to the effect that upon the face of the pleadings, the plaintiff could recover only those damages actually sustained by herself and not those sustained by her minor son. After some argument, counsel for plaintiff moved to amend the complaint by inserting in the title the additional words, "For Herself and on Behalf of Her Minor Son, W. E. Trask," and also proposed other amendments. Counsel for both parties consented to these amendments and also consented to certain amendments to the answer. Thereafter additional instructions were agreed upon and given to the jury by the court covering the amendments. It appears that forms of verdict had been prepared by the court and were ready to be handed to the jury before these amendments to the complaint and answer were made and were not changed after the amendments, and that is evidently the reason why the title was not changed to conform to the amendments.

A motion for a new trial was made and on the hearing of this motion, defendants raised for the first time the proposition that the minor was not bound by the judgment and that the defendants could not be bound. At that time W. E. Trask applied to the court for the appointment of a guardian *ad litem* by an order *nunc pro tunc*, as of the date of the beginning of the trial. Thereupon the court issued the order authorizing the minor to apply for the appointment of some suitable person as guardian *ad litem*, which appointment was made, and also an order was made authorizing Mrs. Trask to file a disclaimer of any interest in the judgment in excess of $1,000, and authorizing the guardian *ad litem* to file a disclaimer on the part of the minor of any sum in excess of $4,000. The court concluded to reduce the judgment from $8,000 to $5,000 or grant a new trial, and concluded to apportion the judgment of $5,000 as above indicated. Thereupon Theodore Daniels was appointed as guardian *ad litem* for the minor and the disclaimers required by the court were duly filed.

The court thereupon entered judgment in favor of Mrs. Trask in the sum of $1,000 and in favor of the minor in the sum of $4,000.

It is not contended that the amendments so consented to involved the introduction of any further evidence or involved any new state of facts. The evidence establishing Mrs. Trask's cause of action in favor of herself as well as the evidence establishing the cause of action in favor of the minor had been submitted for consideration by the jury and upon that state of facts the case comes to this court.

It may be conceded in the outset that the objections here urged are well taken had they been timely and seasonably raised in the lower court. The appellant is now in the position, however, of urging a reversal of the judgment on errors that have been consented to or invited. It is contrary to the uniform holdings of the courts to allow a case to be reversed under such circumstances. Parties cannot stand by and permit the court to act with their consent, and without objection, and thereafter successfully wage objection on appeal. (*Nobach v. Scott*, 20 Ida. 558, 119 Pac. 295.) In this case counsel for the defendants recognized the minor son as the real plaintiff in the case throughout the trial of the case, and so the addition of his name after the trial was over was not in fact the addition of either a new party or a new cause of action in so far as it would have any tendency to either mislead or prejudice the adverse party. Under the provisions of sec. 4229, Rev. Codes, "the court may, in furtherance of justice and on such terms as may be proper, allow a party to amend any pleading or proceeding by adding or striking out the name of any party."

This action was admittedly filed and prosecuted on the theory that the mother as plaintiff, under the provisions of sec. 4099, Rev. Codes, could recover for the damages sustained by her minor son, as well as for those sustained by herself. The complaint alleged the general guardianship of the mother, and the defendants were notified by the allegations that the mother was suing for damages not only sustained by herself but by her minor son. Defendants came into court and answered upon the same theory advanced by the plaintiff in her complaint, and the case was tried from the beginning to the time of giving instructions to the jury on that theory. The defendant should have raised this question by demurrer, but failed to do so. Under the provisions of sec. 4178, Rev. Codes, the failure to raise the questions here involved by demurrer must be deemed to have been a waiver.

It has been held by this court as well as by other courts that if there is a defect or misjoinder of parties, or lack of capacity to sue, that such question should be raised by demurrer, and if not so raised it is a waiver. (*Bonham Nat. Bank v. Grimes Pass Placer Min. Co.*, 18 Ida. 629, 633, 111 Pac. 1078; *Porter v. Title Guaranty & Surety Co.*, 21 Ida. 312, 121 Pac. 548.)

It must also be conceded that the action of the court was irregular, if not erroneous, in appointing a guardian after the case had been tried.

In *Rima v. Rossic Iron Works*, 120 N. Y. 433, 24 N. E. 940, it was held that the omission to appoint a guardian *ad litem* of an infant plaintiff before the bringing of an action is not a jurisdictional defect, but is an irregularity merely. To the same effect, see *Clowers v. Wabash etc. Ry. Co.*, 21 Mo. App. 213; *Wolford v. Oakley*, 43 How. Pr. (N. Y.) 118.

In *Drew v. Farnsworth*, 186 Mass. 365, 71 N. E. 783, the supreme court of Massachusetts suggests that the power to allow amendments in that state was a sufficient justification for granting relief "when some error has been made in a writ bringing a suit for a minor."

While the minor would not have been bound by the judgment had he not subsequently had a guardian appointed, he is bound where the guardian has been duly and regularly appointed and has come into court and accepted the judgment, and thereby bound himself and his ward by the results of the trial previously had. This binds the minor.

In *Watkins v. Lawton*, 69 Ga. 671, the court, considering a kindred question, held that where one, for himself and as next of kin of certain minors, and to protect their interests, filed a bill in equity, to which a cross-bill was filed, the entire matter litigated and a decree rendered, in the absence of all allegation or proof of fraud, the minor would be bound thereby, and persons acquiring rights thereunder would be protected, though no formal order appears appointing the complainant as guardian *ad litem* for the minors.

Counsel also contends that the verdict is uncertain and that the court erred in entering judgment upon it. It is an established rule that "A general verdict must be responsive to the issues made by pleadings sufficient in themselves, be consistent with the case, supported by the law and the evidence, in conformity with the instructions, sufficiently definite to support the judgment, and not in excess of the amount asked for in the pleading or of the amount proven. Mere informality will not vitiate a verdict if it appear that no injustice is done and the meaning is clear. . . . . A verdict should receive a reasonable construction, aided by the petition, and in the light of the instructions." (14 Current Law, pp. 2340, 2341.) Measured by this rule, we think the verdict is amply sufficient, as, between the parties, it finds for the plaintiff; it designates clearly the amount of the recovery and the judgment based upon this verdict does not go beyond it in any essential particular. It is not claimed by appellants that the verdict is not supported by the evidence. The most claimed is that it is indefinite, and that is not a ground for granting a new trial under the provisions of sec. 4439, Rev. Codes.

Under the provisions of sec. 4439, Rev. Codes, the verdict or other decision may be vacated and a new trial granted on the application of the party aggrieved, for any of the causes enumerated in that section "materially affecting the substantial rights of such party." Sec. 4231, Rev. Codes, provides that "The court must, in every stage of an action, disregard any error or defect in the pleadings or proceedings which does not affect the substantial rights of the parties and that no judgment shall be reversed or affected by reason of such error or defect."

It does not appear that any substantial rights of the appellants have been materially affected by any error or defect that occurred in the proceedings or trial of this case. (*Fegtly v. Village Blacksmith Mining Co.*, 18 Ida. 536, 111 Pac. 129; *Rowley v. Stack-Gibbs Co.*, 19 Ida. 107, 112 Pac. 1041; *Nobach v. Scott*, 20 Ida. 558, 119 Pac. 295.)

In this case the jury rendered a verdict in favor of the plaintiffs for $8,000 and the court reduced it to $5,000, and apportioned that $5,000 between the minor and his mother. Both the mother and the minor are bound by the judgment as it comes here. It does not appear that the appellants were in any way injured by the action of the court in apportioning the judgment between the mother and the minor.

Not finding any reversible error in the record, the judgment should be affirmed, and it is so ordered, with costs in favor of the respondents.

Sullivan, J., concurs.

Petition for rehearing denied.

————————

(July 18, 1914.)

THE VILLAGE OF AMERICAN FALLS, a Municipal Corporation, Respondent, v. W. A. WEST, Appellant.

[142 Pac. 42.]

NUISANCE—ACTION TO ABATE NUISANCE—MUNICIPAL CORPORATION—
PARTY PLAINTIFF—CREATION OF NEW COUNTIES—NEW COUNTIES—
PROHIBITION TERRITORY—LICENSED SALOON LAWFUL BUSINESS—
LICENSED SALOON MAY NOT BE ABATED AS A NUISANCE.

1. A village is a proper party plaintiff to bring an action in the district court to obtain the abatement of a public nuisance causing special injury to the rights, morals or interests of such village, even though such nuisance be outside the village boundaries.

2. Where a new county is created from territory which was formerly comprised in "dry" counties and also territory that was formerly part of a "wet" county, and the legislature makes no pro-

vision as to whether the new county shall be a "wet" or "dry" county until a local option election is held in such county, *held*, that the whole of the new county so created becomes a "wet" county and subject to the license system until such time as the voters of the county shall vote the county "dry" under the provisions of the local option statute.

3. A saloon regularly licensed to sell intoxicating liquor within wet territory is thus expressly authorized by law to sell such liquor. And even though the results of such business be disastrous and deplorable, and are the direct cause of what would amount to a public nuisance had such license not been granted, the running of such saloon in the usual and regular manner authorized by law under such license cannot legally be abated as a nuisance, because sec. 3659, Rev. Codes, provides that "Nothing which is done or maintained under the express authority of a statute can be deemed a nuisance."

4. If the owner of a saloon takes an unfair advantage of his opportunity to handle liquor, and goes beyond his rights, granted under his license, to do things that amount to a public nuisance, such things should be abated, even though they are done in connection with a licensed saloon or are an effect thereof. The proper conduct of a lawful business cannot be enjoined, but its abuses and excesses may be prevented.

APPEAL from the District Court of the Fifth Judicial District for the County of Power. Hon. Alfred Budge, Judge.

Action to abate a nuisance. Judgment for plaintiff. Defendant appeals. *Reversed.*

P. E. Cavaney and Baird & Davis, for Appellant.

Within its territorial limits the right of a municipality to maintain the action depends upon the same condition as the right of the individual or private corporation; it must have suffered some special injury. (*Morris Canal & C. Co. v. Jersey City*, 12 N. J. Eq. 252, 547.)

Even in cases where municipalities have been, by their charters, duly authorized to pass ordinances to remove and abate any nuisance injurious to the public health, it is recognized that such provision delegates authority to abate a nui-

sance only within its corporate limits. (*Village of Pine City
v. Munch,* 42 Minn. 342, 44 N. W. 197, 6 L. R. A. 763.)

If Blaine county was wet prior to the formation of Power
county, that portion of Power county taken from Blaine
county would remain wet as part of Power county until the
individuals of Power county, as a county, should hold the
necessary election, as provided by the laws of the state for
determining the question as to whether Power county should
be wet or dry. (Woollen & Thornton, Intox. Liquors, sec.
548, note 25; *Prestwood v. State,* 88 Ala. 235, 7 So. 259;
Oxley v. Allen, 49 Tex. Civ. App. 90, 107 S. W. 945; *Ex parte
Pollard,* 51 Tex. Cr. App. 488, 103 S. W. 878; *In re Cunningham,* 21 Can. Prac. 459; *Ex parte McCleaver,* 21 N. B. 315.)

"If a local option county be divided and an entirely new
one created, local option continues in force in the new
county." (Woollen & Thornton, sec. 548, note 25; *Parker
v. State,* 126 Ga. 443, 55 S. E. 329; *Moore v. State,* 126 Ga.
414, 55 S. E. 327; *Amerker v. Taylor,* 81 S. C. 163, 62 S. E.
7.)

"Where the statute designates who may maintain a proceeding to abate a liquor nuisance it can only be maintained
by the person designated." (Joyce on Intoxicating Liquors,
sec. 624; *Applegate v. Winebrenner,* 66 Iowa, 67, 23 N. W.
267; Thornton & Woollen, Intoxicating Liquors, sec. 585.)

Equity will not enjoin a criminal nuisance merely to sub-
serve the public welfare. There must be a statute declaring
the criminal act to be a nuisance *per se.* (*State v. Vaughan,*
81 Ark. 117, 118 Am. St. 29, 98 S. W. 685, 11 Ann. Cas. 277,
7 L. R. A., N. S., 899; *Marshall v. Board of Managers,* 201
Ill. 9, 66 N. E. 314; *Indian Land & Trust Co. v. Shoenfelt,*
135 Fed. 484, 68 C. C. A. 196; *Stevens v. De La Vaulx,* 166
Mo. 20, 65 S. W. 1003; *Hedges v. Dixon Co.,* 150 U. S. 182,
14 Sup. Ct. 71, 37 L. ed. 1044.)

If the court should find that a nuisance exists in this case,
only a qualified decree could be entered prohibiting the particular acts complained of and not to close up the entire business. (*Lorenzi v. Star Market Co.,* 19 Ida. 674, 115 Pac.
490, 35 L. R. A., N. S., 1142.)

The lower court in the case at bar made a decree absolutely prohibiting the selling of intoxicating liquors at the said Doc West saloon. The court cannot restrain the business carried on on said premises in a lawful way. (*Fresno v. Fresno Canal etc. Co.*, 98 Cal. 183, 32 Pac. 944, 37 Cent. Dig. "Nuisance," 199; *Georgia R. R. & B. Co. v. Maddox*, 116 Ga. 54, 42 S. E. 315; *Green v. Lake*, 54 Miss. 540, 28 Am. Rep. 378; *Cleveland v. Citizens' Gas Co.*, 20 N. J. Eq. 201; *Chamberlain v. Douglas*, 24 App. Div. 582, 48 N. Y. Supp. 710; *Weaver v. Kuchler*, 17 Okl. 189, 87 Pac. 600; *Wilcox v. Henry*, 35 Wash. 591, 77 Pac. 1055; *Minke v. Hopeman*, 87 Ill. 450, 29 Am. Rep. 63; *Richards v. Holt*, 61 Iowa, 529, 16 N. W. 595; *Sawyer v. State Board of Health*, 125 Mass. 182; Dec. Dig. "Nuisance," secs. 35–84; 29 Cyc. 1249; *Haggart v. Stehlin*, 137 Ind. 43, 35 N. E. 997, 22 L. R. A. 577.)

Bissell & Baum, for Respondent.

"Where the complaint alleges the corporate capacity of the plaintiff and that by some threatened act defendant will create a nuisance or is about to commit some act that will endanger the health of the inhabitants of the city or village or that it will result in the damage to the property of the city or village or may be the means of causes of action for damage against the city or village, equity will grant relief." (*Village of Sandpoint v. Doyle*, 11 Ida. 642, 83 Pac. 598, 4 L. R. A., N. S., 810.)

"A municipal corporation, as such, has a right to invoke the aid of equity to prevent a threatened injury to its corporate property or to the lives, health and comfort of its citizens, even though the source of such threatened injury is outside of the corporate limits of the municipality." (*Baltimore v. Warren Mfg. Co.*, 59 Md. 96; *Indianapolis Water Co. v. American Straw Board Co.*, 57 Fed. 1000; *McCallum v. Germantown Water Co.*, 54 Pa. 40, 93 Am. Dec. 656.)

DAVIS, District Judge.—This is an action wherein the village of American Falls prays for an injunction to prevent the running of a saloon by the defendant outside the limits

of such town but near-by and easily accessible therefrom, on
the ground that said saloon is within what should be "dry"
territory, and, although licensed, that it has no legal right
to exist, and that it results in a public nuisance injuriously
affecting the decency, good name and reputation of the inhabitants of American Falls, and has become a menace to
the peace, health, safety and morals of the citizens thereof.

The district court found for the plaintiff and issued the
injunction sought, from which judgment the defendant
appeals.

The most serious questions raised are as to the sufficiency
of the complaint; the right of a village to sue to abate a
nuisance outside of its limits; as to the jurisdiction of the
court in such cases; whether the territory where the saloon
was located was wet or dry; and whether or not the saloon
as conducted resulted in a public nuisance causing special
injury to plaintiff.

A village is a corporate entity with the right to sue in a
proper court, if necessary to protect or secure its rights.
(Sec. 2236, Rev. Codes.)   Such a village is a municipal corporation created to assist in the civil government of its people
and the territory within its limits.   It has the power and duty
of preserving the health and protecting the personal rights,
morals and property of its inhabitants, and as an effective
means of doing so such village may bring an action in the
district court in order to secure the removal and abatement of
a public nuisance causing special injury to the rights, morals
or interests of such village.   If the people within a village, in
their aggregate capacity, are specially injured by a public
nuisance, such village is directly interested in having such
nuisance abated.   And while a village itself might abate a
nuisance within its limits, in order to abate a public nuisance
outside its boundaries it is probably necessary, and undoubtedly proper, for it to apply to a court of equity for aid in
protecting it from such harmful influence.   (1 Dillon, Mun.
Corp., par. 379; *Village of Sandpoint v. Doyle*, 11 Ida. 642,
83 Pac. 598, 4 L. R. A., N. S., 810; *Village of Pine City v.
Munch*, 42 Minn. 342, 44 N. W. 197, 6 L. R. A. 763; *Mayor*

etc. of Baltimore v. Warren Mfg. Co., 59 Md. 96; *Indianapolis Water Co. v. American Strawboard Co.*, 57 Fed. 1000; *McCallum v. Germantown Water Co.*, 54 Pa. 40, 93 Am. Dec. 656.)

The complaint states a cause of action, and the district court had jurisdiction to try the case.

The next question is: Was the saloon attacked as a nuisance legally authorized to exist? It had a license from the county to run, but the authority of Power county to issue such license is denied, on the ground that Power county was created out of portions of Bingham, Cassia and Oneida counties, theretofore dry, and a smaller portion, with fewer people, from Blaine county, previously wet. And it is held by the trial judge and contended by the plaintiff that the new county should therefore be dry in its entirety. But there is no law in Idaho, nor implied power, whereby a portion of a wet county may be made dry merely by joining it with an area of dry territory, however large or populous, when creating a new county. The provisions of the local option law are made applicable only by a vote of the people of the territory affected, and there is no showing here that the people of Power county had indicated their desire for a dry county by a majority vote in favor thereof, or otherwise, at the time this action was brought.

And yet I dissent from the other extreme view adopted by a majority of this court, and announced in paragraph 2 of the syllabus, to the effect that a new county created from other counties becomes wet automatically by virtue of such creation, even though such area had been dry theretofore. The most logical position to hold is that where a new county is created out of portions of other counties, some of which have adopted the provisions of the local option law, and some are operating under the license system, that portion of the new county which was subject to the license system at the time of the creation thereof continues subject to the law permitting licensed saloons to exist, and the dry area remains dry, until the status of such new county in its entirety relative to the liquor question is legally determined.

The legal status of an area relative to the liquor question should not be changed by a law·on another subject entirely, when such question is not involved or directly considered. And when a community has settled the question, its action should not be set aside until some direct action by the inhabitants of such area may be taken on the subject.

Under the decision rendered by a majority of this court, the liquor question will hereafter be a direct issue in every county division fight, and although either is in itself a serious problem, when considered together it may reasonably be anticipated that in the future practically all of the time of the legislature will be occupied struggling with such controversies. And in addition to being supported by reason, this view is maintained by a large majority of the authorities. (Woollen & Thornton, Intoxicating Liquors, sec. 548, cases there cited and notes.)

While the evidence is not before this court, it appears from the findings of fact made by the district court that the people of American Falls may well be solicitous as to the peace, morals and property interests of their community. The saloon which the plaintiff seeks to abate is undoubtedly a menace to the welfare of the inhabitants of American Falls and is a public nuisance in the ordinary sense of the expression. Probably some of the evil results complained of would flow naturally and regularly from the saloon as such, although it were conducted according to law, and the same things in effect may emanate from any saloon, but they are probably greater in degree in this instance because of the monopoly of business enjoyed by the defendant over a large territory and the local conditions under which he operates. It appears, however, that some of the injuries complained of flow from improper and illegal acts of the defendant because of the manner of conducting his saloon.

The officers vested with authority to license a saloon may properly consider the moral effect of such business upon the community where located, and the people of the county and the state are entitled to debate the advisability of allowing saloons to exist. but this court can neither exercise discretion as to what law shall be invoked, nor consider the propriety of the law applicable. It is our duty to enforce the law which governs the matter just as it is written in the codes, and if the law ought to be changed in order to afford full relief from the evils alleged, or if the terms of some other law should be made applicable, then the judgment and action of those who have authority to make or apply other laws must be appealed to for such relief.

The local option prohibitory law is not applicable to the territory where the saloon complained of is located and the law authorizing a license to sell liquor is in force therein. And a saloon regularly licensed to sell intoxicating liquor within wet territory is expressly authorized by law to sell such liquor. And even though the results of such business be disastrous and deplorable, and are the direct cause of what would amount to a public nuisance had such license not been granted, the running of such saloon in the usual and regular manner authorized by law under such license cannot legally be abated as a nuisance, because sec. 3659, Rev. Codes, provides that "Nothing which is done or maintained under the express authority of a statute can be deemed a nuisance."

Where the legislature expressly authorizes a thing to be done, under certain conditions, and thereby legalizes it, the doing of that thing as authorized would not be a public nuisance subject to abatement, although it inevitably results in a great public injury; but to justify acts that would amount to a public nuisance, if not expressly authorized, they must be the natural, probable and reasonable result of the thing authorized.

However, if the saloon owner takes an unfair advantage of his opportunity to handle liquor, and goes beyond the rights granted under his license, to do things that amount to a public nuisance, such things should be abated, even though such things are done in connection with a licensed saloon or are an effect thereof. The proper conduct of a lawful business cannot be enjoined, but its abuses and excesses may be prevented. (*Lorenzi v. Star Market Co.*, 19 Ida. 674, 115 Pac. 490, 35 L. R. A., N. S., 1142.)

It appears, therefore, that the saloon involved in this action has a lawful right to exist so long as it is run properly within the terms of the law, but that all acts and things done or permitted outside of the regular and proper operation of the saloon and the natural results therefrom, that cause a public nuisance specially affecting the plaintiff, may and should be abated.

The judgment of the district court is reversed, and the case is remanded with directions to the trial court that such court enter a judgment authorizing and permitting the defendant to conduct the saloon referred to in the pleadings and to sell intoxicating liquor therein in the manner allowed by his license and the law applicable thereto. But that he be enjoined from operating said saloon in any manner other than that authorized by law and the license granted him by Power county; from running said saloon in a disorderly manner; from urging, inducing or compelling persons purchasing liquor from him to convey the liquor outside the building into American Falls, or to drink the same upon the highways, byways or in the streets, alleys or public or private buildings of said town; from allowing women or minors in said saloon; from selling liquor to intoxicated persons or minors; from allowing children to resort to said saloon for any purpose; and that in case he does not comply strictly with the foregoing terms of said injunction while engaged in so conducting said saloon, that he shall not operate or maintain said saloon at all.

Each party to pay one-half the costs on appeal.

SULLIVAN, J., Dissenting in Part and Concurring in Part.—(1) I am unable to concur in the conclusion reached by Judge Davis, to the effect that the village is a proper party plaintiff in this action. Under the law the village is not authorized to maintain an action to abate a public nuisance, such a one as is alleged in the complaint, since it clearly appears that the nuisance, if one exists, affects all of Power county and several other counties in southeastern Idaho, and is not located within the corporate limits of the Village of

American Falls. Under the provisions of sec. 3666, Rev. Codes, a public nuisance may only be abated by "public body or officer authorized thereto by law." We have no statute whatever authorizing a village to bring an action for the abatement of a nuisance such as the one alleged in this case, outside of its corporate limits. Under the 4th section of the local option act (Sess. Laws 1911, p. 30), the prosecuting attorney of any county is authorized to bring an action in the name of the state to abate and perpetually enjoin the common nuisance of selling liquor in a prohibition district. Since the trial court found that said Power county was a prohibition district, it is clear under the law that the village had no right to maintain the action, as it should be brought by the prosecuting attorney in the name of the state. After the trial court had concluded that said Power county was "dry," it was error for it not to dismiss the case and permit the prosecuting attorney of said county to institute the action authorized by said section 4 of the local option act.

(2) I cannot concur with Judge Davis in holding that said Power county, having been created out of parts of "dry" counties and a part of a "wet" county, that the territory taken from the said "dry" counties remains "dry" and the territory taken from the "wet" county remains "wet." Under the provisions of our local option statute, no county can become "dry" except by a majority vote of all the people of such county. That law does not provide for a county part "wet" and part "dry," under any conditions or circumstances.

(3) I concur in the conclusion reached by Judge Davis that the judgment of the trial court must be reversed and that a judgment should be entered in favor of the defendant permitting him to conduct his saloon under the laws of the state. Of course, if he is conducting his business in a way and manner not authorized by law and is creating a public nuisance, he may be enjoined from those specific acts which he is not authorized to do under the intoxicating liquor and other laws of this state, by the state or persons authorized by law to bring an action for that purpose.

AILSHIE, C. J., Concurring in Part and Dissenting in Part.—I agree with Judge Davis that the city of American Falls can maintain this action, and I agree with Justice Sullivan that when a new county is created by act of the legislature, it becomes a "wet" county or a "dry" county in its entirety and not in spots. The legislature has a right to say whether the new county will be wet or dry until an election takes place under the local option law, but if the legislature fails to provide which it will be, then, under the general law, it would be subject to the license system.

I dissent from a reversal of the judgment. The record brought before us shows that the appellant was maintaining a nuisance, and the trial court has the right and power to abate a nuisance. A lawful business may degenerate into a nuisance or be so conducted as to become a nuisance, and the same may be true of a business conducted on mere sufferance of the state.

(September 19, 1914.)

In re DRAINAGE DISTRICT No. 1 of CANYON COUNTY.

[143 Pac. 299.]

CONSTITUTIONAL LAW—JOURNALS OF THE HOUSE—EVIDENCE—PASSAGE OF BILLS—WHAT JOURNAL ENTRIES MUST AFFIRMATIVELY SHOW—PRESUMPTION.

1. Under the provisions of sec. 15, art. 3, of the constitution, it is provided that no bill shall become a law unless the same shall have been read on three several days in each House previous to its final passage; provided, however, in case of urgency two thirds of the House where such bill may be pending may, upon a vote of the yeas and nays, dispense with that provision.

2. Under the provisions of sec. 13, art. 3, each House is required to keep a journal of its proceedings, and the yeas and nays of the members of each House on any question may be, at the request of three members, entered on the journal.

3. The journal entries made by either House may be resorted to as evidence to prove either the regularity or the irregularity of the passage of a law.

4. . It will not be presumed in any case from the mere silence of the journals that either House has exceeded its authority or disregarded a constitutional requirement in the passage of legislative acts, unless where the constitution has expressly required the journals to show the actions taken, as, for instance, where it requires the yeas and nays to be entered.

5. Unless the journal shows affirmatively that the legislature has failed to comply with each step required to be taken in the passage of an act under the provisions of the constitution, the presumption is that the legislature did comply with all of such provisions.

6. The case of *Cohn v. Kingsley*, 5 Ida. 416, 49 Pac. 985, 38 L. R. A. 74, modified.

APPEAL from the District Court of the Seventh Judicial District for Canyon County. Hon. Ed. L. Bryan, Judge.

Action to determine the validity of what is known as the "Drainage Law." Judgment *reversed*.

H. S. Kessler, for Appellant.

The present members of this bench have not hesitated to express disapproval of the majority opinion in the Cohn-Kingsley case. (*Swain v. Fritchman*, 21 Ida. 783, 125 Pac. 319.)

The omissions in the journal that have been held fatal to any bill have been omissions of facts which the constitution expressly requires should be entered in the journal. The true rule and the one now almost universally accepted by those authorities which recognize the journal as evidence was stated by Judge Cooley in Cooley's Const. Limitations, 7th ed., p. 193.

"Unless expressly so stated the journal is not required to show that a bill was read at the times and in the manner prescribed by the constitution." (*Mass. Mut. Life Ins. Co. v. Colorado Loan & Trust Co.*, 20 Colo. 1, 36 Pac. 793; *Weyand v. Stover*, 35 Kan. 545, 11 Pac. 355; *In re Ellis*, 55 Minn. 401, 43 Am. St. 514, 56 N. W. 1056, 23 L. R. A. 287; *New Hanover County v. De Rossett*, 129 N. C. 275, 40 S. E. 43; *Commissioners of Stanley Co. v. Snuggs*, 121 N. C. 394, 28 S. E. 539, 39 L. R. A. 439; *Mumford v. Sewall*, 11 Or. 67, 50 Am. Rep. 462, 4 Pac. 585; *Illinois v. Illinois Cent. Ry. Co.*, 33 Fed.

730, affirmed in 146 U. S. 387, 13 Sup. Ct. 110, 36 L. ed. 1018;
Hollingsworth v. Thompson, 45 La. Ann. 222, 40 Am. St. 220,
12 So. 1; *Rash v. Allen,* 1 Boyce (Del.), 444, 76 Atl. 370;
Ridgely v. Mayor, 119 Md. 567, 87 Atl. 909; *Webster v. City
of Hastings,* 59 Neb. 563, 81 N. W. 510; *People v. Leddy,* 53
Colo. 109, 123 Pac. 824; *State v. Erickson,* 39 Mont. 280, 102
Pac. 336; notes in 40 L. R. A., N. S., 1; 20 Am. & Eng. Ann.
Cas. 350; 36 Cyc. 950.)

John C. Rice, for Respondents.

It is conceded that the district court correctly followed the
law as laid down by this court in the case of *Cohn v. Kingsley,*
5 Ida. 416, 49 Pac. 985, 38 L. R. A. 74, but this court is now
asked to overrule that case. In cases of this kind it is uniformly held in this state that journals of the two Houses of
the legislature are not only proper, but are conclusive evidence of the facts therein shown. (*Burkhart v. Reed,* 2
Ida. 503, 22 Pac. 1; *Clough v. Curtis,* 2 Ida. 523, 22 Pac. 8;
Blaine County v. Heard, 5 Ida. 6, 45 Pac. 890; *Brown v.
Collister,* 5 Ida. 589, 51 Pac. 417.)

This principle is quite generally adhered to by the courts
of the different states of the Union. (*Union Bank of Rich-
mond v. Commissioners of Oxford,* 119 N. C. 214, 25 S. E.
966, 34 L. R. A. 487.)

"A cardinal rule in dealing with written instruments is
that they are to receive an unvarying interpretation, and that
their practical construction is to be uniform. A constitution
is not to be made to mean one thing at one time, and another
at some subsequent time when the circumstances may have so
changed as perhaps to make a different rule in the case seem
desirable." (Cooley's Const. Lim., 6th ed., p. 68; *McCulley
v. State,* 102 Tenn. 509, 53 S. W. 134, 46 L. R. A. 567; *Baker
v. Lorillard,* 4 N. Y. 261.)   Since the decision was announced
in the case of *Cohn v. Kingsley,* both Houses of the legislature of this state have accepted the construction of the constitution there laid down as binding, and have re-enacted
practically all statutes passed prior to that decision in order

that the question of their constitutionality might not be successfully raised. Therefore, there is every reason for adhering to the rule as announced in the case of *Cohn v. Kingsley,* and the cases subsequent thereto decided by this court.

SULLIVAN, C. J.—This appeal involves the constitutionality of what is known as the "Drainage District Law" of this state, passed at the twelfth session of the legislature and found in 1913 Session Laws, p. 58. It is contended that said act was not passed by the legislature in accordance with the provisions of sec. 15, art. 3, of the constitution. Said section of the constitution is as follows:

"No law shall be passed except by bill, nor shall any bill be put upon its final passage until the same, with the amendments thereto, shall have been printed for the use of the members; nor shall any bill become a law unless the same shall have been read on three several days, in each House, previous to the final vote thereon.

"*Provided,* In case of urgency, two thirds of the House where such bill may be pending, may, upon a vote of the yeas and nays, dispense with this provision. On the final passage of all bills, they shall be read at length, section by section, and the vote shall be by yeas and nays upon each bill separately, and shall be entered upon the journal; and no bill shall become a law without the concurrence of a majority of the members present."

It is contended that it does not appear from the journal entries of the House of Representatives that said bill was read on three several days in said House or that it was read at all, and that the journal entries do not show that the provisions of said section of the constitution requiring a bill to be read on three several days had been dispensed with.

The only other section of the constitution referring to legislative journals is sec. 13, art. 3, which is as follows:

"Each House shall keep a journal of its proceedings; and the yeas and nays of the members of either House on any question shall at the request of any three members present be entered on the journal."

That section requires that each House shall keep a journal of its proceedings, and specifically provides that at the request of three members the yeas and nays must be entered on the journal.

The journal entries of the Senate in regard to the passage of this bill by the Senate are not attacked in this proceeding, but the attack is directed against the journal entries of the House of Representatives. The House journal shows that Bill 92, containing the act in question, was introduced by Elliott and the entries in regard thereto are as follows:

"January 25, 1913.   Page 78.

". . . . INTRODUCTION, FIRST READING AND REFERENCE OF BILLS, JOINT RESOLUTIONS AND JOINT MEMORIALS.

"H. B. No. 92, by ELLIOTT.   .

"An Act entitled 'An Act to provide for the establishment of drainage districts, and the construction and maintenance of a system of drainage, and to provide for the means of payment of the costs thereof, and declaring an emergency.'

.   .   .   .

"The following bills were referred to their respective committees: . . . . H. B. No. 92.   Water Ways and Drainage.

" (Seal)   . . . .

"January 27, 1913.   Page 81.

.   .   .   .

"REPORT OF STANDING COMMITTEES.

.   .   .   .

"Mr. Speaker: We, your Committee on Water Ways and Drainage, beg leave to report that we have considered H. B. No. 92 and recommend that same be printed.

"GILCHRIST, Chairman.

"Report adopted.

.   .   .   .

"January 30, 1913.   Page 103.

"REPORT OF STANDING COMMITTEES.

"Mr. Speaker: We, your Committee on Printing, beg leave to report that we have had correctly printed H. B. Nos . . . . 92. . . . .

"WRIGHT, Chairman.

"Report adopted.

• • • • • ▪ ▪ ▪ ʋ ▪ • • •

"February 3, 1913.   Pages 112–114.

"REPORT OF STANDING COMMITTEES.

• • • • • • • • • • •

"Mr. Speaker: We, your Committee on Waterways and Drainage, beg leave to report that we have considered H. B. Nos. 92 and . . . . recommend that they do pass.

"GILCHRIST, Chairman.

"Report adopted.

"(Seal)   . . . .

"MOTIONS AND RESOLUTIONS.

• • • • • • • • • • • •

"Moved by Elliott that all rules of the House interfering with the immediate passage of H. B. Nos. 92 . . . . be suspended; that the portions of section 15 of article 3 of the Constitution of the State of Idaho, requiring all bills to be read on three several days, be dispensed with, this being a case of urgency, and that H. B. Nos. 92 . . . . be read the second time by title and the third time at length, section by section, and be put upon their final passage.

"Seconded by Farmin.

"Moved by Ferguson as a substitute motion that the House Bills Nos. 92 . . . . be made a special order of business Wednesday, February 5th, at 3:00 o'clock P. M.

"Seconded by Dickinson.

"Motion for suspension of rules withdrawn by Elliott with the consent of his second.

"Moved by Elliott as a substitute to all pending motions, that House Bills Nos. 92 . . . . be made a special order of business Tuesday, February 4th, at 3:00 o'clock P. M.

"Seconded by Shattuck.

"Moved by Ferguson as an amendment to the substitute offered by Elliott that the two bills referred to be made a special order of business Wednesday afternoon at 3:00 o'clock, February 5th.

"Seconded by Parks.

"Motion lost.

"The question being, 'Shall the two bills be made a special order of business Tuesday, February 4th, at 3:00 o'clock P. M.,' a vote was taken with the result that the motion carried.

*   *   *   *   *   *   *   *   *   *   *   *   *

"February 4, 1913.   Page 127.

*   *   *   *   *   *   *   *   *   *   *   *

"MISCELLANEOUS AND UNFINISHED BUSINESS.

"House Bill No. 92 having been made a special order of business for the hour of 3 o'clock P. M., same is now before the House for consideration. The question being, 'Shall the bill pass?' The roll was called with the following result: [Here follows the names of those voting.]

"Total number of votes, 48. Ayes, 48. Nays, none. Absent and not voting, 12.

"And so the bill passed, title approved and the House Bill No. 92 was ordered transmitted to the Senate.

*   *   *   *   *   *   *   *   *   *   *   *

"February 18, 1913.   Page 214.

*   *   *   *   *   *   *   *   *   *   *   *

"CONSIDERATION OF MESSAGES FROM THE GOV-
ERNOR AND SENATE.

*   *   *   *   *   *   *   *   *   *   *   *

"The following communication was received from the Senate:

"Mr. Speaker: I have the honor to transmit herewith House Bills Nos. 92 . . . . , which have passed the Senate.

"J. LOYAL ADKISON,

"Assistant Secretary of the Senate.

"February 19, 1913.   Pages 222, 224.

•   •   •   •   •   •   •   •   •   •   •   •   •   •

"REPORT OF STANDING COMMITTEES.

"Mr. Speaker: We, your Committee on Enrolled Bills, beg leave to report that we have had correctly enrolled House Bills Nos. . . . . 92. . . . .

"CHANDLER, Chairman.

"Report adopted.

•   •   •   •   •   •   •   •   •   •   •   •   •   •

"In the presence of the House, Speaker signed House Bills Nos. . . . . 92. . . . .

•   •   •   •   •   •   •   •   •   •   •   •   •

"February 20, 1913.   Page 226.

"REPORT OF STANDING COMMITTEES.

•   •   •   •   •   •   •   •   •   •   •   •   •   •

"Mr. Speaker: We, your Committee on Enrolled Bills, beg leave to report that we have had correctly enrolled House Bills Nos. . . . . 92 . . . . signed by the Speaker of the House and the President of the Senate and transmitted same to the Governor at 11 A. M. today.

"CHANDLER, Chairman.

"Report adopted.

•   •   •   •   •   •   •   •   •   •   •   •   •

"February 21, 1913.   Page 241.

•   •   •   •   •   •   •   •   •   •   •   •   •   •

"CONSIDERATION OF MESSAGES FROM THE GOV-
ERNOR AND THE SENATE.

•   •   •   •   •   •   •   •   •   •   •   •   •

"Also a communication from the Governor received and read, advising that he had signed House Bills Nos. 92 . . . . , both by Elliott.

"Filed Oct. 23, 1913."

Said entries clearly show that the House of Representatives intended to and did pass said bill. There was no opposition to it; it was unanimously adopted; the yeas on its final passage were entered on the journal; there were no nays. The bill was duly enrolled and signed by the officers of the two Houses, approved by the Governor and filed in the office of the Secretary of State.

Now, under that state of fâcts, is it the duty of this court to hold that said law was not enacted in accordance with said provisions of the constitution?

In the case of *Cohn v. Kingsley*, 5 Ida. 416, 49 Pac. 985, 38 L. R. A. 74, in a majority opinion it was expressly held that the journal must affirmatively show that the provisions of the constitution in regard to the passage of any law were substantially followed by the legislature in the passage of an act, and that it will not be presumed that the legislature complied with the provisions of the constitution in the passage of an act unless it appears on the journal that it did so, and the failure of the journal to show that each step was taken is "conclusive evidence that it was not taken." In other words, it is there held that there is no presumption that the legislature complied with the provisions of the constitution in regard to the passage of a law unless the record on its face shows that it did so. The rule laid down in that decision is not in accord with the decided weight of authority upon this question. There are two distinct lines of authorities in regard to resorting to legislative journal entries to establish the passage of a law, and they establish two well-known rules which have been aptly termed by the courts as the "Enrolled Bill Rule" and the "Journal Entry Rule." The former was adopted from England, where there is no written constitution, and is followed by the supreme court of the United States and several of the states of the Union. This rule is that the enrolled bill, when properly signed by the presiding officer of both Houses and approved by the Governor, is conclusive evidence of the regularity of the passage of the law. Under that rule journal entries cannot be resorted to as evidence to prove the irregularity of the passage of a law.

In 36 Cyc., p. 950, it is declared: "Unless expressly so stated the journal is not required to show that a bill was read at the times and in the manner prescribed by the constitution.''

In the case of *In re Ellis' Estate,* 55 Minn. 401, 43 Am. St. 514, 56 N. W. 1056, 23 L. R. A. 287, the court said: ''The absence from the journal of either House of an entry showing that a particular thing was done, is no evidence that it was not done, unless the constitution requires the entry to be made.''

It was held in *Hollingsworth v. Thompson,* 45 La. Ann. 222, 40 Am. St. 220, 12 So. 1, that if the constitution does not require the legislative journals to show that a particular thing necessary to the validity of the legislative act was done, silence will not invalidate the act. (*Ridgely v. Mayor,* 119 Md. 567, 87 Atl. 909; *People v. Leddy,* 53 Colo. 109, 123 Pac. 824; *State v. Erickson,* 39 Mont. 280, 102 Pac. 336.)

An extended note is appended to the case of *Atchison T. & S. F. Ry. Co. v. State,* 40 L. R. A., N. S., 1, which cites and groups many authorities touching upon the question under consideration.

After reviewing the authorities, the unquestioned weight of authority is to the effect that unless the journal affirmatively shows that some requirement of the constitution in the passage of a bill has been omitted, the presumption is that such requirement has been complied with, although the journal be silent in regard thereto, except when the constitution commands that such act be entered on the journal.

Under the journal entry rule, journal entries may be resorted to as evidence to prove either the regularity or the irregularity of the passage of a law. This court has adopted that rule. In the Cohn-Kingsley case, *supra,* it was held that the court might resort to the journal entries to ascertain whether a law has been properly passed. (See, also, *Swain v. Fritchman,* 21 Ida. 783, 125 Pac. 319.)

The journal entry rule concedes that the enrolled bill is *prima facie* evidence of the regularity of the passage of the law, but this line of authorities holds that the journal entries may be resorted to, and are proper evidence to determine whether or not a law was passed in accordance with the con-

stitutional requirements. This rule seems to be the accepted
law in about thirty states of the Union.

In the case of *Rash v. Allen*, 1 Boyce (Del.), 444, 76 Atl.
370, the court has exhaustively discussed said rules.

In *State v. Hocker*, 36 Fla. 358, 18 So. 767, the court holds
that if the journals of the legislature show explicitly, clearly
and affirmatively that any essential constitutional requirement has not been complied with, "or if they fail to show
any essential step in the process of enactment that the constitution expressly requires them to show—such, for example,
as the entry of the ayes and noes upon the final passage of
any bill in either House—then such journals would prevail as
evidence, and the enrolled bill, as evidence of the law, would
have to fall."

It is stated in Cooley's Constitutional Limitations, 7th ed.,
p. 195, that "it will not be presumed in any case, from the
mere silence of the journals, that either House has exceeded
its authority, or disregarded a constitutional requirement on
the passage of the legislative acts, unless where the constitution has expressly required the journals to show the action
taken, as, for instance, where it requires the yeas and nays
to be entered."

As stated by Judge Cooley, it will not be presumed in any
case from the mere silence of the journals that the legislature
exceeded its authority or disregarded a constitutional requirement in the passage of legislative acts. The journal of the
House, as above quoted, does not show that in the passage of
said act the provisions of the constitution requiring it to be
read on three several days in each House prior to its passage
had been dispensed with, but since the provisions of the constitution do not expressly require the entry of such suspension on the journal, it will not be presumed that the House
disregarded said provisions of the constitution in the passage
of said act; but it will be presumed that said constitutional
provision was complied with by the House in the passage of
said act, and the rule laid down in the Cohn-Kingsley case,
supra, is hereby modified to the extent that the legislature
will be presumed to have done each act required by the con-

stitution in the passage of an act, unless it affirmatively appears by the journal that it has failed to do so. Since the journal of the House does not show affirmatively that said provisions of the constitution were not complied with in the passage of the act under consideration, this court presumes that it did comply with said provisions in the passage of said act and that said act was passed in accordance with the provisions of the constitution, and is valid.

The judgment of the trial court is therefore reversed and the cause remanded for further proceedings in accordance with the views expressed in this opinion.

Costs awarded to the appellant.

Truitt, J., concurs.

(September 23, 1914.)

FRANK J. SMITH, Appellant, v. W. A. BERGSTRESSER, Respondent.

[143 Pac. 402.]

CLAIM AND DELIVERY—SALE OF PERSONAL PROPERTY—AGENT FOR SALE OF PERSONAL PROPERTY NOT IN HIS POSSESSION NOT A BROKER— LIENS PROVIDED FOR BY SEC. 3446, REV. CODES, DO NOT APPLY IN THIS CASE—EVIDENCE—SUFFICIENCY OF—COMMON-LAW LIENS.

1. Where an agent is employed to sell certain personal property but is not given possession thereof and has no authority to fix the price, determine the terms, close the sale of the same, or receive the purchase price, said agent does not have a lien upon the note and mortgage offered as a part of the purchase price of said personal property and delivered by the purchaser to the owner of said property in connection with the sale thereof, then by him placed in the hands of the agent simply and only to have him examine the same as to their value, see if the land mentioned in the mortgage is properly described therein, and determine from the abstract of title whether there were other liens or encumbrances upon it; the agent does not have a lien upon said note and mortgage for a commission for the sale of said personal property only.

2. Under the provisions of sec. 3446, Rev. Codes, an agent who sells personal property of which he does not. have possession and upon which he has rendered no service to the owner thereof, by labor, or skill, employeḍ for the protection, improvement, safe-keeping, or carriage thereof, has no lien for the purchase price, or any part thereof, which may come into his hands in connection with such sale.

3. *Held*, that under the evidence in this case, respondent is not entitled to a lien upon the note and mortgage described in the complaint.

APPEAL from the District Court of the Third Judicial District for Ada County.   Hon. Chas. P. McCarthy, Judge.

Action in claim and delivery to recover possession of a certain note and mortgage described in the complaint, of the alleged value of $1,800.   *Modified.*

J. C. Johnston and J. J. McCue, for Appellant.

Respondent cannot claim a statutory lien, because he does not come within that law, and does not allege that the property was delivered or consigned to him for sale; nor to perform labor or skill, or expend money upon the identical property detained.   (Rev. Codes, sec. 3446; *Mendilie v. Snell*, 22 Ida. 663, 127 Pac. 550, 43 L. R. A., N. S., 965.)

Respondent cannot establish a common-law lien upon the property of the appellant detained by him.

"A particular lien at common law is a right to retain the property of another on account of labor employed or money expended on that specific property."   (19 Am. & Eng. Ency. of Law, 2d ed., 8; 1 Jones on Liens, p. 26; 2 Bouvier's Law Dictionary, 227; *Scott v. Mercer*, 98 Iowa, 258, 60 Am. St. 188, 67 N. W. 108; Mechem on Agency, sec. 685.)

Respondent cannot claim a common-law lien as a factor nor as a broker, because he did not have delivered to him the possession of the goods and merchandise fot sale, nor was the property consigned to him for sale.   (Mechem on Agency, sec. 980; Clark & Skyles on Agency, secs. 745, 822; Story on Sales, 91; *Slack v. Tucker*, 23 Wall. 321, 23 L. ed. 143;

Barry v. Boninger, 46 Md. 59; *Peterson v. Hall*, 61 Minn. 268, 63 N. W. 733.)

Smead, Elliott & Healy, for Respondent.

An agent has a lien on the papers or property of his principal to secure payment of his compensation. (*Gresham v. Galveston Co.* (Tex. Civ. App.), 36 S. W. 796; *Dowell v. Cardwell*, 4 Saw. 217, 7 Fed. Cas. No. 4039; *Vinton v. Baldwin*, 95 Ind. 433; Jones on Liens, sec. 422; *Byers v. Danley*, 27 Ark. 77.)

There exists a particular right of lien in the agent for all his commissions, expenditures, advances and services, (Mechem on Agency, sec. 684; *Barry v. Boninger*, 46 Md. 59, *Richards v. Gaskill*, 39 Kan. 428, 18 Pac. 494; *Carpenter v. Monsen*, 92 Wis. 449, 65 N. W. 1027, 66 N. W. 692; *Peterson v. Hall*, 61 Minn. 268, 63 N. W. 733.)

"Where an agent has a lien on property for his security, the general owner cannot replevin against him for it until the lien be discharged." (*Newhall v. Dunlap*, 14 Me. 180, 30 Am. Dec. 43; *Matthias v. Sellers*, 86 Pa. 486, 27 Am. Rep. 723.)

TRUITT, J.—In this case an action of claim and delivery was brought by appellant against respondent to recover the possession of a note for $1,800 and a mortgage upon certain real property in Canyon county, Idaho, given to secure the same.

On or about October 1, 1912, the appellant, Frank J. Smith, sold to one Dan Barnidge a certain stock of merchandise, saloon fixtures and liquors, located at 702 Main St., Boise, Idaho. This note and mortgage were a part of the purchase price of said personal property, and at the time of the commencement of said action they were in the possession of the defendant, and he admitted that the plaintiff was the owner of them. The defendant filed his answer to the complaint and affidavit of the plaintiff, denying certain allegations therein but admitting the sale of the personal property to said Dan Barnidge by plaintiff, that said note and mortgage were part of the purchase price of the same, and alleged therein that they were delivered to him by plaintiff for his examination in connection with the abstract of title to the real property described in said mortgage.

Said defendant, as a further answer, defense and cross-complaint, among other things, alleged that "on or about the 28th day of August, 1912, the said plaintiff, Frank J. Smith, entered into an agreement with the said defendant, W. A. Bergstresser, wherefor, in the consideration of $200 to be paid by the said plaintiff to the said defendant, the said defendant agreed to negotiate the sale of, sell and dispose of a certain stock of merchandise and fixtures, consisting of intoxicating liquors and saloon fixtures, and entirely of intoxicating liquors and saloon fixtures, described in the said complaint herein, and to draw all contracts for the transfer of said property and agreements to transfer the same, make all invoices, examine all instruments and perform all other services as an attorney at law in connection with the said sale and transfer." This is the contract upon which issue was joined, for the plaintiff in his reply denies making it or any contract with defendant for the sale of said property, or for any other purpose whatever.

The defendant further alleges in said answer that he effected a sale of said personal property to said Dan Barnidge for the purchase price of $3,500; that $1,700 thereof was paid in cash and said note and mortgage for $1,800 were turned over to the plaintiff as the remaining part of said purchase price; and that by reason of his services in effecting said sale the plaintiff became indebted to him in the sum of $200, and asked that it be adjudged and decreed by the court that he have a lien upon said note and mortgage and the possession of them until the amount of $200, as above stated, for said services, be paid to him. All of the material allegations of this answer were denied by plaintiff.

Upon the issues thus joined, the cause was tried before the court with a jury, and the jury returned the following verdict:

"We, the jury in the above-entitled action, find that the defendant is entitled to a lien upon the note and mortgage described in the complaint for the sum of $175, and is entitled to the possession of the same until said sum is paid him by the plaintiff, and so we find for the defendant."

The court, in accordance with this verdict, entered judgment against the plaintiff, and ordered, adjudged and decreed that the defendant, W. A. Bergstresser, do have and has a lien upon the note and mortgage described in the complaint in this action for the sum of $175, and that he is entitled to the possession of the same until said sum is paid him by the plaintiff with interest thereon at the rate of seven per cent per annum from the date of said judgment until paid and for costs and disbursements of the action. From this judgment the plaintiff appeals.

A number of errors have been assigned by the appellant, which, under our view of the case, it will not be necessary to pass upon, for the main and vital question presented by this appeal is as to whether or not the defendant had a lien on the note and mortgage for the services he had rendered plaintiff, and a decision of this question will dispose of the case. But in order to decide this question, it will be necessary to consider the first and second assignments of error as set forth in appellant's brief, for these two assignments of error are so connected that they must be considered together.

The case is somewhat peculiar as presented to this court, in the fact that the testimony at the trial in the court below did not keep well within the issues raised by the pleadings. The contract alleged in the defendant's affirmative defense or cross-complaint is materially different from the one he testified to as having been made with the plaintiff in regard to the sale of said personal property. The contract set out in his answer is that defendant agreed with plaintiff to negotiate the sale of and sell the property described in the complaint, and also to draw the contracts for the transfer of said property and agreements to transfer the same, make all invoices, examine all instruments, and perform all other services as an attorney at law in connection with the sale and transfer of said property. But in his testimony, at page 97 of the transcript, when asked to give the terms of the employment he made with plaintiff, he answered: ''The terms of employment were when we got down to the sale that he was to pay five per cent of the valuation of the stock, and he finally cut down the price and said, 'I will not take less than $4,000,' after the invoice was made, so when he fixed that, and he was to pay me for the services in procuring Dan Barnidge a license if he would accept the stock and pay for it, a reasonable compensation, that part of it.'' In this contract he says plaintiff was to pay him five per cent of the valuation of the stock and then a reasonable compensation for procuring a liquor license for Dan Barnidge, which is materially different from the contract set out in the cross-complaint. The plaintiff denied that he had any contract of any kind whatever with defendant, and as the defendant's own testimony concerning it does not agree with the allegations of his cross-complaint, there is some uncertainty as to whether or not there ever was any contract between these parties for the sale of said property, but as there is some testimony that such contract was made, and the jury have so found in order to reach the verdict, that question may be considered as settled.

Coming now to the consideration of the assignments of error by the appellant heretofore mentioned, they are as follows:

''1. Insufficiency of the evidence to justify the verdict.

''2. That the verdict is against the law in this: That the evidence shows that the defendant did not at any time ever have the possession of the property for sale described in the complaint of the plaintiff, and that the evidence of the defendant shows that the property for sale was never at any time delivered to him for sale, nor that the defendant ever at any time had possession of the title papers to the property for sale, and does not show that the defendant was in law entitled to a common-law lien upon the papers in question in this case.''

All the facts necessary to entitle the plaintiff to recover in said action are alleged in the complaint; that is, that he was the owner of the note and mortgage described in the complaint, that the same was in the possession of defendant at the commencement of said action, that prior to the commencement of the action plaintiff demanded the possession of said note and mortgage, that they were in the possession of defendant at said time, and that he refused to deliver the possession thereof to plaintiff, for the sole and only reason that he asserted a lien upon them for a certain amount of money that he claimed to be due from the plaintiff to him as commission for negotiating the sale of said property. Conceding, then, that plaintiff did owe him the amount of money found due him by the verdict of the jury, this brings up the one vital question in the case, Did he have such lien upon said property?

The evidence of how the note and mortgage got into the possession of Bergstresser is somewhat vague, but we think it shows that Smith himself did not give him possession of them to be held as a part of the purchase price of said property, nor as a direct transaction in connection with the sale thereof. At page 59 of the transcript, the plaintiff testifies as follows: "Did you ever deliver to Bergstresser the property described in the complaint? A. No, sir. Q. Did you ever at any time authorize or consent that Bergstresser should hold this note and mortgage for you? A. No, sir." Dan Barnidge, who purchased the property of Smith, in his testimony at page 83 of the transcript, says that he turned the note and mortgage over to Smith, and Smith handed it to Bergstresser, "he told me he had to have an abstract and he wanted Bergstresser to pass on it." Bergstresser himself, at page 104 of the transcript, testifies as follows: "Before leaving the office, Smith said, 'There is the note and mortgage. I want you to keep it, and you look over the abstract and see that it is all right, because this is no sale unless that is all right.' "

From all the testimony and from the circumstances in connection with the alleged agency and the sale of said property, we do not think the plaintiff ever delivered to defendant this note and mortgage as part of the purchase price, and that if plaintiff did put them into defendant's hands, he put them there simply to have the mortgage examined in connection with the abstract to see if the title to the land described in the mortgage was good and clear of other encumbrances.

The important instruction of the court below bearing upon this question is as follows:

"If the owner of personal property employs another person to procure a purchaser for said property for a commission, and the latter procures a purchaser who purchases said property from the owner upon terms accepted by the owner, then the latter has a right to the agreed commission. If, under such circumstances, the purchase price, or any part thereof, is delivered to the person procuring said purchaser by the owner, such person has a lien upon said purchase price or any part thereof so delivered to him for his commission, dependent on possession, that is, he has a right to hold the same until his commission is paid."

We do not pass upon the question of the correctness of this instruction as a principle of law under other and different facts than appear in this case, but we hold that the testimony here does not bring this question within the purview of such principle. The defendant was not a factor, nor broker in regard to said property, but, giving his testimony the most favorable construction as to the terms of his employment in the premises, he was not in possession of the property, he had no authority to close a sale thereof, no authority to deliver possession of the same to the purchaser or to receive the purchase price therefor. And if, as defendant asserts, the plaintiff, in connection with closing said sale, did put these papers into his hands incidentally, and only to have him examine the mortgage, pass upon its value, and in connection with the abstract, see if the description of the land in the mortgage was correct, and also if it was free of other encumbrances, defendant could not hold them as against the demand of the plaintiff, nor was he entitled to a lien upon them for any commission which might be due from the plaintiff to him in negotiating the sale of said property.

The facts in this case clearly show that the defendant did not have a statutory lien upon said note and mortgage under the laws of this state. (Sec. 3446, Rev. Codes; *Mendilie v Snell*, 22 Ida. 663, 127 Pac. 550, 43 L. R. A., N. S., 965.)

The respondent in his brief, however, admits that under the facts in this case he could not maintain a statutory lien, but contends that he has a common-law lien upon said papers. A number of authorities in support of this position are cited, and we have briefly examined some of them, but do not think those examined sustain his contention.

Gresham v. Galveston County (Tex. Civ. App.), 36 S. W. 796, is a case where the county entered into a specific contract with Gresham and entered an order or decree of the commissioners' court of Galveston county, Texas, appointing him as agent of that county to sell or lease four certain leagues of land granted said county for public school purposes, describing the same; that the said Walter Gresham, in pursuance and by virtue of the power and authority of said order and decree, had sold various tracts of land out of the four-league grant, and as compensation therefor he was to receive ten per cent commission on all lands sold, and he had power and authority to sell or to lease said lands, or any part thereof, upon such terms and for such prices as to him might seem best for the interests of said county. There were some of the notes taken for sales of these lands that were not collected at the time the controversy about them arose which was terminated by the judgment in said action, and Gresham claimed that he was entitled to hold these notes until certain sums which he claimed as commissions on sales made, for which said notes were taken by him, were paid to him by the county. In that case the court held that he would be entitled to retain the notes while acting in good faith within the scope of his agency for the purpose of collecting them, and in that way securing his commission for their collection. We do not think this case sustains the contention of the respondent.

Vinton v. Baldwin, 95 Ind. 433, was a case where there was a contract made between the parties whereby the appellant, Vinton, was appointed agent for the appellee, Baldwin, to procure a loan, and for his services for procuring such loan promised to pay him for said services five per cent commission on the amount of the loan obtained. After the loan was effected, Vinton refused to pay over to Baldwin a certain part of the money, as he claimed it for his commission in effecting the loan, and in that case it was held that a broker has a lien for his commission, and that an agent or broker having money or property in his hands may retain the amount of his lien out of it. But this is not in point on the question of the lien in the case at bar.

In *Shaw v. Ferguson*, 78 Ind. 547, it was held that, "One who carries on the business of slaughtering hogs and curing, storing and selling the product, as well for himself as for others, and makes advances to such customers, continuously holding possession of their product until he sells it, is a factor, and has a lien on the product of the customer, for services and advances." It will be seen that this authority does not apply to the case at bar, for the reason that the defendants in that case were conducting a slaughtering and pork-packing establishment in the city of Indianapolis Ind., and, as it is held in the case, were factors in the possession of the property delivered to them, and all the proceeds of the products of said slaughtering and packing-house was received by them from their customers.

The authorities cited by appellant seem to uniformly hold that a common-law lien is a right to retain the property of another on account of labor performed or money expended upon that specific property. The law as to common-law liens is well and we think fully expressed in American & Eng. Ency. of Law, vol. 19, 2d ed., pp. 8 and 9, as follows:

"It is a principle of the common law that every man who has lawful possession of a chattel upon which he has expended his money, labor, or skill, at the request of its owner, thereby enhancing its value, may detain it as security for his debt. This right extends to all such manufacturers, tradesmen, and laborers, as receive chattels for the purpose of repairing or otherwise improving their condition, and also to common carriers, innkeepers, warehousemen, and wharfingers."

There are a number of other authorities referred to by appellant in his brief, but we deem it unnecessary to comment upon them further, for the reason that we hold that the court erred in entering judgment against the plaintiff and in holding that the amount found by the jury for defendant was a lien upon said note and mortgage. And it is hereby ordered that said judgment be modified as follows: Let the court below enter a judgment for the defendant in the sum of $175, with interest thereon at the rate of seven per cent per annum from date of original judgment and also enter a judgment in favor of the plaintiff that he is the owner and entitled to the immediate possession of the specific personal property described in the complaint, and that the same be delivered to him. Costs awarded to the appellant.

Sullivan, C. J., concurs.

———

(September 26, 1914.)

STATE OF IDAHO, to and for the Use and Benefit of J. F. McFARLAND et al., Appellants, v. PIONEER NURSERIES CO. and FIDELITY & DEPOSIT CO., of MARYLAND, Corporations, Respondents.

[143 Pac. 405.]

CONSTITUTIONAL LAW — HORTICULTURAL ACT — TITLE OF — PROVISIONS GERMANE.

1. Under the provisions of sec. 16, art. 3, of the state constitution, every act should embrace but one subject and matters properly connected therewith, which subject must be expressed in the title.

2. The purpose of said constitutional provision is to prevent fraud and deception in the enactment of laws, to avoid inconsistent and incongruous legislation and to reasonably notify legislators and the people of the legislative intent in enacting a law.

3. An act of the legislature, known as the Horticultural Act, approved February 27, 1903 (Sess. Laws 1903, p. 347), creates and defines the duties of the state board of horticultural inspection and provides for the appointment of a state horticultural inspector and deputies, provides money for their expenses, and provides penalties for the failure to comply with the provisions of said act.

4. Sec. 8 of said act provides, among other things, that no person, firm or corporation shall engage in or continue in the business of importing and selling within the state any fruit trees, etc., without first making application therefor to said board; and also provides that such application must be in writing and accompanied by a good and satisfactory bond in the sum of $1,000, conditioned on the faithful observance of all the provisions of said act and of the laws of the state of Idaho by such applicant or applicants, their agents and representatives.

5. Sec. 10 of said act provides, among other things, penalties for the violation of said act.

6. Sec. 13 provides that persons shipping fruit trees or trees of any kind, within the state, shall affix to each package, bundle or parcel a distinct mark, stamp or label showing the name of the shipper, the locality where grown and the variety of the tree or shrub.

7. *Held,* that the title to said act is sufficient to cover every section and provision of said act.

8. *Held,* that sec. 13 deals directly and primarily with horticultural matters, and comes within the purview of said title and is germane to the subject of horticulture.

9. The bond required to be given under the provisions of said act requires the dealer to fully comply with all the provisions and laws in anywise relating to or concerning nursery stock.

10. *Held,* that if a dealer violates the provisions of said act in regard to placing the proper name of the variety upon his trees, the sureties on said bond are liable for any damages that may be caused thereby to the amount of the bond.

11. *Held,* that the provisions of said sec. 13 clearly come within the title to said act and are germane to the subject of horticulture.

APPEAL from the District Court of the Third Judicial District for Ada County.   Hon. Charles P. McCarthy, Judge.

Action to recover damages for falsely labeling fruit trees. Demurrer to complaint sustained and judgment entered for the defendant.   *Reversed.*

J. H. Peterson and T. S. Risser, for Appellants.

Section 16, art. 3 of the constitution must be given a reasonable construction.   It is sufficient if the act treats of but one general subject, and that subject is expressed in the title, directly or indirectly.   The constitution should be liberally

construed to sustain legislation not within the mischief intended to prevent. (*State v. Doherty*, 3 Ida. 384, 39 Pac.
855; *Putnam v. St. Paul*, 75 Minn. 514, 78 N. W. 90; Cooley's
Const. Lim. 172; *Winters v. Duluth*, 82 Minn. 127, 84 N. W.
788; *Pioneer Irr. Dist. v. Bradley*, 8 Ida. 310, 101 Am. St.
201, 68 Pac. 295; Lewis' Sutherland, Stat. Const., secs. 115-
118.)

The provisions of the statute involved in this appeal are
germane to the subject expressed in the title. The general
object and purpose of the law deals with horticulture and the
duties of the state board of horticulture, and that is fairly
indicated by the title and is sufficient. There is no fraud,
deception or "log-rolling" legislation in the act, nor can any
be implied. (*Kessler v. Fritchman*, 21 Ida. 30, 119 Pac. 692;
State v. Dolan, 13 Ida. 693, 92 Pac. 995, 14 L. R. A., N. S.,
1259; *Maule Coal Co. v. Partenheimer*, 155 Ind. 100, 55 N. E.
751, 57 N. E. 710.)

The provisions of the act of 1903 all relate, directly or indirectly, to the same subject, have a natural connection, and
are not foreign to the subject expressed in the title, and hence
they may be united in the same act. (*Pioneer Irr. Dist. v.
Bradley, supra; People v. Mullender*, 132 Cal. 217, 64 Pac.
299; *Inhabitants of Montclair v. Ramsdell*, 107 U. S. 147, 2
Sup. Ct. 391, 27 L. ed. 431.)

The constitution does not mean that the title must be an
index of the act. (*City of Wilson v. Herink*, 64 Kan. 607,
68 Pac. 72; *Lancy v. King Co.*, 15 Wash. 9, 45 Pac. 645, 34
L. R. A. 817; *Abeel v. Clark*, 84 Cal. 226, 24 Pac. 383; *Ex
parte Liddell*, 93 Cal. 633, 29 Pac. 251; Lewis' Sutherland,
Stat. Const., sec. 121.)

The constitutional provision was intended to simply expe-
dite and facilitate proper legislation, and in order to do so
the constitution will not be interpreted in a strict, narrow or
technical sense, but reasonably. (*Parkinson v. State*, 14 Md.
184, 74 Am. Dec. 522; *Ryerson v. Utley*, 16 Mich. 269; *State
v. Ranson*, 73 Mo. 78; *Municipality No. 3 v. Michoud*, 6 La.
Ann. 605; *Montgomery Mutual Bldg. Assn. v. Robinson*, 69
Ala. 413).

This court will only determine the question as to whether the title expresses the subject of the act, and will not criticise the degree of particularity with which the subject of the act is expressed in the title, for that is a matter which is left to the discretion of the legislature. (*In re Meyer*, 50 N. Y. 504; *State v. Town of Union*, 33 N. J. L. 350; *Whiting v. Mt. Pleasant*, 11 Iowa, 482; *Indiana Central Ry. Co. v. Potts*, 7 Ind. 681; *State v. Bowers*, 14 Ind. 195.)

Wyman & Wyman, for Respondents.

"The framers of the constitution evidently meant that the title to the act should indicate both to the lawmaker and the citizen the general scope and purpose of the legislation intended, and such title should put the citizen upon notice of the proposed legislation." (*Katz v. Herrick*, 12 Ida. 1, 86 Pac. 873; *Turner v. Coffin*, 9 Ida. 338, 74 Pac. 962; *State v. Dolan*, 13 Ida. 693, 92 Pac. 995, 14 L. R. A., N. S., 1259; *Gerding v. Commissioners*, 13 Ida. 444, 90 Pac. 357; *State v. Butterfield L. S. Co.*, 17 Ida. 441, 134 Am. St. 263, 106 Pac. 455, 26 L. R. A., N. S., 1224; *Kessler v. Fritchman*, 21 Ida. 30, 119 Pac. 692; *Hailey v. Huston*, 25 Ida. 165, 136 Pac. 212; Lewis' Sutherland, Stat. Const., pp. 193, 198.)

SULLIVAN, C. J.—This action was brought to recover damages in the sum of $1,000 on a surety company bond, given under the provisions of an act creating the state board of horticulture (Sess. L. 1903, p. 347), for the alleged failure of the respondent Pioneer Nurseries Company to properly mark and label packages of apple trees with the label or mark showing the true variety of the trees, as required by the provisions of sec. 13 of said act.

The action was brought by the state of Idaho and J. F. McFarland, for the reason that the bond provided by sec. 8 runs to the state as obligee, no provision being contained in the act that any person aggrieved or injured by the fact of a nursery company's failure to comply with the requirements of said sec. 12 can sue thereon as provided by the chapter on "Official Bonds."

On demurrer to said complaint, the trial court held that the object and purpose of sec. 13 was not expressed in or embraced within the title of said act, and that said section of the act was unconstitutional for that reason, the court holding that said section was in contravention of sec. 16, art. 3, of the constitution, which section reads as follows:

"Every act shall embrace but one subject, and matters properly connected therewith, which subject shall be expressed in the title; but if any subject shall be embraced in an act which shall not be expressed in the title, such act shall be void only as to so much thereof as shall not be embraced in the title."

It has been repeatedly held by this court that the title to an act under the provisions of said section of the constitution is sufficient if the act treats of but one general subject and that subject is expressed in the title. · (*State v. Doherty*, 3 Ida. 384, 39 Pac. 855; *Pioneer Irr. Dist. v. Bradley*, 8 Ida. 310, 101 Am. St. 201, 68 Pac. 295; *State v. Jones*, 9 Ida. 693, 75 Pac. 819; *Turner v. Coffin*, 9 Ida. 338, 74 Pac. 962; *Katz v. Herrick*, 12 Ida. 1, 86 Pac. 873; *Gerding v. Board of Commrs.*, 13 Ida. 444, 90 Pac. 357; *State v. Dolan*, 13 Ida. 693, 92 Pac. 995, 14 L. R. A., N. S., 1259; *State v. Butterfield L. S. Co.*, 17 Ida. 441, 134 Am. St. 263, 106 Pac. 455, 26 L. R. A., N. S., 1224; *Kessler v. Fritchman*, 21 Ida. 30, 119 Pac. 692; *Hailey v. Huston*, 25 Ida. 165, 136 Pac. 212.)

The purpose of said constitutional provision is to prevent fraud and deception in the enactment of laws; to prevent log-rolling legislation; to avoid inconsistent and incongruous legislation and to reasonably notify legislators and the people of the legislative intent to be enacted in the law. (Cooley's Const. Lim., 6th ed. 172; Lewis' Sutherland on Constitutional Construction, 184.)

The question presented is whether the provisions of said sec. 13 are germane to the subject expressed in the title. The general object and purpose of said law deals with horticulture and the duties of state boards of horticulture. It was intended to protect fruit-growers and the people of the state. The title of the act is as follows:

"An act to create and define the duties of a state board of horticultural inspection and the appointment of a state horticultural inspector and deputies; to appropriate money for their expense and defining the duties thereof; to prevent the gift, sale, distribution, transportation, importation or planting of infected trees, vines, plants, cuttings, scions, grafts, pits, buds or other articles and to provide for the disinfection or destruction of the same; to provide for the extirpation of insect pests or fungus diseases found on trees, shrubs, vines, plants, fruit; to provide penalties for failure to comply with the provisions of this act."

Said act creates and defines the duties of the state board of horticultural inspection and provides for the appointment of state horticultural inspector and deputies and appropriates money for their expenses, and provides penalties for the failure to comply with the provisions of the act.

The 8th section of the act provides that no person, firm or corporation shall engage in or continue in the business of importing or selling within the state any fruit trees, etc., without first making an application therefor to said board. Such application must be in writing and accompanied by a good and satisfactory bond in the sum of $1,000, to be approved by said board, "conditioned on the faithful observance of all the provisions of this act and of the laws of the state of Idaho by such applicant or applicants and their agents and representatives."

Sec. 10 of said act is as follows: "Any person, persons, firms or corporations, his or their agents, who shall bring or import into the state fruit trees, forest trees, vines, plants, shrubs, scions, pits, or other nursery stock with intent to sell or dispose of the same, without first making application to the state board of horticultural inspection, filing the necessary bonds and securing the certificate provided for in section 8 of this act, or who, having imported said fruit trees, forest trees, vines, plants, shrubs, scions, pits or other nursery stock into the state with intent to sell or dispose of the same or any part thereof, without first notifying the state horticultural inspector or the deputy district inspector thereof, or having said fruit trees, forest trees, vines, plants, shrubs, scions, pits or other nursery stock fumigated, as provided in section 9 of this act, or where found infested shall fail or refuse to destroy or disinfect the same, shall be deemed guilty of a misdemeanor and upon conviction thereof, shall be punished as provided by section 14 of this act.''

Sec. 13 of said act provides as follows: "Any person or persons shipping fruit trees or trees of any kind, shrubs, vines, scions, cuttings or plants within the state shall affix to each package, bundle or parcel containing the same a distinct mark, stamp or label, showing the name of the shipper or grower, the locality where grown, and the variety of said trees, shrubs, vines, grafts, scions, cuttings, plants or buds; . . . . ''

Section 14 provides, among other things, as follows: "Any person, persons, dealers or shippers . . . . who shall sell or offer for sale, gift, distribution, transportation or planting . . . . or who shall refuse or neglect to attach a distinct mark or label as hereinbefore provided, shall be deemed guilty of a misdemeanor and upon conviction thereof shall be fined not less than twenty-five or more than three hundred dollars. All sums so collected shall be paid into the state treasury.''

It will be observed from the provisions of said act that it prohibits not only the importation and sale of infected fruit trees, but it requires the person shipping fruit trees into the state to "affix a distinct mark, stamp or label showing the name of the shipper or grower and the locality where grown and the variety of said trees,'' and in addition to a civil action which the injured person has in the bond provided for by sec. 8 of the act, the state has a criminal action against the shipper "who shall refuse or neglect to attach a distinct mark or label as herein provided.'' The bond required by the provisions of sec. 8 is "conditioned for the faithful observance of all the provisions of this act and of the laws of the state of Idaho by said applicant or applicants and their agents and representatives.'' Now, said act provides that the person or persons shipping fruit trees within the state shall affix to each package, etc., the name of the shipper or grower, the locality where grown and the variety of said trees, etc. It is clear that said act deals directly and only with horticulture and horticultural interests of the state, and especially fruit horticulture. It clearly embraces but one subject and matters properly connected therewith, and that subject is certainly expressed in the title. The subject of the act deals generally with horticulture, creates and defines the duties of the state board of horticultural inspection, etc. It would have been sufficient if all of the title had been left out except the following: "An act to create and define the duties of a state board of horticultural inspection and the appointment of a state horticultural inspector and deputies; to appropriate money for their expense and defining the duties thereof; and to provide penalties for failure to comply with the provisions of this act." The title as above given would be sufficient to cover every section of said act, since the act deals with horticulture and the creation of a state board, etc.

Said sec. 13 deals directly and primarily with horticultural matters and clearly comes within the purview of said title. The legislature evidently undertook to index some provisions of the act but did not index all of them.

The bond in question is in conformity with and contains the conditions required to be contained therein by the provisions of said sec. 8. Among other things, it contains the following provisions: "The conditions of this obligation are as follows: If the above-bound principal shall faithfully demean himself as a dealer in fruit trees, forest trees, ... and shall as such dealer fully comply with all of the provisions of an act of the legislature of the state of Idaho, entitled [here follows the title of the act] approved February 28, 1903, and shall fully comply with the provisions of all the laws of the state of Idaho in any wise relating to or concerning nursery stock and dealers therein, then this obligation to be void; otherwise to remain in full force and effect."

The conditions of that bond are clear and unequivocal. They require the dealer in fruit trees to faithfully demean himself as such and to "fully comply with all the provisions" of said act, and the provisions of sec. 13 of the act require the seller to mark each package with a stamp or label showing the name of the shipper or grower, the locality where grown and the variety of the tree or shrub or vine. This was for the protection of the purchaser as well as to give certain information to the horticultural inspectors. It was just as obligatory under the provisions of said act for the seller to mark the variety of the tree as it was to give the name of the grower and the locality where grown. The legislature no doubt considered it as important to protect the purchaser in obtaining the kind or variety of tree purchased as to protect him from the diseases and pests with which fruit trees are sometimes infected. A purchaser might be injured more by the failure of the seller to deliver him the kind of trees purchased than he would be by delivering him trees infected with insects or disease, since the insects or disease might be gotten rid of while a seedling or some inferior kind of apple tree could not be easily changed to a standard variety.

This court has held in a number of cases that the provisions of an act which relate directly or indirectly to the same subject and have an actual connection and are not foreign to the subject expressed in the title may be united in the same act. (*Pioneer Irr. Dist. v. Bradley,* 8 Ida. 310, 101 Am. St. 201, 68 Pac. 295.) As bearing upon this subject, see, also, *State v. Doherty,* 3 Ida. 384, 39 Pac. 855; *State v. Dolan,* 13 Ida. 693, 92 Pac. 995, 14 L. R. A., N. S., 1259; *Kessler v. Fritchman,* 21 Ida. 30, 19 Pac. 692.

This court held in *Pioneer Irr. Dist. v. Bradley, supra,* that however numerous the provisions of an act may be, if they can be, by fair intendment, considered as falling within the subject matter legislated upon in such act, or necessary as ends and means to the attainment of such subject, the act will not be in conflict with said constitutional provision.

The title to such act is not of such a character as to mislead or deceive either the legislature or the public as to the legislative intent. It is broad enough to cover the subject dealt with in the act, and the provisions of said sec. 13 clearly come within said title, and are not repugnant to said provision of the constitution because of not being included within the title.

It is the well-established rule that where there is a doubt as to the subject expressed in the title, the doubt should be resolved in favor of the validity of the act; but it seems to us there can be no doubt here. Said provisions of sec. 13 clearly come within the subject expressed in the title and are germane to the subject of horticulture.

The trial court therefore erred in holding that said act was unconstitutional and in sustaining said demurrer. The judgment is reversed and the cause remanded for further proceedings in accordance with the views expressed in this opinion. Costs are awarded to the appellant.

Truitt, J., concurs.

(September 28, 1914.)

MRS. A. E. RASMUSSEN, Respondent, v. MARTIN SILK, Appellant.

[143 Pac. 525.]

INJUNCTION—PUBLIC HIGHWAY—VACATION OF—ESTABLISHMENT OF.

1. Where a public highway has run diagonally across a 40-acre tract owned by plaintiff, and the proper authorities have established a new highway along the line of said 40-acre tract, at the instance and request of the owner, and vacated the "diagonal road," conditioned on the plaintiff's placing the newly established highway in a good and passable condition as a public highway, the public has a right to travel the "diagonal road" until such condition is complied with, and the vacation of such "diagonal road" does not take place until the new highway is placed in proper condition.

APPEAL from the District Court of the Fourth Judicial District for Gooding County. Hon. C. O. Stockslager, Judge.

Action to enjoin the defendant from traveling upon a certain road that had been conditionally vacated. Judgment granting the defendant the right to travel upon the "diagonal road" until the newly established road is put in proper condition. *Affirmed.*

Martin Silk, *pro se,* cites no authorities.

A. F. James, for Respondent.

The vacation of highways is not a taking of property for which compensation must be made. (*Swift v. Santa Barbara County,* 16 Cal. App. 72, 116 Pac. 317; *Levee Dist. v. Farmer,* 101 Cal. 178, 35 Pac. 569, 23 L. R. A. 388; *State v. Deer Lodge County,* 19 Mont. 582, 49 Pac. 147.)

SULLIVAN, C. J.—This action was brought to enjoin and restrain the defendant from traveling a certain highway or road passing diagonally across a 40-acre tract of land owned by the plaintiff, and a qualified injunction was granted. The appeal is from the judgment granting such injunction.

It appears from the record that the plaintiff and defendant own adjoining tracts of land, and a highway or road designated in the record as a "diagonal road" runs across a 40-acre tract owned by the plaintiff; that the plaintiff desired to have said highway or road vacated and a highway or road placed on the line of the legal subdivisions owned by the parties, and that on the 20th day of March, 1913, the plaintiff, defendant and others petitioned the board of highway commissioners of the Gooding Highway District for the establishment of a highway on the line between the land of the parties, as above stated, which road was to be located wholly upon the land owned by the plaintiff. It is alleged in the complaint that the plaintiff did by deed of dedication convey and dedicate to the said highway district said strip of land for said road, and that the board of highway commissioners thereafter at a regular meeting established a public highway on and over the land so dedicated, and vacated said "diagonal road" and closed the same from travel of any kind. It is also alleged that immediately thereafter the said board of highway commissioners, acting by and through their road director, opened to public travel and traffic the aforesaid strip of land so conveyed and dedicated to the said highway district, and worked the same, making it suitable for travel and use as a highway.

It is also alleged that the defendant repeatedly tore down the plaintiff's fences placed across said "diagonal road" after said highway board had declared the same closed.

The defendant answered, admitting some of the allegations of the complaint, but denied that the highway as accepted and laid out by the highway commissioners had been put in a suitable condition to travel by the plaintiff, who had promised to put said new highway in a passable and fit condition for general highway purposes, and that the time for the abandonment of said "diagonal road" was contingent on the plaintiff's giving possession of said strip of land and putting it in a safe, fit and passable condition for public use.

The court after hearing the case and hearing the statement made by the defendant, granted a qualified injunction against the defendant's interfering with the plaintiff's fences placed across said "diagonal road," which injunction provided, however, "that a certain highway laid out by the Gooding Highway District adjoining and between plaintiff's and defendant's aforesaid land [here follows a description of the land] shall be made passable and fit for public travel for highway purposes and as suitable for the same as the aforesaid 'diagonal road,' and provided, further, that in case the removal of plaintiff's ditch in the aforesaid highway be necessary to make such highway suitable and fit for highway purposes, then the plaintiff shall remove such portion or portions as may be necessary for the same," etc.

It is evident from said decision or judgment of the court that the defendant is granted the right to travel said "diagonal road" until the new road is put in a fit and suitable condition for public travel. We think that fully protects the rights of the defendant. Under that judgment he has a right to remove any obstructions placed across the "diagonal road" and to travel it as a public highway until said new highway is put in a fit and passable condition for travel. Under the provisions of said injunctive judgment, the defendant is not enjoined from traveling said "diagonal road," and has the absolute right to travel the same until the plaintiff puts the new road in a suitable condition for public travel. It therefore devolves upon the plaintiff to place the new highway in a suitable condition for travel before she can enforce said injunction against the defendant and prevent him from traveling said "diagonal road."

The judgment is affirmed, with costs in favor of the respondent.

Truitt, J., concurs.

————————

(September 29, 1914.)

BEN Q. PETTINGILL, as Receiver of the BOISE STATE BANK, LTD., Respondent, v. W. H. MacWILLIAMS, Appellant.

[143 Pac. 524.]

PROMISSORY NOTE—TITLE TO—VERDICT—SUFFICIENCY OF—ATTORNEY'S FEES.

1. Evidence *held* sufficient to sustain the verdict of the jury and the judgment of the court awarding attorney's fees.

2. *Held,* that the bank came into the possession of said promissory note in due course and before maturity.

APPEAL from the District Court of the Seventh Judicial District for Canyon County. Hon. Ed. L. Bryan, Judge.

Action to recover on a promissory note. Judgment for the plaintiff. *Affirmed.*

I. W. Kenward, J. A. Elston and W. C. Bicknell, for Appellant.

The owner of plaintiff's exhibit "P" does not hold the same in due course of business and the dates of the indorsements thereon are immaterial, the indorsee, Bank of Montreal, not having indorsed the same. For these reasons instruction No. 3 has no application to the facts in this case, and would have the effect to mislead and confuse the jury. (*People v. Dunn,* 1 Ida. 74.)

Claude W. Gibson, for Respondent.

The law presumes the party in possession to be a holder in due course, and this presumption persists in each and every person that has ever been a holder, so that when the last holder brings an action, he can rely on this presumption that each indorser was a holder in due course. (*Sperry v. Spaulding,* 45 Cal. 544; *Brown v. Spofford,* 95 U. S. 474, 24 L. ed. 508; *Craig v. Palo Alto Stock Farm,* 16 Ida. 701, 102 Pac. 393; *Meadowcraft v. Walsh,* 15 Mont. 544, 39 Pac. 914.)

There was enough evidence before the court upon which to adjudge reasonable attorney's fees as provided in the note. (*Broadbent v. Brumback,* 2 Ida. 366, 16 Pac. 555; *Warren v. Stoddard,* 6 Ida. 692, 59 Pac. 540; *Porter v. Title Guaranty etc. & Co.,* 17 Ida. 364, 106 Pac. 299, 27 L. R. A., N. S., 111, *Monroe v. Fohl,* 72 Cal. 568, 14 Pac. 514; *McNamara v. Oakland Bldg. & Loan Assn.,* 131 Cal. 336, 63 Pac. 670, and cases cited; *Woodward v. Brown,* 119 Cal. 283, 63 Am. St. 108, 51 Pac. 2, 542.)

SULLIVAN, C. J.—This action was brought by the receiver of the Boise State Bank to recover on a promissory note executed by the defendant. Said promissory note had been deposited with said bank as collateral security for the payment of a promissory note executed by the Crown Coal & Coke Co. The cause was tried by the court with a jury and the jury rendered a verdict in favor of the plaintiff for $500, on which verdict a judgment was entered. The appeal is from the judgment.

A number of errors are assigned which go to the admission of certain evidence, to the denying of defendant's motion for a nonsuit, and to the giving and refusing to give certain instructions.

After a careful examination of the record, we find no error in the action of the court in admitting evidence, and are fully satisfied that the evidence is sufficient to sustain the verdict. The instructions given by the court fairly cover the case, and under the evidence the court did not err in giving instructions or in refusing to give certain instructions requested by the defendant.

This court does not think it necessary to prepare any extended opinion in this case and specifically pass upon each assignment of error. The evidence shows that the Boise State Bank came into the possession of said promissory note in due course and before maturity; that it transferred said note as collateral to another bank, and that it was thereafter returned to the Boise State Bank and was held by said receiver as collateral at the time this action was tried. Clearly, under the law, the receiver had the right to maintain this action for the collection of said note.

A question is raised in regard to the sufficiency of the evidence to sustain that part of the judgment awarding fifty dollars attorney's fees. We think, under the evidence, the court was fully justified in awarding that amount as attorney's fees.

Finding no reversible error in the record, the judgment must be affirmed, and it is so ordered. Costs awarded in favor of respondent.

Truitt, J., concurs.

(September 30, 1914.)

BOISE DEVELOPMENT COMPANY, LTD., Appellant, v. BOISE CITY, a Municipal Corporation, Respondent.

[143 Pac. 531.]

CONTRACT OF MUNICIPAL CORPORATION—WHEN VOID—WHAT CONSTITUTES DEBT OR LIABILITY UNDER SECTION 3, ARTICLE 8 OF CONSTITUTION — CONSTITUTIONAL CONSTRUCTION — WHAT CONSTITUTES INDEBTEDNESS FOR ORDINARY AND NECESSARY EXPENSES — NEW DEBT.

1. When a city enters into a contract by the terms of which it becomes liable for a large expenditure of money, exceeding in that year the income and revenue provided for it for said year, without fully complying with all the provisions of sec. 3, art. 8 of the constitution of Idaho relating to such expenditure, *held*, that said contract is void.

2. The word "liability," as used in said section, has its ordinary meaning, and signifies the state of being bound in law and justice to pay an indebtedness or discharge some obligation.

3. Where uncertain and contingent claims for alleged damages to the property of a corporation against a city are made a part of the consideration of a contract entered into between them, and said claims have never been liquidated, settled, or reduced to a definite fixed amount of indebtedness against said city, *before* the date of the contract, by a judgment or decree of court, arbitration, compromise, nor in any manner whatever, if these sums are liquidated, settled and fixed as a definite amount of indebtedness against the city for the first time by the contract itself, *held*, that this would constitute a *new debt*.

APPEAL from the District Court of the Third Judicial District for Ada County. Hon. Carl A. Davis, Judge.

Action for damages for breach of contract. Judgment for defendant, dismissing said action. *Affirmed.*

Smead, Elliott & Healy and Hawley, Puckett & Hawley, for Appellant.

A claim for uncertain and unliquidated damages is not a debt. (*Jackson v. Bell*, 31 N. J. Eq. 554.)

Our supreme court has had sec. 3, art. 8 of the constitution
under consideration many times.   On every occasion when the
prohibition has been applied, there has been a true indebtedness involved.   (*Ada County v. Bullen Bridge Co.*, 5 Ida.
79, 47 Pac. 818, 36 L. R. A. 367; *Ball v. Bannock County*, 5
Ida. 602, 51 Pac. 454; *Dunbar v. Board of Commrs.*, 5 Ida.
407, 49 Pac. 409; *Bannock County v. Bunting & Co.*, 4 Ida.
156, 37 Pac. 277.)

The case of *Feil v. Coeur d'Alene City*, 23 Ida. 32, 129
Pac. 643, 43 L. R. A., N. S., 1095, a case cited by the city,
deals with a true indebtedness.

The California court, in which state the section is identical
with our own, and the construction of which court has been
quoted with approval by our own, has construed the section
exactly as we contend for.   (*McBean v. City of Fresno*, 112
Cal. 159, 53 Am. St. 191, 44 Pac. 358, 31 L. R. A. 794; *Smilie
v. Fresno County*, 112 Cal. 311, 44 Pac. 556; *Johnson v. Bank
of Lake*, 125 Cal. 6, 73 Am. St. 17, 57 Pac. 664; *Doland v.
Clark*, 143 Cal. 176, 76 Pac. 958.)

Liability to pay money arising out of tort is not the creation
of an indebtedness.   (*Ft. Dodge Electric Light & Power Co.
v. Ft. Dodge*, 115 Iowa, 568, 89 N. W. 7; *Conner v. Nevada*,
188 Mo. 148, 107 Am. St. 314, 86 S. W. 256; *Lorence v.
Bean*, 18 Wash. 36, 50 Pac. 582; *Bloomington v. Perdue*, 99
Ill. 329; *Rice v. Des Moines*, 40 Iowa, 638; *Little v. Portland*,
26 Or. 235, 37 Pac. 911; *Cook v. Ansonia*, 66 Conn. 413, 34
Atl. 183; *Smith v. St. Joseph*, 122 Mo. 643, 27 S. W. 344.)

The compromise of an action or claim is not the creation of
a debt.   (*Chicago v. Pittsburg etc. Co.*, 244 Ill. 220, 135
Am. St. 316, 91 N. E. 422; *Conyers v. Kirk*, 78 Ga. 480, 3
S. E. 442.)

The contract does not create a new liability.   Indebtedness
already existing may be paid in a given year, though the sum
so paid exceeds the income of that year.   (*Hickey v. Nampa*,
22 Ida. 41, 124 Pac. 280.)

If the right to a compromise is considered best to the city's
interest, the exercise of this discretion vested in the council
will not be reviewed by the courts.   (*Pike v. State Land*

Board, 19 Ida. 268, Ann. Cas. 1912B, 1344, 113 Pac. 447; *Murphy v. Chicago, R. I. etc. Ry. Co.*, 247 Ill. 614, 93 N. E. 381.)

Charles F. Reddoch, for Respondent.

It is safe to presume that if the city had sufficient funds available with which to carry out the scheme of improvement contemplated, an appropriation would have been made for that purpose, and in that event the contract might in some of its phases be legal, but the contrary conclusively appears. It provides for future improvements and future payments of at least $5,000 a year for at least five years, with no provision made at the time of the execution of the contract for defraying this expense, in direct violation of sec. 3, art. 8 of the constitution. (*Hickey v. City of Nampa*, 22 Ida. 41, 124 Pac. 280; *Veatch v. City of Moscow*, 18 Ida. 313, 21 Ann. Cas. 1332, 109 Pac. 722; *McNutt v. Lemhi County*, 12 Ida. 63, 84 Pac. 1054; *Ada County v. Bullen Bridge Co.*, 5 Ida. 79, 47 Pac. 818, 36 L. R. A. 367; *Dunbar v. Board of Commrs.*, 5 Ida. 407, 49 Pac. 409; *Bannock Co. v. Bunting & Co.*, 4 Ida. 156, 37 Pac. 277.)

A city indebtedness incurred during one fiscal year cannot be paid from the income and revenue of a future fiscal year, unless a fund is specially provided for the purpose, and collected therefor in such future year. (*Theiss v. Hunter*, 4 Ida. 788, 45 Pac. 2; *San Francisco Gas Co. v. Brickwedel*, 62 Cal. 641; *Feil v. City of Coeur d'Alene*, 23 Ida. 32, 129 Pac. 643, 43 L. R. A., N. S., 1095; *Ramsey v. City of Shelbyville*, 119 Ky. 180, 83 S. W. 116, 1136, 68 L. R. A. 300; *Eaton v. Mimnaugh*, 43 Or. 465, 73 Pac. 754; *O'Neil Engineering Co. v. Town of Ryan*, 32 Okl. 738, 124 Pac. 19; *Campbell v. State*, 23 Okl. 109, 99 Pac. 778.)

TRUITT, J.—This action was commenced by the appellant as plaintiff in the court below to recover damages from respondent, Boise City, for breach of a written contract entered into between appellant and respondent on the 27th day of December, 1911.

The complaint sets out said contract in full, and, though the same is quite lengthy, for the reason that it is the basis of the action and there is much controversy as to the meaning and legal effect of its terms, we think it proper to give it in full as follows:

"This agreement, made and entered into this 27th day of December, 1911, by and between Boise City, a municipal corporation of the state of Idaho, acting herein by the duly elected and qualified mayor and clerk of said municipal corporation, by and through the authority of its duly elected and qualified common council, and Boise Development Company, Ltd., a corporation organized and existing under and by virtue of the laws of the state of Idaho, with its principal place of business at Boise City, Ada County, Idaho, Witnesseth:

"That whereas the said Boise City is the owner of certain real property commonly known and designated as the Julia Davis Park, lying and being along the north bank of Boise River, between the Ninth Street bridge and the Broadway bridge leading across said river from said city, part of which property is, at the present time bottom land of said Boise river, and being cut up by many small arms of said river, and said land is not in a compact form, and it is the desire of the said Boise City to fill in the wasted parts of said land and to establish a permanent park, and to grade and beautify said land, and otherwise improve the same, in order to get the same in shape, and in order to protect the same from the action of erosion of Boise river, and to place such embankments and structures, and to drive piles, and to do other necessary and proper work in order to protect the said land and to give the said river at this vicinity a uniform width and a uniform bank along the said north bank of said river between the said bridges hereinbefore mentioned;

"And whereas, the said Boise Development Company, Ltd., is owner of certain interests in certain real property lying along the south bank of said river and directly opposite and across said river from the property hereinbefore mentioned, belonging to said Boise City;

"And whereas, the said Boise City is desirous of reclaiming certain lands on the south bank of said Boise River, the same being opposite to the said Julia Davis Park and adjacent to certain property owned by the Boise Development Co., Ltd., and known as Boise City Park Subdivision, situate in Ada County, Idaho;

"And whereas, it is necessary and convenient, and to the best interests of said Boise City to establish a uniform width of said river between the said Broadway bridge and the said Ninth Street bridge, and also to establish uniform banks on the south and north banks of said river between the said bridges;

"And whereas, it is the intention of said Boise City from time to time to do such work and construct such dams, breakwaters and improvements as shall be necessary and proper to establish a uniform width, and to provide uniform banks on the said river between the said Ninth Street and the said Broadway bridges;

"And whereas, there is now pending in the District Court of the Third Judicial District of the State of Idaho, in and for Ada County, a certain action brought by the said Boise Development Co., Ltd., wherein Boise City has been made a party defendant, wherein it is sought to restrain the said city and others from the construction of a proposed wing dam or breakwater in the said Boise River between the said Ninth Street and Broadway bridges;

"And whereas, it is mutually desired between the said parties hereto to effect an amicable settlement of the controversy involved in said action, and to beautify and improve the north and south banks of said river between the said bridges;

"Now therefore, in consideration of the foregoing conditions and in consideration of the covenants, agreements and stipulations hereinafter set out to be kept and performed, it is mutually agreed between the said Boise City, hereinafter known as a party of the first part, and the Boise Development Co., Ltd., hereinafter known as the party of the second part, as follows, to wit:

"I.

"The party of the first part agrees to commence immediately upon the construction of such breakwaters or other structures on the south bank of said Boise river as shall be necessary to give the said Boise river a channel of uniform width between the said Ninth Street bridge and the Broadway bridge, and particularly to protect the said Boise City Park Subdivision, a property of the party of the second part, hereinbefore referred to, from damage which might be incurred to said property due to the usual and ordinary flow of said Boise river. It is further agreed that as a measure preliminary to the construction of said uniform channel, the party of the first part will proceed immediately to construct a wing dam from the south bank of the Boise river at a point on the north line of Boise City Park Subdivision as the same appears from the official plat thereof now on file in the office of the county recorder of Ada county, state of Idaho, opposite the point where the said river is divided by a certain bar or island lying between the said Subdivision and the said Julia Davis Park, said dam to extend from the said point to the head of said bar or island, and to be so constructed as to shut off the flow of water between said bar or island, and the said Subdivision, and to turn the same into the middle of said channel along the north side of said bar or island; and the said party of the first part will at the same time construct along the south bank of said river from the said wing dam to Broadway bridge, a temporary breakwater of rip-rap sufficient to protect the lands lying behind the said temporary protection from overflow or erosion due to the ordinary and usual flow of said river, until the completion of the permanent uniform channel hereinbefore provided for.

"II.

"The party of the first part further agrees to fill in between the south bank of said river as established by the building of the said wing dam provided for in paragraph I hereof, with such solid filling material as earth, sand, gravel, or equally solid fill as it shall have at its disposal, and such

fill shall exclude garbage, sweepings and unsightly or un-
cleanly materials likely to injure the sale of the property
in said subdivision, or detrimental to health; to level the same
after filling, and to plat, grade, construct, maintain and sod
the said property thus reclaimed as a public park. It is further agreed that said reclaimed property shall not be filled
to a higher level at any point of the same than the present
street grade of Earle Street in said subdivision as platted.
The party of the first part further agrees to expend in the
reclaiming, filling and improving the park on the south side
of said Boise river, at least $5,000 each and every year from
and after the date of this agreement for a period of at least
five years and to complete the said work of establishing a
uniform channel, reclaiming the said property and filling,
grading and sodding the same ready for opening as a public
park, at a time not to exceed eight years from the date of
this agreement.

"III.

"The party of the first part further agrees to construct
Riverside Drive as platted, to a grade to be furnished by the
party of the second part, according to official plat of Boise
City Subdivision and field notes thereof; to construct cement
curbs along both sides of said drive and to plant desirable
shade trees on both sides thereof at a distance of from twenty-
five to forty feet apart, from point of intersection of said
drive with Ninth Street Pike to the easterly end of said
subdivision; to construct a cement sidewalk, or cause the
same to be constructed, from the south end of Ninth Street
bridge to the point of intersection of said drive with Ninth
Street Pike, a distance of approximately three hundred to
four hundred feet. Any fill acquired from grading down
said drive shall be placed in the depression at the easterly
end of said subdivision at the point where the old channel
of the Boise river formerly flowed.

"IV.

"The party of the first part also agrees, at some time not
later than five years from the date hereof, to construct a sur-

face for such Riverside Drive of oil macadam or some other hard substance equally durable and desirable.

"Said drive shall be commenced at Ninth Street Pike not later than May 1, 1912, and shall be completed, surfaced, and graded in the style of a turnpike, with the exception of said oil macadam or other hard surface, to Broadway Bridge, not later than October 1, 1912.

"It is further agreed that no part of the cost of construction or of paving or surfacing said drive shall at any time hereafter be assessed against the abutting property in said subdivision, or against the owners thereof.

"The title to the said pile breakwater at present erected along the northerly line of said subdivision shall remain in the party of the second part, with the right to remove the same; if the same is not removed by the party of the second part, the party of the first part shall remove the same with as little destruction of materials as possible, to a level with the surrounding property as soon as the uniform channel is established on the south side of said river as herein provided for.

"V.

"It is further agreed that no franchises for public utilities shall be granted on Riverside Drive or upon the park property along the north line of said subdivision, without the consent of the party of the second part; provided, however, that the party of the second part shall retain the right to lay gas, water, sewer and similar mains and tubing under Riverside Drive and the said park property to Boise river; and the party of the first part hereby agrees that the party of the second part, its agents or assigns, shall be granted the right to cross the said drive and park property at the westerly end thereof with the tracks and rights of way of a railroad which shall connect with the railroad to be built along Ninth Street Pike, pursuant to the franchise heretofore granted by the county of Ada to J. S. Clark and A. R. Smith, and similar trackage on Seventh, Eighth or Ninth streets in Boise City, if the common council of said Boise City shall grant a franchise for such trackage and right of way.

"VI.

"It is further agreed that no scenic railways, merry-go-rounds or other amusement devices of a like nature shall be constructed on said park property, and that no zoological gardens or exhibits shall be established thereon. No pavilions or other structures shall be placed in said park closer to the said subdivision than one hundred and fifty feet from the north line of said Riverside Drive.

"In consideration of the foregoing terms and stipulations on the part of the party of the first part, the party of the second part agrees as follows:

"I.

"To dismiss the action now pending between the parties hereto as set out hereinbefore, at its own proper cost.

"II.

"To furnish for the use of the party of the first part a plat of said Boise City Park Subdivision and adjacent property with surveyors' notes and all data pertaining to the same.

"III.

"Party of the second part further agrees to construct a cement sidewalk along the south line of Riverside Drive and inside the south curb line of the same, to a grade to conform to the grade of said street and the southerly curb thereof, within twelve months after the completion of said curb.

"IV.

"To define the southerly line of Riverside Drive as platted, and stake the same off on the ground, and to establish the grade of the same prior to the time set for its construction.

"V.

"To execute properly and to deliver to the party of the first part, a quitclaim deed to all the right, title and interest of the party of the second part in and to said Riverside Drive, Tract 'A,' and that part of Lots 9, 4, 13, and Tract 'C,' lying northerly from the southerly line of said Riverside Drive as platted, and easterly from the Ninth Street bridge across said Boise River; it being the intention of the party of the second part to convey by said deed, all its right, title and interest in and to any and all lands and riparian rights lying northerly from the said southerly line of said drive and easterly from the said bridge, said land to be used exclusively for park purposes.

"Said deed to be drawn as above set out, properly executed and placed in escrow in the hands of some third party, to be delivered to the party of the first part herein when his contract shall have been executed according to the terms hereof; and in the event of default or failure on the part of the said party of the first part in the execution of this contract, said deed shall be returned to the party of the second part, and this contract shall be null and void, and of no force and effect.

"In witness whereof, The party of the first part has, by resolution of its common council, duly and regularly passed, caused these presents to be executed, signed by its mayor and attested by its city clerk, under the official seal of said Boise City; and the party of the second part has caused these presents to be executed, signed by its president and attested by its secretary, under the corporate seal of the Boise Development Co., Ltd.

"This agreement executed in duplicate at Boise City, Ada county, Idaho, this 27th day of December, 1911."

This contract was duly executed as to form.

The complaint further alleges performance of this contract on the part of plaintiff as far as permitted by the defendant. It alleges a breach of the same by the defendant and claims damages therefor in the aggregate sum of $53,142.70, with costs and disbursements.

To this complaint the respondent interposed a demurrer on the ground that the same does not state a cause of action for various reasons; that two or more causes of action were improperly united; for ambiguity and uncertainty; and also filed a motion to strike out certain portions of the complaint, and a motion requiring appellant to elect as to whether it would proceed upon the alleged breach of said contract or for certain torts alleged to have been committed by defendant both prior and subsequent to the execution of said contract.

There are numerous points raised by the pleadings, and some of them are presented in the briefs of the parties, but only two questions were argued at any considerable length, these being whether the contract sued on is void under sec. 3 of art. 8 of the state constitution, and if not, then whether it is *ultra vires* under the powers granted to the mayor and council by the charter of the city. As either of these points would be a bar to the action if sustained, we deem it unnecessary to pass upon them both if the first one decided in its order is sustained. As the first question presented and argued by respondent is as to whether said contract is void under the inhibition of sec. 3 of art. 8 of the constitution of Idaho, we will consider that in its order, for if the contention of respondent is sustained as to that point, it is decisive of the case. This section is as follows:

"No county, city, town, township, board of education, or school district, or other subdivision of the state, shall incur any indebtedness, or liability, in any manner, or for any purpose, exceeding in that year, the income and revenue provided for it for such year, without the assent of two-thirds of the qualified electors thereof voting at an election to be held for that purpose, nor unless, before or at the time of incurring such indebtedness, provision shall be made for the collection of an annual tax sufficient to pay the interest on such indebtedness as it falls due, and also to constitute a sinking fund for the payment of the principal thereof, within twenty years from the time of contracting the same. Any indebtedness or liability incurred contrary to this provision shall be void. Provided, that this section shall not be construed to apply to the ordinary and necessary expenses authorized by the general laws of the state."

Under this section the point raised by the respondent is that by the terms of said contract an indebtedness or liability is incurred exceeding the yearly income of the city and against said constitutional requirements. The appellant takes issue with respondent on this point and maintains that the city does not incur any indebtedness or liability by the terms and conditions of said contract. But before taking up the propositions of law presented in the case, it may be well to examine the contract in regard to what the city is required to do in order to comply with its provisions and obligations. First, the city agrees to commence immediately upon the construction of breakwaters or other structures necessary to confine the flow of the Boise river to a channel of uniform width between the Ninth street bridge and the Broadway bridge, a distance of about half a mile in length. The Ninth street bridge is 325 feet in length, and the Broadway bridge is something near the same, so that these breakwaters and other structures would be required to confine the waters of the river in a channel of about 300 feet in width, which, owing to the volume of water and the nature of its banks, would in itself be no small job. But the city in the same section of the contract further agrees to proceed immediately to construct a wing-dam from the south bank of the river at a point on the north line of Boise City Park subdivision, opposite the point where the river is divided by the island lying between said subdivision and Julia Davis Park. The city also agrees at said time to construct along the south bank of said river from said wing-dam to Broadway bridge a temporary breakwater of riprap sufficient to protect the lands behind the same from overflow or erosion till the permanent channel is completed.

Now, the construction of these works must immediately commence; and it will be noticed that nothing is said as to their cost or how they are to be paid for, which is a very important matter with the people who will have to pay for them. Then the contract further provides that the city shall fill in between the south bank of the river as established by said wing-dam and breakwater down to or near the Ninth street bridge, making a tract of about forty acres, with such solid filling material as earth, sand, gravel or equally solid fill as it shall have at its disposal; to level the fill, plat and construct it into a public park. Now, if the city did not have the material for this fill at its "disposal," the question will arise as to where or how this material could be obtained; and here is where the first mention is made as to the paying for the expenses of any of this work. The contract says at this point that the city in this reclaiming work shall expend at least $5,000 each year for five years from the date thereof. The city might expend more, and we think it quite probable that it would have to expend much more than the minimum sum in order to complete this work in the five years providing for such yearly payments.

It is further provided that the city shall construct Riverside drive and do various other things, all requiring more or less expense, and it must all be complete within eight years from date of contract. It is true that the appellant corporation agrees to do certain things on its part that are specified in said contract as the consideration for the terms and stipulations on the part of the city, but there is nothing in the record other than the contract itself to enlighten this court as to the value of these things. However, this is unimportant from our viewpoint, because we are not passing upon whether this is a favorable deal for the city, but the question is: Did it incur a debt or liability when it executed the same? And we submit that under a fair and reasonable construction of said section of our constitution, it did. If an agreement to perform this vast amount of work does not incur a liability on the part of the city, then the words "incur" and "liability" must each be given meanings unknown to lexicographers.

Black's Law Dictionary, 2d edition, defines the word "incur" as follows: "Incur. Men contract debts; they incur liabilities. In the one case they act affirmatively; in the other, the liability is incurred or cast upon them by act or operation of law." Bouvier, in his Law Dictionary, defines the word "liability" as follows: "Responsibility. The state of one who is bound in law and justice to do something which may be enforced by action. This liability may arise from contracts either express or implied, or in consequence of torts committed. The state of being bound or obliged in law or justice.''

Coming now to the application of said section of the constitution to the contract in question, it will be observed that it refers in terms to the incurring of indebtedness or liability, not expressly to the payment of the indebtedness or the discharge of the liability.

In the case of *Feil v. City of Coeur d'Alene*, 23 Ida. 32, 129 Pac. 643, 43 L. R. A., N. S., 1095, this section came directly before this court for consideration, as it was urged by the appellant Feil against the validity of an ordinance of the city of Coeur d'Alene providing for the purchase by the city of a waterworks system, at that time in operation in the city. As a very similar question was presented to the supreme court of Washington in *Winston v. City of Spokane*, 12 Wash. 524, 41 Pac. 888, that case was urged by respondent, City of Coeur d'Alene, in support of its ordinance, but the same was held void, for the reason that it would create a *liability* against the city. Mr. Justice Ailshie delivered the opinion of the court and reviewed the Winston case and other cases where it had been followed as authority in construing constitutional provisions of other states similar to sec. 6, art. 8 of the constitution of Washington. Referring to the Winston case in said opinion, this court says:

''Since this decision was announced by the supreme court of Washington, in 1895, a number of very similar cases have arisen throughout the various states, and the opinions of the courts adhering to this view have invariably referred back to the Winston case and relied upon it as an authority, and so by citing that case and the various cases from other states that have followed the doctrine of that case, a line of authorities has been built up within the last fifteen years which tend to support the contention made by the respondent in this case and to sustain the validity of the ordinance here in question. . . . . An analysis and comparison of the constitutional provisions above quoted will at once disclose, however, that none of them were so sweeping and prohibitive in their terms as sec. 3, art. 8, of our constitution above quoted.

We shall not take the time or space here to draw the comparison and analyze the differences existing between those constitutional provisions and our own, but will rather content ourselves with a brief analysis of our own constitutional provision, and point out what seems to us the peculiar and decisive provisions of our own constitution which should be held as conclusive in this case."

And further on in the opinion, this language is used:

"The courts to whose decisions we have above referred have indulged in various subtleties and refinements of reasoning to show that no *debt* or *indebtedness* is incurred where a municipality buys certain property and specifically provides that no liability shall be incurred on the part of the city, but that the property shall be paid for out of a *special fund* to be raised from the income and revenue from such property. The reasoning, however, of those cases utterly fails when applied to our constitution, for the reason that none of those cases deals with the word 'liability,' which is used in our constitution, and which is a much more sweeping and comprehensive term than the word 'indebtedness'; nor are the words 'in any manner or for any purpose' given any special attention by the courts in the foregoing cases. The framers of our constitution were not content to say that no city shall incur any indebtedness 'in any manner or for any purpose,' but they rather preferred to say that no city shall incur any *indebtedness or liability* in any manner, or for any purpose. It must be clear to the ordinary mind on reading this language that the framers of the constitution meant to cover all kinds and character of debts and obligations for which a city may become bound, and to preclude circuitous and evasive methods of incurring debts and obligations to be met by the city or its inhabitants."

In the case at bar, appellant corporation seems to rely mainly on *McBean v. City of Fresno*, 112 Cal. 159, 53 Am. St. 191, 44 Pac. 358, as authority in support of its contention that said contract is valid, and as this case is not referred to in *Feil v. City of Coeur d'Alene*, we will briefly consider it. This was a case where the court, no doubt, had strong equitable grounds in favor of the validity of the contract upon which the action was based. The facts show that the city of Fresno had provided a sewer system for the city, but no natural means were available for the disposition of its sewage. It had provided sewers but had made no provision for the care of their contents. These must necessarily be discharged beyond the city limits, but before the sewers could be used, grounds must be secured for the reception and treatment of the waste matter. In these circumstances, the contract was entered into with McBean. By the terms of this contract he agreed to take care of the sewage of the city for five years for the sum of $4,900 per annum, payable quarterly. He gave a bond in the sum of $10,000 for the faithful performance of the contract on his part. Now, in these circumstances there was an urgent necessity for the city to make some arrangements to dispose of its sewage at once. The quarterly expense was small, and the price was probably very reasonable. Moreover, the charter of the city authorized the levying and collection of a tax not exceeding ten cents on each $100 for a sewer fund, and it was conceded that the tax which would be collected for that fund was ample to meet all sums that might be needed to pay McBean under said contract. Because of the merit of the contract and the pressing necessity for some means to take care of the sewage of the city, we believe the better judgment of the court was somewhat biased by its desire to actually benefit the people of the city. In fact, as a matter of public policy, the execution of this contract might well be justified. But when the court attempts by argument to escape the force and effect of the constitutional provision under consideration and show that the city incurred no *liability* under the contract, we submit that its reasoning is not sound. It says:

"In a certain very restricted sense it may be said that a liability is created by a contract such as this; but to call it a present liability for the aggregate amount of the payments in the contract contemplated thereafter to be made is not legally permissible. A liability to the city would arise upon breach of contract, but the constitution never meant to protect the city from the consequences of its own wilful and tortious acts.''

But if this contract was valid, would not the courts intervene to compel the city authorities to comply with all its terms and provisions? Conceding that it is true that it would not be "legally permissible" to call the aggregate amounts in the contract to be paid a present *debt,* then we submit that it would be a "present *liability*" for such aggregate amounts. If the contract was valid, by its terms $1,225 would become due at the end of each quarter of each year of its existence, as the services were performed, from the beginning of said services to the expiration of the five years for which it was made, and this sum would then be a *debt,* but the city incurred a *liability* for the aggregate sum of $24,500 at the date the contract was executed.

If A by a valid contract employs B to work for him for the term of one year at $50 per month, payable at the end of each and every month, would this contract not be a liability on A as soon as executed? A debt of $50 would accrue thereon at the end of each month, but the liability would be incurred at the time the contract was entered into. But in said opinion the court further says: "A liability to the city would arise upon breach of contract, but the constitution never meant to protect the city from the consequences of its own wilful and tortious acts." It is by no means apparent to this court as to how any liability could arise upon the breach of a contract that neither imposed a *debt* or a *liability.*

But appellant also maintains that the obligations entered into by the city in the contract under consideration do not constitute a *new debt* or *liability,* because it simply assumed and entered into terms for the payment of existing debts or liabilities which grew out of certain torts committed by the city against appellant, and therefore does not come within the inhibitions of said section 3.

In support of this point, appellant in its brief cites the cases of *Hickey v. City of Nampa,* 22 Ida. 41, 124 Pac. 280, *Pike v. State Land Board,* 19 Ida. 268, Ann. Cas. 1912B. 1344, 113 Pac. 447, *Murphy v. Chicago B. & Q. Ry. Co.,* 247 Ill.

614, 93 N. E. 381, and *Carson v. City of Genesee,* 9 Ida. 244, 108 Am. St. 127, 74 Pac. 862. After an examination of these authorities, we are persuaded that none of them sustain appellant's contention, but as we consider *Hickey v. City of Nampa* the nearest in point of these authorities, we will therefore review the case at some length.

The action was brought for the purpose of procuring a writ of injunction restraining the issuance and sale by the city of Nampa of certain municipal coupon bonds in the sum of $37,000. The city owned a water system consisting of a pumping station and a system of wooden pipes. The city also owned certain fire equipments and appurtenances for the fighting and extinguishing of fire. In July, 1909, a disastrous fire broke out in the business section of the city by which about $200,000 worth of property was destroyed. During the fire the water supply was exhausted, the water was pumped directly through the mains, and this resulted in bursting most of the wooden pipes, and the city was left without any fire protection. The mayor and council considered this a casualty within the purview of section 2270 of the Rev. Codes, that the repair and improvement of the water system and fire-extinguishing apparatus was a public necessity calling for immediate action. Under the stress of this necessity, they, by unanimous vote, determined to restore the water system in such a manner as to adequately protect the property in the city. To pay for the material and work for these improvements, city warrants were issued for various items of expense. In August, 1911, an ordinance was duly passed to issue bonds in the sum of $37,000 to pay off the indebtedness represented by these warrants. These were the facts before this court in that case, and it was held that the said bond issue was legal. In the opinion, delivered by Mr. Justice Ailshie, the position of the court is fully stated as follows:

"In the first place, we have no doubt but that the indebtedness which was incurred falls within the purview of sec. 2270 of the Rev. Codes, in that it was entailed as a result of a casualty or accident which could not have been foreseen and provided for by the annual appropriation. The city of Nampa had duly and regularly exercised the power and authority conferred upon it by the provisions of subdivisions 36 and 37 of sec. 2238, Rev. Codes, in acquiring and maintaining a waterworks system and apparatus and appliances for extinguishing fires. In order for this property to be of any value to the city, it was necessary for it to be kept in repair. When the fire came and the waterworks system was impaired and rendered useless, it was necessary that the city repair and restore it. It was also equally necessary to have fire equipment and apparatus to enable it to properly utilize the water in case of fire. The vote of the council to make this expenditure and incur the indebtedness was authorized by unanimous vote, and was therefore a compliance with the requirements of sec. 2270. It appears in this case that the mayor and city council acted in good faith, and that this was a *bona fide* improvement and restoration of property within the purview and meaning of the statute. The city council could certainly not use this as a subterfuge for the construction or purchase of a new system of waterworks or other independent, separate or new property so as to contravene the provisions of sec. 3, art. 8, of the constitution. . . . . The same section, however, closes with this proviso: 'Provided, that this section shall not be construed to apply to the ordinary and necessary expenses authorized by the general laws of the state.' We take it that it was within the power of the legislature under this constitutional provision to say that an *expenditure*, though out of the *ordinary*, which is incurred for the purpose of repairing some damage done to city property or improving it in such manner as to render it serviceable to the city, falls within this proviso to the constitution. The repair and improvement of the property may be 'ordinary and necessary' and yet not occur frequently.''

And further on in said opinion it is stated: ''This was not the creation of any new indebtedness, but was rather the changing of the form of the indebtedness or paying an ordinary debt already incurred.''

We do not think the contention of appellant, that the consideration for the agreements entered into by the city in said contract is not a new debt or liability, is sustained by this authority. In *Hickey v. City of Nampa*, it is held that the debt was legally incurred under the proviso of said section 3, and it was a definite fixed liability on the city. The identical debt as evidenced by city warrants was simply changed into the form of bonds, and it was decided in that case that it was not a new debt. But in the case at bar, it cannot be ascertained from the contract, or anything else in the record, what the amount of the liability is that the city assumes thereby, and when we consider the sums of money claimed by appellant for alleged damages to its property by the city, the fact at once appears that said sums so claimed for such damages are uncertain, and contingent, and have never *before* the execution of said contract been liquidated, settled or in any manner reduced to a definite or fixed amount of indebtedness against the city by decree of a court, by arbitration, compromise or in any manner whatever; and if these sums are liquidated, settled and fixed as a definite amount of indebtedness by the contract itself, this amount would then constitute a *new debt*. Furthermore, if a court should attempt to enforce this contract, its specifications of the work to be done are so meager and indefinite and the sums to be expended thereon are so uncertain, that it would almost inevitably lead to dispute and litigation.

We think it would not be profitable to review the other authorities cited by appellant in support of the proposition that the consideration for the obligations entered into by the city in said contract did not constitute a new debt or liability, for, as we understand them, they are not in point on this proposition.

We are of the opinion, therefore, that under the authority of *Feil v. City of Coeur d'Alene*, the contract upon which this action is based by its terms plainly incurs a liability, if not a debt, upon the city of Boise, that the obligations of said contract do constitute a new debt upon the city, and we therefore hold that said contract is void.

The judgment of the trial court must be affirmed, with costs in favor of the respondent.

Sullivan, C. J., concurs.

———

(September 30, 1914.)

W. D. FALES and ELIZABETH B. FALES, Respondents, v. WEETER LUMBER COMPANY, LTD., a Corporation, Appellant.

[143 Pac. 526.]

EQUITABLE ACTION—JUDGMENT—SETTING ASIDE.

1. *Held,* under the law and evidence, that the court erred in setting aside the judgment sought to be set aside by this action.

2. One who seeks equity in a court of conscience must do equity before any relief will be granted.

3. Where an equitable action is brought to vacate a judgment upon the ground that it was obtained without jurisdiction, it must appear that the judgment sought to be set aside is inequitable and unjust, and that plaintiff has a good defense thereto.

4. If a judgment is regular on its face, it will never be opened up merely for the purpose of letting in the defense of the statute of limitations.

APPEAL from the District Court of the Fourth Judicial District for Gooding County. Hon. Edward A. Walters, Judge.

Equitable action to set aside a judgment. Judgment for plaintiffs. *Reversed.*

James R. Bothwell and Thos. F. Terrell, for Appellant.

As a matter of equity and good conscience, neither of the plaintiffs would be permitted to maintain this action seeking the equitable relief which they do, without first paying to the defendant the balance due to it for lumber and building materials, which it is conceded has not been paid. (*Tracy*

v. Wheeler, 15 N. D. 248, 107 N. W. 68, 6 L. R. A., N. S., 16;
Willits v. Willits, 76 Neb. 228, 14 Ann. Cas. 883, 107 N. W.
379, 5 L. R. A., N. S., 767; *International Land Co. v. Marshall*,
22 Okl. 693, 98 Pac. 951, 19 L. R. A., N. S., 1056; *Booth v.
Hoskins*, 75 Cal. 271, 17 Pac. 227, and cases cited; *Bernhard
v. Idaho Bank & Trust Co.*, 21 Ida. 598, Ann. Cas. 1913E,
120, 123 Pac. 481; *Brandt v. Little*, 47 Wash. 194, 91 Pac.
765, 14 L. R. A., N. S., 213; 1 Black on Judgments, sec. 394.)

"A court of equity will not interfere with the enforcement
of a judgment recovered at law, unless it is unjust and unconscionable; and therefore such relief will not be granted,
unless the complainant shows that he has good and meritorious
defense to the original action." (23 Cyc. 1031.)

"Acquiescence consisting of mere silence may operate as
an estoppel to preclude assertion of legal title and rights of
property." (*Loughran v. Gorman*, 256 Ill. 46, 99 N. E.
886; 2 Pomeroy, Eq. Jur., 3d ed., 818; *Niven v. Belknap*, 2
Johns. (N. Y.) 573.)

In order for the plaintiff to state a cause of action or to
recover in this cause, she must allege in her complaint and
prove as a fact that the defendant Weeter Lumber Co., at the
time when said lien was filed and at the time when said action
to foreclose the same was commenced, knew that the said
property was community property, and also knew that it was
occupied and used as a place of residence. (*Washington
Rock-Plaster Co. v. Johnson*, 10 Wash. 445, 39 Pac. 115.)

There is nothing in the statutes or the laws of Idaho requiring the wife to be made a party defendant in actions to foreclose a lien either upon the homestead or upon other community property occupied as a residence.

"Where a lien attached to real estate before becoming a
homestead, the wife is not a necessary party to an action
foreclosing the same." (*Watkins v. Sproull*, 8 Tex. Civ. App.
427, 28 S. W. 356; Boisot on Mechanics' Liens, sec. 529.)

W. G. Bissell, for Respondents.

The judgment against which we sought to quiet title was a
nullity and void, and thus, as a general proposition of law, is

open to attacks, either direct or collateral, at any time. (*Gapen v. Bretternitz*, 31 Neb. 302, 47 N. W. 918; *Kansas City etc. R. R. Co. v. Moon*, 66 Ark. 409, 50 S. W. 996; *Miles v. Strong*, 68 Conn. 273, 36 Atl. 55; *Yon v. Baldwin*, 76 Ga. 769; *Johnson v. Logan*, 68 Ill. 313; *Powell v. Gisendorff*, 23 Kan. 538; *Mayo v. Ah Loy*, 32 Cal. 477, 91 Am. Dec. 595.)

"In all suits to foreclose mechanics' liens and mortgages, the wife is a necessary party defendant." (McKay on Community Property, 385.) And notwithstanding the husband individually incurred the debt which the lien secures." (27 Cyc. 349; *Sagmeister v. Foss*, 4 Wash. 320, 30 Pac. 80, 744; *Turner v. Bellingham Bay Lumber Co.*, 9 Wash. 484, 37 Pac. 674; *Seattle v. Bacter*, 20 Wash. 715, 55 Pac. 320; *Powell v. Nolan*, 27 Wash. 318, 67 Pac. 712, 68 Pac. 389; *Weston v. Weston*, 46 Wis. 130, 49 N. W. 834; *Gray v. Gates*, 37 Wis. 614; *Hausmann Bros. Mfg. Co. v. Kempfert*, 93 Wis. 587, 67 N. W. 1136; *Northwestern Bridge Co. v. Tacoma Shipbuilding Co.*, 36 Wash. 333, 78 Pac. 996.)

"Legal proceedings to be conclusive against either must embrace both, and the judgment was therefore void." (*Revalk v. Kraemer*, 8 Cal. 66, 68 Am. Dec. 304; *Hefner v. Urton*, 71 Cal. 479, 12 Pac. 486; *Watts v. Gallagher*, 97 Cal. 47, 31 Pac. 626; *Brackett v. Banegas*, 116 Cal. 278, 58 Am. St. 164, 48 Pac. 90; *Ludwig v. Murphy*, 143 Cal. 473, 77 Pac. 150.)

SULLIVAN, C. J.—This is an equitable action brought for the purpose of setting aside a judgment entered in the case of the *Weeter Lumber Co. v. Fales*, which case was appealed to this court, and the decision on appeal will be found in 20 Ida. 255, Ann. Cas. 1913A, 403, 118 Pac. 289. The trial court entered a judgment in favor of the plaintiff setting aside said former judgment and this appeal is from that judgment.

The following facts appear from the record:

William D. Fales entered into a contract with the Gooding Townsite Company on or about April 5, 1909, to purchase lots 19 and 20 in block 38 in the town of Gooding, by the terms of which contract the townsite company reserved title

to said lots and agreed to convey said title to said Fales upon
the payment of certain sums of money.   At the time of the
sale the lots were vacant and unimproved.   After entering
into said contract, Fales entered into a contract with one Mead
to construct a building upon said lots and contracted with
the appellant, the Weeter Lumber Company, to furnish the
building material for the construction of such building.
The lumber company furnished material to the amount of
$1,927.34, which was actually used in the construction of the
building.   On August 6, 1909, the purchase price of said
lumber being due and unpaid, the lumber company filed its
claim of lien upon said premises.   Thereafter certain payments were made to the lumber company by Fales upon the
amount due for said material, and on February 2, 1910, there
remained a balance of $719.82 due the lumber company for
said material, and on that date the lumber company brought
an action to foreclose the materialman's lien for said amount.
On May 17th, William D. Fales filed a separate answer, wherein
he admitted that he was the owner and reputed owner of
said lots, but thereafter, on September 19, 1910, he filed an
amended answer denying that he was the owner or reputed
owner of said premises, and alleged that he held said property under said contract with the Gooding Townsite Company.   Said foreclosure action was then tried and findings
of fact and decree entered in favor of the lumber company,
foreclosing said lien and directing the sale of the premises.
From that judgment Fales took an appeal to the supreme
court, and the opinion of this court therein is found in 20
Ida. 255, Ann. Cas. 1913A, 403, 118 Pac. 289.

It also appears that during the trial of said case Elizabeth
B. Fales, the wife of said Fales, was present as a witness, and
testified in said case on behalf of her husband, that she knew
of the filing of the lien upon said premises and the foreclosure
of said lien and claimed no interest whatever in said premises,
and suffered and permitted judgment to be entered in said
suit without in any manner raising the question as to said
property being community property.   More than a year after
said trial and the entry of said judgment, she filed her motion

in said foreclosure suit to set aside and vacate the judgment
of foreclosure, on the ground that it was community property
and occupied as a residence. That motion was argued and
submitted to the court and denied, and she failed to appeal
from the order denying her motion.

Thereafter this action was commenced by said Elizabeth
B. Fales and her husband to set aside said judgment of foreclosure, on the ground that said property was community
property and that the court had no jurisdiction over the community property and that she had not been made a party to
said foreclosure suit. After the trial of this action the court
set aside said judgment and entered judgment in favor of the
plaintiffs.

The main contention of plaintiffs is that said property being
community property and resided upon by plaintiffs, the court
acquired no jurisdiction in the foreclosure proceedings because service of summons was not made upon the plaintiff
Elizabeth B. Fales. She admits that the defendant furnished the lumber for the construction of said building, and
the record clearly shows that said building was constructed
before she and her husband began to reside therein, and that
if she is successful in this action she no doubt will be able to
appropriate as community property $719.82 worth of the
material used in the construction of said building without
paying for it.

It is a familiar maxim of equity that a party asking equity
must first do equity, and a court of conscience would not
permit her to appropriate said material without paying for
it, which the record shows she has not done. The record also
shows that said lien attached before she began to reside upon
said premises and that she had full knowledge that the Weeter
Lumber Company had furnished said material and that it
had not been paid for. As a matter of equity and good conscience, neither of the respondents would be permitted to
maintain this action without first paying to the appellant the
balance due for said building materials.

It was held in effect in *Tracy v. Wheeler*, 15 N. D. 248,
107 N. W. 68, 6 L. R. A., N. S., 516, that a court of equity

would not cancel a real estate mortgage securing a just debt which it was conceded had not been paid, at a suit of the mortgagor or one standing in his shoes, when the only ground urged for such relief is that the statute of limitations is available as a defense against the foreclosure, and the fact that the plaintiff could not be coerced by legal means to pay the debt affects only the legal character of the obligation; that it does not alter the primary fact that she (the plaintiff), owes the obligation which in equity and good conscience she ought to pay. *Booth v. Hoskins,* 75 Cal. 271, 17 Pac. 225, is to the same effect.

This court held in *Bernhard v. Idaho Bank & Trust Co.,* 21 Ida. 598, Ann. Cas. 1913E, 120, 123 Pac. 481, that where an independent action is brought to vacate a judgment upon the ground that it was obtained without jurisdiction, a showing that the defendant has, or at the time of the judgment, had, a defense, is none the less necessary because the judgment may have been obtained without service of the summons or appearance of the defendants; and that it must be shown that the former judgment is not equitable.

It is stated in Black on Judgments, sec. 394, that "The privilege of vacating judgments is to be used only in furtherance of justice, and a judgment should not be set aside unless it is unjust as it stands. Hence, if it is regular on its face, it will never be opened up merely for the purpose of letting in an unconscionable, dishonest, or purely technical defense."

In 23 Cyc., p. 1031, it is said that "A court of equity will not interfere with the enforcement of a judgment recovered at law, unless it is unjust and unconscionable; and therefore such relief will not be granted unless the complainant shows that he has a good and meritorious defense to the original action."

The plaintiff, Elizabeth Fales, claims in effect that the Weeter Lumber Company failed to make her a party to the action of foreclosure, and not being made a party to that action and the statute requiring that an action to foreclose such liens shall be commenced within six months, as to her said action is barred by the statute of limitations and cannot be maintained.

In such cases where the statute of limitations might be plead against another action brought for the foreclosure of the lien and it is clear that the debt had never been paid, a court of equity will not assist a plaintiff in avoiding a just debt by that means.

The trial court erred in entering judgment for the plaintiffs. That judgment must be set aside, and it is so ordered, and the trial court is directed to enter judgment in favor of the defendant.

Costs awarded to appellant.

Truitt, J., concurs.

(October 1, 1914.)

JULIUS C. MILLER, Respondent, v. ULYSSES G. WALLACE et al., Appellants.

[143 Pac. 524.]

Appeal—Motion to Dismiss—Service of Notice of Appeal.

 1. Under the provisions of sec. 4808, Rev. Codes, the notice of appeal must be served on the adverse party or his attorney.

 2. Under the provisions of said section, the notice of appeal must be served upon every party whose interests might be affected by the reversal of the order or judgment appealed from, irrespective of whether they are plaintiffs, defendants or intervenors.

APPEAL from the District Court of the Third Judicial District, in and for Ada County. Hon. Carl A. Davis, Judge.

Proceeding to set aside sheriff's sale. Motion to dismiss appeal. Granted.

J. C. Johnston and J. J. McCue, for Appellants.

It is true, as this court has often held, that from an appeal from the judgment or decree of the court below the appellant must serve notice of appeal upon all adverse parties to the judgment or decree. But upon reading the decisions of this court, it will be noted that in all the cases there was an appeal taken to reverse or modify the judgment of the court below, but in the case before the court, the action of the appellant is not an appeal from the judgment or decree of the court below, nor does the appellant seek to reverse or modify the decree or judgment of the court below, but it is simply an appeal from the order and judgment of the court below denying and overruling the motion of appellant to set aside the sheriff's sale, and affects no one except the purchaser at the sheriff's sale. (*Mills v. Smiley,* 9 Ida. 325–327, 76 Pac. 783).

Wyman & Wyman, for Respondent.

Both Wallace, the mortgagor, and O'Donnell,. who acquired an interest in the property subsequent to the mortgage, are adverse parties to the appellants here and should have been served with notice. Wallace is vitally interested. There is now no deficiency judgment against him. Should appellant succeed, such a deficiency judgment will probably result. O'Donnell is perfectly satisfied with the decree and the amount found to be due from him. On a resale he might be seriously injured. He is opposed to a reversal of the order appealed from. Both he and Wallace are entitled to their day in court on this appeal. (*Diamond Bank v. Van Meter,* 18 Ida. 243, 108 Pac. 1042, 21 Ann. Cas. 1273; *Coffin v. Edgington,* 2 Ida. 627, 23 Pac. 80, is to the same effect; *Titiman v. Alamance Min. Co.,* 9 Ida. 240, 74 Pac. 529; *Baker v. Drews,* 9 Ida. 276, 74 Pac. 1130; *Reed v. Stewart,* 12 Ida. 699, 87 Pac. 1002, 1152.)

SULLIVAN, C. J.—This action was brought to foreclose a mortgage on real estate given by the defendant Wallace to the plaintiff Miller. Subsequent to the giving of the mortgage and prior to the commencement of the action, certain parties acquired an interest in the premises and were made parties defendant. A decree of foreclosure was entered and a sale thereunder had.

After the giving of said mortgage, the premises had been subdivided and the sale was made in separate parcels. The property sold for enough, so that there remained no deficiency. One of the defendants, Roberts, after the sale, moved to set the sale aside. This motion was overruled and the appeal is from the order denying the motion. He served his notice of appeal on the plaintiff Miller, but not on any of his co-defendants, and the appeal now comes up on the motion of plaintiff Miller to dismiss the appeal on the ground that the notice of appeal was not served on all of the adverse parties.

The record shows that the property sold for sufficient to satisfy the mortgage and costs. The decree of foreclosure provided for a deficiency judgment against Wallace, provided the property did not sell for sufficient to pay the mortgage debt with interest and costs. Thus it is shown that Wallace is vitally interested in the matter and may be injuriously affected provided the sale is set aside and a new sale made. If on a resale the property should not sell for sufficient to pay said indebtedness and costs, a deficiency judgment would be entered up against Wallace. The defendant O'Donnell might also be adversely affected by the setting aside of said sale.

On an appeal either from the judgment or an order, the notice of appeal must be served on all parties to the action, or their attorneys, who might be affected by a reversal or modification of the judgment or order. (See sec. 4808, Rev. Codes.) In the case of *Diamond Bank v. Van Meter,* 18 Ida. 243, 108 Pac. 1042, 21 Ann. Cas. 1273, many of the decisions of this court upon the point under consideration are cited.

· The notice of appeal not having been served upon all of the parties who might be affected by a reversal of the order appealed from, the motion must be sustained and the appeal dismissed, and it is so ordered. Costs awarded to the respondent.

Truitt, J., concurs.

(October 15, 1914.)

McCONNON & CO., a Corporation, Appellant, v. G. R. HODGE et al., Respondents.

[143 Pac. 522.]

VERDICT—INSUFFICIENCY OF EVIDENCE.
1. The evidence *held* not sufficient to sustain the verdict.

APPEAL from the District Court of the Second Judicial District for Latah County. Hon. Edgar C. Steele, Judge.

Action to recover for goods, wares and merchandise. Judgment for defendants. *Reversed.*

Wm. E. Lee, for Appellant, cites no authorities.

William M. Morgan, for Respondents.

It is the universal rule that a contract may be discharged by agreement between the parties. (9 Cyc. 593.)

SULLIVAN, C. J.—This is an action brought to recover the value of certain goods alleged to have been sold to the respondent Hodge, Hughes and Clark, being sureties for the payment of the price of said goods.

The cause was tried by the court with a jury and a verdict rendered in favor of the defendant Hodge for the sum of $94.72 and costs, and in favor of Hughes and Clark for their costs incurred in the trial of the case. The appeal is from the judgment and is based on the insufficiency of the evidence to sustain the verdict.

It appears from the record that the appellant corporation is engaged in the manufacture of spices, flavoring extracts, etc.; that the sale of such products is made to individuals at wholesale prices, and the individuals sell and dispose of the articles in territories assigned to them.

On or about October 12, 1911, the respondent Hodge, desiring to purchase certain goods from the appellant, entered into a written contract with the appellant, the respondents Clark and Hughes signing said contract as guarantors, to the effect that Hodge would pay for the goods purchased. After said contract was signed and delivered, the appellant shipped certain goods to respondent Hodge on his order and he made a number of payments on said goods prior to the 29th of April, 1912, on which date the appellant was notified by Hodge's wife that Hodge had left the country and was not attending to business.

On May 15, 1912, one Norrup, an employee of appellant, visited Moscow for the purpose of trying to adjust or put upon a business basis the business of said Hodge. The record shows that he tried to adjust matters and in doing so an offer was made to sell the business to one Rush. The plan was to have Hodge turn over the remainder of the goods he held and also the accounts still due for goods, to Rush, who was then to enter into a contract with the appellant, and guarantor Clark was to sign the contract as guarantor for Rush. Norrup, Hodge and Rush invoiced the goods and accounts and the goods were turned over to Norrup for Rush, but when the matter was presented again to Clark, he refused to sign as guarantor for Rush. Thereupon the goods were turned back to Hodge, who continued to make certain sales from the goods; but Hodge was not conducting the business satisfactorily to appellant, and appellant demanded payment of the balance due from Hodge and his guarantors. Payment was refused and this action was brought in April, 1913.

The respondents pleaded a counterclaim, alleging that Hodge and Norrup effected a settlement in which Norrup agreed to pay Hodge $105 for his interest in said goods. Upon the issues thus made the case was tried before the court with a jury and a general verdict was rendered in favor of the respondents, including a judgment in favor of Hodge in the sum of $94.72. The respondents' contention was that there had been a settlement between Hodge and Norrup, whereby the guarantors had been released and the appellant had agreed to pay plaintiff $105.

It appears from the record that Rush had been recommended by Hodge as an agent or salesman for the appellant, and he had discussed with Clark and Hodge the matter of taking over Hodge's business and the balance of the goods remaining in his hands.   It also appears that the respondent Clark and the appellant were not satisfied with the action of Hodge, and Clark was anxious to get the goods into the hands of some person who would attend to the business. Certain negotiations were carried on between Rush, Norrup, Hodge and Clark which the respondents insist constituted a settlement between appellant and Hodge.

On the trial Hodge testified on his direct examination that he sold his interest in said goods for $60 to the appellant, through Norrup, its agent; that thereupon they proceeded to invoice the goods, and Hodge testified that when he told his wife what he was getting, "she put up a kick" and said he was not getting enough, and thereupon Norrup agreed to pay the freight on the goods "on top of the $60," and that the freight agreed upon was $35.00. He also testified that Norrup said to him that if a new contract were accepted by the company, Rush would be given credit for the amount of goods Hodge had on hand. He also testified that he had never demanded the payment of the $105, or of any other sum, which he claimed was the contract price of the sale through Norrup. The testimony of respondent Hodge was quite contradictory.

Rush testified that it was his understanding that he was to pay Hodge the freight provided that he (Rush) took the goods. A letter written by Hodge to the appellant the day after the goods had been returned to him, to wit, May 16, 1912, clearly shows the understanding that he had of the transaction and acts that took place on the previous day. He states, among other things, in said letter, as follows:

"I received yours of the 11th yesterday and will say that Mr. A. J. Norrup has just been here, he said you sent him here to try to close a contract with Mr. Joseph Rush not knowing I was here ready to go to work . . . . and I agreed to turn the whole thing over to Mr. Rush providing Mr.

Clark would sign with him instead of me to this Mr. Clark agreed but backed down as soon as they got up there with the goods so they just turned around and brought the goods back to me and I have concluded to get on the road just as soon as possible and if Mr. Clark wont stand for me to order more goods I will try to get different guarantors altogether. . . . . Mr. Clark seems to talk one way to me and to Mr. Norrup another. I don't know how he has written you. I went to see my guarantors just as soon as I got home and they told me it was all right, to go right ahead they were willing to stand by me and I made my arrangements to this effect until Mr. Norrup came but as he failed to make any different arrangements I shall go ahead and will be on the road in a few days."

This letter written the day after Norrup had tried to adjust the matter fully corroborates the testimony of Norrup in regard to said transaction. And that is not all; on June 3, 1912, Hodge wrote another letter to appellant in which he said nothing about the settlement that he swore to on the trial and he did not make any demand for the $95 or $105 which he testified Norrup had promised to pay him. In a letter to appellant dated July 16, 1912, Hodge offered to turn over said goods to any person simply upon the payment of the freight that he had paid on them. Why would he write such a letter as this if he had made a full settlement with Norrup for the appellant, whereby the appellant had agreed to pay him $60 and the freight for his interest in the goods and had taken possession of the goods under such a contract? He certainly would not have done so if he had sold his interest in the goods to the appellant for $60.

On July 25, 1912, Hodge wrote a letter to the appellant in which he stated that he had been trying to dispose of said goods to Rush. Is it not surprising that he would be trying to dispose of the goods to Rush when, if his testimony be true, he had already disposed of them to appellant? On October 9th he wrote another letter to appellant in which he said: "I think if I can turn my goods to some one," etc. On that day he made a payment of five dollars on the account.

Why would he send five dollars on account to appellant if appellant were owing him nearly a hundred dollars? He claims that the settlement was made on the 15th of May, 1912, and as late as October 9, 1912, he remits five dollars on account to the appellant. On October 16th he wrote another letter to appellant in which he stated: "I received one remittance of $1.50 and hope to collect quite a little before the 20th. If you can send a man to get the goods, all right; if not I will ship them back. I assure you I am doing all I can do to make a settlement and will do so at the earliest possible date." His letters and acts corroborate the testimony of Norrup and show that the testimony given by Hodge in regard to said alleged settlement was not true. The evidence shows that he had received no goods from appellant in the meantime. So far as the record shows, Hodge had never intimated to the appellant corporation that he had made a settlement with Norrup for the goods that he had on May 15, 1912, until he filed his answer in this action. It is clear from the record that Rush had discussed with Hodge and Clark the proposition of buying Hodge out, and Rush was willing to do so if Clark would sign Rush's contract as guarantor. Clearly, Norrup's only interest in the matter was to get the matter adjusted and get Rush to take the territory that Hodge had, and when Clark refused to become guarantor for Rush, the attempt at a settlement fell through and the goods were returned to Hodge.

The evidence is not sufficient to sustain the verdict. The judgment must be reversed and a new trial granted. Costs awarded to appellant.

Truitt, J., concurs.

(October 21, 1914.)

STATE, Appellant, v. L. STAFFORD, Respondent.

[143 Pac. 528.]

CRIMINAL LAW—APPEAL ON BEHALF OF STATE—MOTION TO DISMISS—PROBATE COURT—COMPLAINT—INFORMATION—STATUTORY CONSTRUCTION.

1. Where a defendant is tried in the probate court for selling intoxicating liquors without a license, under the provisions of sec. 1518, chap. 33, title 8, of the Rev. Codes, and is convicted and appeals to the district court, *held*, that the district court erred in dismissing said action on the motion of the defendant, on the ground that the probate court had no jurisdiction to try such case but should have held a preliminary examination.

2. *Held*, that the misdemeanor for which the defendant was tried and convicted in the probate court was not the crime of selling liquor in a prohibition district, since the defendant was not charged in the complaint filed in said action with selling intoxicating liquors in a prohibition district, but was charged with selling liquor without first procuring the license required by law.

3. Under the provisions of the first subdivision of sec. 8043, Rev. Codes, the state is authorized to take an appeal from a judgment for the defendant on demurrer to the indictment or information.

4. Under the provisions of sec. 8325, Rev. Codes, when an appeal is taken from a justice's or probate court, the clerk of the district court must file the papers received and enter the action on the calendar in its order with other criminal cases, and such case must be tried anew in the district court at the next term thereof, unless for good cause the same is continued.

5. When a criminal case is appealed from a probate court, the case stands on appeal the same as though it had been begun in the district court. It is there for a new trial on every point in question that could legally be raised therein.

6. Under the provisions of sec. 7509, Rev. Codes, a complaint or information is defined as an allegation in writing made to a magistrate that a person has been guilty of some designated offense.

7. The complaint or information is the name of the pleading by which a criminal action is instituted in a justice's or probate court, and the names "complaint" and "information" are used interchangeably and refer to the same kind of a pleading.

8. On an appeal from the probate court to the district court in a criminal case, the proceedings in the trial *de novo* is substantially

the same as in a case before the district court on indictment or information.

9. *Held*, under the provisions of the statute, the state has the authority to appeal in a case on appeal from the probate court in criminal cases, where the appeal is dismissed on the demurrer or motion of the defendant, on the ground that the probate court had no jurisdiction to try said case.

10. *Held*, that the misdemeanor for which the defendant was convicted in the probate court was one which the probate court had jurisdiction to try, to wit, that of selling liquor without a license, and was not a misdemeanor which required the probate court to hold a preliminary examination, and the defendant could not have been convicted of the misdemeanor of selling liquor in a prohibition district under the complaint filed in this case.

APPEAL on behalf of the state from the District Court of the Second Judicial District for Latah County. Hon. Edgar C. Steele, Judge.

Defendant was convicted in the probate court of selling intoxicating liquor without a license, and on appeal the district court held that the probate court should have held a preliminary examination in said matter, and on motion of the defendant dismissed the action. Judgment *reversed*.

J. H. Peterson, Atty. Genl., J. J. Guheen, T. C. Coffin and E. G. Davis, Assts., for the State.

Sec. 8325, which has to do with appeals from the justice court to the district court in criminal matters, provides that when the appeal papers have been filed in the district court, the clerk must enter the action on his calendar in its order with other criminal cases, and that the same shall be there tried anew. The appeal having been properly effected, the case was in the same situation as one originally instituted in the district court.

"On appeal to the circuit court, the cause was triable *de novo*, and no objection could be made to any inaccuracy or imperfection in the proceedings before the county court." (*Tatum v. State*, 66 Ala. 465.)

Other states have had occasion to obtain from their supreme courts a definition of the word "information" as it affected litigants, and to ask for a determination of the pleadings covered by the term. (*State v. Hewlett*, 124 Ala. 471, 27 So. 18.)

Upon a trial *de novo* in the district court, the complaint takes the place of an indictment or an information. The proceedings had upon it are the same in the district court as upon either an indictment or an information. (*Clepper v. State*, 4 Tex. 242; *Simpson v. State*, 111 Ala. 6, 20 So. 572.)

There is no law prohibiting the issuance of a license to sell intoxicating liquors in Latah county, and therefore any person selling liquors in Latah county without a license can be convicted and punished under the terms of sec. 1518, Rev. Codes.

There will be found in many states laws providing for the issuance of licenses to people engaged in selling liquors and providing penalties for the sale of liquor without a license. These same states also have laws making it a crime to sell liquor on Sunday, either with or without a license.

The courts, however, have been uniform in holding that a charge of selling liquor without a license, even though the sale took place on Sunday, was proper. (*State v. Cox*, 23 W. Va. 797; *State v. Bradley*, 132 N. C. 1060, 44 S. E. 122; *State v. Heibel*, 116 Mo. App. 43, 90 S. W. 758; *Shuler v. State*, 125 Ga. 778, 54 S. E. 689; *O'Brien v. State*, 91 Ala. 25, 8 So. 560; *People v. Krank*, 110 N. Y. 488, 18 N. E. 242, 23 Cyc. 187; *State v. Moeling*, 129 La. 204, 55 So. 764; *Carpenter v. State*, 120 Tenn. 586, 113 S. W. 1042.)

Cannon, Ferris & Swan and Wm. E. Lee, for Respondent.

There having been no indictment or information at any time entered against respondent, it is apparent that this court has no jurisdiction to try the appeal. (*State v. Ridenbaugh*, 5 Ida. 710, 51 Pac. 750; *United States v. Sanges*, 144 U. S. 310, 12 Sup. Ct. 609, 36 L. ed. 445; *State v. Northrup*, 13 Mont 522, 35 Pac. 228; *Territory v. Laun*, 8 Mont. 322, 20 Pac. 652.)

Under sec. 3854, Rev. Codes, the justice court has no jurisdiction in a case like the one at bar, where a misdemeanor is alleged to have been charged for which the maximum penalty exceeds $300. (*State v. West*, 20 Ida. 387, 118 Pac. 773.)

The respondent was never indicted for any crime by a grand jury. His case did not come before the district court on information from the public prosecutor after indictment by a magistrate. He had no preliminary examination. The district court had no jurisdiction, therefore, over respondent. No information could have been filed against respondent until he had had a preliminary examination. (*State v. McGreevey*, 17 Ida. 453, 105 Pac. 1047; *State v. Raaf*, 16 Ida. 411, 101 Pac. 747.)

SULLIVAN, C. J.—The defendant was prosecuted and convicted in the probate court of Latah county for having sold intoxicating liquors without first obtaining the license required by the provisions of chap. 33, title 8, of the Revised Codes. The charging part of the complaint is as follows: "Did then and there, wilfully, knowingly and unlawfully, sell to C. Douglas, then and there being, a quantity of intoxicating liquor, to wit, beer, without first having obtained and procured the license, and executed and filed the bond required by the State of Idaho and in violation of chap. 33, title 8, of the Revised Codes of Idaho," etc.

To that complaint the defendant demurred on the ground and for the reason that the facts stated in the complaint did not constitute a public offense. The demurrer was overruled and the defendant was convicted of said offense and fined in the sum of $250 and costs. The defendant thereupon appealed to the district court, and when the case was called for hearing, the defendant made a motion to dismiss it on the ground and for the reason that the probate court had no jurisdiction to try and determine such cause, which motion was sustained and the action dismissed and judgment of dismissal entered. The state appealed from said judgment.

(1) *In limine,* we are met with a motion by the defendant to dismiss this appeal on the ground that the probate court of Latah county did not have jurisdiction to try and deter-

mine said action. On that motion it was contended that the
crime for which the defendant was prosecuted was for selling
liquor in Latah county, a prohibition district. (The complaint contradicts this contention.) It was contended that
Latah county became a prohibition district because of the
provisions of sec. 7, of an act of the legislature, approved
February 19, 1913 (Sess. Laws, p. 127), which section declares
that a " 'Prohibition District' within the meaning of this act
and all other acts prohibiting the sale of intoxicating liquors
in any prohibition district in this state, is territory in which
the sale of intoxicating liquor is prohibited by law, or where
no liquor license has been issued in accordance with the laws
of this state.'' Latah county did not become a prohibition
district by a vote of the people, but the county commissioners
of that county had refused to issue any liquor licenses whatever, and when this case was appealed to the district court, it
seems that counsel for the defendant concluded to contend
that the defendant had been prosecuted for selling liquor in
a prohibition district, instead of for selling liquor without
first having procured a license, as charged in the complaint
on which he was tried, and the district court agreed with
counsel in this contention and dismissed the case on the
ground as above stated, that the probate court had no jurisdiction to try the defendant for the crime of which he was
convicted.

From the foregoing statement of facts, we will now proceed
to determine said motion.

The trial court, in sustaining said motion and dismissing
the appeal, found "that the probate court of Latah county
did not have jurisdiction to try and determine said cause, and
that this court does not have jurisdiction to determine said
cause except on a commitment from a committing magistrate;
that the said L. Stafford has not been given a preliminary
examination, and that this court does not have jurisdiction to
try and determine said cause,'' and entered judgment dismissing the action.

It is contended by counsel for defendant that the only provisions of the statute authorizing the state to appeal are found

in sec. 8043, Rev. Codes, and that said section does not authorize an appeal by the state from any case appealed from a justice's or probate court. Subdivision 1 of that section is as follows:

"An appeal may be taken by the state:

"1. From a judgment for the defendant on a demurrer to the indictment or information."

And it is contended that since there has been no indictment or information filed in this case, the state has no appeal, and in support of that contention *State v. Ridenbaugh*, 5 Ida. 710, 51 Pac. 750, is cited. This court held in that case as follows: "We have no statute in this state authorizing the state to appeal from a judgment in favor of a defendant in a criminal action rendered in a justice's or probate court; nor have we any statute authorizing the state to appeal in any criminal action except the statute cited *supra*." (Sec. 8043.) In that opinion the court quotes the first subdivision of sec. 8043 as found in the Rev. Stats., as follows: "1· From a judgment for the defendant on a demurrer to the indictment." That subdivision has been amended, and as found in the Rev. Codes, reads: "1· From a judgment for the defendant on a demurrer to the indictment or information." The court in the Ridenbaugh case evidently overlooked the amendment to that subdivision of sec. 8043, or concluded that said amendment had not been properly passed by the legislature under the decision of *Cohn v. Kingsley*, 5 Ida. 416, 49 Pac. 985, 38 L. R. A. 74. On an appeal in a criminal case from a justice's or probate court, sec. 8325 provides that the clerk of the district court must file the papers received and enter the action on the calendar in its order with other criminal cases, and the same must be tried "anew" in the district court at the next term thereof, unless for good cause the same be continued. Under the provisions of that section the case must be tried anew, or *de novo*. That means that the motions and demurrers decided by the justice or probate court must be heard by the district court, provided either the state or the defendant cares to present them, or the defendant may first demur to the complaint in the district court. The defendant in the probate court filed his demurrer based on the ground that the court had no jurisdiction to try said cause. The demurrer was overruled and instead of calling up that demurrer in the district court, after his appeal had been perfected, he took another tack and moved in the district court to dismiss the case, because the probate court had no jurisdiction to try the case. That paper is in effect a demurrer to the jurisdiction of the court, and it must be viewed from the standpoint of its legal effect and not from the name that the court or the pleader may have given it. If that motion had been called a demurrer to the jurisdiction of the court, would it be contended that on sustaining such demurrer and dismissing the case the state would not have the right to appeal? It might be, but we think such contention would be without merit, and not warranted under the provisions of our statute.

A criminal case appealed from a justice's or probate court, after the appeal, stands the same in the district court as though it had been begun there. It is there for a new trial on every point and question that was raised or might have been raised in the justice's or probate court. The name given by the statute to the paper charging the crime and filed in the justice's or probate court is "complaint," and cases involving indictable misdemeanors and felonies are prosecuted in the district court on a paper called an "indictment" or "information." The paper called a "complaint" in the justice's court serves the same purpose as the paper called an "information" in the district court, and those two words are often used synonymously and mean the same thing. An information or a complaint is a paper charging a defendant with a particular offense, and it matters not whether it is called an information or a complaint. The object and purpose in giving the state the right to appeal is the same whether the case has been first tried by a justice's or probate court on a complaint, or whether an indictable misdemeanor or felony is tried in the district court; and the appeal from the probate court or justice's court having been properly perfected and the papers filed in the district court, those statutes which provide the procedure in criminal cases in the district court apply to such appeals as well as to those criminal cases which the district court has original jurisdiction to try and determine.

Under the provisions of sec. 7509, Rev. Codes, a complaint is defined the same as an information. That section is as follows: "The complaint or information is the allegation in writing, made to a magistrate, that a person has been guilty of some designated offense." It is clear that the words "complaint" and "information" as used in the statute are used to represent the name of a pleading by which a criminal action is instituted in a justice's or probate court, or on which a criminal prosecution may be based in the district court; and if the words "complaint" and "information" are not meant to apply to the same thing, it may be said that "complaint" is the name given to the pleading filed by any person other than the prosecutor himself with a justice's or probate court, and that the same pleading is called "information" when the pleading is filed by the public prosecutor. In this case the prosecuting attorney filed the complaint. In form it is an information, such as is used in a preliminary hearing and filed in the district court by the public prosecutor. The term "information" as used in said section 8043 applies to the first pleading which begins a criminal prosecution in a justice's or probate court. Under the provisions of our statute, the paper containing the incriminating charge is clearly an information. Upon a trial *de novo* in the district court, the complaint or information filed in the district court takes the place of an indictment or information filed in that court, and the proceedings upon such an appeal in the district court is the same as upon either an indictment or information.

Upon the question as to the meaning of the word "information," see *Clepper v. State*, 4 Tex. 242; *Tatum v. State*, 66 Ala. 465; *Simpson v. State*, 111 Ala. 6, 20 So. 572; 4 Words and Phrases, p. 3585, defines information as "a complaint or accusation, in writing, exhibited against a person for some misdemeanor."

It is contended that the state has no right to appeal in a criminal case unless the right is given by the statute. We concede that, and are satisfied that the authority is given by the provisions of said sec. 8043. This conclusion is based upon the following reasons: First, that the misdemeanor tried upon appeal in the district court is subject to the same statutes relating to procedure as any other criminal case tried in that court; second, the word "information" as used in said section is intended to apply to the complaint filed in the justice's court originally and in the district court on appeal; third, that the word "information" as used in said section was intended by the legislature to be construed in its generic sense and not in its technical sense. In so far as the Ridenbaugh case is in conflict with the views expressed in this opinion, it is overruled.

In granting said motion to dismiss, the district court erred.

(2) As above stated, the complaint or information filed in the probate court charged the defendant with the crime of having sold intoxicating liquors without a license, contrary to the provisions of chap. 33, title 8, of the Rev. Codes, and he was convicted of that offense and sentenced to pay a fine of $250. The crime of selling liquor without a license, under the provisions of said chapter, is not an indictable misdemeanor, and therefore a justice's or probate court has jurisdiction to try and determine such misdemeanor. The defendant on his motion to dismiss in the district court contended that the crime charged was selling liquor in a prohibition district, which, under the statute, is an indictable misdemeanor, or a misdemeanor of which the justice's or probate court has no jurisdiction, and the trial court took that view of the case and dismissed it.

Under the provisions of sec. 7 of the Laws of 1913, *supra*, Latah county became a prohibition district by reason of the fact that no liquor license had been issued in said county in accordance with the law, and not by reason of a vote of the people, and the defendant was not charged in said complaint with selling liquor in a prohibition district, and hence subject to a penalty of $500, but was charged with the crime of selling liquor without a license contrary to sec. 1518, Rev.

Codes, which is another and distinct crime from that of selling liquor in a prohibition district.

Under the complaint filed in the probate court, a preliminary examination could not have been held, for the reason that it did not charge a crime, for the commission of which defendant could have a preliminary examination and be bound over to the district court. It charged only a crime of which the probate court had jurisdiction, and the court erred in sustaining the demurrer or motion of the defendant and in holding that the probate court had no jurisdiction to try and determine said case. The complaint or information on which the defendant was tried does not intimate in any way that the crime of which the defendant is charged is one of selling liquor in a prohibition district, but specifically charges him with the crime of selling liquor without a license. On that information he could not have been convicted of selling liquor in a prohibition district, because it did not charge him with that crime. The probate court is not required to hold a preliminary examination in cases where it has jurisdiction to try and determine, and when it tries and determines such a case and the case is appealed to the district court, it is the duty of the district court to try such case *de novo.*

The judgment of dismissal is reversed and the cause remanded.

Truitt, J., concurs.

(October 17, 1914.)

FEDERAL MINING & SMELTING CO., Plaintiff, v. THE PUBLIC UTILITIES COMMISSION et al., Defendants.

[143 Pac. 1173.]

UTILITY ACT — UTILITIES COMMISSION — COMPULSORY PRODUCTION OF BOOKS AND PAPERS.

1. In a contest between a patron and a utility corporation in regard to the establishment of reasonable rates, the Utilities Commission has power to require the corporation to produce any and all records, contracts or papers bearing upon the questions in issue and that would throw any light upon the question of reasonable rates; and the commission has full power and authority to pass upon and determine the relevancy or competency of all evidence offered to prove or disprove the issues made by the pleadings, and this authority should be liberally exercised to enable parties to prepare properly for trial.

2. The business of the Washington Water Power Company, the defendant in the original proceeding, is the manufacture and sale of electricity to numerous customers, and the reasonable cost thereof can only be determined by showing the actual value of the plant, the actual cost to manufacture and deliver the electricity and all necessary disbursements for that purpose, including taxes, also the depreciation of the plant, plus a fair return on the money invested; and to determine the questions that must be determined, it will necessitate an examination of the plant and business of the corporation, and for that reason the plaintiff, in order to prepare itself for trial, should have an inspection of all the books, papers and documents of said utility corporation and all of its plants in so far as the same will show, or tend to show, the reasonable value of the plant and what it actually costs to manufacture and deliver electricity and power.

3. The Public Utilities Commission should, under suitable conditions, permit the Federal Mining Company to inspect the books, files and papers of said utility corporation in so far as they contain matter relating to, or in any way connected with, the fixing of the value of the plant and the reasonable rate to be charged for the product, and should give plaintiff ample time and opportunity for that purpose.

4. Under the provisions of sec. 49 of said act, said commission is not bound by the technical rules of evidence, and by the provisions of sec. 29 of said act, said commission is authorized to do all things necessary to carry out the spirit and intent of said act.

Original proceeding in this court for a writ of review to determine the validity of an order of the Public Utilities Commission refusing to require the Washington Water Power Company to permit the plaintiff to examine all of its records, files and papers. The order and action of the Commission *affirmed.*

James E. Babb, A. H. Featherstone, C. W. Beale and John H. Wourms, for Plaintiff.

The opinion of the commission, as to privacy of the power company's books and as to a fishing examination, is based on rules that would be applicable in a suit between private individuals or private corporations and which were established before *Munn v. Illinois* (1877), 94 U. S. 113, 24 L. ed. 77, in which it was first established that any business affected with a public interest is subject to public control and direction— the power to regulate rates and get information necessary being the police power. (*Town of Ukiah v. Snow Mountain Water & Power Co.* See many cases cited in opinion of California Railroad Commission, Feb. 27, 1914, Case No. 483, Decision No. 1309.)

The resulting change in the attitude of the courts in investigating the books and accounts of such corporations is declared in *Wilson v. United States,* 220 U. S. 614, 31 Sup. Ct. 545, 55 L. ed. 610; followed in *Burnett v. State,* 8 Okl. Cr. 639, 129 Pac. 1110, 47 L. R. A., N. S., 1175, notes; *Hammond Packing Co. v. Arkansas,* 212 U. S. 322, 29 Sup. Ct. 370, 53 L. ed. 530, 15 Ann. Cas. 645.

Accounts kept of such a public use belong to the public use, and the consumers have an interest therein, and the facts reposing therein as to the success and failure of the enterprise, which affects the rate to be paid. (*New York Edison Co. v. City of New York,* 133 App. Div. 728, 118 N. Y. Supp. 238; *United Electric Light & Power Co. v. City of New York,* 133 App. Div. 732, 118 N. Y. 240; *Brigham v. Zaiss,* 48 App. Div. 144, 62 N. Y. Supp. 706; *Vciller v. Oppenheim,* 75 Hun, 21, 26 N. Y. Supp. 1051; *Thomas v. Guy B. White Co.,* 113 App.

Div. 494, 99 N. Y. Supp. 297; *People v. American Ice Co.*, 54 Misc. Rep. 67, 105 N. Y. Supp. 650; *Home Telephone Co. v. City of Carthage*, 235 Mo. 644, Ann. Cas. 1912D, 301, 139 S. W. 547, 48 L. R. A., N. S., 1055.)

W. H. Hanson, *Amicus Curiae.*

There is no authority in an equity proceeding where a general and extensive ramifying account is to be taken, but holds that it is necessary to have the inspection and examination before the commencement of the trial. The staying by injunction of a court of equity of trial of law case is a uniform and unquestioned precedent in support of that position. (*Arnold v. Pawtuxt Val. Water Co.*, 18 R. I. 189, 26 Atl. 55, 19 L. R. A. 602; *Hillman v. United States*, 192 Fed. 264, 112 C. C. A. 522; *In re Grant*, 198 Fed. 708; *Simon v. American Tobacco Co.*, 192 Fed. 662; *Dreier v. United States*, 221 U. S. 394, 31 Sup. Ct. 550, 55 L. ed. 784; *Wheeler v. United States*, 226 U. S. 478, 33 Sup. Ct. 158, 57 L. ed. 309; *Burnett v. State*, 8 Okl. Cr. 639, 129 Pac. 1110, 47 L. R. A., N. S., 1175, and notes.)

John P. Gray, for Washington Water Power Co.

"The plaintiff's right to a discovery does not extend to all facts which may be material to the issue, but is confined to facts which are material to his own title or cause of action; it does not enable him to pry into the defendant's case, or find out the evidence by which that case will be supported." (Pomeroy's Eq. Jur., sec. 201; Story's Equity Pleadings, secs. 317, 325; *Newkerk v. Willett*, 2 Caines Cas. (N. Y.) 269; *Cully v. Northern Pac. Ry. Co.*, 35 Wash. 241, 77 Pac. 202; *Carpenter v. Winn*, 221 U. S. 533, 31 Sup. Ct. 683, 55 L. ed. 842; *Owyhee Land & Irr. Co. v. Tautphaus*, 109 Fed. 547, 48 C. C. A. 535; *Oro Water, Light & Power Co. v. Oroville*, 162 Fed. 975; *State ex rel. Boston & M. Con. Copper & Silver M. Co. v. District Court*, 27 Mont. 441, 94 Am. St. 831, 71 Pac. 602; *Ex parte Clarke*, 126 Cal. 235, 77 Am. St. 176, 58 Pac. 546, 46 L. R. A. 835.)

The question of the organization of the defendant company, how its capital stock was issued and how it was paid for, and all kindred questions, is immaterial to the controversy. (*Smyth v. Ames,* 169 U. S. 466, 18 Sup. Ct. 418, 42 L. ed. 819.)

J. H. Peterson, Atty. Genl., J. J. Guheen, T. C. Coffin and E. G. Davis, Assts., for Defendant.

In passing upon requests to examine the books and records of corporations, the test of reasonableness is always applied, and in general, parties litigant who desire to inspect the books and records of opposing parties, must first make some showing as to the necessity of such inspection, and their demands must specify with reasonable exactness the particular books and papers which they desire to examine. (*Hale v. Henkel,* 201 U. S. 43, 26 Sup. Ct. 370, 50 L. ed. 652; *Wilson v. United States,* 221 U. S. 361, Ann. Cas. 1912D, 558, 31 Sup. Ct. 538, 55 L. ed. 771.)

SULLIVAN, C. J.—The Federal Mining and Smelting Company filed its formal complaint with the Public Utilities Commission of this state on the 5th of September, 1913, under the provisions of the public utilities act, approved March 13, 1913 (Sess. Laws 1913, p. 247). The purpose of said proceeding was to litigate the reasonableness of rates for power furnished to the plaintiff by the Washington Water Power Company.

The complaint was answered by the water power company and thereafter the complainant made a motion for the production and inspection of all books and records, or certified copies thereof, of the water power company within the state of Idaho, for examination by the attorneys or expert accountants of the plaintiff or petitioner. It was the purpose of this motion, if favorably acted upon, to secure to the plaintiff company an opportunity to examine the books and records of the defendant company and to obtain therefrom such information as it might consider necessary in preparing itself for the hearing before the commission. That motion was resisted by the Washington Water Power Company on the following specified grounds:

First, that it will be unjust, unfair, unreasonable and work an irreparable damage to the defendant to make any such order.

Second, that the commission is without power to make such an order under chapter 61, Laws of 1913, or any other statute or law in the state of Idaho.

Third, that the making of such an order would be a violation of the defendant's right under and contrary to the provisions of the fourth amendment to the constitution of the United States.

After a hearing, the Utilities Commission denied the motion. Thereafter the plaintiff company filed a petition for a rehearing which was denied. Application was made to this court under the provisions of sec. 63a of said utilities act for a writ of review to review the action of said commission in refusing to grant said motion.

After a consideration of the three grounds above set forth by the Washington Water Power Company against the granting of said motion, we conclude that there is nothing in said first and third grounds. Then the question directly presented is whether it was within the power of the commission to grant said order under said public utilities act, or any other statute or law of the state, and if it possessed the authority and power to grant such order, whether it erred in denying said motion.

Counsel for plaintiff contends that the commission has full power and authority under the provisions of said public utilities act, and especially under sec. 55 thereof, to grant its motion for an inspection of all the books and records of said corporation, and that it erred in refusing to do so. To determine this question several sections of said act must be referred to and construed.

·Sections 26(d), 29, 54 and 55 are as follows:

"Sec. 26(d). No information furnished to the commissioner by a public utility except such matters as are specifically required to be open to the public inspection by the provisions of this act, shall be open to the public inspection or made public except on order of the commission, or by the commission or a commissioner in the course of a hearing or proceeding. Any commissioner, officer or employee of the commission who, in violation of the provisions of this subsection, divulges any such information shall be guilty of felony."

"Sec. 29. The Public Utilities Commission is hereby vested with power and jurisdiction to supervise and regulate every public utility in the state and to do all things necessary to carry out the spirit and intent of the provisions of this act."

"Sec. 54. The commission, each commissioner and each officer and person employed by the commission shall have the right at any and all times to inspect the accounts, books, papers and documents of any public utility, and the commission, each commissioner and any officer of the commission or any employee authorized to administer oaths shall have power to examine under oath any officer, agent or employee of such public utility in relation to the business and affairs of said public utility; *provided,* that any person other than a commissioner or an officer of the commission demanding such inspection shall produce under the seal of the commission his authority to make such inspection; and, *provided, further,* that a written record of the testimony or statement so given under oath shall be made and filed with the commission."

"Sec. 55. The commission may require, by order served on any public utility in the manner provided herein for the service of order, the production within this state at such time and place as it may designate, of any books, accounts, papers or records kept by said public utility in any office or place without this state, or, at its option, verified copies in lieu thereof so that an examination thereof may be made by the commission or under its direction."

Said sec. 54 is the only part of said act which attempts to designate the officers or individuals who may be authorized to inspect the books, accounts and records of a public utility, and applies equally to public utilities whose records are kept within the state and to those whose records are kept without the state.

Sec. 55 relates to the books and records of public utilities doing business within the state but whose books and records are kept without the state. It provides that the commission may require such books and records, or verified copies in lieu thereof, to be produced within the state "so that an examination thereof may be made by the commission or under its direction." The books and records of such corporations kept without the state are clearly subject to the same limitations as is the inspection of such books and records as are kept permanently within the state. There can be no doubt of the right of the complainant to ask that the books and records of this foreign corporation be produced within the state at the time of the hearing, and the right to such facilities as are necessary in order to enable it to inspect the books, records and documents specified by it in order to enable it to meet the issues presented by the case before the commission. Reasonable time for such inspection and examination as may be found necessary under the circumstances of each case must be given by the commission. All of which is conceded by the commission in its written decision in this case denying the motion for such examination and inspection of the records of the defendant company as was asked by the plaintiff in this proceeding; but as we understand it, this motion of the plaintiff calls for the production of any and all documents, books, records, letters and papers of the defendant company, whether the matters contained in them relate to the question in issue or not, and if granted, would permit it to make such use as it might desire of all the records, etc., thus inspected.

The question is then directly presented: What was the purpose intended to be served by the provisions of said sections of said act with reference to the inspection of the books and records of public utilities? It was no doubt for the purpose of enabling the commission to ascertain fully at any time the manner in which any public utility is conducting its business and whether it is violating the law or acting unjustly toward the public in the matter of rates. Those sections were not intended to enable those who complain against public utilities to go on "fishing expeditions" through all the cor-

respondence, papers and records of a utility corporation to
see if they can obtain some evidence against the legality of
the acts of such corporation, or to procure information that
might be valuable to one contemplating the purchase or duplication of such plant, or for the purpose of procuring information that one was not entitled to without the consent of the
corporation. In a contest between a party and a utility corporation in regard to rates, etc., the commission has power
to require the utility to produce any record, contracts or
papers bearing upon the questions in issue in the case, or
that would throw any light upon the question of reasonable
rates. It evidently has full power and authority in the
matter of compelling the production of evidence in the case
before it.

Said section 54 gives the right and authority to the commission, or each commissioner and any officer or person employed by the commission, at any and all times to inspect the
accounts, books, papers and documents of any public utility;
and also provides that any person other than a commissioner
or officer of the commission demanding such inspection shall
produce under seal his authority to make such inspection.
That section refers to persons who are authorized to inspect
the books and records of a utility by the commission, and does
not refer to the production of any books or records required
to be produced and introduced as evidence on the trial of
some question or issue before the commission.

It is provided by sec. 26(d) that no information furnished
to the commissioner by a public utility, except such matters
as are specifically required to be open to public inspection
by the provisions of said act, shall be open to the public inspection or made public except in the course of a hearing or
proceeding, and it is there also provided that any commissioner, officer or employee of the commission who in violation
of the provisions of such section divulges any such information shall be guilty of a felony. What would be the necessity
or reason for making it a felony for a commissioner or an
employee of the commission to reveal certain facts that might
be obtained from an investigation of the books and records

of a utility if it were the right of any and all persons to procure an order from the commission for the inspection of all books, records and files of a utility and not make them guilty of a felony if they should reveal any of the facts which they might discover on such investigation?

The provisions of said act are sufficient to give authority to the commission, and do give it, to make all investigations of books and other documents of public utilities necessary for the decision of all questions that might arise involving the control by the commission of such utilities within the state. Sec. 29 of said act empowers the commission to supervise and regulate every public utility in the state and "to do all things necessary to carry out the spirit and intent of the provisions of this act." It has full power and authority to require the production of all records and documents that may be pertinent and necessary to use as evidence in cases brought before said commission and to grant the litigants time and place sufficient for an examination of the same. The motion of the plaintiff company in this case is based on the ground that the issues raised by the pleadings require an investigation into all of the affairs of the defendant company from its organization to the present time. It no doubt has the right to an examination of all books, contracts and files of the company that would tend in any wise to fix the value of the plant and the cost of the manufacture of electric power, and that would show, or tend to show, reasonable rates to be charged for the same.

The commission has authority under said act to determine or pass upon the relevancy and competency of all evidence offered to prove or disprove the issues made by the pleadings, and this authority vested in the commission should be liberally exercised to enable parties to properly prepare for trial. The plaintiff's business is affected with a public interest and is subject to state control and direction, and the power of the commission to regulate rates and get information necessary for that purpose is a power that has been conferred by said act on said board, and the commission has the legal right to demand information as to the business involved and as to the value of all the property involved therein as a basis for the regulation of its business and the fixing of reasonable rates for its services.

Under the provisions of sec. 46 of said act, the accounts of such corporations are required to be so kept that in case of a controversy over rates or service, there may be reliable evidence to which the consumer may appeal. Each consumer of the product of a utility corporation is a party in interest in its public use, and such corporations' accounts should be subject to the reasonable inspection of the consumer in any matter affecting his relation with the utility, so far as reasonable rates are concerned. The relation established by law between the utility and the consumer is that the consumer must pay a fair return on the value of assets reasonably acquired and necessary for the accomplishment of such utility's object and purpose. The ascertainment of a just rate involves, among other things, the reasonable cost of the plant, the cost of production, transportation to the point of intended use, and so forth.

In *New York Edison Co. v. City of New York*, 133 App. Div. 728, 118 N. Y. Supp. 238, it was held that the defendant was entitled to an inspection of the books and records of the plaintiff company, and an examination of its plant, so far as the same would show, or tend to show, the actual cost of production and distribution of electricity during the time it was alleged to have been furnished. In that case the court said, among other things: "And it is quite apparent that the defendant, unless it can have an inspection and discovery, cannot prepare its case for trial. How can it determine what is the reasonable and fair market value, unless it can ascertain what it actually cost the plaintiff to manufacture and deliver?" And after reviewing a number of cases, the court further said: "Here the plaintiff's business is the manufacture and sale of electricity to thousands of customers, and the reasonable cost thereof can only be determined by showing the amount of capital invested, the actual cost to manufacture and deliver, including taxes and all disbursements for that purpose, and the depreciation of its plant, plus a fair return on the money invested. This will necessitate an examination of its entire business, and for that reason the defendant, in order to prepare itself for trial, should have an inspection of all the books, papers and documents of the plaintiff, and of its plant, in so far as the same will show, or tend to show, what it actually cost it to manufacture and deliver the electricity for which a recovery is sought."

In *Brigham v. Zaiss*, 48 App. Div. 144, 62 N. Y. Supp. 706, the court said:

"Manifestly, the plaintiff has no way of ascertaining what the net amount is, except from the defendants themselves, or from an inspection of their books of account. . . . . No good reason can be suggested why they should not furnish the same to the plaintiff, and, in the interest of justice, we think they should be required, under suitable conditions, to permit the plaintiff to inspect their books and to take copies of them, in so far as they contain entries relating to, or in any way connected with, the subject matter of the action."

In *Hart v. Ogdensburg & L. C. R. Co.*, 69 Hun, 497, 23 N. Y. Supp. 713, the court said: "The discretion vested in the court should be liberally exercised, to enable parties to properly prepare for trial," and then quoted from *Powers v. Elmendorf*, 4 How. Pr. 60, as follows:

"I can see no good reason why a party should be permitted to withhold from the knowledge of his adversary documentary evidence affecting the merits of the controversy, only to surprise him by its production at the trial, unless, for some satisfactory reason to be made apparent to the court, each party ought to be required, when it is desired, to disclose to the other any books, papers and documents within his power which may contain evidence pertinent to the issue to be tried."

In *Interstate Commerce Com. v. Baird*, 194 U. S. 25, 24 Sup. Ct. 563, 48 L. ed. 860, the court said:

"The inquiry of a board of the character of the Interstate Commerce Commission should not be too narrowly constrained by technical rules as to the admissibility of proof. Its function is largely one of investigation, and it should not be hampered in making inquiry pertaining to interstate commerce by those narrow rules which prevail in trials at common law, where a strict correspondence is required between allegation and proof.''

The principle or rule there declared is substantially 'the rule that should govern the Public Utilities Commission in its hearings and investigations as provided by sec. 49 of said act, and it is there provided that in the conduct of investigations before said commission it should not be bound by the technical rules of evidence.

By sec. 29 of said act it is declared that said commission is vested with power and jurisdiction to supervise and regulate every public utility in the state and do all things necessary to carry out the spirit and intent of said act.

In *Matthews v. Board of Corp. Commrs. of N. C.*, 106 Fed. 7, the court said: ''The basis of all calculations as to the reasonableness of rates is the fair value of the property used for the convenience of the public,'' and then proceeded to state what may be taken into consideration in determining such rate.

The commission no doubt will admit all competent evidence offered showing or tending to show what would be a reasonable rate for the service rendered by said public utility, and it must permit the plaintiff to inspect all books and papers of the water power company that would throw any light upon that subject, and we understand from the decision of the commission that it will do so and give the plaintiff ample time and opportunity to examine them.

The defendant corporation has been in existence nearly a quarter of a century, and all of its files and records, contracts and communications cover a great many years, much of which can have no application whatever to the issues made by the pleadings, and it is stated in the opinion of the commission as follows:

''No investigation by the accountants of the commission has as yet been begun, and no examination of the works and premises of the defendant has as yet been undertaken by the engineers of the commission. In view of the present status of the case, we think it would be going rather far for the commission to grant the application in its present form. We doubt very seriously if the statute confers such extreme visit-atorial power to be exercised by the commission over public service corporations, and as the commission will have full power to control the investigation to be had, ample oppor-tunity during the hearing can be granted to the plaintiff company to make such investigation of the books and records of the defendant as will insure a fair hearing of all the issues involved. If after the hearing before the commission has begun it may appear that it will be necessary for the plaintiff company to inspect any book, account, record or other document in the possession of the defendant, and that such record is material to the issues in the case, it will be the duty of the commission to require the production of such document and to grant to the plaintiff company permission to inspect such documents, although the same may have to be inspected by the experts of the plaintiff company and time afforded them for such inspection. Questions will arise dur-ing the hearing, as we imagine, concerning such proceeding, and when they do arise, the commission will consider the same and grant such facilities and opportunities to the plaintiff company to make such examination of the books, accounts and other records of the defendant as may appear just and reasonable.''

The above quoted part of the decision of the commission clearly sets forth the construction placed by the commission on the powers given them by said act in the matter under consideration. The commission has full power and authority to compel the production of all material evidence on the trial of said case, and on proper application no doubt will do so; but in the first instance, it is for the commission to determine whether the documents or evidence demanded is material and necessary, and if the commission concludes that it is not, it is its duty to decline to receive immaterial evidence and to decline to grant any application of the parties for an in-spection of the records and files of a public corporation which it considers is not material to any of the issues involved.

The plaintiff is not entitled to an examination of the records and files of a corporation which can possibly have no bearing on the issues of the case, and to compel the corporation to produce the same would be most unreasonable, and the constitution of the United States, as well as the constitution of the state of Idaho, prohibits unreasonable searches and seizures. (Sec. 17, art. 1, State Const.; *Hale v. Henkle,* 201 U. S. 43, 26 Sup. Ct. 370, 50 L. ed. 652; *Wilson v. United States,* 221 U. S. 361, Ann. Cas. 1912D, 558, 31 Sup. Ct. 538, 55 L. ed. 771.) In general, parties litigant who desire to inspect the books and records of opposing parties must make some showing as to the necessity of such inspection, and their demands must specify with reasonable exactness the particular books and papers which they desire to examine. If it is made to appear that an examination of any of the books, records and files of the corporation is necessary to a proper determination of the issues involved, the commission certainly will require their production on its own motion or on the application of the plaintiff, before or during the hearing, and give ample opportunity for an inspection thereof. But the commission has no authority under said act to permit a party litigant to examine the records and files of a utility corporation that do not pertain to the issues made by the pleadings, and the commission has no authority under said act to permit a party to examine the records and files of the Washington Water Power Company in a case pending before it, which are not pertinent or material to the issues made by the pleadings.

We therefore conclude that the action of the commission in refusing to grant said motion must be affirmed, and it is so ordered, with costs in favor of the commission.

Truitt, J., concurs.

(November 19, 1914.)

ON PETITION FOR REHEARING.

SULLIVAN, C. J.—A petition for rehearing has been filed in this case, and it is contended that in our order affirming the decision of the Public Utilities Commission we overlooked the fact that the plaintiff had made certain specific demands for the examination of particular records, naming them, among which were (1) the balance sheets for the calendar years 1904–1913, inclusive, as shown by the affidavit of Beukers (see p. 36 of record); (2) the ledgers and journals of the power company covering the entire existence of that company; (3) the minute-books of the corporation with reference to the stock issue of one million dollars and the bond issue of $500,000; (4) a complete list of the names of the consumers of the power company in the Coeur d'Alene district in the state of Idaho, both past and present.

It appears that the expert accountants of the plaintiff, by mutual understanding or agreement with the officers of the water power company, commenced an inspection of some of the books and records of said company, but had not proceeded very far before said officers refused any further inspection of their records, claiming that they were unwilling to have any accountant employed by the Federal company or the complainants, or any of them, to make an investigation of any of the books, accounts, papers, records or documents whatsoever of the water power company, but were willing that an examination should be made by the regular official accountant of the Public Utilities Commission or by the regular official engineer of that commission.

We intended to hold in our original opinion, and now hold, that the commission must require the water power company to produce for examination by the Federal Mining Company its expert accountants and others employed by the Federal Mining Company, all books, papers and accounts that would throw any light upon the question of reasonable rates to be charged for electrical energy or power furnished to the Federal Mining Company by the water power company, as well as a complete list of the names of the consumers of electricity furnished by said power company in the Coeur d'Alene District in the state of Idaho, and the books, papers and accounts showing the rate charged each consumer and class of consumers and the amount of electrical power furnished to each, since such matters are proper to be investigated in determining reasonable rates, and the commission must compel the water power company to produce the same and give the Federal company reasonable opportunity and time for a thorough investigation of such books, papers and documents.

In this case it will be necessary to apportion the expenses of the utility supplying the service to the several classes of consumers. Such consumers are divided into well-defined groups or classes, such as street lighting, commercial power, street railway, etc. Each of those classes demands its special equipment or class of service. Some costs are peculiar to certain kinds of service and not to others, and it is only right and proper that the Federal Mining Company should be furnished all the documentary evidence that would throw any light upon the several classes of consumers and the amount charged each consumer for the service given.

As bearing upon this question, see *City of Racine v. Racine Gas Light Co.* (1911), 6 W. R. C. R. 228, 244, 235.

It is stated by counsel in their petition for rehearing that it is not clear to them whether or not it was the intention of this court to disapprove of a portion of the opinion in the case of *New York Edison Co. v. City of New York*, 133 App. Div. 732, 118 N. Y. Supp. 240, which distinguished the cases requiring a specification of the particular books required from the rate cases, where all of the books were required. Counsel quotes from that opinion as follows: "This will necessitate an examination of its entire business, and for that reason the defendant, in order to prepare itself for trial, should have an inspection of all the books, papers and documents of the plaintiff," and there stops the quotation with a period, when, as a matter of fact, in the original opinion a comma follows the word "plaintiff" and the following language is used thereafter: "And of its plant, *in so far as the same will show, or tend to show,* what it actually cost to manufacture and deliver the electricity for which a recovery is sought." That is identically what we intended to hold in the original opinion in this case, and we did hold in effect that it was the duty of the commission to grant to the plaintiff the right to inspect all books, papers and documents of the water power company and of its plant, *in so far as the same will show, or tend to show,* what it actually cost to manufacture and deliver electricity, electrical energy or power.

It is to be supposed that the power company keeps a list of its customers, and that its books indicate the class to which each customer belongs, the amount of electricity furnished to each, and the price charged each customer therefor. Such a list showing the above indicated facts would no doubt bear upon the reasonable rates to be charged. And all such lists, books, records and accounts should be produced by the power company for inspection by the Federal company, and as we understand the decision of the commission, it will require the power company to produce all such books, records and accounts for the inspection of the Federal company, and time and opportunity given for a thorough inspection thereof.

The court does not question the good faith of the Federal company in making the application it did in this case, and it must be distinctly understood that this court holds that it is the duty of the commission, under the law, to require the power company to produce all of its books, records and accounts so far as the same will show, or tend to show, what it actually cost to manufacture and deliver electricity to the plaintiff.

This decision is rendered without prejudice to the rights of the Federal company to renew its application before the commission for the inspection of the books, records, accounts, etc., above indicated, that show or tend to show what it actually cost to manufacture and deliver electricity to the plaintiff. And the commission may permit the Federal company under the present application, through its officers and experts, to examine all such books, accounts and records.

The petition for rehearing is denied.

Truitt, J., concurs.

———————

(October 17, 1914.)

CAPITAL LUMBER CO., a Corporation, Respondent, v. HEZEKIAH SAUNDERS et al., Appellants.

[143 Pac. 1178.]

INSOLVENT DEBTOR—ATTACHING CREDITORS—ASSIGNMENTS—DEEDS HELD MORTGAGES — INSOLVENCY PROCEEDINGS — NATIONAL BANKRUPTCY LAW—COMMON-LAW ASSIGNMENTS—FRAUD.

1. S., an insolvent debtor, executed and delivered several warranty deeds in form to a corporation to which he was largely indebted at the time to secure the debt, and certain attaching creditors of S. appeared in an action wherein said corporation prayed to have said deeds declared mortgages and foreclosed, and alleged the deeds to be fraudulent as to them, and asked that they be set aside; *held*, under the evidence that they were valid and in effect mortgages.

2. *Held*, that title 12 of chapter 17, Rev. Codes, was suspended and superseded by the national bankruptcy law of 1898.

3. *Held*, that sec. 5932 is a necessary part of said title 12 and not now in force.

4. *Held*, that assignments in conformity with the common-law rules relating to them are not void under sec. 3169.

5. *Held*, that under sec. 3171, Rev. Codes, the question of fraudulent intent as to transfers of property is one of fact.

APPEAL from the District Court of the Third Judicial District for Ada County. Hon. Chas. P. McCarthy, Judge.

This action was commenced and prosecuted by respondent as plaintiff in said district court to have certain instruments, in form warranty deeds, declared to be mortgages and foreclosed as such. Judgment for plaintiff. *Affirmed.*

Martin & Cameron, for Appellants.

The deeds in this case from the insolvent Saunders to the Capital Lumber Company were not intended to be or to operate as mortgages.

Such a transaction does not constitute a mortgage, but an assignment for the benefit of two creditors and the debtor. (*White v. Cotzhausen*, 129 U. S. 329, 9 Sup. Ct. 309, 32 L. ed. 677; *Selz v. Evans*, 6 Ill. App. 466; *Northern Nat. Bank v. Weed*, 86 Wis. 212, 56 N. W. 634; *Watkins v. Jenks*, 24 Ga. 431; *Sabichi v. Chase*, 108 Cal. 81, 42 Pac. 29; *Stout v. Watson*, 19 Or. 251, 24 Pac. 230; *Kickbusch v. Corwith*, 108 Wis. 634, 85 N. W. 148; *Marshall v. Livingstone Nat. Bk.*, 11 Mont. 351, 28 Pac. 312.)

Such an assignment as made by Saunders was illegal and void as to the other creditors of Saunders, under sec. 5932, Rev. Codes. (*Chever v. Hays*, 3 Cal. 471; *Adams v. Woods*, 8 Cal. 153, 68 Am. Dec. 313; *Groschen v. Page*, 6 Cal. 139; *Cohen v. Barrett*, 5 Cal. 195; *Barnett v. Kinney*, 2 Ida. 740, 23 Pac. 922, 24 Pac. 624.)

There was shamefaced fraud and connivance in this transaction between Saunders and these two creditors. (*California Consol. Min. Co. v. Manley*, 10 Ida. 786, 81 Pac. 50.)

Intent to defraud is not necessary under sec. 3169. Intent to delay is sufficient to make such a transaction as the one at bar void and of no effect under the terms of that statute. (*Van Nest v. Yoe*, 1 Sand. Ch. (N. Y.) 4.)

This court in *Johnson v. Sage*, 4 Ida. 758, 44 Pac. 641, has held that a transaction such as was planned by Saunders in this case was void as to the other creditors, as it violated the terms of sec. 3019, Rev. Stats., now 3168, Rev. Codes.

Saunders by his secret oral agreement with Ketchen, of the Capital Lumber Co., practically made these creditors trustees of a surplus fund to be sent out of the state to him when they had sold his property and first paid themselves. (*Bryant v. Young*, 21 Ala. 264; *Sims v. Gaines*, 64 Ala. 392, 397; *Campbell v. Davis*, 85 Ala. 56, 4 So. 140; *Chenery v. Palmer*, 6 Cal. 119, 65 Am. Dec. 493; *North v. Belden*, 13

Conn. 376, 35 Am. Dec. 83; *Moore v. Wood,* 100 Ill. 451;
Best v. Fuller etc. Co., 185 Ill. 43, 56 N. E. 1077; *Beidler v.
Crane,* 135 Ill. 98, 25 Am. St. 349, 25 N. E. 655; *Macomber
v. Peck,* 39 Iowa, 351; *Rice v. Cunningham,* 116 Mass. 466;
Sutherland v. Bradner, 116 N. Y. 415, 22 N. E. 554; *Coburn
v. Pickering,* 3 N. H. 415, 14 Am. Dec. 375; *Newell v. Wag-
ness,* 1 N. D. 62, 44 N. W. 1014; *Smith v. Conkwright,* 28
Minn. 23, 8 N. W. 876; *Walkin v. Horswill,* 24 S. D. 191, 123
N. W. 668; *McCulloch v. Hutchinson,* 7 Watts (Pa.), 434, 32
Am. Dec. 776; *Adams v. Dempsey,* 35 Wash. 80, 76 Pac. 538;
Watkins v. Arms, 64 N. H. 99, 6 Atl. 92; *Neubert v. Massman,*
37 Fla. 91, 19 So. 625; *Halcombe v. Ray,* 23 N. C. 340; *Mo-
laska Mfg. Co. v. Steele,* 36 Mo. App. 496; *Winkley v. Hill,*
9 N. H. 31, 31 Am. Dec. 215; *Lukins v. Aird,* 73 U. S. (6
Wall.) 78, 18 L. ed. 750; *Bernhardt v. Brown,* 122 N. C. 587,
65 Am. St. 725, 29 S. E. 884; *Geary v. Porter,* 17 Or. 465,
21 Pac. 442.)

Karl Paine, for Respondents.

This is the test: If a transaction resolve itself into a security, whatever may be its form, and whatever name the parties
may choose to give it, it is in equity a mortgage. (*Brown
v. Bryan,* 6 Ida. 1, 20, 51 Pac. 995; *Bergen v. Johnson,* 21
Ida. 619, 123 Pac. 484; *Boyer v. Paine,* 60 Wash. 56, 110
Pac. 686; 20 Cyc. 502, notes 70, 71; *Hudkins v. Crim*
(W. Va.), 78 S. E. 1043.)

The act of preference being lawful, there is nothing from
which fraudulent motives can be inferred, and any fraudulent
motives the parties may have are wholly immaterial. (20
Cyc. 592; *Dana v. Stanfords,* 10 Cal. 269.)

When the paramount jurisdiction of Congress has once
been exercised in the enactment of a bankruptcy law, all
state insolvency laws are suspended in so far as they relate
to the same subject matter and affect the same persons as
the bankruptcy law. (5 Cyc. 240.)

The right of an insolvent debtor to prefer one or more
creditors over others is not an open question in this state.

(*Wilson v. Baker Clothing Co.*, 25 Ida. 378, 137 Pac. 896, 50 L. R. A., N. S., 239.)

If the preference is otherwise unobjectionable, the particular form of the transaction by which it is made appears to be immaterial so far as the rights of other creditors are concerned, except where some positive statutory prohibition intervenes. (20 Cyc. 580, 581, note 96; *Ross v. Duggan,* 5 Colo. 85; *McClure v. Smith,* 14 Colo. 297, 23 Pac. 786; *Haseltine v. Espey,* 13 Or. 301, 10 Pac. 423.)

Such conveyances, where given in good faith and to secure an actual indebtedness, are not constructively fraudulent. (*Samuel v. Kittenger,* 6 Wash. 261, 33 Pac. 509; *Ritz v. Rea,* 155 Iowa, 181, 135 N. W. 645; *Merchants' State Bank v. Tufts,* 14 N. D. 238, 116 Am. St. 682, 103 N. W. 760; *Mc-Cormick Harvesting Machine Co. v. Caldwell,* 15 N. D. 132, 106 N. W. 122.)

The rule relied upon by appellants to the effect that a mortgage cast in the form of an absolute deed is void *per se* as to existing creditors is universally rejected in those states having a statute similar to sec. 3171. (*Huntley v. Kingman & Co.,* 152 U. S. 527, 14 Sup. Ct. 688, 38 L. ed. 540; *Dana v. Stanfords, supra.*)

TRUITT, J.—The respondent is a corporation engaged in the business of selling lumber and building material in the city of Boise, Idaho, and had been so engaged for a long time prior to the commencement of said action. Hezekiah Saunders for some years before July 1, 1912, had been a builder and contractor in said city and was at that time engaged in said business, and on account of lumber and other building materials purchased he became largely indebted to the plaintiff corporation, so that as found by the lower court the defendants, Hezekiah Saunders and Lucy Saunders, were indebted to the plaintiff in the total sum of $3,077.21 on July 1, 1912. Said Lucy Saunders is the wife of defendant Hezekiah Saunders. For the purpose of securing this indebtedness as contended by respondent, said Hezekiah Saunders and his wife, Lucy Saunders, on July 2, 1912, executed and

delivered to respondent the certain instruments in question
in this case. They were in form warranty deeds, but respondent, as plaintiff below, brought action to have them
declared mortgages and foreclosed as such. The other defendants who appealed, at the time said instruments were
executed and delivered to respondent, were also creditors
of Saunders, and on or about December 31, 1912, they commenced an action against him and his wife, Lucy Saunders, to
collect the amount due and owning to them. At the time of
commencing said action, a writ of attachment was issued in
their favor and the real property conveyed by said instruments to respondent was duly levied upon. Said appellants
are attaching creditors, and they appeared in the court below
as defendants. They prayed in their cross-complaint that
said deeds be declared fraudulent and void as against them,
and asked that they be set aside. The trial court, however,
found these deeds to be mortgages and declared a foreclosure
of them and entered judgment accordingly. From this judgment respondents appeal.

A number of very interesting legal questions are submitted
by the briefs and arguments of counsel, and we have therefore given them as careful consideration as our time would
afford. The appellants' brief shows much research and care
in its preparation, and in deciding the case we find it logical
and convenient to consider the points of argument on the
several questions presented as arranged in the brief. There
are eight alleged errors presented, based upon findings of the
court at the trial, but these are included in and presented
quite fully by the four points of argument urged as grounds
for the reversal of said judgment, which are as follows:

(1) "The deeds in this case from the insolvent Saunders
to the Capital Lumber Co. were not intended to be or to
operate as mortgages."

(2) "This transaction was a voluntary assignment by an
insolvent debtor to two creditors with a secret interest
reserved for himself."

(3) "Such an assignment as made by Saunders was illegal
and void as to the other creditors of Saunders under section
5932, Idaho Revised Codes; and

(4) "That such transaction as made by Saunders, whether held by this court to be an assignment under sec. 5932 or not, was illegal and void as to the remaining six creditors under the terms, intent and spirit of sections 3168 and 3169, Idaho Revised Codes, and the well-established common-law rule covered and protected in intent and spirit by said sections."

Appellants in support of the first point presented quote sec. 3388, Rev. Codes, which defines a mortgage as follows: "A mortgage is a contract by which specific property is hypothecated for the performance of an act without the necessity of a change of possession," and also sec. 3391, Rev. Codes: "Every transfer of an interest in property other than in trust, made only as a security for the performance of another act, is to be deemed a mortgage, except when in the case of personal property it is accompanied by an actual change of possession, in which case it is to be deemed a pledge." In applying these sections to this case, it is urged that by the general rule of law and by these statutes, the instruments in question must have been given for the performance of an *act*, and that these instruments do not provide that Saunders shall perform any *act* or pay any money.

Sec. 3388, *supra*, gives a very concise definition of a mortgage, and by this definition we are unable to say that these instruments are not mortgages. In the transaction of business it often happens that a mortgage is given to secure a debt already incurred, and even in such case no *act* on the part of the mortgagor is required for its consideration: it would of course require an act, that is, the payment of the consideration to release it. But suppose the instrument, though in fact given to secure an existing debt, be in form a deed, as our statute declares it would be only a mortgage, the actual result as to the remedy is the same as if it had been in the usual form of a mortgage. However, sec. 3391, *supra*, and sec. 3392 we think bear directly upon this point, the last named section being as follows:

"The fact that a transfer was made subject to defeasance on a condition, may, for the purpose of showing such transfer to be a mortgage, be proved (except as against a subsequent purchaser or encumbrancer for value and without notice), though the fact does not appear by the terms of the instrument.''

The testimony shows and the court below found that "plaintiff demanded security for the debt due it, and the defendants, Hezekiah Saunders and Lucy Saunders, elected to furnish security in the form of deeds instead of in the form of a mortgage without plaintiff's knowledge or consent, ... and that said deeds, as to the answering defendants and all the world, are valid and *bona fide;* that they were not executed and delivered to plaintiff in virtue of any secret agreement, scheme, or plan to hinder, delay or defraud any creditor or creditors of the defendants Hezekiah Saunders and Lucy Saunders, but were given solely to secure the said claim of plaintiff.''

But this court had this question before it in *Kelly v. Leachman*, 3 Ida. 392, 29 Pac. 849. In that case the deed and assignment to reconvey were held to be a mortgage. In *Brown v. Bryan*, 6 Ida. 1, 51 Pac. 995, the court held a trust deed to be a mortgage, and announced the broad doctrine that "any hypothecation of property made by the debtor by his own voluntary act, as security for the payment of a debt which he owes to his creditor, whether made with or without the intervention of a third party as trustee, is, under the statutes quoted above, a mortgage, and to be so regarded and treated, whether the instrument by which such property is hypothecated is called a mortgage, deed, or trust deed, irrespective of its form or provisions.'' And then the test of a transaction of this kind is given as follows: "If a transaction resolves itself into a security, whatever may be its form and whatever name the parties may choose to give it, it is in equity a mortgage.''

Again, in the recent case of *Bergen v. Johnson*, 21 Ida. 619, 123 Pac. 484, it was held that, "Where an instrument in writing in the form of a deed or conveyance is executed and delivered as security for a debt, such instrument becomes a mortgage and not a deed, notwithstanding the form of the

instrument.'' Said sec. 3391 seems to have been considered
and construed in connection with the decision in this case.
We think these authorities and the facts as found by the
lower court dispose of appellant's first point as not well taken.

The next point presented, that the transaction was a voluntary assignment by an insolvent debtor with a secret interest reserved for himself, will now be considered.   The first
authority cited in support of this point is *White v. Cotzhausen,* 129 U. S. 329, 9 Sup. Ct. 309, 32 L. ed. 677.   An
examination of this case shows that the Illinois voluntary
assignment act was then in force, and the supreme court
of the United States, was dealing with the provisions of that
act in deciding the case.   It will be found by an examination
of this voluntary assignment act that it is similar to the
proceedings in insolvency of this state and other states that
had insolvency or bankruptcy laws prior to the enactment
of the national bankruptcy law.   For this reason *White v.
Cotzhausen* cannot be accepted as authority in the case at
bar, but even in the opinion in that case Mr. Justice Harlan
says: ''We would not be understood as contravening the general principle, so distinctly announced by the supreme court
of Illinois, that a debtor, even when financially embarrassed,
may in good faith compromise his liabilities, sell or transfer
property in payment of debts, or mortgage or pledge it as
security for debts, or create a lien upon it by means even of
a judgment confessed in favor of his creditors.''   But he
adds that when a debtor is hopelessly insolvent, he will not
be permitted to evade the statute by a preference in favor of
only a part of his creditors and leave the others with no
share in his estate.   But in this he was simply construing
said assignment act.

In *Northern National Bank v. Weed,* 86 Wis. 212, 56 N. W.
634, the decision was controlled by the statutes of Wisconsin
then in force, and cannot be authority in this case.   We have
not had time to carefully examine the many other authorities cited by appellants in support of their second point,
but all those that we have glanced over seem to have been controlled by the statutes of the states where they were tried,

and if this is really the fact, then unless such statutes were substantially like the statutes of this state touching the question under consideration, or if they are so connected with insolvency laws as to be only used in administering such laws, they would not assist in its determination. But even if left in doubt as to the weight of these authorities, the trial court passed directly upon what seems almost decisive of this question in the fact that it found as facts in the case that "said transfer was not made with a secret understanding or with any secret or other agreement or understanding that the plaintiff should hold said property until the defendants should see fit to sell the same, or with any agreement or understanding that in the event they should see fit to sell said property, the plaintiff should convert said property into cash and take from the proceeds enough to satisfy its said claims and turn the surplus over to the defendants." The trial court heard the evidence, saw the witnesses, and determined the weight of their testimony, and having then made these findings of fact, we are not inclined to disturb them. Moreover, we do not think the authorities presented by appellants sustain their contention on this point.

The third point presented by appellants is that such an assignment as they allege the one made by Saunders to respondent to be, was illegal and void as to his other creditors under sec. 5932, Rev. Codes. This raises a very interesting question, and one that has never been passed upon by this court, and we have found no authority that we regard as directly in point from other states. Under the common law, a debtor in failing circumstances could convey or assign his property to one creditor, notwithstanding it might work a preference in favor of such creditor and leave other creditors unpaid. The alert and diligent creditor might secure his debt as a reward for his diligence, and wherever the rights of creditors in this respect have been restrained or entirely taken away, it has been by statute, and in derogation of the common law. "By the common law a debtor has an absolute right to prefer in payment one creditor over another, and such a preference, in the absence of fraud, is perfectly valid

as against other creditors. This right arises from the right
of disposition which is incident to the absolute ownership of
property. It is well settled, therefore, that in the absence
of express statutory provisions to the contrary, a debtor,
although insolvent or in failing circumstances, may prefer
one or more of his creditors by payment in money or other
property or by giving security for the debt, and that the
preference thus given will be valid, notwithstanding that
the claims of other creditors will thereby be delayed or defeated; provided, however, that the debt is actual, that the
property transferred does not greatly exceed the amount of
the claim, and that the transaction is not a mere device to
secure an advantage to the debtor or to hinder, delay, or
defraud other creditors. Such a preference, although it may,
in paying one creditor, exhaust or so reduce the assets of the
debtor as to leave other creditors unpaid and without the
means of collecting their claims, does not of itself 'hinder,
delay or defraud' creditors within the meaning of the general
statutes on this subject. The transaction 'does not deprive
other creditors of any legal right, for they have no right
to a priority'; and it 'is not fraudulent either in law or in
fact.' A creditor has a legal right to influence his debtor
to give him a preference, and 'violates no rule of law when
he takes payment or security for his demand, although others
are thereby deprived of all means of obtaining satisfaction
of their equally meritorious claims.' "   (20 Cyc. 572.)

The right of an insolvent debtor to prefer one or more
creditors over others seems to have been directly passed upon
by this court in *Wilson v. Baker Clothing Co.,* 25 Ida. 378,
137 Pac. 896, 50 L. R. A., N. S., 239.   In that case it was held
that, "An insolvent corporation is not prohibited by the statutes of this state from preferring certain creditors over
others in the due course of business where such preference is not collusively or fraudulently made. A corporation,
although insolvent, holds its assets just as a natural person
holds his property, with the same power to dispose of it to
secure or pay its debts, and neither a private person nor a

corporation can fraudulently dispose of his or its property to the injury or damage of his or its creditors.''

Having held that the deeds in controversy were mortgages, it follows that they are not assignments within the meaning of said section 5932, as they could not be both mortgages and assignments at the same time. But, assuming that said deeds were in fact assignments, then said section is suspended by the national bankruptcy law.

It occurred to us in reading said section that the phrase "provided in this title" is somewhat significant. The *title* referred to is title 12 of the Idaho Revised Codes, which contains the complete proceedings in insolvency of this state. Now, it may be interesting to inquire whether or not a section of an act which in order to be enforced must be assisted by, and taken in connection with, other sections of an entire act upon one specific subject or proceeding, in order to have its force and effect, can be detached from the other sections of the act and invoked as a remedy when the other sections thereof are suspended. Prior to the passage of the national bankruptcy law of July, 1898, said section 5932 was in force, because the insolvency law of this state of which it is a part was in force, and the deeds involved in this case would have been illegal and void as against the creditors of Saunders under said section, regardless of the question whether said deeds were otherwise made in good faith and without any intent to hinder, delay or defraud his other creditors. And this brings before this court the important and somewhat novel question as to whether the enactment of the national bankruptcy law *ipso facto* suspended our state insolvency law including said section. The provision of the constitution of the United States conferring upon Congress the power "to establish uniform laws on the subject of bankruptcies throughout the United States," of necessity constitutes any act of Congress passed upon that subject the supreme law of the land, and it was determined by the courts at an early day that a national bankruptcy law suspended and superseded the operation of any and all state insolvency laws whenever there was a conflict between them.

Appellant cites *Duryea v. Guthrie,* 117 Wis. 399, 94 N. W. 865, as a case "much in point," and we have, therefore, given the opinion in the case quite a careful reading, but it does not sustain the contention of appellant as we understand it. Christopher Guthrie was a resident of the city of Superior, Wisconsin. He was hopelessly insolvent at the time, and on October 16, 1901, he made and delivered to one W. E. Muse, who was then a citizen of Chicago, Ill., an instrument in writing whereby he assigned and delivered to Muse all his property, consisting of merchandise of the value of $5,000, situated in the city of Superior, for the express purpose, as stated in said instrument of assignment, that Muse would receive the same in trust and would sell the property, reduce the same to money, and distribute the proceeds thereof among the creditors of Guthrie *pro rata* without preference. Duryea, the plaintiff, was one of these creditors, and he, not being satisfied with said assignment, commenced an action for his debt and at the same time garnished Muse. Duryea urged a statute of the state of Wisconsin to defeat the said assignment, that statute being as follows: "All voluntary assignments, or transfers whatever of any real estate, chattels real, goods or chattels, rights, credits, moneys or effects for the benefit of or in trust for creditors shall be void as against the creditors of the person making the same unless the assignee shall be a resident of this state and shall, before taking possession of the property assigned and before taking upon himself any trust conferred upon him by the instrument of assignment, deliver to the county judge or court commissioner of the county in which such assignor or some one of the assignors at the time of the execution of such assignment shall reside, not being a creditor of such assignor, a bond duly executed." The said assignee, Muse, was a resident and citizen of Illinois, and he also failed to give a bond as required by the statute. For the reason that said assignee was not a citizen of the state of Wisconsin, the court held this assignment void under the provisions of said statute. The assignee urged that the said statute was *ipso facto* suspended by the national bankruptcy law, but the court decided that said statute "only assumes to regulate and control the manner in which such assignments shall be made and executed," and that it only dealt with the making and administration of common-law assignments, and was not in conflict with the national bankruptcy law.

It will be observed that a clear distinction is drawn between proceedings under a general insolvency statute of a state and one that simply permits and regulates general assignments for the benefit of creditors. This distinction between a state insolvency statute and a statute permitting and regulating general assignments for the benefit of creditors is clearly pointed out in *In re Sievers*, 91 Fed. 366. In that case, which was in Missouri, the contention hinged on the question as to whether the national bankruptcy law suspended the voluntary assignment statutes of the state, and the court on this subject said:

"Concerning these different contentions, it appears to me that there is a substantial difference between a proceeding under a general insolvency statute and one under a statute permitting general assignments. The one administers upon the estate of an insolvent as a proceeding in the courts, derives its potency from the law, winds up the estate judicially, and discharges the debtor. Such is essentially a proceeding in bankruptcy, and such is undoubtedly superseded by the act of Congress in question. . . . . It results from these views that, while proceedings under the insolvency laws, as such, are now void whether proceedings in bankruptcy follow or not, proceedings under the general assignment laws of states, like Missouri, or under the common-law deed of assignment, are not void or voidable, unless proceedings in bankruptcy are subsequently instituted."

We think it will be found on examination of the later authorities cited by appellant that these are in line with the case of *In re Sievers* as to the distinction there pointed out between the insolvency statutes of a state and statutes regulating general assignments. The cases cited by appellant that date prior to the enactment of the national bankruptcy law, such as the early California cases, dealt entirely with statutes in the nature of insolvency laws, or statutes regulating general assignments under the common law. But, without further examination of authorities on this point, we are decidedly of the opinion that sec. 5932 cannot be detached from the body of the insolvency laws of this state, of which it is a part, and made effective to defeat the object and intent of the deeds given by Saunders to respondent. If it is a necessary part of said law, it is suspended by the national bankruptcy law, and if it is not a part of said insolvency law, it was from its passage delusive and ineffective for the purpose for which it was intended, for it has no power whatever if detached from the act or title to which it evidently belongs. It cannot authorize an insolvent debtor to make any kind of an assignment "otherwise than provided in this title," and "this title" is the proceedings in bankruptcy of this state; therefore, it cannot authorize an assignment except when a person as an insolvent debtor avails himself of the insolvency law. Moreover, this section relates back to sec. 5884 of said title 12, and that section is as follows:

"As soon as the assignee is appointed and qualified, the clerk of the court must, by an instrument under his hand and seal of the court, assign and convey to the assignee all the estate, real and personal, of the debtor, with all his deeds, books, and papers relating thereto, and such assignment relates back to the commencement of the proceedings in insolvency, and by operation of law vests the title to all such property and estate, both real and personal, in the assignee. Such assignment vests in the assignee all the estate of the insolvent debtor not exempt by law from execution, subject to the lawful and *bona fide* liens and encumbrances thereon."

This is the only part of the act that provides for the assignment of a debtor's property, and this is made by operation of law through the clerk of the court, not by the debtor himself; thus it will at once be seen that said section is a vain and useless thing, without purpose or power, unless taken as a necessary part of the state insolvency law.

Counsel for appellants in his argument suggested that as this is an equity case, this court should take a broad and equitable view of the matter and endeavor to do substantial justice between the parties, but from this angle of the case, we fail to see any just or reasonable cause for the law or this court, under the claim of preventing a preference in favor of one creditor, to take from him what his diligence has secured, and turn it over to another creditor who will then enjoy the same preference to the exclusion of all others. Furthermore, the national bankruptcy law court was open to appellants, and at any time within four months after said deeds were given and placed on record, they might have gone into said court and had them set aside under section 60 of the national bankruptcy law, and then the estate would have been administered by said court and equitably distributed among all creditors including appellants.

The fourth and last point of the argument of counsel for appellants is addressed to specifications of errors numbers 7 and 8, and these are based upon sections 3169 and 3168, Rev. Codes. It is urged as to said sec. 3169 that the mere execution, delivery and placing on record of the deeds in question without a defeasance rendered them fraudulent, *per se*, and that the trial court had no right to hear evidence or make findings of fact as to the intent with which they were made. But without going into a lengthy review of the numerous authorities cited on this point by the brief of appellants, we think sec. 3171, Rev. Codes, determines this contention:

"In all cases arising under the provisions of this title, except as otherwise provided in the last section, the question of fraudulent intent is one of fact, and not of law; nor can any transfer or charge be adjudged fraudulent solely on the ground that it was not made for a valuable consideration."

But counsel for appellants attempts to evade this section by urging that sec. 3169 makes a transfer of property void when "taken with intent to delay or defraud," and that *intent* to *delay* is not within the purview of said sec. 3171. But we think the word "delay" would have been out of place and incongruous in that section. While there may be certain acts, the mere commission of which would be a fraud *per se*, we are not advised of any authority that imports damage or injury to delay of any kind as a question of law.

Delay and its consequences are questions of fact, and in any case where injury or damage was alleged to have been sustained by *delay,* that would raise a question of fact and require proof. The court below heard evidence on the question as to whether these deeds were made with intent to delay or defraud the creditors of Saunders, and it found as a fact, "that said transfer was not made or taken with intent to hinder, delay or defraud the answering defendants or either of them, or the other creditors of Hezekiah Saunders and Lucy Saunders." There is nothing new presented on this point; said sec. 3169 substantially puts in to our statutory law the long-established rule of the common law upon the same subject. Under the common-law rule and under statutes similar to ours, the test question as to the validity of a conveyance of a debtor to a creditor is: Was it a *bona fide* transaction? If made with an intent to delay or defraud the courts would set it aside if such an intent was proved in proceedings before them. To reverse the case at bar on this point, we would have to set aside the findings of the trial court, and under the evidence and the law we are not justified in doing this. Sec. 3168 relates, as suggested by counsel for respondent, to personal property only, and has no bearing on the point last presented for consideration.

The judgment is affirmed, with costs to respondent.

Sullivan, C. J., concurs.

(October 17, 1914.)

IDAHO HARDWARE & PLUMBING CO., a Corporation, Respondent, v. HEZEKIAH SAUNDERS et al., Appellants.

[143 Pac. 1183.]

APPEAL from the District Court of the Third Judicial District for Ada County. Hon. Charles P. McCarthy, Judge.

This action was commenced and prosecuted in said district court to have certain instruments, in form warranty deeds, declared mortgages and foreclosed as such. Judgment for the plaintiff. *Affirmed.*

Martin & Cameron, for Appellants.

Karl Paine, for Respondent.

TRUITT, J.—The facts in this case are substantially the same as in *Capital Lumber Co. v. Hezekiah Saunders et al.* Briefs of counsel included both cases. The points of law in each case are identical, and they were presented and argued before this court at the same time by the same counsel. The following statement in the brief of respondent explains this matter:

"Before beginning the perusal of the statement of the Idaho Hardware & Plumbing Co., the court should understand that the case of *Capital Lumber Co. v. Saunders et al.*, is in no wise connected with the case of *Idaho Hardware & Plumbing Co. v. Saunders et al.* For the convenience of counsel and the trial court, the action of the *Idaho Hardware & Plumbing Co. v. Saunders et al.* was tried immediately following the trial of the Capital Lumber Co. The writer has consented that the appellants might present to this court in a single brief the points relied on by them in both of these cases, believing that such a course will save both court and counsel time and labor, but it must be borne in mind that the facts of the two cases differ somewhat and that each case stands upon its own bottom.''

The theory of appellants in this case was exactly the same as in the *Capital Lumber Co. v. Saunders et al.*, and the decision of the lower court was similar. The only material difference in the testimony in the two cases is that there was no testimony in this case touching the point that there was an agreement or secret understanding of any kind by which the hardware company was to reserve any interest in said property for the benefit of Saunders. The opinion and the judgment in *Capital Lumber Co. v. Saunders et al.* therefore disposes of this case.

The judgment is affirmed, with costs to respondent.

Sullivan, C. J., concurs.

———————

(October 23, 1914.)

BANK OF OROFINO, a Corporation, Appellant, v. W. A. WELLMAN and P. E. McROBERTS, Copartners Doing Business Under the Firm Name and Style of WELL-MAN-McROBERTS CO. and ORA WELLMAN, Respondents.

[143 Pac. 1169.]

MARRIED WOMAN—SEPARATE PROPERTY—FRAUD—PROOF—COMMUNITY PROPERTY—CREDITORS OF HUSBAND—ATTACHMENT—IMPROVEMENTS ON WIFE'S SEPARATE PROPERTY—ESTOPPEL IN PAIS—EVIDENCE—FINDINGS OF FACT.

1. *Held*, that the finding of facts in this case to the effect that the property in controversy was the separate property of the wife was sustained by the evidence.

2. *Held*, that to constitute estoppel *in pais*, there must have been either false representation as to material facts or wrongful, misleading silence. (Bigelow on Estoppel, p. 602.)

3. *Held*, that a husband when free from debts and liabilities may make a gift to his wife from their community property, and that the same will then become her separate property and will not be liable for debts subsequently contracted by him.

APPEAL from the District Court of the Second Judicial District for Clearwater County, from a judgment and decree in favor of respondent, Ora Wellman. Hon. Edgar C. Steele, Judge.

Action to determine the title to a certain lot situate in the city of Lewiston, Idaho, and claimed to be owned as her separate property by the said Ora Wellman; and not to in any way or manner interfere with the validity of appellant's judgment heretofore entered in said court. *Affirmed.*

John R. Becker, for Appellant.

The separate character of the property must be established by something more than a mere preponderance of the evidence. It is hardly possible for a creditor to prove, or to offer any evidence tending to prove, that the sister of the debtor did not, at one time, make the debtor's wife a present of several hundred dollars in cash.

It is not only necessary for these respondents to satisfactorily show that the wife came into possession of separate funds through one of the recognized sources of separate acquisition, but those identical funds must be traced into the investment which she claims is a part of her separate estate. (*Patterson v. Bowes*, 78 Wash. 476, 139 Pac. 225; McKay, Community Property, sec. 265; *Riebli v. Husler*, 7 Cal. Unrep. 1, 69 Pac. 1061; *Ramsdell v. Fuller*, 28 Cal. 37, 87 Am. Dec. 103; *Chapman v. Allen*, 15 Tex. 278; *Claiborne v. Tanner*, 18 Tex. 69; *Dominquez v. Lee*, 17 La. 295; *Webb v. Peet*, 7 La. Ann. 92; *Smith v. Smith*, 12 Cal. 216, 73 Am. Dec. 533; *Meyer v. Kinzer*, 12 Cal. 247, 73 Pac. 538; *Smith v. Weed*, 75 Wash. 452, 134 Pac. 1070; Ballinger, Community Property, sec. 40.)

"A spouse who has by his or her acts or conduct induced third persons to deal with property as separate will be estopped afterward to deny that it is separate, where to permit him to do so would operate to the prejudice of such third persons. And the same principle is applicable to property represented or treated as community property." (21 Cyc. 1654; *Patton v. Gates,* 67 Ill. 166; *Coon v. Rigdon,* 4 Colo. 275; *Roberts v. Bodman etc. Lumber Co.,* 84 Ark. 227, 105 S. W. 258; *Hobbs v. Frazier,* 61 Fla. 611, 55 So. 848; *Million v. Commercial Bank,* 159 Mo. App. 601, 141 S. W. 453.)

"In the states where the wife has the control of her separate property, there would seem to be no reason why creditors of the community might not at any time subject to the payment of their claims funds applied to the wife's separate benefit, with her express or implied consent." (McKay, Community Property, sec. 250; *Maddox v. Summerlin,* 92 Tex. 483, 49 S. W. 1033; *Collins v. Bryan,* 40 Tex. Civ. App. 88, 88 S. W. 432.)

George W. Tannahill, for Respondents.

The improvements became a permanent part of the wife's property and no creditor then existed to challenge the same. (*Ware v. Seasongood,* 92 Ala. 152, 9 So. 138; McKay on Community Property, sec. 250.) In the case at bar, the record is silent of any indication of fraud.

"Where the husband erects a building on land of his wife, the law presumes that he intended it for her benefit." (*Appeal of Connecticut Humane Society,* 61 Conn. 465, 23 Atl. 826; *Metropolitan Nat. Bank v. Rogers,* 47 Fed. 148.)

"The mere fact that a husband, by his labor, has improved the real estate of his wife, will not render it subject to his debts." (*Cox v. Bishop,* 2 Ky. Law Rep. 310; *McFerrin v. Carter,* 62 Tenn. (3 Baxt.) 335; *Webster v. Hildreth,* 33 Vt. 457, 78 Am. Dec. 632.)

"In order to estop a married woman from asserting her claim to real estate, it is essential that she be guilty of positive fraud, or some act of concealment or suppression equivalent to fraud." (*Williamson v. Gore* (Tex. Civ. App.), 73 S. W. 563; *McClain v. Abshire,* 72 Mo. App. 390; *William-*

son v. Jones, 43 W. Va. 562, 64 Am. St. 891, 27 S. E. 411,
38 L. R. A. 694; *Kemp v. Folsom,* 14 Wash. 16, 43 Pac. 1100;
Harris v. Van De Vanter, 17 Wash. 489, 50 Pac. 50; *Steed
v. Petty,* 65 Tex. 490; *Johnson v. Bryan,* 62 Tex. 623.)

TRUITT, J.—In this case the Bank of Orofino, situated
in the town of Orofino in Clearwater county, in this state,
recovered a judgment for $2,542.13 and for costs in the dis-
trict court for said county on December 8, 1913, from W. A.
Wellman and P. E. McRoberts, copartners doing business in
said town of Orofino under the firm name of the Wellman-
McRoberts Co. This company had been engaged in business
for some years prior to December 4, 1913, and at that date
the company was financially in failing circumstances, and
for the purpose of making a distribution of their property
among all their creditors said W. A. Wellman and P. E. Mc-
Roberts at said date made an assignment of their stock of
merchandise, together with all accounts receivable, to one
J. B. Campbell, as assignee, and also deeded to said Campbell certain real property in said town of Orofino. At the
commencement of the action of said bank in which said judgment was obtained against Wellman and McRoberts, an
attachment was issued and levied upon said merchandise and
said real property in Orofino, and also upon certain real property in Nez Perce county, Idaho, standing on the records of
said county in the name of said W. A. Wellman, and upon
lot 1 of block 13 of Riverview addition to the city of Lewiston, in said Nez Perce county, standing on record in said
county in the name of his wife, Ora Wellman, which is the
subject of the controversy in this case. The testimony is not
disputed to the effect that this property was purchased by
said Ora Wellman with her own money in March, 1906, and
that the improvements thereon were put upon the property
during the spring of the same year. On December 11, 1913,
a stipulation in writing was entered into by and between all
the parties interested by which the said bank released its
attachment on all the said property and agreed to share the
estate *pro rata* with all the other creditors of said Wellman

and McRoberts, and also to the property in Lewiston claimed by Ora Wellman, the said stipulation being as follows as to the property claimed by said Ora Wellman:

"It is further agreed that the title to the said property claimed by Ora Wellman may be tried out in the above-entitled cause upon complaint in intervention, and answer thereto, the parties hereto waiving any objections on the ground that the complaint in intervention was not filed prior to the entry of judgment or default, it being considered that the sole purpose of the complaint in intervention is to try out the title to the lot situate in the city of Lewiston, and claimed to be owned as separate property by the said Ora Wellman, and not to interfere in any way or manner with the validity of the plaintiff's judgment heretofore entered."

According to the terms of this stipulation, on December 18, 1913, said Ora Wellman filed her complaint in intervention in said district court, in which she recited the facts of the attachment of said lot 1 of block 13, Riverview addition to Lewiston, Idaho, and claimed the same as her sole and separate property; she alleged that the attachment was a cloud upon her title, and asked that it be removed, and that said bank be enjoined from selling the property. To this complaint the bank filed its answer, denying the material allegations of the complaint, and setting up as a separate and affirmative defense certain facts tending to defeat plaintiff's claim of title to said property as alleged in her complaint. On the issues thus made by the pleadings the cause was tried by the court without a jury on March 13, 1914, and the court's findings of fact relating to the property in controversy are as follows:

"III. That the intervenor, Ora Wellman, is the owner of lot 1 of block 13 of Riverview Addition to the city of Lewiston, Idaho, which is the separate property of the intervenor, Ora Wellman."

And as to the material allegations of intervenor's complaint, the court found as follows:

"V. That all the material allegations of intervenor's complaint in intervention are found to be supported by the evidence and true, and all the material denials and affirmative matter alleged in plaintiff's amended answer thereto are found to be unsupported by the evidence and untrue."

The principal question presented in this case is as to whether the respondent has the title to the property in controversy, and whether she secured it so as to make it her sole and separate property within the meaning of sec. 2676, Rev. Codes, and this was the main question presented to this court in *Stewart v. Weiser Lumber Co.*, 21 Ida. 340, 121 Pac. 775, and in the case of *Baldwin v. McFarland*, decided May 15, 1914, and reported *ante*, p. 85, 141 Pac. 76, the same question was again presented to it and briefly disposed of in this way:

"Our examination and consideration of the record and briefs in the case, and the law applicable thereto, satisfies us that the trial judge reached the correct conclusion, and that this property is the separate property of the wife, and was not subject to execution for the collection of the husband's debt. To our minds, this case falls within the rule announced in *Stewart v. Weiser Lumber Co.*, 21 Ida. 340, 121 Pac. 775, and the long line of cases from this court followed in the Stewart-Weiser Lumber Co. case."

But there are two other questions raised by appellant's brief and oral argument in the case at bar that are not directly passed upon in this line of cases as we understand them. These are (1) whether community funds put into improvements on the wife's separate property can be traced and recovered by a creditor of the husband; and (2) if not, whether in this case the respondent is estopped from claiming this property as her sole and separate estate by reason of having permitted her said husband to use, improve and deal with it as it is alleged he did in appellant's said answer to intervenor's complaint. Under sec. 2676, Rev. Codes, it is provided that, "All property of the wife owned by her before marriage, and that acquired afterwards by gift, bequest, or descent, or that which she shall acquire with the proceeds of her separate property, shall remain her sole and separate property, to the same extent and with the same effect, as the property of a husband similarly acquired." The evidence conclusively shows that the said lot was purchased with said Ora Wellman's own money, and $100 of her own money went into improvements thereon, but the improvements except as to the $100 were placed upon said property with community funds. It is not claimed that these improvements were made with said Ora Wellman's separate money, but her husband testified that the part of these improvements put on the lot with community funds was a gift from him to his said wife. On this point W. A. Wellman, the husband, testified as follows: "Q. What was your idea in moving the building on this lot and putting it upon Mrs. Wellman's lot? A. I had to get it off the Yantis lots and she owned that lot in Riverview Addition, and I gave her that building to put on it as a home. Q. What was your intention as to its being her property? A. It was her property. Q. Did you retain any interest or attempt to retain any interest in the building on the lot? A. Not a dollar. Q. Were you indebted to anyone at that time? A. No, sir. Q. Were you indebted to anyone at the time this building was constructed? A. No, sir. Q. Were you in debt to anyone at the time Mrs. Wellman purchased this lot? A. No, sir."

The case of *Maddox v. Summerlin*, 92 Tex. 483, 49 S. W. 1033, 50 S. W. 567, is relied upon by counsel for appellant in support of this point as a leading case in the line of authorities approving the holding of the court in that case on this question. For this reason we have read and analyzed this opinion and find that this point was presented there, but the case turned upon the vital question embraced in the following quotation from the opinion in that case:

"We conclude that the land of the wife cannot be sold at the suit of the creditor, unless the facts shall show that the husband made the improvements with his own or the community funds, with intent to defraud his creditors, and that the wife, knowing of such intent, participated in the fraud. What may be the proper remedy to accord to the plaintiffs will depend upon the development of the case on another trial, and we refrain from making any suggestions, except to say that the house, when constructed upon the separate property of the wife, if paid for with community funds, did not become her separate property, but remained a part of the community estate, as was the money with which it was built, and, being community property, it is liable, if otherwise subject to sale, to the debts of the husband. If the husband intended the house as a gift to the wife, it was void as to existing creditors, and is subject to their debts as if not given to her, unless she shows that, when the gift was made, he had enough property remaining to pay all of his existing debts. The law will not presume it to be a gift, in the absence of evidence to show such intention.''

The decisive and crucial point is in the one sentence in the above quotation: "If the husband, *being a debtor*, intended the house as a gift to the wife, it was void as to *existing* creditors, and is subject to their debts as if not given to her, unless she shows that, when the gift was made, he had enough property remaining to pay all his *existing* debts.'' The italics are ours, and are intended to emphasize the vital and decisive difference between that case and the case at bar. There is no legal objection to the gift as such of the property in that case made by the court, provided that it was not repugnant to a certain statute which was in force at that time in the state of Texas, this statute being as follows: "Every gift, conveyance, assignment, transfer or charge made by a debtor, which is not upon consideration deemed valuable in law, shall be void as to prior creditors unless it appears that such debtor was then possessed of property within this state subject to execution sufficient to pay his existing debts.'' It will be observed that under this statute as to pre-existing debts, the gift was *prima facie* void and the property was subject to the payment of *pre-existing* debts, unless the donee should make it appear that the person making the gift at the time it was made possessed property within that state subject to execution sufficient to pay all his existing debts, and if this was done the gift would be legal and unobjectionable. Now, the statute of this state as to the property of the wife applies the same rule to her separate property that is applied to the property of the husband similarly acquired. The transfer of property by a husband to his wife in this state stands in the same relation to his creditors as any other transfer or conveyance. If he is out of debt and has no other legal liabilities, he has a perfect right to give his wife any of his property, or all of it if he is so inclined. But sec. 3169 is intended to protect creditors against a debtor conveying his property away to any person, including his wife, if done "with intent to delay or defraud any creditor or other person of his demands, and is void against all creditors of the debtor and their successors in interest." Whether in a given case the transaction is sincere and *bona fide,* or a mere device as a cover to conceal the real ownership of the husband to his property and thus delay or defraud existing creditors is the true test, and this is a question of fact to be determined by a jury or by the court when hearing the case without a jury. (*Knapp v. Smith,* 27 N. Y. 277.)

Another authority relied upon by appellant is *Collins v. Bryan,* 40 Tex. Civ. App. 88, 88 S. W. 432, which is also a Texas case. In that case the trustee in bankruptcy of A. L. Collins brought suit against Sallie Collins, the wife of said A. L. Collins, alleging that when insolvent and just prior to being adjudged a bankrupt, with intent to hinder, delay and defraud his creditors, said A. L. Collins conveyed to his said wife certain real property described in the complaint; and, further alleging, if not entitled to recover the land, that while still seised with the title to said land said A. L. Collins expended $1,000 out of the community estate upon this land in the way of improvements, and asked for a lien for said amount upon such improvements. The lower court found that the land belonged to said Sallie Collins, but that A. L. Collins had expended the sum of $300 of the community funds on improvements on this land, and that to that extent the improvements were community property, and ordered them sold and that the trustee be paid $300 out of the proceeds. Sallie Collins appealed from this judgment, and one of the material points presented on the appeal was as to whether said improvements were a gift from her husband, and the court disposed of that in the opinion in this way: "Improvements erected upon land, the separate property of the wife, by the husband out of community funds, will not be presumed to be a gift, in the absence of evidence to show such intention. There was no pleading or proof in this case that the improvements in controversy were intended by the husband of appellant Sallie Collins as a gift to her." In fact, she alleged in her answer that the improvements were placed on the land by her father and mother prior to the date that they conveyed the same to her, and that her husband, A. L. Collins, did not put said improvements or any part of them upon the property out of either his separate estate or the community property. The very material difference between this case and the one at bar is that the evidence shows that the property claimed by respondent herein was put upon her separate property as a gift from her husband for the purpose of giving her a home, at a time when neither the community nor the husband were in debt in any sum whatever, and the testimony of the husband is that the same was a gift from him to his said wife.

We have examined the three cases referred to in *Maddox v. Summerlin, supra,* in support of the opinion of the court in that case, and find that all relate to and are based upon the material fact that the husband in each case was *insolvent* when the respective improvements were put upon the wife's property.

In *Kirby v. Bruns,* 45 Mo. 234, 100 Am. Dec. 376, it is held that, "The value of improvements placed by the husband on the land of the wife may be reached through appropriate chancery proceedings, and the amount thereof applied to the payment of claims existing against him at the time of such investment." Bruns at the time of making the conveyance to his wife in this case was insolvent, and the suit was brought by his creditors for the purpose of subjecting said property to their claims. In *Lynde v. McGregor,* 13 Allen (Mass.), 182, 90 Am. Dec. 188, the rule is announced that, "If the wife of an insolvent debtor, not knowing his pecuniary condition, mortgages land, which she holds as her separate property, as security for money advanced to him, and he thereafter, within six months before the commencement of proceedings in insolvency, knowing himself to be insolvent, with intent to defraud his creditors, and with the fraudulent participation of the mortgagee, expends money in improving and building upon the land, the assignee in insolvency may maintain a bill in equity against her, her husband and the mortgagee to compel the payment to him of the amount of the increased value of the land, by reason of the husband's expenditures thereon''; and in *Humphrey v. Spencer,* 36 W. Va. 11, 14 S. E. 410, which is a West Virginia case, the court decided this same point, and held that the improvements placed by the husband upon his wife's separate estate as a gift was void as to his *existing debts* under a statute of that state.

We have referred to these authorities presented by appellant to sustain his position in the case, not to approve of the rather extreme doctrine announced by some of them upon this question, but rather to show that if adopted as authority herein, they would not sustain the contention of appellant in this case under the facts as shown by the record. But there is a line of authorities that take a more liberal view of this question as to the rights of married women, and hold that when improvements are put upon a wife's separate property by her husband who is free from debt at the time, it attaches to the realty, becomes a part of it, and cannot be reached by subsequent creditors of the husband unless the wife participated in a fraudulent investment of the funds put into the improvements. However, in deciding this case, we deem it unnecessary to review them.

But we think the case of *Peck v. Brummagim,* 31 Cal. 440, 89 Am. Dec. 195, is almost directly in point on this question as presented in the case at bar. It is announced in that case that the husband ''when free from debts and liabilities may make a gift to his wife of either real or personal property which at the time was the common property of the husband and wife, and the same will become her separate property and will not be liable for debts by him afterward contracted,'' and further, ''if the husband uses money which is the common property of the husband and wife in erecting a house on land which is the separate property of the wife, the house, if it is a part of the realty, becomes the separate property of the wife.''

Now, in the case before this court, the evidence shows that the husband was not in debt, ''didn't owe a dollar,'' at the time this property was purchased, and was not indebted when the improvements were put on it. The lot was purchased with his wife's own money given to her by Mrs. Hurlbert, her sister in law, for her separate property to buy a home with, and the deed was made to her, and the title to the property was still in her name of record when attached by appellant bank for debts which the husband had incurred long after the transaction of purchasing and improving said property. In these circumstances, if W. A. Wellman at the time of the transaction wished to move a certain barn that the testimony shows was upon his own property on to his wife's lot and convert it into a dwelling for their home and gave it to her, it became a part of her said realty, the title to the premises then vested in her, and subsequent debtors of her husband cannot subject it to the payment of their debts. We think the trial court decided correctly on this point.

Coming now to the question of estoppel, we shall dispose of this very briefly. In Bigelow on Estoppel, 6th ed., 602, the author says:

''We have now to consider cases in which one man has, otherwise than by contract, caused another to believe something which afterward it would be unjust for the former to repudiate. There are two classes of cases of this kind, to wit, cases of representation and cases of silence, or, more fully, cases of false representation and cases of wrongful, misleading silence. Representation, as the term must here be understood, imports some word or act; silence, the entire absence, on the part of the person silent, of word or act. And wrongful, misleading silence is here, and for the present, to be understood as silence by a person aware of his rights, and of what is going on, while those rights are being disposed of by another.''

In *McClain v. Abshire*, 72 Mo. App. 390, a distinction is drawn in favor of a married woman as to matters of property between her and her husband, and such matters where the peculiar relationship does not exist. This distinction is expressed as follows:

"Before a married woman can be estopped to claim her separate property against a lien attempted to be created by her husband, she must know of his creating such lien and act in such manner as to induce the other party to rely upon the lien; and in applying the principles of estoppel, the peculiar relationship existing between husband and wife will be considered by the courts."

In *Steed v. Petty*, 65 Tex. 490, the generally received rule on the subject of estoppel *in pais* is announced as follows: "Among other requisites, two must concur to constitute an estoppel. First, there must have been a false representation or a concealment of material facts; second, the party to whom the representation was made or from whom the material facts were concealed must have been ignorant of the existence of the facts concealed or of the falsity of the representation."

We do not think in this case that the facts as shown by the testimony establish an estoppel against respondent, Ora Wellman, regarding her rights to the property in controversy, and, therefore, decline to disturb the findings of the trial court covering this point. The judgment is affirmed, with costs to respondent.

Sullivan, C. J., concurs.

(October 29, 1914.)

THE BOISE ASSOCIATION OF CREDIT MEN, LTD., a Corporation, Appellant, v. T. R. ELLIS and THOMAS BUHL, Respondents.

[144 Pac. 6.]

Constitutional Law—Liberty of Contract—Class Legislation—Sale of Merchandise in Bulk—Due Process of Law—Fixtures—Merchandise—Police Power.

1. *Held*, that chap. 3 of title 10, Rev. Codes, which provides for "sales of goods in bulk," is a constitutional and valid law, that it does not constitute class legislation within the inhibition of the constitution, and that it is a proper and reasonable exercise of the state's police power.

2. *Held*, that a stock of goods, wares and merchandise, when sold in bulk, does not by implication include the fixtures as a part of the sales.

APPEAL from the District Court of the Seventh Judicial District for Washington County. Hon. Ed. L. Bryan, Judge.

In this action appeal was taken from the judgment of the lower court sustaining the demurrer to the complaint of appellant and denying the relief prayed for therein, and rendering judgment in favor of the defendant Thomas Buhl for costs of the action. Judgment *affirmed*.

Raymond L. Givens and Charles E. Winstead, for Appellant.

Statutes regulating the sale of stocks of goods, wares and merchandise in bulk have within a comparatively recent period been enacted in twenty-four states of the Union and by Congress for the District of Columbia.

A statute with the same object attained by a similar remedy has been held valid by the highest courts in Massachusetts, Connecticut, Tennessee, and Washington. (*John P. Squire & Co. v. Tellier*, 185 Mass. 18, 102 Am. St. 322, 69 N. E. 312; *Walp v. Mooar*, 76 Conn. 515, 57 Atl. 277; *Neas v. Borches*,

109 Tenn. 398, 97 Am. St. 851, 71 S. W. 50; *McDaniels v. J. J. Connelly Shoe Co.*, 30 Wash. 549, 94 Am. St. 889, 71 Pac. 37, 60 L. R. A. 947.)   An act declaring such sales presumptively fraudulent was assumed to be valid by the courts of last resort in Wisconsin and Maryland.   (*Fisher v. Herrmann*, 118 Wis. 424, 95 N. W. 392; *Hart v. Roney*, 93 Md. 432, 49 Atl. 661; *Wright v. Hart*, 182 N. Y. 330, 75 N. E. 404, 3 Ann. Cas. 263, 2 L. R. A., N. S., 338; *Jaques & Tinsley Co. v. Carstarphen Warehouse Co.*, 131 Ga. 1, 62 S. E. 82.)

"The Michigan sales in bulk act (Pub. Acts 1905, No. 223), avoiding, as against creditors, sales in bulk otherwise than in the regular course of business, unless an inventory is made at least five days before the sale, and the purchaser receives a list of the seller's creditors, and notifies them of the proposed sale personally, or by registered mail, at least five days before its consummation, and making a purchaser not conforming to the statute a receiver for the benefit of the seller's creditors, is a valid exercise of the police power, and does not deny due process or the equal protection of the laws." (*Kidd, Dater & Price Co. v. Musselman Grocer Co.*, 217 U. S. 461, 30 Sup. Ct. 606, 54 L. ed. 839; sustained in *Noble State Bank v. Haskell*, 219 U. S. 104, 31 Sup. Ct. 186, 55 L. ed. 112, Ann. Cas. 1912A, 487; *Thorpe v. Pennock Mercantile Co.*, 99 Minn. 22, 108 N. W. 940, 9 Ann. Cas. 229; *John P. Squire & Co. v. Tellier*, 185 Mass. 18, 102 Am. St. 322, 69 N. E. 312; *Lemieux v. Young*, 211 U. S. 489, 29 Sup. Ct. 174, 53 L. ed. 295; affirming *Young v. Lemieux*, 79 Conn. 434, 129 Am. St. 193, 65 Atl. 436, 600, 8 Ann. Cas. 452, 20 L. R. A., N. S., 160.)

A sale of the fixtures necessary for the conducting of the business made such sale fraudulent and void as to the creditors unless the notices provided in the statute had been given in the manner prescribed by law, for the reason that by the sale of such fixtures without the purchase of new fixtures to take the place of the old fixtures there was a substantial conveyance of the business or trade of the vendor to the prejudice of the rights of the vendor's creditors, among whom were plaintiffs herein.   (*Parham & Co. v. Potts-Thompson Liquor*

Co., 127 Ga. 303, 56 S. E. 460; *Knapp, Stout & Co. v. Mc-Caffrey*, 178 Ill. 107, 69 Am. St. 290, 52 N. E. 898; *Fitz Henry v. Munter*, 33 Wash. 629, 74 Pac. 1003; *Holford v. Trewella*, 36 Wash. 654, 79 Pac. 308; *Plass v. Morgan*, 36 Wash. 160, 78 Pac. 784.)

Varian & Norris, for Respondent Thomas Buhl.

The bulk sales law is unconstitutional and violates the provisions of sec. 1, art. 1, and sec. 13 of art. 1 of the constitution. (*Off & Co. v. Morehead*, 235 Ill. 40, 126 Am. St. 184, 85 N. E. 264, 14 Ann. Cas. 434, 20 L. R. A., N. S., 167; *Pogue v. Rowe*, 236 Ill. 157, 86 N. E. 207; *Wright v. Hart*, 182 N. Y. 330, 75 N. E. 404, 3 Ann. Cas. 263, 2 L. R. A., N. S., 338; *Miller v. Crawford*, 70 Ohio St. 207, 71 N. E. 631, 1 Ann. Cas. 558; *McKinster v. Sager*, 163 Ind. 671, 106 Am. St. 268, 72 N. E. 854, 68 L. R. A. 273; *Block v. Schwartz*, 27 Utah, 387, 101 Am. St. 971, 76 Pac. 22, 1 Ann. Cas. 550, 65 L. R. A. 308.)

The language of the statute seems to be very plain, and it is evident from the terms thereof that the legislature never intended that fixtures should be embraced within its meaning. (*Gallus v. Elmer*, 193 Mass. 106, 78 N. E. 772, 8 Ann. Cas. 1067; *Lee v. Gillen & Boney*, 90 Neb. 730, 134 N. W. 278; *Albrecht v. Cudihee*, 37 Wash. 206, 79 Pac. 628; *Bowen v. Quigley*, 165 Mich. 337, 130 N. W. 690, 34 L. R. A., N. S., 218; *People's Savings Bank v. Van Allsburg*, 165 Mich. 524, 131 N. W. 101; *Everett Produce Co. v. Smith Bros.*, 40 Wash. 566, 111 Am. St. 979, 82 Pac. 905, 5 Ann. Cas. 798, 2 L. R. A., N. S., 331; *Curtis v. Phillips*, 5 Mich. 112; *Kolander v. Dunn*, 95 Minn. 422, 104 N. W. 371, 483.)

The bulk sales law being in derogation of the common law and of the right to alienate property without restriction is to be strictly construed. (*Yancey v. Lamar-Rankin Drug Co.*, 140 Ga. 359, 78 S. E. 1078; *Taylor v. Folds*, 2 Ga. App. 453, 58 S. E. 683.)

TRUITT, J.—This action was commenced by the appellant corporation, as assignee of two different mercantile companies, against said T. R. Ellis to collect certain accounts against him for goods, wares and merchandise sold and delivered to him by said companies at his place of business in Cambridge, Idaho. The complaint alleges that these accounts were duly assigned by said companies to appellant, who was the owner and holder of them at the time of commencing this action, and that the aggregate sum of said accounts amounting to $285.46 was due and owing from Ellis to appellant, and judgment was demanded for said sum against him.

In said complaint the respondent, Thomas Buhl, is connected with the transaction which is the basis of the action against him as follows: "That on or about December 11, 1912, the said T. R. Ellis sold and transferred all his said stock of goods, wares and merchandise, including fixtures, out of the usual and ordinary course of business and trade, and did thereby substantially sell and convey the entire business and trade thereof conducted by the said T. R. Ellis, said fixtures consisting of counters, scales, shelving, tables, and store fixtures in general. That the said T. R. Ellis particularly sold the said fixtures to the defendant, Thomas Buhl, for the sum of $150." It will be seen from the complaint that Buhl did not buy or receive any of the merchandise.

The respondent Buhl, as defendant therein, interposed a general demurrer to said complaint, and after consideration of the same by the trial court it was sustained and the action dismissed. From the order dismissing said action and the judgment entered against appellant, this appeal is taken. The defendant Ellis did not appear in the court below, and the record is silent as to whether or not he was served with process.

The appellant in his brief presents an argument and cites authorities to show that the claims in this case were assignable and were properly assigned to the plaintiff, and it could therefore legally maintain an action upon them. As to the defendant Ellis, counsel for the respondent Buhl do not dispute the validity of the assignment of these claims, nor the right of appellant to maintain an action to collect the debt which they constitute, as to the defendant Ellis, but do question the manner of the proceeding in said action for the purpose of holding defendant Buhl liable for this debt. But as this only relates to the manner of procedure and not to the real points presented by the appeal, we do not think proper to pass upon it.

The two important points presented by this appeal are, (1) whether the law under consideration imposes such restrictions on sales of goods, wares and merchandise in bulk by persons engaged in that business, as to deprive them of their property without due process of law, and also whether it is class legislation within the inhibition of the constitution on that subject; and, (2), that if the law is constitutional, whether fixtures used in connection with the mercantile business are by implication included within its purview and meaning.

This act, though passed by the legislature in 1903, has never before come before this court for interpretation, and for that reason we have examined a number of the decisions of other courts that have passed upon and construed similar laws with much interest.

It must be conceded that this law does restrict and put some burdens on the sale of the kind of property to which it relates, but it is claimed in its favor that its object is to prevent an abuse of credit extended to debtors engaged in the mercantile business and thus prevent fraudulent sales that would otherwise deprive their creditors of their honest debts.

In *John P. Squire & Co. v. Tellier*, 185 Mass. 18, 102 Am. St. 322, 69 N. E. 312, a case decided by the supreme court of Massachusetts, it is said:

"The statute deals only with sales in bulk of a part or the whole of a stock of merchandise, which are not made in the ordinary course of trade and in the regular and usual prosecution of the seller's business. It does not interfere with the transaction of ordinary business, but relates to unusual and extraordinary transfers. In substance it declares that a sale of this kind shall not be made without first giving to creditors an opportunity to collect their debts, so far as the property to be sold might enable them to collect, or without subsequently making satisfactory provision for the payment of

these debts.   A sale made in violation of the statute is void
as against creditors, and, if the vendor's debts are paid, the
sale cannot be interfered with.   A purchaser, to be safe, has
only to see that the vendor's creditors are provided for.   The
vendor may sell freely, without regard to the statute, if he
pays his debts.''

The purpose of this law is quite similar to that of sec. 3169,
Rev. Codes, against transfers of property with intent to defraud or delay creditors; and under the statute relating to
sales in bulk, the object is to prevent a retail merchant from
disposing of his stock of goods without notice to his creditors
with the intention of doing the same thing, and it is the intention and purpose of this law to prevent that.   It is true that
in doing this, it may work a hardship on honest tradesmen,
but many other laws do the same thing as to honest men that
the designs of the dishonest may be defeated.

Some of the early acts passed upon this subject were held
unconstitutional and void by the supreme courts of the respective states in which they were passed, but the objections
pointed out by the courts in those acts have been corrected
in the later laws enacted on this subject and have now been
held constitutional by the courts of the same states that had
declared the earlier acts unconstitutional.

Block v. Schwartz, 27 Utah, 387, 101 Am. St. 971, 76 Pac.
22, 1 Ann. Cas. 550, 65 L. R. A. 308, is relied on by respondent
to support his contention that the law in question in the case
at bar is unconstitutional and void.   In that case the statute
on this subject in the state of Utah was held unconstitutional, but that statute had two objectionable provisions in it
which are pointed out by Mr. Justice Bartch in his opinion as
follows: ''Under the provisions of this act a sale of any portion or all of a stock of merchandise, made out of the ordinary
course of trade, by any merchant who has creditors, without
a detailed inventory made at least five days before the sale,
showing the cost price of each article, and notice of the proposed sale, the cost price, and selling price, given at least five
days before the sale to each creditor, is not only fraudulent
and void, but also renders both the seller and purchaser guilty

of a misdemeanor, and subjects them to the penalty provided
in the act for that crime." And in the opinion a further
objection is stated as follows: "Now, it will be noticed that
nowhere in its provisions is there any exemption of any sale
by administrators, executors, trustees, assignees for the benefit of creditors, trustees in bankruptcy, or public officers acting under judicial process. There being no such exemption,
it would seem that such sales of merchandise owned by
debtors, made by persons acting in a fiduciary capacity under
judicial process, must also be made in accordance with the
provisions of the act, in order that the seller and purchaser
may avoid the penalties provided. It is evident that such a
law would not only deprive property of one of its chief attri-
butes, but would greatly hamper the administration of estates
and retard the enforcing of judicial process." It is not probable that a law with such drastic and unreasonable provisions
as the Utah statute had would ever be sustained by any court.

It is generally conceded that state legislatures have the right
to enact reasonable laws to prevent fraudulent sales of property and to protect creditors, and that this right falls within
the general scope of police power will not be denied. But
the police power must stop where it comes against the provisions of the constitution. It must be exercised for a reasonable and beneficial purpose to the general public or to a special
class of business.

In the syllabus of *Hirth-Krause Co. v. Cohen*, 177 Ind. 1,
97 N. E. 1, Ann. Cas. 1914C, 708, which is a case decided in
1912, by the supreme court of Indiana, it is stated: "Acts
1909, c. 49, sec. 1, making a sale of goods or merchandise in
bulk void, unless in the ordinary course of trade, and unless
an inventory be made before the sale showing the quantity
of the goods, and the cost of each article, and unless the purchaser demand and receive from the seller a written list of
names and addresses of the seller's creditors, with the amount
of indebtedness, and unless the purchaser before taking possession shall notify personally the creditors named in the list,
or known to him, of the proposed sale, and the price and con-

ditions thereof, is a proper exercise of the state's police power.''

In *Spurr v. Travis*, 145 Mich. 721, 116 Am. St. 330, 108 N. W. 1090, 9 Ann. Cas. 250, which is a leading case, the supreme court of Michigan held that the "sales in bulk" statute of that state did not violate the constitution, and in discussing that point the opinion says: "Does the act conflict with section 32 of article 6 of the constitution? It may be conceded that an act which should prohibit the sale of property of any character, either generally or for a stated time, without any adequate purpose or object, would constitute such an interference with the property and liberty of the individual as is inhibited by this section. The courts have, however, never treated this or similar provisions as prohibitive of legislation in the exercise of the police power which regulates the manner of the use or disposition of property, even though a temporary inconvenience may be suffered by the owner.'' And in the case of *Musselman Grocer Co. v. Kidd etc. Co.*, 151 Mich. 478, 115 N. W. 409, the same court held that the act was not in conflict with any of the provisions of the Michigan constitution, or of section 1 of the fourteenth amendment of the constitution of the United States. The plaintiff in error, being dissatisfied with the decision, carried the case to the supreme court of the United States, which, in 1910, held that the Michigan law was based on a proper and reasonable classification of business and did not violate the fourteenth amendment to the federal constitution. (*Kidd, Dater & Price Co. v. Musselman Grocer Co.*, 217 U. S. 461, 30 Sup. Ct. 606, 54 L. ed. 839.) In this holding, the court followed its previous ruling, made in the case of *Lemieux v. Young*, 211 U. S. 489, 29 Sup. Ct. 174, 53 L. ed. 295, which involved the same question with reference to a similar statute of Connecticut. In delivering the opinion in *Lemieux v. Young*, *supra*, Mr. Justice White said: ''The supreme court of errors, in upholding the validity of the statute, decided that the subject with which it dealt was within the police power of the state, as the statute alone sought to regulate the manner of disposing of a stock in trade outside of the regular course of business, by methods which, if uncontrolled, were often resorted to for the consummation of fraud, to the injury of innocent creditors. In considering whether the requirements of the statute were so onerous and restrictive as to be repugnant to the fourteenth amendment, the court said: 'It does not seem to us, either from a consideration of the requirements themselves of the act, or of the facts of the case before us, that the restrictions placed by the legislature upon sales of the kind in question are such as will cause such serious inconvenience to those affected by them as will amount to any unconstitutional deprivation of property. A retail dealer who owes no debts may lawfully sell his entire stock without giving the required notice. One who is indebted may make a valid sale without such notice, by paying his debts, even after the sale is made. Insolvent and fraudulent vendors are those who will be chiefly affected by the act, and it is for the protection of creditors against sales by them of their entire stock at a single transaction, and not in the regular course of business, that its provisions are aimed.' " And Mr. Justice White further said: "That the court below was right in holding that the subject with which the statute dealt was within the lawful scope of the police authority of the state, we think is too clear to require discussion."

We think the foregoing authorities are decisive as to the first point submitted by appellant, but will say that as the state of Washington has a law substantially like ours on this subject, and as the same question was presented to the supreme court of that state as is here presented in the case at bar, we refer to the case of *McDaniels v. J. J. Connelly Shoe Co.*, 30 Wash. 549, 94 Am. St. 889, 71 Pac. 37, 60 L. R. A. 947, as being directly in point in this case. In meeting the objections there urged to the Washington law, the court said:

"The first objection to the constitutionality of the act is that it deprives persons of their property without due process of law. As we understand the argument, the contention is not that the act deprives an owner of property of his day in court, where his property rights are judicially called in question, or that it in any manner authorizes the actual physical taking by one of the property of another, but it is that as the term 'property,' in legal signification, includes in its meaning the right of any person to possess, use, enjoy or dispose of a thing, the act violates the constitution, inasmuch as it. restricts the right of an owner to dispose of his property. The act, it is true, does prohibit owners of certain kinds of property from disposing of it in a particular way, without complying with certain conditions, but it is not for that reason necessarily unconstitutional. While the legislature may not constitutionally declare that void which in its nature is, and under all circumstances must be, entirely honest and harmless, yet it may, under its police powers, place such reasonable restrictions on the right of an owner in relation to his property as it finds necessary to protect the interests of the public, or prevent frauds among individuals. If this were not so, it would be easy to find many unconstitutional acts on the statute books. . . . .

"It is next said that the act violates that provision of the constitution which prohibits the legislature from granting to a class of citizens privileges and immunities which upon the same terms shall not equally belong to all citizens; in other words, it is class legislation. In *Redford v. Spokane Street Ry. Co.*, 15 Wash. 419, 46 Pac. 650, we held that where a law is uniform so far as it operates, its constitutionality is not affected by the number of persons within the scope of its operation; and, applying this principle, we held in *Fitch v. Applegate*, 24 Wash. 25, 64 Pac. 147, that a law giving laborers in certain enumerated industries liens upon the general property of their employers was constitutional. The same principle is applicable to the case in hand."

In deciding the question as to the constitutionality of the law of this state regulating the purchase, sale and transfer of stocks of goods, wares and merchandise in bulk and prescribing penalties for the violation thereof, we hold both by weight of authority and on principle that said law is constitutional and valid, that it is not repugnant to the constitution as class legislation, and that it is a proper exercise of the police power of the state.

Coming, now, to the other point presented by the appellant to reverse the judgment of the lower court, viz.: That the fixtures of a merchant are in effect a part of his goods, wares and merchandise or stock in trade, and that said statute relating to sales in bulk of such merchandise should be construed to include the word "fixtures" by implication. This statute is clearly in derogation of the common-law rule, in that it prescribes conditions and restrictions regarding the sale of such property, for under the common law a person could sell any of his property at such time and in such manner as he might choose, without notice of the sale to his creditors or any other person, and without doing the things prescribed by said statute. Statutes of this kind should not be extended by implication to supply words that would bring subjects into the purview of the statute not specifically found there and not within its spirit or intention. Can the word "fixtures" be supplied to this statute? Is it germane to the scope, meaning and purpose of the statute? We think not.

The Standard Dictionary defines "fixture" as, "An article of a personal or chattel nature affixed to the freehold by a tenant, and removable by him, if it can be taken away without material injury to the realty, as gas fixtures in a residence, counters, shelving, and store fixtures in a mercantile house, or machinery or apparatus in trade and manufactures." And Bouvier's Law Dictionary defines "fixture" as, "Anything affixed or attached to a building, and used in connection with it, movable or immovable. Whenever the appendage is of such nature that it is not part or parcel of the building but may be removed without injury to the building, then it is a movable fixture and does not pass without conveyance to the freehold." Now, we think that under these definitions it would do violence to the clear meaning and intent of this statute to read the word "fixtures" into it. Merchandise is defined by Webster as, "Objects of commerce; whatever is usually bought and sold in trade or market by merchants." We think that merchandise as used in this statute must be construed to mean such things as are usually bought and sold by merchants. Merchandise means something that is sold every day and is constantly going out of the store and being replaced by other goods, but the fixtures are not a part of the trade or business; they are not sold in the ordinary trade as goods.   They remain from year to year. The merchant could not dispose of them as long as he remains in business.   It is true that shelving, counters, drawers, tables and many other things are necessary in order to conduct the business of the retail merchant, and so are delivery wagons in the larger towns to deliver goods, and clerks to sell the goods, and so is a house or room in which to keep them, but the clerks are not part of the goods, wares or merchandise, and though the business cannot be conducted without a house or place to keep and display the goods, the house or the room where they are sold is not a part of the goods, wares and merchandise.

In *Kolander v. Dunn*, 95 Minn. 422, 104 N. W. 371, 483, it was held that, "Under chap. 291, p. 357, Laws 1899, the sale of the stock of merchandise was presumed to be fraudulent and void, but that act has no application to the sale of 'fixtures." In *Gallus v. Elmer*, 193 Mass. 106, 78 N. E. 772, 8 Ann. Cas. 1067, it is held that, "As used in the Massachusetts statute prohibiting sales in bulk except when made in the ordinary course of trade, the phrase 'stock of merchandise' is applicable only to the articles which the seller keeps for sale in the ordinary course of his business, and is not applicable to a storekeeper's fixtures."

In *Lee v. Gillen & Boney*, 90 Neb. 730, 134 N. W. 278, it was held that, "Section 6048, Ann. St. 1909, commonly called the 'Bulk Sales Law,' relates only to merchandise kept for sale 'in the ordinary course of trade and in the regular and usual prosecution of' business, and does not apply to fixtures or a manufacturer's stock of raw materials used by himself, and not kept or offered for sale in the ordinary course of trade."

It is suggested that to make the law apply to fixtures as well as to the goods would strengthen the retail merchant's credit.   Perhaps it would, and it might also strengthen his credit to make it include all his other personal property, or his store building, if he owned it, or his farm, but that is beyond the scope and reasonable purpose of the law, which is not primarily to strengthen the retailer's credit but to make him pay his honest debts.

A very peculiar feature of this case is that the complaint does not charge that the goods, wares or merchandise were sold to respondent Buhl, but in effect claims that he should pay for them because he bought the fixtures, and this theory of the case would make the goods, wares and merchandise a *part* of the *fixtures* instead of the *fixtures* being a *part* of the goods. We hardly think this is permissible.

Having thus decided that the points relied on by appellant to reverse the judgment against it are not well taken, we hold, therefore, with the lower court that said complaint does not state a cause of action against respondent Buhl. The judgment must be affirmed, with costs in favor of respondent.

Sullivan, C. J., concurs.

(November 2, 1914.)

JOHN DAVIES et al., Plaintiffs, v. BOARD OF COUNTY COMMISSIONERS OF NEZ PERCE COUNTY, Defendants.

[143 Pac. 945.]

WRIT OF MANDATE—COUNTY BOARD OF CANVASSERS—SPECIAL ELECTION— CANVASS OF ELECTION RETURNS—STATUTORY CONSTRUCTION—OPEN- ING OF BALLOT-BOX.

1. Where the county board of canvassers rejects certain returns from certain precincts on account of informality, ambiguity or uncertainty, under the provisions of sec. 448, Rev. Codes, the returns rejected must be delivered by the board to the sheriff of the county, who must proceed at once to summon and call together the judges of election of such precinct and inform them that the return made by them has been rejected, and it is made the duty of such judges to meet publicly at the place where the election was held in such precinct and at once proceed to put said returns in due form and certify the same, and for the purpose of so doing they may have

the ballot-box brought in and opened in their presence and the contents thereof inspected, and when such returns have been duly corrected, they must be delivered into the hands of the sheriff.

2. Sec. 442, Rev. Codes, provides what must be done by the judges of election after the canvass of the votes, and further provides that the poll-box and ballots must be kept with the seal unbroken for at least eight months, unless the same is required as evidence in a court of law in any case arising under the election laws of the state, and then only when the judge having the ballot-box in charge is served with a subpoena to produce the same.

3. *Held,* that the provisions of said section are applicable when the returns are properly made and are not returned to the judges for correction. In that case the ballot-box must not be opened except as directed in said section; but where returns have been rejected, as provided by statute, and returned to the judges of election for correction, they may, under the provisions of sec. 448, open the ballot-box for the purpose of correcting the returns.

4. *Held,* that the provisions of secs. 442 and 448 must be construed together in order to ascertain and carry out the true intention of the legislature.

5. *Mandamus* will lie in a proper case to compel action on the part of a canvassing board, but it will not direct what the result of their action must be.

Original application in this court for a writ of mandate to compel the county commissioners as a board of canvassers of election returns to reassemble and announce the result of the election in a different manner and to a different effect from that which they had already announced and entered of record such announcement. Writ *denied.*

E. O'Neill, P. E. Stookey and F. L. Ulen, for Petitioners.

When it is shown, as in our petition alleged, that the board has not performed the duty imposed upon them by law, of canvassing the legal returns, to wit, those which must be returned under the provisions of sec. 339, Rev. Codes, they have not performed their duty and the court has jurisdiction to compel them to recanvass and perform their duty, and they have no right to canvass changed returns. (*State ex rel. Rice v. Marshall County Judge,* 7 Iowa, 186; *State ex rel. Romig v. Wilson,* 24 Neb. 139, 38 N. W. 31; *State ex rel. Will-*

ard v. Stearns, 11 Neb. 104, 7 N. W. 743; *People ex rel. Mc-
Cauley v. Brooks,* 16 Cal. 11; *State v. Pigott,* 97 Miss. 599,
54 So. 257, Ann. Cas. 1912C, 1254; *State ex rel. Whittemore
v. Peacock,* 15 Neb. 442, 19 N. W. 685; *Welty v. McFadden,*
46 Neb. 668, 65 N. W. 800.)

• "A board authorized to issue the writ of *mandamus* may
compel the board of canvassers to discharge their duties by
canvassing the lawful returns, leaving all questions as to the
validity of the returns for election to the proper tribunal."
(*State v. Van Camp,* 36 Neb. 9, 91, 54 N. W. 113.)

C. L. McDonald, D. E. Hodge, G. W. Tannahill and M. S.
Johnson, for Respondents.

It is a well-settled principle of law that the courts will not,
by *mandamus,* direct an inferior tribunal to act in a certain
way. (*Board of Commissioners v. Mayhew,* 5 Ida. 572, 51
Pac. 411; *Connolly v. Woods,* 13 Ida. 591, 92 Pac. 573.)

This court has also held that the board of commissioners
has jurisdiction to send the returns back to the judges for
correction. (*Lansdon v. State Board of Canvassers,* 18 Ida.
596, 111 Pac. 133.)

"Courts of equity have no inherent power to try contested
elections." (*Toncray v. Budge,* 14 Ida. 621, 95 Pac. 26; 15
Cyc. 397; *Nims v. Gilmore,* 17 Ida. 609, 107 Pac. 79.)

In this case the petition shows that the board of canvassers
has performed the very act sought to be commanded by the
writ, but the result obtained by such performance is what has
displeased the petitioners, and not the failure to perform, and
mandamus cannot lie to afford them any relief. (*State v.
Carney,* 3 Kan. 88; *Sharpless v. Buckles,* 65 Kan. 838, 70 Pac.
886; *Rosenthal v. State Board of Canvassers,* 50 Kan. 129, 32
Pac. 129, 19 L. R. A. 157; *State ex rel. Harmon v. Hammel*
(Ala.), 11 So. 892; *Bach v. Spencer,* 24 Ky. Law Rep. 354,
68 S. W. 442; *People ex rel. Wilson v. Mattinger,* 212 Ill. 530,
72 N. E. 906; *Booe v. Kenner,* 105 Ky. 517, 20 Ky. Law Rep.
1343, 49 S. W. 330; *State ex rel. Ingerson v. Berry,* 14 Ohio
St. 315; *Roberts v. Marshall,* 33 Okl. 716, 127 Pac. 703; *Mad-*

den v. Moore, 228 Pa. 503, 77 Atl. 821; *Orman v. People ex rel. Cooper*, 18 Colo. App. 302, 71 Pac. 430; 26 Cyc. 277.)

"The writ will not issue . . . . where *quo warranto* or a statutory writ of contest or other proceedings at law affords a specific adequate remedy." (*Wright v. Kelley*, 4 Ida. 624, 43 Pac. 565; *Jolly v. Woodward*, 4 Ida. 496, 42 Pac. 512; *Pyke v. Steunenberg*, 5 Ida. 614, 51 Pac. 614; *Blomquist v. Board of Commrs.*, 25 Ida. 284, 137 Pac. 174; *Chemung Min. Co. v. Morgan*, 11 Ida. 232, 81 Pac. 384.)

SULLIVAN, C. J.—This is an application for a writ of mandate to compel the board of county commissioners as a board of canvassers of the election returns of a special election held on May 27, 1914, in Nez Perce county, to reassemble and announce and enter of record the result of said election as claimed by plaintiffs. A demurrer to the petition has been submitted by the defendants.

The petition clearly shows that said board has canvassed the returns of said election; but it is contended that the returns canvassed by the board and the result announced therefrom are not correct returns nor the correct result.

It appears that said board has acted in said matter and in acting rejected some of the returns on account of informality, ambiguity or uncertainty, and placed them in the hands of the sheriff under the provisions of sec. 448, Rev. Codes, and he returned them to the proper precinct election officers for correction, and such election officers proceeded to correct such returns and for that purpose they opened the ballot-box as they were clearly authorized to do by the provisions of said sec. 448. But it is contended that the election officers had no authority to open such boxes under the provisions of sec. 442, Rev. Codes.

We concede that, but they were not acting under the provisions of that section, but were acting under the provisions of sec. 448, which gave them authority to open the ballot-box in correcting the returns.

The provisions of sec. 442, as amended by Laws of 1913, p. 379, apply when the returns are properly made out and not returned for correction, but when sent back for correction, under the provisions of sec. 448 the ballot-box may be opened for the correction of the returns.

The provisions of secs. 442 and 448 must be construed together in order to ascertain and carry out the true intent of the legislature. Under the provisions of sec. 448, the board of canvassers had authority to reject the returns for the causes mentioned in said sec. 448, and return them for correction. The allegations of the petition show they did just what that section authorizes them to do. The main contention of the petitioners, however, is that the election judges had no right to open the ballot-boxes for the correction of said returns. That contention is without merit, since sec. 448 authorizes them to open the ballot-box for that purpose.

A writ of mandate is for the purpose of compelling the performance of an act which the law especially enjoins as a duty resulting from an office, trust or station; but the writ cannot be used to correct errors made in passing upon questions regularly submitted to a board for its determination, provided it keeps within the law. The writ will not lie for the purpose of having the action of a canvassing board declared incorrect and to compel it to recanvass the votes and change the result from what it originally determined. *Mandamus*, however, will lie in a proper case to compel action on the part of a canvassing board, but it cannot direct what the result of the action must be.

This view of the matter disposes of this case without entering into a discussion of the other points raised. We therefore conclude that the demurrer must be sustained and the writ denied. Costs are awarded to the defendants.

Truitt, J., concurs.

(November 4, 1914.)

NORTHERN PACIFIC RAILWAY CO., a Corporation, Appellant, v. COUNTY OF CLEARWATER et al., Respondents.

[144 Pac. 1.]

COMPLAINT — ALLEGATIONS OF — DEMURRER — ILLEGAL ASSESSMENT — OVER-VALUATION — UNDER-VALUATION — ARBITRARY TAXATION — INJUNCTION AGAINST—REMEDY—EQUITY JURISDICTION.

1. Where a railroad company is the owner of about 4,000 acres of land consisting of about one hundred 40-acre tracts distributed over a county and in many different sections, and it is alleged in the complaint that the assessor "by a systematic, intentional and illegal method of assessing said land placed thereon a valuation and assessment which after being equalized by the state board of equalization exceeded the full cash value of the property by 25 per cent," and that other and similar land of the same value in said county was assessed and valued at 75 per cent less than the appellant's lands, and that said valuation and assessment were placed on appellant's lands by the assessor without making any investigation whatever and in violation of law and of the rights of appellant, and said valuation and assessment were made with the design, systematic and illegal effort on the part of the assessor to unjustly and unlawfully discriminate against appellant and its property, *held*, that said allegations show an unlawful, illegal and fraudulent discrimination by the assessor in assessing said property.

2. In this class of cases courts of equity will not interfere to correct mere errors of judgment as to valuation of property, since value is a matter of opinion; but where the allegations of the complaint show that the officer refused to exercise his judgment and by an arbitrary and capricious exercise of official authority has fraudulently attempted to defeat the law instead of enforcing it, a court of equity will relieve against such illegal and fraudulent actions of an assessor.

3. *Held*, that the facts alleged in the complaint, if proven, would establish fraud as a conclusion of law.

4. *Held*, that where an assessor by a systematic, intentional and illegal method assessed property at more than double what he assessed other property of the same class and value, he perpetrates a fraud from which a court of equity, upon proper application, will relieve.

5. In this case it is not a question of a mere difference of opinion as to the value of the property, but it is a question of no

opinion or judgment at all as to the value, since it is admitted by the demurrer that the assessor did intentionally and illegally assess said property at more than double what other property of the same kind and value was assessed, and the law presumes that he intended the natural, inevitable effect of his acts in assessing said property.

6. Equity will not relieve against an assessment merely because it happens to be at a higher rate than that of other property of the same class or kind, for the reason that absolute uniformity under an honest judgment may not be obtained; but where it is made to appear that honest judgment was not used and that an illegal and unlawful value was placed upon the property by the assessor, the injured party may obtain redress in a court of equity.

7. In a case where the valuation is so unreasonable as to show that the assessor must have known that it was wrong and that he could not have been honest in fixing it, *held,* that such a valuation is clearly a fraud upon the owner.

8. In a case of this kind, the trial court should require the plaintiff to pay the amount of taxes which the allegations of the complaint show are reasonable and just before issuing any restraining order against the collection of the portion of the tax alleged to have been illegally assessed.

APPEAL from the District Court of the Second Judicial District for Clearwater County. Hon. Edgar S. Steele, Judge.

Action to restrain the collection of a tax alleged to have been illegally made. Demurrer to complaint sustained by trial court. *Reversed.*

Cannon & Ferris and James E. Babb, for Appellant.

The facts pleaded in the case at bar, admitted as they are by the demurrer, establish fraud as a conclusion of law, and the allegation that these acts were fraudulent would not strengthen the complaint or be in any way essential. (*Louisville Trust Co. v. Stone,* 107 Fed. 305, 46 C. C. A. 299; *Andrews v. King County,* 1 Wash. 46, 22 Am. St. 136, 23 Pac. 409; *Raymond v. Chicago Union Traction Co.,* 207 U. S. 20, 28 Sup. Ct. 7, 52 L. ed. 78, 12 Ann. Cas. 757.)

The appellant has shown that its property has been unfairly assessed by the assessor, and that it has been assessed

in excess of its full cash value. It is therefore entitled to
relief at the hands of a court of equity. (*Atchison etc. R.
Co. v. Sullivan*, 173 Fed. 456, 97 C. C. A. 1; *Humbird Lumber
Co. v. Thompson*, 11 Ida. 614, 83 Pac. 941; *Chicago etc.
R. Co. v. Board of Commissioners*, 54 Kan. 781, 39 Pac. 1039;
Albuquerque Nat. Bank v. Perea, 147 U. S. 87, 13 Sup. Ct.
194, 37 L. ed. 91; *Otter Tail County v. Batchelder*, 47 Minn.
512, 50 N. W. 536; *Dickson v. Kittitas County*, 42 Wash. 429,
84 Pac. 855.)

The discrimination between the property of appellant and
all other property in the county is of such a character as to
constitute constructive fraud, and therefore a court of equity
should grant relief. (*The Railroad Tax Cases*, 13 Fed. 722,
8 Saw. 238; *Santa Clara County v. Southern Pac. R. Co.*, 18
Fed. 385; *Cincinnati Southern Ry. v. Guenther*, 19 Fed. 395;
Northern Pacific Ry. Co. v. Pierce County, 77 Wash. 315,
137 Pac. 433; *Louisville etc. R. Co. v. Bosworth*, 209 Fed.
380, 452; *First Nat. Bank v. Board of Commrs.*, 36 Colo. 265,
84 Pac. 1111; *First Nat. Bank v. Holmes*, 246 Ill. 362, 92
N. E. 893; *Citizens' Nat. Bank v. Board of Commrs.*, 83 Kan.
376, 111 Pac. 496; *Savage v. Pierce County*, 68 Wash. 623,
123 Pac. 1088; 2 Cooley on Taxation, 3d ed., p. 1459; *Ex
parte Ft. Smith & Van Buren Bridge Co.*, 62 Ark. 461, 36
S. W. 1060; *Randell v. City of Bridgeport*, 63 Conn. 321, 28
Atl. 523.)

A. A. Holsclaw, G. W. Tannahill, J. H. Peterson, Atty.
Genl., J. J. Guheen, T. C. Coffin and E. G. Davis, Assts., for
Respondents.

No appeal lies from the decision of the board of county
commissioners, sitting as a board of equalization. (*Feltham
v. Board of County Commissioners*, 10 Ida. 182, 77 Pac. 332;
Olympia Waterworks Co. v. Board of Equalization, 44 Pac.
267; *General Custer Min. Co. v. Van Camp*, 2 Ida. 40, 3 Pac.
22; *Humbird Lumber Co. v. Ramey*, 10 Ida. 327, 77 Pac. 433.)

Nor can mere irregularity in the rightful exercise of the
powers of the board of equalization be reviewed by *certiorari*.

(*Murphy v. Board of Equalization,* 6 Ida. 745, 59 Pac. 715; *Braden v. Union Trust Co.,* 25 Kan. 362.)

The judge of the district court had not jurisdiction of the subject matter. (*People ex rel. Alexander v. District Court,* 68 Pac. 242; *State Railroad Commission v. People,* 98 Pac. 7; *Speer v. People* (Colo.), 122 Pac. 768.)

A taxpayer is not entitled to relief in equity, except upon condition of doing equity on his part, which requires payment of all the taxes assessed, or which should be assessed against him. (*Tacoma Ry. & Power Co. v. Pierce Co.,* (Wash.) 193 Fed. 90.)

Courts of equity are not prone to move for the relief of an individual or single corporation in cases like the one at bar. (*Andrews v. King County* (Wash.), 23 Pac. 409; *Raymond v. Chicago Union T. Co.,* 207 U. S. 19, 52 L. ed. 78; *Taylor v. Louisville Ry.,* 88 Fed. 350; *Washington Water Power Co. v. Kootenai County,* 210 Fed. 867.)

The fact that a valuation is excessive does not entitle the party to relief at equity, such a relief being granted only in cases of fraud or a clear adoption of a fundamentally wrong principle. (*Chicago B. & Q. R. Co. v. Babcock,* 204 U. S. 585, 598, 27 Sup. Ct. 326, 51 L. ed. 636, 640.)

Equity will relieve against discrimination in valuation and assessments where the uniformity of taxation guaranteed by the constitution is violated in two cases only: First, where the statute of the state operates to cause a large class of persons or species of property to be assessed or taxed at a higher rate than all other property; and second, where the revenue officers by a system or scheme adopted in making valuations and assessments discriminate, with the effect of destroying uniformity against a large class of persons or species of property. (*State Railroad Tax Cases,* 92 U. S. 575, 612, 23 L. ed. 663, 673; *People ex rel. Williams v. Weaver,* 100 U. S. 539, 25 L. ed. 705; *Pelton v. Commercial Nat. Bank,* 101 U. S. 143, 25 L. ed. 901; *Cummings v. Merchants' Nat. Bank,* 101 U. S. 153, 25 L. ed. 903; *Board of Supervisors v. Stanley,* 105 U. S. 305, 26 L. ed. 1044, 1120; *Hills v. National Albany Exchange Bank,* 105 U. S. 319, 26 L. ed. 1052; *Evansville Nat. Bank v.*

Britton, 105 U. S. 322, 26 L. ed. 1053; *Boyer v. Boyer*, 113 U. S. 689, 5 Sup. Ct. 706, 28 L. ed. 1089; *German Nat. Bank v. Kimball*, 103 U. S. 732, 26 L. ed. 469; *Exchange Nat. Bank v. Miller*, 19 Fed. 372; *Wagoner v. Loomis*, 37 Ohio St. 571; *Stanley v. Board of Supervisors*, 121 U. S. 535, 7 Sup. Ct. 1234, 30 L. ed. 1000.)

SULLIVAN, C. J.—This action was brought by the Northern Pacific Railway Company against Clearwater county, its assessor, treasurer, taxpayer and auditor, to restrain the collection of certain taxes alleged to have been illegally assessed for the year 1913, on about 4,000 acres of land owned by the appellant in Clearwater county, and for other relief; also for a preliminary writ of injunction to restrain the tax collector of said county and his successors in office from extending said property upon any delinquent list or delinquency certificates, and enjoining the defendants from advertising said property for sale and from selling the same and from making certificates of sale, and other relief.

A demurrer was filed to said complaint on four grounds:

· 1. That the complaint does not state facts sufficient to constitute a cause of action.

2. That the court had no jurisdiction to hear and determine said cause.

3. That it affirmatively appears that the board of equalization of Clearwater county and the state board of equalization have exclusive and original jurisdiction of the matters alleged in the complaint, and that said boards have passed upon the matters alleged and charged in plaintiff's complaint and rendered their judgment thereon, and that the same was filed and was and is *res adjudicata*.

4. That it affirmatively appears that the plaintiff has not tendered the amount of taxes due, owing and unpaid, or the amount alleged in plaintiff's complaint to be just and reasonable, for the taxes due, owing and unpaid, upon said property, for the year 1913.

Said demurrer was sustained by the court and the plaintiff elected to stand upon its complaint in said action and declined to amend, and judgment of dismissal was entered. The appeal is from the judgment.

It is stated by the appellant in its brief that the court sustained the demurrer for the reason that the court was of the opinion that fraud was not alleged in the complaint, and for that reason the complaint did not state facts sufficient to warrant a court of equity in taking jurisdiction of said matter.

It is alleged in the complaint, in substance, that the appellant is the owner of some 4,000 acres of unimproved land situated in Clearwater county, and said land is specifically described by an exhibit attached to the complaint, wherein it appears that said land consists of about 100 forty-acre tracts scattered throughout said county situated in many different sections; that the assessor by a systematic, intentional and illegal method of assessing said property placed thereon a valuation and assessment, which after being equalized by the state board of equalization exceeded the full cash value of the property by twenty-five per cent; that the full cash value of said property was at that time and now is the sum of $62,334.75, and that the valuation placed thereon by the assessor, after being equalized by the state board was and is the sum of $81,000. (The full cash value of each and every subdivision of said land is specifically set forth in the complaint as is also the valuation and assessment placed thereon by the assessor.) It is also alleged that it was the duty of the assessor in assessing said land to actually determine, as nearly as possible, the full cash value thereof, and that the assessor, in direct violation of his duty in this regard, failed and neglected to take any steps whatever to learn the full cash value, but, on the contrary, valued and assessed the same and all thereof at a flat and uniform valuation, and that said lands differ in character and value and have no flat or uniform value; that the valuation and assessment was placed thereon by said assessor without making any investigation whatever to actually determine as nearly as practicable what all the tracts of land and each thereof were worth in money, or the full cash value thereof, as is the duty of said assessor under the law, but, on the contrary, said assessor, disregarding his duty in this regard, adopted a speculative valuation on said lands and all thereof; that said valuations and assessments so made are greater and higher than the assessments and valuations made by said assessor on other lands in Clearwater county of the same general character and of the same full cash value, and are unfair, unjust and unequal as compared with the assessments and valuations made by said assessor on land in the same locality and of the same class, character and full cash value; that all lands in said county, save and except the lands here in controversy, are valued and assessed by said assessor at only 50 per cent of their full cash value; that the valuation and assessment made by said assessor against the property of appellant is 25 per cent more than its full cash value, and is unfair, unequal and unjust, and the plan and scheme adopted by said assessor in assessing appellant's property at 25 per cent in excess of its full cash value, and in assessing all other lands in said county at only 50 per cent of their full cash value is in violation of law and of the rights of appellant, and is the result of design and a systematic effort on the part of said assessor to unjustly and unlawfully discriminate against appellant and its property; that appellant for the purpose of having the said valuation so made by the assessor reduced to the full cash value of said property, as required by law, did on or about the 26th of July, 1913, and within the time required by law, and while the board of equalization of Clearwater county was in session, make application to said board for the reduction of said taxes, but the said board refused to make any reduction whatever from the valuation and assessment placed upon said property, and denied appellant's application and the whole thereof; that the total tax upon said property after being equalized by said state board of equalization has been extended upon the assessment-roll for Clearwater county, and amounts to the sum of $1,293.99, and that a just and fair proportion of said tax of $1,293.99, as compared with the valuation and assessment of all other lands in the county of Clearwater, is the sum of $485.25, which sum was tendered by appellant and refused prior to the commencement of this action. The appellant also alleges that the assessor threatens to claim a penalty of ten per cent in addition to the said tax of $1,293.99, and further threatens to make out delinquent certificates for the year 1913 covering the property here involved, and that said delinquent certificates will be sold by the defendant county auditor, all of which will cause a cloud upon appellant's title and cause great and irreparable damage; that the appellant has no plain, speedy or adequate remedy at law, and that if appellant should pay said alleged tax of $1,293.99, as claimed by defendants, the same would be distributed and apportioned to the clerk of each incorporated city, town or village, and each independent school district, and every other tax district having a treasurer in said county of Clearwater, and also to the state of Idaho; and this would require appellant to bring a multiplicity of suits to recover the sum so paid in excess of $485.25, the amount which appellant alleges is legally and justly due. The complaint contains the usual prayer for relief in an action of this character.

Under the well-established rule, on demurrer to the complaint all facts well pleaded in the complaint are admitted. The question presented is whether or not appellant is entitled to any relief at the hands of a court of equity where it is admitted that appellant's property, consisting of about 4,000 acres of land, embracing many separate tracts in various parts of the county, has been by a systematic, intentional and illegal over-valuation assessed at twenty-five per cent over its full cash value, and at the same time all other lands in said county were assessed at fifty per cent of their full cash value; and where it is also admitted that such assessment so made by the assessor was with the design and systematic effort on his part to unlawfully and unjustly discriminate against appellant and its property. Stated in another way: Is the discrimination alleged in this case, amounting to seventy-five per cent, so unreasonable as to amount to a constructive fraud upon appellant?

It must be borne in mind that this is not a case of occasional or accidental discrimination which might be attributed to the fallibility of human judgment, a mistake or other accidental cause, but it is a case where it stands admitted that the discrimination is due to systematic and intentional and unlawful over-valuation of appellant's hundred or more different tracts of land, and the under-valuation of all other property in the county, and where the difference between the valuation of property so made amounts to seventy-five per cent against appellant.

The trial court in sustaining the demurrer said: "I have no doubt but that a court of equity may take hold of these matters, but it is only on one condition, that is, only when the facts are stated which invoke the powers of a court of equity. There must be either fraud or such facts as show the badge of fraud, or the court will not take hold of it. There is not a single allegation in this case that even squints at a fraud."

While it is true the word "fraud" does not appear in the complaint, the language used in the complaint charges fraud on the part of the assessor as clearly as if it had used it a dozen times, and the using of the word "fraud" would not add anything to the complaint. It is alleged that said discrimination is due to the "systematic, intentional and unlawful valuation" of the property, and the under-valuation of similar property of others situated in said county. A difference of seventy-five per cent is alleged.

The precise question presented here was before the supreme court of Washington in the case of *Andrews v. King County*, 1 Wash. 46, 22 Am. St. 136, 23 Pac. 409. In the complaint in that action it was alleged, among other things, that the assessor uniformly assessed demands secured by mortgages on real estate at their par value, and uniformly assessed lands, improvements and personal property at from one-tenth to one-fourth of their actual cash value. A demurrer was sustained to the complaint, plaintiff elected to stand upon the complaint, and the action was dismissed. The ruling of the court on said demurrer was reversed on appeal, and in the

course of the decision the court stated that in the investigation of the case there were three leading propositions to be
considered, viz.: First, in order to put in issue the question
of fraud, is it necessary to allege in terms that defendants
were guilty of fraud? Second, conceding the allegations in
the complaint to be true, are the facts there stated sufficient
to establish a *prima facie* case of fraud? Third, had the
plaintiff any other remedy than the one invoked? And the
court said: "So far as the first proposition is concerned, we
are clearly of the opinion that, if the complaint alleges a state
of facts which if proved to be true would establish fraud as
a conclusion of law, that it is a sufficient allegation of fraud;
and that the declaration of the pleader that such acts were
fraudulent is in nowise essential or necessary to put the question of fraud in issue." The court then states that the essential idea of the statute is that each person shall pay a tax in
proportion to the value of his property, and the fact that
plaintiff's property is admitted to be assessed at its par value
will not deprive him of the constitutional guaranty if by the
under-valuation of other property he is compelled to bear more
than his just proportion of the burden of taxation, and after
stating two cases or propositions, says: "The just principle
of taxation is equally violated in both cases, and the constitutional mandate that 'all taxes shall be equal and uniform,
and that the assessment shall be according to the value of the
property,' is equally ignored. . . . . Nor will courts of equity
interfere to correct errors in judgment as to valuation, because, as has been well said by Judge Cooley, 'value is matter
of opinion,' and, when the law has provided officers upon
whom the duty is imposed to make the valuation, it is the
opinion of those officers to which the interests of the parties
are referred. But, according to the same learned author,
'it is possible, however, that there may be circumstances
under which the action of the officers will not be conclusive.'
(Cooley, Taxation, 218.) And one of those circumstances is
where the officer refuses to exercise his judgment, and, by
an arbitrary and capricious exertion of official authority, seeks
fraudulently to defeat the law, instead of enforcing it. In

such a case the taxpayer will not be left completely at the mercy of the assessor.'' And the court further concludes from the allegations of that complaint that ''the conclusion is inevitable that the honest judgment of the officer was not exercised; and that a rule or system of valuation was adopted by the assessor, and confirmed by the board of equalization, which was designed to discriminate unfairly against one class of taxpayers, and which was in plain contravention of the constitutional law, which provides that 'all taxes shall be uniform, and that the assessment shall be according to the value of the property.' '' The court there states that the uniform rule of the higher courts has been that while equity will not interfere to correct mere mistakes or inadvertencies, or to contravene or set aside the judgment of assessors or boards of equalization in relation to values, it will interfere when the officers fraudulently, capriciously or tyrannically refuse to exercise their judgment by adopting a rule or system of valuation designed to operate unequally and to violate a fundamental principle of the constitution.

The complaint under consideration does not use the words ''fraudulently,'' ''capriciously'' or ''tyrannically,'' but uses language equally as strong. The assessor is charged with a systematic design and effort to unjustly and unlawfully discriminate against appellant and its property. If that language does not mean that the officer fraudulently, capriciously and tyrannically did the acts complained of, then we are not able to understand the English language. The facts pleaded in the case at bar established fraud as a conclusion of law, and had the complaint contained the allegations that these acts were fraudulent, capricious and tyrannical, it would not strengthen the complaint or be in any way essential.

It was said in *Louisville Trust Co. v. Stone*, 107 Fed. 305, 46 C. C. A. 299, that ''if the allegations of the bill are made out, there exists in respect to the property of complainant, and others similarly situated, a systematic, intentional and illegal under-valuation of other property by the taxing officers of the state, which necessarily effects an unjust discrimination against the property of which the plaintiff is the owner, and a bill in equity will lie to restrain such illegal discrimination, and that in such cases federal jurisdiction will arise because of the equal protection of the laws guaranteed by the fourteenth amendment.''

When an assessor does by a systematic, intentional and illegal method assess one owner's property at more than double what he assesses other property of the same class and value, he perpetrates a fraud from which a court of equity on proper application will relieve. Here is alleged an illegal and fraudulent discrimination on the part of the assessor in making said assessments; that he did not exercise the judgment required by law to be exercised by him in making such assessments. Said assessments were designed to operate unequally and to violate a fundamental principle of the constitution and statute, and equity may properly interfere to restrain the operation of this fraudulent and illegal exercise of power by the assessor. Said assessment was not made because of any defect or difference in judgment, but was made intentionally and illegally in order and for the purpose of effecting an unjust discrimination against the property so assessed. It is not a question of mere difference of opinion as to the value of the property, but it is a question of no opinion or judgment at all as to its value. It is admitted that it was made intentionally and illegally at more than double what other property of the same kind was assessed.

It was held in *Humbird Lumber Co. v. Thompson*, 11 Ida. 614, 83 Pac. 941, that ''If the plaintiff has shown by its complaint that its property has been unfairly assessed by defendant, Thompson, as assessor of Kootenai county, in any manner whatever, or that it has been assessed in excess of its actual cash value, then it certainly has a remedy.''

It is admitted by the demurrer that appellant's property has been unfairly assessed—that it has been assessed at more than double what other similar property has been assessed in said county, and that such assessment was made illegally and intentionally so, with intent to disregard the law.

In *Atchison etc. R. Co. v. Sullivan*, 173 Fed. 456, 97 C. C. A. 1, referring to the assessor, the court said:

"His acts, nevertheless, were in violation of the statute, their natural and inevitable effect was to diminish the burden of taxation upon the property within his jurisdiction and to increase it upon the railroad property, and, however innocent in actual intent he may have been, his acts were as injurious to the owners of railroad property as if he had actually intended to discriminate against them, and the law conclusively presumes that he intended the natural and inevitable effect of his deeds." And referring to the assessor and county commissioners acting as a board of equalization, the court said: "It was sufficient to sustain its cause that they intended to disregard the law, and that the natural and inevitable effect of that violation was the increase of its share of the burden. . . . . A systematic and intentional under or over assessment of one or more classes of property in violation of the law whereby one or more classes of property is to be made to bear an undue proportion of the burden of taxation, presents a good cause of action for relief from the payment of the unjust part of the proposed tax," and the court holds that the acts shown there amounted either to intentional fraud upon the complainant or to such a gross mistake that it was a fraud in law.

The discrimination alleged in this complaint does not come or result from a mistake in judgment, but does, as in effect alleged, result from a systematic, intentional and illegal disregard of the law by the assessor.

The case of *Taylor v. Louisville etc. R. Co.*, 88 Fed. 350, 31 C. C. A. 537, is an instructive case and reviews many cases upon the subject under consideration, and says: "They [the cases reviewed] merely emphasize the point that equity will not relieve against an assessment merely because it happens to be at a higher rate than that of other property; that such inequalities, due to mistake, to the fallibility of human judgment, or to other accidental causes, must be borne, for the reason that absolute uniformity cannot be obtained; that, in other words, what may be called 'sporadic cases of discrimination' cannot be remedied by the chancellor," and holds that the chancellor can only interfere when it is made clear that there is with respect to certain species of property a systematic, intentional and unlawful under-valuation of property for taxation by the taxing officers which necessarily effects an unjust discrimination against the species of property of which the complainant is an owner. And further on the court said: "The interference by the chancellor in the case at bar and in the Cummings case rests on something equivalent to fraud in the tribunal imposing the tax."

In that case the property of the plaintiff was only assessed at its full value, while here it is admitted that the property of the appellant is assessed at twenty-five per cent in excess of its full cash value, and other property of a similar character and value is assessed at fifty per cent less than its full cash value, and both cases, to wit, the assessment of appellant's property at twenty-five per cent more than its cash value, and the assessment of similar property at fifty per cent less than its cash value, show a systematic, intentional and illegal discrimination from which a court of equity ought to grant relief.

While exact equality and uniformity may not be had in the assessment of property, and while the mistakes and omissions of the assessor may not at all times be the subject of adequate remedy of the courts, yet for the gross injustice and violation of the law complained of in this action there ought to be some remedy, and there is a remedy. The discrimination alleged in the complaint is so unreasonable, so unjust—so intentionally unjust, as to amount in law to constructive fraud upon the appellant.

There is a clear distinction between this case and the *Humbird Lumber Co. v. Thompson, supra.* In that case there was no contention that the discrimination there charged was the result of systematic, intentional and unlawful effort on the part of the assessor to illegally assess the property there involved.

It is contended by both the attorney general and the other attorneys for respondent that since this case does not involve

a class of persons or a class of property, the court has no
jurisdiction to grant relief; that a court can only grant relief
where there is a class of property or the interests of a number
of property owners involved.

In *Otter Tail County v. Batchelder,* 47 Minn. 512, 50 N. W.
536, it was sought to be shown that while the lands in general
in the township referred to were assessed at less than one-half
of their value, the unimproved lands of the defendants were
assessed at nearly fifty per cent above their value. The defendants owned a number of different tracts of land and the
court held that such proof should be considered in connection
with the circumstances that this inequality was not with respect to a single tract of land, which might more readily be
accounted for on the ground of error of judgment, but to
nearly sixty different tracts owned by those nonresident,
defendants, and the court said: "Such facts being shown, it
would be difficult, in the absence of opposing proof or explanation, to escape the conclusion that the assessment had been
intentionally made, without regard to the requirements of
the law, and upon a basis of systematic inequality," and thereupon reversed the case.

In the case at bar there are at least one hundred distinct
40-acre tracts distributed over Clearwater county involved,
and that brings this case virtually within the rule above
stated. (See, also, *Dickson v. Kittitas County,* 42 Wash. 429,
84 Pac. 855.)

It was held in *First National Bank v. Holmes,* 246 Ill. 362,
92 N. E. 893, that if property is arbitrarily assessed fraudulently at too high a valuation, a court of equity will interfere
to protect a taxpayer in his constitutional rights. It was also
there held that where the property of corporations was assessed so far above the property of individuals as to justify
the inference of intent to require them to pay more taxes in
proportion to the value of the property than private owners,
a court of equity would grant relief.

Common experience teaches that the judgment of reasonable men will differ as to the value of property, and mere
under-valuation or over-valuation, unless glaring and gross,

is not sufficient evidence of fraudulent intent; but in a case where the valuation is so unreasonable as to show that the officer must have known that it was wrong and that he could not have been honest in fixing it, such a valuation is clearly a fraud upon the owner.

As touching upon the relief against discriminating assessments in state courts, see Judson on Taxation, sec. 470 et seq.; *Louisville & N. R. Co. v. Bosworth,* 209 Fed. 380.

The allegations of the complaint show that there has been a systematic, intentional and illegal discrimination against appellant in the assessment of its said lands, and that appellant cannot pay the alleged tax under protest and thereafter recover back the excess without bringing a multiplicity of suits because of the distribution which is made of taxes when collected by the proper officers; and it further appears from the allegations of the complaint that the action taken by the assessor therein alleged casts a cloud upon the title of said land. Under the decision of the supreme court of the United States in *Raymond v. Chicago Union Traction Co.,* 207 U. S. 20, 22, 28 Sup. Ct. 7, 52 L. ed. 78, 12 Ann. Cas. 757, appellant is entitled to proper relief upon establishing the allegations of his complaint.

In this class of cases the court should require the plaintiff to pay the amount of taxes which the allegations of the complaint show are reasonable and just before issuing any order restraining the collection of said taxes.

We do not think there is any danger of a large number of taxpayers going into court to restrain the collection of taxes if the taxing officers will carefully and conscientiously perform the duties imposed on them by law. The proceedings in courts will only be resorted to when illegal and fraudulent methods are resorted to in the assessment of property.

The judgment must be reversed, and it is so ordered, and the cause is remanded, with instructions to overrule the demurrer and permit the defendants to answer. Costs are awarded to the appellant.

Truitt, J., concurs.

(November 5, 1914.)

R. L. CHENEY, Respondent, v. MINIDOKA COUNTY et al., Appellants.

[144 Pac. 343.]

PUBLIC LANDS—RECLAMATION ACT—CONSTITUTIONAL AND STATUTORY LAW—HOMESTEAD ENTRYMAN—INTEREST OF ENTRYMAN—PROOF OF RESIDENCE AND CULTIVATION—TAXATION.

1. Where a homestead entryman of land included within a government reclamation project presents proof to the proper government officer that he has complied with the law in relation to residence and cultivation of said land and secures a certificate from the United States that his proof has been accepted, further residence on the land is not required in order to obtain final certificate and patent, and patent will issue upon proof that at least one-half of the irrigable area in the entry as finally adjusted has been reclaimed and that all the charges and fees and commissions due on account thereof have been paid to the proper receiving officer of the government.

2. Where such entryman, in addition to establishing his residence on, and cultivation of, such land, has paid the United States five annual instalments on his water right amounting to $11 per acre, as provided by the reclamation act and the rulings of the Secretary of the Interior thereunder, and the entryman still owes the United States five annual instalments in payment of what is known as the construction charge for the irrigation canals and other works constructed by the United States for the purpose of furnishing water to the land entered, he has an equitable interest in such land, which is "property" within the meaning of that word as used in the constitution and laws of this state, and the matter then rests wholly with the entryman whether he will make the deferred payments and the additional proof required by said reclamation act.

3. Under the provisions of secs. 2, 3 and 5, art. 7 of the state constitution, and sec. 1, Sess. Laws 1913, p. 173, all "property" within the state is liable to taxation, unless expressly exempted.

4. Under said reclamation act, where a person has so far complied with the provisions of said law as to residence and cultivation of the land for more than five years, he can complete his title at any time by making final proof and paying the deferred payments on his water right and the fees provided by law to be paid. Under said act the government simply retains title as security for the pay-

ment of the money owing on the purchase price of the water right for such land.

5. *Held*, under the facts of this case, that plaintiff's interest in said lands is "property," and subject to taxation.

6. The possessory right referred to in secs. 4554 et seq., Rev. Codes, is a squatter's right on public lands, and there is a clear distinction between such right and the right acquired by a formal homestead or other entry of public land under the laws of the United States.

7. When public land is surveyed by the government and filed upon by a qualified entryman it ceases to be public land, and if such entryman complies with the law and thereafter makes proper final proof and payments, he is entitled to a patent.

8. When such entryman makes his proof of residence and cultivation and there only remains the lien of the government for deferred payments on the water right for such land, the entryman's interest in such land is taxable.

9. The interest of the entryman in such land can be sold at delinquent tax sale and the lien of such sale foreclosed and the title thereto obtained, under the provisions of the present revenue law, chap. 58, Laws of 1913, p. 173.

10. Nothing that the taxing authorities have done or could do can or will affect the lien, rights or interests of the United States in such land for the deferred payments on the water right.

APPEAL from the District Court of the Fourth Judicial District for Minidoka County. Hon. C. O. Stockslager, Judge.

Action to restrain Minidoka County from levying and collecting taxes on certain lands in said county. Demurrer to the complaint overruled and judgment and decree entered in favor of the plaintiff. *Reversed.*

Sweeley & Sweeley and H. B. Redford, for Appellants.

All property is liable to taxation unless expressly exempted. (*Salisbury v. Lane*, 7 Ida. 370, 63 Pac. 383.) And when a claim of exemption is made, it must clearly appear, and the party claiming it must be able to point out some provision of law plainly giving the exemption. (*People v. Coleman*, 135 N. Y. 231, 31 N. E. 1022; note to *Herrick & Stevens v. Sargent & Lahr*, 132 Am. St. 293, and cases cited.)

The term "property" as applied to land comprehends every species of title, inchoate or complete. It is supposed to embrace those rights which lie in contract—those which are executory as well as those which are executed. (*Soulard v. United States,* 4 Pet. (U. S.) 511, 7 L. ed. 938; *King v. Gotz,* 70 Cal. 236, 11 Pac. 656.)

The interest of the settler is recognized as property by the statutes of the United States, which permit him to sell and mortgage.

And the fact that the government has some interest in the property is no reason why taxes on the interest of the settler cannot be laid. (*Baltimore Shipbuilding etc. Co. v. Baltimore,* 195 U. S. 375, 25 Sup. Ct. 50, 49 L. ed. 242, and cases cited.)

A similar question is presented by the taxation of what is known as Carey act lands prior to the issuance of a patent and was determined by the case of *Bothwell v. Bingham County,* 24 Ida. 125, 132 Pac. 972.

He who has the right to property and is not excluded from its enjoyment shall not be permitted to use the legal title of the government to escape his just share of taxation. (*Northern Pac. R. Co. v. Patterson,* 154 U. S. 130, 14 Sup. Ct. 977, 38 L. ed. 934; *Maish v. Territory of Arizona,* 164 U. S. 599, 609, 17 Sup. Ct. 193, 41 L. ed. 567, 571; *Northern Pac. R. Co. v. Myers,* 172 U. S. 589, 601, 19 Sup. Ct. 276, 43 L. ed. 564, 568; *Stearns v. Minnesota,* 179 U. S. 223, 21 Sup. Ct. 73, 45 L. ed. 162.)

Where a person has so far complied with the provisions of the homestead law, by residing upon and cultivating the land for more than five years, that he can complete his title at any time by making final proof and paying the fees provided by law, the land covered by his entry is taxable. (*Bellinger v. White,* 5 Neb. 399; *Iowa R. R. Land Co. v. Fitchpatrick,* 52 Iowa, 244, 3 N. W. 40; *Northern Pac. R. Co. v. Myers,* 172 U. S. 589, 19 Sup. Ct. 276, 43 L. ed. 564.)

Under the law as it originally stood, what are known as "possessory rights" to public lands were taxable. (*People v. Owyhee Min. Co.,* 1 Ida. 409; *Quivey v. Lawrence,* 1 Ida. 313.)

In no just sense can lands be said to be public lands after they have been entered at the land office and certificate of entry obtained. (*Herrick & Stevens v. Sargent & Lahr, supra.*)

This court has stated in effect that land covered by a possessory right is a part of the public domain. (*Maydole v. Watson,* 7 Ida. 66, 60 Pac. 86.)

Surveyed land filed on as a homestead is private property and not public land. (*Johnson v. Oregon Short Line R. Co.,* 7 Ida. 355, 63 Pac. 112, 53 L. R. A. 744; *Brown v. Kennedy,* 12 Colo. 235, 20 Pac. 696.)

"When the entry of land is made and the certificate given, the particular land is segregated from the mass of public lands and becomes private property." (*Witherspoon v. Duncan,* 4 Wall. (U. S.) 210, 18 L. ed. 339; *Bardon v. Northern Pac. R. R. Co.,* 145 U. S. 535, 12 Sup. Ct. 856, 36 L. ed. 806; *Hastings & Dakota R. R. Co. v. Whitney,* 132 U. S. 357, 10 Sup. Ct. 112, 33 L. ed. 363.)

W. R. Hyatt, for Respondent.

Under the general public land laws of the United States, until patent has issued or a final receipt showing the holder entitled to a patent, the land or any equity or interest therein is not subject to taxation for state, county, etc., purposes. (*Bothwell v. Bingham County,* 24 Ida. 125, 132 Pac. 972; *Oregon Short Line R. R. Co. v. Quigley,* 10 Ida. 770, 80 Pac. 401.)

Taxation cannot apply in any case until the right to a patent is complete and the equitable title fully vested in the party without anything more to be paid or any act to be done going to the foundation of the right. (Cooley on Taxation, pp. 135, 137; *Kansas Pac. Ry. Co. v. Prescott,* 16 Wall. (U. S.) 603, 21 L. ed. 373; *Union Pacific R. R. Co. v. McShane,* 22 Wall. (U. S.) 444, 22 L. ed. 747; *Central Colorado Imp. Co. v. Board of County Commissioners,* 95 U. S. 259, 24 L. ed.

495; *Northern Pac. R. Co. v. Rockne,* 115 U. S. 600, 6 Sup. Ct. 201, 29 L. ed. 477; *Wisconsin Central R. Co. v. Price County,* 133 U. S. 496, 10 Sup. Ct. 341, 33 L. ed. 687; *Hussman v. Durham,* 165 U. S. 144, 17 Sup. Ct. 253, 41 L. ed. 664; *Stearns v. Minnesota,* 179 U. S. 223, 21 Sup. Ct. 73, 45 L. ed. 162; *Diver v. Friedheim,* 43 Ark. 203; *Kohn v. Barr,* 52 Kan. 269, 34 Pac. 880; *Durham v. Hussman,* 88 Iowa, 29, 55 N. W. 11; *Pitts v. Clay,* 27 Fed. 635; Judson on Taxation, p. 23.)

For the purpose of the act, the mere possessory right of the settler does not remove the land from the legal classification as public lands of the United States, and the homestead settler under the provisions of the reclamation act has certainly nothing more than a possessory right prior to the time when he shall have paid for the land and the water charges as provided in the act. (*United States v. Minidoka & Southwestern R. Co.,* 190 Fed. 491, 111 C. C. A. 323.)

"Lands belonging to the state are exempt from taxation, and no title can be acquired to the same by a tax deed." (*State v. Stevenson,* 6 Ida. 367, 55 Pac. 886.)

SULLIVAN, C. J.—This suit was brought to determine the legality of a certain tax levy upon plaintiff's interest in certain land which he had entered under the homestead laws and statutes of the United States commonly known as the reclamation act. Said land is situated under the government reclamation project in Minidoka county. A general demurrer was interposed to the complaint and overruled by the court. Defendants elected to stand on their demurrer and judgment was thereafter entered in favor of the plaintiff. This appeal is from the judgment.

All of the material facts alleged in the complaint are admitted as true under the general demurrer. The following are among the admitted facts: The plaintiff entered the land on which said taxes were levied, on November 14, 1904, and settled thereon, and on October 21, 1910, offered evidence to the United States that he had complied with the law in relation to residence and cultivation of said land, and secured a certificate from the United States certifying that his proof had been accepted. In said certificate the commissioner of the general land office, among other things, states as follows: "Further residence on the land is not required in order to obtain patent and final certificate, and patent will issue upon proof that at least one-half of the irrigable area in the entry as finally adjusted has been reclaimed, and that all of the charges, fees and commissions due on account thereof have been paid to the proper receiving officer of the government."

The plaintiff, in addition to establishing a residence and cultivating said land, had paid the United States the five annual instalments amounting to $11 per acre, as provided by said reclamation act and the rulings of the Secretary of the Interior thereunder, and still owes the United States five annual instalments amounting to $11 per acre. Said annual instalments are in payment of what is known as the "construction charge" for the irrigation canals and other works constructed by the United States for the purpose of furnishing the plaintiff with water with which to reclaim and irrigate said land. In addition to said deferred payments, the plaintiff will be required to make certain proof to the proper officers of the United States.

It appears that the matter rests now wholly with the plaintiff himself whether he makes the deferred payments and the additional proof required by said reclamation act. The board of equalization of Minidoka county at its July meeting, 1913, made the following order:

"In regard to the homestead entries on the Minidoka Project on which final residence proof has been made and approved, up to the second Monday in January, 1913, and upon which no application for patent has been made prior to said date. It is hereby ordered that all the equity or interest of the owner of said land be segregated and separated from the equity or interest of the United States government in said land and that taxes be charged on all the settler's interest or equity therein and not on the equity or interest of the United States government in said land and the assessor is hereby ordered to change his assessment-roll to conform herewith."

The assessor of said county thereafter complied with said order and levied an assessment upon the equitable interest of the plaintiff in said lands for the purposes of taxation for state, county and school purposes. The plaintiff declined to pay the taxes so levied and the tax collector was about to advertise said land for sale for such delinquent taxes.

Upon that state of facts the trial court held that the equity of the plaintiff in said land was not assessable, and entered a decree perpetually enjoining and restraining the collection of said taxes.

Under the constitution and laws of this state all property is liable to taxation unless expressly exempted. (Secs. 2, 3 and 5, art. 7, Const. of Idaho; sec. 1, Sess. Laws 1913, p. 173.) When a claim of exemption from taxation is made, the party claiming it must be able to point out some provision of law plainly giving the exemption. The respondent has not done so in this case. Since the plaintiff claims and has an equitable interest in the land in question, it is an interest in real estate. The interest of the plaintiff in the land in question is recognized as "property" by the statutes of the United States which permit him to sell and mortgage it. (See act of Congress approved June 23, 1910, 36 U. S. Stats. 592, as amendatory of the act of Congress of June 17th, 1902, 32 U. S. Stats. 388. See, also, General Reclamation Circular, approved by the Secretary of the Interior, Feb. 6, 1913, as amended to Sept. 6, 1913, p. 28.)

Under the reclamation law the plaintiff made proof of the five years' residence and cultivation required by the law, which proof was submitted to and approved by the government, and under the law the government still retained the right to withhold patent until final payment for the water right had been made. Under the law the right to a patent by the plaintiff can be defeated only through his own default, and cannot come about by an affirmative act of the government, and the fact that the government has some interest in the property, that of a lien for deferred payments on a water right, is no reason why taxes on the interest of the plaintiff cannot be laid. (See *Baltimore Shipbuilding & Dry Dock*

Co. v. Baltimore, 195 U. S. 375, 25 Sup. Ct. 50, 49 L. ed. 242, and cases cited. See, also, as bearing on the question, *Bothwell v. Bingham County*, 24 Ida. 125, 132 Pac. 972.)

The second section of an act of Congress entitled "An act providing for patents on reclamation entries and for other purposes," approved August 9, 1912, 37 U. S. Stats. at Large, p. 265, provides that every patent and water right certificate issued under such act of Congress shall expressly reserve to the United States a prior lien on the land patented, or for which water right is certified, etc., and upon default of payment of any amount so due title to the land shall pass to the United States free of all encumbrance, subject to the right of the defaulting debtor or any mortgagee, lienholder, judgment debtor, or subsequent purchaser to redeem the land within one year after the notice of such default shall have been given by payment of all moneys due with interest, and the United States, at its option, acting through the Secretary of the Interior, may cause the land to be sold at any time after such failure to redeem, and from the proceeds of the sale there shall be paid into the reclamation fund all moneys due, with interest; and the balance of the proceeds, if any, shall be the property of the defaulting debtor, or his assignee, etc.

Under that act, if the respondent would make proper proof of the reclamation of one-half of the irrigable land in his entry, he would then be entitled to a patent and the deferred payments to the government would become a lien on the land; and if the government sold said land under the provisions of said act, to recover said deferred payments, and there was any balance after paying the same, that would go to the respondent, or his assignee, etc. Under the reclamation law, the entryman has a property interest in the land when he has made his final proof of residence and cultivation, and is entitled to a patent upon making the additional proof that he has reclaimed the portion of said land required to be reclaimed under said act. The reclamation law is very favorable to the entryman, and his neglect and refusal to make the proof required to obtain a patent when he has complied with the law sufficiently to authorize him to do so will not protect him from the payment of legally assessed taxes.

Under the reclamation law, where a person has so far complied with the provisions thereof by residing on and cultivating the land for more than five years, he can complete his title at any time by making the final proof required and paying the fees provided by law. While it is true the government retains the title, this is done simply as a security for the payment of the money still to become due on the purchase price of the water right. The purchaser under that law has an equitable interest in such land which will ripen into a title in fee, and he may receive a patent if he complies with the law.

It was held in *Iowa R. R. Land Co. v. Fitchpatrick*, 52 Iowa, 244, 3 N. W. 40, that where a corporation is entitled to have certain land certified to under a grant, it cannot escape taxation by failing to have such certification made. In *Herrick & Stevens v. Sargent & Lahr*, 140 Iowa, 590, 132 Am. St. 281, 117 N. W. 751, it was held that where one is entitled to make final proof under a homestead entry, the failure to do so is no reason why the land should be exempt from taxation. (See, also, *Bellinger v. White*, 5 Neb. 399.)

The complaint shows that the plaintiff has done all that is required under the law as regards residence, cultivation and improvement. He can at any time complete the irrigation of at least half of the area in the entry, if he has not already done so, and make final payment of the charges, fees and commissions due and receive his patent. Under that state of facts his interest in said land is subject to taxation. (See *Northern Pac. R. Co. v. Myers*, 172 U. S. 589, 19 Sup. Ct. 276, 43 L. ed. 564.)

Considering the authorities above referred to in connection with the reclamation act, which act provides that the entryman may sell, assign and mortgage the lands after the five years' proof has been made and accepted by the government, necessarily leads to the conclusion that when the requirements as to residence, improvement and cultivation have been met, the government recognizes that the settler has a valid and

substantial property right in and to his land, since it permits
him to sell and give the purchaser the same right that he
has, and to obtain patent by making proof of reclamation and
final payment, and does not require the purchaser or assignee
to be a qualified entryman.   In like manner it protects the
mortgagee and the grantee of the entryman.   It clearly recognizes that if the entryman has fully complied with the law,
he has a complete equitable title which by his affirmative
action can be made at any time into a full legal title and obtain
a patent.   He therefore has such an interest in said land as
is taxable under the constitution and laws of this state.

The plaintiff's interest in said land is not such as is referred
to in the statutes of this state as a possessory right to public
lands.   Such possessory rights thus referred to are recognized
by sec. 4552 et seq. of the Code of Civil Procedure of Idaho.
The right referred to there was a squatter's right upon unsurveyed land and the squatter had no legal or equitable interest
in the land.   There is a clear distinction between a "possessory right" which is initiated and made good by occupancy
and settlement and filing a notice thereof as required by sec.
4554, Rev. Codes, and the right which accrues to a person
through the making of a formal homestead or other entry of
the land under the laws of the United States.   When the public land is surveyed by the government and filed upon by a
qualified entryman in the usual way, it ceases to be public
land; and if the entryman complies with the law thereafter,
he is entitled to a patent, and when he makes his proof of
residence and cultivation and makes proof of reclamation of
one-half of the irrigable land contained in his entry, he is
entitled to a patent from the government.

In the case of *Shiver v. United States,* 159 U. S. 491, 16
Sup. Ct. 54, 40 L. ed. 231, which was a case involving the
cutting of timber from a homestead entry, the court said:
"While we hold in this case that, as between the United States
and the settler, the land is to be deemed the property of the
former, at least so far as is necessary to protect it from waste,
we do not wish to be understood as expressing an opinion
whether, as between the settler and the state, it may not be

deemed the property of the settler, and therefore subject to taxation.''

The interest held by the plaintiff in said lands is private property and is recognized as private property by the laws of the United States and by the laws of this state. If the interest of the settler on such lands is not subject to taxation until patent finally issues, it would permit the settler to enjoy for years, and perhaps for an ordinary lifetime, all the rights and privileges of his property without sharing in the burden of taxation. He is permitted under the law to lease, mortgage or sell his interest in such land; is not required to reside on it after the period of five years has expired; in fact, has all the privileges of possession and ownership, and clearly has such an interest in the land as is subject to taxation under the constitution and laws of this state.

The record shows that he has made five payments on his water right and there are five deferred payments remaining unpaid. Congress passed an act extending the period for payment under reclamation projects, which was approved August 13, 1914. Under that act the time for making payment was extended to twenty years, and if the plaintiff takes advantage of the liberality of the government as expressed in that act, he may, by declining to make proof of reclamation and final payment on his water right, be protected from paying taxes on his interest in said land for twenty years, provided the contention of counsel for plaintiff be correct. And during that time his interest in said land will no doubt become more and more valuable and he has a right therein that he may assign, sell or mortgage and that may be sold under judicial sale. Such a settler clearly has a vested and private interest in the land, a right separate and distinct from that of the government, and such an interest or right is taxable under the laws of this state.

The record shows that plaintiff has made proof showing that he has complied with the requirements of the general homestead law, and if it were not for the fact that his land is on a reclamation project and that he owes the government certain payments for his water right, he would now be entitled to a patent, upon making proof of reclamation of one-half of the irrigable land in his entry and making the deferred payments. The real interest of the government in the land at the present time is that of a mortgagee and lienholder only, which lien the government is not required to go into a court to foreclose, under the reclamation law.

Counsel for plaintiff suggests that there is no method of enforcing the collection of the tax against the interest of a settler in such lands. That certainly need not worry him, since the land is subject to taxation. Clearly the interest of the entryman can be sold at tax sale and the lien of such sale foreclosed and title thereto obtained, under the provisions of the present revenue law found in secs. 127–144, chap. 58, Sess. Laws 1913.

The settler has the right under the reclamation act to mortgage or sell and convey his interest in said land, and may lose it through the foreclosure of a mortgage. The county may tax his interest, and if the taxes become delinquent, may sell his interest in the land. Nothing that the county authorities have done or could do can or will affect the rights or interests of the United States in such lands, since the right to enforce its claim for deferred payments on water rights exists unchanged and unimpaired, whether the land remains the property of the original entryman or has passed by voluntary conveyance or judicial sale from him to a grantee, or whether it has been sold and transferred by the county for the payment of delinquent taxes.

We therefore conclude that the court erred in sustaining the demurrer to the complaint and entering judgment perpetually, or at all, enjoining and restraining the county from assessing said interest of the plaintiff in said land and from selling or disposing of such interest as the plaintiff has in such lands for delinquent taxes.

The cause is remanded, with directions to sustain the demurrer and enter judgment in favor of the defendants. Costs awarded to defendants.

Truitt, J., concurs.

Points Decided.

(November 6, 1914.)

BOISE BUTCHER CO., LTD., a Corporation, Respondent, v. ANNA V. ANIXDALE, Appellant.

[144 Pac. 337.]

CREDITOR'S BILL—PROCEEDINGS SUPPLEMENTARY TO EXECUTION—SUFFI-
CIENCY OF COMPLAINT—SEPARATE PROPERTY OF MARRIED WOMAN—
COMMUNITY PROPERTY—ESTOPPEL.

1. *Held*, that a complaint on a judgment brought against a person alleged to have money of the judgment debtor in her possession,
under the authority of the order provided for in sec. 4510, Rev.
Codes, which substantially shows that the judgment was rendered
by a court of competent jurisdiction, its date, amount and the
parties thereto, and then alleges facts showing that proper proceedings under the provisions of chap. 2 of title 9, providing for proceedings supplementary to execution, had been taken, that the
order provided for in said sec. 4510 had been duly obtained, and
further alleges that the defendant has money belonging to the
judgment creditor subject to execution in her possession, is sufficient when tested by a general demurrer.

2. A married woman bought a meat market which was personal
property, placed her husband in possession of the shop, authorized
him to manage and control the business, buy and sell meat, receive
the money from sales and pay the bills incurred in the business and
thereafter her husband, as manager of the business, went to a
wholesale butcher company, represented himself as the proprietor of
said meat market, bought meat there, and obtained credit from
said company, which was given under the belief that he owned the
shop and the business, and his wife never notified said company of
her ownership of the property, and the company had no knowledge
of it. *Held*, that under these circumstances she is estopped from
asserting ownership to the property when it would result in the
loss of a debt contracted by her husband.

APPEAL from the District Court of the Third Judicial
District for Ada County. Hon. Carl A. Davis, Judge.

Action in the nature of a creditor's bill brought by the
respondent.to subject certain money alleged to be in the hands
of the appellant to the payment of a judgment obtained
against Alfred Anixdale, her husband, under the provisions

of sec. 4510, Rev. Codes. Defendant appealed. Judgment *affirmed.*

J. C. Johnston and J. J. McCue, for Appellant.

This evidence shows that Alfred Anixdale was the agent of appellant and acted under instruction from his principal not to contract any bills upon credit, but to pay cash and do business only upon the cash basis, and that she never gave her agent any authority to buy on credit. The authority to · buy does not include buying on credit. (*Berry v. Barnes,* 23 Ark. 411; *Jaques v. Todd,* 3 Wend. (N. Y.) 83; Mechem on Agency, sec. 363.)

"A principal is not bound by the acts of his agent unless authorized." (*Lewis v. Bourbon County Commrs.,* 12 Kan. 186.)

"A person who deals with an agent is bound to inquire into the extent of his authority, ignorance of which is no excuse." (*Thorsen v. Babcock,* 68 Mich. 523, 36 N. W. 723; *Baxter v. Lamont,* 60 Ill. 237; *Saginaw etc. R. Co. v. Chappell,* 56 Mich. 190, 22 N. W. 278; 1 Clark & Skyles on Agency, sec. 452.)

"Where an indebtedness is contracted by the husband and the credit given to him, the wife cannot be held liable therefor." (*Larson v. Carter,* 14 Ida. 511, 94 Pac. 825.)

"The law does not favor the divestiture of the wife's separate estate by her implied consent." (*Dozier v. Freeman,* 47 Miss. 647.)

Harry S. Kessler and Hawley, Puckett & Hawley, for Respondent.

The property and business in Boise was acquired after marriage; therefore, the *prima facie* presumption at once arises under our statute that this property was community property. (*Douglas v. Douglas,* 22 Ida. 336, 125 Pac. 796; *Humbird Lumber Co. v. Doran,* 24 Ida. 507, 135 Pac. 66; 6 Am. & Eng. Ency. of Law, 2d ed., 327, and authorities cited in note.)

The appellant, so far as respondent knew, had nothing whatever to do with the shop. She never notified the plaintiff that she was the owner and respondent probably never heard of her until it had secured a judgment against Mr. Anixdale and then she appeared on the scene and claimed it as her separate estate. Under every principle of equity, appellant is estopped from claiming the proceeds of the business adversely to the claims of respondent. (Jones on Evidence, secs. 275, 276; 11 Am. & Eng. Ency. of Law, 2d ed., 421, 422, and cases cited; *Bowen v. Howenstein,* 39 App. Cas. (D. C.) 585; Ann. Cas. 1913E, 1179.)

"An estoppel *in pais* requires, as to the one against whom the estoppel is claimed, opportunity to speak, duty to speak, failure to speak, and reliance in good faith on such failure." (*Sheffield Car Co. v. Constantine Hydraulic Co.,* 171 Mich. 423; Ann. Cas. 1914B, 984, 137 N. W. 305.)

TRUITT, J.—This action is in the nature of a creditor's bill and was brought by the Boise Butcher Co., a corporation engaged in business in the city of Boise, Idaho, to subject certain money alleged to be in the hands of the appellant, Anna V. Anixdale, to the payment of a judgment for $205.96, obtained against Alfred Anixdale, the husband of said Anna V. Anixdale, in the justice's court for Boise precinct, Ada county, Idaho, on April 18, 1913. The cause of action against said Alfred Anixdale in the said justice's court, as alleged in the complaint therein, was for meat and goods in that line of trade sold and delivered to him by the respondent company in February, 1913, while he was conducting the O. K. Meat Market in Boise, Idaho. Execution on said judgment was thereafter issued, placed in the hands of the constable of said Boise precinct, and by him returned *nulla bona.* Thereafter proceedings supplementary to the execution were had under chap. 2, title 9, Rev. Codes, in said justice's court. As provided for under the provisions of said chap. 2, the said Anna V. Anixdale and her said husband appeared in said court and were examined under oath regarding the property of said Alfred Anixdale. After this examination on or about April 29, 1913, complaint was filed in said justice's court against said Anna V. Anixdale, and the result of said examination is stated therein in connection with other material allegations as follows: "That an order was duly made and entered by G. G. Adams, justice of the peace of said precinct, that an action be instituted against said Anna V. Anixdale for the recovery of such money, and forbidding the transfer of the same until an action be commenced and prosecuted to judgment. That plaintiff is informed and believes from the evidence produced at the examination aforesaid that this defendant has in her possession certain money in the sum of about $900 which is the community property of this defendant and the said Alfred Anixdale, and that this defendant wrongfully and fraudulently claims said money as her sole and separate estate."

Though, as above stated, the complaint in this action was filed in the said justice's court, it was for some reason transferred from there to the probate court of said Ada county, and the subsequent proceedings in the case were in that court. The appellant appeared therein and filed a demurrer to the complaint. This was overruled, and then she filed her answer in which the allegations of the complaint were denied, and she alleged that the said money in her hands was her separate property. The case was tried in the probate court with a jury, a verdict was rendered by said jury in favor of said company for the amount claimed in the complaint, and upon this verdict the court entered judgment in favor of said company for said amount and for costs of the action. The said Anna V. Anixdale, appellant herein, appealed from said judgment to the district court of the third judicial district of this state for Ada county. The case was tried de novo before the court with a jury. This jury returned the following verdict, to wit: "We, the jury in the above-entitled cause, find for the plaintiff and against the defendant and assess plaintiff's damages at $205.96, and interest amounting to $4.80, making a total of $210.76 and costs of suit." The court entered judgment against the said Anna V. Anixdale, and in favor of said Boise Butcher Co. in accordance with said verdict, and also ordered her to pay from said money in her possession the amount of said judgment so entered against her. From this order and judgment this appeal is taken by said Anna V. Anixdale as appellant.

There are seven errors specified by appellant on the motion for a new trial and urged upon the trial court as grounds for setting aside the judgment, and these errors are set out at great length in appellant's brief herein. The first error presented by the brief of appellant is that the complaint does not state facts sufficient to constitute a cause of action; that it is ambiguous and uncertain; and, further, that there is another action pending.

The complaint is brought under the provisions of sec. 4510, Rev. Codes, and we think it states a cause of action as specially provided for by that section. In substance, it alleges that the plaintiff obtained a judgment to secure the payment of which the action was brought, states the court wherein it was obtained, the date, and the amount of the judgment. It also alleges that execution was issued on said judgment and placed in the hands of the officer for service, and that he returned it *nulla bona;* that thereafter the defendant and her husband, Alfred Anixdale, appeared in court on proceedings supplementary to execution, and were examined under oath regarding the property of the said husband. It further alleges that an order was then duly made directing that an action be instituted against said defendant, Anna V. Anixdale, for the recovery of the amount of money necessary to satisfy said judgment. It then alleges that from the evidence produced at said examination the plaintiff is informed and believes that said defendant has in her possession $900 which is community property of the defendant and said Alfred Anixdale, that she wrongfully and fraudulently claims the same as her separate property. It states the amount of the judgment sued on and demands a judgment such as is provided for by said statute. We think the complaint sufficient when tested by a general demurrer. (*High v. Bank of Commerce,* 95 Cal. 386, 29 Am. St. 121, 30 Pac. 556; *Spaulding v. Coeur D'Alene Ry. etc. Co.,* 6 Ida. 638, 59 Pac. 426.)

The complaint does not seem to be ambiguous, and the objection that another action was pending was set up in the answer and disposed of at the trial.

The second and third errors assigned are as to the sufficiency of the evidence to sustain the verdict of the jury. This calls for an examination of the evidence in the case as brought up by the transcript. The principal witness at the trial in the court below was appellant, Anna V. Anixdale. Her testimony details the lives and business transactions of herself and husband, Alfred Anixdale, from about the time of their marriage at Bellingham, Wash., in 1907, to the time that they arrived in Boise, Idaho, which was sometime in May, 1912. But we do not think for the purpose of reaching a conclusion in this case that it is necessary to review or consider that part of her testimony in this opinion. When she and her husband arrived in Boise, she had about $1,800, which she deposited in her own name in the Boise City National Bank. She testifies that this was her sole and separate property, and we think the weight of the testimony fully proves that it was her own separate property. She and her husband had for a good part of the time during their married life been engaged in the retail butcher business at places where they had resided, and she seems to have been inclined to engage in that business again. However that may be, she did soon after arriving in Boise purchase in her own name and take charge of the fixtures of the O. K. Meat Market in this city. She also bought a residence, also situated in Boise, in the same trade by which she secured the meat market. She at once opened up the market and engaged in the retail butcher business, and continued it until sometime in April, 1913, when the shop in which she did business with all its fixtures and stock in trade was destroyed by fire. The Anixdales seem to have made a kind of family arrangement at the time the meat market was opened for business, whereby she put her husband in full charge and management of the market and she kept the home and did the ordinary housework. Concerning the business of the market or shop, Mrs. Anixdale testified as follows: "Q. Now, who took charge of the shop? A. I had my husband run it for me. Q. Who did all the buying? A. He did. Q. Who paid the bills? A. He did. Q. Who was in charge of the business? A. He was running it for me. Q. Did you pay any bills by check? A. Yes, sir. Q. Who signed the checks? A. He signed the checks for me. Q. How did he sign them? A. A. V. Anixdale. Q. Didn't put it by him? A. I don't understand. Q. He didn't sign his name after yours? A. No, sir. Q. He just signed the checks A. V. Anixdale? A. Yes, sir. Q. And did you ever go to the Boise Butcher Co. to buy any meat? A. No, I have never been inside it. Q. Did you ever notify the Boise Butcher Co. that you were the owner of the business? A. I had no occasion to.''

It further appears from the testimony that Alfred Anixdale immediately after taking charge of the O. K. Meat Market went to the appellant company's office for the purpose of making arrangements to secure meats and other goods which he might need in the retail butcher business of them. And in connection with this point in the case, William Lomax, who was the secretary and treasurer of the Boise Butcher Co., testified as follows:

''Q. Are you acquainted with Mr. Alfred Anixdale? A. Yes, sir. Q. When did you first become acquainted with Mr. Anixdale? A. First got acquainted with Mr. Anixdale in May, 1912, the first time I ever saw him to know him. He was in the market speaking with Mr. Sweitzer, and I came to the wholesale counter where they were talking and Mr. Sweitzer introduced Mr. Anixdale to me as being the proprietor—the new proprietor of the O. K. Market. That is the first time I ever remember meeting Mr. Anixdale to know him. Q. You say that was in May, 1912? A. That was in May, 1912. Q. What was his business? A. He was running the O. K. Meat Market at that time, that is, he had just bought it from Mr. Beemer. Q. What was his particular business in your shop at that time? A. He was making arrangements with Mr. Sweitzer about buying meats and wanting to commence to trade there with us. Q. Did your company sell him meat after that? A. Yes, we did business with Mr. Anixdale from that time on up to the time he burned out, which was in February, well, we did business with him up to February 22d, I think that was our last statement. He burned out on the 23d. We were doing business with him at that time. Q. What year? A. 1913. . . . . Q. Who was in charge of the market? A. Mr. Anixdale. Q. Who paid the bills? A. Mr. Anixdale. Q. How did he pay them? A. Why, usually he would come in and pay with cash or an accumulation of checks which he might have taken in; he generally paid cash that way. Sometimes there would be some money and some checks. Those he happened to have taken in during Saturday perhaps or during the week.''

It must be borne in mind that these were the only witnesses that testified concerning this part of this business matter, that there is no conflict in their testimony and that it stands absolutely unimpeached.

From this testimony and all the circumstances of the case, it does not appear that the respondent company had any knowledge or information or that there was anything unusual in connection with this whole transaction that would put a careful, prudent man on inquiry as to the ownership of the business of the O. K. Meat Market. The company knew the property had been sold by its former owner Beemer; Alfred Anixdale came to the company's place of business to arrange for buying stock for the trade of his meat market. He was introduced to Mr. Lomax, an officer of the company, as ''the new proprietor'' of the O. K. Meat Market; he then and there arranged to buy meats of the company and continued to order such stock of it from time to time as he needed the same for the business. He was managing the business, he bought and sold, he collected for goods sold, and paid the company each week for goods purchased of it. In short, he had all the *indicia* of ownership, and there was absolutely nothing to arouse suspicion or put the company on inquiry. It probably had numerous customers, and it is not likely that any other one of them conducted a business for his wife. Such a thing is unusual. But the said company acted on the presumption that Alfred Anixdale was in fact the owner of the

O. K. Meat Market, and all his actions were consistent with that presumption. His manner of transacting the business was in no way unusual. It was similar to that of other customers of the company. If the appellant wanted the company to know the real facts regarding the ownership of the property, it was her duty to inform it. The officers of the company never thought of going to her to inquire if she owned the property. There was nothing whatever to suggest such an inquiry. Moreover, this meat market was only personal property, and there was no record, as in case of real property, to give notice of her ownership. But it is submitted by appellant that as the testimony shows that Alfred Anixdale sometimes turned in checks signed "A. V. Anixdale," that should have caused the officers of the company to make some inquiry concerning them. But we see nothing in this fact to arouse suspicion or cause inquiry. These checks were made in his own handwriting, and signed by Alfred Anixdale with his wife's initials. If the officers of the company gave the matter any thought at all, they must have thought that Alfred Anixdale signed them with his own initials and that they were his own checks on his own bank account.

The jury in the court below must have found their verdict in this case on the theory that either this money in controversy was community property, or that if it was not community property, then the appellant by her actions and silence while her husband was managing and conducting the O. K. Meat Market as the proprietor and owner thereof, induced the respondent to believe him to be such, and for that reason to give him credit for the goods sold to him, and that therefore she is now estopped from denying that it is community property to the injury and loss of the respondent. We think the evidence is sufficient to sustain the verdict on that theory and that this was a proper question for the jury. "What is said in the hearing of a party is evidence, but it is the province of the jury to draw proper inference from his conduct or silence." (*Morrill v. Richey*, 18 N. H. 295.)

It is perfectly evident from the testimony that by her neglect in not notifying the Boise Butcher Co. that she owned the O. K. Meat Market, and that by allowing her husband to manage and represent himself to said company as the proprietor thereof, she caused it to make the mistake of charging this bill to him, and to its loss of the amount of the bill if she is now permitted to take advantage of this mistake. Conceding, then, that this was only her neglect and that she did not wilfully intend to cheat or defraud the company, still, as was said in *Hill v. Lowe*, 6 Mackay (D. C.), 428, "This would, therefore, seem to be a plain case for the application of the well-known rule that if a loss is to fall on one of two innocent parties, the one whose neglect or lack of foresight made the loss possible is the one who must bear the burden." However, it is by no means certain that appellant can be said to be an innocent party, or that she would actually suffer loss if compelled to pay the judgment in this case, for it is very questionable whether she has not actually in her possession enough money received from the sale of the very meat for which this charge was made during the week before said fire, and for the insurance money paid for the loss of the fixtures and goods in the shop, to pay this company the amount of its judgment against her. Her testimony shows that the amount of money received from insurance for loss of fixtures and stock on hand in the shop at the time of the fire was $1,000, and her testimony further shows that the fixtures at the very most only cost her $950; therefore a part of this insurance must have been for the loss of goods. Then it also appears that the fire occurred on Saturday night or Sunday morning, so that the amount of meat bought from respondent that week and sold by the O. K. Meat Market had not been paid for, and as appellant had the proceeds from sales of the market that week placed in the bank to her account, part of the $900 in controversy in this action must have been received by her from sales of said meat purchased of respondent and not paid for, and from said insurance money. But respondent company made the mistake of thinking that her husband owned the meat market and of bringing the original action in the justice's court to collect its bill for this meat and other goods sold to her husband, and delivered at said market, against him instead of bringing it against her. If it had brought the action against her, there is no question but that a judgment against her for the debt would have been obtained. So far as appears from the record, neither the appellant nor her husband attempted to correct that mistake of said company, neither one of them went to it and offered to pay the bill, though they must both have known it was unpaid, but they allowed the company, which was still ignorant of the real facts in the matter, to commence an action in said justice's court against appellant's husband and recover judgment in said court against him for the full amount of its said bill; and that judgment is now the basis of this action against appellant. The original debt is merged into said judgment and cannot be inquired into here; it is now *res adjudicata.* If the mistake made by respondent in giving credit, and also in bringing the action against the wrong party was caused by the actions and by the silence of appellant, and no lack of ordinary business prudence and reasonable diligence can be attributed to respondent, then we think appellant should be estopped from denying that the appellant's ownership of the O. K. Meat Market was not real, and from now asserting that it was in fact her separate property and not community property, to the loss of said company.

In *Johnson v. Byler,* 38 Tex. 606, it is held that, "A party is estopped by his acts whenever he has gained an undue advantage and has caused his adversary a loss or injury." In the case at bar, if appellant is allowed to dispute the apparent facts which respondent relied on as real when it extended credit to her husband, she will certainly gain an advantage, and the respondent will suffer a loss. Bigelow on Estoppel, 6th ed., 607, gives the rule in regard to estoppel by conduct as follows: "It is now a well-established principle that where the true owner of property, for however short a time, holds out another, or, with knowledge of his own right, allows another to appear, as the owner of or as having full power of disposition over the property, the same being in the latter's *actual* possession, and innocent third parties are thus led into dealing with such apparent owner, they will be protected. . . . . This rule applies to married women doing business for themselves under the statutes.''

The fourth error assigned by appellant is in substance that the verdict is contrary to law because the jury had no right to find a judgment against the defendant under the facts proved by the evidence in the case. This point is, we think, sufficiently covered by what we have held in regard to the sufficiency of the evidence to sustain the verdict. The fifth and sixth assignments of error relate to instructions of the court given to the jury, and to instructions asked for by the defendant and refused by the court. The instructions given to the jury by the court perhaps to some extent went beyond the questions properly embraced in the issues made by the pleadings, but, taken as a whole, we do not think they show error sufficient to warrant us in concluding that they misled the jury as to the law of the case to the prejudice of the defendant. It is not proper to detach one instruction from the others and assail it on the ground that it, taken alone, does not fully or accurately state the law, when, if taken and construed with the other instructions given, there is no error sufficient to mislead the jury as to the law relating to the material issues of the case. We do not think these instructions taken together show any prejudicial error for which the verdict should be disturbed. As to the instructions asked for by defendant and refused by the court, having held that there is no reversible error in the instructions that were given, we find no reversible error in the refusal of the court to give said instructions asked for by defendant.

We have examined defendant's seventh and last assignment of error, which relates to the sufficiency of the complaint to state a cause of action, to the overruling of defendant's motion to have the jury instructed to bring in a verdict for the defendant, and as to alleged errors which occurred at the trial, and we conclude that the same is without merit.

From an examination of the entire record in this case, we do not find that it shows prejudicial error against the appellant, and the judgment of the court below is, therefore, affirmed. Costs are awarded to respondent.

Sullivan, C. J., concurs.

(November 7, 1914.)

JOHN R. KENNEDY, Respondent, v. JESSE B. TUTTLE, THE HOME LAND CO., HESTER A. DAVIS et al., Appellants.

[144 Pac. 336.]

TITLE TO LAND—ACTION TO QUIET—SUFFICIENCY OF EVIDENCE.

    1. The evidence *held* sufficient to sustain the findings of the court.

APPEAL from the District Court of the Third Judicial District for Ada County. Hon. Carl A. Davis, Judge.

Action to quiet title to certain islands in Boise river. Judgment quieting title to part of the land involved in favor of plaintiff and a part of the land in favor of some of the defendants. Judgment *affirmed.*

B. S. Crow, C. S. Hunter, Richards & Haga, Hawley, Puckett & Hawley, for Appellants.

Milton G. Cage and Frawley & Block, for Respondent.

SULLIVAN, C. J.—This action was commenced by the plaintiff to quiet title to a tract of land situated in sections 4 and 5 of township 2 north, range 2 east, and sec. 32 of township 4 north, range 2 east, said tract consisting of islands in Boise river and embracing a portion of what was officially surveyed by the government on October 31, 1868, and thereafter officially platted as lot 17. Said lot 17 as officially surveyed and platted was situated in section 5 of said township 3.

The appellants were made defendants by reason of their claiming some right or interest in and to said land. They answered, setting up their interest, and it appears therefrom that the Home Land Company claims some rights under contract with the appellant Davis, and that appellant Tuttle claims under a squatter's homestead right, alleging that said land is unsurveyed, a part of the public domain and subject to settlement by a homesteader. There were other defendants who disclaimed any interest in said land.

The court by its judgment quieted title to a portion of said land in the respondent Kennedy and to a part in Hester A. Davis and the Home Land Company, and decreed that appellant Tuttle had no right or interest in and to any portion of said land. The appeal is from the judgment.

Several errors were assigned which are to the effect that the court erred in finding that appellant Davis was not entitled to all of the land described in her cross-complaint, and in finding that any portion of the land claimed had accreted to lot 17 in sec. 5, and in finding that the boundary of lots 4 and 5 of sec. 4 and lot 17 of sec. 5 was not the section line, and in not finding that the middle of the stream was the boundary line between said lots.

The evidence consists of about 400 typewritten pages, besides numerous exhibits.

It appears that the islands involved have been greatly changed since the survey of 1868, and the main channel of the river has also changed, and the questions of accretion and reliction are presented by counsel in their briefs as bearing upon the decision in this case under the evidence. After an examination of the evidence and the findings of the court, we are satisfied that the evidence sustains the findings of the court and that the court did not err in its findings of fact, conclusions of law and judgment.

Finding no reversible error in the record, the judgment must be affirmed, and it is so ordered, with costs in favor of the respondent.

Truitt, J., concurs.

(November 14, 1914.)

R. F. BLUCHER, Respondent, v. MARY J. SHAW et al.,
Appellants.

[144 Pac. 342.]

REAL ESTATE MORTGAGE—FORECLOSURE—COMMUNITY PROPERTY—UN-
RECORDED DEED.

  1. Where M. J. G., daughter of J. H. G., made an entry of 160
acres of land under the homestead laws of the United States, with
an understanding that her said father should assist her in improving said land and that she would thereafter convey to him one-half
of said land, and after procuring patent from the government for
such land she conveyed to her said father by deed in October, 1904,
eighty acres of said land, and her said father withheld said deed from
record until January 27, 1913, and procured a loan of over $4,000
from B. on the representation and as shown by the abstract of
title to said land that the said daughter, M. J. G., was the owner
of said land, and the said B. had no knowledge or information
which would put her on inquiry as to whether said J. H. G. and his
wife had any interest in said land, *held*, that the said mortgage is
a valid and subsisting lien on said land and that the trial court did
not err in granting the foreclosure thereof.

  2. Under the provisions of sec. 3160, Rev. Codes, every conveyance of real property other than a lease for a term not exceeding
one year is void as against any subsequent purchaser or mortgagee
of the same property, or any part thereof, in good faith and for a
valuable consideration, whose conveyance is first duly recorded.

  3. The evidence *held* sufficient to show that neither B. nor her
agent had any notice, constructive or otherwise, of the existence
of said deed conveying one-half of said land from M. J. G., the
daughter, to J. H. G., the father, prior to the execution of said
mortgage, and that said mortgage was procured in good faith and
for a valuable consideration.

APPEAL from the District Court of the Third Judicial
District for Ada County. Hon. Carl A. Davis, Judge.

Action to foreclose a mortgage on real estate. Judgment
for plaintiff. *Affirmed.*

Frank Butler, for Appellants.

The actual possession of land with the exercise of the usual acts of ownership and dominion over it, operates in law as a constructive notice to all the world of the claim of title under which the purchaser holds. (*Talbert v. Singleton*, 42 Cal. 390; *Scheerer v. Cuddy*, 85 Cal. 270, 24 Pac. 713; note in 13 L. R. A., N. S., 49.)

The claim of Grimmett to the ownership of the 80 acres of this property used as his residence is fully substantiated by the evidence and fulfills all the requirements laid down in the general rule. (*International Harvester Co. v. Myers*, 86 Kan. 497, 121 Pac. 500, 39 L. R. A., N. S., 528; Century Dig., secs. 344–353; Dec. Dig., sec. 154.)

Having readily accessible means of acquiring knowledge of a fact, which subsequent purchaser might have ascertained by inquiry, is equivalent to notice and knowledge of it. (*Montgomery v. Keppel*, 75 Cal. 128, 7 Am. St. 125, 19 Pac. 178; *Beattie v. Crewdson*, 124 Cal. 577, 57 Pac. 463; *Eversdon v. Mayhew*, 65 Cal. 163, 3 Pac. 641; *Wilhoit v. Lyons*, 98 Cal. 409, 33 Pac. 325.)

"Possession under apparent claim of ownership is notice to purchasers of whatever interest the person actually in possession has in the fee." (*Kirby v. Tallmadge*, 160 U. S. 379, 16 Sup. Ct. 349, 40 L. ed. 463; *Carr v. Brennan*, 166 Ill. 108, 57 Am. St. 119, 47 N. E. 721; *Cornell v. Maltby*, 165 N. Y. 557, 59 N. E. 291.)

"Constructive notice of a prior unrecorded title is as effectual as actual notice to defeat title of a subsequent purchaser." (*Anthony v. Wheeler*, 130 Ill. 128, 17 Am. St. 281, 22 N. E. 494; *McAlpine v. Resch*, 82 Minn. 523, 85 N. W. 545.)

John F. Nugent, for Respondent.

If the person in possession of realty himself misleads the prospective mortgagee and by words and acts induces him to believe that the land belongs to the holder of the apparent title, he cannot afterward be heard to say that the fact of his possession was notice of his rights or that it was a circumstance putting the prospective mortgagee upon inquiry as to such rights. Grimmett cannot claim the benefit of the rule, and is estopped from now asserting ownership of the premises in himself. (*Eastwood v. Standard Mines & M. Co.*, 11 Ida. 195, 81 Pac. 382; *Farber v. Page & Mott Lumber Co.*, 20 Ida. 354, 118 Pac. 664; *Froman v. Madden*, 13 Ida. 138, 88 Pac. 894; *Filipini v. Trobock*, 134 Cal. 441, 66 Pac. 587.)

SULLIVAN, C. J.—This action was brought by the respondent to foreclose a mortgage upon certain real estate situated in Ada county, which mortgage was given to secure a principal of $4,450 and interest. The mortgage also provides for an attorney's fee. The court made findings of fact, conclusions of law and entered a decree in favor of the respondent for the foreclosure of said mortgage and for a deficiency judgment against all of the appellants except Bellzina Grimmett in case the land did not sell for sufficient to pay the amount of the judgment. The appeal is on behalf of J. H. Grimmett and Bellzina Grimmett, his wife.

It appears from the record that the mortgage and notes involved in this action were executed by J. H. Grimmett, Guy Shaw and Mary Jane Shaw, his wife. The title of record of said land stood in the name of Mary J. Grimmett, she having entered it as a homestead under the land laws of the United States. Mary J. Shaw is the daughter of J. H. Grimmett and his wife, Bellzina Grimmett. She entered said land in the year 1902 and thereafter procured title from the government. There was an understanding or agreement between the father and daughter that they would all reside upon the land, and after the daughter had procured title thereto she would convey to J. H. Grimmett one 80-acre tract of the land included in said entry, and in compliance with said contract, Mary J. conveyed to her father 80 acres of said land, about the month of October, 1904. J. H. Grimmett withheld said deed from record until the 27th of January, 1913, and the abstract of title to said land showed the title to be in Mary J. Grimmett.

In about the month of November, 1904, Mary J. Grimmett and the defendant Guy Shaw were married, and soon thereafter removed from said land, and with the exception of a few months have not resided on it since.

On December 14, 1908, the plaintiff and her brother loaned to Mary J. and Guy Shaw and J. H. Grimmett $4,000 and took a promissory note for said sum of money so loaned, signed by said defendants, the payment of which promissory note was secured by said mortgage on said land and a water right which had been procured in the name of J. H. Grimmett and used for the purpose of irrigating said land. Said promissory note became due on December 14, 1911, and was not paid, and new notes, one in the sum of $4,000, representing the principal, and one in the sum of $450, representing the accrued interest and costs, were executed by said Mary J. and Guy Shaw and J. H. Grimmett for the purpose of having the first mortgage canceled, and a mortgage was executed by said defendants upon said land and water right to secure said two promissory notes, and the mortgage given in 1908 was satisfied of record.

The defense of Bellzina Grimmett is based upon the ground that she and her husband were residing upon said land at the time the said mentioned mortgages were executed, and that she had no knowledge or information in regard to the execution of said mortgages and that the 80 acres of land conveyed to her husband by her daughter was community property and her home and residence.

Considerable testimony was taken by the trial court upon the several issues made by the pleadings and the court made findings of fact and conclusions of law in favor of the contentions of the plaintiff, and concluded that said mortgage was executed and delivered to plaintiff by the defendants, Mary J. Shaw, Guy Shaw and J. H. Grimmett, and that neither the plaintiff, her brother, nor her agent had notice of said unrecorded deed from Mary J. Grimmett to J. H. Grimmett for 80 acres of said land, and that plaintiff loaned said sum of money to the defendants in good faith and without any knowledge or information that the appellant, Bellzina Grimmett, had any interest whatever in said land. It appears from the record that in the month of October, 1904,

Mary J. Grimmett conveyed eighty acres of land to her father, J. H. Grimmett, and that he withheld the deed from record from that time until January 27, 1913, and it also appears that neither the plaintiff nor her agent had any information in regard to said conveyance, and the evidence clearly shows that the respondent is a mortgagee in good faith. Sec. 3160, Rev. Codes, provides as follows:

"Every conveyance of real property other than a lease for a term not exceeding one year, is void as against any subsequent purchaser or mortgagee of the same property, or any part thereof, in good faith and for a valuable consideration, whose conveyance is first duly recorded."

The abstract of title furnished by J. H. Grimmett to the respondent showed the title in Mary J. Grimmett, and the evidence shows that J. H. Grimmett informed the respondent and her agent that Mary J. (Grimmett) Shaw owned said land. After the husband, J. H. Grimmett, had so informed the respondent and her agent, it certainly would have been presumptuous on their part to go to Bellzina Grimmett, his wife, and inquire of her whether she owned any interest in said land, since they had no notice or intimation whatever that she had any interest in said land.

We find the evidence amply sufficient to sustain the findings and judgment. The judgment must therefore be affirmed, and it is so ordered, with costs in favor of the respondent.

Truitt, J., concurs.

(November 9, 1914.)

GEORGE E. WYCOFF, Plaintiff, v. J. R. STRONG, Clerk of the City of Moscow, Defendant.

[144 Pac. 341.]

CITY CLERK—DUTIES OF—MINISTERIAL—SEWER CONTRACT—ACCEPT-
ANCE OF SEWER BY CITY—FISCAL YEAR—TAXES LEVIED FOR.

1. Where a city council allows a claim and directs the city clerk to draw a warrant in payment thereof, and he refuses to do so, he may be compelled to issue and countersign such warrant by writ of mandate, as such duty is merely ministerial and requires no exercise of discretion on the part of the clerk.

2. Where a contract is within the exercise of the powers and duties of a city council, and the city accepts the work done under such contract, it must pay for it.

3. The fiscal year of certain municipalities under the law commences on the first Tuesday in May, and the enactment of a law allowing one-half of the taxes levied for city purposes to be paid before the first Monday in January following and the other half before the first Monday in July following, only changes the time of the payment of the taxes and does not deprive the city of the amount of taxes levied for the fiscal year, even though such taxes were not collected during the fiscal year for which they were levied.

Original application for a writ of mandate to compel the city clerk of the city of Moscow to issue and countersign a certain warrant. Writ granted.

C. J. Orland, for Plaintiff.

Mandamus is the only remedy open to the plaintiff. The council has audited and allowed the claim of the plaintiff, and ordered a warrant drawn therefor, and the clerk, assuming that the claim is illegal, has refused to perform the ministerial duty, required of him by law, of issuing such warrant. (*Rice v. Gwinn,* 5 Ida. 394, 49 Pac. 412; *Wood v. Strother,* 76 Cal. 545, 9 Am. St. 249, 18 Pac. 766; *People v. Flagg,* 16 Barb. (N. Y.) 503; *Ireland v. Hunnel,* 90 Iowa, 98, 57 N. W. 715; *Idaho Power etc. Co. v. Stephenson,* 16 Ida. 418, 101 Pac. 821; *Montgomery v. State,* 35 Neb. 655, 53 N. W. 568.)

Where there is no lack of power upon the part of a municipality to make a contract for the performance of labor, or the
furnishing of material in its behalf, upon a contract which
is irregular, and fatally defective, but it is performed, the
municipality receiving and retaining the benefit thereof will
be held liable upon an implied contract for the reasonable
value of such labor or service.   (*Moore v. Hupp,* 17 Ida. 232,
105 Pac. 209; *Schipper v. Aurora,* 121 Ind. 154, 22 N. E. 878,
6 L. R. A. 318; *Hitchcock v. Galveston,* 96 U. S. 341, 24
L. ed. 659; *Moore v. Mayor etc. of N. Y.,* 73 N. Y. 238, 29
Am. Rep. 134; *Rogers v. Omaha,* 76 Neb. 187, 107 N. W. 214;
City of Logansport v. Dykeman, 116 Ind. 15, 17 N. E. 587;
Ward v. Town of Forest Grove, 20 Or. 355, 25 Pac. 1020;
Miles v. Holt County, 86 Neb. 238, 125 N. W. 527, 27 L. R. A.,
N. S., 1130; 1 Abbott on Municipal Corporations, p. 623.)

G. G. Pickett, for Defendant, files no brief.

SULLIVAN, C. J.—This is an original application for a
writ of mandate to J. R. Strong, city clerk of the city of
Moscow, for the purpose of requiring him to issue and countersign a warrant on the treasurer of said city for the sum
of $5,500 which has been allowed by the city to the plaintiff
upon his claim for material and labor in the construction of
certain sewers in the said city of Moscow.

After the material had been furnished and the work done,
the plaintiff filed with the city his verified claim therefor,
which was audited and allowed by the city council and the
defendant was directed to draw and countersign a warrant
on the city therefor, and the clerk thereupon refused to draw
said warrant and entered upon the minutes the following:
"The city clerk at this time gave notice to the city council
of his refusal to comply with the order of the council and
hereby does refuse to draw such warrant for the reason that
he is informed and believes that the said claim was and is
illegal and void." And said clerk has ever since refused to
draw said warrant, and this proceeding was instituted for
the purpose of procuring a mandate commanding the clerk
to issue such warrant to the plaintiff.

The act required to be done by the clerk in this matter is a duty pertaining to his office; it is merely ministerial and requires the exercise of no discretion on the part of the clerk after the council has directed him to draw the warrant. (See Ord. No. 6 of the City of Moscow; also sec. 2262, Rev. Codes.) It is not the duty of the clerk to supervise the action of the city council in allowing the claims against the city. If their action did not meet with the approval of the clerk, he cannot defeat or control the council's action in making contracts or in the expenditure of money by refusing to issue or countersign warrants that the council directs him to issue. (As applicable to the point here in question, see *People v. Flagg,* 16 Barb. (N. Y.) 503; *Rice v. Gwinn,* 5 Ida. 394, 49 Pac. 412.)

If the city clerk may decide whether a warrant shall be drawn or not in payment of a claim against the city, then the act of council in allowing or disallowing the claim would be an idle act. The city under the provisions of the law has the right to construct sewers and to pay for the same out of the general fund or by special assessments. The record shows that the city contracted for said improvements; that they were constructed by the plaintiff; that the city accepted them; that it allowed the claim of plaintiff therefor, and ordered the warrant drawn for the payment of the same. Even if the law were not technically complied with in letting said contract and in doing the work, and the city thereafter accepted it and appropriated the work to its benefit, it certainly must pay for it, especially where there is no fraud charged in the letting of such contract. A contract because of some irregularity or informality in the time or manner of its execution may be illegal and incapable of enforcement, but where such contracts are within the usual exercise of the powers and duties of the city council and the work and materials are accepted by the city, it must pay for them.

Some question is raised by the answer, out of what funds this claim must be paid. It is conceded that there is sufficient in the general fund for that purpose and more than sufficient, and the question is mooted, as to levies made in 1913, when half of the taxes realized therefrom are paid in

January and the other half in July, whether the half paid
in July is subject to the payment of debts accruing during
the former fiscal year of the city.   Under the law the fiscal
year of certain municipalities commences on the first Tuesday
in May, and the enactment of the law allowing one-half of the
tax to be paid before the first Monday in January and the
other half before the first Monday in July only changes the
time of the payment of the taxes and cannot deprive the city
for each fiscal year of the amount of taxes levied for that
year.   The fact that the time for the collection of taxes may
be made after the commencement of a fiscal year from that
in which they were levied would not deprive the city of the
taxes levied for any fiscal year, even though they were collected in a succeeding fiscal year.

For the reasons above stated, the peremptory writ as
prayed for must be granted, and it is so ordered, with costs
in favor of the plaintiff.

Truitt, J., concurs.

————————

(November 16, 1914.)

LILLIE THIESSEN, Appellant, v. THE CITY OF LEWIS-TON, Respondent.

[144 Pac. 548.]

PUBLIC HIGHWAY—COMMON-LAW DEDICATION—ACCEPTANCE AND USER
BY THE PUBLIC—ACCEPTANCE OF PART DEDICATION—STATUTORY
DEDICATION.

1.   Where a strip of land is by parol agreement dedicated to the
public for a highway, and the public by user accepts of such portion
thereof as is in condition to be traveled but does not accept by user
the part thereof over which travel is prevented by a steep bluff or
hill; *held,* that the dedication only applies to the portion of said
tract accepted and used by the public.

2.   Where obstructions are placed wrongfully upon a part of a
street or highway, they do not work a forfeiture of any rights of the
public to the portion of such street or highway obstructed, however
long continued.

APPEAL from the District Court of the Second Judicial District for Nez Perce County. Hon. Edgar C. Steele, Judge.

Action to quiet title to a portion of a certain street in the city of Lewiston, Idaho. Both parties appeal. Judgment *affirmed.*

Dwight Hodge, for Appellant Thiessen.

It is clear from *Boise City v. Wilkinson*, 16 Ida. 150, 102 Pac. 148, as well as *Boise City v. Hon*, 14 Ida. 272, 94 Pac. 167, and *Hanson v. Proffer*, 23 Ida. 705, 714, 132 Pac. 573, that this court is committed to the doctrine that a municipal corporation may be estopped to assert a claim to streets. The character of the acts which the municipality must have done or neglected to do may from these decisions be fairly defined to be such as indicate a disclaimer and, in the absence of estoppel, such as would work injury or practical fraud to the claimant.

Examined from this point of view, the acts of commission and omission on respondent's part cannot sustain the trial court's findings.

"Where the right to a highway depends solely upon user by the public, its width and the extent of the servitude imposed on the land are measured and determined by the character and extent of the user, for the easement cannot upon principle or authority be broader than the user." (13 Cyc. 488; *Montgomery v. Somers*, 50 Or. 259, 90 Pac. 674.)

Fred E. Butler, for Appellant City of Lewiston.

The acceptance of a dedicated highway may be either express or implied. "Where the acceptance is by long continued user, then, of course it is not necessary to produce record evidence." (Elliott, Roads & Streets, secs. 151, 153.)

It is not necessary that every foot of the dedicated highway, both in width and in length, be used as a highway; and it is not necessary that every foot of such dedicated road be worked at the public expense to show an acceptance. (*Meservey v. Gulliford*, 14 Ida. 133, 93 Pac. 780; Elliott on Roads and Streets, 2d ed., sec. 174.)

It being unnecessary to use this strip for its entire length, the respondent did not make a cut in the hill any more than it would be required to bridge a stream which crossed a public highway, until such time as it was deemed necessary by the public authorities. (*Boise City v. Hon,* 14 Ida. 272, 94 Pac. 167.)

"It is not necessary to an acceptance of an offer to dedicate land for a street that every street, or all of any street, should be forthwith opened and used when platted." (13 Cyc. 464, 465, 469; *Stewart v. Conley,* 122 Ala. 179, 27 So. 303; *Brewer v. City of Pine Bluff,* 80 Ark. 489, 97 S. W. 1034; *Augusta v. Tyner,* 197 Ill. 242, 64 N. E. 378.)

After Mr. Thompson and his grantees acted upon the express dedication of Mr. Phillips they have the right to demand that Mr. Phillips and his grantees keep their portion of the street open and especially so when the city is ready to improve.

"Where a dedication has been made, whether under statute or under the common law, and accepted by the public, it becomes irrevocable . . . . One can dedicate land as a street or alley that cannot be traveled in any manner until the proper authorities work it or prepare it for travel." (*Hanson v. Proffer,* 23 Ida. 705, 132 Pac. 573.)

TRUITT, J.—This action was commenced by the appellant, Lillie Thiessen, against the respondent, the city of Lewiston to quiet title to a certain tract of land within the limits of said city. At the time the road about which the controversy in this case arose was opened for travel, said land was not within the limits of the city, but some years ago the city limits were extended over and beyond this land. To the complaint the respondent filed its answer and specifically pleaded that the respondent city is the owner of an easement for street and highway purposes over a strip of land twenty-five feet in width and east of the west line of sec. 32, township 36 north, range 5 west of Boise Meridian, and extending from the southern line of Main street in said city in a southerly direction for a distance of forty rods, more or less, to the southern extremity of the land alleged in the complaint

to be owned by the appellant in this case, said strip being
the west twenty-five feet of said land. The principal question involved in this case is whether the said city is the owner
of an easement over this strip of land for street and highway purposes. The title of the other portion of the land
described in the complaint is not questioned in this case. The
action was duly tried by the court below, and after consideration thereof it made certain findings of fact and conclusions
of law and entered a judgment in accordance therewith,
wherein and whereby it was adjudged and decreed that the
title to the following portion of said land be forever quieted
in the plaintiff and that the defendant and its successors in
interest be and forever are barred from all right, claim and
title thereto, to wit: "A strip of land twenty-five feet wide
off the west side of the heretofore described premises, beginning at a point 540 feet south from the point where the west
line of said section thirty-two (32), township thirty-six (36)
north, range five (5) west of Boise Meridian intersects the
south line of said Main street, extending to the southern end
of said premises." And it was further adjudged and decreed
by the court, "that the defendant has a right of way for
street purposes over a strip of land twenty-five feet wide off
from the west side of the hereinbefore described premises,
beginning at a point where the west line of said section thirty
two aforesaid intersects the south line of Main street in the
city of Lewiston and extending southward along said section line, a distance of five hundred and forty (540) feet."
Briefly stated, the judgment and decree awards the northern
540 feet of said strip to the city for street or highway use,
and quiets the plaintiff's title to the remainder of said strip
extending south from the southern end of the 540 feet thereof
awarded to the city. This part awarded to the plaintiff is
about 125 feet in length. Both parties claim the whole of
said strip of land; the plaintiff claimed title in fee to it, and
the defendant claimed an easement over it for use as a street
or public highway. Therefore, they were both dissatisfied
with said judgment and decree. The plaintiff appealed from
the part thereof unfavorable to her, and the city took a cross-

appeal as to the part thereof deemed unfavorable to it. In regard to the appeal of the city, the following stipulation was made and filed:

"It is hereby stipulated by and between the parties to the above-entitled action, by their respective attorneys, that the defendant, the city of Lewiston, may take its cross-appeal in said action entirely upon the record to be furnished by the plaintiff in said action, and that said defendant will not be required to take any steps to make up the record in said case, and shall be required duly to file its briefs within the time required of a respondent.

"Dated at Lewiston, Idaho, this 25th day of February, 1914.

"DWIGHT E. HODGE,
"Attorney for Plaintiff.
"FRED E. BUTLER,
"Attorney for Defendant."

Whether the judgment of the trial court in regard to the rights of the respective parties to the said strip of land is correct or not depends upon the correctness of its findings of fact upon which said judgment is based. And for that reason we deem it proper to give said findings to which objections are made by either party in their respective assignments of error. No objection is made to the first one of said findings, and No. 2 simply finds the plaintiff to be the owner of the land described in her complaint, and then adds that said land is "subject to easement of the defendant for street purposes hereinafter described." And to this part of said finding appellant objects. Findings Nos. 4, 5, 6, 7, and 8 are as follows:

"(4) That prior to the year 1881 one William Phillips was the owner of the tract of land described and referred to in paragraph No. 2 of these findings; that at that time one S. C. Thompson was the owner of the land lying immediately south for a distance of more than forty rods; that while the said William Phillips was the owner of said land described in paragraph No. 2 of these findings, and while S. C. Thompson was the owner of the land lying immediately west and adjoining the land of the said William Phillips, the said William Phillips and S. C. Thompson agreed to give and dedicate, and did offer to give and dedicate to the public a highway extending from the highway now known as Main street southerly twenty-five feet in width on each side of the west line of section 32, township 36, north, range 5 west of Boise Meridian for a distance of forty rods.

"(5) That said highway was continuously, openly and uninterruptedly traveled by the public as a highway, for a distance of 540 feet southerly from the south side of Main street for a period of more than ten years prior to January 1, 1893; that there was a fence upon each side of said highway so traveled for more than ten years prior to the year 1893.

"(6) That the remainder of the strip of land in controversy in this suit, viz., a strip of land twenty-five feet in width and about 125 feet long, measured along the west line of said property described and belonging to the plaintiff in this action and southward from the strip of land last described, and never having been used by the public as a highway, was never accepted by the defendant as a highway and never used by the public at all as a highway but was always in the open, notorious and continuous possession of the plaintiff and her predecessors in interest.

"(7) That prior to the year 1898 said strip of land twenty-five feet by 540 feet hereinbefore found to be used as a public highway has been fenced by J. D. C. Thiessen, the husband of the plaintiff, in his lifetime and by said J. D. C. Thiessen, since the time of the erection of the said fence, and this plaintiff, claimed openly, notoriously and continuously, that the telephone poles in said Twenty-first street were erected along the line of said fence; that the said defendant, since the inclusion of the property belonging to the plaintiff within the corporate limits of the city of Lewiston, has done no work upon said twenty-five strip as a public highway until the year 1913.

"(8) That ever since the erection of said fence by the said J. D. C. Thiessen, as in the preceding paragraph found, that portion of said public highway and Twenty-first street lying immediately west of said fence has been continuously used by the public as a highway and street.''

There were a large number of witnesses called at the trial of said case and the testimony is quite voluminous. Some of the witnesses testified from their memory regarding the strip of land in controversy and the length and direction of the old traveled road between the lands of Thompson and Phillips and other matters in connection therewith, twenty-five or thirty years ago. After so many years they could not be expected to remember very clearly about these matters. However, after reading and considering all the evidence taken together, we conclude that it is sufficient to support the finding of the lower court in paragraph four of said findings to the effect that William Phillips, the owner of said land, at that time dedicated as a public highway said strip of land twenty-five feet wide and forty rods in length off the west side of the land now owned by appellant.

The question of the dedication of a street by the owner of the land to the public was before this court in *Boise City v. Hon,* 14 Ida. 272, 94 Pac. 167, and the whole subject carefully considered and numerous authorities bearing upon the proposition were referred to and reviewed. The conclusion of the court in that case is stated as follows:

"It is useless for us to cite other cases upon this proposition, but there are many well-considered cases holding that dedication is complete when a plat is filed showing streets and alleys thereon and sales are made with reference thereto, and that such dedication is irrevocable, and does not require an acceptance on the part of the city, and we will content ourselves with citing a few of those cases: *Steel v. City of Portland,* 23 Or. 176, 31 Pac. 479; *Hogue v. City of Albina,* 20 Or. 182, 25 Pac. 386, 10 L. R. A. 673; *Carter v. City of Portland,* 4 Or. 339; *Evans v. Blankenship,* 4 Ariz. 307, 39 Pac. 812; *Bartlett v. City of Bangor,* 67 Me. 460; *Great Northern Ry. Co. v. City of St. Paul,* 61 Minn. 1, 63 N. W. 96, 240.''

However, the facts in the case at bar are very different from the facts presented in *Boise City v. Hon, supra,* for in that case the land in controversy had been dedicated as a street by being marked as such on a plat of a certain addition to Boise City. This plat had been regularly filed and sales made of lots in the addition; but in this case the dedication as claimed by the respondent, and as stated in the findings of the trial court, was an oral dedication of a strip of land for the purpose of a rural or country highway near the city of Lewiston, and as there is no writing or record in regard to a dedication of this kind such as there is in case of a dedication by the plat of a city or town, or by a written instrument of some kind, from which the intention of a dedicant can be definitely ascertained, it is sometimes difficult to determine his real intention in regard to the dedication, and the same difficulty also exists as to ascertaining the intention of the public in regard to the acceptance of such dedication. But when properly established by evidence an oral dedication is valid and binding upon the person making it when duly accepted by the public. It is announced in a note to the case of *Morgan v. Chicago & A. R. R. Co.*, 96 U. S. 716, 24 L. ed. 743, that "A parol dedication is good, as well as one by deed or by unsealed writing. . . . . An acceptance may be proved by parol, by long public use, and by acts of recognition on the part of proper public officers; or it may be presumed from the beneficial nature of the dedication." And in *Rector v. Hartt*, 8 Mo. 448, 41 Am. Dec. 650, it is held that, "The doctrine seems well-settled in America, that an owner of land may, without deed or writing, dedicate it to public uses. No particular form or ceremony is necessary in the dedication: all that is required is the assent of the owner of the land, and the fact of its being used for the public purposes intended by the appropriation." However, the respondent contends that the dedication in this case included the entire strip of land in controversy and that the trial court erred in only giving to it the said 540 feet thereof mentioned in the judgment. This presents a rather novel question, viz.: Could the public accept such part of the dedication as it might use or need for the purpose intended at that time, and tacitly decline to accept such part as it could not under the existing circumstances use? The authorities all hold that to complete the dedication, it must be accepted, but, as in the matter of the dedication, no formal acceptance is required. "User by the public is a sufficient acceptance of a dedication for the purpose of a way to invest a right of way to the public." (*Buchanan v. Curtis,* 25 Wis. 99, 3 Am. Rep. 23; *Holdane v. Cold Spring,* 23 Barb. (N. Y.) 103; *Green v. Canaan,* 29 Conn. 157; *Hanson v. Taylor,* 23 Wis. 548; *State v. Tucker,* 36 Iowa, 485.) Now, if user is a sufficient acceptance of a dedication and the public only sees proper to use a portion of the land dedicated to it, and the person making such dedication acquiesces in such partial acceptance thereof, we think the dedication is complete and irrevocable as to the part of the land accepted and that the unoccupied part is not affected by the unaccepted offer to dedicate it.

In *State v. Trask,* 6 Vt. 355, 27 Am. Dec. 554, touching this point, it is said: "From what has already been said, it will be inferred, that to render a dedication to public use binding, it is necessary, not only that there be some act of dedication on the part of the owner, but there must also be something equivalent to an acceptance on the part of the public. . . . . If this position be correct, it follows that there may be an acceptance and appropriation in part, and not for the whole. A piece of land may be dedicated to public use and yet the public convenience may not require the whole of it; a part may be in fact appropriated, and the residue may by common consent, be relinquished."

In the case at bar, it was not practicable for the public to make use of the entire length of said strip of land as a road at the time of said dedication, for the reason that a steep bluff or hill obstructed the travel at a point about 125 feet from the southern end thereof. The 540 feet extending from the north end of said strip down to that point was accepted and traveled as a road continuously by the public, but at that bluff or hill the roadway turned abruptly off to the southeast away from said strip of land, and extended on in a southwesterly direction, or, according to some testimony, it passed around the bluff and then swung back and intersected the main traveled road leading out into the Tammany and Waha country. However, that may be, the testimony proves that the road did not pass over any part of said strip of land after it turned off therefrom at said bluff. The court below at paragraph 6 of its findings says regarding this part of said strip that it "was never accepted by the defendant as a right of way and never used by the public at all as a highway but was always in the open, notorious and continuous possession of the plaintiff and her predecessors in interest."

But the appellant contends that because for a number of years the 540-foot tract which the city now claims as part of one of its streets was inclosed by a fence and obstructed by telephone poles, it should now be estopped from asserting any right or title thereto. In support of this contention, a quotation is given from 13 Cyc. 488 as follows: "But where the right to a highway depends solely upon user by the public, its width and extent of the servitude imposed on the land are measured and determined by the character and extent of the user, for the easement cannot upon principle or authority be broader than the user." We do not think this authority applies in this case, for the reason that the trial court found that there was an express dedication of said land and an acceptance thereof by the public. Therefore, as to the part that was accepted by the public for use as a road, it would take its easement over the land for the full width agreed upon by the dedication and accepted by the public. No obstructions wrongfully placed in said road would work a forfeiture of the title to the city thereto, however long they might be suffered to remain there. But as to the proposition of establishing a public road by mere user, this court in *Meservey v. Gulliford*, 14 Ida. 133, 93 Pac. 780, quotes with approval from Angell on the Law of Highways, sec. 155, as follows: "Where there is no other evidence of dedication than mere user by the public, the presumption is not necessarily limited to the traveled path, but may be inferred to extend to the ordinary width of highways; or, if the road be inclosed with fences, to include the entire space so inclosed." And after reviewing other leading authorities upon this same proposition, the court announced its conclusion as follows: "It would seem that the right acquired by prescription and user carries with it such width as is reasonably necessary for the reasonable convenience of the traveling public, and where the public have acquired the easement, the land subject to it has passed under the jurisdiction of the public authorities for the purpose of keeping the same in proper condition for the enjoyment thereof by the public." We think this authority fully disposes of appellant's contention upon this point.

As to the contention of the respondent that there was a statutory dedication of the 540 feet of said strip awarded by the judgment of the trial court to it, we have not carefully considered that feature of the case, for the reason that we think the evidence supports the findings and judgment of the court on the theory of a common-law dedication. However, we think from the evidence and from the findings of the court that the judgment and decree of the court might also be sustained upon that theory. There were some points presented on both sides of this case in the argument that from our view it is not deemed necessary to specifically refer to in this opinion, but we have examined the evidence and think it is sufficient to support the findings of fact made by the trial court upon the material issues presented and that its conclusions and judgment and decree should be sustained. The judgment is affirmed, and as both parties appealed, each party must pay half of the costs on this appeal.

Sullivan, C. J., concurs.

(November 21, 1914.)

MARY KISSLER, Appellant, v. J. H. MOSS and CONRAD
KISSLER, Defendants. J. H. MOSS, Respondent.

[144 Pac. 647.]

APPEAL—MOTION TO DISMISS—DEMURRER—MISJOINDER OF PARTIES DE-
FENDANT.

1. A party who is named as one of the defendants in a complaint and on whom it does not appear that summons has been served
nor that he appeared in the action, on an appeal from a judgment
entered in favor of his codefendant, is not an adverse party on whom
the notice of appeal must be served, under the provisions of sec. 4808,
Rev. Codes.

2. Where an action is brought against M. and K. and it is
alleged in the complaint that K. acted as the agent and trustee of
the plaintiff in bringing an action and procuring a judgment against
M., and the prayer as to K. is that he be declared to be the agent
and trustee of the plaintiff in procuring such judgment, and that
the plaintiff is the owner thereof, and as to M. that the plaintiff
have a judgment against him for the identical debt included in the
other judgment in favor of K., and K. demurs to the complaint on
the ground that there is a misjoinder of parties defendant and
that the complaint does not state a cause of action as to him, *held*,
that the court did not err in sustaining said demurrer and entering a judgment of dismissal as to defendant M.

APPEAL from the District Court of the Fifth Judicial
District for Power County. Hon. Alfred Budge, Judge.

Action to have defendant K. declared a trustee of the plaintiff and for judgment against defendant Moss for a certain
sum of money. Demurrer on the part of M. sustained and
judgment of dismissal entered as to him.   *Affirmed.*

O. M. Hall, for Appellant.

It is not necessary to show any reason for commencing the
second suit, other than that the first judgment has not been
paid. (*Ames v. Hoy*, 12 Cal. 11; *Stuart v. Lander*, 16 Cal.

372, 76 Am. Dec. 538; *Rowe v. Blake,* 99 Cal. 167, 37 Am. St. 45, 33 Pac. 864.)

The complaint states a cause of action against defendant Moss and his demurrer should have been overruled on that ground. The demurrer on the ground that there is a misjoinder of parties defendant does not specify, or attempt to specify, wherein misjoinder exists, and for that reason alone it should have been disregarded. (*Irwin v. Wood,* 7 Colo. 477, 4 Pac. 783; *Gardner v. Samuels,* 116 Cal. 84–88, 58 Am. St. 135, 47 Pac. 935; *O'Callaghan v. Bode,* 84 Cal. 489, 24 Pac. 269.)

With regard to the motion to dismiss the appeal, on the ground that adverse party was not served, a judgment in favor of or against defendant Kissler would not bind defendant Moss and a reversal of the judgment appealed from could not affect in any way any judgment that could be entered against or for defendant Kissler, but such judgment would stand regardless of the result on this appeal. (*Randall v. Hunter,* 69 Cal. 80, 10 Pac. 130; *Hinkel v. Donohue,* 88 Cal. 597, 26 Pac. 374; *Foley v. Bullard,* 97 Cal. 516, 32 Pac. 574; *Aulbach v. Dahler,* 4 Ida. 522, 23 Pac. 192; *Boob v. Hall,* 107 Cal. 160, 40 Pac. 117.)

O. R. Baum and W. G. Bissell, for Respondents.

In the complaint wherein suit is brought upon a judgment the plaintiff must allege and afterward prove that she is the owner of the judgment and that the same is unsatisfied.

A complaint in which the plaintiff fails to allege that she is the owner of the judgment is fatally defective, and does not state facts sufficient to constitute a cause of action. (*Ryan v. Spieth,* 18 Mont. 45, 44 Pac. 405.)

SULLIVAN, C. J.—This is an appeal from a judgment entered on sustaining a demurrer to the complaint.

In limine, we are met with a motion to dismiss the appeal on the ground that the notice of appeal was not served on the defendant Conrad Kissler. The action was brought against

J. H: Moss and Conrad Kissler for the purpose of having a judgment which had been entered in favor of Conrad Kissler and against said Moss transferred or decreed to belong to the plaintiff.

The demurrer was sustained on two grounds, to wit: (1) That there was a misjoinder of parties defendant; and (2) that the complaint does not state facts sufficient to sustain a cause of action against the defendant Moss.

From the record it does not appear that the defendant Kissler was ever served with summons or appeared in the action. The demurrer was filed by the defendant Moss and the name of the defendant Conrad Kissler is not mentioned in the judgment. It is provided in the judgment as follows: "That the plaintiff recover nothing herein from the defendant Moss and that the said defendant do have and recover from the plaintiff his costs and disbursements herein expended taxed at $——."

The defendant Conrad Kissler not having been served with summons and not appearing in the action, it was not necessary to serve the notice of appeal on him, as the judgment entered in such action could in no manner affect him. A person may be named as a party to the action in the complaint, but if he is neither served nor appears in the action and no judgment is entered either for or against him, he is not an "adverse party" within the meaning of that term as used in sec. 4808, Rev. Codes. That being true, it was not necessary to serve the notice of appeal on him and the motion to dismiss must therefore be denied.

Now as to the merits of the case: The action of the trial court in sustaining the demurrer and entering judgment in favor of Moss is assigned as error. It is alleged, among other things, in the complaint, that the plaintiff is the owner of a well-drilling outfit and engaged in the well-drilling business; that in the operation of said business she employed the defendant Conrad Kissler as her agent and attorney in fact to conduct said business for her; that said Conrad Kissler. as her said agent, entered into a contract with the defendant Moss to drill for him a certain well on land owned by him in

Oneida county, Idaho; that the said Conrad Kissler, under said contract, in performing plaintiff's part of said contract, used the plaintiff's said well-drill and appliances; that the plaintiff supplied all money for carrying out and executing said contract; that Conrad Kissler had no interest in said contract other than as the agent and attorney in fact of the plaintiff; that Moss, having failed to pay the contract price for the drilling of said well, a suit was commenced by the said Conrad Kissler in his own name in the district court of Oneida county to recover the amount due for drilling said well, which action resulted in a judgment in favor of the said Conrad Kissler and against Moss for the sum of $860.00 and $28.75 costs; that said action was prosecuted in the name of Conrad Kissler for the use and benefit of the plaintiff and that he holds said judgment in trust for the use and benefit of the plaintiff; that no part of said judgment has been paid, and plaintiff prays for judgment to the effect that she is the owner of said judgment and the defendant Conrad Kissler has no interest or title therein or thereto, and that she have judgment against Moss for said sum of $860 with interest from November 22, 1911, and costs.

Under the allegations of the complaint the trial court sustained the demurrer on the two grounds above mentioned. It is contended by counsel for the respondent that since the defendant Moss was not in any way interested in the outcome of this suit as to which one owned said judgment, Conrad Kissler or Mary Kissler, and that since the judgment had been obtained against him by the agent of Mary Kissler, and since said judgment had been duly rendered against the defendant Moss for the full amount claimed, the plaintiff had no right to another judgment against him for the same debt.

This contention appears reasonable since under the demurrer of the defendant Moss he admits all of the allegations of the complaint which are well plead, and one of those allegations is that Conrad Kissler, as agent of the plaintiff, the appellant here, obtained a judgment against Moss for the identical service for which the plaintiff is seeking to obtain a judgment in this case. Since the defendant Moss admits that said judgment was a valid judgment, the only controversy now is between the plaintiff and the defendant Conrad Kissler as to whether he or she is the owner of said judgment, and whether he as her agent now holds the same in trust for her use and benefit. This controversy appears only from the allegations of the complaint, and under those allegations it does not appear that Moss is a necessary party.

It is a little remarkable that the appellant did not require her agent to transfer the judgment he held in trust for her to her, rather than bring this action seeking to get another judgment against Moss.

The trial court did not err in sustaining said demurrer and entering judgment dismissing the case, so far as Moss was concerned.

The defendant Conrad Kissler, since this case was appealed, filed in this court his written waiver of notice of appeal and states in said waiver, among other things, as follows: "that he has no interest in said appeal or the judgment appealed from adverse to appellant or at all." Under that state of facts the cause will be remanded to the trial court with instructions to enter judgment in favor of the appellant to the effect that she is the owner of said judgment against J. H. Moss for the sum of $860, with interest, and costs of suit taxed at $28.75, and that the defendant Conrad Kissler has no interest therein.

Costs of this appeal are awarded to the respondent.

Truitt, J., concurs.

(November 28, 1914.)

ALFRED BUDGE, Plaintiff, v. W. L. GIFFORD, as Secretary of State, Defendant.

[144 Pac. 333.]

MANDAMUS—JUSTICE OF SUPREME COURT—VACANCY IN OFFICE—BALLOTS —ELECTION TO FILL VACANCY—APPOINTMENT TO FILL—DUTY OF GOVERNOR—CONSTITUTIONAL CONSTRUCTION.

1. · An election to fill a vacancy in the office of justice of the supreme court is not authorized under the constitution of this state, and no attempt at a special election to fill such vacancy by writing in the name of the office to be filled and the person to be voted for would be legal and valid.

2. Under the provisions of sec. 6, art. 4 of the state constitution, when a vacancy occurs in the office of justice of the supreme court, it becomes the duty of the governor to fill the same by appointment, and such appointee shall hold such office until the end of the term for which the original incumbent was elected.

3. Certain provisions of the constitution cited and commented on.

4. All provisions of the state constitution relating to a given subject must be construed together, and where certain provisions are definite and explicit, they must be given precedence over expressions which are merely of a general character.

5. *Held,* under the facts of this case the peremptory writ must issue.

Original application for writ of mandate to compel the Secretary of State to issue a commission for the appointment of Honorable Alfred Budge to fill the full term of vacancy caused by the death of Justice Stewart. Writ *granted.*

Cavanah, Blake & MacLane, Martin & Martin and Budge & Barnard, for Plaintiff.

Where a term of office is fixed by the constitution, the legislature has no power to change the length of the term. (29 Cyc. 1397; *State v. Thoman,* 10 Kan. 191; *Commonwealth v. Sheatz,* 228 Pa. St. 301, 77 Atl. 547, 21 Ann. Cas. 54, 50 L. R. A., N. S., 374.)

If a judge now takes his seat as successor to Justice Stewart the office is in no sense vacant either under sec. 317 Rev.

Codes or under the commonly accepted meaning of the term, at the general election of 1916; and if a successor may then be elected, it is because Judge Budge's term ends, and not because there is a vacancy in the term either of Justice Stewart or of Judge Budge. (*Knight v. Trigg,* 16 Ida. 256, 100 Pac. 1060; *State v. Howe,* 25 Ohio St. 588, 595, 18 Am. Rep. 321; *Collins v. State,* 8 Ind. 344; 8 Words & Ph. 7259; *State v. Howell,* 59 Wash. 492, 110 Pac. 386, 50 L. R. A., N. S., 336.)

The provision of sec. 320, that a vacancy in the supreme court "shall be filled by appointment by the governor until the next general election, etc., refers to the next general election at which the particular term of office in the supreme court is to be filled. (*People v. Mathewson,* 47 Cal. 442; *People v. Budd,* 114 Cal. 168, 45 Pac. 1060, 34 L. R. A. 46, *People v. Col,* 132 Cal. 334, 64 Pac. 447; *State v. Smith,* 35 Mont. 523, 90 Pac. 750, 10 Ann. Cas. 1138; *State v. Collins,* 2 Nev. 351; *State v. Cobb,* 2 Kan. 32; *Matthews v. Board of Commissioners,* 34 Kan. 606, 9 Pac. 765; *Wainwright v. Fore,* 22 Okl. 387, 97 Pac. 831; *People v. Hardy,* 8 Utah, 68, 29 Pac. 1118; *State v. Gardner,* 3 S. D. 553, 54 N. W. 606; *People* v. *Wilson,* 72 N. C. 157; *State v. Philips,* 30 Fla. 590, 11 So. 922; *Ransdell v. Ariail,* 13 La. Ann. 459; *Smith v. Halfacre,* 6 How. (Miss.) 582.)

It is to be observed, as held in *Kenfield v. Irwin,* 52 Cal. 164, cited and followed in *State v. Howell, supra,* that an election to fill a vacancy, though held at the same time as a general election, is a special election. The only elections to fill vacancies which the statute provides for are for vacancies in the office of members of the legislature and of members of Congress. (Secs. 325, 326.) By sec. 331, an appointee as well as one elected to fill a vacancy possesses "all the rights and power" of the officer whose vacancy he fills. (*Sheen v. Hughes,* 4 Ariz. 337, 40 Pac. 679.)

J. H. Peterson, Atty. Genl., J. J. Guheen, T. C. Coffin and E. G. Davis, Assistants, for Defendant.

No valid election could be held in this state under the circumstances of writing in a few names on the ballot such as was done at the last general election in an attempt to thereby elect a member of this court. (*People v. Porter*, 6 Cal. 26; *People v. Kerwin*, 10 Colo. App. 472, 51 Pac. 531; *Beal v. Morton*, 18 Ind. 346; *Wood v. Barthing*, 16 Kan. 109; *Cook v. Mock*, 40 Kan. 472, 20 Pac. 259; *Wilson v. Brown*, 109 Ky. 229, 139 Ky. 397, 58 S. W. 595; *Commonwealth v. Smith*, 132 Mass. 289; *Secord v. Foutch*, 44 Mich. 89, 6 N. W. 110; *Adsit v. Board of Canvassers*, 84 Mich. 420, 48 N. W. 31, 11 L. R. A. 534; *State ex rel. Bates v. Thayer*, 31 Neb. 82, 47 N. W. 704; *State ex rel. Bolton v. Good*, 41 N. J. 296; *People ex rel. Davies v. Cowles*, 13 N. Y. 350; *People ex rel. McKune v. Weller*, 11 Cal. 49, 70 Am. Dec. 754; *Foster v. Scarff*, 15 Ohio St. 532; *In re Contested Election of Lawlor*, 180 Pa. St. 566, 37 Atl. 92; *State ex rel. Sampson v. Superior Court*, 71 Wash. 484, Ann. Cas. 1914C, 591, 128 Pac. 1054; *State ex rel. Peacock v. Orvis*, 20 Wis. 235; *State ex rel. Chase v. McKinney*, 25 Wis. 416.)

People v. Budd, 114 Cal. 168, 45 Pac. 1060, 34 L. R. A. 46, is a case upon which considerable reliance seems to be placed by the plaintiff in this action. A careful reading of that case will show, however, that instead of being a case in favor of his contention, it is one against it. (See, also, *People v. Babcock*, 123 Cal. 307, 55 Pac. 1017; *People, etc. v. Col*, 132 Cal. 334, 64 Pac. 477.)

In the case of *Rice v. Stevens*, 25 Kan. 302, the court lays down the proposition that "the theory of our law is that officers shall be elected whenever it can be conveniently done, and that appointments to office will be tolerated only in exceptional cases."

In *State v. Mechem*, 31 Kan. 435, 2 Pac. 816, the court construes certain sections of the compiled laws of that state, and sets out at length, two sections of such laws, one of which is identical with sec. 320 of our code, and the other is practically word for word with sec. 329. These compiled laws of Kansas were enacted in 1879, and it is a reasonable assumption that sec. 329, which appears to·have been first enacted in 1899, was copied bodily from the compiled laws of Kansas of 1879. In the latter case, construing the section of the

Kansas compiled laws which is practically identical with sec. 329, the Kansas court said: "By this last section it was the evident intention of the legislature to provide that where officers are elected to fill vacancies, they are to hold during the unexpired term of the former incumbent; but if appointed they are not to hold for the unexpired term, but only until their successors are elected and qualified."

No matter what may be read into the other sections of our code, nothing can be read into sec. 329 without doing violence to every principle of statutory construction. (*Matthews v. Board of Commissioners*, 34 Kan. 606, 91 Pac. 765; *State v. Cobb*, 2 Kan. 32; *McIntyre v. Iliff*, 64 Kan. 747, 68 Pac. 633.) See, also, *State v. Johns*, 3 Or. 533, in which is discussed, not only the tenure of appointed officers, but the theory under which appointments of this nature are permitted, and *Joy v. Gifford*, 22 Ida. 301, 125 Pac. 181.

In no case which we have been able to examine is there a single indication that if the court had been construing language similar to that contained in our statutes it would have held that vacancies filled by appointment could continue beyond the next general election at which the vacancy could be filled according to the provisions of the law.

SULLIVAN, C. J.—This is an original proceeding in this court for a writ of mandate to compel the Secretary of State to issue to the plaintiff, Alfred Budge, a commission as justice of the supreme court, under an appointment made by the governor to fill the vacancy occasioned by the death of Justice Stewart, whose term of office will not expire until the first Monday in January, 1919.

The defendant appeared at the time of filing the complaint and waived the issuance of the alternative writ and thereafter made return as if such writ had been issued. The plaintiff demurred to the return and also interposed a motion to quash and upon the issues thus made the cause was presented to the court.

The facts set forth in the petition and return are undisputed and leave nothing for decision but questions of law.

It appears from the record that the governor on the 17th of November, 1914, appointed Honorable Alfred Budge to fill the vacancy caused by the death of Justice Stewart, and recited in the letter of appointment that the appointment would continue for the remaining part of the unexpired term for which Justice Stewart was elected, or until the first Monday in January, 1919, and until a successor was duly elected and qualified, and on the same date the Secretary of State declined to issue a commission to the plaintiff, for two reasons, namely: (1) That the secretary was advised that such appointment could only continue until the next general election to be held in the year 1916, and until a successor to such appointee is elected and qualified; and, (2) because at the general election held November 3, 1914, ballots were cast upon which were written or attached with stickers names of persons for the office of justice of the supreme court to succeed the late Justice Stewart, and for the reason that he is advised that the person receiving the highest number of votes thus cast for that position is entitled to a certificate of election, and for those reasons there is no vacancy to be filled by appointment.

Thus it will be observed that two questions are presented for determination: (1) Was there a vacancy in the supreme court at the time of the appointment of Alfred Budge which the governor could fill by appointment, or was such vacancy filled at the general election by casting ballots in the forms hereinafter stated: (2) If there was a vacancy, does the appointment so made run for the balance of the unexpired term of Justice Stewart, which may be called for convenience a four-year term, or simply until the next general election and the qualification of a successor thereunder, which may be called a two year term?

The facts are substantially as follows: At the general election held in 1912, Honorable George H. Stewart was elected as one of the three justices of the supreme court of this state for a term of six years commencing on the first Monday of January, 1913, and ending on the first Monday of January, 1919. On the 25th of September, 1914, thirty-eight days before the election held on November 3d of this year, Justice Stewart died and a vacancy in his office was thereby created. The primary election for nominations for state officers occurred on the first day of September, 1914, twenty-five days before the death of Justice Stewart. No nominations were made to fill the vacancy thus created and no names of candidates to fill this vacancy were printed upon the official ballots, nor was there any space designated or left upon the ballots for electors to write in names to fill said vacancy, and the election proceeded upon the presumption, so far as the state and election officials and the general public were concerned, that but one justice of the supreme court, to wit, a successor to Justice Truitt holding the term of Justice Ailshie, resigned, which expires on the first Monday in January, 1915, was to be elected at said election.

Notwithstanding these facts, in four counties of the state there were 232 votes cast for W. H. Holden to fill said vacancy; in two counties there were 129 votes cast for T. H. Bartlett to fill said vacancy; in one county 97 votes were cast for C. L. McDonald to fill said vacancy, and in two counties there were 67 votes cast for Carl Davis to fill said vacancy, making the total number of votes cast to fill said vacancy 525. All of said votes were cast in four counties, thus leaving twenty-nine counties in which no votes were cast to fill said vacancy. The total number of votes cast at such election, as shown by the votes cast for governor was 107,913, and the total number of votes cast for the two candidates for justice of the supreme court to succeed Judge Ailshie was 47,162; the total number of votes cast for all of said candidates to fill said vacancy occasioned by the death of Justice Stewart was 525, and the highest number cast for any one of them was 232. This clearly shows that said election, so far as filling said vacancy was concerned, was not a full and free expression of the public will to fill said vacancy at said election.

In voting for some of said candidates the electors used stickers upon which were printed the words, "For Justice of the Supreme Court to fill the vacancy of former Justice George

H. Stewart,'' and wrote or had printed under such stickers the name of the person for whom they desired to vote. Other electors wrote substantially the same words upon the ballots and below the words wrote in the name of the person for whom they desired to vote.

The first question presented is as to whether there was a vacancy in the supreme court at the time the governor made the appointment above referred to, or was such vacancy filled by the votes cast as above indicated?

It is sufficient to say that we have no statute for filling vacancies as was attempted to be done in this case. Under the provisions of sec. 353 the governor is required to issue an election proclamation, which proclamation must contain a statement of the time of election and the offices to be filled. The governor issued such proclamation and mentioned all state officers therein to be filled, but did not notify the electors that the vacancy occasioned by the death of Justice Stewart was to be filled at that election, and, in fact, it could not have been done had the proclamation been issued at least forty days before the election, as required by statute, since the death of Justice Stewart occurred only thirty-eight days before the election. Therefore, the electors were not notified in any manner that said vacancy was to be filled at said election; no candidate was nominated in any way at said election to fill said vacancy and no person publicly announced himself or advertised himself as a candidate to be voted for at said election to fill said vacancy, through the press of the state or otherwise. The said votes procured to be cast for the four persons above stated were procured quietly by said candidates or their friends and in such a manner as not to give notice to the public generally. The official ballot used at said election did not contain any mention of said office and contained no space wherein the name of a candidate to fill such vacancy might legally be written. It clearly appears that the electors of the state generally had no notice or knowledge that such vacancy was to be filled, since only 525 votes were cast out of 107,913 cast for governor at said election.

While it thus appears that the notice required by the statutes of this state, as a preliminary requisite to the holding of
a valid and legal election, was not given, and while we should
not hesitate to hold, in any case in which the question might
be squarely presented, that no special election to fill a vacancy
could legally be had under such circumstances as those presented in this case where a few scattered voters write upon
their ballots both the name of the vacancy to be filled and the
person to be voted for, yet under the view we have taken of
the constitutional power of the governor to fill vacancies occurring in the office of justice of the supreme court, that
particular question does not arise in this case and need not
be definitely passed upon at this time.   Under our views upon
the appointive power of the governor in cases of this character,
no election to fill this particular vacancy could have legally
been held in any event.

The other question presented is: Does the appointment of
Honorable Alfred Budge, made by the governor on the 17th
of November, 1914, run or continue for the balance of the
unexpired term of Justice Stewart?   In deciding this question, certain provisions of our state constitution must be
referred to.

Art. 5 of the constitution treats of the judicial department
of the state.   Sec. 2 of that article is as follows: ''The judicial
power of the state shall be vested in a court for the trial of
impeachments, a supreme court, district courts, probate courts,
courts of justices of the peace and such other courts, inferior
to the supreme court, as may be established by law, for any
incorporated city or town.''

Section 6 provides that the supreme court shall consist of
three justices, a majority of whom shall be necessary to make
a quorum or pronounce a decision.   The term of office of such
justices is fixed at six years, except the first three elected
who were to draw for terms.   Sec. 11 provides for the creation
of the office of district judge.   Sec. 14 provides for the establishment of municipal courts.   Sec. 21 relates to the jurisdiction of probate courts.   Sec. 22 provides for the election
of justices of the peace.   Said article, then, may be said to

provide for the following courts and judges: State senate as a court of impeachment; justices of the supreme court; district judges; probate judges; justices of peace and municipal judges.

Under the provisions of sec. 19 of said art. 5, it is provided that vacancies in any of said offices must be filled as provided by law and if that were the only provision of the constitution with reference to vacancies, the contention of the defendant as to the plenary power of the legislature in filling such vacancies would be correct. But in determining this question we must take into consideration a part of sec. 6 of art. 4 of the constitution which relates to the filling of vacancies, and is as follows:

"If the office of a justice of the supreme court or district court, Secretary of State, state auditor, state treasurer, attorney general, or superintendent of public instruction, shall be vacated by death, resignation or otherwise, it shall be the duty of the governor to fill the same by appointment, and the appointee shall hold his office until his successor shall be elected and qualified in such manner as may be provided by law."

Under that provision of the constitution, whenever a vacancy occurs in the office of the justice of the supreme court, it becomes the duty of the governor to fill the same by appointment. This is an absolute grant of appointive power to the governor by the constitution itself and does not depend upon legislative action or legislative sanction. That power given the governor is not limited or controlled in any manner by the provisions of said section 19 of art. 5. If that were so, the legislature might provide that when a vacancy occurs in the office of a justice of the supreme court, or any other office named in said section 6, such vacancy should be filled by special election or by the legislature or in any other manner than by appointment by the governor, and thus deprive him of that power, the exercise of which is not merely permitted but is made mandatory by the provisions of said section. The language there used with reference to the vacancy is that the governor "shall fill the same by appointment" and with reference to the appointee, that he "shall hold his office until his successor shall be elected and qualified in such manner as may be provided by law."

After the vacancy has once been filled, there is no vacancy to be filled. The vacancy caused by the death of Justice Stewart extended from September 25, 1914, the date of his death, until the first Monday in January, 1919, or until a successor should be duly elected and qualified, a little over four years, and the governor is authorized to fill that vacancy, and at the end of the term to which the deceased incumbent was elected the successor of such appointee shall be elected and qualified in such manner as may be provided by law. Since the governor is empowered to fill such vacancy—not a part of it—the appointee holds the office until the term of vacancy expires, or until his successor is elected and qualified as provided by law. The words "his office" and "his successor" clearly indicate that the appointee succeeds to all the rights in the office held by the original incumbent and that he shall continue to hold and exercise them until the time arrives for the election of his successor in the manner provided by law, for the next succeeding term of the office in question.

In view of these considerations, it must be held that said sec. 19 has no application whatever to a vacancy in the office of the supreme or district courts, but that it relates wholly to vacancies in other offices provided for by art. 5, the filling of which is not otherwise provided for by the constitution.

It is a well-recognized rule of construction that all provisions of a statute or constitution relating to a given subject must be construed together. It is also a well-recognized rule of construction that expressions which are perfectly definite and explicit in their character must be given precedence in any case over those expressions which are of a general character only; and construing said section 19 with said section 6 of article 4, the indefinite provisions of the former must be governed and controlled by the specific and definite provisions of the latter. In the light of these well recognized rules of construction, said sec. 19 must be understood and interpreted as though it read as follows: All vacancies occurring in the offices provided for in this article of the constitution shall be filled as provided by law "unless otherwise provided for in this constitution." The appointment to fill a vacancy in the office of supreme justice being otherwise provided for in the constitution, and such appointment being vested solely in the governor, it must be held that sec. 19 has no application whatever to such vacancy and that the legislature is given no power whatever by the constitution to deprive the governor of the right of such appointment. The absolute grant of that right to the governor is prohibitive on the legislature to attempt to limit or restrict the full exercise thereof.

Having reached that conclusion, it follows that the provisions of secs. 320 and 329 of the Revised Codes, in so far as those sections attempt to provide a manner of filling a vacancy in the office of the justice of the supreme court to hold only until the next general election, are necessarily repugnant to the constitution and in derogation of the specific power of appointment to fill vacancies in that office granted by the constitution to the governor, unless the term "next general election" be construed to mean until the next general election to fill the particular office in question.

Many authorities have been cited where it has been held that the terms "general election" and "regular election" mean the next general or regular election for the filling of the office referred to, and the provisions of sec. 324, Rev. Codes, with reference to the filling of vacancies occurring thirty days prior to the general election, in so far at least as the issues of this particular case are concerned, may be held to apply only to elections at the end of the term when the particular office would ordinarily be filled. However, under our view of the constitutional provisions cited, and having held that the governor is authorized thereby to fill such vacancies for the entire unexpired term of the office vacated, it is not necessary to further pass upon or construe the sections of the statute above referred to.

The peremptory writ must therefore issue requiring the Secretary of State to issue a commission to the Honorable Alfred Budge, as prayed for in his petition, for the full term of the vacancy occasioned by the death of Justice Stewart.

Truitt, J., concurs.

(December 1, 1914.)

L. H. CAUTHORN, Trustee of the Estate of A. C. DUNNING and GUY OLIN, Partners Doing Business Under the Firm Name and Style of "THE TOGGERY," in Bankruptcy, Appellant, v. BURLEY STATE BANK, a Corporation, Respondent.

[144 Pac. 1108.]

BANKRUPTCY—CHATTEL MORTGAGE—PREFERENCE—CAUSE OF ACTION—
REASONABLE CAUSE TO BELIEVE TRANSFER WILL EFFECT PREFERENCE
—PLEADING.

1. In an action by a trustee in bankruptcy to set aside a transfer, on the ground that it effects a preference, and also that it is voidable as a fraud upon other creditors, under subdivision "e" of sec. 67 of the present bankruptcy law; the question as to a preference is determined from the facts and circumstances, and unless these are such as to produce a reasonable cause of belief in the mind of the person receiving the transfer that its enforcement would effect a preference, the transaction must be held valid. On the question as to whether a certain transfer is void because it is a fraud upon other creditors, the question must be determined by the evidence in each case.

2. *Held*, a chattel mortgage on a stock of goods which provides that the mortgagors may retain possession of the goods, sell them in the usual course of business, and each week pay a certain per cent of the gross proceeds of sales on the mortgage debt, is not void *per se*, but the question of its validity must be determined by the good faith or lack of good faith of the parties to the transaction.

APPEAL from the District Court of the Fourth Judicial District for Cassia County. Hon. Edward A. Walters, Judge.

Action by a trustee in bankruptcy to have a certain chattel mortgage declared illegal and void, and to have the mortgaged property turned over to the bankrupt's estate. Judgment for defendant. Plaintiff appeals. Judgment *affirmed.*

W. E. Abraham and James H. Wise, for Appellant.

"It does not now depend upon the purpose of intention of the debtor or creditor. It is implied that the debtor intended the transfer to be a preference at the time it was made." (*In re Andrews,* 144 Fed. 922, 75 C. C. A. 562; *In re First National Bank,* 155 Fed. 100, 84 C. C. A. 16; *Kimmerle v. Farr,* 189 Fed. 295, 111 C. C. A. 27.)

"The trustee need not prove knowledge or belief, only reasonable cause to believe that a preference was intended." (*Lampkin v. People's National Bank,* 98 Mo. App. 239, 71 S. W. 715.)

"This phrase includes reasonable cause to believe that the debtor is insolvent, for this is one of the elements of preference." (*Thomas v. Adelman,* 136 Fed. 973; *In re Kullberg,* 176 Fed. 585.)

"A person is always presumed to intend what is the necessary consequence of his act." (*Western Tie & Timber Co. v. Brown,* 196 U. S. 502, 25 Sup. Ct. 39, 49 L. ed. 571; *English v. Ross,* 140 Fed. 630; *Wilson v. Nelson,* 183 U. S. 191, 22 Sup. Ct. 74, 46 L. ed. 147; *Forbes v. Howe,* 102 Mass. 427, 3 Am. Rep. 475.)

"Whatever fairly puts a party upon inquiry is sufficient notice where the means of knowledge are at hand, and if the party under such circumstances omits to inquire and proceeds to receive the transfer or conveyance, he does so at his peril, as he is chargeable of knowledge and of all the facts, which by a proper inquiry he might have ascertained." (*Crittendon v. Barton,* 59 App. Div. 555, 69 N. Y. Supp. 559, 5 Am. Bankr. Rep. 775; *Wager v. Hall,* 16 Wall. (U. S.) 584, 21 L. ed. 504; *Hackney v. Hargreaves Bros.,* 68 Neb. 624, 94 N. W. 822, 99 N. W. 675; *Andrews v. Kellogg,* 41 Colo. 35, 92 Pac. 222; *Walker v. Tenison Bros. Saddlery Co.* (Tex. Civ. App.), 94

S. W. 166; *Whitwell v. Wright,* 115 N. Y. Supp. 48; *Stevens v. Oscar Holway Co.,* 156 Fed. 90.)

"Where a mortgage is given to secure a present loan in a pre-existing debt, it is invalid as a preference and to the extent of the pre-existing debt secured thereby." (*City National Bank v. Bruce,* 109 Fed. 69, 48 C. C. A. 236; *Stedman v. Bank of Monroe,* 117 Fed. 237, 54 C. C. A. 269; *In re Hull,* 115 Fed. 858; *In re Wolf,* 98 Fed. 84; *In re T. Furse & Co.,* 127 Fed. 690, 62 C. C. A. 446.)

"Possession of a stock of merchandise by the mortgagor, with power to sell and retail the same, without requiring the proceeds to be applied to the payment of the debt due the mortgagee is void as to attaching creditors of the mortgagor." (*Lewiston National Bank v. Martin,* 2 Ida. 734, 23 Pac. 920; *Robinson v. Elliott,* 22 Wall. (U. S.) 513, 524, 22 L. ed. 758; *Lyon v. Council Bluffs Sav. Bank,* 29 Fed. 566, 578.)

"Knowledge on the part of the mortgagee that the mortgagor is disposing of his stock at retail in the usual course of business without devoting the proceeds to the payment of the debt is sufficient evidence of the mortgagee's consent to such sales to warrant a conclusion of fraudulent intent and avoid the mortgage." (*Hayes Woolen Co. v. Gallagher,* 58 Minn. 502, 60 N. W. 343; *Scott Hardware Co. v. Riddle,* 84 Mo. App. 275, 282; *Ryan v. Rogers,* 14 Ida. 309, 94 Pac. 427.)

T. Bailey Lee, for Respondent.

"If the trustee fail to prove any one of the elements necessary to constitute a preference, the transfer cannot be set aside." (*Utah Assn. of Credit Men v. Boyle Furniture Co.,* 39 Utah, 518, 117 Pac. 800; *Crook v. People's Nat. Bank,* 18 Am. Bankr. Rep. 684, note; *McNaboe v. Columbian Mfg. Co.,* 153 Fed. 967, 83 C. C. A. 81.)

"Mere knowledge that a debtor is behind in his payments is insufficient to put his creditors upon inquiry, and charge them with facts an inquiry might disclose. Nor will the mere fact of taking security for a loan do so." (Loveland on Bankruptcy, p. 1003, note 47 and citations; *Grant v. First National Bank,* 97 U. S. 81, 24 L. ed. 971.)

"Creditor is not bound to trace or investigate suspicious circumstances which come to his attention." (*Blankenbaker v. Charleston State Bank*, 111 Ill. App. 393.) Doubt or suspicion is insufficient. (*Summerville v. Stockton Milling Co.*, 142 Cal. 529, 76 Pac. 243; *Stuckey v. Masonic Sav. Bank*, 108 U. S. 74, 27 L. ed. 640.)

"An adjudication of bankruptcy soon after the transfer is insufficient to show reasonable cause to believe insolvency." (Loveland on Bankruptcy, sec. 506, note 68, and citations.)

And the burden of proof to show this "reasonable cause to believe" lies upon the trustee. (*Kimmerle v. Farr*, 189 Fed. 295, 111 C. C. A. 27; *Arkansas Nat. Bank v. Sparks*, 83 Ark. 324, 103 S. W. 626.)

Even had the partners been insolvent, this respondent must, under the language of sec. 11 of the Amendatory Act of 1910, have had "reasonable cause to believe that the enforcement of such transfer would effect a preference." (Loveland on Bankruptcy, sec. 492 and citations.)

"If a mortgage executed at the time the loan is made creates a lien on specific chattels, no preference is created." (Loveland on Bankruptcy, sec. 519; *First Nat. Bank of Holdredge v. Johnson*, 68 Neb. 641, 94 N. W. 837, 4 Ann. Cas. 485.)

In order to invalidate a mortgage such as the one involved here, actual fraud must be proven. The old common-law rule holding such mortgages fraudulent *per se* has been abolished by American jurisdictions which have recognized the utter impossibility amid modern business conditions of carrying on business under its restriction. (*Etheridge v. Sperry*, 139 U. S. 266, 11 Sup. Ct. 565, 35 L. ed. 171; *Williams v. Mitchell*, 9 Kan. App. 627, 58 Pac. 1025; *Whitson v. Griffis*, 39 Kan. 211, 7 Am. St. 546, 17 Pac. 801.)

TRUITT, J.—This action was brought in the lower court by the appellant, L. H. Cauthorn, trustee in bankruptcy of the estate of A. C. Dunning and Guy Olin, bankrupts, against the Burley State Bank, a corporation engaged in the banking business at the town of Burley, Idaho, to have a certain chattel mortgage on a stock of merchandise and fixtures appertaining thereto, also located at said town, declared illegal and void and that the property described in said mortgage be turned over to said trustee as a part of the estate of said bankrupts.

The complaint sets up two separate causes of action. In the first cause set up therein, it is alleged that said A. C. Dunning and Guy Olin were on the 16th day of October, 1911, engaged in business as copartners under the firm name and style of "The Toggery" at said town of Burley; that said firm was at said date insolvent and that it was indebted to the defendant bank in the sum of $1,700. It further alleges that at said date said firm and said A. C. Dunning and Guy Olin executed and delivered to the defendant a promissory note in said sum of $1,700; that to secure the same they also at said time executed a chattel mortgage upon their entire stock of merchandise and fixtures used in the business and for no other consideration whatever; that said $1,700 was at said time a pre-existing, unsecured indebtedness, and that the transfer of said property was made for the benefit of said defendant with the intent to give it a preference as a creditor, and with intent to hinder, delay and defraud the other creditors of said parties, thereby making it possible for said defendant to obtain a greater percentage of its said debt than any other creditor in the same class. The complaint further alleged that at the time said chattel mortgage was given and said property transferred to the defendant, it had reasonable cause to believe that said parties were insolvent, that a preference was intended, and the transfer of said property was received by defendant with the intent and purpose to hinder, delay and defraud the other creditors of said parties of the same class. It further alleges that the defendant at the time of this transaction was and for more than one year prior thereto had been the banker for said firm, and as such had full knowledge of its financial standing and condition, that its liabilities greatly exceeded its assets and resources of all kinds; that said firm and said A. C. Dunning and Guy Olin were insolvent and unable to pay all their creditors in full, that said mortgage was intended as a preference over other creditors of the same class; that the same was made, executed and delivered for the purpose of hindering, delaying and defrauding the other creditors of said parties of a like class.

The complaint also alleges that on the 9th day of December, 1911, a petition in involuntary bankruptcy was filed against the partnership composed of said A. C. Dunning and Guy Olin by a large number of their creditors representing claims of about $5,000, and that thereafter on the 13th day of December, 1911, the property of said partnership was placed in the hands of L. V. Gallogly, as receiver; that on the 7th day of March, 1912, an adjudication was had in the matter of said petition in bankruptcy, and said A. C. Dunning and Guy Olin were duly declared bankrupts; that thereafter on the 24th day of April, 1912, said L. H. Cauthorn was appointed as trustee in bankruptcy of their estate; that he at said date duly qualified as such trustee and has been acting as such ever since. It was further alleged that a notice to said bank was given by said trustee, L. H. Cauthorn, of the first meeting of the creditors of such bankrupts; that said bank by its agent appeared at said meeting and was requested by said trustee to surrender said chattel mortgage and property therein described and to share with the other unsecured creditors in the distribution of the estate, but it then refused to do so and has ever since refused to surrender the mortgage or said property.

From the record here presented, there seems to have been some irregularity in the proceedings by which the adjudication in bankruptcy in this case was effected, in this, that though the petition was against the partnership doing business under the firm name and style of "The Toggery," the adjudication was against A. C. Dunning and Guy Olin as individuals. And yet the only property that was taken possession of by authority of said proceedings and adjudication was the property of said partnership. However, as no question regarding the matter is presented by this appeal, if there was any irregularity in the proceedings by which said A. C. Dunning and Guy Olin were declared bankrupts as individuals when the petition was against them as copartners, it could not be raised in this court for the first time.

In the second cause of action, plaintiff alleges the execution of said note and mortgage set out in its first cause of action, as above mentioned, and then alleges that said mortgage was and is illegal and void, for the reason that the bank permitted the mortgagors to retain possession of said merchandise, conduct a retail business from day to day, and sell goods from the stock of merchandise so mortgaged without requiring the receipts from the sales of the same to be applied to the extinguishment of said mortgage indebtedness, that no payments were made on said mortgage, and that the same was made, executed and delivered to the bank for the purpose and with the intent to hinder, delay and defraud the other creditors of said copartnership, and that the defendant had full knowledge of such intent on the part of the mortgagors, and was a party thereto. The answer joined issue upon the material allegations of the complaint, and the cause was tried before the court without a jury. Both parties by a stipulation in writing waived findings of fact and conclusions of law, and thereafter the court duly entered judgment against the plaintiff and awarded costs to the defendant. From this judgment this appeal is taken.

As there were no findings of fact by the trial court, it is necessary for this court to examine the evidence and determine for itself what facts are established thereby and from these facts conclude whether the principles of law upon which the judgment rests are sustained by the evidence. There were only two witnesses, S. G. Rich and L. B. Gallogly, who testified in regard to the controlling points in the case. The only other witness called was the county recorder, and he was called simply to identify some records required to be used in the case. Mr. Rich testified that he was cashier of the Burley State Bank and had dealings with A. C. Dunning and Guy Olin while they were engaged in business as copartners under the firm name of "The Toggery" at Burley. He testified that said note and mortgage for $1,700 given on the 16th of October, 1911, were executed and delivered to take up an unsecured note for $1,500 and some interest thereon that the firm owed to the bank. This $1,700 was deposited to the credit of the firm and $1525.25 checked from its account at said date so that $174.75 of this $1,700 note and mortgage was a new debt, and as to that sum the mortgage in any event would be valid so far as the question of preference might affect it. This witness further testified that during the month of October, 1911, he inquired into the condition of this firm and went over their books, but made no inventory of the goods and fixtures; that its account at the bank was overdrawn during the months of September and October, and this led him to inquire into the condition of the business. He also stated that the firm during October and November of said year deposited to its credit at various times a total sum of $579.23, the last deposit being made November 18th, but this sum was all checked out so that on that date there was an overdraft of $8.79 on the account of said firm. During this time $55 was credited on the $1,700 note. The mortgage provided that the mortgagors should each week apply 50% of the gross proceeds of the sales of merchandise covered by said mortgage in payment of the $1,700 indebtedness, and this witness testified that he went to the store each week, asked for a statement of the receipts from sales of the week and for 50% of the money received; he further testified that he went each week and had an accounting but did not get any money for some weeks. He explained this by saying that, "I am not certain but there were some weeks when the amounts applied to new stock and exhausted their funds and they had nothing to pay." The witness was asked about the individual property of Guy Olin, and though he testified that he owned fifteen or twenty thousand dollars' worth of property, he admitted on cross-examination that, "He had his title in such shape that it could not be used for security. . . . . He had not perfected title to his real estate."

It would seem from this explanation in regard to this property owned by Guy Olin that he could not use it for securing his creditors or raising money to pay them, and if this is so, we do not see how they could reach it by any legal process. In *Louisiana Nat. Life Assur. Soc. v. Segen*, 28 Am. Bankr. Rep. 19, it is stated that: "In order to determine the solvency of a bankrupt, the assets ought to be such as a creditor could realize on if he obtained a judgment against him in the ordinary course of judicial procedure.'' It is admitted that Dunning had no property other than his interest in this store, except a diamond ring. The amount of indebtedness presented by the unsecured creditors to the trustee in bankruptcy was $4,954, the mortgage in controversy amounted to $1,700, and there was another mortgage against the firm for about $1,000, making a total indebtedness of about $7,600 at the date of the filing of the petition in bankruptcy. At the time of the execution of this mortgage, the said goods and fixtures were estimated to be of the value of $3,500 to $4,000, and though this did not include book accounts, as the items of indebtedness within a short time after the date of said mortgage amounted to $7,600 as above stated, we think the record shows that this copartnership was insolvent at the date on which this mortgage was executed and delivered to the bank. Moreover, while it is true that secured creditors are not bound by an adjudication in bankruptcy and may litigate the same issues in another proceeding, still the adjudication is as to them *prima facie* evidence of what is therein decreed, and the adjudication was made March 7, 1912, so that it is *prima facie* evidence in this case that these parties were insolvent at that date or a little over four and one-half months after the date of the mortgage. And this fact might be considered as of some weight in determining whether the copartnership was insolvent at the date of said transfer.

The other witness, L. B. Gallogly, in this case testified that some months prior to the date of this mortgage, he was employed as a salesman by ''The Toggery'' firm and was so employed at that time; that on the 13th day of December, 1911, he was appointed receiver of the business of said firm by the federal court and took charge of the property on said date. He further testified that on the date of said mortgage he would estimate the stock of goods and fixtures to be worth from $3,500 to $4,000, though he did not take an inventory thereof, but when he took charge of the property as receiver, he then made an inventory of the merchandise and fixtures,

and this showed the value to be about $3,000. He further
testified that during the month of October, 1911, the firm
appeared to be doing a "very prosperous business," and was
making sales of about $50 or $60 a day.

The foregoing statement includes the material facts in this
case, as stated by the witnesses and as shown by the record.

Based upon the facts as thus shown to exist, it now becomes
necessary to apply the principles of law applicable to them
in order to reach a correct decision of the case. The appellant only complains of two errors, (1) "That the evidence
conclusively shows that said mortgage was given with the
intent to prefer the defendant bank, mortgagee, over other
creditors of the same class, and was given to secure an antecedent debt; and (2) that said mortgage was illegal and void,
for the reason that the same permitted the mortgagors to
remain in possession of the same in the regular course of
business without accounting to the mortgagee for the proceeds
of said daily sales, and that the mortgagee knew and had
reason to believe that the mortgagors were at the time insolvent." The first alleged error raises the question of a preference as defined by the National Bankruptcy Law now in force.
The Bankruptcy Act of 1898, in regard to preferences, made
the result obtained by the creditor, and not the intent of the
debtor, the essential fact; if a transfer to a creditor within
four months of the bankruptcy was received which would give
him an advantage over other creditors of the same class, it
was a preference without regard to the intent or motive of
either debtor or creditor. As a large part of the mercantile
business of this country is done upon a credit system, this
law in its result materially restricted trade, for it to a large
extent eliminated credit, and the retail merchant was limited
in his purchases to such amount of goods as he could pay for
in cash. So much complaint was made against this law and
its evil effects on business were so apparent that the amendatory act of 1903 was passed by Congress. Subdivision "b"
of sec. 60 of said act was further amended by act of Congress,
approved June 25, 1910, and this subdivision so far as it
relates to this case is as follows:

"If a bankrupt shall have procured or suffered a judgment to be entered against him in favor of any person or have made a transfer of any of his property, and if, at the time of his transfer, or of the entry of the judgment or of the recording or registering of the transfer if by law recording or registering thereof is required, and being within four months before the filing of the petition in bankruptcy or after the filing thereof and before the adjudication, the bankrupt be insolvent and the judgment or transfer then operate as a preference, and the person receiving it or to be benefited thereby, or his agent acting therein, shall then have reasonable cause to believe that the enforcement of such judgment or transfer 'would effect a preference, it shall be voidable by the trustee, and he may recover the property or its value from such person."

Under the Bankruptcy Act as amended in 1903, an essential element to a preference was that the creditor "had reasonable cause to believe that it was intended thereby to give a preference," and in a number of cases it was held that the debtor must also intend the transfer as a preference, because such intention might be presumed from the necessary result of the transaction, and much refinement of argument as to the meaning of the word "intended," as used in this section, was indulged in by the courts in construing it. Probably on this account the language of this section was changed by the amendment of 1910, as will be noticed in the foregoing quotation, so as to eliminate the question of intention as to either creditor or debtor. As the law now is, if the creditor had reasonable cause to *believe* the enforcement of the transfer would *effect* a preference, it shall be voidable by the trustee. And, as already stated, this makes the intent of the debtor immaterial and predicates this element of a preference upon the *belief* of the creditor. And this belief must be based upon reasonable cause. We apprehend that the courts will find about as much difficulty in defining a "reasonable cause" as they have had in construing the word "intended" in this section before the last amendment thereto. The controlling question presented by appellant's first assignment, then, is whether he has, by the weight of the proof, established the fact that the bank had reasonable cause to believe that the enforcement of this transfer would effect a preference.

Collier on Bankruptcy, 10th ed., p. 790, gives the essential elements of a preference under the present law as follows:

"Since the amendatory act, a preference consists in a person, (1) while insolvent and (2) within four months of the bankruptcy, (3) procuring or suffering a judgment to be entered against himself or making a transfer of his property, (4) the effect of which will be to enable one creditor to obtain a greater percentage of his debt than any other creditor of the same class. Such a preference is voidable at the instance of the trustee, if (5) the person recovering it or to be benefited thereby has (6) reasonable cause to believe that the enforcement of the judgment or transfer will result in a preference. If the transfer was made or the judgment procured or suffered while the debtor was insolvent and the effect of such transfer or judgment was to enable one creditor to obtain a greater percentage of his debt than any other creditor of the same class, such transfer or judgment is a preference. The burden of proving the existence of the essential elements of a transfer is upon the trustee seeking to avoid it."

The first authority cited in the brief of appellant on the question of a preference is *Swarts v. Fourth National Bank,* 117 Fed. 1, 54 C. C. A. 387, and the quotation given therefrom as the test of a preference is as follows: "The test of a preference under the act is the payment out of the bankrupt's property of a greater percentage of the creditor's claim than other creditors of the same class." But it will be found upon examination of this case that it presents a different state of facts from the one at bar, and moreover it was determined in 1902, which brought it under the provisions of the law of 1898, and for that reason, even if the facts had been identical with the facts before us in this case, the rule as to the test of a preference is not the same under the present law as it was under the statute of 1898. Under that statute, if the transfer was made within four months before the bankruptcy, it was voidable by the trustee because of that fact without regard to the intentions of the parties to the transaction. But, under the present law, even though the transfer is made within the four months preceding bankruptcy, it is not voidable, unless the person receiving it has reasonable cause to believe that the enforcement thereof would effect a preference.

There are a number of authorities also cited by appellant upon the question of the intentions of the parties to a transfer that might effect a preference under subdivision "b" of sec. 60 of the present law, but we do not deem it profitable to review these authorities at length because they are not in point upon the question of a preference under the present law.

The vital question upon the point under consideration is whether the officers of the bank had reasonable cause to believe at the time of its execution that the enforcement of the $1700 mortgage given by said firm to it would effect a preference, and this must be ascertained from the facts connected with the transaction. This mortgage was executed by "The Toggery" and by Guy Olin and A. C. Dunning as individuals, upon the entire stock of goods and the fixtures of the store known as "The Toggery." The firm had been in business in the town of Burley for some considerable time and did its banking with the respondent bank. Prior to the date of the mortgage in controversy, the cashier of the bank investigated the business of the firm and concluded it was solvent, and the witness Gallogly testified that when he was employed there as a salesman it was making sales of from $50 to $60 per day prior to and about the time of the execution of said mortgage, and that the business seemed to him to be in a prosperous condition. If the facts and circumstances were such as to constitute in the mind of the officers of the bank a reasonable cause to believe when this transfer was given to it that the enforcement thereof would effect a preference, then it is voidable, but if from said investigation of the assets and the business of "The Toggery" made by the cashier of the bank, and with his knowledge of its financial affairs, a man of ordinary prudence and business experience would not have had a reasonable cause therefrom to believe that the enforcement of said mortgage would effect a preference, then we think the contention of the appellant on this point must fail. The fact that this firm was unable to meet all its obligations as they fell due alone was not sufficient to cause a belief that it was insolvent.

In *Wilson v. City Bank*, 17 Wall. (U. S.) 473, 486, 21 L. ed. 723, it is said: "Many find themselves with ample means, good credit, large business, technically insolvent; that is, unable to meet their current obligations as fast as they mature. But by forbearance of creditors, by meeting only such debts as are pressed, and even by the submission of some of their property to be seized on execution, they are finally able to pay all, and to save their commercial character and much of their property. If creditors are not satisfied with this, and the parties have committed an act of bankruptcy, any creditor can institute proceedings in a bankrupt court. But until this is done, their honest struggle to meet their debts and to avoid the breaking up of all their business is not, of itself, to be construed into an act of bankruptcy, or a fraud upon the act." And in *Grant v. First National Bank*, 97 U. S. 81, 24 L. ed. 971, as a proposition of importance in discussing the question, it is said: "The debtor is often buoyed up by the hope of being able to get through with his difficulties long after his case is in fact desperate; and his creditors, if they know anything of his embarrassments, either participate in the same feeling, or at least are willing to think that there is a possibility of his succeeding."

But there is some testimony in the record in this case that we think has an important bearing on this question. The cashier of the bank testified that Guy Olin was worth between fifteen and twenty thousand dollars at the time this mortgage was executed, and although it further appeared that his title to this property was not in such condition that he could mortgage it, still the rule given by Loveland for determining insolvency includes all of the assets of the creditor of every kind. "In computing the assets of the debtor to determine the solvency or insolvency, all his property which has value should be included. In determining the question of the solvency, there should be included property exempt under the state law, and property transferred in payment of or as security for a just debt, irrespective of whether it constitutes a preference or not." However, whether this property which this witness testifies to as being of the value of from fifteen to twenty thousand dollars should have been considered in determining the question of the solvency of this firm or not, the knowledge that it was owned by one of the partners would very probably have great weight upon the mind of a person in forming an opinion upon the financial conditions of the firm. After carefully considering the evidence and the circumstances in this case, we conclude that a reasonable cause to believe that the enforcement of this transfer would effect a preference in favor of appellant cannot be attributed to the respondent.

The second alleged error complained of by the appellant is that said mortgage was illegal and void, for the reason that the same permitted the mortgagors to remain in possession of the mortgaged goods and sell and dispose of the same in the regular course of business, without accounting to the mortgagee for the proceeds of the sales, and that the mortgagee had reason to believe that the mortgagors were at the time insolvent. But before taking up the argument of this question, perhaps it is well to pass upon the error alleged by the respondent in regard to the ruling of the trial court in not sustaining his motion to strike out the amendment made to the original complaint by adding thereto an additional cause of action. The trustee brought the action to have the said mortgage declared void, and in addition to the allegations in the first cause of action to the effect that it was void under subd. "b" of sec. 60 of the bankruptcy law, he had the right in the second cause of action to also demand that it be declared void under subd. "e" of sec. 67 of said law. We think the trial court did not err in overruling said motion.

The appellant cites a number of authorities to sustain his contention that this mortgage is void, for the reason that the mortgagors remained in possession of the goods and continued in possession of the property and to sell the goods upon which it was given in the regular course of business, with the knowledge and consent of the bank, without applying the proceeds of the sales to the reduction of the mortgaged debt. But there was a provision in the mortgage that was intended to meet this objection. This provision is as follows:

"And it is hereby further mutually agreed by and between the respective parties hereto, that the mortgagors may continue to conduct a retail mercantile business heretofore and now being conducted by said mortgagors, in the said building aforesaid, and to sell and dispose of any portion or part of said stock for cash, in the conduct of said business, and to replace and replenish said stock by purchases from time to time, investing a portion of the proceeds of said sales in the purchase of goods for the replenishing and maintaining of said stock; provided, however, that 50% of the gross proceeds of said sales shall be applied upon and in discharge of said mortgage indebtedness, as evidenced by said note; to which end and for which purpose it is further mutually agreed that 50% of said sales shall be paid to the said mortgagee once each and every week until the said mortgage indebtedness together with the interest thereon shall have been paid off and discharged."

It would serve no useful purpose for us to review the earlier authorities that follow the common-law rule, holding that to allow the mortgagors to remain in possession of a stock of merchandise and sell it out in the usual course of business renders the mortgage void *per se*, for the reason that since the decision in *Etheridge v. Sperry*, 139 U. S. 266, 11 Sup. Ct. 565, 35 L. ed. 171, that rule has been greatly modified or abolished by a well-considered line of authorities. The cases of *Robinson v. Elliott*, 22 Wall. (U. S.) 513, 22 L. ed. 758, and *Means v. Dowd*, 128 U. S. 273, 9 Sup. Ct. 65, 32 L. ed. 429, were frequently cited in support of the common-law rule, but in *Etheridge v. Sperry, supra*, these cases were analyzed and held not to control in that case. In the opinion Mr. Justice Brewer says: "In neither of those cases is it affirmed that a chattel mortgage on a stock of goods is necessarily invalidated by the fact that either in the mortgage, or by parol agreement between the parties, the mortgagor is to retain possession, with the right to sell the goods at retail. On the

contrary, it is clearly recognized in them that such an instrument is valid, notwithstanding these stipulations, if it appears
that the sales were to be for the benefit of the mortgagee.
What was meant was that such an instrument should not be
used to enable the mortgagor to continue in business as theretofore, with full control of the property and business, and
appropriating to himself the benefits thereof, and all the while
holding the instrument as a shield against the attacks of unsecured creditors.''

The appellant cites *Ryan v. Rogers*, 14 Ida. 309, 94 Pac. 427,
in support of his contention. But in this class of cases good
faith is the controlling principle in testing the validity of
the conveyance. And this must be in each case decided upon
the evidence. The facts in the case at bar are very different
from the facts in the Ryan case. In that case the mortgage
was executed July 21, 1903, and no attempt on the part of
the mortgagee to take possession thereof was made until July
8, 1904, and during all that time there was only $37.50 paid
upon said mortgage. However, in that case the mortgage was
not held void *per se*, but the court after reviewing the facts
presented by the record said: "The fact that the mortgagee
permitted the mortgagor to remain in possession of the property, which was within itself something like double the value
of the debt secured, for a period of one year, and for at least
nine months after breach of the conditions named in the mortgage, and sell and dispose of the property, without any
attempt to collect any part of the mortgage debt, or take possession of the property, would, as a matter of law, be such
a fraud upon attaching creditors and purchasers as to avoid
the mortgage.'' In the case at bar, it appears from the evidence that the mortgage was executed on the 16th day of
October, 1911, and that on the 9th day of December, 1911,
bankruptcy proceedings were instituted against said firm and
the possession of the property placed in the hands of a receiver under such proceedings. The cashier of the bank testified that he went to the business place of the mortgagors
each week and required them to make an accounting and pay
the amount of the proceeds of their sales, as provided in said

mortgage, and although the payments amounted to only $55 during said time, there were some weeks when the amounts of their sales had been applied to new stock, and in that way their funds were exhausted and they had nothing to pay. But his testimony also is to the effect that they were making sales and paying their current bills and expenses and conducting the business in the usual way until the bankruptcy proceedings were commenced, and we think these facts clearly distinguish this case from *Ryan v. Rogers, supra.*

After a careful consideration of the facts and circumstances in this case, we are disposed to think that the respondent was acting in good faith, that its cashier did not believe and did not have reasonable cause to believe that the firm was insolvent at the time of the execution of this mortgage or during the time thereafter until said proceedings in bankruptcy were commenced. We think the evidence shows that he hoped by giving the mortgagors reasonable indulgence in the matter of this indebtedness to the bank, it would pull through its financial stress and in the course of time be able to meet all its indebtedness. The trial court heard the testimony, weighed the evidence, and found in favor of the respondent, and we do not find from the record, as presented, that the judgment of that court should be disturbed. The judgment is therefore affirmed and costs awarded to the respondent.

Sullivan, C. J., concurs.

(December 1, 1914.)

L. H. CAUTHORN, Trustee of the Estate of A. C. DUN-
NING and GUY OLIN, Partners Doing Business Under
the Firm Name and Style of "THE TOGGERY," in
Bankruptcy, Appellant, v. ANDREW LOUNSBURY,
Respondent.

[144 Pac. 1113.]

APPEAL from the District Court of the Fourth Judicial
District for Cassia County. Hon. Edward A. Walters, Judge.

Action by a trustee in bankruptcy to have a certain chattel
mortgage declared illegal and void, and to have the mortgage
properly turned over to the bankrupt's estate. Judgment
for defendant. Plaintiff appeals. Judgment *affirmed.*

W. E. Abraham and James H. Wise, for Appellant.

The mortgagee Lounsbury, defendant herein, permitted
the bankrupts, Dunning and Olin, to remain in possession
of the property for a period of six months, and to sell and
dispose of the property without collecting any part of the
mortgage debt, or taking possession of the property, or having the mortgagors account to him and collecting the proceeds of sales and applying upon his indebtedness. This was
as a matter of law, such a fraud upon creditors and purchasers as to avoid the mortgage *in toto.* (*Lewiston National
Bank v. Martin,* 2 Ida. 734, 23 Pac. 920; *Ryan v. Rogers,* 14
Ida. 309, 94 Pac. 427; *Stevens v. Curran,* 28 Mont. 366, 72
Pac. 753; *Wilson v. Voight,* 9 Colo. 614, 13 Pac. 726; *Roch-
eleau v. Boyle,* 11 Mont. 451, 28 Pac. 872; *Martin v. Holloway,*
16 Ida. 513, 102 Pac. 3, 25 L. R. A., N. S., 110; *In re Hicker-
son,* 162 Fed. 345.)

"Knowledge on the part of the mortgagee that mortgagor
is disposing of his stock at retail in the usual course of business without applying the proceeds to the payment of the
debt, is sufficient evidence of the mortgagee's consent to such

a sale to warrant a conclusion of fraudulent intent and avoiding the mortgage.'' (*Hayes Woolen Co. v. Gallagher*, 58 Minn. 502, 60 N. W. 343; *Scott Hardware Co. v. Riddle*, 84 Mo. App. 275, 282.)

S. T. Lowe, for Respondent.

The plaintiff must show three things, in addition to the insolvency of the bankrupt at the time of the execution of the mortgage, to wit: (1) That the mortgage was given for a fraudulent purpose and that the mortgagee had notice of the fraudulent intent on the part of the mortgagors; (2) That the mortgage was given for a past consideration and for a present consideration; (3) That the consideration was paid with knowledge of the fraud. (*Galbreath v. Cook*, 30 Ark. 417; *Carnahan v. McCord*, 116 Ind. 67, 18 N. E. 177; *Hedman v. Anderson*, 6 Neb. 392.)

The plaintiff failed to plead negligence or misconduct on the part of the mortgagee in foreclosing the mortgage, and the facts of the case as shown by the record, do not support the rule therein laid down.

TRUITT, J.—This case is controlled in its principles of law by the decision just announced in *L. H. Cauthorn, Trustee v. Burley State Bank*, ante, p. 532, 144 Pac. 1108. The facts, however, are more favorable to the defendant in this case than in that. In *Cauthorn v. Burley State Bank*, the mortgage was given to secure a pre-existing indebtedness, but in this case the court found that ''the certain note and mortgage were executed and delivered to the defendant, Andrew Lounsbury, for money loaned by the said Andrew Lounsbury to A. C. Dunning and Guy Olin at the time the said note and mortgage were executed, and not for a pre-existing indebtedness; that the money for which the said note and mortgage were executed and delivered was paid to the said A. C. Dunning and Guy Olin and by them used in carrying on their mercantile business aforesaid.'' We think the evidence fully sustains this finding; and upon the authority of said case of *Cauthorn v. Burley State Bank,* the judgment of the lower court is affirmed in this case, and costs awarded to respondent.

Sullivan, C. J., concurs.

(December 2, 1914.)

F. NETTIE RICE, as Treasurer and Ex-Officio Tax Collector of POWER COUNTY, Appellant, v. HENRY ROCK, Respondent.

[144 Pac. 786.]

TAX CERTIFICATE—TAX DEED—STATUTORY CONSTRUCTION—NOTICE— WHEN GIVEN.

1. Under the provisions of sec. 1763, Rev. Codes, as amended at the special session of the legislature (Laws 1912, p. 43), no purchaser or assignee of such purchaser of any land at a tax sale shall be entitled to demand a tax deed therefor until the notice therein required shall be given.

2. Under the provisions of sec. 1649, Rev. Codes, the levy of a tax has the same effect as a judgment and becomes a lien upon the property, which lien can only be divested by the payment of the tax or the sale of the property.

3. Under the provisions of sec. 1762, Rev. Codes, on filing the certificate of tax sale with the *ex-officio* auditor and recorder, the lien vests in the purchaser and is only divested by the payment to the county treasurer, on certificate of the auditor, for the use of the purchaser, of the whole amount of money paid for such certificate, together with interest thereon.

4. At the time said certificates were issued, the law did not require the giving of any notice to the owner of the property, but the legislature has authority to change the remedy provided for the enforcement of certificate contracts provided they do not impair the obligation of the contract, so long as the obligation of performance remains in full force.

5. Provision of said sec. 1763 which requires said notice to be given at least three months and not more than five months before the expiration of the term of redemption is directory.

6. A period of time in which said notice is required to be given was made for the purpose of ending the period in which redemption could be made and not for the purpose of divesting the holder of his lien on the property described in his tax sale certificate.

7. *Held*, that after the expiration of the three-year period and up to the time the notice is given, the owner may redeem the property from tax sale.

APPEAL from the District Court of the Fifth Judicial District for Power County. Hon. Alfred Budge, Judge.

Action to determine the right of a tax certificate holder to the deed without giving the notice required by sec. 1763, Rev. Codes, as amended. Judgment for plaintiff. *Reversed.*

J. H. Peterson, Atty. Gen., J. J. Guheen, T. C. Coffin, and E. G. Davis, Assts., and O. R. Baum, for Appellant.

Cases precisely similar to the case at bar have arisen in many jurisdictions in this country and without exception those jurisdictions now hold that it is incumbent upon the holder of a tax sale certificate, under such circumstances, to publish the notice required by the statute. (*Curtis v. Whitney*, 80 U. S. (13 Wall.) 68, 20 L. ed. 513; *Oullahan v. Sweeney*, 79 Cal. 537, 12 Am. St. 172, 21 Pac. 960; *Gage v. Stewart*, 127 Ill. 207, 11 Am. St. 116, 19 N. E. 702; *Herrick v. Niesz*, 16 Wash. 74, 47 Pac. 414; *State v. Krahmer*, 105 Minn. 422, 117 N. W. 780, 21 L. R. A., N. S., 157; *Coulter v. Stafford*, 56 Fed. 564, 6 C. C. A. 18.)

T. S. Becker and McDougall & Jones, for Respondent.

The plaintiff in this case, by virtue of the tax certificate, obtained a vested right in the property which could only be divested by the redemption from said sale by the owner of the lots within three years. (*Lawrence v. Defenbach*, 23 Ida. 78, 128 Pac. 81.)

The right of the owner and purchaser at a tax sale must both be governed by the law as it existed at the time of the sale. (Black on Tax Title, sec. 175; *Merrill v. Dearing*, 32 Minn. 479, 21 N. W. 721; *Johnson v. Taylor*, 150 Cal. 201,

119 Am. St. 181, 88 Pac. 903, 10 L. R. A., N. S., 818; *Teralta Land etc. Co. v. Shaffer,* 116 Cal. 518, 58 Am. St. 194, 48 Pac. 613; *Allen v. Allen,* 95 Cal. 184, 30 Pac. 213, 16 L. R. A. 646.)

The enforced sale of property on execution or for the non-payment of taxes, constitutes a contract with the purchaser which cannot be materially altered, without his consent. (*Lawrence v. Defenbach, supra; Welsh v. Cross,* 146 Cal. 621, 106 Am. St. 63, 81 Pac. 229, 2 Ann. Cas. 796.)

If the remedy afforded be qualified and restrained by conditions of any kind the right of the owner may indeed subsist and be acknowledged, but it is impaired and rendered unsecure according to the method and extent of such restrictions. (*Green v. Biddle,* 8 Wheat. (U. S.) 1, 5 L. ed. 547; *San Diego Inv. Co. v. Shaffer,* 137 Cal. 323, 70 Pac. 179.)

It is settled that all the laws of a state existing at the time a contract is made which affect the rights of the parties to the contract enter into and become a part of it, and are as obligatory upon all courts which assume to give a remedy on such contracts as if they were referred to or incorporated in the terms of the contract. (*Ford v. Durie,* 8 Wash. 87, 35 Pac. 595, 1082; *Stein v. Hanson,* 99 Minn. 387, 109 N. W. 821; 37 Cyc. 1452, and cases cited.)

Kansas has repeatedly held that the amendment of a statute of tax sale certificates cannot affect certificates previously issued. (*Richards v. Board of Commrs.,* 28 Kan. 326; *Coonradt v. Myers,* 31 Kan. 30, 2 Pac. 858; *Pounds v. Rodgers,* 52 Kan. 558, 39 Am. St. 360, 35 Pac. 223; *Morgan v. Board of Commrs.,* 27 Kan. 89.)

SULLIVAN, C. J.—This is an appeal from the judgment of the district court of Power county whereby the treasurer and *ex-officio* tax collector was directed to issue a treasurer's tax deed to the respondent Rock conveying to him certain town lots situated in the village of American Falls on tax sale certificates procured by said Rock at a tax sale duly held in said county on July 8, 1910, for taxes assessed against such lots for the year 1909.

It appears from the record that the respondent in the month of August, 1913, applied to the defendant as treasurer and *ex-officio* tax collector of said county for tax deeds to the several lots that he had purchased at said tax sale, and she refused to execute such deeds. Thereupon the respondent made application to the district court of the fifth judicial district for a writ of mandate to compel the appellant to execute such deeds. To said petition or complaint a demurrer was interposed and overruled by the court, and the defendant thereafter stood on her demurrer and refused to answer and the court thereafter heard certain proofs and made findings of fact and conclusions of law and entered judgment in favor of the respondent.

It appears from the record that the respondent had not complied with the requirements of sec. 1763 as amended at the special 1912 session of the legislature (Sess. Laws 1912, p. 43). That section provides, among other things, that thereafter no purchaser or assignee of such purchaser of any land at tax sale shall be entitled to a tax deed therefor until the notice therein required shall have been given as provided by said section, which notice, it is conceded, was not given in this case.

Counsel for appellant contends that said law as amended is applicable to the facts of this case even though the said land was sold for taxes long prior to the time that the act of 1912 went into effect; that it is necessary for the respondent to comply with the terms of said law in giving notice before she would be justified or authorized to execute the deeds demanded.

The question then directly presented to the court is whether under the law the respondent is required to give such notice as that statute requires before he is entitled to tax deeds. The law in force at the time said tax sale was made did not require any notice to be given of the application for a deed. Under the provisions of sec. 1649, Rev. Codes, the levy of a tax in this state has the same effect as a judgment and becomes a lien upon the property, which lien can only be divested by the payment of the tax or the sale of the property. Sec.

1762, Rev. Codes, transfers that right to the purchaser at the tax sale and creates a vested right and provides the method and manner by which such right may be divested. Sec. 1763 provides that a tax deed may issue at the expiration of three years to the owner of the certificate. Sec. 1770 limits the time for redemption to three years. The law in force at the time of said tax sale required nothing of the purchaser except to pay the amount of the purchase price, then to await the expiration of three years and pay to the treasurer two dollars for the deed. That is the procedure where the sale is made to a private party and not the county. Under the law, the respondent, by virtue of his tax certificate, obtained a vested right in said lots which could only be divested by redemption. But regardless of the provisions of said section of the statute, must the respondent give the notice provided for in said sec. 1763 as amended?

It is contended that said section imposed new obligations and duties on the owner of such tax certificate and the giving of such notice and the publication thereof in a newspaper where it is required will greatly enhance the cost of a tax deed over the cost under the law that was in force at the time said tax sales were made and certificates issued; that it places upon the certificate owner added burdens and obligations.

It is clear that in some cases the value of the property involved might be less than these added burdens forced on the certificate owner by said statute. But it is held by the great weight of authority that the legislature may pass a remedial statute providing for the different methods of enforcing a contract from that which the law required at the time the contract was entered into, and that a law that would deprive a party of all legal remedy on a contract or impose impossible conditions would be absolutely void. It was held in *Gage v. Stewart,* 127 Ill. 207, 11 Am. St. 116, 19 N. E. 702, that it is competent for the legislature in its discretion to regulate or change the methods of conducting the public business and to impose such restrictions and conditions on those having contracts with the state as public policy may demand, although such restrictions, conditions or changes may require

the observance of new forms by the officer or by the party
to the contract, and that the exercise of such power is the
same as that which may be exercised in respect to remedies
for the enforcement of contracts which, within the limitation
that the right itself shall not be impaired, is to be regarded
as within the legislative control, and that "no new condition
could be imposed requiring the payment of an additional
consideration or that would hinder the purchaser or his
assignees from acquiring title or extending the time of redemption."

In *Curtis v. Whitney,* 13 Wall. (U. S.) 68, 20 L. ed. 513,
the supreme court of the United States had under consideration the Wisconsin statute which provided that a holder of a
certificate of tax sale should give notice to whomever might
be found in possession of the land before taking a deed.
That statute is similar to the one under consideration, and
in disposing of that case, the court said:

"That a statute is not void because it is retrospective has
been repeatedly held by this court, and the feature of the
act of 1867, which makes it applicable to certificates already
issued for tax sales, does not of itself conflict with the constitution of the United States. Nor does every statute which
affects the value of a contract impair its obligation. It is
one of the contingencies to which parties look now in making
a large class of contracts, that they may be affected in many
ways by state and national legislation. For such legislation
demanded by the public good, however it may retroact on
contracts previously made, and enhance the cost and difficulty
of performance, or diminish the value of such performance
to the other party, there is no restraint in the federal constitution, so long as the obligation of performance remains
in full force."

As bearing upon this question, see, also, *Coulter v. Stafford,*
56 Fed. 564, 6 C. C. A. 18; *State v. Krahmer,* 105 Minn. 422,
117 N. W. 780, 21 L. R. A., N. S., 157, and the authorities
there cited.

Under the authorities above cited, it is made quite clear
that the plaintiff must give the notice required by said sec.

1763, and that the provisions of said section do not impair the obligations of the contract entered into in the purchase of said tax certificate.

The next question presented is whether the provisions of said sec. 1763, which require the notice therein referred to to be given "at least three months and not more than five months before the expiration of the time of redemption of such sale" is mandatory or merely directory.

We are clearly of the opinion that said provisions are directory and not mandatory and that the certificate owner is not entitled to receive a deed under such certificate until he has given the required notice. It would certainly impair the obligation of the contract to forfeit the plaintiff's right to receive a deed under the law existing at the time said tax sales were made to him, since under that contract he had a lien upon the land or lots which could not be divested by an act of the legislature requiring him to give notice before receiving a deed from the proper officer. Under said statute the service of notice must be made as therein required before the issuance of a tax deed for property sold prior to the taking effect of the act, but that requirement of said section as to service of notice within a fixed period of time was made for the purpose of ending the period in which redemption could be made and not for the purpose of divesting the holder of the tax sale certificate of his right to a deed for all time. In other words, the holder of the tax certificate may give the notice required after the expiration of the three-year period and up to the time it is given the owner may redeem the property from such tax sale.

The judgment must therefore be reversed and the cause remanded for further proceedings in accordance with the views expressed in this opinion. Costs awarded to the appellant.

Truitt, J., concurs.

(December 3, 1914.)

W. R. WILKERSON, as Trustee in Bankruptcy, Respondent, v. MYRTLE F. AVEN, Appellant.

[144 Pac. 1105.]

COMMUNITY PROPERTY—TRUSTEE IN BANKRUPTCY—ACTION TO QUIET
TITLE—STATUTORY CONSTRUCTION.

   1. *Held,* under the facts of this case that the land involved is
the separate property of the wife and not subject to the payment
of the husband's indebtedness.

APPEAL from the District Court of the Seventh Judicial
District for Canyon County. Hon. J. M. Stevens, Presiding
Judge.

Action to quiet title in a trustee in bankruptcy to real
estate standing in the wife's name. Judgment for trustee.
Reversed.

Griffiths & Griffiths and Thomas D. Griffin, for Appellant.

The fact that the husband managed the investment for appellant does not constitute a presumption of community property. The husband could only hold this property in trust
for his wife. (*Title Ins. & Trust Co. v. Ingersoll,* 153 Cal.
1, 94 Pac. 94; *Stickney v. Stickney,* 131 U. S. 227, 9 Sup. Ct.
677, 33 L. ed. 136; *Denny v. Denny,* 123 Ind. 240, 23 N. E.
519; *Chadbourn v. Williams,* 45 Minn. 294, 47 N. W. 812;
Carter v. Becker, 69 Kan. 524, 77 Pac. 264; *Jones v. Davenport,* 44 N. J. Eq. 33, 13 Atl. 652.)

Upon the question of a wife's earnings constituting a part
of her separate estate under an agreement with her husband,
see *Dobbins v. Dexter Horton & Co.,* 62 Wash. 423, 113 Pac.
1088; *Wren v. Wren,* 100 Cal. 276, 38 Am. St. 287, 34 Pac.
775; *Gage v. Gage,* 78 Wash. 262, 138 Pac. 886.

The presumption that property acquired during marriage
is community property may be rebutted. (*Stewart v. Weiser*

Lumber Co., 21 Ida. 340, 121 Pac. 775; *Heney v. Pesoli,* 109 Cal. 53, 41 Pac. 819.)

It is only by giving effect to sec. 2677, Rev. Codes, that sec. 2680, which defines community property, and sec. 4479, which exempts the rents, issues and profits of the wife's separate property and her personal earnings from execution against her husband, can be reconciled. (*Thorn v. Anderson,* 7 Ida. 421, 63 Pac. 592; *Humbird Lumber Co. v. Doran,* 24 Ida. 507, 135 Pac. 66.)

Jackson & Walters, for Respondent Wilkerson.

Where separate property has by investment or otherwise, undergone changes or mutations, as in the case at bar, it is indispensable in order to maintain its separate character that the wife shall trace and identify it, and rebut the presumption that the property acquired during marriage belongs to the community. (*Hamilton Brown Shoe Co. v. Lastinger* (Tex. Civ. App.), 26 S. W. 924; *Morris v. Hastings,* 70 Tex. 26, 8 Am. St. 570, 7 S. W. 649; *Brown v. Lockhart,* 12 N. M. 10, 71 Pac. 1086; *Yesler v. Hochstettler,* 4 Wash. 349, 30 Pac. 398, and cases cited.)

At the time of the purchase of the property involved in this action appellant was a married woman living with her husband, thus raising the presumption that the property so acquired was community property, and placing the burden on the appellant to establish the contrary. (*Humbird Lumber Co. v. Doran,* 24 Ida. 507, 135 Pac. 66; *In re Niccolls Estate,* 164 Cal. 368, 129 Pac. 278.)

SULLIVAN, C. J.—This action was brought by the plaintiff as trustee of the estate of H. B. Aven, a bankrupt, to quiet title to a tract of land consisting of about eleven acres in Orchard Heights Addition to the town of Caldwell, Canyon county. The cause was tried by the court without a jury and findings of fact, conclusions of law and judgment entered in favor of the plaintiff, quieting the title in him as trustee. The appeal is from the judgment.

The principal assignment of error is that the evidence is not sufficient to support findings Nos. 3, 5, 6 and 7.

The evidence shows that the appellant, Myrtle F. Aven, was the wife of the bankrupt H. B. Aven; that they were married in the year 1893; that they lived on a homestead in Deer Flat not far from the town of Caldwell for a period of about nine years, beginning in 1894; that shortly after their marriage the appellant's father gave her $100 in cash which she invested in one cow with a suckling calf, a heifer, three brood sows and a dozen chickens, which were taken to and kept on said homestead; that during that time the husband managed, controlled and cared for said livestock and its increase, selling a part of it at times and accounting to the appellant; that the husband retained the money from the sale of the stock so sold and used the same in the operation of said farm; that after leaving the ranch in about 1903, they took some of the stock with them to Caldwell and kept it there and finally sold the last of it in 1907, some three or four years after they had left the ranch; that after the last of it was sold, a settlement was had between the husband and wife and the amount due appellant was agreed upon; that both husband and wife testified that there was a settlement between them about 1907, and according to their best recollection it was agreed that there was between twelve and thirteen hundred dollars due appellant; that they kept a book part of the time of the amount received from the sales of such property and what it cost to feed the stock; that the cost of the feed was deducted from the price the cattle, hogs, etc., brought; that no other cattle, hogs or chickens were kept on the homestead but those purchased with said $100 and their increase; that the husband began to repay the appellant in small sums; that there was an agreement between them that the appellant should have as her separate property her personal earnings which she might derive from keeping roomers and a part of what she might derive from keeping boarders. and the sums for which said property sold, less the cost of the feed they consumed.

The evidence shows that appellant opened a savings account with the Caldwell Banking & Trust Company, the predecessor in interest of the Caldwell Commercial Bank, on July 24, 1907, and at the time she purchased the land in question, viz., December 27, 1909, she had in that savings account $726.94; that the purchase price of said land was about $1650 and in order to make a cash payment of $1000 at the time she purchased the land, she borrowed $250 from the bank on her note and her husband paid her $50 on the debt he owed her, the appellant later paying the note of $250 to the bank from her savings, and she thereafter mortgaged the land for $650, from the proceeds of which loan she paid the balance of the purchase price. It appears that her said husband signed said mortgage with her. About the time, or shortly after, of removing from the ranch to the town of Caldwell, the husband entered into some kind of merchandising and was engaged in that business up to the 30th day of January, 1912, when he was adjudged to be a bankrupt under the bankrupt laws of the United States. From the time plaintiff's said husband entered into the mercantile business until he was declared a bankrupt, his indebtedness to the bank varied from four to about eight thousand dollars. The cashier of the bank was one of the parties who made the sale of this land to the appellant and knew all about her husband's indebtedness to the bank and her savings account as kept in said bank.

Under that state of facts the question is directly presented as to whether said land was community property and as such whether the trustee in bankruptcy was entitled to take and apply the proceeds thereof in the satisfaction of the bankrupt's indebtedness.

It is provided by sec. 2676, Rev. Codes, that all property owned by the wife before marriage, and that acquired afterward by gift, bequest or descent, or that which she shall acquire with the proceeds of her separate property, shall remain her sole and separate property, to the same extent and with the same effect, as the property of a husband similarly acquired. Sec. 2679 provides that all property owned by the husband before marriage, and that acquired by gift, bequest, devise or descent is his separate property. Sec.

2680 provides that all other property acquired after marriage by either husband or wife, including the rents and profits of the separate property of the husband and wife, is community property, unless by the instrument by which any such property is acquired by the wife it is provided that the rents and profits thereof be applied to her sole and separate use. Sec. 4479 provides for exemptions in favor of a married woman and that all real and personal estate belonging to her at the time of her marriage, or to which she subsequently becomes entitled in her own right, and all rents, issues and profits thereof, and all compensation due and owing her for personal service is exempt from execution against her husband.

Said sections all construed together contemplate that the wife's separate property and the increase thereof cannot be applied to the payment of her husband's debts on execution. A bankruptcy proceeding places the estate of the bankrupt under the control of the law as effectually as it could be placed by an execution or attachment, and clearly the law does not contemplate that the property of a married woman or the rents, issues and profits thereof, can be applied by judicial proceeding in the form of a judgment and execution in the payment of her husband's debts.

The appellant's father gave her $100 in cash and she purchased with it a cow, calf, heifer, three sows and a dozen chickens. That livestock was taken upon the homestead of the appellant and her husband and it was cared for, and its increase, which must have amounted to considerable in twelve or thirteen years, was fed and nurtured on the products raised on the farm, and as we gather from the evidence, the value of the grain and hay fed the stock was deducted from the total sales, and in the settlement between the husband and wife in regard thereto, it was agreed that the wife was entitled to between twelve and thirteen hundred dollars for the money that the husband had received on such sales.

So far as the evidence shows, up to the time she purchased said land in 1909, she had saved from her own earnings with what her husband had paid her on what he owed her, about

$726, and on the day she purchased the land the husband paid her $50 on the indebtedness of between twelve and thirteen hundred dollars. At that time she borrowed from the bank $250 and applied that, together with $750 of her savings account in the bank, in the payment of $1,000 on said land. Thereafter she mortgaged said land for about $650 and·paid the balance of the purchase price therefor from the proceeds of such loan.

It does not appear from the evidence that any fraud or deception was practiced on the bank or on either of the husband's creditors whereby they were induced to give him credit by reason of the appellant's savings account in said bank or by reason of her having purchased said land. There is not a syllable of evidence that tends to show any credit was given to the bankrupt under the representations either from the wife or her husband that said land or said savings account was community property or the property of the husband, and it could not become the property of the husband without some intent on the part of the wife to transfer it to him as and for his property.

In *Title Ins. & Trust Co. v. Ingersoll*, 153 Cal. 1, 94 Pac. 94, it was held that the mere acquirement of the possession of the wife's separate property by the husband and his subsequent management and control of the same, all done with her consent, does not show any intent on the part of the wife to make a gift of such property to the husband or to change its status from separate to community property; that the presumption in such a case appears to be that the property continues to be the separate property of the wife and the husband takes it in trust for his wife.

If the husband borrowed money from the wife, we fail to understand why he would not have as valid a right to pay her the money borrowed as he would to pay any of his creditors, and since it does not appear from the evidence that the husband used either her money in the bank or said land as a basis of credit in his mercantile business, the bank certainly did not give the husband any credit because of the savings deposit of the wife or the land which stood in her name.

Further than that, the bank through its cashier personally made the sale of said land to the appellant, the wife, and not to the husband, and received from her the pay therefor and he knew at the time of the sale just where the thousand dollars came from which was used in making the first payment on the land. And he also knew that the balance of about $650 was raised by giving a mortgage by the wife and husband on said land, and the wife and husband are liable for the payment of said mortgage debt. Certainly if the wife pays it out of her own money, the land ought not to be taken from her and given to the creditors of the husband. If there were any indications of fraud or a conspiracy between the husband and wife to procure credit for the husband because of the property involved, then a very different question would be presented. But everything was done openly and above-board, and the cashier of the bank knew of the husband's indebtedness to the bank and also of the wife's savings account in said bank and where she procured the money to pay the purchase price for said land.

Counsel for the trustee contends that there was such a confusion of property in this case that it works a forfeiture, and that there has been no attempt to trace the separate property of appellant or its proceeds. The evidence does not show that there was any confusion of property. The evidence shows that the husband had no cattle or hogs or chickens on said ranch—that all that were ever kept there were bred from the animals purchased by the wife with the $100 given her by her father. It is true the husband in selling the property was permitted to retain the money, with the understanding that he would account for all of it after deducting the cost of the feed and grain used in feeding such animals. There is no element of confusion in this case.

We therefore hold that the land in dispute is the separate property of the appellant and that the judgment must be reversed and it is so ordered, with directions to the trial court to enter judgment in favor of the appellant in accordance with the views expressed in this opinion.

Costs awarded in favor of appellant.

(December 8, 1914.)

MYRTLE F. AVEN, Appellant, v. CALDWELL COM-
MERCIAL BANK, Respondent.

[144 Pac. 1108.]

Griffiths & Griffiths and Thos. D. Griffin, for Appellant.

Under any state of facts the bank would be estopped to
deny that the person making a deposit is the owner of it.
(*Booth v. Oakland Bank of Savings*, 122 Cal. 19, 54 Pac.
370; 5 Cyc. Law and Proc. 517.)

John C. Rice, for Respondent.

By sec. 2680, Rev. Codes, the rents and profits of the separate property of the husband and wife is community property, unless by the instrument by which any such property
is acquired by the wife, it is provided that rents and profits
thereof be applied to her sole and separate use. (*Howard v.
York*, 20 Tex. 670; *Wolford v. Melton*, 26 Tex. Civ. App.
486, 63 S. W. 543; 21 Cyc. 1647.)

The earnings of the wife while living with the husband are
also community property. (2 Am. & Eng. Ency. of Law, 311;
Wren v. Wren, 100 Cal. 276, 38 Am. St. 287, 34 Pac. 775;
Cooke v. Bremond, 27 Tex. 457, 86 Am. Dec. 626. *In re
Cudworth's Estate*, 133 Cal. 462, 65 Pac. 1041; *Yesler v.
Hochstettler*, 4 Wash. 349, 30 Pac. 398.)

SULLIVAN, C. J.—This case involves the right and title of
the wife to certain money deposited in the defendant bank
by herself, and the contention was made in this case that said
savings deposit was community property and could be applied by the bank on its claim on the husband's indebtedness,
on the theory that the same was community property subject
to the husband's debts.

On the authority of the case of *W. R. Wilkerson, Trustee
in Bankruptcy, Respondent, v. Myrtle F. Aven, Appellant*,
just decided by this court, the judgment entered in this case

must be reversed and the cause remanded with instructions to enter judgment in favor of appellant.

Costs awarded to appellant.

Truitt, J., concurs.

———

(December 17, 1914.)

STATE, Respondent, v. WILLIAM C. JANKS, Appellant.

[144 Pac. 779.]

LARCENY—INFORMATION—POSSESSION OF STOLEN PROPERTY—RECENTLY STOLEN PROPERTY—INSTRUCTIONS.

1. Where the information charges three persons with receiving stolen property, without stating whether the receiving of the same was joint or several, and one of the defendants asks for and receives a separate trial; *held*, that said defendant is not prejudiced by such defect in the information.

2. Any incriminating inference to be drawn from the possession of stolen property is not a presumption of law but is a deduction of fact to be considered by the jury.

3. Unless the fact is undisputed, the question whether stolen property found in the possession of a person has been "recently" stolen should be left to the jury to decide like any other material fact. It is error for the court to instruct the jury that possession of stolen property immediately after the theft is sufficient to warrant a conviction, and especially so where the evidence does not show that the defendant was in the possession of the·property immediately after the theft.

APPEAL from the District Court of the Fourth Judicial District for Twin Falls County. Hon. Chas. O. Stockslager, Judge.

Prosecution for receiving stolen property. Verdict and judgment of conviction. Defendant William C. Janks appeals. Judgment *reversed*.

W. P. Guthrie and J. C. Rogers, for Appellant.

"The inference arising from the possession of stolen property is said to be one of fact, and not of law. It never rises to the dignity of a conclusive presumption." (*State v. Pome-roy*, 30 Or. 16, 46 Pac. 797; *State v. Hodge*, 50 N. H. 510.)

"Even the recent, exclusive, unexplained possession of recently stolen property constitutes a mere circumstance, to be considered by the jury." (*Cooper v. State*, 29 Tex. App. 8, 25 Am. St. 712, 13 S. W. 1011.)

"Possession itself, without evidence tending to show guilty knowledge, could have no tendency to establish guilt." (*Durant v. People*, 13 Mich. 351; *Commonwealth v. Phelps*, 192 Mass. 591, 78 N. E. 741.)

"There is a distinction between possession as evidence of larceny and possession as evidence of unlawful receiving. In the latter offense the possession is held to be no evidence of the guilt of the person receiving them." (10 Ency. of Evidence, 671.)

"But in no case will possession sustain the conviction, on a charge of receiving stolen property." (Wharton's Criminal Law, par. 985; Wharton's Criminal Evidence, 758; *People v. Chambers*, 18 Cal. 383.)

The jury in this case arrived at their verdict by illogically drawing conclusions from assumed and unproven facts, and by reason of the misdirection by the court in giving the law in its instructions and by erroneous rulings upon the admission of evidence. Where error is shown injury is presumed unless the contrary appears affirmatively. (Hayne New Trial and Appeal, Rev. ed., par. 287, p. 1608.)

J. H. Peterson, Attorney General, J. J. Guheen, T. C. Coffin and E. G. Davis, Assistants, for Respondents.

A particular ground of error cannot be urged for the first time on appeal. (*People v. Fitzpatrick*, 80 Cal. 538, 22 Pac. 215.)

Where the information charges three persons with receiving stolen goods without stating whether the receipt was joint or several, but one receipt can be proved, and if the persons receiving were several, but one defendant can be convicted. The failure to allege whether the receipt was joint or several, however, is not a ground for demurrer. (Sec. 988, Bishop's

New Crim. Proc., 2d ed.; *Commonwealth v. Slate*, 11 Gray (Mass.), 60; *State v. Smith*, 37 Mo. 58.)

The unexplained possession of recently stolen property is sufficient to warrant a conviction for receiving stolen goods. (*State v. Weston*, 9 Conn. 527, 25 Am. Dec. 46; *State v. Raymond*, 46 Conn. 345; *Davis v. State*, 50 Mass. 86; *Knickerbocker v. People*, 43 N. Y. 177; *State v. Guild*, 149 Mo. 370, 73 Am. St. 395, 50 S. W. 909; *Goldstein v. People*, 82 N. Y. 231; *Slater v. United States*, 1 Okl. Cr. 275, 98 Pac. 110; *Huggins v. People*, 135 Ill. 243, 25 Am. St. 357, 25 N. E. 1002.)

In Idaho, the possession of recently stolen property raises a presumption of guilt upon the part of the person in possession thereof, unless the circumstances are such as to show in themselves that such possession was innocent. (*State v. Marquardsen*, 7 Ida. 352, 62 Pac. 1034; *State v. Sanford*, 8 Ida. 187, 67 Pac. 492; *State v. Seymour*, 7 Ida. 257, 61 Pac. 1033.)

TRUITT, J.—The defendant, William C. Janks, was convicted in the lower court of the crime of buying and receiving stolen property for his own gain, knowing the same to have been stolen, and was convicted and sentenced to imprisonment in the penitentiary for the term of not less than six months and not more than five years, and to pay the costs of the prosecution. From this judgment and from the order denying the motion for a new trial defendant appeals to this court.

The errors relied upon for the reversal of said judgment of conviction as presented by the brief of appellant are as follows:

"1st. The overruling of the demurrer to the information.

"2d. Overruling defendant's motion to advise the jury to acquit the defendant when the state rested, and refusing to so advise the jury.

"3d. Giving to the jury over defendant's exceptions erroneous instructions.

"4th. The insufficiency of the evidence to justify the verdict.

"5th. Errors in admission of evidence.

"6th.   Error in overruling motion for a new trial."

The statute upon which this prosecution is based is sec. 7057, Rev. Codes, and reads as follows:

"Every person who, for his own gain, or to prevent the owner from again possessing his property, buys or receives any personal property, knowing the same to have been stolen, is punishable by imprisonment in the state prison not exceeding five years, or in the county jail not exceeding six months, or by fine not exceeding one thousand dollars, or by both such fine and imprisonment."

The charging part of the information is as follows:

"The said William C. Janks, Charley Janks, and J. S. Kirkbride, on or about the 18th day of November, 1912, in the county of Twin Falls, state of Idaho, did then and there wilfully, unlawfully, knowingly, and feloniously and for his own gain, buy and receive one red steer, branded half circle six on left ribs, and of the personal property of H. P. Larsen, and one white-faced cow, branded half circle six on left ribs, and of the personal property of said H. P. Larsen, said William C. Janks, Charley Janks and J. S. Kirkbride then and there well knowing the said steer and cow to have been stolen."

The first error named in the foregoing list of errors relied upon by appellant was not urged except as to one point, which is that the information charges three persons with receiving the property jointly, but if the property was not received jointly and one received it from another, then each receiving would constitute a separate offense and could not stand in the same information.   It is claimed that the information should set out how these three persons received the property, that is, whether it was received by them jointly or severally.   This point does not appear to have been raised by the defendant's demurrer to the information in the court below.   The grounds for demurrer, as specifically stated therein, are that the information does not state facts sufficient to constitute a cause of action in this, that the information does not show that the property was stolen before it was received; that it does not show that the property had been

stolen within the jurisdiction of the court; and that it does
not show who stole the property, or from whom the defendants received it. We do not think it necessary to pass upon
the question of whether or not this objection to the information could have been raised by demurrer in the court below
or not, for the record shows that it was not raised there,
and we think it is not such an objection as could be heard
in this court for the first time. Moreover, before the trial
of the cause in the lower court, this defendant asked for and
was granted a separate trial so that we fail to see how he
was in any way prejudiced by this fault or ambiguity in the
information. In order to convict the defendant of buying
and receiving the property described in the information, the
jury must have found that the crime charged was attributable
to him individually. Counsel for appellant have not even
suggested, either in the brief or by oral argument, that the
defendant in the court below was in any manner prejudiced
by this defect or ambiguity in the information. We think
the contention as to this point is without merit.

Substantially the same question is presented by the second
and fourth assignments of error. They both are based upon
the insufficiency of the evidence to convict the defendant,
and we think may for this reason be considered together in
whatever we may feel called upon to say upon the question
presented by them.

The third objection relates to alleged errors of the trial
court in its instructions to the jury. These instructions are
very long, being divided into thirty-three numbered paragraphs and covering thirty-three pages of the transcript.
We mention this because we think it has some bearing upon
the question as to whether a defective instruction or an erroneous instruction is cured by subsequent instructions correcting such defect or error. If there were only a few
tersely stated principles of law given as instructions, there
would be less chance for the jury to be confused or misled,
if the law was not correctly or fully stated in one or more
paragraphs of the first part of the instructions, although subsequently corrected, than where so many are given. The

appellant in the third specification of error argues that the instructions from one to eight, inclusive, were erroneous and prejudicial to the defendant.

The first of these instructions is as follows:

"Instruction No. 1: You are instructed, gentlemen of the jury, that the state must prove beyond a reasonable doubt all of the material allegations of the information which are as follows: First, that the property set forth in the information was stolen; second; that the defendant in this case purchased or received such property of his own knowledge knowing the same to have been stolen; and, third, that such property was purchased or received by the defendants as hereinbefore defined, in the county of Twin Falls, state of Idaho, at the time set forth and alleged in the information herein, to wit: on or about the 18th day of November, 1912: Regarding the first essential herein set forth, to wit: the fact that such property was stolen, it is not essential that the thief must have been convicted or that the name of the person from whom such property was stolen should be proven; and in this connection you are instructed that the larceny of such property, and consequently the fact that such property was stolen, may be proven by the unexplained possession of recently stolen property, this being a fact and circumstance from which the jury may infer that the property was in fact stolen. And you are further instructed that in determining the question of whether the property was stolen you have the right to consider the fact that the possession of recently stolen property is in law a strong incriminating circumstance tending to show such larceny, unless the evidence and the facts and circumstances proved show that such property came honestly into the possession of the one, the evidence may disclose having possession of the same; and you are therefore instructed that the possession of recently stolen property, the possession being unexplained, is a circumstance from which guilt may be inferred; this is especially true where the charge is larceny and is a circumstance you may consider in the charge in this case, in determining the guilt or innocence of the defendants."

It is urged by appellant that this instruction is erroneous in two particulars: (1) It does not correctly state the elements of the crime charged, and omits to mention the question of motive; and (2) because the court invades the province of the jury by that part of the instruction which says: "The larceny of such property and consequently the fact that such property was stolen may be proved by the unexplained possession of recently stolen property." It is elementary and trite to say that there must be a wrongful or wicked motive back of every crime of this character. This statute makes the buying or receiving of any personal property by a person, knowing the same to have been stolen, the motive or gravamen of the crime therein designated. In this instruction the court first assumes to tell the jury specifically what the state must prove in order to convict the defendant of the crime charged in the information, but wholly fails to mention one of the material elements of the crime. If the information had stated no more than this instruction specifies, it would not have stated a crime under the statute, and if the proof at the trial had established the three propositions enunciated by the court beyond a reasonable doubt, it would not be sufficient to convict the defendant. In said section 7057, the crime specified is predicated upon the very element that this instruction omits to give. A person might buy or receive personal property, knowing the same to have been stolen, but unless he buys or receives it "for his own gain or to prevent the owner from again possessing his property," it is not a crime. Concerning the motive necessary to constitute the crime charged in this case, Bishop says: "Some of the statutes require the receiving to be for the 'gain' of the receiver. But in the absence of any term of this sort, the motive of personal gain is not essential; it is enough, for example. that he did it to aid the thief. . . . . Still the intent must be, in some way, fraudulent or corrupt." (2 Bishop, New Criminal Law, sec. 1138.)

Illinois has a statute similar to ours in all its essential provisions, and in *Aldrich v. People,* 101 Ill. 16, which was a prosecution for receiving stolen property, this identical point was presented, and in passing upon it the court said:

"The intent, as in larceny, is the chief ingredient of the offense. Thus, where A authorizes or licenses B to receive property lost or stolen, and B receives the property from the thief knowing it to be stolen, with a felonious intent, he is guilty of a felony in receiving the property, notwithstanding the license. (Wharton, sec. 1891.)

"Under our statute there is another essential fact to be proven—that is, that the defendant, for his own gain, or to prevent the owner from again possessing his property, bought, received or aided in concealing stolen goods. There is no doubt, from the evidence in this case, in regard to the fact that the defendants knew the goods were stolen. Their knowledge is a conceded fact. It is also an undisputed fact that the stolen goods, in passing from the custody of the thieves to Morrow, the agent of the owners, passed through the hands, first, of defendant Isaacs, and, second, through the hands of defendant Aldrich. The question in the case is then narrowed down to this: Whether defendants received the goods for their own gain, or to prevent the owner from again possessing his property. This, in our judgment, is the turning point upon which the decision of the case must hinge."

In this case the judgment was reversed and the case remanded, not because the court failed to instruct as to the point in question but because the proof failed to show that the defendant received the property for his own gain. We think the court in the case at bar erred in omitting to include as one of the elements of the crime that the defendant must have bought or received the property for his own gain or to prevent the owner from again possessing it. But there are two reasons why this error did not prejudice the rights of the defendant, viz.: First, the court in instruction numbered nine clearly stated the three elements of the crime as specified in said sec. 7057, and alleged in the information, and charged the jury that in order to convict the defendant these three elements of the crime must be proved beyond a reasonable doubt; and, second, the testimony clearly proved that if defendant took the property at all, he bought and received it, partly, at least, for his own gain.

In *People v. Morine*, 61 Cal. 367, it was held that, "It is not necessary that each instruction should fully state the law of the case, but any instruction may be helped out and explained by another on the same point; and in such a case the court will look to all the instructions *in pari materia* for the purpose of determining whether the law has been correctly given." In *State v. Marren*, 17 Ida. 766, 107 Pac. 993, after considering an instruction given in that case by the trial court, it is said: "Although the instruction referred to contains matter which should not have been given to the jury, we are, however, of the opinion that the appellant could have been in no way prejudiced by the giving of such instruction." And it has been held by this court in a number of cases that substantial prejudice must be shown in order to constitute reversible error. And unless that can be shown, the case will not be reversed for errors which fall short of that test. We do not think the error complained of in the first objection to the instruction under consideration could have been prejudicial to the defendant under the circumstances of the case and the evidence found in the record. But the second objection urged to said instruction, to the effect that the fact that said property was stolen may be proved by the unexplained possession of *recently stolen* property, presents a more serious question. In the first place, the use of the phrase "*recently stolen*" as applied to the property in question was not warranted by the evidence, and even if it was, it was not proper for the court to decide this matter. The question as to whether, if this property was stolen, it was "*recently stolen*," should have been left to the jury to decide from the evidence in the case, because it has an important bearing upon the question of the guilt of the person found in possession of the stolen property. If the adverb "recently" does not have some bearing on the question of the guilt of the person who has received stolen property, why not just say *in the possession of stolen property?* Why add the limiting adverb as to time if it has no relevancy to the guilt of the person accused? It will be found from an examination of the authorities relating to prosecutions for buying or receiving stolen property, that whether the property was recently stolen, or whether a long time has elapsed since the larceny, makes a very material difference in determining the guilty knowledge of the person having such possession. If the property in a few hours, or in a few days, after it was stolen from its owner, was found in the possession of a person, the presumption that he received it from the thief would usually be much stronger than if it was received weeks or months after the theft. In the case at bar, the time when this property was stolen, if it was stolen, is vague and uncertain. The owner of the property, H. P. Larsen, testified that he was present at the roundup or gathering of his cattle in the fall of 1912, and further said: "I think I had in this gathering the animals whose hides I discovered at this time." But he also testified that he had from 250 to 300 head of cattle. Now it is apparent that in gathering and looking over this number of cattle he might easily be mistaken about seeing these two cattle in the herd at the time he mentions. The hides of the cattle claimed to have been received and slaughtered by the defendant were mainly identified by the brand on them, so there is much uncertainty as to the actual time of the larceny if they were stolen. If the owner did not see them at the 1912 round-up, then the thief, if they were stolen, may have stolen them a year or two before they were delivered at the slaughter-house of the Robinson-Janks Packing Co.

Goldstein v. People, 82 N. Y. 231, is a case relied on to sustain the court's instructions in this case, to the effect that the possession of recently stolen property, unless explained, will warrant a conviction, but the facts were so different in that case from the facts in this case, that we do not think it sustains the point contended for by the state. In that case the court instructed: "That the possession of stolen goods *immediately* after the larceny, *if under peculiar and suspicious circumstances,* when there is evidence tending to show that some other person or persons stole the property, such possession not being satisfactorily explained, would warrant the jury in convicting the accused of receiving stolen goods, knowing them to have been stolen.'' The italics in this instruction are ours for the purpose of distinguishing this instruction from the instructions under consideration in the case at bar.

The facts upon which this instruction was based were given in the opinion of the court as follows: "It was proven by satisfactory evidence that the goods were the property of Morris and had been stolen from him by some persons other than the prisoners. The theft was at once discovered, and upon instant search they were found in a small room of which Bernard Goldstein had the right of temporary possession for a special purpose, adjoining a room occupied by himself and wife, and into which a door from their room opened." And we may gather what was meant by the phrase *"immediately after the larceny"* in said instruction from what the court further said in the opinion: "If the goods came to the possession of the prisoners or either of them, it was within a very short time, an hour or two at most, after the larceny, and as early as 5 o'clock in the morning, and this, with other incidents which happened in its connection were of an unusual character, fully justifying in that respect the hypothesis submitted, of 'peculiar and suspicious circumstances.' " But in this case there is very slight, if any, evidence in the record to support the hypothesis of "peculiar and suspicious circumstances" that was presented to the jury in that case.

But a more weighty objection to this part of the instruction is that the court plainly told the jury that, "You are instructed that the larceny of such property, and consequently the fact that such property was stolen may be proven by the unexplained possession of recently stolen property, this being a fact and circumstance from which the jury may infer that the property was in fact stolen. . . . . You have the right to consider the fact that the possession of recently stolen property is in law a *strong* incriminating circumstance, tending to show such larceny . . . . and you are, therefore, instructed that the possession of recently stolen property, the possession being unexplained, is a circumstance from which guilt may be inferred." And in the third instruction this point is further impressed upon the jury by the court as follows: "Possession of stolen property *immediately* after the theft is sufficient to warrant a conviction. . . . . And in this case if the jury *believe* from the evidence as herein defined, first, that the property was stolen, and further find that the defendant was possessed of such property *soon* after it was stolen, then such *possession* is in *law* a fact tending to show the guilt of defendant, and from which an inference may be drawn tending to show the guilt of the defendant if such possession remains unexplained." The italics are ours. We think these instructions were erroneous and prejudicial to the defendant. In fact, under these instructions, the jury could hardly do otherwise than find a verdict of guilty.

Thompson on Trials, 2d ed., sec. 2536, in discussing the rule as to the presumption arising from the possession of recently stolen property, says:

"This rule, it is perceived, is a branch of the law of *circumstantial evidence;* and the value of a rule which ascribes to a particular circumstance the character of conclusive evidence of guilt, unless rebutted or explained, may well be questioned under a system of trial which commits to the jury in every criminal case the conclusive power of judging of the existence of the criminal intent. The sounder view is, that it is better that twelve men, sitting in the jury box, should apply their collective experience in the affairs of everyday life to such a circumstance, in view of its surroundings, as shown by the evidence, and say whether a conclusion of guilt is to be drawn from it or not. If this view is correct, it must follow that a peremptory instruction, laying down the rule in the language in which it is formulated in the books, must have the effect of depriving them of that independent judgment of the facts, which the law, under our modern system of trial by jury, intends to give them. The sound view is that, whether the recent, unexplained possession of stolen goods is conclusive evidence that the possessor committed the larceny, is a question of fact exclusively for the jury."

In *People v. Chambers*, 18 Cal. 382, it was held that: "It is well settled that the possession of the fruits of a crime is a circumstance to be considered in determining the guilt of the possessor, but the authorities seem to hold that this circumstance is not of itself sufficient to authorize a conviction. . . . . There are many cases in which an explanation would be impossible; and in such cases to throw the burden of explanation upon the accused would be to slam the door of justice in his face. We think the true rule upon the subject is that laid down by Greenleaf in the section referred to. 'It will be necessary,' says he 'for the prosecutor to add the proof of other circumstances indicative of guilt in order to render the naked possession of the thing available toward a conviction.' "

The case of *Askew v. United States*, 2 Okl. Cr. 155, 101 Pac. 121, is a leading case on the question involved in the instructions that we are now considering, and as the point is so fully and ably discussed in the opinion in that case, we quote at length from said opinion as follows:

"The fifth assignment of error presented by appellant is that 'the court erred in its instructions to the jury in the following: "The unexplained possession, if there should be such unexplained possession, of recently stolen property, is *prima facie*, but not conclusive, evidence of his guilt." ' .

"Exception was taken to this charge of the court at the time it was given, and in view of the holding of this court in the case of *Slater v. United States*, 1 Okl. Cr. 275, 98 Pac. 110, in which the opinion was rendered by Chief Justice Furman, it is not considered necessary in presenting this case to do more than call the attention of the court to that case, which held: 'It is error to instruct a jury that the possession of property recently stolen raises a presumption against the party having such possession, which requires an explanation from him; this being a charge upon the weight of the evidence.'

"The case under consideration here is even stronger than that of *Slater v. United States*, for in the case at bar the court instructed the jury that the possession of recently stolen property is *prima facie* evidence of his guilt, whereas, in the Slater case, the trial court in its instructions went no farther than to state that the possession of recently stolen property is a presumption against the party having possession. The court held in the latter case that: 'The effect of this instruction is to inform the jury that the possession of property recently stolen raises a legal presumption of guilt against the party having it in his possession, and that the law requires an explanation from him of such possession. We do not so understand the law. In the case of *Oxier v. United States*, 1 Ind. Ter. 91, 38 S. W. 332, Judge Lewis says: "The later and the sounder and better rule is believed to be that which makes the presumption, arising from the possession of recently stolen property, not a presumption of law, but of fact; in other words, an inference to be drawn or not, as the jury may determine in the light of all the evidence." '

"This court cites with approval in this connection the case of *Blair v. Territory*, 15 Okl. 550, 82 Pac. 653, and holds: 'The instruction complained of was upon the weight of the evidence, which is for the determination of the jury, and was therefore error.'

"It follows, therefore, if the court adheres to the rule laid down in *Slater v. United States*, and the rule therein enunciated by the court seems to be both forceful, and logical, that fatal error was committed by the trial court in giving the jury the instruction complained of under the head of fifth assignment of error, and that this case should be reversed and remanded."

But these authorities are only given to show the rule regarding this question adopted by other courts and the reason therefor, as set out in their opinions, for the question under consideration was before this court in *State v. Seymour*, 7 Ida. 257, 61 Pac. 1033, and in that case the court after considering some other alleged errors in the record said: "The only question remaining is,. Was the possession of the animal by the defendant a felonious possession? The bare possession of property recently stolen is not conclusive evidence of guilt. Especially is this so of property of the kind involved in this case." The property involved in that case was of the same kind as the property involved in this case. In *State v. Sanford,* 8 Ida. 187, 67 Pac. 492, the court said: "The first error assigned is as follows: 'The court erred in his charge to the jury in reference to the possession of recently stolen property—more particularly the words "is a guilty circumstance, and should be considered by you." ' A careful examination of the instruction to which this error apparently refers shows that the instruction was not erroneous. The language used is somewhat unfortunate, but the instruction conveyed to the jury, who could get no different idea therefrom, the rule of law that possession of recently stolen property is a circumstance from which, when unexplained, the guilt of the accused may be inferred." But this case cannot be accepted as authority in support of the instructions under consideration, although it is referred to by respondent in its brief for that purpose. The court told the jury that under the evidence in that case the possession of recently stolen property was a circumstance from which the guilt of the accused may be inferred. But that is very different from telling the jury that, "the possession of stolen property immediately after the theft is sufficient to warrant a conviction," which the court did in the case at bar.

In *State v. Sanford, supra,* the instruction simply said the possession of recently stolen property was a *circumstance,* from which the guilt of the defendant might be *inferred.* The court did not tell the jury that such possession was "in law a fact tending to show the guilt of defendant," or that "possession of stolen property immediately after the theft is sufficient to warrant a conviction." But in this case the jury was instructed that it might *conclude* that the defendant was guilty from the fact of having in his possession recently stolen property. And every time the court used the phrase "recently stolen property" it was assuming a fact as established that should have been left to the jury to decide. The difference in the meaning of the words *inference* and *conclusion* is well known. The Standard dictionary defines these words as follows: "A *conclusion* is the absolute and necessary result of the admission of certain premises; and *inference* is a *probable conclusion* toward which known facts, statements, or admissions point, but which they do not absolutely establish."

Before a defendant can be convicted in a case like this, four things must be established to the satisfaction of the jury beyond a reasonable doubt: (1) That the property was stolen; (2) that either the thief delivered it to the defendant, or to someone else who delivered it to him; (3) That at the time the defendant received the possession of the property he knew it was stolen, or that it was received under such circumstances that any reasonable person of ordinary observation would have known that it was in fact stolen property; and (4) that he received it for his own gain or to prevent the owner from again possessing it.

The second and fourth assignments of error presented by appellant are based upon the insufficiency of the evidence to convict the defendant, and as we have heretofore stated in this opinion, these assignments of error may be considered together. But we do not deem it necessary in deciding the case to go into an extensive review of the testimony in the record as we think there was prejudicial error in the instructions which we have considered. However, we may say that the initial and vital point in order to convict the defendant, namely, that the property was *stolen*, has very meager support from the evidence. Karl Falk was the most important witness on this point in the case. He testified that twenty-three head of cattle were brought to the slaughter-yards of the Robinson-Janks Packing Co. on Sunday evening, November 17, 1912, by one Frank Dolen. The cattle were received by Falk, Charley Janks and J. S. Kirkbride. The defendant was not there when they were received. There is no evidence that Dolen had stolen these cattle, or that he had received them from the thief if they were stolen. Dolen never seems to have been charged with the larceny of this property, and he did not act like a guilty man so far as the record shows, for Falk says he saw him in the office of said packing company on December 7, 1912, which was about twenty days after he delivered these cattle to the packing company. It is only claimed that two head of these cattle were stolen, and a number of different ways may readily be suggested to account for them being there without any criminal act or intent on the part of Dolen.

But without directly holding the evidence as to whether or not said property was in fact stolen insufficient to support the verdict of the jury, we think there was reversible error in the instructions of the court on the point that we have considered. The judgment must, therefore, be reversed and a new trial ordered.

Sullivan, C. J., concurs.

(May 11, 1914.)

ZACHARIAH MONTGOMERY, Respondent, v. G. R. GRAY, Appellant.

[144 Pac. 646.]

VERDICT—EVIDENCE——SUFFICIENCY OF—EXCESSIVE DAMAGES—INSTRUCTIONS.

    1. *Held*, that the evidence is sufficient to sustain the verdict.

    2. *Held*, that there is no evidence indicating that the verdict was rendered under the influence of passion and prejudice.

    3. *Held*, that the court did not err in giving or refusing to give certain instructions.

APPEAL from the District Court of the Eighth Judicial District for Bonner County. Hon. John M. Flynn, Judge.

Action to recover the value of certain timber alleged to have been sold and delivered to the defendant. Judgment for plaintiff. *Affirmed.*

Allen & Allen and Ezra R. Whitla, for Appellant.

E. W. Wheelan and O. J. Bandelin, for Respondent.

Counsel cite no authorities on points decided.

SULLIVAN, J.—This action was brought to recover the sum of $3,769.80 alleged to be the value of certain timber sold by the plaintiff, who is respondent here, to the defendant, who is appellant here. The written contract under which the sale of said timber was made is attached to the complaint and made a part thereof, where it is agreed, among other things, that the appellant shall have three years in which to cut and remove all of the merchantable timber on said land and that the payments under the contracts were to be made thirty days after each carload of timber was shipped.

The answer put in issue many of the allegations of the complaint, and the cause was tried by the court with a jury and resulted in a verdict in favor of the plaintiff for $1732.31 with interest at 7% from August 18, 1909, on which verdict a judgment was entered for that amount.

A motion for a new trial was denied and the appeal is from the order denying a new trial.

A number of errors are assigned, going to the sufficiency of the evidence to justify the verdict, excessive damages given under the influence of passion and prejudice, and the admission and rejection of certain testimony offered, and the giving and refusing to give certain instructions.

The main controversy arises over the amount of timber taken from said land by the defendant. The defendant took possession of the half section of land on which said timber stood, and, as we view the contract, it was incumbent upon him to scale the logs or measure the timber taken from said tract of land, which he failed to do.

No good purpose can be served in this opinion by analyzing the vast amount of testimony given on the trial, but we are satisfied that the verdict of the jury is fully sustained by the evidence and that the verdict was not given under the influence of passion or prejudice. We find no prejudicial error in the record made by the trial court in the admission or rejection of evidence, nor in the giving or refusing to give certain instructions. The instructions given fairly cover the law of the case as based on the evidence, and the court did not err in refusing to grant a new trial because of newly discovered evidence.

The judgment is therefore affirmed and it is so ordered, with costs in favor of respondent.

Ailshie, C. J., concurs.

(December 17, 1914.)

ON REHEARING.

[144 Pac. 646.]

CONFLICT IN EVIDENCE—DISCRETION OF TRIAL COURT—CUMULATIVE EVIDENCE—ORDINARY DILIGENCE.

.1. Where there is a substantial conflict in the evidence, the verdict of the jury will not be disturbed on appeal.

2. The granting or denying of a new trial rests in the sound discretion of the trial court.

3. Where affidavits filed in support of a motion for a new trial contain a recital of such alleged facts as are merely cumulative, or it clearly appears that the facts contained in the affidavits might have been, by the exercise of ordinary diligence, procured at the trial, the trial court will be justified upon that ground, if upon no other, in denying the motion for a new trial.

BUDGE, J.—On the 25th day of March, 1914, the above entitled cause was by counsel for the respective parties argued, submitted, and by the court taken under advisement. Thereafter, on the 11th day of May, 1914, the court announced its opinion, in which the judgment of the trial court was affirmed.

On the 3d day of June, 1914, a petition for rehearing was filed by the appellant herein, which said petition was on the 13th day of June, 1914, granted. On the 8th day of December, 1914, at the regular term of said court sitting at Coeur d'Alene, said cause was reargued and by the court taken under advisement.

We have carefully considered the questions submitted in this case. There are possibly two additional propositions involved that might be briefly mentioned in connection with the final determination of this cause. From a careful reading of the record it is apparent to us that there is a serious conflict in the testimony of the witnesses, particularly with reference to the amount and kind of timber that was upon the land of the plaintiff, at the time the contract upon which this action was brought was entered into between the parties to this litigation. Where there is a substantial conflict in the evidence the verdict of the jury will not be disturbed upon appeal. (*Baker v. First National Bank,* 25 Ida. 651, 139 Pac. 565; *Tilden v. Hubbard,* 25 Ida. 677, 138 Pac. 1133; *Henry Gold Mining Co. v. Henry,* 25 Ida. 333, 137 Pac. 523; *Hufton v. Hufton,* 25 Ida. 96, 136 Pac. 605.)

We have considered the affidavits filed by the appellant in support of his motion for a new trial, and we are unable to reach the conclusion that the trial court erred in denying counsel's motion for a new trial. The granting or denying of a new trial rests in the sound discretion of the trial court, and where the affidavits filed in support of the motion contain a recital of such alleged facts as are merely cumulative, or it clearly appears that the facts contained in the affidavits might have been, by the exercise of ordinary diligence, procured at or prior to the trial of the cause, the trial court would be justified, if upon no other ground, in denying the motion for a new trial.

The instructions given to the jury by the court in this case, when considered together and as a whole, fairly and correctly state the law of the case.

We therefore hold that the conclusion reached in the original opinion in this case must be affirmed, and it is so ordered, with costs of this appeal in favor of respondent.

Sullivan, C. J., and Truitt, J., concur.

(December 19, 1914.)

STATE, Respondent, v. JOHN BOGRIS, Appellant.

[144 Pac. 789.]

LARCENY OF CHECKS FROM PAYEE—EVIDENCE—ADMISSIBILITY OF TO
PROVE HANDWRITING—INSTRUCTIONS—BURDEN OF PROOF IN DEFENSE
OF ALIBI—CONSIDERATION OF NECESSITY FOR INTERPRETER IN PRES-
ENCE OF JURY—IMPEACHMENT OF DEFENDANT'S TESTIMONY—POSSES-
SION OF RECENTLY STOLEN PROPERTY.

1. Upon a prosecution for larceny of a check for a certain amount
of money, no proof of actual value is required, according to the
provisions of sec. 7053, Rev. Codes, as the law presumes that the
face value of the check is the actual value.

2. In a prosecution for the larceny of certain checks it is not
incumbent upon the state, for the purpose of establishing the value
of the checks stolen, to offer proof of their due execution by the
payer, or to prove the fact that they were never endorsed by the
payee.

3. *Held*, that Exhibits "A" and "B," consisting of checks charged
to have been stolen by the defendant in this case, and to have been
endorsed by him with the name of the payee, were admitted in evidence in the first instance, not for the purpose of comparison of
handwriting, but for the purpose of establishing the crime committed.

4. The question, whether or not a witness requires an interpreter,
is a question for the court, and where counsel for defendant neglects
to request the court to pass upon this question without the presence
of the jury, he cannot afterward assign as error the action of the
court in not excusing the jury while this matter was being considered.

5. The state cannot be deprived of the right to cross-examine a
witness by the mere statement that such witness does not speak the
English language; and, if it is afterward established that such witness speaks and understands the English language, he is estopped
from taking any advantage of his conduct in asserting his inability
to speak and understand said language.

6. Where the court instructs the jury to the effect that if any
witness wilfully testified falsely as to any material fact, the jury
were at liberty to disregard the entire testimony of such witness, except in case his testimony should be corroborated by other and reliable witnesses, the testimony of defendant having been impeached
by the prosecution, but it appearing, so far as the record shows, that

such instruction applied generally to all of the witnesses testifying in the case, the giving of such instruction was not error.

7. The following instruction, "Where the state proved such a case as would sustain a verdict of guilty, and the defendant then offers evidence, the burden of proof is on said defendant to make out his defense, and when the proof is all introduced then the primary question is, in the light of all the evidence, is the defendant guilty beyond a reasonable doubt," is not prejudicial to the defendant, by merely making it incumbent upon him to offer sufficient proof to raise a reasonable doubt in the minds of the jury as to his guilt.

8. If the defendant relies upon an *alibi* for the defense the burden of establishing such *alibi* is upon him. (*State v. Webb*, 6 Ida. 428, 55 Pac. 892, cited and approved.)

9. In giving the following instruction, the trial court did not trespass upon the right of the jury to pass upon all questions of fact, in accordance with the provisions of subd. 6, sec. 7855, Rev. Codes:

"You are further instructed that if you believe from the evidence beyond a reasonable doubt that the property described in the information was stolen and that the defendant was found in the possession of the property after it was stolen, then such possession is, in law, a strong, incriminating circumstance, tending to show the guilt of the defendant unless the evidence and the facts and circumstances thereunder show that he may have come honestly in possession of the same.

"In this connection I further instruct you that if you find from the evidence beyond a reasonable doubt that the property described in the information was found in the possession of the defendant, then in determining whether or not the defendant is guilty you should take into consideration all of the circumstances attending such possession."

10. The possession of recently stolen property is a circumstance from which, when unexplained, the guilt of the accused may be inferred. (*State v. Sanford*, 8 Ida. 187, 67 Pac. 492, cited and approved.)

11. *Held*, that no error was committed by the trial court in the giving of instructions in this case or refusal to give certain instructions offered by the defendant.

APPEAL from the District Court of the First Judicial District for the County of Shoshone. Hon. W. W. Woods, Judge.

Conviction for the crime of grand larceny. Defendant appeals. *Affirmed.*

Chas. E. Miller and W. W. Bixby, for Appellant.

Proof of handwriting by comparison with other handwriting not relevant to any issue, aside from similarity with that in question, is not permissible under the laws of Idaho. (Wharton's Criminal Evidence, sec. 555; *Castor v. Bernstein,* 2 Cal. App. 703, 84 Pac. 244; *Moore v. United States,* 91 U. S. 270, 23 L. ed. 346; *Bane v. Gwinn,* 7 Ida. 439, 63 Pac. 634.)

A witness cannot be impeached on collateral matters, or upon matters not at all material to the issue. (Wharton's Criminal Ev., secs. 482–484; *Hilbert v. Spokane etc. R. R. Co.,* 20 Ida. 54, 60, 116 Pac. 1116; *Western Union Oil Co. v. Newlove,* 145 Cal. 772, 79 Pac. 542; *State v. Deal,* 41 Or. 437, 70 Pac. 532.)

If, by proof of an *alibi,* a defendant is able to raise a reasonable doubt as to his being at a certain place about the time in question he is entitled to an acquittal. (*State v. Conway,* 55 Kan. 323, 40 Pac. 661; *People v. Dick,* 32 Cal. 213; *State v. Mackey,* 12 Or. 154, 6 Pac. 648; *State v. Porter,* 74 Iowa, 623, 38 N. W. 514; *Deggs v. State,* 7 Tex. App. 359.)

The judge must not charge the jury in respect to matters of fact, and, besides, does not state the law correctly in instruction No. 6. (*State v. Walters,* 7 Wash. 246, 34 Pac. 938, 1098; *State v. Bliss,* 27 Wash. 463, 68 Pac. 87.)

The presumption that the person found in possession of recently stolen property is the thief, is not a presumption of law, but one of fact. There is no legal rule on the subject; but much depends on the nature of the property stolen and the circumstances of each particular case. (*Smith v. State,* 58 Ind. 340; *State v. Hodge,* 50 N. H. 510; *State v. Jennett,* 88 N. C. 665; *Stover v. People,* 56 N. Y. 315; *Bellamy v. State,* 35 Fla. 242, 17 So. 560; *Ingalls v. State,* 48 Wis. 647, 4 N. W. 785; *Jones v. State,* 26 Miss. 247; *State v. Pomeroy,* 30 Or. 16, 46 Pac. 797; *State v. Walker,* 41 Iowa, 217; *People v. Fagan,* 66 Cal. 534, 6 Pac. 394; *Considine v. United States,* 112 Fed. 342, 50 C. C. A. 272.)

The burden of proof does not shift on the establishing of a *prima facie* case by the state, but continues on the state throughout the trial and until the verdict is rendered, and defendant's guilt is established beyond a reasonable doubt. (12 Cyc. 379; *People v. Perini*, 94 Cal. 573, 29 Pac. 1027; *State v. Schweitzer*, 57 Conn. 532, 18 Atl. 787, 6 L. R. A. 125; *Trogdon v. State*, 133 Ind. 1, 32 N. E. 725; *State v. Brady* (Iowa), 91 N. W. 801; *People v. McWhorter*, 93 Mich. 641, 53 N. W. 780; *State v. Hardelein*, 169 Mo. 579, 70 S. W. 130; *Davis v. State*, 54 Neb. 177, 74 N. W. 599; *People v. Downs*, 123 N. Y. 558, 25 N. E. 988; *State v. Carland*, 90 N. C. 668; *Turner v. Commonwealth*, 86 Pa. St. 54, 27 Am. Rep. 683; *Agnew v. United States*, 165 U. S. 36, 17 Sup. Ct. 235, 41 L. ed. 624.)

J. H. Peterson, Attorney General, T. C. Coffin, and E. G. Davis, Assistants, for Respondent.

Prima facie the value of a check which has become the subject of larceny is the amount of money for which it passed current, or its face value. (*State v. Hinton*, 56 Or. 428, 109 Pac. 24; *Pyland v. State*, 36 Tenn. (4 Sneed) 357; *State v. Collins*, 49 La. Ann. 1198, 22 So. 357; *Peterson v. State*, 6 Ga. App. 491, 65 S. E. 311; *Whalen v. Commonwealth*, 90 Va. 544, 19 S. E. 182; Rev. Codes, sec. 7053.)

Exemplars of handwriting are admissible in evidence for the sole purpose of comparison with handwriting which is in dispute, when the exemplar is admitted to be genuine or is proved to be such to the satisfaction of the judge. (*Bane v. Gwinn*, 7 Ida. 439, 63 Pac. 634; *State v. Seymour*, 10 Ida. 699, 79 Pac. 825 (dissenting opinion); *Colonel Algernon Sydney's Case*, 9 How. St. Tr. 818; *Horne Tooke's Case*, 25 How. St. Tr. 19; *University of Illinois v. Spalding*, 71 N. H. 163, 51 Atl. 731, 62 L. R. A. 817; 15 Am. & Eng. Ency. of Law, 270 (note 2); *Baker v. Haines*, 6 Whart. (Pa.) 284, 36 Am. Dec. 224; *Moody v. Rowell*, 17 Pick. (Mass.) 490, 28 Am. Dec. 317; *Smith v. Hanson*, 34 Utah, 171, 96 Pac. 1087, 18 L. R. A., N. S., 520.)

When the natural and adequate mode of expression of the defendant, in a criminal action, is not intelligible, he is entitled to an interpreter. In each instance, whether this need exists, is to be determined by the court. (Wigmore on Evidence, sec. 811.)

It is within the sound discretion of the court to allow the state to inquire into the necessity for an interpreter, when the court has reason to feel that he has been imposed upon. (3 Ency. of Evidence, 807.)

All the instructions upon a particular point must be considered together in determining whether or not an instruction is misleading. (*People v. Bernard*, 2 Ida. 193, 10 Pac. 30; *State v. Bond*, 12 Ida. 424, 86 Pac. 43.)

Where instructions fully and fairly state the law upon the questions involved it is not error for the court to refuse further instructions requested by the state or the defendant. (*United States v. Camp*, 2 Ida. 231, 10 Pac. 226; *State v. O'Neil*, 24 Ida. 582, 135 Pac. 60.)

When the state has proved such a case as would sustain a verdict of guilty, that is to say, has proved its case to the satisfaction of the jury beyond a reasonable doubt, and the defendant offers evidence, the burden is upon him to prove facts sufficient to create, in the minds of the jury, a reasonable doubt as to his guilt. (2 Thompson on Trials, 2d ed., sec. 2436, p. 1708; *State v. Thornton*, 10 S. D. 349, 73 N. W. 196, 41 L. R. A. 530; 2 Am. & Eng. Ency. of Law, 56; *Flanagan v. People*, 214 Ill. 170, 73 N. E. 347; *State v. Howell*, 100 Mo. 628, 14 S. W. 4; *Cochran v. State*, 113 Ga. 726, 39 S. E. 332; *Kirksey v. State*, 11 Ga. App. 142, 74 S. E. 902; *Commonwealth v. Choate*, 105 Mass. 451; *Wilburn v. Territory*, 10 N. M. 402, 62 Pac. 968; *State v. Maher*, 74 Iowa 77, 37 N. W. 2; *State v. Brauneis*, 84 Conn. 222, 79 Atl. 70; *State v. Reitz*, 83 N. C. 634; *State v. Jackson*, 36 S. C. 487, 31 Am. St. 890, 15 S. E. 559; *Pate v. State*, 94 Ala. 14, 10 So. 665; *State v. Waterman*, 1 Nev. 543; *State v. Lee*, 1 Boyce (Del.), 18, 74 Atl. 4; *State v. Webb*, 6 Ida. 428–435, 55 Pac. 892.)

The unexplained possession of recently stolen property is a circumstance tending to incriminate the accused, and where the jury believe that the accused had possession of recently stolen property and the accused denied such possession, the same rule is true. (*People v. Fagan*, 66 Cal. 534, 6 Pac. 394;

State v. Graves, 72 N. C. 482; *State v. Drew,* 179 Mo. 315,
101 Am. St. 474, 78 S. W. 594; *Goldstein v. People,* 82 N. Y.
231; *State v. Marquardsen,* 7 Ida. 352, 62 Pac. 1034; *State
v. Sanford,* 8 Ida. 187, 67 Pac. 492.)

BUDGE, J.—The defendant and appellant herein was, on
the 2d day of May, 1914, convicted of the crime of grand
larceny in the district court of the first judicial district in and
for Shoshone county, and on the 5th day of May, 1914, was
sentenced to serve an indeterminate term of imprisonment in
the state penitentiary for not less than one nor more than
fourteen years. This appeal is from the judgment and from
the order overruling defendant's motion for a new trial.

The facts in this case, briefly stated, are about as follows:
John Bogris, the defendant below and appellant here, together with his brother Tony Bogris, George Paragos, Anton
Chukas, Gust Drakos and Pete Drakos, comprised a section
gang employed by the Chicago, Milwaukee & St. Paul Railway Company at Falcon, Shoshone county. On the night of
December 26, 1913, George Paragos was employed as a track
walker by said railway company, and his duty as such track
walker required him to walk one and one-half miles east
and three and one-half miles west of the section-house where
these men lived. Paragos began work at 6 o'clock in the evening and finished at 5 o'clock in the morning. On this evening when Paragos went to work his suitcase was under the
bed in the room where he slept, and where all of the other
employees slept, with the exception of Tony Bogris, who was
the section foreman, and had a separate room in the same
shack or building.

At 5 o'clock in the morning when Paragos came off duty and
reached the bunk-house he found his coemployees already up,
and learned from them that a burglary had been committed
during the night; that two suitcases, one of which belonged
to Paragos, and two pairs of trousers, one of which belonged
to the appellant, had been stolen. A search was instituted,
tracks were followed, and later the two suitcases were found
at the bake-house near the section-house in which these men

lived. Both of the suitcases had been cut open and three
pay checks belonging to George Paragos had been taken from
his suitcase. The trousers were subsequently found, and
there was testimony to the effect that the pockets of the same
were cut and that certain moneys were taken therefrom.

The pay checks in question had been delivered to Paragos
by the Chicago, Milwaukee & St. Paul Railway Company for
wages earned during the months of October and November,
and either September or August, and were for the following
amounts, $62.37, $52.30 and $43.90, respectively. At the time
of the theft of these checks they were not indorsed.

On February 7, 1914, about forty-three days after the
checks were stolen, John Bogris, the defendant below and
appellant here, went to Missoula, Montana, arriving there in
the evening. Practically at the same time that Bogris reached
Missoula, Warren R. Shopp cashed two pay checks of the Chicago, Milwaukee & St. Paul Railway Company, one for $62.37
and the other for $43.90. Upon the trial of this cause Shopp
identified Bogris as the man who presented the checks to him
and who indorsed the same by writing thereon the name of
Paragos, the complaining witness. At the same time that
the two checks above referred to were cashed, Shopp was
asked by the same party to cash a third check of like kind,
which, however, was not cashed, for the reason, as stated by
Shopp, that he did not have sufficient money on hand in his
place of business to cash the third check. Thereafter the defendant was arrested and charged by the information of the
county prosecuting attorney with the crime of grand larceny.

Upon the trial of the cause the state offered in evidence,
and the same were admitted over appellant's objection, pay
checks of the Chicago, Milwaukee & St. Paul Railway Company, marked State's Exhibits "A" and "B," which checks
were identified by the witness Shopp as being the identical
checks that he cashed for the defendant. The state also
offered in evidence Exhibit "D," over the objection of appellant, which was a pay check of a similar kind that had been
given by Paragos to the defendant a short time prior to the

theft of the checks in question for the purpose of having the same cashed, and which Paragos had directed the defendant to indorse by writing the name "G. Paragos" on said time check, which appellant did, and thereafter presented the same to the manager of the Western Commissary Company at Avery, Idaho, who cashed the same.

The state, for the purpose of proving that the indorsements on the back of the checks Exhibits "A" and "B" were made by the defendant, and to corroborate the testimony of Shopp, introduced Exhibit "D"; and to further identify the indorsements upon Exhibits "A" and "B" the state offered, and was permitted to introduce, a trip pass issued by the Chicago, Milwaukee & St. Paul Railway Company and used by the defendant on his trip from Falcon, Idaho, to Missoula, Montana. The signature upon the trip pass was positively identified by D. L. McKay, as well as by other witnesses, as the signature of the defendant. The pass was in regular form and marked State's Exhibits "E," "F" and "G." The payrolls of the Chicago, Milwaukee & St. Paul Railway Company for the months of September and November were shown to the defendant prior to the trial, who identified his signature thereon. These payrolls were also offered by the state and admitted, marked State's Exhibits "H" and "H-1." The purpose that the state's attorney had in introducing these various exhibits was to prove that the indorsements on Exhibits "A" and "B" were in the handwriting of the appellant. To the introduction of all of these exhibits, heretofore referred to, the able counsel for appellant objected and assigned the same as error. There are numerous assignments of error to the introduction of these exhibits, which we will not undertake to discuss separately, because we think they might all be considered together, and we will so discuss them.

The first contention made by counsel for appellant is that Exhibits "A" and "B" should not have been admitted in evidence without proof of their execution and genuineness. Sec. 7053, Rev. Codes, provides:

"If the thing stolen consists of any evidence of debt, or other written instrument, the amount of money due thereupon, or secured to be paid thereby, and remaining unsatisfied, or which in any contingency might be collected thereon, or the value of the property the title to which is shown thereby, or the sum which might be recovered in the absence thereof, is the value of the thing stolen."

We think the general rule to be, that when the larceny of a certain check for a certain amount of money is charged, no proof of the actual value is required, the law presuming that the face value is the actual value. In this instance there was no question so far as the value of these checks to the thief was concerned, who experienced little trouble in procuring the face value of the same. For the purpose of establishing the value of the checks stolen, we do not think that it was incumbent upon the state to offer proof of their due execution by the officers of the company by whom they were issued; neither was it necessary for the state to prove the fact that they were never indorsed by the payee.

The serious question for our consideration is what we will designate as the remaining four assignments of error, which all go to the introduction of the exhibits mentioned for the purpose of comparison of handwriting, Exhibits "A" and "B" being the checks cashed at Missoula, Exhibit "D" being the check cashed by the appellant at the request of Paragos, Exhibits "E," "F" and "G" being the railroad pass on which appellant traveled to Missoula, Montana, and Exhibits "H" and "H-1' being the payrolls.

In the case of *Bane v. Gwinn*, 7 Ida. 439, 63 Pac. 634, this court said:

"In this state, in an action involving the genuineness of a signature, only such papers as are admitted in evidence in the case for *other purposes*, and such as are *admitted to be genuine*, should, except in very exceptional cases, be admitted for the purpose of comparison." (See, also, *State v. Seymour*, 10 Ida. 699, 79 Pac. 825.)

Exhibits "A" and "B" were admitted in this case in the first instance, not for the purpose of comparison of handwriting, but for the purpose of establishing the crime committed. It was the only method that could be adopted in order to prove whether or not the crime of larceny had been committed, and if so, whether it was grand or petit larceny. It therefore follows that Exhibits "A" and "B" were properly admitted for this purpose, and once being properly admitted, become competent evidence for all purposes.

The indorsement on Exhibit "D" made by the defendant was admitted by him to have been made, as testified to by the state's witnesses, also the signature written upon Exhibits "E," "F" and "G," the railroad pass, was not denied. This signature of defendant was positively identified by the witness McKay, and when compared by the witness, Milton J. Flohr, Vice-President of the First National Bank of Wallace (who from the testimony appears to have occupied the position of cashier and Vice-President for approximately nineteen years) with Exhibits "A" and "B," as well as the other exhibits mentioned, such witness testified that all of the indorsements made upon said exhibits were made by one and the same person.

As stated in the case of *Baker v. Haines*, 6 Whart. (Pa.) 284, 36 Am. Dec. 224: "We conceive it to be very material that strict proof of the genuine or test paper should be first given; that no reasonable doubt should remain on that point; and nothing short of evidence of a person who saw him write the paper, or an admission of being genuine, or evidence of equal certainty, should be received for that purpose."

It would seem to us, taking all of the testimony into consideration touching the admissibility of these exhibits which were offered for the purpose of comparison, it was proven to the satisfaction of the trial judge conclusively that the signature upon these exhibits was genuine, and that it was the signature of the defendant.

In the case of *Bane v. Gwinn*, 7 Ida. 439, 63 Pac. 634, this court, speaking through Chief Justice Huston, says:

"We are inclined, in the absence of any statute establishing a different rule, to hold with the lower court upon this proposition; although we think occasions may arise where the latitude of the rule should be extended."

We think this case could be well said to come under the above rule, this being a case where the checks that had been stolen were the subject of the larceny and were the property of the complaining witness and offered in explanation and confirmation of his testimony. The proof of the larceny might have been sustained in the absence of the indorsements, and had it been established by the state beyond a reasonable doubt that the defendant stole the checks, even though he had not indorsed the same, still he would have been guilty of the crime of larceny. There is nothing in the record that is seriously in contradiction of the testimony to the effect that the defendant indorsed Exhibits "A" and "B," offered and received in evidence in this case, and that he secured the money represented by the checks.

We have therefore reached the conclusion that the exhibits were properly introduced and that the court committed no error in permitting the same to be used in the trial of this cause for the purpose of comparison of handwriting.

Defendant's counsel complains and assigns as error the action of the court in permitting the county attorney to call certain witnesses during the trial for the purpose of proving that the appellant did not require the services of an interpreter. It appears from the record that when the defendant was called as a witness on his own behalf and was requested by his counsel to be seated, he made the remark that he "did not understand," whereupon the court asked the following question: "This man wants an interpreter?" to which the county attorney responded that "he does not need an interpreter; he talks English," and to which defendant's counsel replied, "I always talked to him through an interpreter. He does not talk English to me," and to which the court responded, "Well, call Tony." Witness Tony had theretofore been used as an interpreter during the trial of the cause. Later on the county attorney, in the course of the trial, called three witnesses who testified in substance that the appellant talked the English language without any impediment, except the foreign accent common to all persons of his nationality. It may have been, possibly would have been, the better prac-

tice had this testimony been offered without the hearing of
the jury. The question of whether or not the witness required an interpreter was a question for the court, but counsel
for appellant failed to request the court to pass upon this
question without the presence of the jury, and we do not believe that any substantial right of the defendant was jeopardized by reason of the action of the court in this respect.
When counsel for defendant takes the position that his client
is unable to speak the English language, he puts in issue that
question and it is subject to contradiction. The state cannot
be deprived of the right to cross-examine a witness by the
mere statement that he does not speak the English language,
and if it is afterward established that he does speak the English language and that he understands it, he cannot take
advantage of his conduct in this respect and secure any advantage in this court.

In this connection counsel for the defendant complains of
instruction No. 10, which is to the effect that "if any witness
wilfully testified falsely as to any material fact you (the jury)
are at liberty to disregard the entire testimony of such witness," etc., except his testimony be corroborated by other and
reliable witnesses. Counsel urges that the jury applied this
instruction to the testimony offered by the state touching the
knowledge or lack of knowledge upon the part of the defendant of the English language, and that being an immaterial
issue in the case, and there being no further explanation of
this instruction made by the court, the defendant suffered
thereby. We do not think, in view of all the instructions
given by the court, that the jury could possibly have taken that
view of this instruction, but considered and applied this instruction generally to all of the witnesses who testified for the
defendant and the state. No doubt had counsel for defendant
offered an instruction in explanation of the one given by the
court the same would have been given. Having failed to do
so, he ought not to be heard to complain.

Counsel for appellant assigns as error the conduct of the
prosecuting attorney in making the following statement to
the jury: "The convincing fact is that the three checks were

cashed in Missoula when the defendant was there.'' From
the record this is absolutely established. The checks were
cashed in Missoula, the very evening, and within a very short
time after the defendant arrived there. The county attorney
did not say that these checks were cashed by the defendant,
but did say that the checks were cashed in Missoula when the
defendant was there. There is no merit in this contention.

We will next consider propositions 5 and 7 of appellant's
brief, which attack instruction No. 8 as given by the court
at the request of the state, and involve the question of the
burden of proof, which is as follows:

''Where the state proved such a case as would sustain a
verdict of guilty, and the defendant then offers evidence, the
burden of proof is on said defendant to make out his defense,
and when the proof is all introduced then the primary question is, in the light of all the evidence, is the defendant guilty
beyond a reasonable doubt.''

The appellant contends that under this instruction the burden of proof was shifted from the state to the defendant.
We do not so understand the instruction. As we construe the
instruction, the court says that it is incumbent upon the state
to prove the defendant guilty beyond a reasonable doubt, and
when the state has done that, if the defendant offers proof in
support of his defense of *alibi,* it is incumbent upon him to
introduce such proof, not to establish the *alibi* beyond a reasonable doubt, but merely to offer sufficient proof to raise a
reasonable doubt in the minds of the jury as to his guilt. As
stated in sec. 2436, Thompson on Trials, 2 ed., vol. 2, p. 1708:

''The burden of proving it (an *alibi*) certainly cannot be
upon the State; and if it does not rest upon the defendant,
upon whom does it rest? Certainly not on the judge or the
court crier. The courts which so reason seem to forget that
the *burden* of proof—which is merely another name for the
necessity of proof—is one thing, and that the *quantum* of
evidence to sustain the burden is another thing. Certainly
the burden of establishing this defense is upon the defendant,
in spite of all the casuistry by means of which judges have
led themselves to the contrary conclusion. Suppose the de-

fendant is indicted for a crime committed at a given date in St. Louis, and his defense is that on that date he was in Chicago. If he is not to prove this, by whom is it to be proved? Is the State to undertake the task of proving that he was not in ten thousand different places at the time when the crime was committed? But upon the most unshaken grounds, this burden is sustained, and an adequate *quantum* of proof produced by the defendant, when he succeeds in raising a reasonable doubt in the minds of the jurors as to whether or not he was at the place of the crime when it was committed." (*State v. Thornton*, 10 S. D. 349, 73 N. W. 196; 41 L. R. A. 530.)

"The true doctrine seems to be that where the state has established a *prima facie* case, and the defendant relies upon the defense of *alibi*, the burden is upon him to prove it, not beyond a reasonable doubt, nor by a preponderance of the evidence, but by such evidence, and to such a degree of certainty, as will, when the whole evidence is considered, create and leave in the mind of the jury a reasonable doubt of the guilt of the accused." (2 Am. & Eng. Ency. of Law, p. 56; *Ackerson v. People*, 124 Ill. 563, 16 N. E. 847; *Carlton v. People*, 150 Ill. 181, 41 Am. St. 346, 37 N. E. 244; *Flanagan v. People*, 214 Ill. 170, 73 N. E. 347; *State v. Howell*, 100 Mo. 628, 14 S. W. 4.)

This court held, in the case of *State v. Webb*, 6 Ida. 428, 55 Pac. 892:

"It is incumbent upon the state to establish the guilt of the defendant in a criminal action to the satisfaction of the jury, by competent evidence, beyond a reasonable doubt. If the defendant relies upon an *alibi* for his defense, the burden of establishing such *alibi* is upon him. If he succeeds, by competent evidence, in raising a reasonable doubt in the minds of the jury as to the fact of his presence at the place and at the time the offense was committed, he is entitled to an acquittal."

Instruction 8, when considered with all the other instructions given by the court in this case, fairly states the law of the case and is not subject to the objections urged.

We will now briefly discuss proposition 6, which deals with instruction 6 given by the court at the request of the state, which reads as follows:

"You are further instructed that if you believe from the evidence beyond a reasonable doubt that the property described in the information was stolen and that the defendant was found in the possession of the property after it was stolen, then such possession is, in law, a strong, incriminating circumstance tending to show the guilt of the defendant unless the evidence and the facts and circumstances thereunder show that he may have come honestly in possession of the same.

"In this connection I further instruct you that if you find from the evidence beyond a reasonable doubt that the property described in the information was found in the possession of the defendant, then in determining whether or not the defendant is guilty you should take into consideration all of the circumstances attending such possession."

To this instruction counsel for appellant takes exception, upon the ground and for the reason, as counsel contends, the court trespassed upon the right of the jury to pass upon all questions of fact, which was in violation of subdiv. 6, sec. 7855, Rev. Codes. Subdiv. 6 provides that the court "must not charge the jury in respect to matters of fact." This instruction, in substance, has been approved by a great number of the courts of last resort in this country, notably by the supreme court of California in the case of *People v. Fagan,* 66 Cal. 534, 6 Pac. 394. (See, also, *State v. Drew,* 179 Mo. 315, 78 S. W. 594.) A full discussion of this question, with numerous citations of authorities, will be found in 101 Am. St. 474.

We are of the opinion that the instruction is also fully supported by the case of *State v. Sanford,* 8 Ida. 187, 67 Pac. 492, which announced "the rule of law that possession of recently stolen property is a circumstance from which, when unexplained, the guilt of the accused may be inferred."

We have carefully examined propositions 8 and 9 of appellant's brief, being the remaining assignments of error urged by the appellant. The former involves instruction

No. 11, given by the court, upon the question of admissions against interest. From a careful consideration of this instruction we have concluded that there is no necessity for a discussion of this assignment of error, and that the court correctly stated the law.

We have given careful consideration to all of the instructions given by the court in this case, as well as those offered by the defendant and refused by the court, and we are of the opinion that the instructions given by the court fully and fairly state the law on all of the important questions involved in this case and that there is no error in the record.

The judgment of the trial court is affirmed.

Sullivan, C. J., and Truitt, J., concur.

(December 21, 1914.)

C. T. WARD, Assessor and Tax Collector, Appellant, v. C. W. HOLMES, Auditor and Recorder of Adams County, Respondent.

[144 Pac. 1104.]

DUTY OF COUNTY COMMISSIONERS TO FIX SALARIES—CONSTITUTIONAL AMENDMENT—EFFECT OF ON TERMS AND COMPENSATIONS OF OFFICERS —AUTHORITY OF COUNTY COMMISSIONERS TO INCREASE OR DECREASE THE MINIMUM OR MAXIMUM SALARIES OF COUNTY OFFICERS.

1. Sec. 2118, Rev. Codes, as amended by Sess. Laws. 1911, chap. 103, p. 345, provides that, "It shall be the duty of the county commissioners to fix the annual salaries of all county officers at their regular session in April next preceding any general election, except the annual salary of county attorney."

2. The adoption of sec. 6, art. 18 of the constitution, as amended (Ex. Sess. Laws 1912, p. 53), which provides, "That that sentence of sec. 6 of art. 18 of the constitution of the State of Idaho reading: 'The legislature by general and uniform laws shall provide for the election biennially in each of the several counties of the State, of county commissioners, a sheriff, a county treasurer, who is ex-officio public administrator, a probate judge, a county superintendent of public instruction, a county assessor, who is ex-officio tax col-

lector, a coroner and a surveyor,' be amended by striking out the
words 'who is *ex-officio* tax collector' after the words 'a county
assessor' and inserting the words 'and also *ex-officio* tax collector'
after the words 'public administrator,'" in no way affects the
terms of such officers, the time of their election, or their compensation.

3. County commissioners have no authority to increase or decrease
the maximum or minimum compensation of county officers in
anticipation of the adoption of a constitutional amendment.

4. A writ of mandate should not be denied where a board of
county commissioners exceed their authority in fixing the annual
salaries of county officers below the minimum provided by law.

APPEAL from the District Court of the Seventh Judicial
District for the County of Adams. Hon. Ed. L. Bryan,
Judge.

Application for a writ of mandate. Demurrer to defendant's answer overruled. Plaintiff appeals. *Reversed.*

L. L. Burtenshaw, for Appellant.

A board of county commissioners is a tribunal created by
statute, with limited jurisdiction, and only *quasi*-judicial
powers, and cannot act except in strict accordance with the
statute. (*Gorman v. Board of Commrs.*, 1 Ida. 553; *Pro-
thero v. Board of Commrs.*, 22 Ida. 598, 127 Pac. 175.)

Where a board of county commissioners is not acting
within its jurisdiction, the action of the board is void, and
may be attacked, directly or collaterally, at any time or place.
(*Dunbar v. Board of Commrs.*, 5 Ida. 407, 49 Pac. 409; *Fremont County v. Brandon*, 6 Ida. 482, 56 Pac. 264; *Stookey v.
Board of Commrs.*, 6 Ida. 542, 57 Pac. 312.)

B. J. Dillon, for Respondent.

It was the intention of the board of commissioners that if
the assessor ceased to be *ex-officio* tax collector he should
receive but $600 per year for his services. The salary of
the county assessor alone had not been provided for by the
legislature. "In the construction of statutes, when the intention of the legislature can be gathered from the statute,
words may be modified, altered or supplied to give to the

enactment the force and effect which the legislature intended." (*Territory v. Clark*, 2 Okl. 82, 35 Pac. 882.)

"The remedy to correct errors and irregularities in the action of a board of commissioners acting in a matter over which such board has jurisdiction is solely by appeal." (*Dunbar v. Board of Commrs.*, 5 Ida. 407, 415, 49 Pac. 409.)

The writ of mandate should not issue in any case where there is a plain and adequate remedy in the ordinary course of law. (High on Extraordinary Remedies, sec. 341; Merrill on Mandamus, sec. 67; *Graham v. Gillett*, 156 Cal. 113, 103 Pac. 195; *Taylor v. Marshal*, 12 Cal. App. 549, 107 Pac. 1012; *State v. Boerlin*, 30 Nev. 473, 98 Pac. 402; *Lindsey v. Carlton*, 44 Colo. 42, 96 Pac. 997; *State v. Edwards*, 40 Mont. 287, 106 Pac. 695, 20 Ann. Cas. 239; *Steward v. Territory*, 4 Okl. 707, 46 Pac. 487.)

"To authorize a writ of *mandamus* against a public officer, relator must show a clear right to the performance of the act with the corresponding duty upon the officer to perform it." (*State v. Morehouse*, 38 Utah, 234, 112 Pac. 169; *Gray v. Mullins*, 15 Cal. App. 118, 113 Pac. 694; *Curtis v. Moody*, 3 Ida. 123, 27 Pac. 732; *Wright v. Kelley*, 4 Ida. 624, 43 Pac. 565.)

BUDGE, J.—C. T. Ward, assessor of Adams county, made application to the district court of said county for an alternative writ of mandate to compel C. W. Holmes, clerk of the district court and *ex-officio* auditor of said county, to issue to him a warrant for the sum of $91.66 in payment of one-twelfth of his annual salary, for the month of January, 1914, that being the amount claimed to be due under an order made by the board of county commissioners of Adams county fixing the salary of assessor and *ex-officio* tax collector, at their regular April, 1912, meeting.

An alternative writ was issued and on the return day thereof the said Holmes, in his official capacity, appeared and answered said writ, admitting that Ward was the duly appointed and acting assessor of Adams county, that at the regular April, 1912, meeting of the board of commissioners

of Adams county said board made an order fixing the salary
of the assessor and *ex-officio* tax collector at $1,100 per annum
for "the period from January the 13th, 1913, to the second
Monday in January, 1915," the order of said board being as
follows:

"In the matter of fixing salaries for the period January
13, 1913, to the second Monday in January, 1915.

"The Board orders that the following be and is hereby
adopted as the salary schedule for the above period. . . . .

"Assessor and tax collector......$1100.00 per year

Assessor only ....   600.00 per year"

And after fixing in the above order the annual salaries of
all county officers there was added thereto and made a part
thereof the following:

"The salaries of the Assessor and Tax Collector . . . . are
made contingent upon the adoption of the constitutional
amendment making the treasurer the tax collector."

This latter part of the order so made by the commissioners
no doubt referred to the following proposed constitutional
amendment which was submitted to the voters by the legislature at a special session thereof in 1912. Said amendment
is as follows:

"That that sentence of Section 6 of Article 18 of the Constitution of the State of Idaho reading: 'The legislature by
general and uniform laws shall provide for the election biennially in each of the several counties of the State, of county
commissioners, a sheriff, a county treasurer, who is *ex-officio*
public administrator, a probate judge, a county superintendent of public instruction, a county assessor, who is *ex-
officio* tax collector, a coroner and a surveyor,' be amended by
striking out the words 'who is *ex-officio* tax collector' after
the words 'a county assessor' and inserting the words 'and
also *ex-officio* tax collector' after the words 'public administrator.' "

This amendment was adopted, thereby requiring the duties
of tax collector to be performed by the county treasurer instead of the county assessor, except as later provided under

secs. 149 to 169 inclusive, Sess. Laws 1913, p. 221, which in part are as follows:

"Sec. 149. It is hereby made the duty of the Assessor, immediately upon assessing personal property whereon the tax is not a lien on real property of sufficient value, in the judgment of the assessor, to insure the collection of such tax, to compute the amount of taxes due on such personal property . . . . and at the same time, the Assessor must collect such taxes and issue a tax receipt therefor, upon blanks in the form supplied by the State Auditor. . . . .

"Sec. 150. If the payment of any tax due on personal property, as prescribed in the preceding section, is refused, the Assessor must then and there distrain and sell in the manner provided for the distraint and sale of personal property for taxes, so much of such property as may be necessary to pay such taxes, or forthwith bring suit with attachment in aid of such suit, for the amount, or estimated amount, of such taxes due."

It will therefore appear that for certain purposes the assessor is still the tax collector. It was no doubt the intention of the board of county commissioners to provide that in the event the constitutional amendment, *supra,* was adopted and became self-executing the assessor would be relieved of the duties of tax collector and therefore should receive as compensation for his services as such assessor $600 per annum instead of $1,100. But in this connection we must consider chap. 103, Sess. Laws 1911, at p. 345, amending sec. 2118, Rev. Codes, which provides:

"It shall be the duty of the board of county commissioners of each county, at its regular session in April next preceding any general election, to fix the annual salaries of the several county officers . . . . to be elected at said general election, for a term commencing on the second Monday in January next after said meeting, and in no case shall the salary of any county officer be less than the lowest amount hereafter designated for such officer, and in no case shall it be higher than the highest amount hereafter designated for such officer. . . . .

"The assessor and *ex-officio* tax collector shall receive a salary of not less than Eight Hundred Dollars ($800) per annum and not to exceed Three Thousand Dollars ($3000) per annum."

It will be observed from the above statute, as amended, that the salary of assessor and *ex-officio* tax collector could not be fixed at less than $800 per annum, or to exceed $3000 per annum. (*Guheen v. Curtis*, 3 Ida. 443, 31 Pac. 805.)

In the case of *Cleary v. Kincaid*, 23 Ida. 789, 131 Pac. 1117, the court in construing sec. 6, art. 18, *supra*, held that said constitutional amendment was self-executing and transferred the duties of tax collector from the office of the county assessor and imposed such duties upon the office of county treasurer, but that the office of county assessor and county treasurer were in no way affected as to the terms of such officers or the time of the election of such officers or their compensation.

The maximum and minimum salaries to be paid county officers, as well as the time when their salaries shall be fixed, are provided by law. The county commissioners have no authority to change the maximum or minimum so fixed, either by increasing or decreasing the same during the term for which said officers were elected or appointed, or to anticipate that a constitutional amendment would be adopted, and therefore in keeping with their anticipation fix the salary of a county officer below the minimum fixed by law.

The amendment to art. 18, sec. 6, was adopted November 5, 1912. The board of county commissioners fixed the salary of all the county officers, including the appellant's predecessor, for a period from January 13, 1913, to the second Monday of January, 1915, at their regular April meeting, 1912. When the amendment was adopted the assessor was relieved of the duties of tax collector which had theretofore been performed by him by reason of his election to the office of assessor, but this could in no way affect his compensation, nor was the compensation of the county treasurer increased or decreased by reason of the adoption of said amendment. The attempt on the part of the commissioners to fix the salary of the assessor, who was then *ex-officio* tax collector, below the minimum provided by law, was clearly, in our opinion, void and of no force or effect. That portion therefore of the order made by the board of county commissioners of Adams county at their regular April meeting, 1912, which provides, "Assessor only, $600.00 per year," made contingent upon the adoption of the constitutional amendment making the treasurer the tax collector, was null and void and of no force or effect.

We have concluded that it is not necessary for us to determine the constitutional question suggested by counsel for the respondent. This question was not raised in the trial court, and a determination of that question is not essential to a full disposition of the issue involved in this case. The real question that we are called upon to consider here is not when the officer shall be paid, but what compensation he is entitled to receive under the order of the board of county commissioners, *supra*. The fact that the assessor elected at the November election, 1912, resigned, and subsequently thereto the appellant was appointed to fill out the unexpired term of his predecessor, in no way affects the question of compensation.

We are therefore of the opinion that the trial court erred in overruling the demurrer to the defendant's answer and that a writ of mandate should issue. Said cause is remanded, with instructions to the trial court to issue said writ.

Costs awarded to appellant.

Sullivan, C. J., and Truitt, J., concur.

(December 22, 1914.)

STATE, Respondent, v. GUST JOHNSON, Appellant.

[144 Pac. 784.]

RAPE—ASSAULT WITH INTENT TO COMMIT—PUBLIC TRIAL—ADMISSION AND REJECTION OF EVIDENCE—INSTRUCTIONS—SUFFICIENCY OF EVIDENCE.

1. The defendant in a prosecution for the crime of assault with intent to commit rape was not deprived of a public trial as provided by art. 1, sec. 13, of the state constitution, and the statutes of the state, when the court in its discretion required all spectators and all persons except those necessarily in attendance to retire from the courtroom during the trial.

2. *Held,* under the facts of this case that the court erred in not permitting the defendant to answer the following question: "How did you and your wife get along upon the ranch? Did you have any difficulty or quarrel?"

3. *Held,* that the court did not err in giving certain instructions to the jury.

4. *Held,* that the court erred in refusing to give the following requested instruction to the jury: "You are also instructed that in order to convict the defendant of the crime charged it will be necessary for you to find that he made an assault upon this young girl and actually intended to use whatever force was necessary to rape or carnally know her, and that he was prevented therefrom by the resistance of or force used by her, the said Anna Johnson, or by some other reason than that of his own inclination or determination to desist therefrom."

5. The evidence *held* insufficient to support the verdict.

APPEAL from the District Court of the Eighth Judicial District for Kootenai County. Hon. Robert N. Dunn, Judge.

The defendant was charged with the crime of assault with intent to commit rape and convicted and sentenced to imprisonment for a term of not less than seven and not more than fourteen years. *Reversed.*

McFarland & McFarland, for Appellant.

It was reversible error for the trial court to make the order for the exclusion of spectators during the trial. *(People v.*

Yeager, 113 Mich. 228, 71 N. W. 491; *People v. Murray,* 89 Mich. 276, 28 Am. St. 294, 50 N. W. 995, 14 L. R. A. 809; *People v. Hartman,* 103 Cal. 242, 42 Am. St. 108, 37 Pac. 153; *State v. Dreany,* 65 Kan. 292, 69 Pac. 182; *State v. Osborne,* 54 Or. 289, 103 Pac. 62, 20 Ann. Cas. 627.)

In this class of cases courts and juries should be more particular in requiring the state to prove by sufficient evidence every necessary element of constituting the offense than in almost any other case. (*State v. Baker,* 6 Ida. 496, 56 Pac. 81; *State v. Anderson,* 6 Ida. 706, 59 Pac. 180.)

J. H. Peterson, Attorney General, J. J. Guheen, T. C. Coffin, and E. G. Davis, Assistants, and N. D. Wernette, County Attorney, for Respondent.

"Public trial," as used in sec. 13, art. 1, of the Idaho constitution, is used in the sense of distinguishing the trial from secret. (Cooley, Const. Limitations, 7th ed., p. 441; Abbott's Trial Brief, Criminal Causes, 2d ed., pp. 160–162; *People v. Swafford,* 65 Cal. 223, 3 Pac. 809; *Benedict v. People,* 23 Colo. 126, 46 Pac. 637; *People v. Hall,* 51 App. Div. 57, 64 N. Y. Supp. 433; *State v. Nyhus,* 19 N. D. 326, 124 N. W. 71, 27 L. R. A., N. S., 489; *Robertson v. State,* 64 Fla. 437, 60 So. 118; *Reagan v. United States,* 202 Fed. 488, 120 C. C. A. 627, 44 L. R. A., N. S., 583.)

The defendant by his failure to object to the order excluding spectators from the courtroom at the time the order was made, will be presumed to have assented thereto, unless he can show that he was prejudiced. (*People v. Douglass,* 100 Cal. 1, 34 Pac. 490; *People v. Bell,* 4 Cal. Unrep. 522, 36 Pac. 94.)

When the rule excluding witnesses is enforced, it is within the discretion of the trial court to take any witness without the operation of the rule. A deputy sheriff, being an officer of the court, is not generally considered as within the rule. (*People v. Nunley,* 142 Cal. 441, 76 Pac. 45; *Brite v. State* (Tex. Crim.), 43 S. W. 342.)

SULLIVAN, C. J.—The defendant was convicted of the crime of intent to commit rape upon his eleven year old daughter, and sentenced to serve a term at hard labor in the state penitentiary for a period of not less than seven years and not more than fourteen years. The appeal is from the judgment and order denying a new trial.

The action of the court in excluding the spectators from the courtroom during the trial and thus not giving the defendant a public trial is assigned as error, also the action of the court in refusing to admit certain evidence offered by the defendant; in giving and refusing to give certain instructions and the insufficiency of the evidence to justify the verdict and judgment, and in denying appellant's application for a new trial.

The first assignment discussed by counsel for appellant is the action of the court in excluding all spectators from the courtroom during the trial. In that regard the court made the following order: "During the trial of this case, all spectators will be excluded from the courtroom. Before beginning to examine the jury, all spectators will retire. The bailiff will remain at the door and see that nobody comes in or remains where they can hear the proceedings."

Art. 1, sec. 13, of the state constitution provides that in all criminal cases the party accused shall have the right to a speedy and public trial. It is also provided by sec. 7355, Rev. Codes, that the defendant in a criminal case is entitled to a speedy and public trial. It appears that said order was made by the court without the suggestion or request of the defendant, and even had the defendant consented, the question is presented whether he could have waived the right to what he claimed was a public trial.

There seems to be a diversity of opinion on this question. Judge Cooley in his work on Const. Limitations, p. 441, 7th ed., states:

"It is also requisite that the trial be public. By this is not meant that every person who sees fit shall in all cases be permitted to attend criminal trials; because there are many cases where, from the character of the charge and the nature of the evidence by which it is to be supported, the motives to attend the trial on the part of portions of the community would be of the worst character, and where a regard to public morals and public decency would require that at least the young be excluded from hearing and witnessing the evidences of human depravity which the trial must necessarily bring to light. The requirement of a public trial is for the benefit of the accused; that the public may see he is fairly dealt with and not unjustly condemned, and that the presence of interested spectators may keep his triers keenly alive to a sense of their responsibility and to the importance of their functions; and the requirement is fairly observed if, without partiality or favoritism, a reasonable proportion of the public is suffered to attend, notwithstanding that those persons whose presence could be of no service to the accused, and who would only be drawn thither by a prurient curiosity, are excluded altogether."

Counsel for the state cites many decisions sustaining the views of Judge Cooley above set forth, and counsel for the defendant cites a number of cases, and particularly some from the state of Michigan, which hold directly to the contrary. (See *People v. Yeager*, 113 Mich. 228, 71 N. W. 491.)

In *Reagan* v. *United States*, 202 Fed. 488, 120 C. C. A. 627, 44 L. R. A., N. S., 583, the court held upon this question that, in a prosecution for rape, the defendant was not deprived of a public trial by an order clearing the courtroom of spectators, but permitting all persons connected with the court, either as officers or members of the bar, and all persons in any manner connected with the case as witnesses, etc., to remain.

In cases like the one at bar, where the evidence is of a very immoral and disgusting nature, we do not think the court erred in excluding the general public from the courtroom during the trial. Of course, the friends of the defendant who desired to be present and the officers of the court, including members of the bar, ought not to be excluded; but to exclude the general public who only have a curiosity to hear the revolting details of a rape case, does not deprive a defendant of a public trial as provided by the constitution and statutes above cited. The court therefore did not err in making said order.

The next assignment of error goes to the action of the court in refusing to admit certain evidence. The girl had testified that the defendant and her mother had frequent quarrels and when the defendant was on the witness-stand he was asked this question: "How did you and your wife get along upon the ranch? Did you have any difficulty or quarrel?" Since the prosecutrix had testified that the father and mother had frequent quarrels, we think the court erred in not permitting the defendant to answer said question, as it might tend to show the ill-feeling of the wife toward the defendant in having him prosecuted.

The following question was propounded to the defendant: "What is the fact, if you know, as to whether or not before you married your wife, she had her father arrested for the same offense that you are arrested for now." Under the state of the record presented here, we think the court did not err in refusing to permit defendant to answer that question. If he wished to show that the wife in urging this prosecution desired to get rid of him by putting him in the penitentiary, and that that was the motive in having him arrested, that evidence might have been admissible; but the proper foundation was not laid for the introduction of such evidence and the court did not err in refusing to permit the defendant to answer said question.

Certain instructions given by the court are assigned as error. After a careful consideration of those instructions, we are satisfied that there was no reversible error in giving them, as they fairly cover the case.

The refusal to give certain instructions is also assigned as error. The court erred in refusing to give requested instruction No. 4, which instruction correctly states the law when applied to the facts of this case, but did not err in refusing to give other requested instructions.

The next assignment of error goes to the insufficiency of the evidence to support the verdict.

The record shows that the defendant had resided at Turner Bay, near Coeur d'Alene City, in Kootenai county, for fifteen or sixteen years; that in December, 1913, his family consisted of his wife, his daughter Anna, aged 11 years (the prosecutrix in this action), and three boys, aged one, five and eight years, respectively. The family lived in a house on a ranch in which they had but two beds. In one bed the mother slept with the baby boy and in the other the father slept with the other two boys and the daughter.

The daughter testified that about two weeks before Christmas, 1913, the defendant began to take improper liberties with her; that he did such acts almost every morning up to and including the 19th of February, 1914, when the act for which the defendant was convicted she testified was committed. She also testified that she told her mother nearly every day about the improper acts of her father and that, regardless of this information, the mother permitted her to continue to sleep in the same bed with the father and the two boys. On February 18, 1914, the defendant took his family to Coeur d'Alene City to attend the wedding of his wife's sister, at whose house the defendant and his family stayed that night. The same sleeping arrangement was observed that night, the father, the girl and the two boys slept together, the mother, babe and grandmother slept together. The girl testified that she slept next the wall and one of the brothers slept between her and her father and the other boy slept at the foot of the bed. She detailed minutely the actions and conduct of her father, but testified positively that he did not have sexual intercourse with her, that "he didn't get it in." She also testified that about two hours after they got up the morning of the 19th, she told her mother of the conduct of her father, and her mother went down town that forenoon and saw the county attorney, and then in the afternoon she went down again to see the county attorney and took the child with her. Thereafter the county attorney and the deputy sheriff called the defendant to the attorney's office and the deputy sheriff testified that in the conversation that followed the defendant admitted that he had done some things to his daughter that he ought not to have done and would not do them again, but that he intended no harm and denied that he intended to commit rape. This was the only corroboration of the daughter's testimony as to the acts committed by her father. The daughter also testified that the mother and the defendant had a good many quarrels prior to the time the defendant was arrested. The mother of the prosecutrix did not testify in the case.

The defendant testified in his own behalf and denied the testimony of the daughter and denied that he took any indecent liberties with her, and denied any intention of raping her. He also produced at least four witnesses who were neighbors of his and lived near him at Turner Bay for a number of years, who testified that the reputation of the defendant in the neighborhood where he lived was good.

If we concede that all of the acts and conduct of the defendant as testified to by the girl were true, we do not think the testimony is sufficient to sustain the verdict of the jury. The defendant is charged with an assault with intent to commit rape. According to the girl's testimony, the father had her in his power for at least eight weeks, commencing with two weeks prior to Christmas, 1913, and until the morning of February 19, 1914, and could have carried out his intent had he desired to do so; yet the girl testified that he did not accomplish his intent.

While the acts testified to by the girl, if true, show the defendant to be a degenerate, they are not sufficient to convict him of assault with intent to commit a rape, when it so clearly appears that he could have carried out that intention almost any day for eight weeks prior to his arrest. It also seems remarkable that the mother, if she had any regard for the daughter at all, would have permitted her to sleep with the father several weeks after the girl had informed her of the conduct of the father toward her. The evidence shows that she said nothing to the father about those acts and did not attempt to prevent the girl from sleeping with him. The mother and the babe slept in one bed and the father, the two boys and the girl in another. It would seem that if the mother knew of the father's conduct toward the daughter, she would have had the daughter sleep with her and the babe, or at least not permit her to continue to sleep with the father.

It is a well-recognized fact that such a crime charged against a father by a daughter greatly prejudices the public mind against him, and such charges are so easy to be made and so hard, many times, to disprove, that juries ought to be very careful in convicting a man of such a crime unless the evidence is amply sufficient to prove his guilt beyond a reasonable doubt; especially ought that to be the rule where the defendant himself goes upon the stand and denies the acts constituting the crime. In such a case as that the complainant's testimony ought to be corroborated by reputable evidence or physical facts of the commission of the crime.

In the case at bar the girl was only 11 years of age, and had the defendant committed an assault upon her with intent to commit rape, the state should have been required to produce more substantial corroboration of the prosecutrix than it did before a conviction could be legally had.

For the reasons above given, a new trial must be granted, and it is so ordered.

Truitt and Budge, JJ., concur.

(December 23, 1914.)

MARIE D. RISCHAR, Respondent, v. W. W. SHIELDS et ux., Appellants.

[145 Pac. 294.]

ACTION TO QUIET TITLE TO REAL ESTATE—CONTRACT OF PURCHASE—PAYMENT IN INSTALMENTS—TIME OF THE ESSENCE OF THE CONTRACT—FORFEITURE OF CONTRACT—DEMURRER TO COMPLAINT—ANSWER AND CROSS-COMPLAINT—MOTION TO STRIKE—JUDGMENT ON PLEADINGS.

1. *Held*, that the complaint states a cause of action, and that the allegations and denials contained in the amended answer and cross-complaint contain no defense to the action.

2. Where S. and wife contract to purchase certain land from R. and to pay the purchase price in instalments at certain dates, and also agree to pay the taxes and assessments levied against said land and' time is expressly made of the essence of the contract, and S. and wife fail to make the payments as provided by the contract, and R. serves notice of forfeiture after a default in the payments, it is no defense to an action to quiet title and to recover possession of the premises for the defendants to allege a defect in title and ask to have the money paid returned to them; and the vendor may rescind the contract for the failure to pay any of the instalments preceding the last without tender of the deed, since 'the payment of the last instalment and the delivery of the deed are mutual, concurrent and dependent obligations.

3. *Held,* that the court did not err in entering judgment on the pleadings.

APPEAL from the District Court of the Eighth Judicial District for Kootenai County. Hon. John M. Flynn, Judge.

Action to quiet title and regain possession of certain real estate. Judgment for the plaintiff. *Affirmed.*

James H. Frazier, for Appellants.

"When the vendor insists that the vendee is in default to such an extent as to entitle him to have the contract rescinded, he must allege and prove that he had tendered to the vendee a deed conveying to him all the land according to the terms of the agreement on the part of the vendee, and must have notified him that the contract would be rescinded unless purchase money was paid within a reasonable length of time." (*Frink v. Thomas,* 20 Or. 265, 25 Pac. 717, 12 L. R. A. 239; *Kessler v. Pruitt,* 14 Ida. 175, 93 Pac. 965; 39 Cyc. 1375, d, (2).)

A party who is unable to show good title cannot insist upon a forfeiture. (*Tharp v. Lee,* 25 Tex. Civ. App. 439, 62 S. W. 93; *King v. Seebeck,* 20 Ida. 224, 118 Pac. 292.)

"A forfeiture is a harsh remedy and will not be allowed except upon clear proof of a breach of the terms of the contract upon which such forfeiture was to be declared." (*Harris v. Reed,* 21 Ida. 364, 121 Pac. 780; *Hall v. Yaryan,* 25 Ida. 470, 138 Pac. 339; *Lytle v. Scottish-American Mortgage Co.,* 122 Ga. 458, 50 S. E. 402.)

"In order to recover possession of the premises on the ground of rescission of contract the plaintiff must allege a repayment or a tender of the amount paid by the defendant at the execution of the contract." (*Morrison v. Lods*, 39 Cal. 381; *Bohall v. Diller*, 41 Cal. 532; *Heilig v. Parlin*, 134 Cal. 99, 66 Pac. 186; *Wilson v. Sturgis* (Cal.), 16 Pac. 772; *Minah Consol. Mining Co. v. Briscoe*, 47 Fed. 276; *Gay v. Alter*, 102 U. S. 79, 26 L. ed. 48.)

When a party in whose favor a contract runs is guilty of laches, or acquiesces in the waiver of the conditions of a contract, he is estopped from later claiming the benefit of the conditions relating to time. (*Hogan v. Kyle*, 7 Wash. 595, 38 Am. St. 910, 35 Pac. 399; *Scheftel v. Hays*, 58 Fed. 457, 7 C. C. A. 308; *Rugan v. Sabin*, 53 Fed. 415, 3. C. C. A. 578; *McLean v. Clapp*, 141 U. S. 429, 12 Sup. Ct. 29, 35 L. ed. 804; *Grymes v. Sanders*, 93 U. S. 55, 23 L. ed. 798.)

C. H. Potts, for Respondent.

The defendants could not remain in possession of these lands under a contract and at the same time refuse to pay the purchase price. They could not be allowed to use and enjoy what they had agreed to buy and also retain in their hands the price they had agreed to pay. (*Rhorer v. Bila*, 83 Cal. 51, 23 Pac. 274; *Worley v. Nethercott*, 91 Cal. 512, 25 Am. St. 209, 27 Pac. 767; *Gates v. McLean*, 70 Cal. 42, 11 Pac. 489; *Gervaise v. Brookins*, 156 Cal. 103, 103 Pac. 329; *Harvey v. Morris*, 63 Mo. 475, 477; *McIndoe v. Morman*, 26 Wis. 588, 7 Am. Rep. 96; *Taft v. Kessed*, 16 Wis. 273; *Brock v. Hidy*, 13 Ohio St. 306; *Dunn v. Mills*, 70 Kan. 656, 79 Pac. 146, 502, 3 Ann. Cas. 363.)

"The law will not allow a vendee to obtain possession of property under a contract of sale, and while in possession, to defend an action for the purchase money upon the ground of the title being defective." (*McLeod v. Barnum*, 131 Cal. 605, 63 Pac. 924; *Peabody v. Phelps*, 9 Cal. 213; *Gross v. Kierski*, 41 Cal. 111; *Hicks v. Lovell*, 64 Cal. 14, 49 Am. Rep. 679, 27 Pac. 942; *Wyatt v. Garlington*, 56 Ala. 576; *Lane v.*

George, 84 Kan. 823, 115 Pac. 589; *Newmyer v. Roush*, 21 Ida. 106, Ann. Cas. 1913D, 433, 120 Pac. 464.)

It is only where the giving of the deed and the payment of the purchase money are mutual, concurrent and dependent covenants that the tender of the deed is a condition precedent to the right of the vendor to declare a forfeiture. (39 Cyc. 1376; *Bryson v. Crawford*, 68 Ill. 362; *Kiefer v. Carter Contracting etc. Co.*, 59 Wash. 108, 109 Pac. 332; *Reddish v. Smith*, 10 Wash. 178, 45 Am. St. 781, 38 Pac. 1003; *Brentnall v. Marshall*, 10 Kan. App. 488, 63 Pac. 93; *Voight v. Fidelity Investment Co.*, 49 Wash. 612, 96 Pac. 162.)

It is only the payment of the last instalment and the delivery of the deed that are mutual, concurrent and dependent obligations. (*Lewis v. Wellard*, 62 Wash. 590, 114 Pac. 455; *Reese v. Westfield*, 56 Wash. 415, 105 Pac. 837, 28 L. R. A., N. S., 956.)

SULLIVAN, C. J.—This action was brought by the respondent to quiet her title to a certain lot situated in or near Coeur d'Alene City, and to recover possession thereof. A demurrer to the complaint was filed and overruled by the court. Thereafter an answer, an amended answer and a cross-complaint were filed and a motion to strike the amended answer and counterclaim and for judgment on the pleadings was made by the respondent, which was granted by the court. A motion was also made to amend the answer, which was denied by the court, and judgment was entered in favor of the plaintiff for the possession of said lot and quieting her title thereto. The appeal is from the judgment and from the order denying the defendant's motion to amend the answer.

The following facts appear from the record:

On April 28, 1911, the plaintiff and defendants entered into a contract whereby the plaintiff agreed to sell, and the defendants agreed to purchase, the tract of land in controversy. The defendants agreed to pay to the plaintiff $4,000 for said land as follows: $500 on the execution of the contract (which was paid); $1,500 on the 1st of May, 1911, and $2,000 on the 1st of May, 1914, with interest at the rate of 7% per annum, payable semi-annually; and to pay all taxes and assessments that might be legally levied against said land, and in case of failure by the defendants to make either payment, or any part thereof, or to perform any of the covenants by them to be performed, the contract, at the option of the plaintiff, might be forfeited and the defendants should forfeit all payments made on the contract, and such payments might be retained by the plaintiff in full satisfaction and liquidation of the damages sustained by her, and she should have a right to enter into the possession of the premises in case of the default in making such payments. The plaintiff agreed to furnish a complete abstract of title to the defendant and convey said lot clear of all encumbrances by good and sufficient warranty deed upon the completion of said contract. It was mutually agreed that the time of making the payments was of the essence of the contract.

The defendants did not make the $1,500 payment agreed to be made on the 1st of May, 1911, but thereafter paid $1,000 on said payment, and the defendants failed to pay the taxes legally levied on said premises for the years 1911, 1912 and 1913, and failed and refused to make any other payments on the purchase price of said land.

On December 13, 1913, the plaintiff notified the defendants in writing that she intended to declare said agreement and contract forfeited and ended, on January 1, 1914, unless they should comply with the terms of said contract and make the payments due for said land on or before January 1, 1914. Defendants neglected and refused to make such payments and thereafter in March, 1914, this action was brought.

The assignments of error are to the effect that the court erred in overruling the demurrer to the complaint and in sustaining the plaintiff's motion to strike the answer and affirmative defense, and denying the defendant's right to amend their answer and affirmative defense.

On an examination of the complaint we find that it states a cause of action and the court therefore did not err in overruling the demurrer to the complaint.

As above stated, this action was based on a contract for the purchase of real estate, by the terms of which, if the appellants failed to make the payments as stipulated and to pay all taxes and assessments against said land, the plaintiff was authorized to declare a forfeiture of the contract and time was made of the essence of said contract. By the answer and cross-complaint of the defendants, they admitted that they entered into said contract; that they had failed and neglected to make the payments as stipulated, but undertook to justify such failure by alleging that the plaintiff did not have title to a part of said lot and hence could not convey it to them by warranty deed as she had agreed to do, and could not furnish them an abstract of title showing a clear title in her. By their cross-complaint they sought to recover back the amount of money paid and a further sum by reason of the removal of certain electrical fixtures.

Under a well-established rule of law the allegations contained in said amended answer and cross-complaint were no defense to this action. The defendants ought to have tendered a compliance on their part with the provisions of said contract; they ought to have tendered the purchase price as stipulated and then if the plaintiff failed to produce an abstract of title showing a clear title and a warranty deed, as provided in the contract, they would have been in a position to recover back whatever damages they had sustained by reason of the plaintiff's failure or inability to comply on her part with its provisions. The vendees could not retain possession of said land and refuse and neglect to pay the price when due, or offer to pay it, since the failure of title would not give them the right to continue in possession and also the right to recover back the payments made on the land.

In *Brentnall v. Marshall,* 10 Kan. App. 488, 63 Pac. 93, it was held that where payments are to be made in instalments and deed given on the payment of the last instalment, the vendor may rescind for failure to pay any of the instalments preceding the last without tender of a deed. A similar case is that of *Voight v. Fidelity Inv. Co.,* 49 Wash. 612, 96 Pac. 162, wherein it was held that the covenant to pay the first instalment and the covenant to convey were not concurrent; hence a forfeiture of the contract for the nonpayment of the instalment might be made without tendering a deed. It is only the payment of the last instalment and the delivery of the deed that are mutual, concurrent and dependent obligations. (*Lewis v. Wellard,* 62 Wash. 590, 114 Pac. 455. To the same effect is *Reese v. Westfield,* 56 Wash. 415, 105 Pac. 837, 28 L. R. A., N. S., 956.)

In the case at bar there was a written notice of intention to declare a forfeiture given to the defendants and more than a month given to them to make payment and defeat the proposed forfeiture. Under that state of facts and under the terms of the contract of sale, the defense set up in the answer and cross-complaint are no defense, since the payment of the last instalment and the delivery of the deed and abstract were mutual, concurrent and dependent obligations, and in case the plaintiff failed to produce the proper abstract and the deed upon the tender of the last payment, then the defendants would have placed themselves in a position to demand and recover damages they had sustained by reason of such failure on the part of the plaintiff.

In this view of the case, it is not necessary to pass specifically upon the question of whether the court erred in striking out the amended answer and cross-complaint, since the defendants could not recover from the plaintiff until she had defaulted in some of her covenants embodied in said contract.

The judgment of the trial court must therefore be affirmed, and it is so ordered, with costs in favor of the respondent.

Truitt and Budge, JJ., concur.

(December 24, 1914.)

H. O. FRAZIER, Plaintiff, v. F. W. HASTINGS et al., Defendants.

[144 Pac. 1122.]

1. Under the provisions of sec. 10 of an act of the legislature to create and organize the county of Gooding, and for other purposes (Sess. Laws 1913, p. 13), the county commissioners of Gooding county should make provision for the payment of the bonded indebtedness apportioned to it by levy and taxation at the times fixed by law for so doing, and in the same manner that the commissioners of Lincoln county could or should have done had Gooding county not been created.

2. Under the provisions of said section, the legislative intent was to give the same power and authority to the commissioners of Gooding county in dealing with said bonded indebtedness that the county commissioners of Lincoln county had prior to the creation of Gooding county.

3. Under the provisions of sec. 1960, Rev. Codes, the board of county commissioners of Lincoln county was authorized to issue negotiable coupon bonds of their county for the purpose of paying, redeeming, funding or refunding the outstanding indebtedness of the county, and after said Lincoln county debt had been apportioned to Gooding county, the board of commissioners had full authority to issue funding or refunding bonds in payment of said apportioned indebtedness.

4. *Held*, that the plaintiff is not entitled to a writ of injunction to restrain the county commissioners from issuing and selling such funding or refunding bonds.

Original application to this court for a writ of injunction to prohibit the board of county commissioners of Gooding county from issuing and selling certain county bonds for the funding or refunding of that portion of the indebtedness of Lincoln county which was apportioned to Gooding county on the creation of the latter county. Writ denied.

W. G. Bissell, for Plaintiff.

P. T. Sutphen, County Attorney of Gooding County, for Defendants.

Counsel cite no authorities.

SULLIVAN, C. J.—This is an original application by the plaintiff, who is a citizen, resident and taxpayer of the county of Gooding, for a writ of injunction to restrain the board of county commissioners of said county from selling or disposing of county bonds in the sum of $10,000, issued for the purpose of funding a portion of the bonded indebtedness of the county of Lincoln which was apportioned to Gooding county at the time of its creation out of a portion of the territory of Lincoln county. On the filing of the petition or complaint, said board of county commissioners in writing waived the issuance of service of a citation in this matter, and expressly waived the provisions of the statute relative to the giving of a bond by the plaintiff, and asked leave to file an answer *instanter*, which they did, admitting the principal allegations of the complaint but denying that they as a board were about to issue said bonds without any warrant or authority of law, and averred that said bonds were regularly and legally issued in accordance with the provisions of the statutes of the state of Idaho in such cases made and provided.

In the act creating the county of Gooding out of a portion of Lincoln county (Sess. Laws 1913, p. 13), it is provided by sec. 10 thereof as follows:

"The county commissioners of Gooding county shall make provision for the payment of the bonded indebtedness apportioned to it, by levy and taxation at the times fixed by law for so doing, and in the same manner as the county commissioners of Lincoln county could or should have done had Gooding county not have been created. . . . . "

That section clearly contemplates that the county commissioners of Gooding county should make provision for the payment of its proportion of bonded indebtedness in the same manner as the county commissioners of Lincoln county could or should have done had Gooding county not been created. The legislature meant to give the county commissioners of Gooding county all the power and authority in dealing with its proportion of said bonded indebtedness that the county commissioners of Lincoln county would have had had Gooding county not been created. Then, how could the county commissioners of Lincoln county have provided for said bonded indebtedness? They might do so by levy and taxation at the time fixed by law for that purpose, or they might have provided for it as contemplated by sec. 1960 of the Rev. Codes, which is as follows:

"The board of county commissioners of any county in this state, may issue negotiable coupon bonds of their county for the purpose of paying, redeeming, funding or refunding the outstanding indebtedness of the county, as hereinafter provided, whether the indebtedness exists as warrant indebtedness, or bonded indebtedness. . . . . ''

Said section 1960 was amended by an act approved February 25, 1913 (Sess. Laws 1913, p. 132), but the only change made by said amendment provided that the bonds referred to might be redeemed at any time after five years instead of after ten years, as formerly provided, which amendment did not have an emergency clause, hence did not go into effect until sixty days after the adjournment of the session, while the act creating Gooding county contained an emergency clause and went into effect the date of its approval, January 30, 1913.

It was the intention of the legislature in the act creating Gooding county to place it upon a parity with other counties of the state in regard to its indebtedness, whether it be indebtedness created by said county or indebtedness assumed as its proportionate part of the indebtedness of the mother county.

We therefore hold that the county commissioners have authority under the law to issue the bonds referred to and to sell and transfer them for the purpose of taking up and paying said bonded indebtedness apportioned to Gooding county.

The writ of injunction is denied.

Budge and Truitt, JJ., concur.

(December 28, 1914.)

CAMERON LUMBER CO., Appellant, v. STACK-GIBBS LUMBER CO., Respondent.

[144 Pac. 1114.]

REHEARING—FORMER DECISION — JURISDICTION — SUFFICIENCY OF EVI-
DENCE—NAVIGABLE STREAM—SORTING WORKS—BOOMS—OBSTRUC-
TIONS TO THE NAVIGATION OF PUBLIC STREAMS.

1. Granting a rehearing of a case does not *ipso facto* reverse a former decision, but it is suspended by the order of rehearing.

2. Where a rehearing is granted and the court fails to agree upon a decision in the case, it does not lose jurisdiction, and under section 3820, Rev. Codes, another hearing must be ordered.

3. Where there is a substantial conflict in the evidence, this court will not undertake to weigh the proof to ascertain which side has the preponderance, and where there is such conflict in the evidence, it will not disturb the findings of the trial court.

4. The navigable streams of this state are public highways, over which every citizen has a right to carry commerce in such manner and by such means as are best adapted to serve the purposes of the business in which he is engaged, but in doing this he must have due consideration and reasonable care for the rights of others to a like use of the waters of such stream.

5. Where booms and sorting works for logs placed in the river do, to some extent, form a hindrance to the free navigation of the river at times, such hindrance should be considered only an incident to the reasonable use of the stream for floating and securing logs.

6. For such purpose and as incident to the reasonable use of the river for running and securing logs, parties may use temporary sheer or guide booms to direct the logs or lumber into proper places into which to detain them for use.

7. If an obstruction merely impairs or renders more difficult the navigation of a stream without destroying it, an individual has no right for cause of complaint, because he has no right to insist upon the best possible accommodation.

APPEAL from the District Court of the Eighth Judicial District for the County of Kootenai.   Hon. Robert N. Dunn, Judge.

Action in equity by the plaintiff corporation, the owner of certain booms and sorting works near the mouth of Coeur d'Alene river, to enjoin the defendant, also the owner of certain booms and sorting works at the mouth of said river, from maintaining and operating said booms and sorting works. Judgment was entered in favor of defendant, and from this judgment and an order overruling a motion for a new trial, plaintiff appealed. Judgment *affirmed.*

McFarland & McFarland, for Appellant.

The granting of the rehearing did not set aside the decision rendered by Justices Ailshie and Stewart, reversing the judgment of the court below. It stands to reason that the decision of this court, reversing the judgment of the lower court, still stands. (*Ashley v. Hyde,* 6 Ark. 92, 42 Am. Dec. 685; *Rawdon v. Rapley,* 14 Ark. 203, 58 Am. Dec. 370; *Morrow v. Weed,* 4 Iowa, 77, 66 Am. Dec. 122; *Hauser v. Hobart,* 22 Ida. 749, 127 Pac. 1002, 43 L. R. A., N. S., 410.)

An equal division of the court on a motion for rehearing, of a judgment of reversal previously rendered, leaves that judgment in force, and does not result in affirming the judgment of the lower court. (*Carmichael v. Eberle,* 177 U. S. 63, 20 Sup. Ct. 571, 44 L. ed. 672.)

Where the waters of a navigable river are so used as to deprive a riparian holder of all access to the river from the land, or to the land from the river, or so as to injure the benefits or enjoyment of the riparian land or the business thereon, such use may be enjoined. (*Ferry Pass Inspectors' & Shippers' Assn. v. White River Inspectors' & Shippers' Assn.,* 57 Fla. 399, 48 So. 643, 22 L. R. A., N. S., 345; *Smart v. Aroostook Lumber Co.,* 103 Me. 37, 68 Atl. 527, 14 L. R. A., N. S., 1083; *Reyburn v. Sawyer,* 135 N. C. 328, 102 Am. St. 555, 47 S. E. 761, 65 L. R. A. 930; *Powell v. Springston Lumber Co.,* 12 Ida. 723, 88 Pac. 97; *Hobart Lee Tie Co. v. Stone,* 135 Mo. App. 438, 117 S. W. 604; *Union Mill Co. v. Shores,* 66 Wis. 476, 29 N. W. 243.)

The only right that the Stack-Gibbs Lumber Co. had on the river between the lands of appellant was the right of navigation, but that right, though it gives the right to raft logs down the river, does not involve the right of booming them upon private property for safekeeping and storage, any more than the right to travel the highways justifies the leaving of wagons standing in front of private dwellings or stores. (*Lorman v. Benson*, 8 Mich. 18, 77 Am. Dec. 435; *Watkinson v. McCoy*, 23 Wash. 372, 63 Pac. 245; *Reeves v. Backus-Brooks Co.*, 83 Minn. 339, 86 N. W. 337; *Shephard v. Coeur d'Alene Lbr. Co.*, 16 Ida. 293, 101 Pac. 591; *La Veine v. Stack-Gibbs Lumber Co.*, 17 Ida. 51, 134 Am. St. 253, 104 Pac. 666.)

E. R. Whitla and Voorhees & Canfield, for Respondent.

As a part of its appellate jurisdiction, the court may order a cause resubmitted for further argument, whenever it feels that it needs further light, or deems, for any reason, such rehearing necessary to a just decision.

"The power to grant rehearings is inherent—is an essential ingredient of jurisdiction, and ends only with the loss of jurisdiction." (*In re Jessup*, 81 Cal. 408, 21 Pac. 976, 22 Pac. 742, 1028, 6 L. R. A. 594; *Fair v. Angus*, 6 Cal. Unrep. 283, 57 Pac. 385; *Mateer v. Brown*, 1 Cal. 231; *Grogan v. Ruckle*, 1 Cal. 193; *Hasted v. Dodge* (Iowa), 39 N. W. 668.)

When the original order for rehearing was made, the opinion previously delivered became nugatory and without further force and effect, unless put into operation again by a subsequent order of this court. (*Argenti v. City of San Francisco*, 16 Cal. 256, 277; *Pitkins v. Peet*, 99 Iowa, 314, 68 N. W. 705; *Stewart v. Stewart*, 96 Iowa, 620, 65 N. W. 976; *New York v. Miln*, 9 Pet. (U. S.) 85, 9 L. ed. 60; *Richards v. Burden*, 59 Iowa, 723, 7 N. W. 17, 13 N. W. 90.)

Respondent had the right to erect booms and works over the bed of the river or lake, wherever necessary to a reasonable enjoyment of the right of transportation of logs over the river, even though such bed had been owned by appellant. (*Small v. Harrington*, 10 Ida. 499, 79 Pac. 461; *Powell v. Springston Lbr. Co.*, 12 Ida 723, 730, 88 Pac. 97; *Johnson v. Johnson*, 14 Ida. 561, 95 Pac. 499, 24 L. R. A., N. S., 1240;

Idaho Northern R. Co. v. Post Falls Lumber & Mfg. Co., 20 Ida. 695, 119 Pac. 1098, 38 L. R. A., N. S., 114; *Mashburn v. St. Joe Improvement Co.*, 19 Ida. 30, 113 Pac. 92, 35 L. R. A., N. S., 824; *Gaston v. Mace*, 33 W. Va. 14, 25 Am. St. 848, 10 S. E. 60, 5 L. R. A. 392; *Weise v. Smith*, 3 Or. 445, 8 Am. Rep. 621; *Harold v. Jones*, 86 Ala. 274, 5 So. 438, 3 L. R. A. 406; *Davis v. Winslow*, 51 Me. 264, 81 Am. Dec. 573; *Brown v. Kentfield*, 50 Cal. 129; *Lancey v. Clifford*, 54 Me. 487, 92 Am. Dec. 561.)   If any inconvenience or damage falls upon the appellant thereby, the appellant cannot complain, and it is *damnum absque injuria.* (*Small v. Harrington, supra; Idaho Northern R. Co. v. Post Falls Lumber & Mfg. Co., supra; Attorney General v. Evart Booming Co.*, 34 Mich. 462; *Gaston v. Mace, supra.*)

It is necessary to float logs clear into the mouth of the river in order to reasonably enjoy the use of the Coeur d'Alene river.

"There must be facilities for regaining possession of the property after·it has once been turned into the stream.   For this purpose custom has recognized the right to make use of booms and sorting works." (1 Farnham on Waters and Water Rights, p. 426, par. 94; *Powell v. Springston Lumber Co., supra.*)

Where there is a substantial conflict in the evidence, the findings of the lower court are taken as conclusive. (*Robbins v. Porter*, 12 Ida. 738, 88 Pac. 86; *Robertson v. Moore*, 10 Ida. 115, 77 Pac. 218; *Deeds v. Stephens*, 10 Ida. 332, 79 Pac. 77; *Abbott v. Reedy*, 9 Ida. 577, 75 Pac. 764; *Stuart v. Hauser*, 9 Ida. 53, 72 Pac. 719; *Pine v. Callahan*, 8 Ida. 684, 71 Pac. 473; *Sabin v. Burke*, 4 Ida. 28, 37 Pac. 352; *Miller v. Blunck*, 24 Ida. 234, 133 Pac. 383.)

"Temporary sheer or guide booms, though obstructions to navigation, may be used, as incident to the reasonable use of a river for running and securing logs, for the purpose of directing the logs or lumber into proper places in which to detain them for use; but the stream may not be permanently obstructed and converted into permanent places of deposit for logs by the construction of piers and booms." (*Gerrish v. Brown,* 51 Me. 256, 81 Am. Dec. 569; *Davis v. Winslow,* 51 Me. 264, 81 Am. Dec. 573.)

"Every person has an undoubted right to use a public highway, whether upon the land or water, for all legitimate purpose of travel and transportation; and if, in doing so, while in the exercise of ordinary care, he necessarily and unavoidably impede or obstruct another temporarily, he does not thereby become a wrongdoer, his acts are not illegal, and he creates no nuisance for which an action can be maintained." (*Davis v. Winslow,* 51 Me. 264, 81 Am. Dec. 573.)

TRUITT, J.—This action was brought in the lower court by the appellant, a corporation, the owner of certain booms and sorting works near the mouth of the Coeur d'Alene river, to enjoin the respondent, a corporation, and also the owner of other certain booms and sorting works at the mouth of said river below appellant's works, and in Lake Coeur d'Alene, adjacent to its said sorting works, from maintaining and operating said booms and sorting works.

The first question presented to this court is raised by appellant's objection to a rehearing of the case, and upon his motion that a *remittitur* reversing the judgment of the lower court herein be sent down and transmitted to the clerk of said court. The grounds and reason for such objection and motion are specifically stated therein. For the purpose of considering this motion and appellant's objection to a rehearing at this time, it is only necessary to state that this cause was heard on appeal on December 5, 1913, by this court, Chief Justice Ailshie and Justices Sullivan and Stewart then composing the court and sitting at the hearing of said case; and that thereafter, on January 17, 1914, the judgment of the court below was reversed, Justice Stewart handing down the opinion, which was concurred in by Chief Justice Ailshie, but Justice Sullivan did not concur in the decision and filed a dissenting opinion thereto. The respondent made application for a rehearing, and after due consideration of said application a rehearing was granted, and on March 23, 1914, the case was reheard and reargued before this court, which at that time was composed of Chief Justice Ailshie, Justices Stewart and Sullivan. After this rehearing and before a decision and determination was had in the case, Justice Stewart was stricken with a serious illness and was removed from the state for medical treatment, and on the 25th day of September, 1914, he died without having participated in the decision or consideration of the case after such rehearing. After the first rehearing and sudden illness of Justice Stewart, which incapacitated him from further consideration of the case, it seems that no agreement or decision of the case was reached by Chief Justice Ailshie and Justice Sullivan, and that on June 30, 1914, they concurred in and made an order directing that the cause be resubmitted for further argument at the next Coeur d' Alene term of this court, this being the only order that was made or entered in the record.

Counsel for appellant concedes that this court can in the exercise of its sound discretion grant one rehearing for good and sufficient reasons shown, but they contend that, in the first place, the petition or application for a rehearing was in this case insufficient and that, from a strictly legal standpoint, respondent was not entitled to a rehearing upon any ground or reason stated in such application, and that after having been granted a rehearing and this court having failed to agree upon a determination of the case after such rehearing, it does not have jurisdiction to order another hearing.

As to the point in support of appellant's motion which in effect is that respondent was not entitled to the first rehearing upon any ground or reasons stated in the application, it is without merit, for this court in its sound discretion granted the rehearing, and that question is therefore settled and cannot be considered at this time. In regard to the other contention in support of said motion, which is in substance that because this court failed to decide the case after the first rehearing it lost jurisdiction to act further in the matter, and having lost power to change the former adjudication that must in effect leave or affirm this adjudication as the decision of the case, we cannot reach the conclusion contended for by appellant. It is true that the granting of a rehearing does not *ipso facto* reverse the former decision, but we think that from the very moment a rehearing is ordered in any given case the original decision is thereby suspended. By that order the court throws doubt upon the correctness or justness of its decision. It in effect says by such order that it is not fully satisfied to let that decision stand as the final determination of the case. Then, if the court is not satisfied with the decision, the only way to be satisfied with it is to rehear and re-examine it. Until this is done, the decision is tainted with doubt and cannot be taken as the ultimate conclusion of the court. The order of rehearing does not either affirm or reverse the former opinion, but simply suspends it for further consideration. It would be just as permissible to say that the order of rehearing reverses the opinion as to say that it affirms it. If, after the examination of a petition for rehearing, the court decides that it is without merit, a rehearing is denied, and the court then adheres to its former decision that *becomes* the final determination of the case. But if after consideration of the petition and a further examination of the record, the court has some doubt as to the correctness of the determination it has reached, a rehearing is ordered, its former decision is by this order suspended until the rehearing is had, and then the case is disposed of as may seem just and proper without regard to the former decision. If, upon a rehearing, this decision still merits the approval of the court, it is affirmed; if not, it may be modified, or in effect entirely reversed. Of course, if the decision is approved after this rehearing, it would be a useless task to formulate another opinion in the case where the court was convinced that its former opinion correctly expressed its views as to the proper determination of the case.

In *Argenti v. City of San Francisco,* 16 Cal. 277, we think Chief Justice Field correctly states the rule in regard to rehearings as follows: "A rehearing was granted in that case, and no one is better aware than the learned counsel for the defendant, that when a rehearing is granted, the opinion previously delivered falls, unless reaffirmed after the reargument. Until such reaffirmance, the opinion never acquires the force of an adjudication, and is entitled to no more consideration than the briefs of counsel. The opinion subsequent to the reargument constitutes the exposition of the law applicable to the facts of the case, and the only one to which the attention of the court can be directed.''

Hauser v. Hobart, 22 Ida. 749, 127 Pac. 1002, 43 L. R. A., N. S., 410, is a case referred to in the brief of appellant on this motion. In that case a rehearing had been granted, and after such rehearing this court said: ''After a most careful · reconsideration of the case, we are convinced that there is no reason for changing our former opinion.'' This clearly indicates that the case had been reconsidered and re-examined, and if the court had not been convinced of the correctness of its former opinion it would have reached a different determination of the case.

In the case at bar, while Justice Stewart was out of the state, on June 30, 1914, Chief Justice Ailshie and Justice Sullivan having failed to agree upon a decision in the case after the first rehearing, ordered that it be again resubmitted for further argument at the next regular Coeur d'Alene term. Now, it seems to us that under sec. 3820, Rev. Codes, it was the plain duty of the court, under this condition of the case to order this rehearing. That section says: ''The concurrence of two justices is necessary to pronounce a judgment; if two do not concur, the case must be reheard.'' It seems from the record that after this rehearing and the sudden illness of Justice Stewart, there were only two justices who could decide this case, and when they failed to agree upon a decision, under that statute they were *required* to make the order of rehearing, which they did.

We think this rehearing was properly ordered and that the case must be now disposed of upon its merits. The objection to the rehearing of the case is therefore overruled, and the motion herein denied.

This brings us to a consideration of the case upon its merits. The action was brought by appellant, the Cameron Lumber Co., a corporation, the owner of certain booms and sorting works near the mouth of the Coeur d'Alene river, to enjoin the respondent, the Stack-Gibbs Lumber Co., also a corporation and the owner of certain other booms and sorting works at or near the mouth of said river, below appellant's works and in Lake Coeur d'Alene adjacent to its said sorting works, from maintaining and operating said booms and sorting works.

The complaint in this action in substance alleges the incorporation of the plaintiff company, appellant herein, and the incorporation of the defendant, and that plaintiff was at all times mentioned in the complaint and now is the owner and entitled to the immediate and exclusive possession of certain lands situated in Kootenai county, state of Idaho, described as follows: Lots 1, 2, 3 and 4, in sec. 36, township 48 north, range 4 west of Boise meridian; and a portion of lot 1, all of lot 2, and a portion of lot 3 in sec. 1, township 47 north, range 4 west, Boise meridian. These lands border on and along the Coeur d'Alene river, which is a navigable stream and runs through said lands.

It further alleges that plaintiff kept and maintained on said lands along the source of the river certain sorting works and a log-race constructed of piling and timber for receiving and sorting sawlogs and other timber for its own use and for the use of the public generally for compensation; that said pilings, sorting works and log-race are necessary for the use of plaintiff in its business of handling logs and timber products for the public and for its own use; that in the construction, maintenance and operation of said sorting works and log-race, the plaintiff has never and does not now interfere with the free navigation on said river for boats, logs or timber, and that at all of the times herein mentioned, said river at said sorting works has been free and clear of all obstructions and has been and now is open for navigation of boats, logs and all kinds of timbers; that on or about March 16, 1912, defendant without plaintiff's permission wrongfully obstructed its navigation of said river at and along where its lands border thereon, by driving pilings and maintaining across said river booms, and by then and there, without the consent of plaintiff and against its will, attaching booms to pilings and trees, owned and maintained by plaintiff and upon its own lands, and by constructing other sorting works which were tied to the sorting works of plaintiff and to trees or other objects upon its lands, and by stretching sheer booms along and on plaintiff's land and on its sorting works in said river and lake, thereby depriving it of the free use and enjoyment of its lands and sorting works and preventing it from carrying on its business of receiving, sorting and booming logs for itself and for the public; that defendant gave out and threatened that it would continue to maintain its works and booms, thereby interfering with the sorting works of plaintiff, and that unless restrained by an injunction, defendant will continue so to do and plaintiff will thereby suffer great and irreparable damage; that the acts mentioned constitute a nuisance by interfering with the free navigation of said river and preventing the use by plaintiff of its said sorting works.

The answer of defendant, respondent herein, denies mainly the averments of the complaint and affirmatively alleges that it was and is the owner of a large quantity of sawlogs, tributary to said river and above the sorting works of plaintiff; that it became necessary for defendant by means of its said sorting works to receive, sort and boom its logs, and the logs of the public generally, coming down said river at the point of plaintiff's sorting works; that there is no other suitable place on said river at which defendant could maintain its works or sort logs for itself or the public, and that plaintiff was endeavoring to create a monopoly by means of its sorting works in handling and sorting logs for the public generally.

The answer also alleges that plaintiff did not keep its said sorting works in repair and that they were virtually worthless, that the logs or other material coming down said river would slip through said sorting works and become lost. The answer further alleges that along the shore of Lake Coeur d'Alene, beyond the point where the Coeur d'Alene river empties into the lake and beyond the lands of the plaintiff, the defendant is in process of securing a tract of land from the government of the United States bordering on said lake, and in conjunction with others, has driven piling into the lake-bed along the lake shore of said lake, in front of said last mentioned land, for the purpose of receiving logs belonging to it and to others, as they come out into the mouth of the river and are carried into the lake by the current of the river; that the water begins to rise in March of each year and continues to rise until the month of June, and during that period of high water, especially during said months, timber products, such as logs, poles, stulls, and ties cut along said river and its tributaries, are placed in said river and tributary streams and floated down into Lake Coeur d'Alene, where they are cut as herein alleged; that at the time of the commencement of this suit the Coeur d'Alene river was at its flood and in many places overflowing its banks, and many millions of feet of logs were floating down the river for the purpose of being put into the booms of Lake Coeur d'Alene; that at the time the defendant commenced the construction of its receiving booms, there was in said river and along the banks tributary thereto for the purpose of being flooded down the river and caught in said receiving booms during the high-water season of the year 1912 between thirty and thirty-five millions of feet of logs and other timbers which were caught in defendant's receiving booms; and that it is necessary that all of said logs be floated down said river during the high water, for the reason that during other seasons of the year the tributaries of said river become so shallow that sawlogs cannot be floated therein; that the logs floated down in high water and caught and sorted in defendant's sorting works were of the value of $300,000; that the volume of logs floated down the Coeur d'Alene river will increase each year, and there now exists along said river and its tributaries many billions of feet of logs, timber and its products, which will have to be floated down said river, through its booms at or near the mouth thereof, in said lake, and defendant has constructed its receiving booms and sorting works in the position in which they now are, for the purpose of catching and receiving said logs as they float out on said lake, it being the owner of a large part of the saw timber yet tributary to said Coeur d'Alene river, and which must be floated down to said lake; that prior to the construction of said booms and sorting works by defendant the plaintiff went upon said river at the mouth thereof and erected a log-race and sorting works, and for that purpose drove numerous piles into the bed of the river, which said piling, sorting works and log-race of the plaintiff occupy from one-third to one-half of the width of the said river; but that plaintiff is not at the present time and was not at the time of commencing this suit or during the spring of 1912 or at the time the defendant's booms were constructed, using or attempting to use its sorting works or log-race for any purpose; that the plaintiff has driven its piling out into Lake Coeur d'Alene for a distance of from six hundred to one thousand feet from the mouth of the river, and in order to protect the logs of defendant and the logs of other owners from floating down the river and from having their logs entangled with the logs of plaintiff through and by reason of its openings in its booms and sorting works, and to prevent such obstruction to the free floating of the logs into said lake, defendant constructed a boom parallel to the booms of plaintiff, and for this purpose only.

The answer further denies that it attached said booms or any booms to pilings or other property owned or maintained by plaintiff; denies any wrongful acts on its part in connection with the erection or maintaining of its said booms and sorting works or that plaintiff has been deprived of the use or enjoyment of said river at said point or elsewhere, and denies that plaintiff has been deprived of the use or enjoyment of the right of ingress or egress from its said lands to the river or that it has been deprived of any rights whatever or damaged by the acts of defendant in any sum whatever, or at all.

Some affirmative matter was set up by the defendant as a defense to plaintiff's complaint to the effect that the Coeur d'Alene river from the point where it empties into Lake Coeur d'Alene extends eastward for a distance of about sixty miles and is a large navigable river open to the navigation of steamboats and other water craft and also for the floating of saw-logs and other timbers from the headwaters of said river down into said lake. But, as we understand it, there is no issue made by plaintiff as to the fact that said river is navigable and that said river and its tributaries are largely used for the purpose of floating down logs from adjacent timber to Lake Coeur d'Alene. But the defendant also set up as affirmative matter that the plaintiff's sorting works were constructed for, and resulted in delaying defendant and others from receiving logs and collecting the same for others and for themselves when floated down the river, in order that plaintiff might compel defendant and other owners of timber along said river and its tributaries to pay plaintiff the large, exorbitant and unreasonable rental or toll for the use of its sorting works and receiving booms constructed as aforesaid at the mouth of the river; that theretofore a toll or rental of five cents per thousand feet had been charged for using the sorting works and booms of plaintiff which sum was a fair and reasonable amount to be charged for the use thereof, in addition to the actual cost of the labor of sorting and handling said logs, but that during the season of 1912 plaintiff demanded twenty cents per thousand feet for the use of its booms and sorting works in floating and sorting logs, and that this charge was and is exorbitant and unjust; that the defendant made no charge whatever to any person for the use of its receiving booms and sorting works, except the actual expense of handling and sorting the logs.

The pleadings were quite long in this case, but we think the foregoing summary thereof substantially shows the material issues upon which it was tried.

This being an action in equity, it was tried to the court upon the issues made in the pleadings. At the commencement of the trial, it was agreed and stipulated between the parties thereto that this cause and the case of *Stack-Gibbs Lumber Co. v. Cameron Lumber Co.* should be consolidated for the purpose of the trial and tried at one and the same time, and that the evidence in one case should be considered and tried by the court as evidence in the other. After the trial the court made findings of fact and conclusions of law in favor of respondent and against appellant, and thereupon entered judgment ordering that appellant was not entitled to the relief sought, denying its application for an injunction and dismissing the cause. In due course of time appellant regularly gave notice of motion and motion for a new trial. The application of appellant for a new trial was regularly denied, and from the judgment entered against it and the order denying a new trial this appeal is taken.

As grounds for reversing said judgment, the appellant assigns and distinctly specifies seventeen alleged errors of the court that occurred at said trial. These relate to the admission of certain evidence, insufficiency of evidence to support the findings of fact made by the court, conclusions of the court that were contrary to law, that the judgment is contrary to the evidence, that the judgment is against law, that the court erred in entering judgment against appellant and in denying its motion for a new trial.

The first error relied upon by appellant is that the court permitted respondent to prove that logs could not be taken down the Coeur d'Alene river profitably or successfully in booms or tows. Appellant contends that this evidence was immaterial as the fact it tended to prove if established would not give respondent the right to interfere with its property, but we think there was no error in this ruling of the court, for the reason that the Coeur d'Alene river is navigable and open to public use, and the respondent had a right to use the river for transporting to market or to its place of business its logs and timbers in the most convenient and least expensive manner, so long as it did not unnecessarily interfere with the rights of appellant.

As to the second error assigned by appellant to the effect that the court erred in admitting certain testimony on behalf of respondent, tending to prove that the point on the Coeur d'Alene river at which appellant maintained its sorting works was the only practicable place on the Coeur d'Alene river for intercepting, receiving and sorting sawlogs and for sorting works intended for that purpose, we think that the court did not err in admitting this evidence, for the reason that the right to use the river for the purpose of transporting logs and other timbers also carries with it the right in a reasonable manner to intercept them when they reach their destination at the most feasible and convenient place to receive them, so long as this does not unnecessarily interfere with the rights of others to the use of the river. To hold otherwise would render the right to the use of said river for navigating logs and other timbers of little practical value.

Assignment of error No. 3 relates to the ruling of the court in permitting the respondents to show the prevailing winds and the direction of the current of the river during the season for floating logs down the river. We do not think this was error. The respondent in the affirmative part of its answer alleges that appellant's sorting works were not kept in repair and that its logs as they floated down the river, went out through holes in said works and were lost on the lowlands beyond, or on the lakeshore. We therefore think that if the prevailing winds, or currents of the stream, tended to carry logs floating down the same over and against these works and through holes therein, this fact might be shown. Assignments of errors Nos. 4 and 5 alleged that the court erred in permitting respondent to show how many logs it owned in the years 1912 and 1913 and sorted during those years, but we think this testimony was permissible under the issues made by the pleadings and that there was no error in admitting the same.

Assignment of error No. 6 was as to the admission of evidence by the court tending to show that the Coeur d'Alene river was jammed and obstructed with logs in the year 1910, because appellant's sorting works were too small to handle them, but we think there was no error in the admission of this testimony.

The appellant's seventh alleged error, to the effect that the court erred in not separately stating its findings of fact and conclusions of law, we think is without merit. The court made its findings of fact and divided them into nineteen distinct numbered paragraphs, and then based upon them it specifically stated its conclusions of law in six numbered paragraphs.

We see no ground for complaint as to the *form* of these findings and conclusions.

The other assignments of error relate to three principal points of objection against these findings and conclusions, namely, (1) that the findings of fact, or at least most of them, are not supported by the evidence; (2) that said conclusions of law are contrary to the evidence; and (3) that said conclusions of law and judgment are against the law. Before going into the consideration of the objections pointed out by appellant relating to the insufficiency of the evidence to support said findings of fact, we will say that this court has in a number of well-considered cases approved and held to the doctrine that the findings of the lower court are conclusive, where there is a substantial conflict in the evidence upon questions of fact, and in support of this we refer to *Sabin v. Burke*, 4 Ida. 28, 37 Pac. 352, *Pine v. Callahan*, 8 Ida. 684, 71 Pac. 473, *Stuart v. Hauser*, 9 Ida. 53, 72 Pac. 719, and a number of other cases decided by this court, down to the later cases of *Robbins v. Porter*, 12 Ida. 738, 88 Pac. 86, and *Heckman v. Espey*, 12 Ida. 755, 88 Pac. 80. This we accept as the settled doctrine of this court, and, therefore, where there is a substantial conflict of the evidence upon which any certain finding of fact is based, we will not disturb such finding.

Finding No. 7 is the first finding of fact to which appellant objects and assigns as the reason therefor that it is not supported by the evidence. In substance, this finding is that the defendant has not gone upon plaintiff's land and has not deprived it of the free use of the river at or along its banks, and has not prevented it from ingress to or egress from said lands by way of the river, and that defendant has not deprived plaintiff of the use or enjoyment of any of its piling, sorting works, log-race or lands or any of its property. Without going into any analysis of the testimony in support of this finding for the purpose of deciding as to the weight of the evidence, we think the record shows that this finding is not without substantial evidence to support it. The witness Strathorn testified on direct examination that the defendant's works were fastened to the works of the plaintiff, but on cross-examination he was asked: "Q. You do not know of your own knowledge, do you, that the boom that was pointed out to you as the Stack-Gibbs boom was attached to the piling belonging to the Cameron Lumber Co.? A. I do not. Q. It was told to you that it was, was it not? A. I took it for granted, yes. Q. Who told you? A. Mr. Smith,—Mr. Crego was on the boat but it was Mr. Smith that told me. Q. You say that the defendant company attached to the works of the Cameron Lumber Co., the only attachment that was made was at the upper end of the jack where the sheer boom was attached to the piling? A. Yes. Q. It was in the water, was it not? A. Yes." Harrie Deroshie testified in regard to the gaps in respondent's works being open in March, 1912, and said that logs were running through the gaps of appellant's sorting works before the sheer boom was placed along parallel thereto by the respondent company; and this witness also testified that the piling to which said sheer boom of respondent was tied or attached was a piling driven in the river by the Stack-Gibbs Lumber Co., the evidence of this witness upon this point being as follows: "Q. Whose piling is that, if you know? A. Stack-Gibbs. Q. Who drove it? A. Stack-Gibbs." This witness also testified as follows: "What is the fact as to the defendant's boom being attached to any piling constituting part of the Cameron Lumber Co. works? A. Not tied to any of their piling." The record shows that on the trial the respondent went into this question fully as to what was done in connection with this matter and how their works were operated, and we think the evidence shows that the appellant did not use its sorting works in 1912 and was not using them at the time respondent placed its sheer boom in the river, and that all of the logs received by the respondent company passed by the appellant's works down the channel of the river and into the receiving booms of the works of the respondent. The said sheer boom placed on the south side of the river parallel with the works of the appellant was placed there by the respondent to keep their logs from going through the openings of the respondent's works, which was out of repair, and being lost in the lake or the lowlands beyond. It further appears that the appellant was notified that if they would keep these openings closed, then this sheer boom would be removed by the respondent, and that they neglected to do so.

Finding No. 8, which is also objected to by appellant, is in effect disposed of by what we have said in regard to No. 7, and we think the objections to this finding are without merit. Finding No. 9, in which the court finds that no act of the defendant has caused the plaintiff any pecuniary loss whatever and that plaintiff has not been deprived of any business and has not been deprived of the full opportunity to use its sorting works, if it so desired, by reason of the acts of the defendant, and has not lost any profits in the use of its sorting works by reason of any acts of defendant, and that plaintiff has not been damaged in anywise whatever by the acts of defendant, and will not be damaged by any acts which defendant has done or is now doing, we think is supported by substantial evidence and should not be disturbed by this court.

Finding No. 10 is in substance that in the driving of piling in the bed of the river by defendant and in stretching booms upon said river, as defendant has done, said defendant has not prevented the navigation of the river and has not prevented and has not interfered with the navigation of said river, and that defendant has not tied its boom to the sorting works or piling of the plaintiff, and that defendant has not created and has not maintained and is not now maintaining or creating any nuisance or damage to the plaintiff. There was some evidence tending to show that the stretching of the boom referred to in this finding would, to some extent, delay boats and logs that were navigating or being floated in said river, but we think that the respondent had a right to make a reasonable and prudent use of this river, for navigation, and to its use in connection with collecting its logs and passing them through its sorting works to their destination, as long as it conducted its operations in a reasonable and prudent manner and with due regard to the rights of others to exercise an equal privilege thereto. Some inconvenience or damage might thereby fall upon the appellant, but any inconvenience or damage that might be caused by such reasonable use of the stream by respondent would be *damnum absque injuria*. (*Small v. Harrington*, 10 Ida. 499, 79 Pac. 461.)

The question of the reasonable use of a navigable stream, and to what extent the same may be obstructed by persons in exercising such reasonable use, is very fully discussed in *Davis v. Winslow*, 51 Me. 264, 81 Am. Dec. 573, which is a leading case upon this question. In that case, after reviewing numerous authorities, the court said:

"The general doctrine to be deduced from the authorities collated in reference to the use of navigable rivers or public streams as public highways is, that each person has an equal right to their reasonable use. What constitutes reasonable use depends upon the circumstances of each particular case; and no positive rule of law can be laid down to define and regulate such use, with entire precision, so various are the subjects and occasions for it, and so diversified the relations of parties therein interested. In determining the question of reasonable use, regard must be had to the subject matter of the use, the occasion and manner of its application, its object, extent, necessity and duration and the established usage of the country. The size of the stream, also, the fall of water, its volume, velocity, and prospective rise or fall, are important elements to be taken into the account. The same promptness and efficiency would not be expected of the owner of logs thrown promiscuously into the stream, in respect to their management, as would be required of a ship-master in navigating his ship. Every person has an undoubted right to use a public highway, whether upon the land or water, for all legitimate purposes of travel and transportation; and if, in doing so, while in the exercise of ordinary care, he necessarily and unavoidably impede or obstruct another temporarily, he does not thereby become a wrongdoer, his acts are not illegal, and he creates no nuisance for which an action can be maintained."

Appellant makes particular objection to that part of finding No. 12, in which the court states: "That said receiving booms and sorting works of the defendant are placed far out in Lake Coeur d'Alene, far beyond the sorting works of the plaintiff, and do not interfere with the plaintiff's sorting works or other works, or the use there in any manner whatever." This entire finding does not relate to the sheer boom in front of appellant's sorting works, but only to the storage booms and sorting works of respondent located a considerable distance away from appellant's land and sorting works, and we think it is sustained by the evidence.

Counsel for appellant in their brief, at page 28, say that, "Finding No. 13 is to the effect that the works of defendant and respondent do not form a hindrance to navigation; that it can handle all the sawlogs coming down the river without permitting the same to jam, but that plaintiff's and appellant's works are insufficient to handle the logs that come down the river. This is against the weight of testimony that has been introduced touching this matter." There does appear to be some conflict in the testimony of the witnesses upon this point, but, as heretofore stated, this court will not undertake to weigh the proof to ascertain which side has the preponderance, and where there is a substantial conflict in the evidence it will not disturb the findings of the trial court, and, as the record shows at least a substantial conflict upon the main question involved in this finding, we are not disposed to disturb the same. Furthermore, in the judgment or decree in this case, the lower court makes this statement which we think is worthy of consideration by this court in considering the weight of the evidence upon which the various findings herein have been based, to wit: "Oral and documentary evidence was introduced, and thereupon the court personally inspected the booms, sorting works and premises in controversy in this action, and thereupon, upon said testimony and review and personal inspection of said premises so made by the court, the court made and caused to be filed herein its findings of fact and conclusions of law." But even if the booms and sorting works of respondent do in fact to some extent form a hindrance to the free navigation of the river at times, we think that might be considered only an incident to the reasonable use of this public waterway by respondent for floating and securing its logs.

In *Gerrish v. Brown,* 51 Me. 256, 81 Am. Dec. 569, the court says: ''For such purpose, and as incident to the reasonable use of the river for running and securing logs, parties may use temporary sheer, or guide, booms to direct the logs or lumber into proper places, in which to detain them for use.''

In Finding No. 14, the court found that there were no sufficient receiving works in the Coeur d'Alene river to handle the logs that annually came down said river without jamming the river and interfering with navigation, and also that during the spring of 1912 the Cameron Lumber Co. had its sorting works at the mouth of the river along the banks thereof, extending a short distance into the lake, and that said sorting works had jacks or openings on each side thereof for the purpose of attaching bag booms in which logs belonging to different companies and individuals were placed when said sorting works were operated; that during the season of 1912 these sorting works had six of such openings on the north side of the river and these openings were not protected or closed by any sheer booms or jack poles, or any means of preventing sawlogs from floating into the same; that logs floating into these openings from the north side would be, by the force of the current and wind, driven into and through said sorting works into the main waters of Lake Coeur d'Alene beyond, and that by reason of said openings so negligently and carelessly maintained in said sorting works, the logs belonging to the defendant and others became entangled, and were by the force of the current driven through said works and out into Lake Coeur d'Alene beyond. This finding seems to be sustained by substantial evidence. The appellant at said time was not attempting to use its works in any manner whatever, and it refused to keep its jacks closed so that others could have the reasonable use of the river in floating their logs.

In regard to the sheer boom placed along the south side of the river parallel to appellant's sorting works, it was the intention of the respondent, as shown by the record, to only temporarily maintain this boom for the purpose of protecting its logs from being lost by going through said openings in the works of appellant and out into the lake. The evidence shows that the boom placed by respondent on the north side of the river in front of lot 4 was only for a short time attached to some brush or a tree until other arrangements for maintaining it for the purposes then required could be made. Thereafter it was attached to a cluster of piling situated in the river near the south side of the same. This south bank of the river along lot 4 of the land of appellant is low, and during high water was almost entirely submerged thereby, and along this low bank of the river a large quantity of underbrush or shrubbery is growing into which logs coming down the river are carried by force of the current and lodged or lost if not by some means protected from doing so. The record also shows that lot 4 is a low, swampy piece of land through which runs a canal or ditch, known as Howell's ditch, and when the water is high this ditch fills with water and backs out across lot 4, and the evidence shows that said sheer boom was only placed there to prevent logs from going out through said ditch and brush over this swampy land and lodging there or being lost. At that time the appellant was not using this land for any purpose, and the piling to which this sheer boom along the north side of the river was attached did not constitute any part of appellant's works and had not been driven in the river by it, but was placed there by the Northern Pacific Railroad Co. some years before for the purpose of marking the channel of the river. Under such circumstances and conditions as confronted the respondent at the time it placed and maintained said sheer boom in the river, if it had not been permitted to do so, the right to use the river for the purpose of floating logs would have been of no practical benefit to it.

In *Powell v. Springston Lumber Co.*, 12 Ida. 723, 88 Pac. 97, on this question of maintaining a boom on the river in connection with floating and handling logs by parties engaged in that business, the court said: "The construction and use of booms is a necessary adjunct to the floating of logs, without them it would frequently be impossible to handle the logs where wanted for use. The right to float logs down a stream carries with it the necessary resultant right of employing some reasonable means for intercepting them at their destination.'' Without reviewing at length the authorities presented by the briefs of counsel in this case on the subject, we think the doctrine of this court as to the right of obstructing the river by parties engaged in using the same for any legitimate purpose is very clearly stated in *Small v. Harrington, supra,* as follows:

''The rule governing cases of this character is that all parties interested in the free use of a navigable stream are subject to conditions that may exist in each particular case. No one has the right to arbitrarily obstruct a stream to the detriment or injury of his neighbor; each one is entitled to the free and reasonable use of the navigable streams of this state, and may place such reasonable obstructions on the stream so long as they serve a useful and beneficial purpose and leave a reasonable use to others interested. . . . . If an obstruction merely impairs or renders more difficult the navigation without destroying it, an individual has no rightful cause for complaint, because he has no right to insist on the best possible accommodation.''

There are some other objections urged by appellant to the findings of fact and conclusions of the lower court, but we have carefully examined them in connection with the evidence and do not think it would serve any useful purpose in disposing of this case for us to comment upon them, as our views upon the main questions presented by this appeal have been expressed already by what we have said in deciding the points which we have now considered and passed upon. Having reached the conclusion that there is no reversible error presented in this case, the judgment of the lower court is, therefore, affirmed. Costs awarded to the respondent.

Sullivan, C. J., and Budge, J., concur.

(December 28, 1914.)

STACK-GIBBS LUMBER CO., a Corporation, Respondent,
v. CAMERON LUMBER CO., a Corporation, Appellant.

[144 Pac. 1121.]

APPEAL from the District Court of the Eighth Judicial
District for Kootenai County. Hon. Robert N. Dunn, Judge.

Action in equity to enjoin the defendant company from
in any manner interfering with the booms and sorting works
of the plaintiff, at or near the mouth of the Coeur d'Alene
river. Judgment for plaintiff. Defendant appeals. Judgment *affirmed.*

McFarland & McFarland, for Appellant.

Whitla & Nelson and Voorhees & Canfield, for Respondent.

TRUITT, J.—This action was commenced by the respondent, as plaintiff in the lower court, against the appellant, as
defendant in the said court, for the purpose of restraining
and enjoining said defendant from interfering with the plaintiff's receiving booms, sorting works and piling, located in
the Coeur d'Alene river and in Lake Coeur d'Alene, near
and at the mouth of the Coeur d'Alene river in Kootenai
county, Idaho, and to restrain defendant from in any manner
whatever interfering with its receiving and intercepting the
logs floated down said river, and sorting the same and placing
the same in booms. Upon the hearing of this action, this restraining order was granted by the court and made permanent
for the purposes for which it was issued. From this judgment, the defendant appealed.

The same property rights of said plaintiff and defendant
involved in this case were also involved in the case of said
Cameron Lumber Co. against the respondent, Stack-Gibbs
Lumber Co.; and on May 3, 1913, counsel for these respective
parties entered into the following stipulation:

"Whereas, the above-entitled case and the case of Cameron Lumber Co., Ltd., a corporation, plaintiff, against Stack-Gibbs Lumber Co., a corporation, defendant, pending in the above-entitled court, were on, to wit, the 8th day of May, A. D. 1913, consolidated for the purpose of trial in said court, and were thereafter tried together in said court, and,

"Whereas, a judgment was on, to wit, the 21st day of May, A. D. 1913, rendered and entered in said court in said case of Cameron Lumber Co., Ltd., a corporation, plaintiff, against Stack-Gibbs Lumber Co., a corporation, defendant, in favor of said defendant and against said plaintiff, and on June 2, 1913, in said court a judgment was rendered in the above-entitled action in favor of plaintiff, Stack-Gibbs Lumber Co., a corporation, and against said defendant, Cameron Lumber Co., Ltd., a corporation, and

"Whereas, the said Cameron Lumber Co. is desirous of making application and moving for a new trial in each of said cases, and for that purpose, of obtaining the court reporter's transcript of the evidence and proceedings taken upon said trial, and

"Whereas, it is deemed an unnecessary expense to procure and obtain the court reporter's transcript of the evidence and proceedings in each of said cases, and

"Whereas, the plaintiff in the case of Cameron Lumber Co., Ltd., a corporation, plaintiff, against Stack-Gibbs Lumber Co., a corporation, defendant, has procured an order for the court reporter's transcript of the evidence and proceedings, in said case,

"Now, therefore, it is hereby agreed and stipulated by and between the above-named plaintiff and the above-named defendant, by and through their respective attorneys, that the court reporter's transcript of the evidence and proceedings, to be hereafter furnished by said court reporter and lodged with the clerk of said court as required by law, may be used on application and motion of the defendant in the above-entitled action for a new trial herein, and, in the event that a new trial is denied or granted, and an appeal is taken from said order and from the judgment therein to the Supreme

Court of the State of Idaho, that said reporter's transcript may be used on appeal in the above-entitled action in the Supreme Court of the State of Idaho, by either party.

"And it is hereby further stipulated that the defendant in the above-entitled action be not, and it is not hereby required to furnish the reporter's transcript of the evidence and proceedings to be used on motion for a new trial, or on appeal to the Supreme Court of the State of Idaho, in the above-entitled action.

"Dated this 3d day of May, 1913.

"WHITLA & NELSON,

"Attorneys for Plaintiff.

"McFARLAND & McFARLAND,

"Attorneys for Defendant."

The testimony in this case was substantially the same as in the said case of the Cameron Lumber Co. against this respondent, and it is controlled in its principles of law by the decision just announced in that case. We have examined the evidence in this case in connection with the findings of fact by the court and its conclusions of law, and upon the authority of said case of the Cameron Lumber Co. against this respondent, the judgment of the lower court is affirmed, and costs are awarded to the respondent.

Sullivan, C. J., and Budge, J., concur.

(December 31, 1914.)

STATE, to and for the Use and Benefit of CLARA MILLS et al., Respondent, v. AMERICAN SURETY COMPANY OF NEW YORK, Appellant.

[145 Pac. 1097.]

OFFICIAL BOND—ACTION ON—DEFAULT — JURISDICTION—REMOVAL OF
CAUSE—VACATION OF DEFAULT — COMPLAINT — SUFFICIENCY OF
COMPLAINT—STATUTORY CONSTRUCTION—PUBLIC OFFICER—BREACH
OF DUTY—LIABILITY OF SURETY—PARTIES TO ACTION.

1. Where a defendant has been sued in a state court and summons has been served upon him, and, prior to the expiration of the term within which he is required to answer under the statute and without appearing or answering, he files a petition for a removal to the federal court, and an order denying the removal is made by the state court, and the record is thereafter transferred by the defendant to the federal court, when on motion in the latter court the cause is remanded to the state court for want of jurisdiction in the federal court, and the clerk of the district court enters the default of the defendant for failure to appear and answer; *held,* that the action of the clerk in entering the default of the defendant is regular and valid, and within the authority and direction of secs. 4140 and 4360, Rev. Codes, and that such default is not void for want of jurisdiction.

2. Where the default has been entered by the clerk against the defendant, as was done in this case, the court has jurisdiction to hear the proofs submitted by the plaintiff and to enter judgment thereon.

3. Under the above facts, where the defendant moves to have the default vacated on the ground of inadvertence, surprise or excusable neglect, *held,* that under the excuse presented and the facts of this case, as shown by the record, the trial court did not err in refusing to set aside said default.

4. Sec. 4140, Rev. Codes, fixes the time within which a defendant shall appear and answer, and the fact that prior to the expiration of that time the defendant undertook to have the cause removed to the federal court and it was thereafter remanded, such action on the part of the defendant to change the forum will not serve to extend the time for answer in the state court and will not relieve the defendant from a default which it thus allows to be entered against it.

5. The filing of a petition and bond for a removal to the federal court is not an appearance in the state court, under the provisions of the Revised Codes of Idaho.

6. When a defendant attempts to remove an action which he is not entitled to remove, and the state court refuses to surrender its jurisdiction, the state court may proceed with the cause and its subsequent proceedings are valid.

7. *Held*, under the facts of this case, that the default was not prematurely entered.

8. The legislature in enacting sec. 3001, Rev. Codes, making it the duty of the bank commissioner to make an examination of state banks, imposed such duty for the benefit and protection of the depositors as well as the public.

9. A bank commissioner in the exercise of discretionary duties is not responsible to anyone receiving an injury through a breach of his official duty, unless he acts maliciously and wilfully wrong, or clearly abuses his discretion to the extent of acting unfaithfully and in bad faith.

10. In an action by an injured party against the surety on the bond of the bank commissioner executed under sec. 191, Rev. Codes, for failure of said commissioner to faithfully perform his duty, it is not necessary to first proceed and have the damages of the injured party adjudged against the commissioner.

11. Under a joint and several bond executed pursuant to sec. 191, Rev. Codes, it is not necessary to sue jointly the principal and surety, but suit may be maintained against either severally.

12. *Held*, that the complaint herein states a cause of action.

APPEAL from the District Court of the Fourth Judicial District for Blaine County. Hon. Edward A. Walters, Judge.

Action by the state to recover on a surety company's bond. Judgment for the plaintiff. Judgment *affirmed*.

Richards & Haga and McKeen F. Morrow, for Appellant.

When a citizen of another state files a petition and bond in due form and gives the required notice for the removal of a cause to the federal court on the ground of diversity of citizenship, the time within which defendant must plead further is governed by federal law. (Sec. 29, The Judicial Code.)

The attempt of state courts to exercise jurisdiction over causes after the federal court assumed jurisdiction, or while the federal court has the question of its jurisdiction under consideration, has been condemned repeatedly by the higher courts. (*Ches. & Ohio Ry. Co. v. McCabe,* 213 U. S. 207, 29 Sup. Ct. 430, 53 L. ed. 766; *Coeur d'Alene Ry. & Nav. Co. v. Spalding,* 6 Ida. 97, 53 Pac. 107; Dillon, Removal of Causes, 5th ed., p. 158.)

The petition for removal and the accompanying motion or application for an order of removal constitute appearance and pleading within the meaning and intent of the state law governing the authority of the clerk to enter default, and no default can be entered by the clerk until the petition has been finally denied or overruled. (*Mattoon v. Hinkley,* 33 Ill. 208; *State v. Gittings,* 35 Md. 169; *Osprey v. Jenkins,* 9 Mo. 643; *Atchison T. & S. F. Ry. Co. v. Lambert,* 31 Okl. 300, Ann. Cas. 1913E, 329, 121 Pac. 654; 6 Ency. Pl. & Pr. 93; 23 Cyc. 757.)

The petition for removal is a plea to the jurisdiction of the court, and in overruling a petition or motion for the removal of a cause the rule of *respondeat ouster* obtains, and the order should be that defendant plead further within the time fixed by the court, and until the expiration of such time no default can be entered against defendant. (*Kelly v. Van Austin,* 17 Cal. 564; *Reinhart v. Lugo,* 86 Cal. 395, 21 Am. St. 52, 24 Pac. 1089; 6 Ency. Pl. & Pr. 80; 1 Black on Judgments, 2d ed., sec. 13; 1 Freeman on Judgments, 4th ed., sec. 7; *Trow v. Messer,* 32 N. H. 361; *Cooke v. Crawford,* 1 Tex. 9, 46 Am. Dec. 93; *Robb v. Parker,* 4 Heisk. (Tenn.) 58; *Kamp v. Bartlett,* 164 Ill. App. 338.)

A simple default should be vacated in furtherance of justice and on such terms as may be proper. (*McFarlane v. McFarlane,* 45 Or. 360, 77 Pac. 837; *Hall v. McCan,* 62 Or. 556, 126 Pac. 5; *Cutler v. Haycock,* 32 Utah, 354, 90 Pac. 897; *Melde v. Reynolds,* 129 Cal. 308, 61 Pac. 932; *Greene v. Montana Brewing Co.,* 32 Mont. 102, 79 Pac. 693; *Staley v. O'Day,* 22 Cal. App. 149, 133 Pac. 620; *Douglas v. Badger State Mine,* 41 Wash. 266, 83 Pac. 178, 4 L. R. A., N. S., 196.)

The application for vacating the default entered against defendant shows both mistake, inadvertence, surprise and excusable neglect, and the trial court erroneously assumed it had no discretion in the matter.   Statutes should be liberally construed with the view to determining causes on the merits. (Rev. Codes, secs. 4, 4225, 4226, 4228, 4229 and 4231; *Shreve v. Cheesman*, 69 Fed. 785, 16 C. C. A. 413; *Flagg v. Puterbaugh*, 98 Cal. 134, 32 Pac. 863; *Smith v. Whittier*, 95 Cal. 279, 30 Pac. 529; *Wallace v. Okolona Savings' Inst. Co.*, 49 Miss. 616, 620.)

The cause was removable to the federal court, and an order should have been made transferring it.   (*Ex parte Nebraska*, 209 U. S. 436, 28 Sup. Ct. 581, 52 L. ed. 876; *Troy Bank v. Whitehead & Co.*, 222 U. S. 39, 32 Sup. Ct. 9, 56 L. ed. 81; *Illinois Central R. Co. v. Adams*, 180 U. S. 28, 21 Sup. Ct. 251, 45 L. ed. 410.)

The liability of the surety on this bond does not extend to the general public depositing money in the banks of the state. (Ida. Rev. Codes, secs. 191, 194, 3000, 3001, 3003, 3005 and 3004.)   Sec. 191, Rev. Codes, requires all damages against the bank commissioner to be adjudged against such bank commissioner before the surety of such commissioner can be held liable.   (*Umbreit v. American Bonding Co.*, 144 Wis. 611, 129 N. W. 789; *Western Assurance Co. v. Klein*, 48 Neb. 904, 67 N. W. 873; *Blaufus v. People*, 69 N. Y. 107, 25 Am. Rep. 148; *Webb v. Bidwell*, 15 Minn. 484; *United States v. Irwin*, 127 U. S. 125, 8 Sup. Ct. 1033, 32 L. ed. 99; *Sans v. City of New York*, 31 Misc. Rep. 559, 64 N. Y. Supp. 681; *New Orleans Nat. Banking Assn. v. Adams*, 3 Woods, 21, Fed. Cas. No. 10,184; *Brownell v. Greenwich*, 44 Hun (N. Y.), 611, 8 N. Y. St. Rep. 6; *Wirt v. Peck*, 184 Fed. 54, 107 C. C. A. 16; *Tyler Min. Co. v. Last Chance Min. Co.*, 90 Fed. 15, 32 C. C. A. 498; *Browning v. Porter*, 12 Fed. 460, 2 McCrary, 581.)   Sec. 3005 imposes unusually severe penalties on the commissioner if he proceeds against a bank without reasonable cause.   In view of such penalties a very strong showing should be required before any court would be justified in holding the commissioner liable for an abuse of discretion in failing to close a bank.   (*Reed v. Conway*, 20 Mo. 22; *Jenkins v. Waldron*, 11 Johns. (N. Y.) 114, 6 Am. Dec. 359.)

On official bonds there can be no liability and no recovery without malice alleged and proved. (*Wheeler v. Patterson*, 1 N. H. 88, 8 Am. Dec. 41; *Weaver v. Devendorf*, 3 Denio (N. Y.), 120; *Wilson v. Mayor*, 1 Denio (N. Y.), 599, 43 Am. Dec. 719; *Venderheyden v. Young*, 11 Johns. (N. Y.) 160; *State v. Chadwick*, 10 Or. 465.)

The duties of the bank commissioner under sec. 3005, Rev. Codes, are not ministerial. They are of a highly discretionary character. (*State ex rel. Irvine v. Brooks*, 14 Wyo. 393, 84 Pac. 488, 7 Ann. Cas. 1108, 6 L. R. A., N. S., 750.)

The official is not liable in damages for either error of judgment, incompetency or mistakes of law or fact. (*Hoke v. Henderson*, 15 N. C. 1, 25 Am. Dec. 677; *Edwards v. United States*, 103 U. S. 471, 26 L. ed. 314; *United States v. McClane*, 74 Fed. 153; *Gould v. Hammond*, 10 Fed. Cas. No. 5636; *Pratt v. Gardner*, 2 Cush. (Mass.) 63, 48 Am. Dec. 652; *Stone v. Graves*, 8 Mo. 148, 40 Am. Dec. 131; *Rains v. Simpson*, 50 Tex. 495, 32 Am. Rep. 609; *Spalding v. Vilas*, 161 U. S. 483, 16 Sup. Ct. 631, 40 L. ed. 780.)

J. H. Peterson, Attorney General, for the State, and Sullivan & Sullivan, for Respondent.

Default cannot be set aside by reason of mistake of law. (1 Black on Judgments, secs. 335, 340a; Freeman on Judgments, secs. 58, 508; 17 Am. & Eng. Ency. Law, 831, 833; 6 Ency. Pl. & Pr. 167; 23 Cyc. 938, 939; *Smith v. Pelton Water Wheel Co.*, 151 Cal. 394, 90 Pac. 934; *Allen v. Continental Ins. Co.*, 97 Ill. App. 164; *Keenan v. Daniells*, 18 S. D. 102, 99 N. W. 853; *Plano Mfg. Co. v. Murphy*, 16 S. D. 380, 102 Am. St. 692, 92 N. W. 1072; *McDaniels v. Bank of Rutland*, 29 Vt. 230, 70 Am. Dec. 406, 412; *Phifer v. Travelers' Ins. Co.*, 123 N. C. 405, 31 S. E. 715.)

There can be no relief against mistake of law. (*Wilmerding v. Corbin Banking Co.*, 126 Ala. 268, 28 So. 640; *Early v. Bard*, 93 App. Div. 476, 87 N. Y. Supp. 650; *City of Noblesville v. Noblesville Gas etc. Co.*, 157 Ind. 162, 60 N. E. 1032; *Mouser v. Harmon*, 96 Ky. 591, 29 S. W. 448; *Cox v. Arm-*

strong (Ky.), 43 S. W. 189; *Mantle v. Casey,* 31 Mont. 408, 78 Pac. 591; *Donlan v. Thompson Falls Copper etc. Co.,* 42 Mont. 257, 112 Pac. 445; *Willoburn Ranch Co. v. Yegen,* 45 Mont. 254, 122 Pac. 915.)   The early decisions of California, under a statute identical with ours, should be followed in construing the word "mistake" in sec. 4229, Rev. Codes.   (*Chase v. Swain,* 9 Cal. 130; *People v. Rains,* 23 Cal. 128.)

This court in *Morbeck v. Bradford-Kennedy Co.,* 19 Ida. 83, 113 Pac. 89, has passed upon this question of a "mistake of law" not being sufficient to set aside a default.   (See, also, *Donovan v. Miller,* 12 Ida. 600, 88 Pac. 82, 10 Ann. Cas. 444, 9 L. R. A., N. S., 524.)

Under sec. 4229, to set aside simple default, it is necessary to show mistake, inadvertence, surprise or excusable neglect.

"If on the face of the record, including the petition for removal of a cause, the suit does not appear to be a removable one, the state court is not bound to surrender jurisdiction, but may proceed as if no application for removal had been made." (*Missouri K. & T. Ry. Co. v. Chappell,* 206 Fed. 688; *Phoenix Ins. Co. v. Pechner,* 95 U. S. 183, 24 L. ed. 427; *Yulee v. Vose,* 99 U. S. 539, 25 L. ed. 355; *Kern v. Huidekoper,* 103 U. S. 485, 26 L. ed. 354; *Gregory v. Hartley,* 113 U. S. 742, 5 Sup. Ct. 743, 28 L. ed. 1150; *Stone v. South Carolina,* 117 U. S. 430, 6 Sup. Ct. 799, 29 L. ed. 962, 963; *Crehore v. Ohio etc. Ry. Co.,* 131 U. S. 240, 9 Sup. Ct. 692, 33 L. ed. 144, 145; *Chesapeake & O. Ry. Co. v. McCabe,* 213 U. S. 207, 29 Sup. Ct. 430, 53 L. ed. 765; *Springer v. Howes,* 69 Fed. 849; *Monroe v. Williamson,* 81 Fed. 977, 984; *Eisenmann v. Delemar's Nevada Gold Min. Co.,* 87 Fed. 248; *Fife v. Whittell,* 102 Fed. 537; *Dalton v. Milwaukee M. Ins. Co.,* 118 Fed. 881; *McAlister v. Chesapeake & O. Ry. Co.,* 157 Fed. 740, 85 C. C. A. 316, 13 Ann. Cas. 1068; *Phillips v. Western Terra Cotta Co.,* 174 Fed. 873; *Mannington v. Hocking Val. Ry. Co.,* 183 Fed. 133; *Stevenson v. Illinois Cent. R. Co.,* 192 Fed. 956; *Hansford v. Stone-Ordean-Wells Co.,* 201 Fed. 185; *Texas & P. Ry. Co. v. McAllister,* 59 Tex. 349; *McWhinney v. Brinker,* 64 Ind. 360; *Illinois Cent. R. R. Co. v. Le Blanc,* 74 Miss. 626, 21 So. 748; *Hickman v. Missouri etc. Ry. Co.,* 151 Mo. 644, 52 S. W.

351; *White v. Holt*, 20 W. Va. 792; *Hayes v. Todd*, 34 Fla.
233, 15 So. 752; *Western Union Tel. Co. v. Griffith*, 104 Ga.
56, 30 S. E. 420; *Bixby v. Blair*, 56 Iowa, 416, 9 N. W. 318;
Stone v. Sargent, 129 Mass. 503, 510; *Howard v. Southern Ry.
Co.*, 122 N. C. 944, 29 S. E. 778; *Howard v. Stewart*, 34 Neb.
765, 52 N. W. 714; *Southern Pac. R. Co. v. Superior Court*,
63 Cal. 607, 612; *Knott v. McGilvray*, 124 Cal. 128, 56 Pac.
789; *Golden v. Northern Pac. Ry. Co.*, 39 Mont. 435, 104 Pac.
549, 18 Ann. Cas. 886, 34 L. R. A., N. S., 1154; *Debnam v.
Southern Bell Tel. etc. Co.*, 126 N. C. 831, 36 S. E. 269, 65
L. R. A. 915; *Western Coal & Min. Co. v. Osborne*, 30 Okl.
235, 119 Pac. 973; *Chicago etc. Ry. Co. v. Brazzell*, 33 Okl.
122, 124 Pac. 40; Black's Dillon, Removal of Causes, secs. 190,
191; Faust on Federal Procedure, 579; Moon's Removal of
Causes, sec. 177; 2 Foster's Fed. Prac., sec. 391; 2 Rose's Code
of Fed. Prac., sec. 1138 (e), (g); 10 Ency. of U. S. Sup. Ct.
Reps. 704, 705; 18 Ency. Pl. & Pr. 338, 351; 34 Cyc. 1305,
1308; A Federal Equity Suit (Simkins), 806; *Coeur d'Alene
Ry. etc. Co. v. Spalding*, 6 Ida. 97, 53 Pac. 107.)

"If a litigant desires to have a cause removed from the state
court to the United States court, he has the right to have it
so removed if he has sufficient grounds therefor; but if he has
not sufficient grounds, and undertakes to secure a removal and
fails, he must take the consequences." (*Finney v. American
Bonding Co.*, 13 Ida. 534, 90 Pac. 859, 91 Pac. 318; *Mills v.
American Bonding Co.*, 13 Ida. 556, 91 Pac. 381.)

The rule under the cases cited by appellant, where individuals are sureties, does not apply to companies engaged in
the surety business for hire. (23 Am. & Eng. Ann. Cas. 1087;
Atlantic Trust etc. Co. v. Laurinburg, 163 Fed. 690, 90 C. C. A.
274; *American Surety Co. v. Pauly*, 170 U. S. 133, 18 Sup. Ct.
552, 42 L. ed. 977; *Hull v. Massachusetts etc. Ins. Co.*, 86 Kan.
342, 120 Pac. 544; *Rule v. Anderson*, 160 Mo. App. 347, 142
S. W. 358.)

"In an action on a joint and several bond, all or any of the
sureties may be sued." (*State v. McDonald*, 4 Ida. 468, 95
Am. St. 137, 40 Pac. 312.)

The amendment to sec. 29 of the New Judicial Code does not contemplate that the state court must accept a petition for removal, sufficient or insufficient, but the procedure remains the same. (*Goins v. Southern Pac. Co.*, 198 Fed. 432; *Hansford v. Stone-Ordean-Wells Co.*, 201 Fed. 185; *United States v. Sessions*, 205 Fed. 502, 123 C. C. A. 570; *Missouri K. & T. Ry. Co. v. Chappell*, 206 Fed. 688; *Loland v. Northwest S. Co.*, 209 Fed. 626; *Wanner v. Bissinger & Co.*, 210 Fed. 96; *Johnson v. Butte etc. Copper Co.*, 213 Fed. 910; 2 Foster's Fed. Prac., p. 1829, note.)

W. B. Davidson and Wm. C. Bristol, *Amici Curiae.*

An individual has no right of action against a public officer for breach of duty owing to the public only, even though such individual is specially injured thereby. (*Gorman v. Commissioners*, 1 Ida. 655; *Worden v. Witt*, 4 Ida. 404, 95 Am. St. 70, 39 Pac. 1114; *People v. Hoag*, 54 Colo. 542, 131 Pac. 400, 45 L. R. A., N. S., 824; *Miller v. Ouray E. L. & Power Co.*, 18 Colo. App. 131, 70 Pac. 447; *Colorado Paving Co. v. Murphy*, 78 Fed. 28, 23 C. C. A. 631, 37 L. R. A. 630; *Ryus v. Gruble*, 31 Kan. 767, 3 Pac. 518; *State v. Harris*, 89 Ind. 363, 46 Am. Rep. 169; *Moss v. Cummings*, 44 Mich. 359, 6 N. W. 843; *School District No. 80 v. Burress*, 2 Neb. Unof. 554, 89 N. W. 609; *Board v. Bladen*, 113 N. C. 379, 18 S. E. 661; *Lowe v. Guthrie*, 4 Okl. 287, 44 Pac. 198; *Dysart v. Lurty*, 3 Okl. 601, 41 Pac. 724; *McPhee v. United States Fidelity etc. Co.*, 52 Wash. 154, 132 Am. St. 958, 100 Pac. 174, 21 L. R. A., N. S., 535; *Foster v. Malberg*, 119 Minn. 168, Ann. Cas. 1914A, 1116, 137 N. W. 816; *Cottam v. Oregon City*, 98 Fed. 570; *South v. Maryland*, 18 How. (U. S.) 396, 15 L. ed. 433.)

TRUITT, J.—This action was brought by the state of Idaho for the use and benefit of fifty-five depositors, or their assignees, in the Idaho State Bank at Hailey against the American Surety Company of New York as surety on the bond of William G. Cruse, former bank commissioner of the state of Idaho, for the failure of said Cruse to faithfully discharge the duties of his office. Said depositors are among those who made deposits during the last four months the bank was open, and subsequent to the time said Cruse had knowledge of its unsafe and insolvent condition and subsequent to May 12, 1910, which latter date was one year after said bank commissioner's last examination of said bank.

It is not claimed in this action that the deposits of these depositors or other depositors prior to May 12, 1910, could be recovered. On May 15, 1909, a bond was executed by said William G. Cruse, as principal, and the American Surety Company of New York, as surety, as required by sec. 191, Rev. Codes, conditioned as follows:

"Now, therefore, if the said William G. Cruse shall well, faithfully and impartially discharge the duties of his office and pay over to the person entitled by law to receive it, all money coming into his hands by virtue of his office, and that he will pay any and all damages and costs that may be urged against him, under the provisions of chap. 12, title 2, Political Code, and chap. 13, title 4, of the Civil Code of Idaho, and shall well and truly perform all the duties of such office required by any law to be enacted subsequent to the execution of this bond, then this obligation to be void, otherwise to remain in full force and effect."

The plaintiff to and for the use of certain parties claims the right to bring this action under sec. 295, Rev. Codes, which is as follows:

"Every official bond executed by any officer pursuant to law, is in force and obligatory upon the principal and sureties therein to and for the state of Idaho, and to and for the use and benefit of all persons who may be injured or aggrieved by the wrongful act or default of such officer in his official capacity, and any person so injured or aggrieved may bring suit on such bond, in his own name, without an assignment thereof."

It is alleged in the complaint that on August 31, 1910, the Idaho State Bank of Hailey closed its doors and suspended payment and had been unable to meet the demands of its creditors and has been in the hands of a receiver ever since; that William G. Cruse was appointed state bank commissioner on March 6, 1909; that said Cruse and the American Surety Co. executed a bond conditioned as required by said sec. 191, Rev. Codes.

The 7th and 8th paragraphs of said complaint are as follows:

"VII.   That, under the provisions of chap. 12, title 4 of the Civil Code of Idaho, it was, among other things, provided that it shall be the duty of the bank commissioner, when he shall deem it necessary, and at least once in each year, without previous notice, to visit and make complete report and examination of the affairs of each bank falling within the provisions of said chapter, which included the said Idaho State Bank.

"VIII.   That, notwithstanding the obligations of said bond, the said William G. Cruse, after the making of said bond and during and before the expiration of his said office, as aforesaid, did not well, faithfully, and impartially discharge the duties of his said office, according to law and the provisions of said chapter, nor did he observe, fulfill and perform the said conditions of said bond, but, on the contrary, he wholly failed, neglected, omitted and refused so to do, and acted unfaithfully, improperly and illegally in this:

"First, That said W. G. Cruse did not, at least once in each year during his said term of office, without notice, visit and make a complete report and examination of the affairs of said bank, as he made an examination on the 12th day of May, 1909, and did not thereafter visit and make another examination thereof until the 31st day of August, 1910, the day he caused said bank to close its doors and suspend payment;

"Second, That, further, on or about the 12th day of May, 1910, and for some time prior thereto, said William G. Cruse had knowledge of the unsafe condition of said bank, and that the same was being conducted contrary to the provisions of said chapter 13, title 4, of the Civil Code of Idaho, and that the books and accounts of said bank were being falsified, which should have caused him to deem it necessary to visit and make a complete report and examination of its affairs, but, nevertheless, he failed, neglected and omitted so to do."

It is also alleged in said complaint that if said Cruse had at least once in each year and when he had cause to deem it necessary, made an examination of said bank, he would have found that it had been and was then guilty of violating each and every duty and requirement prescribed by our banking laws, and would have found that the books were then falsified in many items and accounts, these items being specifically enumerated, and that he would have then and there found reasonable cause to consider said bank insolvent; that when he had found such a condition, which he would have found had he made an examination, it would have been obligatory upon him in the discharge of his duties to have closed said bank and applied immediately in his official capacity for the appointment of a receiver of said bank; that by reason of the failure of said Cruse to faithfully and impartially discharge his duties, certain depositors, for whose benefit this action was brought, who had deposited certain sums in said bank subsequent to May 12, 1910, suffered loss and damage in certain specified amounts by reason of the failure, neglect and omission of said Cruse to faithfully and impartially discharge the duties of his office. Then followed the usual allegations of ownership of the amount in controversy, and the demand, and that the sums had not been paid, that no dividends had been declared by any of the receivers of said bank, and that the different amounts due said depositors had been wholly lost to them.

There are forty-seven separate and distinct causes of action stated in 'said complaint, and each cause of action is for an amount less than $2,000.

The record in this case shows that the defendant before its time for appearance had expired in the lower court, filed a petition and bond for the removal of said cause to the United States district court, but did not file any demurrer or appearance in the state court therewith, or within the statutory time allowed to plead in said court; that the time for appearance in the state court expired on October 14, 1912; that on October 7th plaintiff was served with notice of a motion for removal and in said notice the plaintiff was notified that the defendant would, on October 14, 1912, at 1:30 P. M., at the courthouse in Hailey, move for an order of removal of said cause to the United States district court of Idaho. In response to said notice, counsel for plaintiff went from Boise to Hailey to appear on the day designated in said notice, to protest against and oppose an order for said removal. At the time noted, to wit, 1:30 P. M., of October 14th, counsel for plaintiff appeared before the district court at Hailey, Idaho. No one appeared on behalf of defendant, and the hearing upon defendant's motion was continued at the request of counsel for plaintiff until the following 'ay at 1:30 P. M., for the purpose of giving counsel for defendant an opportunity to be present at said hearing. Counsel for plaintiff again appeared in said court at the time fixed for hearing said motion on that day, but no one appeared therein for the defendant. The court then heard counsel for plaintiff, and being of the opinion that the cause was not removable, it made an order denying the removal, a part of which order is as follows: "It is hereby ordered that the said petition and application on behalf of said defendant be, and the same is, hereby denied. Upon request of counsel for plaintiff, it is further ordered that this court, upon proper showing, will again hear the matter on a motion of defendant to vacate and set aside the order herein made, if said motion be made within proper time."

It thus appears that the plaintiff could have had default in said case entered on October 15, 1912, because no appearance had been made by answer, demurrer or otherwise, in said court at that time by the defendant. On October 16th, no appearance by the defendant having been made, plaintiff filed a *praecipe* for default which was duly entered by the clerk of said court, and thereupon judgment of default was entered by said clerk. On October 17th, three days after plaintiff was noticed for the hearing on removal, counsel for defendant telegraphed or telephoned requesting a hearing to set aside the order of the court theretofore made denying the removal of said cause, which request was granted. The matter was thereafter duly argued by respective counsel and at the close thereof counsel for plaintiff, in the presence of counsel for defendant, stated in open court that a default had already been entered by the clerk in said case.

The court on October 30th refused to alter its former order of October 15th or to set the same aside, and an order to this effect was thereafter duly entered. The defendant then proceeded on October 28th and filed its record of removal of said cause in the United States district court. The plaintiff thereupon moved to remand to the state court, which motion was granted by the United States district court, and an order to that effect transmitted and filed in said federal court on December 10, 1912. On December 10, 1912, after the United States court had remanded said cause and after the state court had refused to set aside the default therein, and fifty-seven days after its time had expired to appear in the state court, being ninety-seven days after defendant was served, for the first time it entered its appearance in the state court by filing a demurrer. On December 10, 1912, the defendant, besides going on with its removal proceedings in the United States district court, filed a motion in the state court to set aside said default. A hearing was had on said motion on November 9, 1912, and the court on December 11th refused to set aside the default of the clerk, but granted the motion of defendant to set aside the judgment on said default entered by the clerk. On December 12, 1912, the defendant filed a renewal of said motion in the state court to set aside said default. Objections to a hearing of the renewal motion were filed by plaintiff, but were overruled by the court and a full hearing granted. Upon this hearing, all of the grounds urged by defendant were fully presented and considered by the court, and another order was thereafter entered by it, denying the renewal motion to set aside said default.

On May 20, 1913, during the next term of the state court, a hearing was had for the purpose of having the court assess the damages in said case. Proofs were submitted over the objection of counsel for the defendant who was present, and the damages were assessed by the court on each cause of action and judgment entered, and from that judgment this appeal was taken.

Appellant assigns the following errors: (1) That the court · erred in not holding and deciding that, appellant having filed a petition for removal of the cause to the federal court and given the required bond and notice, the time for defendant to plead was extended until the cause was remanded to the state court; (2) That the court erred in refusing to vacate or set aside the simple default entered against appellant by the clerk of the court on October 16, 1912; (3) That the court erred in not making an order transferring the cause to the federal court; (4) That the court erred in entering any judgment against appellant; and (5) That the court erred in not dismissing the action at plaintiff's costs, because the complaint did not state facts sufficient to constitute a cause of action against the defendant.

These assignments of alleged error are so related that they may be considered under three heads, viz.: (1) Error of the court in refusing an order of removal of the cause to the federal court, and error of the clerk in entering the default against defendant; (2) Error of the court in refusing to set aside said default; and (3) Error of the court in holding that the complaint stated a cause of action.

The alleged error of the court as to refusing the order of removal and alleged error in regard to the entering of default against defendant by the clerk of the court may be considered together. The record shows that the default was taken after the expiration of the statutory time to plead had expired. But counsel for appellant contend that the default was prematurely taken because of the removal proceedings in the state court; that the filing of the petition and bond for removal of the cause to the United States court constituted a legal appearance in said action in the state court; that when the state court entered an order refusing to grant the removal, it should have ordered that the defendant plead further within the time fixed by said court, or, in other words, that the rule *respondeat ouster* obtained, and that the filing of said petition and bond for removal suspended the juris-

diction of the state court until the cause had been remanded
to said court, and therefore the default entered by the clerk
of said court was null and void because it was entered between the filing of the petition for removal and the order of
the federal court remanding the cause.

The above contentions of appellant are without merit for
the reason that the filing of the petition for removal and the
bond is not an appearance in the state court, and does not
extend the time to appear therein. The defendant might have
demurred or answered at the time it filed its petition for
removal, which is the usual practice, without prejudice to
its petition for removal, and it would have waived no right
by doing so.

These points were distinctly in issue in the case of *Morbeck
v. Bradford-Kennedy Co.*, 19 Ida. 83, 113 Pac. 89, and after
full consideration it was in that case held as above set forth,
and the court there laid down the correct rule. Not having
made any appearance in the state court within the time required by our statute, the entry of default by the clerk was
within the scope of his authority. (*Morbeck v. Bradford-
Kennedy Co., supra.*)

The contention of appellant that the filing of the petition
and bond on removal was an appearance, and that the default
was prematurely entered, is also without merit. The rule of
respondeat ouster does not apply in such cases. If the state
court had signed an order for removal and thereby voluntarily relinquished its jurisdiction, appellant might with some
force claim that a default entered between the time of the
filing of the order granting a removal and the filing of the
order of the federal court remanding the cause was entered by
the clerk without authority.

In this respect there is a marked difference between the
case at bar and the Morbeck-Kennedy case. In that case the
state court voluntarily relinquished its jurisdiction for a time
by signing an order for the removal, while in the case at bar
the state court considered the matter and refused to relinquish its jurisdiction, entered an order refusing a removal
and thereby claimed and retained its jurisdiction. This dif-

ference makes the reason stronger in favor of sustaining the default herein than it was in that case, since in the case at bar there was at no time a break in the jurisdiction of the state court. The trial court all the time had jurisdiction of this action; it refused to surrender such jurisdiction; it acted consistently throughout, and all of its proceedings were valid. The rule is well settled that if an action is removable and a proper petition and bond filed for removal, it makes no difference whether the state court signs an order removing the cause or refusing to remove it. In fact, no order whatever is necessary or required by the federal law, but the defendant can proceed and file his record for removal to the federal court within the required time and the state court cannot legally proceed further in the matter, and if it does proceed, all of such proceedings are void in case the cause is removed. On the other hand, if the action is one which the defendant is not entitled to remove, and the state court, as in this case, refuses to relinquish its jurisdiction by ordering a removal, then the defendant acts at his peril if he proceeds with the removal and does not protect himself in the state court, as all proper proceedings in the state court will be regular and valid if the case is remanded. So the contention that the mere filing of a petition and bond on removal, whether the same be a case which the defendant is entitled to remove or not, prevents the state court from proceeding further in the action, is untenable. The contentions of appellant are in conflict with all the state and federal decisions which hold that a state court is not bound to surrender its jurisdiction upon petition for removal until a case has been made which on its face shows that the petitioner has a right to a transfer, and not until such a showing is made is the state court prohibited by the federal statutes from proceeding further in the cause; and if the petition in connection with the pleadings does not show that the cause is removable, the jurisdiction of the state court is not ousted and its subsequent proceedings are valid. (*Phoenix Ins. Co. v. Pechner,* 95 U. S. 183, 24 L. ed. 427; *Amory v. Amory,* 95 U. S. 186, 24 L. ed. 428; *Gregory v. Hartley,* 113 U. S. 742, 5 Sup. Ct.

743, 28 L. ed. 1150; *Stone v. State of South Carolina*, 117
U. S. 430, 6 Sup. Ct. 799, 29 L. ed. 962; *Burlington etc. Ry.
Co. v. Dunn*, 122 U. S. 513, 7 Sup. Ct. 1262, 30 L. ed. 1159;
Crehore v. Ohio etc. Ry. Co., 131 U. S. 240, 9 Sup. Ct. 692,
33 L. ed. 144; *Brown v. Nelson & Co.*, 43 Fed. 614; *Chesapeake
etc. Ry. Co. v. McCabe*, 213 U. S. 207, 29 Sup. Ct. 430, 53 L. ed.
765; *Springer v. Howes*, 69 Fed. 850; *Monroe v. Williamson*,
81 Fed. 977 (984); *Mannington v. Hocking Valley Ry. Co.*,
183 Fed. 133; *Golden v. Northern Pac. Ry. Co.*, 39 Mont. 435,
104 Pac. 549, 18 Ann. Cas. 886, 34 L. R. A., N. S., 1154;
Debnam v. Southern Bell Tel. Co., 126 N. C. 831, 36 S. E. 269,
65 L. R. A. 915; *Chicago etc. Co. v. Brazzell*, 33 Okl. 122, 124
Pac. 40; Dillon on Removal of Causes, sec. 136; Moon on Removal of Causes, sec. 177; Foster's Fed. Prac., sec. 391; 2
Rose's Code of Fed. Prac., sec. 1188 (c and g); 18 Ency. Pl.
& Pr. 388, 351; 39 Cyc. 1305, 1308.)

The federal court having decided that the cause was not
removable, we conclude that the default was not prematurely
entered, and that the clerk had authority to enter the same.
In our opinion, the Morbeck case is conclusive upon the question above discussed, to wit, the legality of the default and
the question of the removal of said cause.

Counsel for appellant also contend that the court erred in
refusing to vacate and set aside said default entered by the
clerk.

The appellant based its first motion to set aside the default
on the ground of inadvertence, surprise and excusable neglect.
The excuse offered was that counsel for appellant was of the
opinion that it was not necessary for it to plead, answer or
demur in said cause in the state court, and that it would
have thirty days after duly certified copies of the record had
been filed in the federal court to plead in that court. This
excuse was one of a mistake of law.

In 1 Black on Judgments, sec. 335, it is stated: "When
statutes authorize the vacation of a judgment entered against
a party through his 'mistake,' it is to be understood that they
mean a mistake of fact. Mistake of law—that is, the party's
ignorance of the law, or mistake as to his legal rights or duties

in the premises—will not warrant the setting aside of the judgment.'' And in the case of *Plano Mfg. Co. v. Murphy,* 16 S. D. 380, 102 Am. St. 692, 92 N. W. 1072, it is held: ''Where a defendant suffered a default by reason of his belief that the service of summons made by plaintiff's agent was invalid because not made by an officer, the default was the result of a mistake of law and therefore not ground for setting aside the judgment as procured through defendant's mistake or excusable neglect.''

A motion to renew its motion to vacate said default was thereafter filed by appellant, and a further excuse offered, namely: That there was a uniform practice and custom in said state court that when motions, demurrers and interlocutory matters were ruled on not to take default without inquiry from opposing counsel if he intended to proceed further. This was met by plaintiff with an affidavit of a practicing attorney in said district court to the effect that no such custom or practice prevailed in said district court. But even if this excuse had not been met by a counter-affidavit, we question whether the practice or custom in a state court could be considered by this court. (*Powell v. Springston Lumber Co.,* 12 Ida. 723, 88 Pac. 97.)

It was recited in the renewal motion that it would be based upon the records and files and upon the affidavit filed in the first motion. On said renewal motion the additional excuse of a mistake of fact and the excuse of a mistake of law above referred to were fully argued and considered by the court. The court, on hearing said renewal motion, considered each and every ground of said motion and thereupon overruled the same.

Counsel cites many cases dealing with defaults where the defendant did not appear within the statutory time and some valid excuse for not appearing was offered. These cases were not applicable to one like the case at bar where the defendant did come into court before his time had expired to plead, and attempted to take the wrongful procedure.. In such a case another principle is involved; that is, What are the rights of the plaintiff where the defendant does appear and attempts to gain what it thinks is an advantage over the plaintiff and a benefit to defendant? In such cases, the defendant becomes an actor; it is aggressive in its own interests and seeks to use its time in an unlawful procedure for its own advantage. It is then that courts considering the rights of both parties hold that the plaintiff cannot be charged with such acts of the defendant, and in dealing with substantial justice will require the defendant to assume the risk and consequences that follow its wrongful and unsuccessful procedure. Under the facts of this case, we hold that the trial court did not err in refusing to set aside said default.

As stating these views and showing that the defendant takes his chances when he attempts to remove a case not removable, and that this question is well settled in this state, see *Finney v. American Bonding Co.,* 13 Ida. 534, 90 Pac. 859, 91 Pac. 318, *Mills v. American Bonding Co.,* 13 Ida. 556, 91 Pac. 381, and *Morbeck v. Bradford-Kennedy Co., supra.* The views of this court on this question are well stated in the Morbeck case, as follows: "It seems to us proper and entirely just to both litigants to hold that when a defendant petitions for the removal of a cause from a state to a federal court, he becomes the actor in that particular, and that he must assume the risk and consequences that follow if he is unsuccessful and in the meanwhile has failed to protect and preserve his right under the state statute and rules of practice prevailing in the state court. . . . . The fact that appellants exhausted a part of their time in a vain endeavor to get out of the state court into the federal court is neither the fault of the law, the courts, nor the adverse party. If they saw fit to exhaust a part of their 'day in court' in an effort to get into another forum and failed, the consequence should justly and properly fall upon them and upon no one else. It should not serve as a means of extending the time allowed them by statute or of delaying the adverse party in getting his case to trial after the question of jurisdiction has been determined."

We will next consider the question whether the complaint is sufficient and states a cause of action. The appellant contends that the complaint is insufficient in the following particulars: (1) That it is not alleged that the bank commissioner neglected any duty that he owed to plaintiff; (2) that a public officer invested with certain discretionary powers is not liable when acting within the scope of his authority, unless he acts maliciously or wilfully wrong; (3) that the words used in sec. 3001, Rev. Codes, "at least once in each year," refer to a calendar year; (4) that it is not alleged that the damages claimed have been "adjudged against him," the said bank commissioner.

The first question above enumerated involves a construction of sec. 3001, Rev. Codes, which, in part, is as follows: "It shall be the duty of the bank commissioner, when he shall deem it necessary, and at least once in each year, without previous notice, to visit and make complete report and examination of the affairs of each bank falling within the provisions of this chapter." The law seems to be well settled that an individual has no right of action against a public officer for breach of a duty which he owes to the public only, even though such individual is specifically injured thereby. (*Gorman v. Commrs.*, 1 Ida. 655; *Worden v. Witt*, 4 Ida. 404, 95 Am. St. 70, 39 Pac. 1114; *People v. Hoag*, 54 Colo. 542, 131 Pac. 400, 45 L. R. A., N. S., 824; *Miller v. Ouray E. L. & Power Co.*, 18 Colo. App. 131, 70 Pac. 447; *Colo. Paving Co. v. Murphy*, 78 Fed. 28, 23 C. C. A. 631, 37 L. R. A. 630; *Ryus v. Gruble*, 31 Kan. 767, 3 Pac. 518; *State v. Harris*, 89 Ind. 363, 46 Am. Rep. 169; *Moss v. Cummings*, 44 Mich. 359, 6 N. W. 843; *School Dist. No. 80 v. Burress*, 2 Neb. Unof. 554, 89 N. W. 609; *Board v. Bladen*, 113 N. C. 379, 18 S. E. 661; *Lowe v. Guthrie*, 4 Okl. 287, 44 Pac. 198; *Cottam v. Oregon City*, 98 Fed. 570; *South v. Maryland*, 18 How. (U. S.) 396, 15 L. ed. 433.)

But it is equally well settled that if the plaintiff can show that the duty was imposed for his benefit and that the legislature had in mind his protection in passing the act in question, and intended to give him a vested right in the discharge of that duty, then this will give him such an interest as will support an action.

In *State v. Harris*, 89 Ind. 363, 46 Am. Rep. 169, it was held: "In general, a public officer is liable only to the person to whom the particular duty is owing, and the ruling question in all cases of the kind is as to whether the plaintiff shows the breach of a particular duty owing to him." We think the rule is well settled that in cases of this kind the plaintiff must show that he has an interest in the performance of the duty by the public officer, and that the duty was imposed for his benefit. But the above does not imply that the duty was imposed for his sole benefit; it is sufficient if it appears that besides having in mind a public duty, the legislature also has in mind an additional duty to the individual.

In *Moss v. Cummings*, 44 Mich. 359, 6 N. W. 843, it is stated: "The failure to perform a public duty can constitute an individual wrong only when some person can show that in the public duty was involved also a duty to himself as an individual, and that he has suffered a special and peculiar injury by reason of its nonperformance."

In *School Dist. No. 80 v. Burress*, 2 Neb. Unof. 554, 89 N. W. 609, on this point it is stated: "On the other hand, though there may also be a duty, or even a primary duty, to the public, if there is in addition a duty to and right in the individual, he may maintain an action." Here, then, the real question is, whether the legislature, in passing sec. 3001, Rev. Codes, had in mind the depositors solely, or in connection with the public, and intended that the duty it was imposing on the bank commissioner to make examination was for the benefit of the depositors, thereby making them interested parties in his performance of such duty. In determining this, and in construing said sec. 3001, we must take into consideration the subject matter with which the legislature was dealing, the language used, and the object and purpose of the law being enacted, and the particular duty in question. The matter of consideration in such a case is well stated in vol. 1, Street's Foundations of Legal Liability, p. 175, quoting from *Atkinson v. Newcastle etc. Waterworks Co.*, as follows: "that the question whether or not the breach of a statutory duty gives a private right of action in any case must always depend upon the object and language of the particular statute.'' In reading said sec. 3001 and taking such matters into consideration, as just above referred to, we think it is clear that the legislature in prescribing this particular duty of the bank commissioner had uppermost in its mind the protection of depositors and people dealing with state banks, or at least had in mind a double duty, one owing to the public, and one owing to the depositors; or stating it in still another way, that in the public duty was involved also a duty to depositors as individuals; that the duty of examining state banks was one of the most important elements in our banking law; that the examinations required by law were of particular interest to the depositing public; that the duty prescribed was for the benefit of depositors, although it might not have been for their sole benefit; that it was intended by said sec. 3001 to give the depositors a vested right in the discharge of the duty therein prescribed.

It must be borne in mind that the respondent does not contend that the bank commissioner, under the facts of this case, would be liable to all the depositors of said bank at the time it is alleged he should have closed said bank, by reason of his failure to faithfully perform said duty, or that his surety is a guarantor thereof, but said respondent contends that the depositors who may recover are those that made deposits after the time, May 12, 1910, when said bank commissioner should have closed the bank, that such depositors suffered loss by reason of his unfaithfulness in the performance of a duty, which, if performed, would have prevented their loss, and that the duty violated by him was one which was imposed for their benefit; and that thus being interested parties and intended to be such by the legislature, in the performance of the duty of examination, as prescribed in said sec. 3001, the surety is then liable on its bond for the violation of a duty covered by said bond.

This court has already held in *Palmer v. Pettingill*, 6 Ida. 346, 55 Pac. 653, that where the plaintiff is a party whom the statute was intended to benefit or protect, then the surety is liable. It was also held that ''The sureties of an officer mentioned in sec. 403 of the Revised Statutes [same as 295, Rev. Codes] are liable to any person injured or aggrieved by a wrongful act done by the officer in his official capacity.''

We will now consider the question of the liability of a public officer and his surety for a breach of a discretionary duty. Here we may say that the cases cited by appellant, and in the brief of counsel appearing as *amici curiae* herein, do in the main lay down the correct principle of law applicable to such cases, which is quoted from *Reed v. Conway*, 20 Mo. 43, as follows: ''The doctrine that a ministerial officer, acting in a matter before him with discretionary power, or acting in a matter before him judicially, or as a *quasi* judge, is not responsible to anyone receiving an injury from such act, unless the officer act maliciously and wilfully wrong, is most clearly established and maintained.'' (*Wheeler v. Patterson*, 1 N. H. 88, 8 Am. Dec. 41; *Weaver v. Devendorf*, 3 Denio (N. Y.), 117; *Wilson v. Mayor of New York*, 1 Denio (N. Y.), 595, 43 Am. Dec. 719; *Vanderheyden v. Young*, 11 Johns. (N. Y.) 150; *Jenkins v. Waldron*, 11 Johns. (N. Y.) 114, 6 Am. Dec. 359; *Wilkes v. Dinsman*, 7 How. (U. S.) 89, 12 L. ed. 618; *Gould v. Hammond*, 10 Fed. Cas. No. 5636; 29 Cyc. 1443 et seq.; *United States v. Clark*, 31 Fed. 710; *Kendall v. Stokes*, 3 How. (U. S.) 87, 11 L. ed. 506.)

In the beginning of the discussion on this point, it may be well to divide acts of negligence into two classes, namely: (1) Acts of commission, or positive wrong; and (2) acts of omission, or breach of duty. In other words, the division would be along the lines of affirmative commission and negative omission.

In examining the cases above cited, it will be found that most all of them involve acts of commission, and in alleging a breach of duty by acts of commission, it was charged that the acts were committed maliciously or wilfully. In other cases, however, and especially where the breach alleged was an act of omission, such words were used as ''abuse of discretion,'' ''bad faith,'' ''did not act in good faith,'' ''illegally,'' ''fraudulently,'' ''unlawfully,'' ''wrongfully,'' ''unfaithfully,'' ''knowingly,'' and words of like meaning.

So from all the cases, including the cases where the breaches were acts of commission and acts of omission, the sound rule seems to be that some words beyond the mere allegations of negligence and failure to perform should be alleged, showing intent to act wrongfully, wilfully, maliciously, unfaithfully, or in bad faith, or, in other words, showing evil intent, and then allege such facts as did constitute such intent.

It then follows that it is necessary to examine the complaint herein and determine whether there are sufficient allegations therein to show not only neglect or failure of the public officer to perform a discretionary duty, but also that he clearly abused his discretion to the extent of acting unfaithfully and in bad faith, and with a wilful design not to perform his duty as such officer.

In paragraph 8 of the complaint, as will appear from the copy thereof heretofore set out in this opinion, it is alleged that said William G. Cruse "did not well, faithfully and impartially discharge the duties of his said office," but "on the contrary he wholly failed, neglected, omitted and refused so to do, and acted unfaithfully, improperly and illegally," and then sets forth the particular breach of his duty complained of. The word "unfaithfully" signifies "bad faith." (8 Words & Phrases, 7174.) The word "improperly" implies such conduct as a man of ordinary and reasonable care and prudence would not, under the circumstances, have been guilty of. The word "illegally" means "unlawfully" and "contrary to law."

In the second breach set forth in the complaint, it is further alleged that said Cruse, prior to the time and at the time it is claimed he should have closed said bank, had knowledge of its unsafe condition, that the same was being conducted contrary to the provisions of said chap. 13, title 4, of the Civil Code of Idaho, being our banking law at that time, and that the books and accounts of said bank were being falsified, which should have caused him to deem it necessary to visit and make a complete examination of its affairs. Said allegations of knowledge of such facts were sufficient to show such a condition in said bank as would make it necessary under sec. 3001 for him to make an examination of said bank, and when taken in connection with the words "wholly failed," "neglected," "unfaithfully," "improperly" and "illegally," as used in the complaint herein, are sufficient to charge an evil and wrong intent with a wilful design to refrain from performing his duty which would amount to bad faith, if he then, under such circumstances, failed or refused to make an examination of said bank.

Having held that said bank commissioner abused his discretion and acted in bad faith when he did not deem it necessary, and wilfully failed to examine said bank under the circumstances as alleged in the complaint, we now pass to a consideration of the further question as to whether the allegations in the complaint as to the condition he would have found there had he made an examination of the bank on or before May 12, 1910, were sufficient to give him reasonable cause to consider said bank insolvent, and then if so, was he required to close the bank and immediately apply for a receiver?

Sec. 3004, Rev. Codes, treats of the duty of the bank commissioner when it appears that the capital of a bank is reduced by impairment, or otherwise, below the amount required by sec. 2970; and sec. 3005 provides that if the bank commissioner shall find that a bank is violating its charter, or the provisions of the chapter relating to banks, he shall by an order direct the discontinuance of such illegal practices.

Appellant contends that the condition alleged may have been of such a character that it would have justified a notice to the bank, as provided in sec. 3004, or an order to said bank to discontinue such illegal practices, as is provided for in sec. 3005. But we cannot agree with this contention, as said sec. 3004 and the first part of sec. 3005 deal with conditions which the legislature evidently did not consider as reaching insolvency.

In the next part of said sec. 3005, following the above, the legislature dealt with a condition of insolvency and provided a remedy where the bank commissioner has reasonable cause to consider a bank insolvent. This part of said sec. 3005 referred to, is as follows:

"If such bank shall refuse or neglect to comply with such order, or whenever such commissioner has reasonable cause to consider such bank insolvent, he may immediately apply, in his official capacity, to the district court of the county in which such bank has its principal place of business, for the appointment of a receiver for such bank, who, if he be appointed, shall proceed to administer the assets of the bank in accordance with law."

Here, again, in so far as the matter of the bank commissioner having reasonable cause to consider a bank insolvent is concerned, we have to deal with what may be termed another discretionary duty of the commissioner, and the general rules as hereinbefore discussed would apply. We must, therefore, in considering this question, again go to the complaint to see what the allegations are as to what condition the bank commissioner would have found if he had made an examination on or before May 12, 1910.

In paragraph 9 of the complaint, it is alleged as follows:

"That if said William G. Cruse had, at least once in each year, after his examination of May 12, 1909, or on or about the 12th day of May, 1910, when he had cause to deem it necessary to make an examination of the affairs of said bank, as aforesaid, visited said bank and made a complete report and examination thereof, as was his duty so to do, as aforesaid, he would have found that said bank had been, and was then, guilty of violating each and every duty and requirement prescribed in the provisions of the different sections of said chapter 13, title 4, and would have further found that the books of said bank had been, and were then, falsified in respect to accounts and items of Loans and Discounts, Overdrafts, Bonds and Warrants, due to and from Bank and Bank Accounts, Cash on Hand, Surplus Funds, Undivided Profits, Individual Deposits, Time Certificates of Deposit, Accounts of Officers and Directors and their liabilities, so as to make a proper legal report under date of April 27, 1910, which had been called for a short time prior thereto by said William

G. Cruse, as such Bank Commissioner, in accordance with law, and said William G. Cruse, from an examination of said bank, at said time, would then and there had reasonable cause to consider said bank insolvent.''

If the bank was in fact violating ''each and every'' provision of the banking law, it would indeed be a serious matter and would call for immediate action by the bank commissioner; and we must take it as true that this condition of the bank as alleged in said paragraph of the complaint was true, because in passing upon the sufficiency of the complaint such would be the rule. And further, if the bank, besides violating ''each and every'' provision of the banking law, was also falsifying almost, if not all, of the principal items and accounts, it would be still more serious and require immediate and drastic action by the commissioner; and following these charges, it is alleged that said William G. Cruse from an examination of said bank at said time would then and there have had reasonable cause to consider said bank insolvent.

These allegations present a condition which should have caused him to consider the bank insolvent. Such being the case, what was his duty? It clearly was to adopt the only remedy given him under the law, and close the bank and apply for the appointment of a receiver. And if he failed so to do, then it would be a clear abuse of his discretion, and under such facts and circumstances as alleged, would amount to bad faith and show a wilful design not to perform his duty.

The argument that the word ''may'' in said section 3005 is not mandatory and does not mean ''must'' is without force under such allegations as are contained in this complaint. When such conditions arose under the old banking law, under which this action is brought, in a bank of this state, as alleged in the complaint herein, then the word ''may'' should be construed to mean ''must,'' otherwise the power of the bank commissioner would have been absolute and there would be no such thing as an abuse of discretion, or of holding him liable for bad faith and corruption.

This court has already in effect held in *Blomquist v. Board of County Commissioners*, 25 Ida. 293, 137 Pac. 177, that certain duties of the assessors involved the exercise of their legal discretion or individual judgment, but that such legal discretion must be exercised in good faith, and if not, then an officer who fails to perform his duty is liable for such failure to faithfully perform his duties. In that case the court says: "If an officer exercises his legal discretion in good faith and without fraud, then he is performing his duty under the law, otherwise not; and if not, then he fails to perform his duty and is liable for a failure to faithfully perform his duties."

The next question for consideration is, whether the words "at least once in each year" as used in sec. 3001, Rev. Codes, refer to a calendar year. The complaint in paragraph 8 alleges two breaches of duty under sec. 3001 as to examination by the bank commissioner: (1) That said W. G. Cruse did not, at least once in each year, make an examination of said bank, and that his last examination before the bank was closed on August 31, 1910, was made on May 12, 1909; and (2) that on or before the 12th day of May, 1910, said Cruse had knowledge of the unsafe condition of said bank, its violation of the banking law, and its falsification of the books, and other acts of said bank, as hereinbefore more particularly set forth. We have already discussed the second breach set out in paragraph 8 of the complaint, and held that the facts alleged in regard thereto were sufficient to constitute a breach of the duty of the bank commissioner under sec. 3001, wherein it is provided that it shall be the duty of the bank commissioner, when he shall deem it necessary, to make an examination of state banks. From the conclusion we there reached, it follows that a cause of action is stated in the complaint regardless of the first breach of duty by said commissioner alleged in said paragraph. It is, therefore, unnecessary to discuss or consider the breach of duty first alleged in said paragraph to determine whether or not the phrase "at least once in each year" means a calendar year or once in twelve months.

There still remains for consideration the question as to whether or not in this action it was necessary that the damages claimed should be first adjudged against the bank commissioner. Sec. 191, Rev. Codes, provides that the bank commissioner shall execute a bond with three conditions, as follows: (1) That he shall faithfully and impartially discharge the duties of his office; (2) pay over to the persons entitled by law to receive it all money coming into his hands by virtue of his office; and (3) conditioned further for the payment of all damages and costs that may be adjudged against him under the provisions of title 2, chap. 13 of the Political Code, and under title 4, chap. 13 of the Civil Code.

The legislature intended by the enactment of said sec. 191 to require a bond covering the faithful and impartial discharge of the duties of said office as a distinct subject matter or condition of the bond; and it next intended to require the bond to cover the paying over of all moneys coming into the hands of the commissioner, as a second distinct subject matter or condition; and, lastly, having in mind that in sec. 3005, Rev. Codes, it had provided that where the commissioner had proceeded maliciously or without reasonable cause in closing a bank and having a receiver appointed, he was liable to such bank on his official bond for any damages, expenses and costs resulting therefrom. The legislature further intended to require a bond covering such damages and costs specifically mentioned in said section 3005, or in any other section of said chapter, and did not intend anyone injured or aggrieved by the failure of the commissioner to faithfully perform his duties, to first proceed and have his damages adjudged against the bank commissioner before he could bring suit against the sureties on said bond. Said three conditions required are separate and distinct. The first words "and conditioned further" imply that it is an additional condition to the two former conditions.

We do not in this decision, in passing upon said third condition, hold that even in a cause brought thereunder, that the injured party would be required to have his damage first adjudged against the bank commissioner before proceeding against his sureties. We reserve a decision on this question until it is properly before us. Under the bond in question, the principal and surety are jointly and severally liable, and an action on said bond might be brought jointly against said bank commissioner and his sureties, or might have been brought against either of them severally.

We do not consider that the other questions presented in the brief of *amici curiae,* not raised by appellant and not dealing with the sufficiency of the complaint, are properly before us, and we will, therefore, not pass upon these questions further than to state that from our examination of the same, the points are not well taken when applied to this case.

The judgment of the court below must therefore be affirmed, and it is so ordered, with costs in favor of respondent.

Budge, J., and Guheen, District Judge, concur.

(February 4, 1915.)

ON PETITION FOR REHEARING.

GUHEEN, District Judge.—A petition for rehearing has been filed by counsel for the appellant in the above-entitled action.

The court, after carefully considering the same, finds that all of the material questions discussed by the learned counsel for the appellant in his petition for rehearing were fully covered in the briefs and oral arguments upon the original hearing of said cause, and upon a re-examination of the entire record, we are fully satisfied that we understood the facts and applied the law to the particular facts in this case; that the decision of this court was correct and in harmony with the decisions of this court as heretofore announced.

The petition for rehearing is denied.

Budge, J., concurs.

(January 20, 1915.)

M. L. HARE and JAMES JUST, Administrator of the Estate
of N. A. JUST, Deceased, Respondents, v. W. R. YOUNG,
ANDREW LARSON & SONS, a Copartnership, Com-
posed of ANDREW LARSON, J. B. LARSON and J. R.
LARSON; YOUNG & SORENSON, a Copartnership,
Composed of ROY YOUNG and ANDREAS SOREN-
SON, Appellants.

[146 Pac. 104.]

LEASES OF LIVESTOCK—FILING FOR RECORD—COMITY BETWEEN STATES
—BURDEN OF PROOF—POSSESSION OF PERSONAL PROPERTY—PRE-
SUMPTION OF OWNERSHIP—ATTORNEY'S FEES—IMMATERIAL ISSUES
—FINDINGS OF FACT.

1. Leases of more than ten head of livestock contracted in another state by citizens of another state, if said livestock is afterward brought by the lessee into Idaho, and thereafter and while
the property and the lessee are in Idaho, by agreement between
the parties, the original lease is continued for a longer term than
was originally agreed upon, the new agreement is such a contract
as is required to be filed for record by section 1263 of the Political
Code of Idaho.

2. In order to invoke the doctrine of comity between states with
respect to contracts, it is incumbent upon the party claiming such
a benefit to show that his is such a contract as is contemplated by
the doctrine. He must produce proof that the contract in behalf
of which he seeks to invoke this rule is a foreign contract contemplated by the rule.

3. Where the evidence shows that the mortgagor of personal
property had, for many years, been in possession of the property,
dealt with it as his own, sold and otherwise disposed of portions of
it and mortgaged other portions of it without objection, although
there is evidence tending to show that his interest was that of a
lessee, the finding of the trial court that the mortgagor was the
owner of the property at the time he gave the mortgage is sustained by the evidence.

4. The facts in this case examined and found to justify the
allowance of $750 as an attorney's fee to be awarded to plaintiffs
under the terms of the note and mortgage.

5. Allegations in an answer that a portion of the amount of
money secured by a mortgage was a pre-existing debt, and that no

levy was made on the property by the mortgagee, and that the mortgagee did not take nor attempt to take possession of it, *held*, to be immaterial, and that it was not error for the trial court to fail to make a finding of fact upon them.

APPEAL from the District Court of the Sixth Judicial District, in and for the County of Bingham. Hon. J. M. Stevens, Judge.

Suit to foreclose chattel mortgage. Judgment for plaintiffs. *Affirmed.*

J. W. Jones and Budge & Barnard, for Appellants.

The registration act provides that the lease "must be filed of record in the same county recorder's office or offices and within the same time and manner and for the same fee, as are chattel mortgages."

There is no statutory provision for filing foreign chattel mortgages when the chattels are subsequently brought into this state. The chattel mortgage registration acts apply only to property in Idaho when the mortgage is executed and have no extraterritorial effect. (Secs. 3406–3410, Rev. Codes.) By analogy, a foreign lease of animals, which are subsequently brought to this state, is not required to be placed of record in this state. (*Shapard v. Hynes*, 104 Fed. 449, 45 C. C. A. 271, 52 L. R. A. 675; *Creelman Lumber Co. v. Lesh*, 73 Ark. 16, 83 S. W. 320, 3 Ann. Cas. 108; *Greenville Nat. Bank v. Evans-Snider-Buel Co.*, 9 Okl. 353, 60 Pac. 249.)

"The statutes of one state requiring mortgages and other instruments dealing with personal property to be recorded in the town or county where the mortgagor resides do not apply to mortgages made in another state where the parties and the property are at the time. The *lex loci contractus* governs." (24 Am. & Eng. Ency. Law, 2d ed., 94; *Pyeatt v. Powell*, 51 Fed. 551, 2 C. C. A. 367.)

Hansbrough & Gagon, for Respondents.

The person who has the possession and control of a chattel and the person in possession and control of an article of personal property and who holds himself out as the owner thereof, is presumed to be the owner. (29 Cyc. 1550; *Keith v. Maguire*, 170 Mass. 210, 48 N. E. 1090; *Hornbein v. Blanchard*, 4 Colo. App. 92, 35 Pac. 187.)

The leases in question should have been recorded within a reasonable time after the statute in question, to wit, sec. 1263, Rev. Codes, went into effect. (*Moline Plow Co. v. Witham*, 52 Kan. 185, 34 Pac. 751.) By comity between the states, mortgaged property being removed from one state to another and the mortgage not recorded in the latter state, the mortgagor is permitted to retain possession under the terms of the mortgage, but such comity should not be extended to cases wherein it appears that the mortgagee consented to such removal. (*Newsum v. Hoffman*, 124 Tenn. 369, 137 S. W. 490; *Snyder v. Yates*, 112 Tenn. 309, 105 Am. St. 941, 79 S. W. 796, 64 L. R. A. 353; *Greene v. Bentley*, 114 Fed. 112, 52 C. C. A. 60; *Dawes v. Rosenbaum*, 179 Ill. 112, 53 N. E. 585.)

Where a true owner of property holds out another, or allows him to appear as the owner of or as having full power of disposition over the property, and innocent third parties are thus led into dealing with such apparent owner, or person having such apparent power of disposition, they will be protected. (16 Cyc. 773, 774; *Anderson v. Armstead*, 69 Ill. 452; *Wells v. Higgins*, 1 Litt. (Ky.) 299, 13 Am. Dec. 235; *Craig v. Turley*, 86 Ky. 636, 6 S. W. 648; *Wilson v. Scott*, 13 Ky. Law Rep. 926; *Hostler v. Hays*, 3 Cal. 302; *B. F. Avery & Sons v. Collins* (Tex. Civ. App.), 131 S. W. 426.)

MORGAN, J.—This is an appeal from the district court of the sixth judicial district of the state of Idaho, in and for the county of Bingham, and arises out of an action commenced in said court to foreclose a certain chattel mortgage made and executed by W. R. Young in favor of Anderson Brothers Bank, a corporation.

Prior to the commencement of this action, the said note and mortgage were assigned to M. L. Hare and N. A. Just, and subsequent thereto and prior to the trial in the district court, the said N. A. Just died, and thereafter the respondent, James

Just, as administrator of the estate of N. A. Just, deceased, was substituted as a party plaintiff.

On Dec. 19, 1910, the said W. R. Young, being indebted to Andérson Brothers Bank in the sum of $1,000, and desiring further advancements of money from that institution, made, executed and delivered to said bank his promissory note for $5,000, and, to secure the payment of the same, made, executed and delivered a chattel mortgage in the usual form upon all that remained in his possession of the sheep hereinafter mentioned and in said mortgage described as follows:

"3,000 head of ewes branded with circle on back, wool brand O—, 6 months to seven years old, being all the sheep owned by me. Kept on my ranch on Wolverine Creek in Bingham County, Idaho."

Said mortgage was, on Dec. 21, 1910, duly filed in the office of the county recorder of Bingham county, Idaho. Which said note and mortgage were assigned, as above stated, and sued upon and sought to be foreclosed in this action.

At the time of extending credit to Young and of accepting the mortgage to secure the loan, the officers and agents of the bank had no knowledge nor notice that anyone other than Young claimed any interest in the property mortgaged.

The appellants, Young & Sorenson, a copartnership, claim a portion of the sheep by purchase from Jones and Anderson in June, 1911, and the appellants, Andrew Larson & Sons, a copartnership, claim the remainder of them by purchase from Lund and the Christensens on or about July 1, 1911.

The trial of the case in the district court resulted in a decree that the defendant, W. R. Young, whose default for failure to answer had been entered, is indebted to the plaintiffs (respondents here) in the sum of $6,033.33, together with $750.00 attorney's fee, found by the court to be a reasonable amount to be allowed for that purpose under the terms of the note and mortgage, together with costs of suit, that the said sums are secured by the chattel mortgage, and that said mortgage is a prior lien upon the property therein described and superior to any right or rights of the defendants or either of them.

From this decree the appellants, Andrew Larson & Sons and Young & Sorenson have prosecuted this appeal.

The other facts in the case necessary to a decision thereof will appear in the opinion.

Counsel for the appellants contend that the evidence is insufficient to support certain findings of fact made by the trial judge, and assign the following errors of law:

1. That the court erred in not deciding as a matter of law from all the evidence that all of the sheep in the possession of the defendant W. R. Young were leased to him, in the state of Utah, by residents of Utah, while all of said sheep were in Utah, and that the leases were valid where executed, and said defendant, W. R. Young, had no interest therein or title thereto subject to encumbrance by him.

2. The court erred in not deciding as a matter of law from the evidence that sec. 1263 of the Political Code of Idaho had no application to this controversy, in that the leases in question did not concern property in this state and were not executed in this state, but concerned only Utah property and were executed in Utah, by residents of Utah, prior to the passage of said act, except as to 1100 head leased by Andrew Anderson to said defendant in the year 1910.

Sec. 1263, Rev. Codes, referred to in the second assignment, is as follows:

"All leases of more than ten head of livestock must be in writing and must be acknowledged in like manner as grants of real property, and filed for record in the same county recorder's office or offices, and within the same time and manner, and for the same fee, as are chattel mortgages; and the failure to comply with the provisions of this section renders the interest of the lessor in the property subject and subsequent to the claims of creditors of the lessee, and of subsequent purchasers and encumbrancers of the property in good faith and for value."

It is urged by counsel for the appellants that this section has no application to this case, because the leases in question were made in Utah by citizens of Utah and were leases of property then situated in Utah, which was thereafter brought into the state of Idaho; that such leases in the state of Utah were, at the time they were made, recognized as valid, and that there was no statute in that state requiring them to be recorded, and that the registration acts of Idaho have no extraterritorial effect; that comity requires that the state to which the property is removed recognize and adopt the *lex loci contractus*. Also that the leases were made prior to the passage of the act and that the act can have no retroactive effect.

The doctrine of comity between states cannot be successfully applied to any of the contracts in question.

It is contended by appellants that Jones, in 1903, leased sheep to Young for a period of 5 years. At that time both parties lived in Utah and the sheep were in that state. The lease, however, if such it may be called, was superseded by a written instrument which was dated at Shelley, Idaho, October 9, 1904, and prior to that date Young had removed with the sheep to Idaho. Furthermore, at the expiration of the lease in 1908 and, while Young resided in this state and the sheep were here, the parties reached an agreement whereby he was to continue to hold them.

It is further contended that Anderson in 1904 leased certain sheep to Young for a period of 5 years. At that time the contracting parties and the sheep were in Utah. This agreement was in writing and when it expired in 1909, was renewed by another written instrument. At that time the sheep were in Idaho and Young was a resident of this state.

Appellants further contend that in 1902 or 1903, Young, by an oral agreement, leased from J. M. Christensen, Mary Christensen and P. C. Lund certain sheep for a period of 5 years, and at the date of the transaction the parties all lived in Utah and the sheep were in that state. The terms' of this lease were thereafter changed and some uncertainty exists in the record as to the exact date of the change, but it appears from the testimony of Young that the new agreement was to take effect at the expiration of the old one which testimony, taken as a whole, shows to have been in the year 1908. At the time this new agreement was made, the property was in Idaho. as was also Young.

In this case it makes very little difference whether these subsequent agreements which were entered into after Young removed to Idaho and brought the sheep into this state be considered new leases or continuations of the old ones, or whether, as contended by respondents, Young actually owned the sheep, for if it should be found Young did not own the sheep, the new leases, or continuations of the old ones, are contracts entered into with a resident of the state of Idaho about livestock situated in Idaho, each referring to the leasing of more than ten head, and are such contracts as are required to be recorded by sec. 1263, Rev. Codes.

It is further contended that on or about July 15, 1910, Young, who since 1904 had resided in and had been engaged in the sheep business in Idaho, leased from Anderson 1100 head of sheep then in Utah, and removed them to his ranch in Idaho where they were repossessed by Anderson in April, 1911. The written instrument made as evidence of this lease is dated September 15, 1910, and the record does not disclose definitely whether the sheep were in Utah or Idaho at that time. In order to invoke the doctrine of comity between states with respect to contracts, it is incumbent upon a party claiming such a benefit to show that his is such a contract as is contemplated by the doctrine. He must produce proof that the contract in behalf of which he seeks to invoke this rule is a foreign contract contemplated by the rule. This the appellants fail to do with respect to the instrument dated September 15, 1910. Upon the other hand, the evidence, taken as a whole, invites the conclusion that the property was in Idaho when the document was executed. None of these leases or agreements were recorded in Idaho.

The foregoing conclusions dispose of appellants' contention that the trial judge gave to sec. 1263, Rev. Codes, a retroactive effect in his application of it to these contracts. That section was enacted in 1907 and the new agreements, or renewals of the leases, were all subsequent to its enactment.

The finding of the trial judge, that at the time of the execution of the mortgage the defendant Young was the owner of said sheep, is assigned by the appellants as error.

The word "owner" has been frequently defined by courts and text-writers.

"The owner of property is one who has dominion of a thing, real or personal, corporeal or incorporeal, which he has the right to enjoy and to do with as he pleases—either to spoil or destroy it as far as the law permits—unless he be prevented by some agreement or covenant which restrains his right."

. "An owner is one who has dominion over that which is the subject of the ownership. He has the right to make such use of it, consistently with the rights of others, as he may see fit. The ownership may extend to the entire thing, or may be limited to an interest in it, and whatever is the subject of the ownership is held by the owner for his own individual benefit." (6 Words & Phrases, 5135.)

In the case of *Keith v. Maguire,* 170 Mass. 210, 48 N. E. 1090, construing a statute which provided for the sale of personal property on which there is a lien for work and labor, or for money expended, if the amount due is not paid within sixty days after demand; and also providing for notice of the intended sale to the owner, it was held that a married woman whose goods were stored in her husband's name with her full knowledge and approval was not entitled to such notice, the court says:

"The word 'owner' is not a technical term. It is not confined to the person who has the absolute right in the chattel, but also applies to the person who has the possession and control of it."

According to the contention of the appellants in this case, the sheep were leased to Young, but the record fully discloses that for many years Young had the property in his possession, dealt with it as his own, sold and otherwise disposed of portions of it, and mortgaged it without objection upon the part of the lessors. The finding of the trial court that he was the owner of the sheep is, therefore, fully sustained by the evidence.

It is also assigned as error that the trial judge found $750 to be a reasonable attorney's fee to be allowed to plaintiffs in this action, and it is asserted that the evidence does not justify the allowance of to exceed $500 for this purpose.

The evidence upon this point consists of the testimony of Mr. W. A. Lee, an attorney at law, whose qualifications to testify upon the point having been admitted by the appellants, testified that $750 is a reasonable amount to be allowed as an attorney's fee under the circumstances disclosed by a hypothetical question which fairly disclosed the work and responsibility involved. Upon cross-examination he fixed the minimum fee at $500 and the maximum fee at $1,000. We think this finding fully supported by the evidence.

Assignments of error are also predicated upon the failure of the trial judge to find that the said mortgage was given to secure an antecedent debt to the amount of $1,000, and upon his failure to find that no levy was made on said sheep by the mortgagee and that the mortgagee did not take nor attempt to take possession of them.

The allegations in the answer wherein these points were presented to the court were immaterial, and to fail to make findings of fact upon them was not error.

Since the foregoing conclusions are decisive of the case, the court deems it unnecessary to pass upon the question of estoppel presented by the respondents.

The decree of the trial court is affirmed, and costs are awarded to the respondents.

Sullivan, C. J., concurs.

Budge, J., did not sit at the hearing nor take part in the decision of this case.

(January 20, 1915.)

M. L. HARE and JAMES JUST, Administrator of the Estate
of N. A. JUST, Deceased, Respondents, v. W. R. YOUNG,
ANDREW LARSON & SONS, a Copartnership Com-
posed of ANDREW LARSON, J. B. LARSON and J. R.
LARSON; YOUNG & SORENSON, a Copartnership,
Composed of ROY YOUNG and ANDREAS SOREN-
SON, Appellants.

[146 Pac. 107.]

CHATTEL MORTGAGES—DESCRIPTION OF PROPERTY—AFFIDAVIT OF GOOD
FAITH—POSSESSION OF PROPERTY—PRESUMPTION OF OWNERSHIP.

1. Personal property described in a chattel mortgage as "1333
early spring lambs, branded O—" is a sufficient description as between the mortgagor and the mortgagee.

2. A chattel mortgage, although not accompanied by an affidavit that it is executed in good faith and without any design to
hinder, delay or defraud creditors, is valid as between the mortgagor and the mortgagee.

3. Possession of personal property is *prima facie* evidence of
ownership.

4. The evidence in this case examined and the conclusion
reached that the trial court was justified in finding that the presumption of ownership created by the possession of the property,
under the facts and circumstances in this case, is not overcome by
the testimony introduced to rebut it.

APPEAL from the District Court of the Sixth Judicial
District, in and for the County of Bingham. Hon. J. M.
Stevens, Judge.

Suit to foreclose chattel mortgage. Judgment for plaintiffs.
Affirmed.

J. W. Jones and Budge & Barnard, for Appellants.

This registration act provides that the lease "must be filed
of record in the same county recorder's office or offices and
within the same time and manner and for the same fee, as are
chattel mortgages."

There is no statutory provision for filing foreign chattel mortgages when the chattels are subsequently brought into this state. The chattel mortgage registration acts apply only to property in the state of Idaho when the mortgage is executed and have no extraterritorial effect. (Secs. 3406–3410, Rev. Codes.) By analogy, a foreign lease of animals, which are subsequently brought to this state, is not required to be placed of record in this state. (*Shapard v. Hynes*, 104 Fed. 449, 45 C. C. A. 271, 52 L. R. A. 675; *Creelman Lumber Co. v. Lesh*, 73 Ark. 16, 83 S. W. 320, 3 Ann. Cas. 108; *Greenville National Bank v. Evans-Snyder-Buel Co.*, 9 Okl. 353, 60 Pac. 249.)

"The statutes of one state requiring mortgages and other instruments dealing with personal property to be recorded in the town or county where the mortgagor resides do not apply to mortgages made in another state where the parties and the property are at the time. The *lex loci contractus* governs." (24 Am. & Eng. Ency. Law, 2d ed., 94; *Pyeatt v. Powell,* 51 Fed. 551, 2 C. C. A. 367.)

The mortgage sought to be foreclosed by this action is void as to the defendant copartnerships because of the insufficiency of the description of the property attempted to be mortgaged. The sole description of the property attempted to be mortgaged is "1333 early spring lambs, branded O—." The location of the property is not stated nor the ownership, nor does the mortgage specify the county or state where the property attempted to be mortgaged is located. (*Huse v. Estabrooks*, 67 Vt. 223, 48 Am. St. 810, 31 Atl. 293; *Barrett v. Fisch*, 76 Iowa, 553, 14 Am. St. 238, 41 N. W. 310.)

"A mortgage of a specific number of sheep out of a herd comprising a much larger number of sheep which does not separate or designate the sheep mortgaged is void for uncertainty." (*Jacobsen v. Christiansen*, 18 Utah, 149, 55 Pac. 562; *South Omaha Nat. Bank v. McGillin*, 77 Neb. 6, 108 N. W. 257; *Wattles v. Cobb*, 60 Neb. 403, 83 Am. St. 537, 83 N. W. 195; *Clark v. Voorhees*, 36 Kan. 144, 12 Pac. 529; *Everett v. Brown*, 64 Iowa, 420, 20 N. W. 743.)

The mortgage is void because the property attempted to be described was not *in esse* and the mortgagor had no potential interest in or title to the ewes from which the lambs were subsequently born. (Jones on Chattel Mortgages, 2d ed., sec. 140; *New England Nat. Bank v. Northwestern Nat. Bank,* 171 Mo. 307, 71 S. W. 191, 60 L. R. A. 256; *Townsend Brick etc. Co. v. Allen,* 62 Kan. 311, 84 Am. St. 388, 62 Pac. 1008, 52 L. R. A. 323; *First Nat. Bank v. McIntosh & Peters Livestock etc. Co.,* 72 Kan. 603, 84 Pac. 535, and *Robinson v. Haas,* 40 Cal. 474.)

Mortgage is void as to defendant copartnerships because of lack of affidavit of good faith. (*Reynolds v. Fitzpatrick,* 23 Mont. 52, 57 Pac. 452; 2 Cobbey, Chattel Mortgages, sec. 583; 6 Cyc. 1002.)

Hansbrough & Gagon, for Respondents.

The person who has the possession and control of a chattel and the person in possession and control of an article of personal property and who holds himself out as the owner thereof, is presumed to be the owner. (29 Cyc. 1550; *Keith v. Maguire,* 170 Mass. 210, 48 N. E. 1090; *Hornbein v. Blanchard,* 4 Colo. App. 92, 35 Pac. 187.)

The leases in question should have been recorded within a reasonable time after sec. 1263, Rev. Codes, went into effect. (*Moline Plow Co. v. Witham,* 52 Kan. 185, 34 Pac. 751.)

By comity between the states, mortgaged property being removed from one state to another and the mortgage not recorded in the latter state, the mortgagor is permitted to retain possession under the terms of the mortgage, but such comity should not be extended to cases wherein it appears that the mortgagee consented to such removal. (*Newsum v. Hoffman,* 124 Tenn. 369, 137 S. W. 490; *Snyder v. Yates,* 112 Tenn. 309, 105 Am. St. 941, 79 S. W. 796, 64 L. R. A. 353; *Greene v. Bently,* 114 Fed. 112, 52 C. C. A. 60; *Dawes v. Rosenbaum,* 179 Ill. 112, 53 N. E. 585.)

Where a true owner of property allows another to appear as the owner of or as having full power of disposition over the property, and innocent third parties are thus led into dealing with such apparent owner, or person having such apparent power of disposition, they will be protected. (16 Cyc. 773, 774; *Anderson v. Armstead*, 69 Ill. 452; *Wells v. Higgins*, 1 Litt. (Ky.) 299, 13 Am. Dec. 235; *Craig v. Turley*, 86 Ky. 636, 6 S. W. 648; *Wilson v. Scott*, 13 Ky. Law Rep. 926; *Hostler v. Hays*, 3 Cal. 302; *B. F. Avery & Sons v. Collins* (Tex. Civ. App.), 131 S. W. 426.)

The mortgage is good between the parties. (*Marchand v. Ronaghan*, 9 Ida. 95, 72 Pac. 731; *Chase v. Tacoma Box Co.*, 11 Wash. 377, 39 Pac. 639; *Marcum v. Coleman*, 8 Mont. 196, 19 Pac. 394; *Reynolds v. Fitzpatrick*, 23 Mont. 52, 57 Pac. 452; *Darland v. Levins*, 1 Wash. 582, 20 Pac. 309.)

MORGAN, J.—This case was tried in the district court immediately following the trial of that just decided by this court, in which the same parties appellant and respondent appeared, and in which case the foreclosure of a mortgage made by W. R. Young in favor of the Anderson Brothers Bank was involved. (See *ante*, p. 682, 146 Pac. 104.)

In this case it was stipulated that the testimony of the witnesses John O. Jones, Andrew Anderson, J. B. Larson, W. R. Young and W. A. Lee given on behalf of the defendants in the case involving the Anderson Brothers bank mortgage and all exhibits introduced on defendants' behalf in said case be considered as evidence for the defendants herein, subject to objections made as to its competency, relevancy and materiality, with like effect as if said witnesses had been sworn and said evidence had been introduced.

The two cases came on to be heard in this court at the same time and were argued together. This case, however, presents some questions of law which do not occur in the other and which require, in order that the conclusions of this court be made clear, an additional discussion of the facts.

On January 7, 1911, W. R. Young being indebted to the Shelley Banking Company of Shelley, Idaho, in the sum of $4,000, for moneys theretofore advanced to him, gave to said banking company his promissory note in said amount, and to secure the payment thereof made, executed and delivered to said bank a chattel mortgage upon the property described as follows: "1333 early spring lambs, branded O—."

By assignment, in like manner as in the case just decided, the respondents became the owners of said note and mortgage and, the indebtedness not having been paid when due, this suit was instituted to foreclose the mortgage.

The defendants (appellants here) Andrew Larson & Sons, a copartnership, and Young & Sorenson, a copartnership, answered and the default of the defendant, W. R. Young, for failure to answer was entered. The trial resulted in a decree foreclosing the mortgage and adjudging and decreeing it to be a valid lien upon the property described therein prior and superior to any right or rights of the defendants or either of them. From said decree this appeal was taken to this court.

In so far as the facts discussed in the case involving the Anderson Brothers Bank mortgage are decisive of this case, they will not be restated here but, as before indicated, this case presents some additional questions which require the consideration of some portions of the evidence not found necessary to be discussed in the other.

It is contended by the appellants that the trial judge erred in not finding that the lambs, not being *in esse* at the time of the execution of the mortgage, and Young having no potential interest in the ewes subsequently giving birth to them, said chattel mortgage was wholly void; also in not finding that the description of the property in the mortgage is so indefinite as to render it void; that the appellants being purchasers of the property in good faith and for value, the mortgage, as against them, was void because it was not accompanied by an affidavit that it was executed in good faith and without any design to hinder, delay or defraud creditors. Other assignments of error were made but they go to the points above stated.

These assignments of error are all based upon the theory that the appellants were purchasers of the property without notice of the mortgage, in good faith and for value, from Jones, Anderson, Lund and the Christensens, and that at the time the purchases were made the said vendors were the actual owners of the property and Young, the mortgagor, was not, for if Jones, Anderson, Lund and the Christensens were not the owners of the property, it is clear the appellants could not acquire ownership by purchase from them. This mortgage as between the mortgagor and the mortgagee is valid and the description is sufficient.

In the case of *Marchand v. Ronaghan*, 9 Ida. 95, 72 Pac. 731, this court, after holding that between mortgagor and mortgagee the affidavit of good faith is unnecessary, commenting upon the defense that the description in a chattel mortgage was insufficient, said:

"It was proper for the plaintiff to prove where the property was located and identify it as the property mortgaged. It could in no way injure the mortgagor. The strictness of the rules applied to chattel mortgages where disputes arise between the mortgagee and attaching creditors and subsequent encumbrancers and purchasers in good faith is never applied where the differences arise between the mortgagor and mortgagee; and the courts will not look with favor upon the efforts of a mortgagor to defeat the security given his creditors upon such flimsy pretexts." (See, also, *Rea v. Wilson*, 112 Iowa, 517, 84 N. W. 539.)

One of the questions determined by the trial judge and here to be decided is, Was the mortgagor at the time the mortgage was made the owner of the property mortgaged?

While it appears from the testimony of Jones, Anderson and Young that Young leased the sheep in question from Lund, the Christensens, Jones and Anderson, and that said parties owned them up to the time they were sold to the appellants, the conduct of said parties, with respect to the property, tends to contradict this testimony. According to the testimony the other parties above named had known Young in the state of Utah for a number of years, and from 1902 or 1903 until 1910 they, from time to time, placed in his possession about 6,700 head of sheep upon contracts or agreements, whereby he was to make payment in some instances in cash and in other instances in wool and lambs for the use of the sheep. Some of these contracts were oral and others, while called leases in the testimony, are very informal. Two of these documents were introduced in evidence and are as follows:

"Shelley, Idaho, Oct. 9/1904.

"I the undersiner received of John O. Jones 956 ewes and 240 ewes lambs and 17 bucks to be kept for the terms of four years at the yearly rent of two lbs of wool for each head and six lambs on each one hundred head of sheap to be added yearly. And said sheep are to young good sheep at the time of delivery.

"Remarks.

"John O. Jones stood one half of expence of shipment on said sheep said amount was $99.00.

"Should John O. Jones at time of receiving said sheep return them to Utah by rail I agree to pay the same amount And in addishon I have allready gave to John O. Jones one contract writen in year 1903 and for the terms of 5 years on the same said sheep. It was sined by W. R. Young and lost by said John O. Jones. Should said contract ever be found it shall be null and void and of no effect.

"Signed by W. R. YOUNG."

"Maroni, Utah, Sept. 15, 1910.

"Received from Andrew Anderson of Maroni, Utah Eleven Hundred head of Stock Sheep to be kept by me for the term of three years, for which I agree to pay 50 cts in cash for each sheep per year as rent, said cash to be payed July 1st of each year and at the end of said three years I agree to deliver to Andrew Anderson, his heirs or order, the said Eleven Hundred (1100) head of stock sheep in good condition.

"W. R. YOUNG."

Young removed from Utah to Idaho about 1904 and engaged in the livestock business. He always dealt with the sheep in question as his own. His testimony is in part as follows:

"Q. In April, 1911, how many sheep all told did you have in your possession? A. Something over 3,000 in April.

"Q. Three thousand in April? A. Somewhere near 6,000.

"Q. How many sheep did you have about March, 1911, in your possession that you claimed to lease from Jones and Anderson in Sand Peak county? A. Over 3,000.

"Q. And in March of that same year 1911 counting the Christensen sheep and the Anderson and Jones sheep you had something over 6,000? A. No, I didn't say that.

"Q. How many did you have? A. Close to 6,000.

"Q. What sheep was it you mortgaged to the Anderson Brothers Bank on December 19, 1910? A. These same sheep.

"Q. Which sheep do you refer to by these same sheep? A. All that I had.

"Q. That would cover the Christensen and Lund sheep and also the Jones and Anderson sheep? A. Yes.

"Q. How many sheep, if you know, did you describe in that mortgage? A. Three thousand.

"Q. But you had in your possession about that time about 6,000? A. I did not.

"Q. How many did you have? A. About 3,000 or a little over.

"Q. Where were those others? A. I didn't count the lambs.

"Q. The lambs of what season? A. In 1911, this was in December, 1910, that mortgage to Anderson.

"Q. In December, 1910, you say you had only about 3,000 head of sheep? A. Yes.

"Q. I understood you to say you got about 3,000 sheep under lease from Lund and Christensen? A. I said so.

"Q. Did you have them in December, 1910? A. Not all of them.

"Q. How many did you have? A. Not all of them.

"Q. How many old ones did you have of the Christensen sheep? A. They were all old ones at that time.

"Q. Going back to the spring of 1910, how many sheep did you have in your possession in the spring of 1910? A. Over 6,000.

"Q. How many old ones? A. Over 3,000.

"Q. That was counting the lambs the spring of 1910? A. Yes.

"Q. What I am trying to get at how many old sheep belonging to Young and Christensen you had in the spring of 1910? A. You can figure that out yourself. I had about 3,000 old sheep; 3,100 belonging to other people, then 3,400 would belong to these people; how many would that make?

"Q. Did you have 3,100 old sheep that you leased from Anderson and Jones? A. No.

"Q. How many old sheep did you have that you leased from Jones and Anderson in the spring of 1910? A. Must have had about 1500.

"Q. How many old sheep did you have in the spring of 1910 of the Christensen and Lund sheep? A. About 1,500.

"Q. Then you didn't have 3,000 and you didn't lease that many sheep from Christensen, did you? A. Yes, I did.

"Q. What have you done with them? A. Sold them and ate them up.

"Q. And what? A. Sold them.

"Q. How many sheep did you sell out of these two herds. A. I can't tell; I sold the increase every year.

"Q. How many old ones did you sell? A. I sold from two to five hundred old ones at different years.

"Q. What I am trying to get at now is the number of old sheep say nothing about their increase at the time you made the first lease from the Christensens and Lund—got from them under that lease. A. About 2,000, I guess, old ones.

"Q. And how many lambs? A. About 1,800 old ones and about 1,600 lambs.

"Q. What time in the year did you get them? A. Got them in August.

"Q. That was 3,400 head of grown sheep that you had that fall? A. Yes.

"Q. Did you ever sell any of those sheep? A. Yes.

"Q. When did you sell them? A. Sold some that fall and some the next year.

"Q. And still continued to sell? A. Yes.

"Q. Do you know how many you sold that fall? A. About 200.

"Q. And how many the next year? A. I couldn't tell.

"Q. Do you know how many old sheep you had at the expiration of that verbal lease you took from Christensen and Lund when you say you wrote a letter and changed the terms of the lease belonging to them? A. I don't think I had over 2,000. I don't think the old ones had increased any.

"Q. You had been selling the lambs right along? A. Yes.

"Q. Treated these sheep from the time you got them until you turned them back as your own? A. Had full charge of them.

"Q. Sold them when you wanted to and sold the wool when you wanted to? A. With their permission, their part of it.

"Q. But sold those sheep any time you wanted to? A. Yes.

"Q. Any part of them? A. Yes."

The testimony of Anderson is in part as follows:

"Q. Were those dealings with reference to the leasing of certain sheep to W. R. Young? A. Yes.

"Q. On how many occasions did you lease him sheep? A. I don't know how many times.

"Q. When was the first occasion when you had dealings with him of that nature? A. 1904, I think.

"Q. What did you do at that time? A. I leased him 500 head of sheep.

"Q. Where were the sheep at that time? A. They were in his herd, I think.

"Q. In what place? A. I don't know whether they would be in Sand Peak or where."

From other portions of Anderson's testimony it appears that he leased sheep to Young on but two occasions; 1,000 head in 1904 and 1,100 head in 1910.

Anderson further testified as follows:

"Q. When did you first know that Mr. Young had mortgaged those sheep to the Anderson Brothers bank and the Shelley Bank? A. I think he told us about the first of April.

"Q. You said in your direct examination that he told you he had mortgaged some of them? A. He told us he had mortgaged some of them. I don't remember how many.

"Q. That was about the first of April? A. Yes.

"Q. 1911? A. Yes.

"Q. Where were you when he told you that? A. At Goshen.

"Q. Did he tell you to whom they were mortgaged? A. I don't remember whether he did or not.

"Q. Did you make any effort at that time to ascertain who he had mortgaged these sheep to? A. No.

"Q. You didn't care whether they were mortgaged to the Anderson Brothers Bank or Shelley Bank or anybody else? A. Not at that time."

In another place in the record Anderson testified as follows:

"Q. What were you getting under that lease? A. Straight 50 cents a head.

"Q. In cash? A. Yes.

"Q. When were those payments made? A. At the proper shearing time.

"Q. You never were up here when the sheep were shorn? A. No.

"Q. You never had any agent here to claim any wool or wool money for you? A. No.

"Q. And never did anything about putting anybody on their guard as to who owned those sheep, did you? A. Never was up here.

"Q. Never wrote anybody? A. No.

"Q. And so far as you know no one knew but what W. R. Young owned those sheep? A. I don't know as to that."

Without quoting further from the record it may be said that the testimony is intended to show that the sheep claimed by Anderson and Jones were taken from the possession of Young in April, 1911, and by them turned over to Andreas Sorenson, by whom they were kept as the agent of Anderson and Jones until in June, 1911, when they were sold to said Andreas Sorenson and one Roy Young, who, it was admitted in the oral argument, was a relative of W. R. Young, the mortgagor. Prior to this pretended sale the relations between Andreas Sorenson and Anderson and Jones were such that Sorenson issued checks against the funds of his principals in the bank to cover the expense of caring for the sheep and the checks were presented and paid. The sheep repos-

sessed by Lund and the Christensens were taken over by them
in July, 1911, and immediately transferred to Larson & Sons.

It seems nearly incredible that the owners of sheep would
deliver them over to another under contract of lease, allow
him to remove them from the state, fail and neglect to conform to the recording laws of the state to which they were
conveyed, permit him to treat them as his own, to sell and
otherwise dispose of them until the number had been dimin-
ished from 6,700 to 3,000, and then to mortgage the 3,000,
without exciting the curiosity of the owners sufficiently to
prompt them to inquire as to the amount of the mortgage or
to whom it had been given.

These are some of the circumstances disclosed by the record
which probably prompted the trial judge to scrutinize the
testimony critically and to reach the ultimate conclusion that
W. R. Young was the owner of the sheep and that Anderson,
Jones, Lund and the Christensens were not.

"Possession of personal property is *prima facie* evidence
of ownership." (*Goodwin v. Garr*, 8 Cal. 615; *Courtright
v. Deeds*, 37 Iowa, 503; *Trevorrow v. Trevorrow*, 65 Mich. 234,
31 N. W. 908.)

The case last above cited is from the supreme court of
Michigan and the syllabus is as follows:

"In an action by an administratrix against the intestate's
father to determine the ownership of a team of horses, evidence that the intestate used the team as his own for over
one year justified the instruction to the jury that 'the possession of the team under a claim of ownership was presumptive
evidence of the ownership, not conclusive, but sufficient until
proof was introduced to the contrary,' although it also appeared from the evidence that the father had originally
bought and paid for the team."

In this case the trial judge, who heard the testimony and
had an opportunity to observe the demeanor of the witnesses
on the witness-stand, reached the conclusion that W. R. Young,
the mortgagor, was the owner of the property. An examination of the record convinces us that he was justified in this
finding and that the presumption of ownership created by

the possession of the property, under the facts and circumstances of this case, is not overcome by the testimony introduced to rebut it.

The decision appealed from is accordingly affirmed and costs are awarded to the respondents.

Sullivan, C. J., concurs.

Budge, J., did not sit at the hearing nor take part in the decision of this case.

Petition for rehearing denied.

(January 20, 1915.)

E. H. JENNINGS, Respondent, v. IDAHO RAILWAY, LIGHT & POWER COMPANY et al., Appellants.

[146 Pac. 101.]

FOREIGN CORPORATIONS—NONRESIDENT ALTHOUGH COMPLYING WITH LAWS OF STATE — NOT EXEMPT FROM ATTACHMENT — IMMATERIAL ASSIGNMENTS OF ERROR WILL NOT BE CONSIDERED AND DETERMINED.

1. Under sec. 2792, Rev. Codes, which provides "That foreign corporations complying with the provisions of this section shall have all the rights and privileges of like domestic corporations, including the right to exercise the right of eminent domain, and shall be subject to the laws of the state applicable to like domestic corporations," such corporation is not a citizen or resident of this state within the meaning of the foreign attachment laws, and is not exempt from attachment as a nonresident.

2. A corporation organized under the laws of a foreign jurisdiction, although engaged in business in this state and having complied with the constitution and all the laws of this state affecting foreign corporations, is a nonresident and subject to attachment as such.

3. Where counsel for respective parties agree that should the conclusion of the court be adverse to the contention of appellant upon one question, the remaining objections assigned become immaterial, and when it appears from the record that a consideration

of said questions is not necessary to a final determination of the cause under consideration, the same will not be decided by the court.

APPEAL from the District Court of the Third Judicial District, in and for Ada County. Hon. Chas. P. McCarthy, Judge.

Action to recover on a promissory note. Attachment issued and the court refused to discharge the attachment. *Affirmed.*

Cavanah, Blake & MacLane, for Appellants.

No attachment can be issued against a domestic corporation in an action on a secured debt, and, therefore, if foreign corporations have the same rights and privileges, and are subject to like laws, no attachment can be issued against them in such cases. (6 Thompson on Corporations, ed. 1895, p. 6420, sec. 8060; *Farnsworth v. Terre Haute etc. Ry. Co.,* 29 Mo. 75; *Martin v. Mobile etc. R. Co.,* 7 Bush (Ky.), 116; *Burr v. Co-operative Construction Co.,* 162 Ill. App. 512; *Hackettstown Bank v. Mitchell,* 28 N. J. L. 516.)

Nonliability to attachment is a right or privilege of domestic corporations, and it is further certain that the attachment law is one of the laws of the state applicable to domestic corporations. If the statute is to be given meaning and effect, the construction here suggested would seem to be the only possible one. Furthermore, this construction is in harmony with the spirit of the attachment laws against nonresidents, the purpose of which is to enable a citizen of the state to acquire jurisdiction against a nonresident defendant to the extent of property of the nonresident within the state. The attachment is allowed in order to compel the defendant to come forth and allow his indebtedness to be litigated. (*Blair v. Winston,* 84 Md. 356, 35 Atl. 1101; *Herbert v. Herbert,* 49 N. J. Eq. 70, 22 Atl. 789; *Munroe v. Williams,* 37 S. C. 81, 16 S. E. 533, 19 L. R. A. 665.)

Richards & Haga and McKeen F. Morrow, for Respondent.

The authorities are uniform that the domicile, residence and citizenship of a corporation are in the state where it is created, and that where the corporation is not·domesticated, that is, reincorporated in other states where it does business, it can have but one domicile, one residence, and one citizenship, and that is in the state issuing its charter and maintaining supervision and control over the corporation. (*Cowardin v. Universal Life Ins. Co.*, 32 Gratt. (Va.) 445; *Barbour v. Paige Hotel Co.*, 2 App. Cas. (D. C.) 174.)

"A corporation chartered by a foreign state is a foreign corporation and is liable to attachment as a nonresident debtor, although it may have an office and do business in the state in which the attachment is issued." (*Boyer v. Northern Pacific Ry. Co.*, 8 Ida. 74, 66 Pac. 826, 70 L. R. A. 691; Shinn on Attachments, sec. 105; *New York Life Ins. Co. v. Pike*, 51 Colo. 238, 117 Pac. 899; 5 Thompson on Foreign Corporations, 2d ed., sec. 6629; Cook on Corporations, 7th ed., sec. 1.)

The domicile, residence and citizenship of a corporation are in the state where it is created. (Beale on Foreign Corporations, secs. 111, 113, 211; *Waechter v. Atchison, T. & S. F. Ry. Co.*, 10 Cal. App. 70, 101 Pac. 41; *Voss v. Evans Marble Co.*, 101 Ill. App. 373.)

Appellants should not be heard to contend that respondent holds security and cannot therefore attach the railway company's property. The evidence is uncontradicted that the appellant railway company has done everything in its power to destroy the security which it pledged with respondent. The lien must be a lien of a fixed, determinate character, capable of being enforced with certainty, and depending on no conditions. (*Porter v. Brooks*, 35 Cal. 199; *Watson v. Loewenberg*, 34 Or. 323, 56 Pac. 289; *Bowman v. Wade*, 54 Or. 347, 103 Pac. 72.)

BUDGE, J.—On the 6th of November, 1911, the Idaho Railway, Light & Power Company, a corporation organized under the laws of the state of Maine, made, executed and delivered its promissory note to one E. H. Jennings for $180,000, payable two years after date, bearing interest at the rate of six per cent per annum from July 6, 1912. In order to secure

the payment of the above obligation, the Idaho Railway, Light
& Power Company deposited with the said Jennings as collateral security 1,200 shares of the preferred stock and 2,884
shares of the common stock of the Boise Railroad Company,
Ltd. After the loan had been negotiated and the stock of
the Boise Railroad Company pledged, as aforesaid, the Idaho
Railway, Light & Power Company, being then the owner of
all of the stock of the Boise Railroad Company, elected its
employees or officers as directors and officers of the Boise
Railroad Company, and immediately thereafter caused said
officers to convey by proper conveyance all of the property,
assets, franchises and privileges of the Boise Railroad Company to the Idaho Railway, Light & Power Company. This
being done, the necessity for the existence of the Boise Railroad Company as a corporation ceased, and thereafter the
annual license tax of said company was not paid to the state
by either the Boise Railroad Company or the Idaho Railway,
Light & Power Company, and on the 1st of December, 1913,
the charter of the said Boise Railroad Company was forfeited
to the state.

At the date of the commencement of this action in the trial
court, the capital stock of the Boise Railroad Company, which
had theretofore been pledged as collateral security for the
payment of the respondent's note, was the stock of a corporation which had forfeited its charter and conveyed all of
its physical properties, rights, assets and franchises to the
appellant corporation herein. The Idaho Railway, Light &
Power Company, by its officers, executed a mortgage or deed
of trust to the Guaranty Trust Company of New York, securing an issue of bonds aggregating thirty millions of dollars,
which said mortgage or deed of trust covered all the property then owned by the Idaho Railway, Light & Power Company, or which it might thereafter acquire, and under which
bonds of said company of the par value of about $9,095,000
had been actually issued. The property transferred to the
Idaho Railway, Light & Power Company, which had previously constituted the security as represented by the stock
pledged to Jennings, was now claimed by the Idaho Railway,

Light & Power Company as owner, and by the Guaranty Trust Company of New York as trustee under the thirty million dollar mortgage above referred to.

On December 23, 1913, a receiver for the Idaho Railway, Light & Power Company was duly appointed by an order of the United States court for the district of Idaho, southern division.

The answer of the appellant admits the indebtedness of $180,000 to the respondent, and also admits the appointment of a receiver by an order of the United States district court, and the insolvency of the appellant corporation.

This is a brief statement of what appears to be the facts in this case:

At the time of the issuance of summons in this action, the respondent, upon affidavit and sufficient bond, secured a writ of attachment and caused to be attached all of the properties, assets and franchises of the Idaho Railway, Light & Power Company. On May 28, 1914, appellant by its counsel moved in the trial court to discharge the attachment theretofore issued, for the following reasons, to wit:

1. That the affidavit of attachment shows upon its face that the debt upon which action is brought was secured by pledge of stock of the Boise Railroad Company, and fails to show that such security has become valueless.

2. That the defendant Idaho Railway, Light & Power Company is not a nonresident of the state of Idaho within the meaning of the attachment law, but is a foreign corporation that has complied with the constitution and all the laws of Idaho respecting foreign corporations, and as such, by the terms of such statutes is entitled to all the rights and privileges, and subject to the laws applicable to domestic corporations.

3. That the undertaking for attachment is insufficient.

It was conceded upon the argument of this cause that the appellant corporation had fully complied with the constitution and laws of this state respecting foreign corporations. That being true, the appellant insists that it is exempt from attachment under the laws of this state authorizing the attachment of the property of nonresidents.

Sec. 4302, Rev. Codes, as amended by Sess. Laws 1913, page 160, provides, that

"The plaintiff at the time of the issuing of summons, or at any time afterward may have the property of the defendant attached, as security for the satisfaction of any judgment that may be recovered, unless the defendant gives security to pay such judgment as in this chapter provided, in the following cases: . . . .

"2. In an action upon a judgment, or upon contract, express or implied, or for the collection of any penalty provided by any statute of this state, against a defendant not residing in this state."

Sec. 2792, Rev. Codes, provides, among other things:

"That foreign corporations complying with the provisions of this section shall have all the rights and privileges of like domestic corporations, including the right to exercise the right of eminent domain, and shall be subject to the laws of the state applicable to like domestic corporations."

The pertinent question for our consideration, therefore, is; Do the provisions of our statute exempt foreign corporations from attachment within the meaning of sec. 4302 and subd. 2, *supra,* for the reason that said nonresident corporation has fully complied with the constitution and all of the laws of the state affecting foreign corporations? In other words, when foreign corporations comply with the constitution and laws of our state, do they occupy the same position with reference to our attachment laws that domestic corporations do, or is their property liable to attachment irrespective of their compliance with the constitution and laws affecting nonresidents?

Should this court reach the conclusion that a foreign corporation is not exempt from attachment by reason of having complied with the constitution and laws of this state affecting foreign corporations, it would be unnecessary to discuss or determine any other question involved in this case.

It is conceded that the appellant is a foreign corporation organized and existing under the laws of the state of Maine, and unless when it applied to the state of Idaho for admission to do business within this state and by a full compliance with the constitution and laws of this state affecting foreign corporations it thereby became a resident corporation within the meaning of the attachment law, and thereby became exempt from attachment within the meaning of the statutes above cited, it could at this time be considered in no other light than a nonresident.

In the case of *Boyer v. Northern Pac. Ry. Co.*, 8 Ida. 74, 66 Pac. 826, 70 L. R. A. 691, the court says:

"Both upon principle and authority, private corporations are residents of the state in which they are created. They have, and can have, but one domicile—that the state of their birth, and which is fixed by the charter of incorporation. They may migrate into other countries and jurisdictions for the purpose of business, and may be permitted to carry on business in other states; yet, so far as jurisdiction of courts is concerned, they are treated both by our federal courts and by our state courts as residents of the state in which created, and nonresidents of other states. The appellant in this case is a foreign corporation. . . . . Foreign corporations are and remain, to all intents and purposes, so far as jurisdiction of actions is concerned, nonresidents of the state."

In the case of *New York Life Ins. Co. v. Pike*, 51 Colo. 238, 117 Pac. 899, the supreme court of Colorado says:

"The authorities, both court and text-writers, announce as settled doctrine that a corporation organized under the laws of one state is a resident of the state under whose laws it was created; that it cannot be a resident of any other state; and, though such a corporation be permitted by another state, upon compliance with its laws, to carry on its business there, such permission and compliance does not make it a resident of such other state. . . . . To hold otherwise would be to ingraft upon the statute an exception which is wholly foreign to its plain terms, and would be only an amendment thereof."

In Cook on Corporations, 7th ed., sec. 1, it is said: "The domicile, residence, and citizenship of a corporation are in the state where it is created."

To grant to a foreign corporation the right to hold property, to do business, maintain actions, enjoy the benefits of eminent domain, does not make it a domestic corporation, and notwithstanding the right to the enjoyment of all of these privileges, and such others as the legislature may from time to time provide, the residence or citizenship of a foreign corporation would not be changed and it would still, under the great weight of authority, be subject to attachment as a foreign corporation. (*Barbour v. Paige Hotel Co.*, 2 App. Cas. (D. C.) 174; *Cowardin v. Universal Life Ins. Co.*, 32 Gratt. (Va.) 445; *Merrick v. Van Santvoord*, 34 N. Y. 208; *Blackstone Mfg. Co. v. Blackstone*, 13 Gray (Mass.), 488; *Bank of Augusta v. Earle*, 13 Pet. (U. S.), 519, 10 L. ed. 274; *Shaw v. Quincy Min. Co.*, 145 U. S. 444, 12 Sup. Ct. 935, 36 L. ed. 768.)

The supreme court of California in *Waechter v. Atchison, T. & S. F. Ry. Co.*, 10 Cal. App. 70, 101 Pac. 41, had under consideration the question of venue in a suit brought against a foreign corporation, involving the same principle that we are called upon to consider. The court held that "Its primary purpose was apparently to place foreign railway and transportation companies upon an equal standing in this state with domestic corporations, in respect to building railways and exercising the right of eminent domain, and the rights and privileges incident thereto. To construe it as taking such companies out of the operation of the provisions of the general section relating to the place of trial of actions would be to create a specially privileged class of nonresident corporations who would be favored above, not only nonresident natural persons, but all other foreign corporations that might be doing business in the state. This would not only result in creating a special class of corporate defendants in civil actions, but would also arbitrarily discriminate in favor of corporations against natural persons who were nonresidents."

The authorities are uniform that the domicile, residence and citizenship of a corporation are in the state where it is created, and that where the corporation is not domesticated, that is, reincorporated in other states where it does business, it can have but one domicile, one residence and one citizenship, and that is in the state issuing its charter and maintaining supervision and control over the corporation. (5 Thompson on Foreign Corp., 2d ed., sec. 6629.)

In Drake on Attachments, 7th ed., sec. 80, the proposition is stated as follows:

"The foreign character of a corporation is not to be determined by the place where its business is transacted, or where the corporators reside, but by the place where its charter was granted. With reference to inhabitancy, it is considered an inhabitant of the state in which it was incorporated." These general principles respecting residency or inhabitancy of corporations cannot be denied or questioned. (*Cowardin v. Universal Life Ins. Co.*, 32 Gratt. (Va.) 445.)

It must be conceded that it is beyond the power of the state to forfeit or extend the corporate existence of a foreign corporation. It can exercise no power or control over the corporation as such. A foreign corporation by compliance with the constitution and laws may do business within the state at its pleasure, and when dissatisfied can withdraw at will.

The provisions of our attachment law provide for no such exemption as contended for by appellant, and even though the legislature should attempt to make some such provision looking to the exemption of foreign corporations from attachment by a compliance with the constitution and laws, such legislation might be seriously questioned upon the ground and for the reason that it would be class legislation, or an attempt on the part of the legislature to confer special privileges upon a particular class of persons which could not be enjoyed by all alike. We do not think that the legislature ever intended that a foreign corporation, by complying with the constitution and laws of this state permitting it to do business should be regarded as a resident of this state within the meaning of our attachment laws, and that its property should be exempt from attachment. (*Voss v. Evans Marble Co.*, 101 Ill. App. 373.)

In view of the conclusion reached by this court upon the second ground of objection urged to the validity of the attachment of the property of appellant, it becomes immaterial whether or not the stock pledged by the Idaho Railway, Light

& Power Company to respondent is or became valueless by the fault of respondent or the conduct of appellants.

. The third objection urged, namely, that the undertaking for attachment was insufficient, was not discussed by counsel for appellants, either during the oral argument or in the brief filed on appellants' behalf.

The order of the district court refusing to dissolve the attachment is hereby affirmed. Costs awarded to respondent.

Sullivan, C. J., and Morgan, J., concur.

(January 21, 1915.)

THE SOUTHERN IDAHO CONFERENCE ASSOCIATION OF SEVENTH DAY ADVENTISTS, a Corporation, Appellant, v. THE HARTFORD FIRE INSURANCE CO., a Corporation, Respondent.

[145 Pac. 502.]

Policy of Insurance—Nonsuit—Evidence—Sufficiency of—Rejection of Evidence—Proof of Loss—Waiver of.

1. Upon motion for nonsuit, as provided by sec. 4354, Rev. Codes, the defendant admits the existence of every fact which the evidence tends to prove or which could be gathered from any reasonable view of the evidence, and plaintiff is entitled to the benefit of all inferences in his favor which the jury would be justified in drawing from the testimony.

2. The refusal of the court to admit certain evidence on the trial *held* reversible error.

3. Where a waiver of proof of loss is an issue in a case, all evidence tending to establish such waiver ought to be admitted.

APPEAL from the District Court of the Third Judicial District for Ada County. Hon. Charles P. McCarthy, Judge.

Action to recover on a policy of insurance. Judgment of nonsuit for the defendant. *Reversed.*

Richard H. Johnson, for Appellant.

. The rule of law which governs on a motion for nonsuit is clearly laid down by this court in *Later v. Haywood*, 12 Ida. 78, 85 Pac. 494, and *Bank of Commerce v. Baldwin*, 12 Ida. 202, 85 Pac. 497, to the effect that such a motion admits the existence of every fact in favor of the plaintiff which the evidence tends to prove or which could be gathered from any reasonable view of the evidence. (See, also, *Shank v. Great Shoshone & Twin Falls Water Power Co.*, 205 Fed. 836, 124 C. C. A. 35; *Culver v. Kehl*, 21 Ida. 596, 123 Pac. 301; *Allen v. Phoenix Assur. Co.*, 12 Ida. 653, 88 Pac. 245, 10 Ann. Cas. 328, 8 L. R. A., N. S., 903; *Pratt v. Dwelling-House Fire Ins. Co.*, 130 N. Y. 206, 29 N. E. 118.)

An agreement to renew insurance in force is presumed to have reference to the terms and conditions of the existing policy. (19 Cyc. 630, and cases cited in note 33.)

Where plaintiff's last insurance was had with the defendant insurance company through the same agent, the word "renew" in an oral contract with such agent to renew the insurance sufficiently designates the company, as well as the property to be insured, and the terms of the policy. (*Abel v. Phoenix Ins. Co.*, 62 N. Y. Supp. 218, 219, 47 App. Div. 81.)

In the following cases there was less evidence than in the case at bar to show a contract of insurance, and in all of them the court held that the question was one for the jury to determine: *Smith v. Provident Sav. Life Assur. Soc.*, 65 Fed. 765, 13 C. C. A. 284; *Dove v. Royal Ins. Co.*, 98 Mich. 122, 57 N. W. 30; *Bowman v. Agricultural Ins. Co.*, 59 N. Y. 521; *Church v. La Fayette Fire Ins. Co.*, 66 N. Y. 222; *Welsh v. Continental Ins. Co.*, 47 Hun (N. Y.), 598; *Hardwick v. State Ins. Co.*, 23 Or. 290, 21 Am. St. 879, 31 Pac. 656; *Long v. North British & M. F. Ins. Co.*, 137 Pa. 335, 21 Am. St. 879, 20 Atl. 1014; *Latimore v. Dwelling-House Ins. Co.*, 153 Pa. 324, 25 Atl. 757; *Nute v. Hartford Fire Ins. Co.*, 109 Mo. App. 585, 83 S. W. 83; *Gerib v. International Ins. Co.*, 1 Dill. 443, Fed. Cas. No. 5298; *Forehand v. Niagara Ins. Co.*, 58 Ill. App. 161; *Phoenix Ins. Co. v. Coffman*, 10 Tex. Civ. App. 631, 32 S. W. 810.

In *Marysville Merc. Co. v. Home Fire Ins. Co.*, 21 Ida. 383, 121 Pac. 1026, the facts are in many respects like the case at bar, and what was said with reference to the agent Kruger in that case applies with equal force to Gardner in this case.

Martin & Martin, for Respondent.

The insurance policy sued upon was properly excluded from evidence, for the reason that appellant ·failed to show that there was a contract of insurance at the time of the fire. (Joyce on Insurance, secs. 41, 1459; Kerr on Insurance, sec. 49, p. 107; 2 Clement on Fire Insurance, p. 522; Wood on Insurance, 2d ed., secs. 5, 6, 15.)

"An oral agreement between plaintiff and defendant's agent in regard to renewing a policy of fire insurance in which the amount of the policy to be taken is not fixed does not constitute a binding contract." (*Sater v. Henry County Farmers' Mut. Fire Ins. Co.*, 92 Iowa, 579, 61 N. W. 209; *Michigan Pipe Co. v. Michigan Fire & Marine Ins. Co.*, 92 Mich. 482, 52 N. W. 1070, 20 L. R. A. 277.)

A parol contract of renewal cannot be established by mere negotiation. The minds of the parties must have met upon terms well agreed upon without anything being left for future determination. (2 Clement on Fire Ins., p. 522; *Zigler v. Phoenix Ins. Co.*, 82 Iowa, 569, 48 N. W. 987; *O'Reilley v. Corporation of London Ins. Co.*, 101, N. Y. 575, 5 N. E. 568; *Healey v. Imperial Ins. Co.*, 5 Nev. 268.)

Where at the time of the fire the policy has not been delivered, although written, the contract is *prima facie* incomplete, and the burden is upon the insured to show there was a valid, binding agreement of insurance prior to the fire. (*Ogle Lake Shingle Co. v. National Lumber Ins. Co.*, 68 Wash. 185, 122 Pac. 990; *Stephens v. Capital Ins. Co.*, 87 Iowa, 283, 54 N. W. 140; *Davis Lumber Co. v. Scottish Union & Nat. Ins. Co.*, 94 Wis. 472, 69 N. W. 156; *Ferguson v. Northern Ins. Co.*, 26 S. D. 346, 128 N. W. 125; *New York Lumber etc. Co., v. People's Fire Ins. Co.*, 96 Mich. 20, 55 N. W. 434; *Hartford Fire Ins. Co. v. Whitman*, 75 Ohio St. 312, 79 N. E. 459, 9 Ann. Cas. 218; *Stebbins v. Lancashire*, 60 N. H. 65.)

SULLIVAN, C. J.—This case was decided by this court on May 26, 1914, and a petition for rehearing was thereafter granted and a rehearing had at the January, 1915, term of court.

The action was brought by the plaintiff, the Southern Idaho Conference of Seventh Day Adventists, a corporation, to recover $3,500 on an insurance policy issued by the defendant, the Hartford Fire Insurance Company, a corporation, covering a school building situated near the village of Eagle in Ada county, which building was destroyed by fire on the night of November 21, 1911.

The complaint alleges that said policy was executed and delivered on November 20, 1911, and the payment of premium of $122.50 was made. The answer denies the execution and delivery of the policy, but on the trial counsel for defendant admitted that the policy was signed by the agent, but denied that it was delivered to the plaintiff. The complaint alleges, and it is admitted by the answer, that at all times mentioned in the complaint, Frank M. Gardner was the duly appointed, qualified and acting agent of the defendant Insurance Company, residing at the village of Eagle, and was authorized to solicit and receive applications for fire insurance and that he was duly licensed as such agent by the insurance commissioner of the state of Idaho, and that he was duly authorized by defendant to countersign and deliver for said defendant contracts or policies for insurance against loss or damage by fire, and to receive on behalf of said defendant payment of premiums therefor.

The case was tried by the court with a jury and before plaintiff had completed the introduction of its evidence, the court refused to permit the insurance policy to be introduced in evidence. The plaintiff then offered other evidence to sustain the remaining allegations of the complaint, much of which testimony was offered for the purpose of showing a waiver on the part of the defendant of any want of authority from plaintiff to Gardner to execute the policy, even if such authority had not been fully shown by the testimony theretofore introduced. This evidence was all ruled out by the court and exceptions taken. The court thereupon sustained a motion for a nonsuit on the part of the defendant and judgment of dismissal was entered against the plaintiff. The appeal is from the judgment.

The assignments of error go to the action of the court in excluding certain evidence offered by the plaintiff and granting a nonsuit at the close of plaintiff's evidence. The motion for nonsuit was granted and judgment of dismissal entered on the ground that no evidence was introduced by the plaintiff showing that the agent of the insurance company had any authority or direction from the plaintiff to execute the policy sued upon, and the court by granting said nonsuit held that it was executed without authority from the plaintiff and therefore did not constitute a binding contract upon the insurance company.

Since in our view of the matter the case must be sent back for a new trial, we shall not comment upon the evidence, but after a careful examination of all the evidence in the record, we are fully satisfied that there was evidence admitted and offered tending to show that the agent of the insurance company was authorized to issue the policy of insurance sued upon in this case, and that it was error for the court to grant a nonsuit and enter a judgment of dismissal.

It is a well-settled rule of this court that on a motion by the defendant for nonsuit, after the plaintiff has introduced his evidence and rested his case, the defendant is deemed to have admitted all of the facts of which there is any evidence, and all of the facts which the evidence tends to prove, and that the evidence must be interpreted most strongly against the defendant. (*Culver v. Kehl*, 21 Ida. 595, 123 Pac. 301, and authorities there cited; *Shank v. Great Shoshone & Twin Falls Water Power Co.*, 205 Fed. 833, 836, 124 C. C. A. 35.)

The policy of insurance on which this action was based was offered in evidence and rejected by the court. That was error. The policy should have been admitted. Other evidence tending to show the understanding or agreement between the insured and the agent of the insurer was offered and rejected by the court. All evidence ought to be received that tends to sustain the material allegations of the complaint.

The record shows that the proof of loss was not made within sixty days after the fire, and the question will be presented on a retrial as to whether the failure to make such proof precludes a recovery in this case. The evidence offered showing or tending to show a waiver by the company of making the proof of loss within the sixty days ought to be received on the trial.

The above is sufficient to indicate the views of the court upon the points discussed.

For the reasons above given, the judgment must be reversed and a new trial granted, and the cause remanded for further proceedings in accordance with the views expressed in this opinion. Costs awarded in favor of appellant.

Budge and Morgan, JJ., concur.

(January 25, 1915.)

WASHINGTON COUNTY LAND & DEVELOPMENT COMPANY, a Corporation, Appellant, v. THE WEISER NATIONAL BANK, a Corporation, Respondent.

[146 Pac. 116.]

APPEAL—UNDERTAKING FILED BUT OMITTED FROM TRANSCRIPT—APPEARANCE—STIPULATION—JURISDICTION—DEFAULT—JUDGMENT — RELIEF DEMANDED.

1. A motion to dismiss an appeal upon the ground that no undertaking on appeal or deposit of money, in lieu thereof, was made or deposited with the clerk of the district court within five days after the service of the notice of appeal, will be denied and the appeal will be heard upon its merits when such an undertaking in due form and in the proper amount was, in fact, filed in time and transmitted to this court but omitted from the transcript through oversight on the part of the clerk.

2. A defendant appears in an action when he answers, demurs or gives the plaintiff written notice of his appearance or when an attorney gives notice of appearance for him.

3. A stipulation that the defendant have until a certain date to make settlement of the amount claimed by plaintiff and containing a promise on the part of the defendant that in the event the settlement is not made by that time, it will confess judgment in the action then pending between the parties, is not an appearance contemplated by sec. 4892, Rev. Codes.

4. In case the defendant fails to appear, answer, demur or otherwise plead within the time prescribed by statute, the district judge has jurisdiction and power at chambers to enter a default and to hear testimony thereon and to enter judgment.

5. In case the defendant fails to answer, the trial court is without power to grant relief not demanded in the complaint, and if there be no prayer accompanying the complaint and no relief demanded, no judgment can be entered in favor of the plaintiff.

APPEAL from the District Court of the Seventh Judicial District for the County of Adams. Hon. Ed. L. Bryan, Judge.

Suit to vacate and set aside judgment and to quiet title. Judgment for defendant. *Affirmed.*

Lynne F. Clinton, for Appellant.

The stipulation filed by appellant and respondent was a voluntary appearance within the purview of sec. 4149, Rev. Codes, and had the jurisdictional effect of an answer or demurrer. (*Cooper v. Gordon,* 125 Cal. 296, 301, 57 Pac. 1006.)

Powers conferred on a court cannot be exercised by a judge in vacation, even by consent of parties, unless a statute so provides. (23 Cyc. 545; *Bates v. Gage,* 40 Cal. 183; *Wicks v. Ludwig,* 9 Cal. 173.)

The omission of any prayer for relief is not a fatal defect. (*Sannoner v. Jacobson,* 47 Ark. 31, 14 S. W. 458; *Parker v. Norfolk etc. R. Co.,* 119 N. C. 677, 25 S. E. 722; *Iowa County v. Mineral Point Ry. Co.,* 24 Wis. 93.)

The prayer for relief is no portion of the statement of facts constituting a cause of action. The entire omission of any demand for judgment does not subject the complaint to a general demurrer. (*Fox v. Graves,* 46 Neb. 812, 65 N. W. 887; *Culver v. Rodgers,* 33 Ohio St. 537, 546.)

"If the facts stated in the complaint are established by the evidence and show that the plaintiff is entitled to any relief, the court may grant him such relief, although not prayed for." (*Anderson v. War Eagle Consol. Min. Co.*, 8 Ida. 789, 72 Pac. 671; *Presson v. Boone*, 108 N. C. 78, 12 S. E. 897.)

The want of a special or general prayer is not a defect involving the power or jurisdiction of a court to render a decree. (*Evans v. Schafer*, 119 Ind. 49, 21 N. E. 448; *Baxter v. Knoxville First Nat. Bank*, 85 Tenn. 33, 1 S. W. 501.)

Ed. R. Coulter, for Respondent, files no brief.

MORGAN, J.—This is an appeal from the district court of the seventh judicial district for Adams county, and is prosecuted from a judgment wherein the court refused to set aside a former judgment entered in a case in which respondent here was plaintiff and this appellant was defendant.

The defendant, Weiser National Bank, named as respondent herein, defaulted in the district court by its failure to answer or otherwise appear, but moved in this court to dismiss this appeal upon the ground that no undertaking on appeal, or deposit of money in lieu thereof, was made or deposited with the clerk of the district court from which this appeal was taken within five days after service of the notice of appeal upon said respondent, and alleges, among other things, that a copy of the said notice of appeal was served upon respondent on the 3d of December, 1913; that no undertaking on appeal was ever filed in said cause, as appears from the transcript on appeal.

An undertaking on appeal in due form and in the proper amount has been transmitted to this court in this case, and, as appears from the filing mark thereon, it was filed on December 6, 1913. As a matter of fact it does not appear in the transcript, probably through oversight on the part of the clerk, but the undertaking being in due form and in the proper amount and having been filed in time, the motion to dismiss will be denied and the appeal will be considered upon its merits.

Although the complaint in this case is not accompanied by a prayer and no relief is demanded, the apparent purpose of the action is to vacate and set aside the former judgment and to remove from the title to plaintiff's real estate the cloud thereby cast upon it.

In the former case the default of the defendant was entered and judgment was thereafter awarded to plaintiff at chambers. The defendant in the former case, plaintiff and appellant in this, has prosecuted this appeal upon the theory that the judge of the district court was without jurisdiction to enter said former judgment at chambers, for the reason, as it contends, that it appeared in said former action and is, therefore, entitled to a judgment in this case vacating and setting aside said former judgment. The document relied upon by appellant as an appearance in the former action is a stipulation between the parties and, omitting the title of the court and cause, is as follows:

"STIPULATION.

"It is hereby stipulated by and between the respective parties to the above-entitled action, and their respective attorneys, that the Washington County Land and Development Company shall have up to and including November 1, 1912, in which to settle said action and have the suit dismissed at the instance of the Weiser National Bank, and that in the event that said suit is not settled and dismissed by November 1, 1912, that the Washington County Land and Development Company will confess judgment for the amount of the said promissory notes involved in said suit, together with interest and attendant costs and attorneys fees in such sum as the Court may adjudge reasonable not to exceed amt. prayed for.

"WASHINGTON COUNTY LAND AND DE-
VELOPMENT COMPANY.

"By LYNNE F. CLINTON,

"Its Attorney in Fact.

"WEISER NATIONAL BANK.

"By ED R. COULTER,

"Its Attorney in Fact.

"Filed Sept. 6, 1912. C. W. Holmes, Clerk."

Appellant cites and relies upon the 17th subdivision of sec. 3890, Rev. Codes, conferring jurisdiction upon district judges at chambers, and the part of said section material to a decision of this case is as follows:

"Sec. 3890. A district judge may sit at chambers anywhere within his district, and when so acting, has jurisdiction and power as follows: . . . .

"17th. To enter defaults and to hear testimony thereon; and to enter judgment in default cases, where there has been no appearance or plea filed within the time prescribed by statute, and to give such judgments the same force and effect as though entered in open court."

In said case the defendant (appellant here) failed to answer, demur or otherwise plead, and unless the stipulation above quoted is an appearance in contemplation of the seventeenth subdivision of said sec. 3890, it made no appearance whatever in said case.

Sec. 4892, Rev. Codes, is as follows:

"A defendant appears in an action when he answers, demurs, or gives the plaintiff written notice of his appearance, or when an attorney gives notice of appearance for him. After appearance, a defendant or his attorney is entitled to notice of all subsequent proceedings of which notice is required to be given. But where a defendant has not appeared, service of notice or papers need not be made upon him unless he is imprisoned in the action for want of bail."

In Words & Phrases, vol. 1, pages 449, 450, the following definitions, among others, of the word "appearance" are found:

"Where a paper, which has been voluntarily executed by the defendants in a suit pending therein filed, contains a recital, 'we hereby enter our appearance to said cause,' such phrase signifies that they make an appearance for every necessary purpose of the cause." (Citing *Mutual Nat. Bank of New Orleans v. Moore*, 50 La. Ann. 1332, 24 So. 304, 306.)

"Appearance is the process by which a person against whom a suit has been commenced submits himself to the jurisdiction of the court." (Citing *Flint v. Comly*, 95 Me. 251, 49 Atl. 1044, 1045.)

"An appearance is the formal proceeding by which a defendant submits himself to the jurisdiction of the court; the prescribed mode of complying with the exigency of the process." (Citing *Crawford v. Vinton*, 102 Mich. 83, 62 N. W. 988, 989.)

The stipulation is not an appearance contemplated by sec. 4892, Rev. Codes. It is an agreement that the appellant should have until Nov. 1, 1912, to make settlement of the claim of the respondent and a promise that, in the event settlement was not made by that time, it would confess judgment in the action then pending between said parties. It in no way bound the appellant to fail to answer, demur or give written notice of its appearance, nor did it bind the respondent to refrain from causing default to be entered for failure to do so. In said case, as shown by the judgment of the court, the appellant was duly served with process within the state of Idaho, and after the time for answering had expired, its default for failure to answer was duly entered. Had the said appellant not been regularly served with process the said stipulation would not be deemed an appearance contemplated by our code, nor would it have been process by which said appellant submitted itself to the jurisdiction of the court and thereby waived the service of the summons upon it, for it expresses no such intention.

Another question presented by this appeal is, Could any relief have been granted to the appellant by the trial court since none was demanded in the complaint and the respondent failed to answer?

Sec. 4360, Rev. Codes, provides for the entry of judgment if the defendant fails to answer the complaint. Subdivision 1 of said section refers to the entry of judgments in actions arising upon contracts for the recovery of money or damages only, and subdivision 2 of said section provides:

"In other actions, if no answer has been filed with the clerk of the court within the time specified in the summons, or such further time as may have been granted, the clerk must enter the default of the defendant; and thereafter the plaintiff may apply at the first or any subsequent term of the court for the relief demanded in the complaint. . . . . '' This section limits the plaintiff in his application to the court in case the defendant has not answered, to the relief demanded in the complaint, and sec. 4353, Rev. Codes, limits the court in granting relief in such case, and is as follows:

"Sec. 4353. The relief granted to the plaintiff, if there be no answer, cannot exceed that which he shall have demanded in his complaint; but in any other case, the court may grant him any relief consistent with the case made by the complaint embraced within the issue." (See *Lowe v. Turner*, 1 Ida. 107; *Wilson v. Boise City*, 7 Ida. 69, 60 Pac. 84.)

Since the defendant failed to answer in this case, the trial court was without power to grant relief not demanded in the complaint. No relief was demanded in the complaint and no judgment could have been entered in favor of appellant.

For the foregoing reasons the judgment appealed from is affirmed and costs are awarded to the respondent.

Sullivan, C. J., and Budge, J., concur.

(January 28, 1915.)

EXCHANGE STATE BANK, a Corporation, Appellant, v. GEORGE C. TABER, Respondent.

[145 Pac. 1090.]

JURY—OPENING AND CLOSING ARGUMENT TO—PROMISSORY NOTES—ALTERATION OF—COLLATERAL SECURITY—CONVERSION OF BY AGENT—NEGLIGENCE OF PLEDGEE—INSTRUCTIONS—ADMISSION AND REJECTION OF EVIDENCE—DIRECTED VERDICT.

1. The order of trial in a civil case is provided by sec. 4383, Rev. Codes, and directs that the trial must proceed in the order there indicated, unless the judge, for special reasons, otherwise directs, and where an action is brought on promissory notes and the respondent admits the execution of such notes but makes special

defenses thereto, it rests in the sound discretion of the trial court to direct the order of addressing the jury, and unless there is a clear abuse of discretion, this court will not disturb the verdict.

2. Where a note appears to have been altered in a material respect, the *onus* is on the party seeking to enforce the payment to show that it is not void, but where the respondent in his answer and counterclaim, in express terms, admits the execution and delivery of the notes, which are set out in full in the complaint, and when introduced in evidence, are in the same condition as they appeared in the complaint, the respondent should not be permitted to introduce evidence tending to establish any alteration, nor should the court instruct the jury upon the law governing the alteration of written instruments.

3. Where the notes are set out in the complaint and when introduced in evidence, are in the same condition as they appear in the complaint, and respondent admits in express terms the execution and delivery of the notes, it will be presumed that any alteration was made prior to the execution of the notes.

4. Where a party by conduct has intimated that he consents to an act which has been done or will offer no opposition thereto, though it could not have been lawfully done without his consent, and he thereby induces others to do that from which they otherwise might have abstained, he cannot question the legality of the action to the prejudice of those who have acted on the fair inference to be drawn from his conduct.

5. A pledgee must exercise ordinary and reasonable diligence to secure the fruits of the collateral, but he is held to no greater degree of diligence, and extraordinary care and efforts in the collection of the collaterals are not necessary.

6. Where a person is jointly agreed upon by the pledgor and pledgee to make collection of collateral notes, he becomes the representative of both parties and neither can charge the other with negligence.

7. Refusal to give certain instructions requested by appellant, *held* to be error.

8. *Held*, that it was error to reject certain evidence offered by appellant.

9. The admission of certain evidence over the objection of the appellant, *held* to be error.

10. Where a party is entitled to have a verdict directed in his favor at the close of the evidence and the case is reversed on his appeal, a new trial will not be ordered. The case will be remanded, with instructions that judgment be entered in his favor.

APPEAL from the District Court of the Fourth Judicial District for the County of Twin Falls. Hon. C. O. Stockslager, Judge.

Action to recover on certain promissory notes. Judgment for defendant. *Reversed.*

Sweeley & Sweeley, for Appellant.

In nearly all the states the order of trial is by statute made subject to conditions, leaving it to the judgment of the court. (15 Ency. Pl. & Pr. 187.)

But that is not true in Idaho. Our statute is identical with that of California, from which state it was copied. (*Benham v. Rowe*, 2 Cal. 387, 56 Am. Dec. 342.)

In those jurisdictions where the order of trial is under the control of the court, the test is that the right to open and close belongs to the party against whom judgment would be rendered if no evidence were introduced by either side. (15 Ency. Pl. & Pr. 184; *Coffman v. Spokane Chronicle Pub. Co.*, 65 Wash. 1, 117 Pac. 596, Ann. Cas. 1913B, 636; *Grisinger v. Hubbard*, 21 Ida. 469, 122 Pac. 853, Ann. Cas. 1913E, 87; *MacDermid v. Watkins*, 41 Colo. 231, 92 Pac. 701; *Rahm v. Deig*, 121 Ind. 283, 23 N. E. 141.)

Where in an action on a note the defendant had admitted its execution without admitting the plaintiff's ownership, the defendant is not entitled to the right to open and close. (*Dodd v. Norman*, 99 Ga. 319, 25 S. E. 650; *Myers v. Binkley*, 26 Ind. App. 208, 59 N. E. 333; *Teller v. Ferguson*, 24 Colo. 432, 51 Pac. 429; *Mastin v. Bartholomew*, 41 Colo. 328, 92 Pac. 682.)

The demand for the right to open and close cannot be made for the first time after the testimony is all in. (*Edwards v. Murray*, 5 Wyo. 153, 38 Pac. 681.)

If either party to this action is more guilty of negligence than the other in the selection of Robinson, it is the defendant. It is not, however, so much a question of negligence as it is a matter of both parties being bound by the acts of the person agreed upon to handle the property. (*Murdock v. Clarke*, 90

Cal. 427, 27 Pac. 275; *Damon v. Waldteufel*, 99 Cal. 234, 33
Pac. 903; *Mt. Vernon Bridge Co. v. Knox Co. Sav. Bank*, 46
Ohio St. 224, 20 N. E. 339; *Wilson v. Carlinville Nat. Bank*,
187 Ill. 222, 58 N. E. 250, 52 L. R. A. 632; *Bank of Lindsborg
v. Ober*, 31 Kan. 599, 3 Pac. 324; *Kershaw v. Ladd*, 34 Or.
375, 56 Pac. 402, 44 L. R. A. 236.)

The notes in suit were set out in full in the complaint. By
his answer the defendant in express terms admitted their
execution. No question or suggestion as to their having been
altered in any respect was contained in the answer. (14
Ency. Pl. & Pr. 656.)

Defendant having admitted that he executed the notes
which were set out in full in the complaint and which, when
they were introduced in evidence, were the same as they appeared in the complaint, could not be heard to claim that they
had been altered. (*Kleeb v. Bard*, 12 Wash. 140, 40 Pac.
733.)

The appellant as pledgee of the collaterals was required to
exercise only ordinary diligence. (*Murphy v. Bartsch*, 2 Ida.
636, 23 Pac. 82; 22 Am. & Eng. Ency. of Law, 2d ed., 902.)

Longley & Walters, for Respondent.

Under our statute the question as to who has the burden
of proof is properly a matter of practice, and the ruling of
the court thereon will not be reviewed unless there is evidence
of an abuse of discretion. (*Viele v. Germania Ins. Co.*, 26
Iowa, 9, 96 Am. Dec. 83.)

Also the court has a discretion in the matter of opening
and closing. (*Names v. Dwelling-House Ins. Co.*, 95 Iowa,
642, 64 N. W. 628; *Goodpaster v. Voris*, 8 Iowa, 334, 74 Am.
Dec. 313; *Shaffer v. Des Moines Coal etc. Co.*, 122 Iowa, 233,
98 N. W. 111.)

It is well settled in the federal courts that the determination of the right to open and close rests in the sound discretion
of the trial court, and is not a proper subject of exception
and review on writ of error. (*Day v. Woodworth*, 13 How.
(U. S.) 363, 14 L. ed. 181; *Hall v. Weare*, 92 U. S. 728, 23
L. ed. 500; *Lancaster v. Collins*, 115 U. S. 222, 6 Sup. Ct. 33,

29 L. ed. 373; *Florence Oil & Ref. Co. v. Farrar*, 109 Fed. 254, 48 C. C. A. 345.)

"A statute which provides that the plaintiff in an action shall open the case and conclude the argument to the jury unless for special reasons the court otherwise directs, has been held to leave the order of trial within the discretion of the trial court." (*Paine v. Smith*, 33 Minn. 495, 24 N. W. 305; *Aultman & Co. v. Falkum*, 47 Minn. 414, 50 N. W. 471.)

"An erroneous instruction which produces no injury will not be ground for reversal." (Haynes, New Trial and Appeal, secs. 132, 286; *Hisler v. Carr*, 34 Cal. 641; *Bradley v. Lee*, 38 Cal. 362; *Satterlee v. Bliss*, 36 Cal. 489.)

In endeavoring to collect the collateral and for a failure to use such diligence, or for his negligence, inexcusable default, wrongful act or omission, the bailee is answerable for the loss resulting to his debtor. (*Montague v. Stelts*, 37 S. C. 200, 34 Am. St. 736, 15 S. E. 968; *Rumsey v. Laidley*, 34 W. Va. 721, 26 Am. St. 935, 12 S. E. 866; *Chemical Nat. Bank v. Armstrong*, 50 Fed. 798; *Lamberton v. Windom*, 12 Minn. 232, 90 Am. Dec. 301.)

One who seeks to rely upon an estoppel must first show that he exercised due and reasonable diligence to know and ascertain the true facts and conditions, and if he failed to do this, he can make no claim of estoppel. (14 Ency. of Law, 117; *Morgan v. Farrel*, 58 Conn. 413, 18 Am. St. 282, 20 Atl. 614; *Blodgett v. Perry*, 97 Mo. 263, 10 Am. St. 307, 10 S. W. 891; Pomeroy's Eq., 1905 ed., sec. 810.)

To constitute an agency, it requires the concurrence of the minds of both the principal and the agent. (*Western Union Tel. Co. v. Northcutt*, 158 Ala. 539, 132 Am. St. 38, 48 So. 553.)

"The bailee cannot justify his conversion upon the ground that the bailment was illegal, and set this up as an excuse for his own default; nor can he deny bailor's title." (3 Ency. of Law, 758; *Allgear v. Walsh*, 24 Mo. App. 134; *Sinclair v. Murphy*, 14 Mich. 392; *Sherwood v. Neal*, 41 Mo. App. 416; *Burton v. Wilkinson*, 18 Vt. 186, 46 Am. Dec. 145.)

Taber parted with all his right of control over the collaterals, and the appellant was bound to employ reasonable diligence in their collection. (*Hanna v. Holton*, 78 Pa. 334, 21 Am. Rep. 20; *McQueen's Appeal*, 104 Pa. 595, 49 Am. Rep. 592.)

BUDGE, J.—This is an action brought in the district court of Twin Falls county, by the appellant Exchange State Bank, a corporation, against George C. Taber, respondent. Judgment upon a verdict of the jury was entered against the appellant for the sum of $3,924.07 upon the respondent's counterclaim. From said judgment an appeal was prosecuted to this court. On the 14th day of March, 1914, a majority and minority opinion was handed down, resulting in a reversal of the judgment of the trial court and remanding said cause for a new trial. Thereafter a petition for rehearing was filed by both the appellant and respondent, which petition was granted.

This action was brought to recover upon two promissory notes, one for $504.49 dated January 1, 1911, payable May 1, 1912; the second note was for $2,393.00, dated October 8, 1911, payable six months after date. Both notes bear interest at six per cent per annum.

The respondent, in his answer, admits the execution and delivery of the two notes, but denies that they were the property of the appellant and that they were unpaid or past due, and alleges affirmatively that each of said notes has been fully paid and discharged by reason of the facts alleged in the affirmative allegations of respondent's answer and the facts as alleged in respondent's counterclaim, which, in substance and effect are, that the appellant had been negligent in its handling of said promissory notes, which had been pledged with the appellant by the respondent as collateral security to respondent's obligation, to his damage in the sum of $6,566.00.

From the record it appears that on April 8, 1907, James T. Robinson, of Jackson county, Missouri, and George C. Taber, the respondent herein, then of Corral county, Illinois, entered into an agreement whereby Robinson and Taber became the owners of a tract of land in Kansas City, Missouri. Taber furnished the purchase price of the land. Robinson was to furnish all material and labor in erecting nine houses and was to pay for all street improvements and to furnish all necessary funds to erect the houses, and on the completion and sale of the houses, Taber was to receive $9,200.00 as his full share and interest in the whole transaction, and to accept payments under the following contract:

"Two-thirds of the second mortgage paper received from the sale of the above described property up to the amount, and not to exceed Nine thousand two hundred dollars, and in event that two-thirds of the second mortgage paper does not amount to $9,200.00 the balance to be in cash.

"James T. Robinson agrees to collect all money paid in on the notes turned over to Geo. C. Taber from the sale of the above described property, and remit to him the 1st of each month the entire life of notes given, free of charge."

On August 2, 1908, the respondent called upon John R. Wolf, assistant cashier of the appellant at Lanark, Illinois, and told Wolf that he had some notes and collaterals and wanted to arrange to borrow some money on these notes; that they were at Kansas City and secured by mortgages; that a Mr. Robinson had been and was collecting the monthly instalments as they became due, and was sending the payments to him; that for Wolf to investigate the matter and that a William Hess who resided in the city was well acquainted with Robinson; that he could see him and that he could write and find out the character of the man, how he was, etc. About two weeks thereafter, respondent met Wolf and it was arranged between them that a loan should be made to the respondent; that the bank would accept the collateral notes, and as they were paid the amounts received would be indorsed upon the respondent's obligation to the bank. On September 7, 1908, a letter was written by Wolf and signed by Taber, addressed to Robinson at Kansas City, which is as follows:

"I have talked with J. R. Wolf asst. cashier with whom I am depositing all my notes as collateral and have concluded the best way will be for you to send (all my notes in your hands) to me at Twin Falls, Idaho. I will endorse them and forward them to Exchange State Bank Lanark then they return them to you for collection the same as I have done and you receipt to Bank instead of me. I enclose your receipts. Please forward notes at once and Oblige.''

In pursuance to the above communication, Robinson forwarded the collateral notes to Taber at Twin Falls, who indorsed them and then sent them to the Exchange Bank at Lanark, and by the bank they were forwarded to Robinson at Kansas City.

It appears that in the construction of nine houses upon the land purchased by Taber, the material was bought from the Belt Line Lumber Company, that within two months after Robinson received the collateral notes from the Exchange Bank, the Belt Line Lumber Company filed notices of materialman's liens, and, in order to avoid foreclosure, Robinson turned over the collateral notes sent to him by the appellant, to the Belt Line Lumber Company in adjustment of its claim, in order to protect the land and houses formerly owned by Robinson and Taber, and which formed the basis of their contract of settlement heretofore referred to. The application of the collateral notes in the adjustment of the Belt Line Lumber Company's claim was not known positively by either the appellant or respondent until November 21, 1911, at which time Robinson wrote a letter to Taber, addressed to Twin Falls, Idaho, in which he admitted in substance, that he had used the collateral notes as above stated. For some time after the collateral notes were diverted by Robinson, he continued to make payments to the bank according to the provision of the collateral notes, first regularly and latterly at irregular periods, and finally ceased to make any payments. The appellant and respondent, as shown by numerous exhibits, persistently urged Robinson to make collections of the collateral notes.

In December, 1911, Taber went to Lanark for a conference with Wolf, which resulted in Wolf making a visit to Kansas City to see Robinson. There is evidence in the record that Taber agreed to go with Wolf. He did not do so. Wolf met

Robinson in Kansas City and made a conditional settlement with him, and then returned to Lanark where he immediately afterwards met Taber. A day or so following, the notes agreed in the settlement to be given by Robinson and his brother, W. S. Robinson, were received by mail at Lanark. The notes were made payable to Taber, who thereafter indorsed the notes and left them with the appellant as collateral security. In the settlement between Taber and the bank, it appears that there was $504.49 still due on the larger of the two notes given to the bank by Taber on September 7, 1908, which is one of the notes in this action. Thereafter Taber returned to Twin Falls.

Upon the trial it was agreed that there was an error in the amount for which Robinson gave his notes at the time of the settlement made in Kansas City of $400. The trial was had before the court with a jury and a verdict was rendered in favor of the respondent in the sum of $3,924.07. This appeal is from the judgment.

Numerous errors are assigned by appellant. The first is that the court erred in holding that the respondent was entitled to open and close the argument to the jury. It rests in the sound discretion of the trial court to direct the order of addressing the jury, and unless there is a clear abuse of discretion this court will not disturb the verdict. (Sec. 4383, Rev. Codes; *Goodpaster v. Voris*, 8 Iowa, 334, 74 Am. Dec. 313; *Shaffer v. Des Moines Coal etc. Co.*, 122 Iowa, 233, 98 N. W. 111; *Brunswick & W. R. Co. v. Wiggins*, 113 Ga. 842, 39 S. E. 551, 61 L. R. A. 513; *Day v. Woodworth*, 13 How. (U. S.) 363, 14 L. ed. 181; *Hall v. Weare*, 92 U. S. 728, 23 L. ed. 500; *Lancaster v. Collins*, 115 U. S. 222, 6 Sup. Ct. 33, 29 L. ed. 373; *Florence Oil & Ref. Co. v. Farrar*, 109 Fed. 254, 48 C. C. A. 345; 38 Cyc. 1300.)

The second assignment is that the court erred in giving the following instruction to the jury:

"You are instructed that if you believe from the evidence in this case, when the notes sued on were originally made or had indorsed thereon by agreement of the parties at any time after making, an agreement or indorsement to the effect that the same were not to be collected from the defendant, and that thereafter said notes or either of them were altered without the knowledge, authority or consent of the defendant, by cutting from said notes such indorsement, then such an alteration would be material, and the plaintiff cannot recover upon said notes, and your verdict should be for the defendant.''

The notes sued upon in this action are set out in full in the complaint. The answer of the respondent admitted the execution and delivery of the notes to the appellant. The respondent did not affirmatively allege in his answer or counterclaim that the notes had been altered in any respect. The alteration of the notes was not an issue in the case. The general rule is that a note which has been altered is not void unless the alteration is material and was made subsequent to its delivery and without the consent of the parties liable. Where a note appears to have been altered in a material respect, the *onus* is on the party seeking to enforce the payment to show that it is not void, but where the respondent in his answer and counterclaim in express terms admits the execution and delivery of the notes which are set out in full in the complaint, and when introduced in evidence were in the same condition as they appeared in the complaint, the respondent should not be permitted to introduce evidence tending to establish any alteration, nor should the court instruct the jury upon the law governing the alteration of written instruments. It will be presumed that the alteration was made before the execution of the instrument. The above instruction as given by the court, was clearly prejudicial error. (14 Ency. Pl. & Pr. 656; *Kleeb v. Bard,* 12 Wash. 140, 40 Pac. 733; 1 Standard Ency. Proc. 822; 2 Am. & Eng. Ency. Law, 2d ed., 185.)

The appellant calls attention to the court's refusal to give instruction No. 5 requested by the appellant, which is as follows:

''In the handling of securities placed with it, the plaintiff was required to exercise only ordinary diligence, and before you will be justified in finding for the defendant on his affirmative defense, or on his counterclaim, it must be established by the evidence that the plaintiff was grossly negligent in handling such securities, and that if it had used reasonable diligence it could have collected the amounts due on said collaterals, and unless you find that through the gross negligence of the plaintiff the defendant was in fact damaged, then the defendant has failed to establish his affirmative defense and counterclaim.''

This instruction seems to be within the rule announced by this court in the case of *Murphy v. Bartsch,* 2 Ida. 636, 23 Pac. 82. It is impossible to prescribe any definite rule applicable to every case of property pledged as collateral security; each case must be determined by the attendant facts and circumstances, rather than by any iron-clad rule, but in view of the peculiar circumstances surrounding this case, it would have been eminently proper for the court to have given this instruction.

The next error that we will consider relates to the refusal of the court to admit certain evidence offered by the appellant touching the disposition of the collateral security sent to Robinson by the bank and by Robinson diverted. There is evidence in the record which shows that these collateral notes had been used by Robinson for the express purpose of protecting the business interests of the respondent and Robinson. If this was true and the respondent had in truth and in fact received the benefits of the collateral security either in whole or in part by the payment of certain debts that were liens on the property formerly owned by respondent and Robinson, and out of which respondent expected to realize upon the collateral notes, appellant should have been permitted to introduce any testimony that might establish the application of the proceeds of the collateral notes to the benefit of the respondent. This testimony would have been admissible, if for no other reason than for the purpose of reducing damages.

We are of the opinion that the court erred in admitting respondent's exhibit No. 15, a letter of August 1, 1912, written by Taber to Wolf. This letter was self-serving and immaterial. It had reference to a business transaction that had been for some considerable time closed and fully settled.

We do not think it necessary to discuss each of the remaining 17 assignments of error separately. They are based upon the refusal of the court to grant appellant's motion to strike out all of the testimony offered by respondent in support of the affirmative allegations of his answer, and the refusal of the court to grant appellant's motion for a nonsuit at the conclusion of the introduction of testimony by respondent in support of his counterclaim. We do not think the court erred in refusing to strike out the testimony offered by respondent in support of the affirmative allegations in his answer.

The serious question that confronts us in this case is: Was there sufficient evidence to justify the court in submitting this case to the jury after all of the testimony was received in support of the affirmative allegations of the answer and counterclaim of respondent? It appears that the respondent prior to his execution of the two notes given to the Exchange Bank in the year 1908, had entered into a contract in the year 1907 with Robinson, of Jackson County, Missouri, whereby they purchased some land in Kansas City for $6,500. Taber furnished the money for said purchase as his part of the enterprise. Robinson was to furnish the material and labor in the erection and construction of nine houses upon the lots. Upon completion and sale of the houses and lots, Taber was to receive $9,200 as his share or interest in the transaction. The evidence shows that they proceeded with the contract. Robinson procured the material for the erection of the houses from the Belt Line Lumber Company, to which company he became indebted, and to which company the collaterals were subsequently turned over in order to avoid foreclosure proceedings against the property. This agreement provided that Robinson should collect all deferred payments for the houses free of charge and remit the money to Taber. When Taber went to the bank, this was the arrangement that existed between him and Robinson, and when he made the loan from the bank, he explained to the assistant cashier Wolf, that he had these notes and the arrangement between Robinson and himself for the collection of the payments as they became due, free of charge. It was Taber who made the bank acquainted with

Robinson, who vouched for his honesty and integrity; who suggested that an investigation of Robinson's character and standing in the community where he lived should be made, that he would be a proper person with whom to place these collateral notes for collection. Taber also referred Wolf to one Hess, a witness in this case, an old acquaintance of Wolf's, who, Taber said, would substantiate what he had said with reference to Robinson as an additional reason why the collateral notes should be sent to Robinson for collection.

Taber signed a letter, exhibit "J," addressed to Robinson, requesting him to forward all the notes that he had belonging to him (Taber) to Twin Falls for indorsement, and that he (Taber) would forward the same to the Exchange Bank at Lanark after indorsing them, to be by said bank returned to Robinson for collection in the same manner as he had theretofore done for Taber. Upon receipt of the notes from Robinson, Taber wrote Wolf of date September 21, 1908; that he had just received the notes from Robinson; that he had indorsed the same and sent them for security; that he supposed Robinson had written him (Wolf) and explained all, and further stated: "And he will remit to you from now on the collections on same."

The bank made statements from time to time to Taber, accounted for all payments made through Robinson, and in numerous letters urged Taber to insist that Robinson make collection upon the collateral notes and forward the same to the bank for credit. Taber was notified by the bank repeatedly that Robinson was behind with the collections. The bank informed Taber that they had requested Hess to call upon Robinson and insist upon the collections of the collateral notes being made. Taber wrote to Wolf in response to these communications and particularly of date December 5, 1910, as follows:

"Mr. Guy Wolf, Lanark, Ill.

"Dear Sir:—Yours rec'd some time ago in regard to Mr. Robinson's delinquence on payments. I have written him and have received no answer from him. I wish you would take this in hand and see what you can do with him. I will write him again this evening.

"Yours respectfully,

"GEO. C. TABER."

There are numerous communications from Taber to the bank in which he states that he has written Robinson insisting upon the collection of the collateral notes and requests the bank to make arrangements with Hess to assist in the collection of these collateral notes. In each and all of these communications, fairly construed, Taber never relinquished ownership or control, or his right to collect the collateral notes. It is quite clear that both Taber and the bank were industrious in their endeavor to bring about the collection of these collateral notes.

On November 21, 1911, Robinson addresses a letter to Taber at Twin Falls, in which he informs Taber that the collateral notes have been diverted. After receiving this information, on December 25, 1911, Taber left Twin Falls for Lanark to consult Wolf. After reaching Lanark a settlement was finally brought about between Robinson and Taber and the notes received from Robinson were put up as collateral security with the bank to secure the payment of the obligations sued upon in this action.

The bank, by the verdict of the jury, has been held responsible for the loss of these collateral notes, upon the ground and for the reason, as appears from the record, that the bank was negligent in handling these collateral notes and their failure to collect the same. We do not think the record supports this conclusion. Within two or three months after the collateral notes were received by Robinson, he diverted them. No effort upon the part of the bank or Taber would have resulted in the recovery of these collateral notes. There could, therefore, be no negligence in the collection of these collateral notes. Robinson had parted with them and was not in a position to collect the payments as they became due. Therefore, if the bank was negligent at all, its negligence consisted in forwarding the notes to Robinson for collection. This, the bank never would have done if it had not been for the conduct of Taber, which consisted in calling the bank's attention to Robinson, recommending him as a man capable and honest, the proper person to be entrusted with the collection of these notes, who would perform the services free of charge and calling the bank's attention to Hess, an old acquaintance, to verify what he (Taber) had said with reference to Robinson.

"Where a party by conduct has intimated that he consents to an act which has been done or will offer no opposition thereto, though it could not have been lawfully done without his consent, and he thereby induces others to do that from which they otherwise might have abstained, he cannot question the legality of the action to the prejudice of those who have acted on the fair inference to be drawn from his conduct." (*Divide Canal & Reservoir Co. v. Tenney* (Colo.), 139 Pac. 1110; *Truesdail v. Ward,* 24 Mich. 117.)

The more consistent position to take, is that Robinson was the person jointly agreed upon by Wolf and Taber to collect these collateral notes; that he became the joint agent of both of the parties; that being true, neither could charge the other with negligence. This fact is further emphasized when we consider the letters written by Taber with reference to this transaction and that Taber ratified the settlement made by Robinson and Wolf; indorsed the notes given by Robinson and thus adjusted his obligations with the bank. (*Murdock v. Clarke,* 90 Cal. 427, 27 Pac. 275; *Damon v. Waldteufel,* 99 Cal. 234, 33 Pac. 903.)

We think that it was the duty of the court, after all of the testimony had been submitted, to have taken the case from the jury and directed that judgment be entered for the appellant. Where a party is entitled to have a verdict directed in his favor at the close of the evidence, and the case is reversed on his appeal, a new trial will not be granted. The case should be remanded with instructions for judgment to be entered in his favor. (Sec. 3818, Rev. Codes; *Bernhard v. Reeves,* 6 Wash. 424, 33 Pac. 873; *Larson v. American Bridge Co.,* 40 Wash. 224, 111 Am. St. 904, 82 Pac. 294.)

"Where a party shows no right to recover under any possible state of proof, the court is not bound to submit the case to a jury." (*Gorman v. Commissioners of Boise County,* 1 Ida. 655.)

For the foregoing reasons the judgment appealed from must be reversed, and the cause is hereby remanded, with instructions to the trial court to enter judgment for the appellant as prayed for in its complaint, in accordance with the views expressed in this opinion. Costs are awarded to appellant.

Sullivan, C. J., and Morgan, J., concur.

(February 3, 1915.)

STATE, Respondent, v. CHARLES DRISKILL, Appellant.

[145 Pac. 1095.]

STATUTORY RAPE — CONVICTION OF — EVIDENCE—SUFFICIENCY OF— IN-STRUCTIONS—PROSECUTRIX—IMPEACHMENT OF — PROSECUTING AT-TORNEY—REMARKS TO JURY.

1. *Held*, that the evidence is sufficient to support the verdict, and that the court did not err in refusing to give certain instructions.

APPEAL from the District Court of the Second Judicial District for Nez Perce County. Hon. Edgar C. Steele, Judge.

Prosecution for statutory rape. Conviction and sentence of defendant. Judgment *affirmed.*

McNamee & Harn, for Appellant.

Admission of testimony as to acts of misconduct and lewdness by the defendant with other girls was clearly reversible error. (*People v. Stewart,* 85 Cal. 174, 24 Pac. 722; *People v. Bowen,* 49 Cal. 654; *People v. Lenon,* 79 Cal. 628, 21 Pac. 967; *People v. McNutt,* 64 Cal. 116, 28 Pac. 64; *People v. Barnes,* 48 Cal. 551; *People v. Elliott,* 119 Cal. 593, 51 Pac.

955; *People v. Lane*, 100 Cal. 379, 34 Pac. 856; *Owens v. State*, 39 Tex. Cr. 391, 46 S. W. 240.)

"Conviction may be had upon the unsupported testimony of the prosecutrix, if believed by the jury, but defendant should not be convicted without corroboration where the testimony of the prosecutrix bears on its face indications of unreliability or improbability, and particularly when it is contradicted by other evidence." (33 Cyc. 1497; *State v. Trego*, 25 Ida. 625, 138 Pac. 1124; *People v. Ardage*, 51 Cal. 371; *People v. Benson*, 6 Cal. 221, 65 Am. Dec. 506; *People v. Hamilton*, 46 Cal. 540; *State v. Goodale*, 210 Mo. 275, 109 S. W. 9; *State v. Tevis*, 234 Mo. 276, 136 S. W. 339.)

J. H. Peterson, Attorney General, J. J. Guheen, E. G. Davis and T. C. Coffin, Assistants, and Miles S. Johnson, for Respondent.

Where two witnesses testify to the same state of facts, and one of them is successfully impeached, nevertheless the verdict will not be disturbed where no attempt has been made to impeach the other. (*Smith v. State*, 13 Ga. App. 32, 78 S. E. 685; *Dozier v. State*, 62 Tex. Cr. App. 258, 137 S. W. 679.)

SULLIVAN, C. J.—The defendant was indicted and convicted of the crime of statutory rape and sentenced to an indeterminate term of imprisonment of from five to ten years in the state penitentiary. A motion for a new trial was denied and this appeal is from the judgment and order denying a new trial.

Fifteen errors are assigned which go to the admission of certain evidence, the refusal of the court to give certain requested instructions, and in permitting the prosecuting attorney to make certain statements during his argument to the jury, the insufficiency of the evidence, and the impeachment of the prosecutrix.

After an examination of the record, we are fully satisfied that the evidence is sufficient to support the verdict and that the court did not err in the admission of evidence. There was a sufficient corroboration of the testimony of the prosecutrix.

The action of the court in permitting a witness on behalf of the state to testify that she had sexual intercourse with the defendant within a very few minutes after he had had intercourse with the prosecutrix is assigned as error. It appears that said witness and the prosecutrix went to a barn with the defendant and another young man and there the acts referred to were committed, and that after the defendant had had intercourse with the prosecutrix it was suggested that the young men change girls, and thereupon the change was made and the defendant had intercourse with the other girl, and the record shows that such acts were not more than fifteen minutes apart. Being so close together and really a part of the *res gestae*, the court did not err in admitting the evidence referred to.

After an examination of the instructions requested by the defendant and refused by the court, we are satisfied that the court did not err in refusing to give said instructions.

As to the impeachment of the prosecutrix and to what extent the jury would give credence to her testimony, that was for the jury to determine, and we do not think if the jury believed the prosecutrix had made contradictory statements, they must of necessity reject all of her evidence as untrue. The jury evidently concluded from all of the evidence that the defendant was guilty of the crime charged beyond a reasonable doubt, and we think all of the evidence taken together would justify that conclusion.

As to the remarks made by the prosecuting attorney in his argument to the jury, we do not think there was sufficient error in those remarks to warrant a reversal of the judgment.

Finding no reversible error in the record, the judgment must be affirmed, and it is so ordered.

Budge and Morgan, JJ., concur.

(February 6, 1915.)

STATE, Respondent, v. DANIEL H. HOPKINS, Appellant.

[145 Pac. 1095.]

ASSAULT WITH INTENT TO COMMIT RAPE—SUFFICIENCY OF EVIDENCE—
ALIBI—ADMISSIBILITY OF EVIDENCE—WITHDRAWAL OF OBJECTION TO
QUESTION.

1. The evidence in this case examined and found to be sufficient to justify the conviction of the defendant of the crime
charged.

2. Where the evidence adduced by the state tends to show that a
crime was committed during a two weeks' vacation in school at the
Christmas holiday season and does not fix the date more definitely
than that, and where the defendant relies upon an *alibi* and produces evidence tending to show his whereabouts from Dec. 24th to
Jan. 1st, inclusive, and that he was not at the place where the evidence produced by the state tends to show the crime was committed,
but produces no evidence tending to show his whereabouts during
the remainder of the two weeks in question, the jury is justified in
reaching the conclusion that the *alibi* relied on was not established.

3. Where there is a substantial conflict in the evidence and the
evidence taken as a whole is sufficient to sustain the verdict, the
verdict will not be disturbed.

4. Where a party to an action does not object to a question
propounded to a witness, or having objected, expressly gives consent that the question may be answered, error cannot be predicated
upon the action of the court in admitting the testimony nor upon
the refusal of the court to strike out the answer if it is responsive
to the question.

APPEAL from the District Court of the Ninth Judicial
District for the County of Fremont.   Hon. James G. Gwinn,
Judge.

The defendant was found guilty of an attempt to commit
rape.   Judgment *affirmed*.

John A. Bagley, for Appellant, cites no authorities.

J. H. Peterson, Attorney General, E. G. Davis and V. P.
Coffin, Assistants, for the State.

There being a substantial conflict in the evidence, and the
jury having passed upon it, under the well-settled rule of

this court, the verdict of the jury will not be disturbed. (*State v. Silva,* 21 Ida. 247, 120 Pac. 835; *Panhandle Lbr. Co. v. Rancour,* 24 Ida. 603, 135 Pac. 558.)

A conviction of the crime of assault with intent to commit rape will be sustained, even though the prosecutrix be uncorroborated, unless her testimony be impeached as to her previous good character and reputation for truthfulness. This is especially so where the circumstances surrounding the commission of the offense are clearly corroborative of the statements of the prosecutrix. (*State v. Anderson,* 6 Ida. 706, 59 Pac. 180; *People v. Wessel,* 98 Cal. 352, 33 Pac. 216.)

MORGAN, J.—In this case the appellant was convicted of the crime of assault with intent to commit rape. The trial resulted in a verdict of guilty, upon which a judgment of conviction was made and entered, from which judgment and from an order of the court denying his motion for a new trial this appeal was taken.

In his brief upon appeal and in his oral argument counsel for the appellant relies upon four assignments of error, in substance as follows:

First: That the evidence is insufficient to support the verdict and judgment;

Second: That the verdict was rendered by the jury on account of bias and prejudice against this class of cases and the additional reason that the court permitted, over the objection of the appellant, the respondent to show that the appellant had been found guilty of the offense charged in this case by a tribunal of the church of which he was a member;

Third: That the appellant proved a full and complete *alibi;*

Fourth: That there is no evidence to corroborate the prosecutrix and she is contradicted by the facts and circumstances proved by the appellant.

The first, third and fourth assignments of error and the first portion of the second may be considered together as denying the sufficiency of the evidence. The latter portion of the second assignment will be considered separately as relating to the admissibility of evidence.

We will first consider the evidence which affects the *alibi* relied upon by the appellant. The testimony of the prosecutrix shows that she attended school during the school year of 1911 and 1912; that there was a vacation, or holiday period, at Christmas time of two weeks; that the crime of which the appellant was convicted was committed during this vacation period, at a haystack in appellant's field some distance from the house. The prosecutrix further testified that she was unable to give the exact date of the assault upon her nor to fix the time any closer than that it occurred at about noon on a day during this two weeks' vacation in school.

The defendant testified as to his whereabouts from the 24th of December, 1911, to and including January 1, 1912, and he produced the testimony of a number of witnesses to corroborate his testimony as to his whereabouts, and that he was not at the place where the prosecutrix testified the crime was committed upon and between said dates. Since the testimony of the prosecutrix does not fix the date of the commission of the crime upon a day between December 24, 1911, and January 1, 1912, inclusive, but does fix it as having occurred on a day during the Christmas holidays of two weeks' duration, it readily appears that the jury was justified in reaching the conclusion that the *alibi* relied upon by the appellant was not established.

Upon many material points in their testimony the prosecutrix and the appellant contradict each other. The prosecutrix testified that on the occasion of the assault the appellant and herself had gone in a sled to a haystack for a load of hay. The appellant testified, and in this he is corroborated by other witnesses, that he did not begin to haul hay from the stack in question until late in January, 1912, and that during the holiday season of 1911 and 1912, no road was broken through the snow to the haystack. In this he is, however, contradicted by testimony other than that of the prosecutrix. "Where there is a substantial conflict in the evidence and the evidence taken as a whole is sufficient to sustain the verdict, the verdict will not be disturbed." (*State v. Downing*, 23 Ida. 540, 130 Pac. 461.)

It is true there are some discrepancies between the testimony given by the prosecutrix at the trial and that given by her at the preliminary examination, but these may be accounted for, to a considerable extent at least, upon the theory that she misunderstood certain questions propounded to her at the preliminary examination.

This court in the recent case of *State v. Driskill, ante,* p. 738, 145 Pac. 1095, commenting upon the effect of contradictory statements made by a prosecuting witness in a case of this kind, said: "As to the impeachment of the prosecutrix and to what extent the jury would give credence to her testimony, that was for the jury to determine, and we do not think if the jury believed the prosecutrix had made contradictory statements, they must of necessity reject all of her evidence as untrue."

The evidence in this case, considered in its entirety, is amply sufficient to justify the jury in reaching the conclusion expressed in its verdict.

Had the trial court, as charged in the second assignment of error, over the objection of the defendant, permitted the state to show that the appellant had been tried and found guilty by a tribunal of his church, such action upon the part of the court would have been reversible error. A careful examination, however, discloses that the said second assignment of error is not borne out by the record.

Mention of this church trial is first found in the testimony of the witness Alfred Hansen and occurs in the cross-examination of the said witness by the attorney for the appellant. The witness was asked if a complaint had been filed against the defendant with the church authorities and, having answered in the affirmative, he was asked whether he made a certain statement on the occasion of the church trial as to his motives in commencing the church proceedings and this case. Upon redirect examination counsel for the state asked the witness as to the result of the church trial, whereupon counsel for the appellant said, "Object to that, if the court please— Oh, well go ahead."

Thereafter, upon recross-examination of the witness Hansen, counsel for appellant went into the question of the proceedings in the church hearing and the result thereof at considerable length.

Upon direct examination of the appellant this church trial was referred to, and upon his cross-examination it was inquired into by counsel for the respondent without objection upon the part of the appellant or his counsel, and upon his redirect examination it was further inquired into.

Where a party to an action does not object to a question propounded to a witness, or having objected, expressly gives consent that the question may be answered, error cannot be predicated upon the action of the court in admitting the testimony nor upon the refusal of the court to strike out the answer, if it is responsive to the question, and the answer of the witness, Hansen, was responsive.

The judgment appealed from is affirmed.

Sullivan, C. J., and Budge, J., concur.

———

(February 6, 1915.)

WILLIAM F. CALLAHAN, Appellant, v. STERLING G. PRICE, Respondent.

[146 Pac. 732.]

PATENT FROM UNITED STATES—LAND BORDERING NAVIGABLE STREAMS—TITLE EXTENDING TO NATURAL HIGH-WATER LINE ONLY—OWNERSHIP IN AND TO BED OF LAKES AND NAVIGABLE RIVERS—ISLANDS NOT PASSING TO STATE—USE OF NAVIGABLE STREAMS FOR BENEFIT OF PUBLIC AS HIGHWAYS—JUDGMENT OF NONSUIT, AFFIRMED.

1. A patent from the United States for land bordering on a navigable lake or stream extends no farther than the natural high-water line.

2. When lands border on a stream, the banks of which are both well-defined and where the stream separates at the head of an island into distinct channels constituting a well-defined stream on either side, the boundary line of the land granted extends only to the natural high-water mark.

3. Where there is no evidence offered at the trial, as in this case, which establishes or tends to establish the fact that the island in controversy was at any time attached to or a part of lots bounded by a stream, it was not error for the court to grant a nonsuit.

4. The United States, since the admission of Idaho to statehood, has the power to dispose of subdivisions or fractional subdivisions of public lands consisting of islands that existed in the territory of Idaho prior to its admission as a state.

5. Islands in existence when Idaho was admitted to the Union did not pass to the state or come within the disposing influences of its laws, but remained the property of the United States subject to disposal by it.

6. It is the settled law of this state that no title to islands, lakes or the beds of streams passes to the patentees of the United States by the sale of border lots; that the state holds the title to the beds of navigable lakes and streams below the natural high-water mark, for the use and benefit of the whole people, subject to the rights vested by the constitution in the United States.

7. The Salmon river is a navigable stream, and is therefore a public highway belonging to the state.

8. Since statehood the state holds the title to the beds of all navigable lakes and streams, subject to the rights of the general government to regulate commerce, and the right by the public to the use of the same as public highways over which every citizen has a natural right to carry commerce, whether by ships, boats, the floating of logs or lumber, having due consideration and reasonable care for the rights of individuals as well as the public in the common use of such public highways.

9. The cases of *Johnson v. Hurst*, 10 Ida. 308, 77 Pac. 785, *Lattig v. Scott*, 17 Ida. 506, 107 Pac. 47, *Johnson v. Johnson*, 14 Ida. 561, 95 Pac. 499, 24 L. R. A., N. S., 1240, and *Ulbright v. Bas-lington*, 20 Ida. 539, 119 Pac. 292, 294, are hereby overruled in so far as they conflict with this opinion.

APPEAL from the District Court of the Sixth Judicial District for the County of Lemhi. Hon. J. M. Stevens, Judge.

Action to quiet title. Judgment of nonsuit for defendant. *Affirmed.*

A. C. Cherry, for Appellant.

The defendant on motion for nonsuit must admit all the facts which the evidence tends to prove; and in determining the propriety of a nonsuit at the close of plaintiff's case, the evidence most favorable to the plaintiff must be accepted as true; for the motion of nonsuit admits the truth of plaintiff's evidence and every inference of fact that can be legitimately drawn therefrom. (*McDaniel v. Moore*, 19 Ida. 43, 112 Pac. 317; *Mineau v. Imperial etc. Co.*, 19 Ida. 458, 114 Pac. 23; *Hoff v. Los Angeles Pac. Co.*, 158 Cal. 596, 112 Pac. 53; *Lawyer v. Los Angeles Pac. Co.*, 161 Cal. 53, 118 Pac. 237.)

The case at bar is not within the purview of the case of *Lattig v. Scott*, but is governed rather by the cases of *Grand Rapids etc. R. R. Co. v. Butler*, 159 U. S. 87, 15 Sup. Ct. 991, 40 L. ed. 85, and *United States v. Chandler-Dunbar Water Power Co.*, 209 U. S. 447, 28 Sup. Ct. 579, 52 L. ed. 881.

F. J. Cowen, for Respondent.

There are no differences which would take this case out of the rule laid down in the *Scott v. Lattig* case and the rule announced in the later case of *Moss & Bro. v. Ramey*, 25 Ida. 1, 136 Pac. 608.

The Salmon river is a navigable stream under the decisions of this state. (*Idaho Northern R. R. Co. v. Post Falls Lbr. Co.*, 20 Ida. 695, 119 Pac. 1098, 38 L. R. A., N. S., 114.)

For the plaintiff to recover in this case it would be necessary for him to show that at the time of the patent to McCain this island was not in fact an island but constituted a part of the land conveyed to McCain by that patent. This the plaintiff has not attempted to do, for the earliest date that a witness of the plaintiff remembers having seen the island in question was about the year 1887 or 1888, and that is stated only from recollection. (29 Cyc. 349, 353; *Fowler v. Wood*, 73 Kan. 511, 117 Am. St. 534, 85 Pac. 763, 6 L. R. A., N. S., 162; 40 Cyc. 625.)

BUDGE, J.—This action was brought in the district court of the sixth judicial district, for Lemhi county, to quiet title to the following described lands, situate, and being in Lemhi county, to wit: All the upper portion of that certain island lying and being in the Salmon river just opposite lot 14, of section 6, and lot 1 of section 7, township 21 N., range 22 E., Boise meridian.

The appellant claims title to the upper portion of said island by virtue of a patent from the United States to Sylvester McCain and to the lower portion of the island by virtue of a deed from Thomas Elder, probate judge of the county of Lemhi to Sylvester McCain; said Elder being the successor in office to one Ellwood T. Beatty, to whom a patent was issued by the United States conveying the land in question to be held in trust for the several use and benefit of the occupants of the townsite of Salmon City; said patents conveying to the patentees the lands bordering along the Salmon river. The particular deed in controversy in this action is appellant's exhibit "C," a deed executed by Thomas Elder, as probate judge, to Sylvester McCain, appellant's predecessor, conveying the land bordering along the bank of the Salmon river described as follows, to wit:

"Commencing at the Witness stake on the right bank of Salmon River and on the section line between Sections 6 & 7, in Township No. 21, North of Range No. 22, East of Boise Meridian, and running thence along said Section line N. 89 degrees 51 minutes East Seventy nine (79) rods and two (2) links, thence North 24 degrees East, Sixteen (16) rods and fourteen (14) links, thence N. 54 degrees 30 minutes West fifty four (54) rods, and thence S. 43 degrees West sixty two (62) rods to the place of beginning. Area (13) Acres and one hundred and twenty seven (127) Rods, in the same more or less."

This cause was tried to the court with a jury upon the complaint of the appellant and the answer and cross-complaint of the respondent. The complaint set out a description of the island in question and a statement of the facts upon which the appellant relied to establish his title to said island and lots 14 and 1. Appellant further alleged that the respondent, Price, claimed and asserted an estate in and to said island and had entered into possession of the island without right, title or license and wrongfully withholds the possession of the same, to appellant's damage in the sum of

$200; that since entering upon said island, respondent has cut a large number of valuable trees into cordwood and hauled the same away, and that by reason thereof large portions of said island are liable to be washed away, to the irreparable loss and injury of the appellant.

Upon filing the verified complaint together with affidavit of C. G. Mathewson, an injunction was issued in this cause and served upon the respondent, restraining him from further committing the acts complained of in the appellant's complaint. Respondent, in his answer, denies that the appellant or his grantors or predecessors in interest, have been or were the owners for a long time hitherto, or at all, of the island as described in the appellant's complaint, or any portion thereof, and alleges that he entered into possession of said island rightfully and is lawfully seised and possessed of the same. The respondent admits that upon entering into possession of the island in controversy he cut timber and trees and hauled the same away, but denies that the appellant has been damaged in the sum of $200 or in any other sum.

In respondent's cross-complaint he alleges that he is the owner, in the possession and entitled to the possession, subject only to the paramount title of the United States, of the following described real estate, situate in the county of Lemhi, to wit: All that certain island consisting of about 100 acres of land lying and being in the Salmon river, just west and opposite appellant's lot 14, in section 6, and lot 1 in section 7, township 21 north, range 22 east, Boise meridian.

After the appellant had introduced his testimony, the respondent moved for a nonsuit, "On the grounds of insufficiency of evidence," which motion was granted and judgment of nonsuit entered.

There are two assignments of error:

First, that the court erred in granting the motion for nonsuit.

Second, that the court erred in striking out the evidence of Chat Mathewson and in sustaining respondent's objection to certain evidence.

The lands lying on the east side of the Salmon river opposite the island involved in this litigation were surveyed in 1881, while the lands lying on the west side of the river opposite the island were surveyed in 1890 or 1891. From the record it would seem that the surveyor who made the survey of the east bank of the river mentioned no islands, while the surveyor who surveyed the lands on the west side of the river noticed two islands and indicated the same upon the map filed with his field-notes.

The evidence offered on the part of the appellant establishes the fact that he is the owner of a considerable tract of land bordering along the eastern bank of the Salmon river and abutting the same, including lots 1 and 14, and is in the possession of all of the lands covered by his patents and deeds except possibly a small portion that may have been eroded away from the main land by the action of the river. The respondent in this case has located upon the island west and across the east branch of the Salmon river from said lots 1 and 14.

The real question involved in this litigation is the west boundary line of appellant's land. If this west boundary line extends to the thread of the stream of the west channel of the Salmon river, appellant would then be entitled to the possession of all of the upper portion of the island in controversy. This island is not contained either in acreage or description, in the patents or mesne conveyances to appellant's predecessors in interest, and if it should be determined that the appellant is entitled to the island, it must be upon the theory that his west boundary line extends across the east channel of the Salmon river. In *Packer v. Bird,* 71 Cal. 134, 11 Pac. 873, it was held that a patent from the United States for land bounded on a river which is actually navigable, extends no farther than the edge of the stream, and does not include an island separated from the upland by a slough forming part of such river, although the slough is not ordinarily navigable, or not navigable at all. In *Steinbuchel v. Lane,* 59 Kan. 7, 51 Pac. 886, it is held that a patent for lands bordering on a stream, both banks of which were

meandered by the government, without any reference to a large
island therein composed of primitive soil, includes no part
of the island opposite such land as an appurtenance thereof,
whether the stream be navigable or not, where it separates
at the head of the island into two distinct channels, constituting a well-defined stream on either side, and it is not necessary to include any part of the island to make up the quantity of land included in the patent; but at most, the boundary
of the land granted extends only to the middle of the thread
of the channel between it and the island. In *Shoemaker v.
Hatch*, 13 Nev. 261, it was held that an unsurveyed island of
considerable size in a river is no part of the land surveyed
on the side opposite one channel, where the two branches of
the river are both well-defined channels and there is no dis-
parity in size, although in low water the one channel carries
all the running water, and at other times more than the other
channel, because it is shorter and has more fall.

We think that the evidence establishes the existence of this
island for a considerable length of time prior to the survey
being made of the lands on the east or west banks of the
river, and before Idaho's admission to the Union. There was
no evidence offered by the appellant in the trial court, that
even tended to establish the fact that the island in controversy was at any time attached to or a part of lots 1 and 14.
On the contrary, the proof offered by appellant, clearly established the fact that the east channel of the Salmon river was
where it now is and where it had been for many years prior
to the time appellant became the owner and went into possession of lots 1 and 14; that the banks of the east channel
of the river are clearly defined; that this island is "Fast
Land," not subject to overflow; that a portion of the same
had been fenced and used, by the predecessor of appellant,
and others, for the pasturage of cattle and that for a period
of years, cordwood was cut on and sold from said island.
While it might be true that for a time the east channel of
the Salmon river between the lands of the appellant and the
island was not the main channel of the river, it was proven
by appellant that by reason of the peculiar characteristics of

the stream, the main body of water during different years ran through the east channel of the river, along which the lands of the appellant abut, eroding and cutting away a small portion of lots 1 and 14. This erosion of appellant's lands by the changing of the main body of the stream from the west to the east channel was, as appears from the record, almost imperceptible.

From all of the evidence offered by appellant, it would seem to be clearly established that an open waterway between the island and the lands of the appellant was found to exist by the first occupant of these lands, and that strenuous efforts were made to divert the main flow of the stream through the west channel of the river by the construction at the upper end of the island and at the intake of the east channel of the river of riprap earth and rock for the express purpose of preventing the water from flowing through the east channel, which undertakings were unsuccessful and all obstructions were subsequently washed out, and the waters, as formerly, flowed down through the east channel.

The evidence further shows that the island opposite lots 1 and 14 contains an area of between forty and fifty acres; that the deed from Elder to McCain and from McCain to appellant contained only 13 acres and 127 rods more or less; that the starting point in the deed is positively located, to wit: Commencing at the witness stake on the right bank of the Salmon river, and on section lines between sections 6 and 7, in township No. 21 north, range No. 22 east, Boise meridian, etc. It therefore, clearly appears that when the appellant purchased this land abutting upon the east side of the river, that there was no intention upon the part of his predecessors to convey to him any portion of the island.

Under the decisions of the supreme court of the United States, the appellant by reason of becoming the purchaser of the lands abutting upon the river would not be entitled, by paying therefor, to additional land on the island. (*Scott v. Lattig*, 227 U. S. 229, 33 Sup. Ct. 242, 57 L. ed. 490, 44 L. R. A., N. S., 107; *Horne v. Smith*, 159 U. S. 40, 15 Sup.

Ct. 988, 40 L. ed. 68; *Niles v. Cedar Point Club*, 175 U. S. 300, 20 Sup. Ct. 124, 44 L. ed. 174.)

If he were entitled to the island or any portion of it, it would be upon the theory that a riparian owner upon a navigable stream takes to the thread of the main stream. That was the doctrine announced by a majority of this court in the cases of *Johnson v. Johnson*, 14 Ida. 561, 95 Pac. 499, 24 L. R. A., N. S., 1240, *A. B. Moss & Bro. v. Ramey*, 14 Ida. 598, 95 Pac. 513, and *Lattig v. Scott*, 17 Ida. 506, 107 Pac. 47. This latter case was appealed to the supreme court of the United States, which reversed the former decisions of this court, holding, among other things, that the error in omitting an island in a navigable stream from the field-notes and plat of the government did not divest the United States of title or interpose any obstacles to a subsequent survey of the island; that the disposal by the United States, after the admission of Idaho to statehood, of fractional subdivisions or islands in the navigable streams, carried with it no right to the bed of said rivers, save as the law of Idaho may have attached such a right to private riparian ownership on a navigable stream, and that islands in existence when Idaho became a state, did not pass to the state upon admission to statehood or come within the disposing influence of its laws, but remained the property of the United States, subject to disposal by it.

This decision was followed by this court in the case of *A. B. Moss & Bro. v. Ramey*, upon rehearing, 25 Ida. 1, 136 Pac. 608, the court holding in effect, that an island which is surrounded by well-defined channels of the stream and which island existed at the time the state was admitted into the Union and was not included in the public land of the survey, but comprised an area larger than a legal subdivision authorized under the United States land surveys, did not pass from the government to the state on the admission of the state, and did not pass to the upland or riparian proprietor by a patent to the abutting lots of a subdivision meandering the channel of the stream.

It is therefore, we think, the settled law of this state, that no title to islands, lakes or the bed of navigable streams passes to the patentees of the United States by the sale of border lots, and that the state holds the title to the beds of navigable lakes and streams below the natural high-water mark for the use and benefit of the whole people, and that the right, title or interest of riparian proprietors or owners of uplands, to such shores are determined by the laws of the state, subject only to the rights vested by the constitution of the United States.

The Salmon river is a navigable stream, and is therefore a public highway belonging to the state upon its admission to the Union, and may be used and disposed of by the state, subject only to the rights of the public in such waters and to the paramount power of Congress to control their navigation so far as may be necessary for the regulation of commerce among the states and of foreign nations. (*St. Clair County v. Lovingston*, 23 Wall. 46, 68, 23 L. ed. 59; *Barney v. Keokuk*, 94 U. S. 324, 24 L. ed. 224; *Illinois C. R. Co. v. Chicago*, 176 U. S. 646, 20 Sup. Ct. 509, 44 L. ed. 622.) In this last-named case it is held that the right of the state to regulate and control the shores of navigable waters and the land under them is supreme; that it depends upon the law of each state as to what waters and to what extent this prerogative of the state over the beds of such streams shall be exercised; that after statehood, the state holds the title to the beds of the navigable streams and may dispose of them if it desires to do so to private owners, but that no such disposition shall interfere with the rights of the general government to regulate commerce on such navigable streams, or in any manner interfere with the right to the use of the navigable lakes, rivers or streams as public highways over which every citizen has a natural right to carry commerce, whether by ships, boats or the floating of logs or lumber; having due consideration and reasonable care for the rights of individuals as well as the public in the common use of such public highways.

The cases of *Johnson v. Hurst*, 10 Ida. 308, 77 Pac. 784, *Lattig v. Scott*, 17 Ida. 506, 107 Pac. 47, *Johnson v. Johnson*, 14 Ida. 561, 95 Pac. 499, 24 L. R. A., N. S., 1240, and *Ulbright v. Baslington*, 20 Ida. 539, 119 Pac. 292, 294, are hereby overruled in so far as they conflict with this opinion.

Upon an examination of the record and the authorities applicable to this case, we are satisfied that our conclusions are not only supported by the great weight of authority, but that this case comes squarely within the rule laid down in the cases of *Scott v. Lattig, supra,* and *A. B. Moss & Bro. v. Ramey,* on rehearing, *supra.*

The trial court did not err in granting a nonsuit in this case. We have also examined appellant's second assignment of error and find that there is no merit in it.

It is therefore ordered that judgment of nonsuit in favor of respondent be and the same is hereby *affirmed.* Costs are awarded to respondent.

Sullivan, C. J., and Morgan, J., concur.

(February 8, 1915.)

STATE ex rel. CANYON COUNTY, Appellant, v. JACOB FORCH, J. FORCH DRUG CO., and UNITED STATES FIDELITY & GUARANTY CO., a Corporation, Respondents.

[146 Pac. 110.]

LIQUOR LAW—DRUGGIST—BOND—CONDITION OF—STATUTORY CONSTRUCTION—ACTION ON BOND.

1. Under the provisions of sec. 4 of an act commonly known as the Haight Liquor Law (1913 Sess. Laws, pp. 121 and 415), a bond conditioned that the one giving it "shall use and dispense with such intoxicating liquors in accordance with the laws of the state of Idaho, then this obligation to be void; otherwise to remain in full force and effect," is a sufficient bond under the provisions of said act.

2. *Held*, that the provisions of said sec. 4 requiring a bond "conditioned that none of said liquors shall be used or disposed of for any purpose other than in compounding or preserving medicines, the sale of which would not subject him to the payment of the special tax required of liquor dealers, by the United States," is surplusage and contradictory to the legislative intent and purpose of said act, inasmuch as the purpose of said act was to permit druggists to sell intoxicating liquors in accordance with the provisions of such act.

3. Said condition of the bond is out of harmony and in conflict with the clear intent and purpose of said act.

4. When a statute contains a clause that is directly contrary to the legislative intent, as collected from the whole act, such clause will be treated as surplusage and be disregarded in the proper construction of such act.

5. The title to an act may be resorted to as an aid in determining the intention of the legislature.

6. *Held*, that the conditions of the bond given by the respondent make him and his sureties liable thereon if he violates any laws of the state of Idaho in the sale of intoxicating liquor.

7. Under the provisions of the Haight Liquor Law, a civil action may be maintained on the bond given in case of a violation of its conditions, and a criminal action may also be maintained for using or selling intoxicating liquors in violation of the provisions of said law.

APPEAL from the District Court of the Seventh Judicial District for Canyon County. Hon. Ed. L. Bryan, Judge.

Action to recover on a bond given by a drug company for the observance of the laws of the state in the sale of intoxicating liquors. Judgment for the defendant. *Affirmed.*

J. H. Peterson, Attorney General, E. G. Davis and T. C. Coffin, Assistants, and B. W. Henry, for Appellants, cite no authorities.

Scatterday & Van Duyn, for Respondents.

Statutes should be construed so as to render them valid and give them force and effect. (36 Cyc. 1111 (e), notes 74 and 75.)

Particular expressions in one part of a statute, not so large and extensive in import as other expressions in the same statute will yield to the larger and more extensive expression when the latter embodies the real intent of the legislature. (36 Cyc., p. 1131, note 70.)

The title of chapter 27 is an aid in determining the intent of the legislature. (36 Cyc., p. 1133 (f); *State v. Paulsen,* 21 Ida. 686, 694, 123 Pac. 588.)

Construction leading to absurdity, injustice or contradiction is to be avoided in interpreting statutes. (*Chandler v. Lee,* 1 Ida. 349; *Ex parte Ellis,* 11 Cal. 223; *Knowles v. Yeates,* 31 Cal. 82; *Greathouse v. Heed,* 1 Ida. 494; *Riggs v. Palmer,* 115 N. Y. 506, 12 Am. St. 819, 22 N. E. 188, 5 L. R. A. 343.)

Sections of statutes should be construed with reference to the purposes and policy of the act and the object intended to be accomplished. (36 Cyc. 1110 (d).)

SULLIVAN, C. J.—This action was brought by Canyon county, whereby the county seeks to recover from Jacob Forch, a druggist, the Forch Drug Company, and the United States Fidelity & Guaranty Company a judgment for $500 on a bond given by Forch for an alleged violation by Mr. Forch of the liquor laws of the state.

It is alleged in the complaint that the defendant Forch had sold alcohol and wine in Canyon county in September, 1913, and that by reason of making said sales he had become liable upon his bond by reason of the fact that the laws of Idaho prohibited the sale of alcohol and wine in a dry territory, and that Canyon county is a dry territory.

Forch and the bonding company answered in substance and effect denying that defendant Forch and the defendant drug company had made any sale of intoxicating liquors in violation of the laws of this state. Upon the issues thus made the case was heard before a jury and the jury returned a verdict in favor of the defendants. The state appeals from that judgment.

The only question presented for consideration is the proper construction of the act known as the Haight Liquor Law (Sess. Laws 1913, chap. 27, p. 121, and chap. 99, p. 415), and involves particularly the provisions of sec. 4 of said act. Said section provides, among other things, that a bond of $500 shall be given, to be approved by the probate judge in the county in which the pharmacy is located, "conditioned that none of said liquors shall be used or disposed of for any purpose other than in compounding or preserving medicines, the sale of which would not subject him to the payment of the special tax required of liquor dealers, by the United States, and that he will not violate any of the provisions of the laws prohibiting the sale or disposal of intoxicating liquors in any prohibition district in this state as herein provided."

Forch filed a bond which had been approved by the probate judge, upon which bond the defendant the United States Fidelity & Guaranty Company was surety, conditioned as follows: "Now, therefore, if the said Jacob Forch, doing business as the J. Forch Drug Company, shall use and dispense with such intoxicating liquors in accordance with the laws of the State of Idaho, then this obligation to be void; otherwise to remain in full force and effect."

This action is brought on that bond.

It is contended by the attorney general that said bond is not sufficient under the provisions of said sec. 4 of the Haight Liquor Law, for the reason that it does not contain the provision that "none of said liquors shall be used or disposed of for any purpose other than in compounding or preserving medicines, the sale of which would not subject him to the payment of the special tax required of liquor dealers, by the United States"; that to condition said bond, as the said bond is conditioned, to wit, that Forch "Shall use and dispense with such intoxicating liquors in accordance with the laws of the state of Idaho, then this obligation to be void; otherwise, to be in full force and effect," is not a compliance with the provisions of said sec. 4; that the defendant Forch is in fact selling intoxicating liquors without first filing a bond containing proper conditions, and is guilty for having failed to file the required bond.

As we view it, the defendant Forch would become liable under said bond if he sold or dispensed any intoxicating liquor contrary to the provisions of any of the laws of the state of Idaho, and if the Haight Liquor Law is a law of the state, which it is, and he violated any of its provisions in selling or dispensing intoxicating liquors, he would be liable on that bond. The condition of said bond under a reasonable construction of said sec. 4, would make the defendant liable upon his bond if he used, dispensed or sold any intoxicating liquor other than in compounding or preserving medicine, ''the sale of which would not subject him to the payment of a special tax required of liquor dealers by the United States.''

Liquor dealers, before they can legally sell or dispose of any kind of intoxicating liquors, must procure a license from the United States, and the intoxicating liquors that druggists use in compounding or preserving medicines are the kind that require the ordinary liquor dealer to procure a license from the United States for the sale thereof. If the druggist is required to give a bond conditioned that he will not use or dispose of any intoxicating liquors for any purpose other than in compounding or preserving medicines, the sale of which would not subject him to the payment of the special tax required of liquor dealers by the United States, he would obligate himself not to sell any intoxicating liquors whatever, since liquor dealers must procure a license from the United States for the sale of the intoxicating liquors referred to in said act.

It is conceded by the attorney general that that construction is not the proper one to be placed upon said language, but nevertheless he contends that such condition and language must be inserted in the bond. Counsel for the state admit that the object and purpose of the Haight Liquor Law was to permit druggists to use intoxicating liquors for compounding and preserving medicines and to sell intoxicating liquors upon being furnished with the proper physician's certificate or the proper affidavit of the purchaser or the certificate of a clergyman. And it is admitted in this case that the defendant Forch has not sold any liquor contrary to the provisions of said act, but it is contended that he has failed to file a bond conditioned that he will not sell any such liquors that would subject him to the payment of a special license required by the United States of liquor dealers, and for that reason has violated said law.

It will thus be seen that under a literal interpretation or construction of said condition of the bond contended for by the state, a druggist could not sell intoxicating liquors at all, and what is the purpose or object of requiring a druggist to give a bond which absolutely prohibits him from selling intoxicating liquor when as a matter of fact it was not the intention of the Haight Liquor Law to absolutely prohibit the sale of such liquors?

Aside from said condition in the bond, there is not a single intimation in the law that a druggist shall not sell intoxicating liquors in accordance with the provisions of said act; but, on the contrary, the Haight Liquor Law clearly permits the sale of intoxicating liquors if they are sold in accordance with the provisions of said act. In other words, it is not a prohibition, but a limited or qualified permission to sell.

The United States law substantially provides that no person shall legally sell distilled spirits or wine in quantities of less than five gallons without paying a $25 revenue license, nor in quantities of more than five gallons without paying $100 for such license. Forch sold intoxicating liquors in less than five gallon quantities, but it is admitted that he sold it in compliance with the laws of the state of Idaho, aside from giving the bond conditioned as above claimed by counsel for the state. The condition that the druggist will not sell any intoxicating liquors which would subject him to the payment of the special tax required of liquor dealers by the United States is clearly contradictory to the entire object and purpose of said law. That clause is out of harmony and in conflict with the entire act. Counsel for the state does not insist upon the court's construing the Haight Liquor Law as a prohibition from selling any intoxicating liquors whatever, and they admit it was the evident purpose of the legislature to allow the sale of such liquors under the safeguard provided by said law.

The rule of statutory construction is that whenever a statute contains a clause which is directly contrary to the legislative intent, as collected from the whole act, such clause will be treated as surplusage and will be disregarded in the proper construction of such act. The condition of the bond above referred to is not in harmony with the clear legislative intent of said act but is directly contrary thereto, hence it must be disregarded. It is stated by the author, 36 Cyc., p. 1131, as follows: "But a particular expression in one part of a statute not so large and extensive in its import as other expressions in the same statute will yield to the larger and more extensive expressions, where the latter embody the real intent of the legislature."

It is a general rule that the title to an act may be resorted to as an aid in determining the intent of the legislature. The title in this act relates to the sale of intoxicating liquors in prohibition districts and prescribes how alcohol and wines may be sold in any prohibition district. (*State v. Paulsen,* 21 Ida. 686, 123 Pac. 588; 36 Cyc. 1133.) Not only the title to said act, but the entire act itself, aside from the clause providing one of the conditions of the bond, shows clearly the intent of the legislature to allow druggists to sell alcoholic spirits and wines in dry counties.

The construction of a statute leading to an absurdity or contradiction should be avoided if possible. (*Chandler v. Lee,* 1 Ida. 349; *Greathouse v. Heed,* 1 Ida. 494; *Riggs v. Palmer,* 115 N. Y. 506, 12 Am. St. 819, 22 N. E. 188, 5 L. R. A. 340.)

The legislature clearly intended by the enactment of said Haight Liquor Law to allow alcoholic spirits and wines to be sold in dry counties of the state under the restrictions therein provided, and the defendant has given a bond conditioned on his selling such intoxicating liquors in accordance with the laws of the state, then the obligations of the bond to be void, otherwise to remain in full force and effect. The conditions of that bond clearly make him and his sureties liable thereon if he violates any laws of the state in the sale of such liquors, and amply cover the object and purpose of said Haight Liquor Act in requiring a bond from druggists. Under the facts of this case, the defendant has complied with the laws of the state in selling the liquors referred to in the record.

We therefore hold that the trial court did not err in entering judgment in favor of the defendant.

It is contended by counsel for respondent that an action on a bond given under the provisions of the Haight Liquor Law cannot be maintained until the violator of the law has been prosecuted for a misdemeanor, found guilty and a fine imposed, since sec. 4 of said act provides, among other things, that "Any person or corporation who shall violate the provisions of this Section shall be guilty of a misdemeanor, and shall be fined not more than Five Hundred Dollars ($500.00) for each offense. It shall be the duty of the County Attorney to bring suit on said bond executed by such person for the recovery of any such penalty and all costs."

There is nothing in this contention. The required bond was executed in the sum of $500, conditioned that Forch should use and dispense or sell intoxicating liquors in accordance with the laws of the state of Idaho, then the obligation to be void; otherwise to remain in full force and effect; and if he should violate any of the laws of the state of Idaho in selling or disposing of such liquors, the obligation of the bond would be broken and the county might immediately bring suit on the bond, or it might prosecute him for a misdemeanor for violating the law in selling intoxicating liquors. And if he were convicted and a sentence imposed, an action might be brought on the bond to recover the judgment or penalty imposed in the misdemeanor action. In other words, both a civil and a criminal action may be maintained under the provisions of said act.

For the foregoing reasons, we conclude that the judgment of the trial court must be affirmed, and it is so ordered, with costs in favor of the respondents.

Budge and Morgan, JJ., concur.

(February 8, 1915.)

W. A. FIFE, Appellant, v. VILLAGE OF GLENNS· FERRY, Respondent.

[146 Pac. 467.]

EJECTMENT—LOCATION OF CITY LOT—FINDINGS OF FACT—SUFFICIENCY
OF EVIDENCE.

1. *Held,* that the evidence is sufficient to support the finding of facts.

APPEAL from the District Court of the Fourth Judicial District for Elmore County. Hon. Edward A. Walters, Judge.

Action in ejectment to recover possession of lot 9 and the west half of lot 10, block 21, Hammer's addition to the village of Glenns Ferry. Judgment for the defendant. *Affirmed.*

Budge & Barnard, for Appellant.

Allen Miller, for Respondent.

SULLIVAN, C. J.—This is an action in ejectment to recover the possession of lot 9 and the west half of lot 10 in block 21 in Hammer's addition to the town of Glenns Ferry.

The village of Glenns Ferry owns lot 8 in said block and has its city jail on said lot 8. The real controversy arises over the exact location of lot 9 and the west half of lot 10 in said block. The cause was tried to the court without a jury and finding of facts and judgment entered in favor of the village, from which judgment this appeal was taken.

The sole question presented for determination is where in the village of Glenns Ferry and in Hammer's addition thereto lot 9 and the west half of lot 10 are located. After hearing the testimony of the civil engineer or surveyor on the part of the plaintiff and of the county surveyor on the part of the defendant, and some other testimony, the court made its findings and judgment as above stated.

There are eight assignments of error, but they all go to the sufficiency of the evidence to support the findings.

After a careful examination of the evidence, we are satisfied that there is sufficient evidence in the record to support the findings of the trial court. The judgment must therefore · be affirmed, and it is so ordered, with costs in favor of the respondent.

Morgan, J., concurs.

(February 10, 1915.)

In the Matter of the Application of HARRY S. KESSLER for a Writ of Habeas Corpus.

[146 Pac. 113.]

MOTOR VEHICLES — CONSTITUTIONAL LAW — REVENUE AND TAXATION — LICENSE OR REGISTRATION FEE.

1. Chapter 179, Sess. Laws 1913, p. 558, is a law intended, among other things, to require those who operate motor vehicles upon the public highways to cause such vehicles to be registered and to pay therefor a license, or registration fee, which is in excess of the amount necessary to be raised for the purpose of policing such vehicles upon the public highways.

2. In matters of taxation the legislature possesses plenary power, except as such power may be limited or restricted by the constitution. It is not necessary that the constitution contain a grant of power to the legislature to deal with the question of taxation.

3. The provisions of the constitution requiring all taxes to be uniform and to be levied and collected under general laws which shall prescribe such regulations as shall insure a just valuation of all property, refer to taxation according to the commonly accepted meaning of that term, and do not apply to license or registration fees.

4. The constitution of Idaho does not prohibit the state from raising revenue in the manner provided for in said chapter 179.

APPEAL from the District Court of the Third Judicial District for the County of Ada. Hon. Carl A. Davis, Judge.

Petition for writ of *habeas corpus*. Petition granted. *Reversed.*

J. H. Peterson, Attorney General, E. G. Davis, T. C. Coffin, Assistants, Raymond L. Givens, Prosecuting Attorney, E. P. Barnes, Jay M. Parrish, for Appellant.

In the case of *Achenbach v. Kincaid*, 25 Ida. 768, 140 Pac. 529, this court has held that every intendment shall be in favor of the constitutionality of the act in question.

The right of the state to pass a law authorizing a license tax under police power for the purpose of revenue has been expressly recognized in the following cases: *Nebraska Telephone Co. v. City of Lincoln*, 82 Neb. 59, 117 N. W. 284; *Salt Lake City v. Christenson Co.*, 34 Utah, 38, 95 Pac. 523, 17 L. R. A., N. S., 898; *City of Buffalo v. Lewis*, 192 N. Y. 193, 84 N. E. 809; *Adler v. Whitlock*, 44 Ohio St. 539, 9 N. E. 672; *Commonwealth v. Boyd*, 188 Mass. 79, 108 Am. St. 464, 74 N. E. 255; *City of Terre Haute v. Kersey*, 159 Ind. 300, 95 Am. St. 296, 64 N. E. 469; Elliott on Roads and Streets, p. 1114.

The use of the roads is a right which by and of itself may be taxed and which does not violate any of the principles of our constitution either as to exempting the automobile from valuation taxes or on the ground that it operates under police power. (*Kaiser Land and Fruit Co. v. Curry*, 155 Cal. 638, 103 Pac. 341; *People v. Grant*, 157 Mich. 24, 133 Am. St. 329, 121 N. W. 300; *Dudley v. Northampton Street Ry. Co.*, 202 Mass. 443, 89 N. E. 25, 23 L. R. A., N. S., 561; *Ex parte Miller*, 13 Cal. App. 564, 110 Pac. 139; *Kellaher v. City of Portland*, 57 Or. 575, 110 Pac. 492, 112 Pac. 1076; *Wiggins Ferry Co. v. East St. Louis*, 102 Ill. 560.)

It is not necessary to determine whether the license fee is for revenue or for purposes of regulation. (*Banta v. City of Chicago*, 172 Ill. 204, 50 N. E. 233, 40 L. R. A. 611; *Price v. People*, 193 Ill. 114, 86 Am. St. 306, 61 N. E. 844, 55 L. R. A. 588; *Bassett v. People*, 193 Ill. 334, 62 N. E. 215, 56 L. R. A. 558; *Raymond v. Hartford Fire Ins. Co.*, 196 Ill. 329, 63

N. E. 745; *Northern Pac. Ry. Co. v. Gifford,* 25 Ida. 196, 136 Pac. 1131; *Kane v. State,* 81 N. J. L. 594, Ann. Cas. 1912D, 237, 80 Atl. 453; *Cleary v. Johnston,* 79 N. J. L. 49, 74 Atl. 538; *Dewitt v. State,* 155 Wis. 249, 144 N. W. 253; *State v. Sheppard,* 79 Wash. 328, 140 Pac. 332.)

Harry S. Kessler, Respondent, *pro se.*

"The power to impose such a tax (license) extends only to the business as contradistinguished from the ownership or possession or right of ownership of the property." (*In re Gale,* 14 Ida. 761, 95 Pac. 679.)

The primary and paramount, if not the only, object of the law, is to obtain revenue. (*Rosenbloom v. State,* 64 Neb. 343, 89 N. W. 1055, 57 L. R. A. 922.)

If the money is to be used particularly for some public improvement it indicates that the exaction is a tax. (*Ellis v. Frazier,* 38 Or. 462, 63 Pac. 642, 53 L. R. A. 454; *Harder's Fireproof Storage & Van Co. v. Chicago,* 235 Ill. 58, 85 N. E. 245, 14 Ann. Cas. 434.)

A fee for a license must be such a fee only as will legitimately assist in the regulation; and it should not exceed the necessary or probable expense of issuing the license and of inspecting and regulating the business which it covers. (Cooley on Taxation, 2d ed., 597; *State v. Moore,* 113 N. C. 697, 18 S. E. 342, 22 L. R. A. 472; *City of Jacksonville v. Ledwith,* 26 Fla. 163, 23 Am. St. 558, 7 So. 885, 9 L. R. A. 69; *City of Jackson v. Newman,* 59 Miss. 385, 42 Am. Rep. 367; *Sipe v. Murphy,* 49 Ohio St. 536, 31 N. E. 884, 17 L. R. A. 184; *Chaddock v. Day,* 75 Mich. 527, 13 Am. St. 468, 42 N. W. 977, 4 L. R. A. 809; *Waters-Pierce Oil Co. v. City of Hot Springs,* 85 Ark. 509, 109 S. W. 293, 16 L. R. A., N. S., 1035.)

An examination of the authorities reveals that an annual fee of three dollars is the maximum that has ever been approved as a legitimate charge for police regulation for automobiles. (*Ayers v. Chicago,* 239 Ill. 237, 87 N. E. 1073; *Cleary v. Johnston,* 79 N. J. L. 49, 74 Atl. 538; *State v. Lawrence* (Miss.), 61 So. 975; *In re Hoffert* (S. D.), 148 N. W.

20, 52 L. R. A., N. S., 949; *Graves v. Janes,* 18 Ohio C. C. (N. S.) 448.)

The registration fees are charged against each motor vehicle, and exempting them from any other taxation shows that the legislature intended to tax them as articles of personal property. (*Vernor v. Secretary of State,* 179 Mich. 157, 146 N. W. 338.)

This method of registration fees just as clearly violates the rule of uniformity as the requirement of valuation. As between the owners of motor vehicles the law is both unfair and unjust. (*High School v. Lancaster Co.,* 60 Neb. 147, 83 Am. St. 525, 82 N. W. 380, 49 L. R. A. 343; *State v. Poynter,* 59 Neb. 417, 81 N. W. 431; *Attorney General v. Winnebago Lake & R. Plank Road Co.,* 11 Wis. 35; *In re Opinion of the Justices,* 195 Mass. 607, 84 N. E. 499; *McCurdy v. Prugh,* 59 Ohio St. 465, 55 N. E. 154; *State v. Case,* 39 Wash. 177, 81 Pac. 554, 1 L. R. A., N. S., 152; *Hawkeye Ins. Co. v. French,* 109 Iowa, 585, 80 N. W. 660.)

MORGAN, J.—This is an appeal from an order of the district court discharging from custody the respondent who had been arrested for and convicted of operating and driving a motorcycle upon the public highways of Ada county, Idaho, in violation of the provisions of chapter 179 of the Session Laws of 1913, in that he had not caused the said motorcycle to be registered nor paid the fee incident thereto.

Said chapter creates a State Highway Commission and provides, among other things, a comprehensive plan of state highway construction and improvement and of policing motor traffic upon the public highways. Sec. 12 thereof is as follows: "Except as hereinafter provided, no motor vehicle shall be operated or driven upon any state or other public highway or upon the public streets of any city or incorporated village in this state until the said motor vehicle shall have been registered with the Secretary of the State Highway Commission." Said chapter provides the manner in which registration shall be applied for and the manner in which a record thereof shall be kept; that the application for registration of a motor vehicle of 30 horse-power or less shall be accompanied by a fee of $15, and of a motor vehicle of over 30 horse-power and up to and including 40 horse-power, by a fee of $20, and of a motor vehicle of over 40 horse-power and up to and including 50 horse-power, by a fee of $25, and a motor vehicle of over 50 horse-power, by a fee of $40, and in case of a motorcycle, by a fee of $5. Said chapter also provides for the issuance to the applicant a certificate of registration and a number.

The fees above mentioned are to be paid annually and shall be in lieu of all taxes, general or local, and the chapter expressly provides that all motor vehicles for which this annual fee is to be paid and which have been so registered shall be exempt from taxation. It is also provided that the violation of any of the provisions of this chapter in question shall be a misdemeanor, punishable by imprisonment in the county jail not exceeding six months, or by a fine not exceeding $300.00, or by both such fine and imprisonment. Under the terms of the chapter all such fines are to be turned over to the Secretary of the State Highway Commission who shall pay them over to the State Treasurer, together with all fees collected under the provisions of said chapter, and said moneys shall go into the state highway fund.

This chapter was before the court for consideration in the case of *Achenbach v. Kincaid et al.*, 25 Ida. 768, 140 Pac. 529, wherein the constitutionality of the law was questioned and it was held to not violate the constitution in the particulars therein considered, but the court held the questions here presented were not properly before it in that case.

In this case the respondent contends that the registration fee on motor vehicles provided for in section 16 of said chapter 179 is an attempted taxation other than by valuation and violates sec. 2, art. 7 of the constitution of Idaho, which is as follows: "The legislature shall provide such revenue as may be needful, by levying a tax by valuation, so that every person or corporation shall pay a tax in proportion to the value of his, her, or its property, except as' in this article hereinafter otherwise provided. The legislature may also impose a license tax (both upon natural persons and upon corporations, other than municipal, doing business in this state); also a per capita tax. *Provided,* the legislature may exempt a limited amount of improvements upon land, from taxation.''

It is contended that the said chapter, in so far as it provides for the payment of fees for registration, in an amount in excess of that necessary to properly police the use of motor vehicles upon the public highways, is a revenue measure. That it does raise considerable revenue in excess of an amount necessary for police purposes, and that it appropriates the money so raised to a fund for the construction and maintenance of public highways, is quite true. In this connection, however, it may be observed that the license, or fee, is exacted not upon the ownership of the motor vehicle, but upon the right to use it upon the public highways.

Respondent also contends that said sec. 16 is an attempted taxation in violation of the rule of uniformity required by sec. 5, art. 7 of the constitution, which is as follows: ''All taxes shall be uniform upon the same class of subjects within the territorial limits, of the authority levying the tax, and shall be levied and collected under general laws, which shall prescribe such regulations as shall secure a just valuation for taxation of all property, real and personal, *provided,* that the legislature may allow such exemptions from taxation from time to time as shall seem necessary and just, and all existing exemptions provided by the laws of the territory, shall continue until changed by the legislature of the state, *provided, further,* that duplicate taxation of property for the same purpose during the same year, is hereby prohibited.''

The respondent, in presenting his petition for a writ of *habeas corpus,* and the district court, in granting it and in ordering him discharged from custody, seem to have proceeded upon one of two erroneous theories; either that the legislature of the state of Idaho possesses no inherent power in matters of taxation but may raise revenue only in conformity to a grant of authority so to do, expressed in the constitution, or that a prohibition against raising revenue in the manner attempted by said chapter 179 is expressed in or is to be implied from the language of the constitution.

In case of *Achenbach v. Kincaid, supra,* this court said: "As to the question of taxation: "The legislature possesses plenary power, except as such power may be limited or restricted by the constitution. It is not necessary that the constitution shall contain a grant of power to the legislature to deal with the question of taxation. It is sufficient proof of its power if there be found in the constitution no prohibition against what the legislature has attempted to do."

As stated by the supreme court of Oregon in the case of the *State v. Cochran,* 55 Or. 157, 104 Pac. 419, 105 Pac. 884: "A state constitution unlike a federal constitution is one of limitation and not a grant of powers, and any act adopted by the legislature not prohibited by the state constitution is valid, and the inhibition must expressly or impliedly be made to appear beyond a reasonable doubt." (See *St. Joe Improvement Co. v. Laumierster,* 19 Ida. 66, 112 Pac. 683; *Walker v. City of Spokane,* 62 Wash. 312, Ann. Cas. 1912C, 994, 113 Pac. 775; *People ex rel. Simon v. Bradley,* 207 N. Y. 592, 101 N. E. 766.)

"In passing on the constitutionality of a statute, every reasonable doubt as to its validity will be resolved in favor of sustaining the statute. (*People v. Rose,* 203 Ill. 46, 67 N. E. 746; *Board of Trustees of House of Reform v. City of Lexington,* 112 Ky. 171, 65 S. W. 350; *Commonwealth v. Barney,* 115 Ky. 475, 74 S. W. 181; *State v. Thompson,* 144 Mo. 314, 46 S. W. 191; *Ex parte Loving,* 178 Mo. 194, 77 S. W. 508.)

"An act of the legislature will not be declared unconstitutional unless in plain violation of some provisions of the constitution. (*Brady v. Mattern,* 125 Iowa, 158, 106 Am. St. 291, 100 N. W. 358.)

"The court in construing a statute must adopt such construction as will sustain the constitutionality of the statute, where that can be done without doing violence to the language thereof. (*State v. Barrett,* 172 Ind. 169, 87 N. E. 7.) The courts must as far as possible uphold and give effect to all statutes enacted by the legislature. (*Commonwealth v. International Harvester Co.*, 131 Ky. 768, 115 S. W. 755.)''

Judge Cooley in vol. 1 of his works on Taxation, third edition, page 9, says:

"Everything to which the legislative power extends may be the subject of taxation, whether it be person or property, or possession, franchise or privilege, or occupation or right. Nothing but express constitutional limitation upon legislative authority can exclude anything to which the authority extends from the grasp of the taxing power, if the legislature in its discretion shall at any time select it for revenue purposes; and not only is the power unlimited in its reach as to subjects, but in its very nature it acknowledges no limits, and may be carried even to the extent of exhaustion and destruction, thus becoming in its exercise a power to destroy. If the power be threatened with abuse, security must be found in the responsibility of the legislature that imposes the tax to the constituency which must pay it. The judiciary can afford no redress against oppressive taxation, so long as the legislature, in imposing it, shall keep within the limits of legislative authority, and violate no express provision of the constitution. The necessity for imposing it addresses itself to the legislative discretion, and it is or may be an urgent necessity which will admit of no property or other conflicting right in the citizen while it remains unsatisfied." (See, also, *Lowe et al. v. Board etc.*, 156 Ind. 163, 59 N. E. 466.)

Certainly our constitution does not expressly prohibit the people of Idaho from raising revenue in the manner provided in chapter 179 of the Session Laws of 1913, and while it is true there are three methods of raising revenue expressed in sec. 2 of art. 7 of the constitution, we cannot infer from this that an implication arises prohibiting the state from also raising revenue pursuant to its inherent power to do so in any other manner its legislature may see fit to adopt.

It is earnestly urged that this is not a property tax, that it is a license and raises more revenue than sufficient to police motor vehicles upon the public highway. We are fully convinced that in this contention respondent is correct, but it does not follow that the law is in contravention of the constitution.

By way of sustaining his contention that this law is intended to raise revenue, respondent quotes from *Rosebloom v. State*, 64 Neb. 343, 89 N. W. 1055, 57 L. R. A. 922, as follows: "We agree with counsel in the view that the primary and paramount, if not the only, object of the law, is to obtain revenue, by imposing a tax upon the business of peddling. The only thing the peddler is required to do is to pay his tax, and exhibit the appropriate evidence of payment to any person who may wish to see it. The only thing he is forbidden to do is to pursue his calling without first having paid the tax. No police inspection or supervision is provided for. If the things commanded and forbidden are to be regarded as features of regulation or repression, they are not, to say the least, so pronounced or conspicuous as to suggest the idea that the law is referable to the police power, rather than the power of taxation."

By beginning to quote from the point in that decision where respondent leaves off, the attitude of the supreme court of Nebraska and of this court upon this question is very clearly stated as follows:

"But granting the contention of counsel for defendant that the statute is a revenue measure, pure and simple, we are not able to discover any valid objection to the enforcement of it in the manner provided by the legislature. It is settled doctrine in this and in every other jurisdiction that courts will not adjudge statutes unconstitutional unless they are plainly so. Now, with what express provision of the higher law does the statute in question clash? We know of none."

Respondent seeks to distinguish from this case that of *Salt Lake City v. Christensen Co.*, 34 Utah, 38, 95 Pac. 523, 17 L. R. A., N. S., 898, where a revenue raising license fee was sustained, and with that end in view quotes from the Utah constitution as follows: "Nothing in this constitution shall be construed to prevent the legislature from providing a stamp tax, or a tax on income, occupation, license, franchise or mortgages." This paragraph of the Utah constitution merely points out the proper construction of that document, which would prevail even in the absence of the paragraph.

In like manner respondent seeks to distinguish from this case that of *Ex parte Schuler,* 167 Cal. 282, 139 Pac. 685, decided by the supreme court of California, which upholds the right of the legislature of California to enact a law exacting from the owners of motor vehicles a revenue for their use upon the public highways, which revenue was to be used for the upkeep of said highways, by reason of this paragraph in the California constitution: "The legislature shall have power to establish a system of state highways or to declare any road a state highway, and to pass all laws necessary or proper to construct and maintain the same, and to extend aid for the construction and maintenance in whole or in part of any county highway." It is perfectly clear that the foregoing provision of the California constitution neither grants to nor takes from the legislature of that state the power to raise revenue. Said paragraph only points out one of the ways in which the moneys of the state may be expended.

The respondent also quotes at considerable length from the case of *Vernor et al. v. Secretary of State,* a Michigan case, reported in 179 Mich. 157, 146 N. W. 338. This case is not in point except to show that the principal purpose of the law was to raise revenue rather than a police regulation. The act was held to be unconstitutional upon the ground that the title was insufficient, not upon the ground that revenue cannot be raised by requiring those who operate motor vehicles upon the public highway to procure and pay for a license so to do.

The respondent maintains that the law under consideration violates sec. 5, art. 7 of the constitution in that the registration fees therein provided for are not uniform upon the same class of subjects and that it does not secure a just valuation of the property thus taxed.

The provision of that section of our constitution, requiring all taxes to be uniform upon the same class of subjects within the territorial limits of the authority levying the tax, and to be levied and collected under general laws which shall prescribe such regulations as shall insure a just valuation for taxation of all property, real or personal, refers solely to taxation according to the commonly accepted meaning of that term, by assessment, levy and collection and does not apply to license or registration fees. It is to be borne in mind that the law under consideration does not impose a tax upon property, but imposes a registration fee, or license, upon the privilege of operating motor vehicles upon the public highways.

It has been frequently held by this court that liquor licenses, pool and billiard table licenses, taxes by way of licenses imposed upon persons and corporations engaged in loaning money within the state, and upon railway and express companies doing business within the state, are not taxes contemplated by secs. 2 and 5 of art. 7 of the constitution, but constitute a separate and distinct way of raising revenue, independent of taxation in the commonly accepted meaning of that term. (*State v. Doherty,* 3 Ida. 384, 29 Pac. 855; *State v. Union Central Insurance Co.,* 8 Ida. 240, 67 Pac. 647; *State v. Jones,* 9 Ida. 693, 75 Pac. 819; *In re Gale,* 14 Ida. 761, 95 Pac. 679; *Northern Pacific Ry. Co. v. Gifford, Secretary of State,* 25 Ida. 196, 136 Pac. 1131. See, also, *Salt Lake City v. Christensen Co., supra,* and *Ex parte Schuler, supra.*)

The respondent complains that, as between the owners of motor vehicles, the law is unfair and unjust; that the owner of such a vehicle worth but a couple of hundred dollars is required to pay the same tax as the owner of one worth two or three thousand dollars, or more, provided, of course, the machines happen to be of the same horse-power. We fail to see wherein the value of the machine affects the value of the right to use it upon the public highway. Even though this act does not fairly distribute the burden of building and maintaining roads among the owners of motor vehicles used upon them, or between that class of persons and other citizens of the state, it may be said with equal force that ever since the dawn of civilization the problem of raising revenue has been with governments, as with individuals, one of the chief causes of concern, and that a scientific and satisfactory solution of it has never been reached. If chapter 179 of the Session Laws of 1913 is unskillfully drawn or the plan to raise revenue therein provided is unscientific, or for any other reason unsatisfactory, recourse for its correction must be had to the legislature and not to the courts, for this branch of the government cannot declare an act of the legislature unconstitutional unless it violates some provision of the constitution.

The supreme court of New Jersey in the case of *Kane v. State,* 81 N. J. L. 594, Ann. Cas. 1912D, 237, 80 Atl. 453, in upholding a statute much like the one under consideration, said: "The imposition is a license or privilege tax charged in the nature of compensation for the damage done to the roads of the state by the driving of these machines over them, and is properly based, not upon the value of the machine, but upon the amount of destruction caused by it."

In the recent decision by the supreme court of the United States in the case of *Hendrick v. Maryland,* 235 U. S. 610, 59 L. ed. 140 (U. S. Sup. Ct. Advance Opinions of February 1, 1915), a case closely resembling this in many important particulars, the opinion delivered by Mr. Justice McReynolds is, in part, as follows: "The movement of motor vehicles over the highways is attended by constant and serious dangers to the public, and is also abnormally destructive to the ways themselves. Their success depends on good roads, the construction and maintenance of which are exceedingly expensive; and in recent years insistent demands have been made upon the states for better facilities, especially by the ever-increasing number of those who own such vehicles. As is well known, in order to meet this demand and accommodate the growing traffic the state of Maryland has built and is maintaining a system of improved roadways. Primarily for the enforcement of good order and the protection of those within its own jurisdiction the state put into effect the above described general regulations, including requirements for registration and licenses. A further evident purpose was to secure some compensation for the use of facilities provided at great cost from the class for whose needs they are essential, and whose operations over them are peculiarly injurious.

Idaho is a mountainous state wherein vast sums of money have been, and still greater sums must in the future, be expended in the construction and maintenance of public highways. The motor vehicle is a conveyance requiring a different and better class of roads than ordinary traffic has heretofore demanded. These motor vehicles have been found to be exceedingly destructive of the highways, and particularly is this true of those propelled by engines of great power especially when driven at a high rate of speed. It seems probable that by reason of these conditions the legislature enacted said chapter 179, but whatever the reason for its enactment may have been, said chapter is not repugnant to the provisions of the constitution.

The order of the district court granting the writ of *habeas corpus* and discharging the defendant from custody is reversed with instruction to said court to quash the writ and to remand the respondent to custody.

Sullivan, C. J., and Budge, J., concur.

(February 15, 1915.)

HARRY M. COON et al., Respondents, v. JAMES A. SOM-
MERCAMP, Treasurer and *Ex-officio* Tax Collector of
Washington County, State of Idaho, Appellant.

[146 Pac. 728.]

POLITICAL CORPORATION—STATE, COUNTY, MUNICIPAL OFFICERS—PROSE-
CUTION OR DEFENSE OF SUITS IN OFFICIAL CAPACITY—UNDERTAKINGS
ON APPEAL—TRANSCRIPTS SERVED ON ADVERSE PARTY—PROOF OF
SERVICE OF TRANSCRIPT—CLERK'S CERTIFICATE INSUFFICIENT—
MOTION TO DISMISS APPEAL SUSTAINED.

1. Sec. 4935, Rev. Codes, which provides that "In any civil action
or proceeding wherein the state or the people of the state, is a party
plaintiff, or any state officer, in his official capacity, or on behalf
of the state, or any county, or city, is a party plaintiff or defendant, no bond, written undertaking, or security can be required
of the state, or the people thereof, or any officer thereof, or of any
county, or city; but on complying with the other provisions of this

code, the state, or the people thereof, or any state officer acting in his official capacity, or any county or city, have the same rights, remedies and benefits as if the bond, undertaking or security were given and approved as required by this code," applies to county treasurers and *ex-officio* tax collectors in prosecuting an action for and on behalf of a rural high school district; said rural high school district being a political corporation of the state.

2. Whenever an action is brought by or against state, county or municipal officers, and such officers prosecute or defend in said action in their official capacity, acting for or defending the rights of the state, county or municipality, or any legal subdivision thereof, they are permitted to so act without furnishing costs or undertakings on appeal. (Sec. 4935, *supra*.)

3. In all cases where an appeal is perfected, a transcript of the record must be served upon the adverse party and filed in this court within sixty days after the appeal is perfected, unless an extension of time be granted; otherwise the appeal will be dismissed.

4. Where it appears from the record on appeal that the transcript was not served upon the adverse party and a motion is made in this court to dismiss the appeal for that reason, and where an affidavit by counsel for appellant, attempting to show service, but uncertain and indefinite in its terms, is filed subsequent to the hearing of the motion to dismiss the appeal, it will not be considered by the court as sufficient proof of service of the transcript and the motion to dismiss will be allowed.

5. Upon an appeal from a judgment, the clerk is required to furnish the court with a copy of the notice of appeal, the judgment-roll and any bill of exceptions or reporter's transcript. Where the clerk certifies that the transcript of the proceedings in the trial court "contains all the papers specified in the *praecipe* filed with me," said certificate is insufficient.

APPEAL from the District Court of the Seventh Judicial District for Washington County. Hon. Ed. L. Bryan, Judge.

Action to enjoin collection of school tax. Motion to dismiss appeal. *Sustained.*

J. H. Peterson, Attorney General, and T. C. Coffin, Assistant, James Harris and Devaney & Carter, for Appellant.

The law in California with regard to the filing of a bond by a public officer is in conflict, but we find another and apparently better rule established in Washington, and a con-

sistent line of decisions follows it. The rule there announced
in the case of *Corbett v. Civil Service Commission of the City
of Seattle*, 33 Wash. 190, 73 Pac. 1116, is that the section of
the code dispensing with the filing of a bond applies to all
cases in which an officer of a legal subdivision of the government is acting in his official capacity. That the appellant in
the case at bar is so acting is sufficiently shown for the purposes of this case by the fact that he is sued in that capacity.
The respondent is endeavoring on this motion to take advantage of mere technicalities in the procedure of taking the
appeal, and those who rely upon technicalities must themselves observe them. The twenty days prescribed by sec.
4809, Rev. Codes, for objecting to the undertaking had expired, and the motion comes too late under the provisions of
this section. (*King v. Seebeck*, 20 Ida. 223, 118 Pac. 292;
Martin v. Wilson, 24 Ida. 353, 134 Pac. 532. See, also, *Kohn
v. Davidson*, 23 La. Ann. 467; *Arrington v. Smith*, 26 N. C.
59; *Saylor v. Marx*, 56 Tex. 90; *Seattle & M. Ry. Co. v. Johnson*, 7 Wash. 97, 34 Pac. 567; *Roberts v. Shelton S. W. R. Co.*,
21 Wash. 427, 58 Pac. 576.)

The signing of a stipulation allowing the respondent more
time in which to file his brief constitutes an appearance in the
supreme court which waives technical defects in the appeal
and in the bond. (*National Safe & Lock Co. v. People*, 50 Ill.
App. 336.)

Wood & Driscoll and Varian & Norris, for Respondents.

Sec. 1058 of California Code of Civil Procedure is identical,
so far as this question is concerned, with our sec. 4935, Rev.
Codes.

The supreme court of California in *Lamberson v. Jefferds*,
116 Cal. 492, 48 Pac. 485, held that it would be applied to
such official in all cases where it appeared that the county
was really the party in interest. But in an earlier case it was
said: "A county officer is not exempted from filing an undertaking on appeal by virtue of the provisions of sec. 1058, Code
Civil Procedure." (*Von Schmidt v. Widber, County Treasurer*, 3 Cal. Unrep. 835, 32 Pac. 532.)

The county treasurer is acting as agent for the school district and not for the county; the county is not the real party in interest, and in fact, has no interest therein. As county treasurer, where the county is not the real party in interest, he is not excused from filing bond. Much less is he excused when he is acting in the interest of and agent for the school district, for the statute makes no mention of them. (*Mitchell v. Board of Education*, 137 Cal. 372, 70 Pac. 180.) The Washington rule is identical with that of California and based on California cases, and the question in this case remains as stated, Is the county here the real party in interest? If not, the bond must be filed.

The record shows the appeal perfected in this case on June 5, 1914, and the transcript was filed in this court on August 29, 1914, eighty-five days later. The record shows no extension of time. It affirmatively appears from the record that there is no reporter's transcript, and but 32 pages of clerk's transcript. It does not appear that appellant filed his *praecipe* for a transcript with the clerk within five days, that he paid the fees, nor does any other matter appear which would excuse the delay, or show that the appellant had proceeded with all the diligence in his power. (*First National Bank of American Falls v. Shaw*, 24 Ida. 134, 132 Pac. 802.)

Chapter 17, Sess. Laws 1911, sec. 3, p. 376, provides that the appellant shall file with the transcript "appropriate affidavit or admission of service." Rule 23 of this court contains substantially the same provision. The record in this case shows absolutely no compliance with the requirement. Under the rule in *Strand v. Crooked River Min. etc. Co.*, 23 Ida. 577–580, 131 Pac. 5, the omission is jurisdictional, and the appeal must be dismissed.

BUDGE, J.—Rural high school district No. 1 of Washington county was composed of school districts Nos. 5 and 8. On the 18th day of January, 1913, the board of county commissioners of Washington county, ordered the segregation of school district No. 5 from rural high school district No. 1.

After said segregation, the board of directors of school district No. 1 levied a tax upon all property situated therein, as it existed prior to the action of the board of county commissioners, segregating the same, which levy was duly reported and certified to the county commissioners, and thereafter entered upon the assessment-roll by the county assessor, who, subsequent thereto, turned over his assessment-rolls to the appellant herein, as county treasurer and *ex-officio* tax collector, for collection. This action was instituted to restrain the appellant as *ex-officio* tax collector from collecting said tax. A general demurrer to respondent's complaint was filed by appellant and thereafter argued and by the trial court overruled. To the complaint of respondent, the appellant filed an answer, to which answer, respondent filed a motion to strike a portion of the same, which motion was sustained by the trial court, whereupon judgment was taken by the respondent. This appeal is from the judgment.

On October 17, 1914, attorneys for respondent filed a notice of motion and motion to dismiss the appeal herein, upon the following grounds, to wit:

First, that the undertaking on appeal was not filed within five days after the service of the notice of appeal, upon the attorneys for the respondent, as required under sec. 4808, Rev. Codes.

Second, upon the ground that the transcript was not accompanied with a certificate of the clerk or of the attorneys, that an undertaking on appeal in due form had been properly filed.

Third, that the transcript was not filed in the supreme court within the statutory time.

Fourth, that proof of service of the transcript was not filed.

Fifth, that the certificate of the clerk to the transcript is insufficient.

The first ground of the motion to dismiss the appeal is based upon the failure of appellant to file an appeal bond or undertaking within the statutory time, or to furnish any other security that he would pay such damages or costs, as might be awarded against him, upon the dismissal of the appeal.

Sec. 4935, Rev. Codes, provides that, "In any civil action or proceeding wherein the state or the people of the state, is a party plaintiff, or any state officer, in his official capacity, or on behalf of the state, or any county, or city, is a party plaintiff or defendant, no bond, written undertaking, or security can be required of the state, or the people thereof, or any officer thereof, or of any county, or city; but on complying with the other provisions of this code, the state, or the people thereof, or any state officer acting in his official capacity, or any county or city, have the same rights, remedies, and benefits as if the bond, undertaking, or security were given and approved as required by this code."

From the record in this case, it appears that notice of appeal was served on June 2, 1914, and filed June 5, 1914, in the district court, and that a writing purporting to be an undertaking on appeal, was filed on the 12th day of June, 1914, which was ten days after the service of the notice of appeal upon the adverse party, and seven days after filing with the clerk.

Under sec. 4808, *supra,* counsel for respondent contends that the appeal is ineffectual for any purpose, for the reason that the undertaking was not filed within the five days after service of the notice of appeal, and calls our attention to a number of decisions by this court, upon the question of the necessity for filing the notice and undertaking on appeal within the statutory time. As we view this case, it is not necessary to determine whether or not the undertaking on appeal is sufficient to meet the requirements of the statute, or that there has been a waiver by respondent of the insufficiency of the undertaking, by reason of his failure to take advantage of sec. 4809, Rev. Codes, which provides: "If any undertaking be insufficient or defective in any respect, such insufficiency or defect shall be deemed waived unless the respondent, within twenty days after the filing of such undertaking, shall file and serve upon the appellant or his attorney a notice, in writing, pointing out specifically the defects and insufficiency of such undertaking. No defect or insufficiency not thus specifically pointed out, shall subsequently be urged against the undertaking or the appeal."

Sec. 1058, Kerr's Codes of Cal., is practically the same as sec. 4935, *supra*, and in the case of *Lamberson v. Jefferds*, 116 Cal. 492, 48 Pac. 485, the court held that "Although county officers are not expressly mentioned in this section, where county officer prosecutes action not in his individual right, but on behalf of the county, he comes within reason of rule and is included within provisions of this section; county itself being real party in interest."

Sec. 4935, *supra*, does not include the words "county official"; neither does sec. 1058, Kerr's Code. However, the supreme court of California, in placing a construction upon this statute, held that where a county official prosecutes or defends in an action in his official capacity and not in his individual right, and the action is maintained or defended on behalf of the county; that such county officer comes within the reason of the rule, and is included within the provisions of the section above cited.

Counsel contends that in any event, the appellant, in the case at bar, would not be protected under the California decisions, or under section 4808, *supra*, for the reason that the county of which appellant is treasurer and *ex-officio* tax collector, is not the real party in interest, or in any sense a party in interest, and that said tax collector acts solely as agent for said high school district.

Session Laws 1911, sec. 137, subdivision "G," p. 537, provides that it is the duty of the board of trustees of rural high school districts "To estimate and vote the amount of tax necessary to support the school, at a meeting previous to September 1st in each year, and report the same to the board of county commissioners, which amount, ... shall be spread upon the tax-roll the same as other district taxes . . . . "

Sess. Laws 1911, sec. 138, p. 537, provides: "The duties of the officers of the board shall be the same as is prescribed by law for similar officers of other boards of school trustees, "

Sess. Laws 1913, sec. 65, p. 530, provides: "The tax for general school purposes, levied for the purpose of establishing and maintaining public schools in the several counties of this state, must be levied by the board of county commissioners at its session when the tax is by it levied for county purposes and must be collected by the same officers and in the same manner as other state and county taxes are collected, and paid into·the county treasury and apportioned to the county school fund."

Sess. Laws 1913, sec. 103, p. 206, provides that "The governing authorities of every city, town, village, school district, or any other district or municipality to which is delegated by law the power to levy taxes must, on or before the third Monday of September in each year, certify to the county auditor the tax rate levied by any such city, town, village, school district or other district or municipality, for the said year upon any property situated therein, and the county auditor shall on or before said date file a certified list of such levies in the office of the assessor and in the office of the tax collector."

In our opinion, a reasonable construction of the sections above referred to, would be that all school taxes, whether they be fixed by the board of trustees of a rural high school district (under Sess. Laws 1911, sec. 137, subdivision "G," p. 537), or by the board of county commissioners (under Sess. Laws 1913, sec. 65, p. 530), are placed upon the tax-roll, as all other taxes, and collected in the same manner and by the same official. Therefore, in an action against, or one maintained by or on behalf of a county treasurer and *ex-officio* tax collector, involving the validity of either a rural high school tax, or a general school tax, the official would be acting on behalf of a legal subdivision of the state government and not as the agent of a rural high school district, as contended by counsel for respondents.

In the case of *Trueman et al. v. Village of St. Maries et al.*, 21 Ida. 632, 123 Pac. 508, wherein the village of St. Maries was appellant, a motion was made to dismiss the appeal on the ground that no undertaking was given as provided by law. Counsel for the village relied upon sec. 4935, *supra,* and

furnished no undertaking upon appeal. Upon the argument
of the motion to dismiss the appeal, counsel for respondent
contended that the word "city" as used in sec. 4935, *supra,* did
not include villages organized under the laws of the state, and
that the statute was only intended as immunity to cities, and
not towns or villages. In that case, the court held "that in
the law regulating the organization and government of cities
and villages in this state, the words 'cities,' 'villages' and
'towns' have been used indiscriminately, and one word for
the other; and we have no doubt whatever but that the legislature intended, in using the word 'city' in the above act, to
include all municipal corporations organized under the laws
of the state governing the organization of cities and villages,
and to exempt the state and county, and all municipalities
organized as such, as cities and villages." The motion to dismiss was denied.

Whenever an action is brought by or against state officers,
and such officers prosecute or defend in said action, in their
official capacity, acting for, or defending the rights of the
state, or any legal subdivision thereof, they are permitted to
so act without furnishing costs or undertakings on appeal.
This same rule applies to all state, county, district and municipal officers, while engaged in protecting the rights of the
people in the courts. This, we think, is but a reasonable construction of sec. 4935, *supra.* Any other rule might seriously
tend to defeat the interest of the public in protecting its legal
rights in the courts.

In the case of *Holmes v. City of Mattoon,* 111 Ill. 27, 53
Am. Rep. 602, we think the rule is there correctly stated, as
follows:

"Public municipalities, such as counties, cities, villages,
towns and school districts, and all officers suing for or defending the rights of the state, or acting for or instead of the
state in respect of public rights, being only instrumentalities
of the state, may constitutionally be authorized to sue without the payment of costs, or conforming to all the requirements imposed by the law upon natural persons or corporations formed for private gain." In that opinion the court

says: "The state, whatever its form or its powers, has the un-questioned right, as representing the sovereign power, to prosecute and defend all suits and maintain all legal proceed-ings without costs or other restrictions, unless imposed by fundamental law, or self-imposed by legislative enactment. .... From and before the organization of the state it has ever prosecuted and defended suits, criminal and civil, with-out liability for costs, damages or forfeitures, and has prose-cuted writs of error without bonds or any restrictions what-ever. .... It is believed that in no government, in ancient or modern times, has it been required to give bond for the payment of the costs of litigation, before bringing suit, or an appeal, or on error. .... This being true of the state gov-ernment, it is necessarily true of all its officers, agents and instrumentalities, while employed in seeking the rights of the government in the courts of justice. Hence, officers suing for or defending the rights of the state are acting for and in the stead of the state, and to that extent not only may but should be permitted to do so on the same terms and for the same reasons the state is permitted to sue for or defend its rights. •

"Again, municipalities, such as counties, cities, villages, towns, school districts .... under the patronage and control of the state, and all public officers when suing or defending in their official capacity for the benefit of the public, are the instruments of the state to carry out its powers for the public welfare, and in exercising their powers and enforcing public rights they act as agents, and may have extended to them the same exemptions in suits as belong to the state."

We are of the opinion that the appellant comes within the provision of sec. 4935, *supra,* and that he was not required to furnish an undertaking on appeal.

The conclusions reached upon this question, dispose of the second ground of respondent's motion to dismiss the appeal.

We come now to the third, fourth and fifth grounds of the motion to dismiss the appeal.

The record shows that the appeal in this case was perfected on June 5, 1914; that the transcript was filed in this court on

August 29, 1914, and that no extension of time was granted
by the court. Rule 23 of this court provides: "In all cases
where an appeal is perfected, ... transcripts of the record
. . . . must be served upon the adverse party and filed in this
court within sixty days after the appeal is perfected . . . .
and the same must be certified to be correct by the attorneys
of the respective parties or by the clerk of the court from
which the appeal is taken. Written evidence of the service
of the transcript upon the adverse party shall be filed therewith." This transcript was not filed until the expiration of
eighty-five days after the appeal was perfected. There was
no *praecipe* filed with the reporter and no transcript of the
testimony appears in the record. However, from the findings
of fact, it appears that "evidence was introduced on behalf
of the plaintiff" and it also appears from the transcript, that
there was one exhibit at least, introduced in evidence, which
is found in the transcript. What the evidence was that was
introduced on behalf of the plaintiff, we are not advised and
we have no means of knowing from the transcript.

It nowhere appears that the appellant filed his *praecipe* for
transcript with the clerk within five days after the filing of
the notice of appeal. There is no stipulation by the attorneys
that the clerk's transcript contains a true and correct transcript of the proceedings had before the trial court. Rule 26
of this court provides: "If the transcript of the record is not
filed within the time prescribed by Rule 23, the appeal . . . .
may be dismissed, on motion, without notice, ... " It was
clearly the duty of the attorney for appellant to use reasonable diligence to the end that the clerk complete his transcript
and that the same be served upon the opposing counsel within
the time prescribed by the rules of this court.

Sess. Laws 1911, sec. 3, p. 376, provides that the appellant
shall file with the transcript "appropriate affidavit or admission of service," and Rule 23 of this court, contains substantially the same provision. The transcript in this case affirmatively shows a failure to comply with these requirements.
We are not unmindful of the fact that an affidavit was filed
with the clerk of this court, by permission, on the 25th day

of January, 1915, subsequent to the argument of the motion
to dismiss the appeal.   We have carefully examined the contents of the affidavit and do not feel warranted in holding
that it is sufficient proof of service of the transcript upon
counsel for respondents, as it is altogether too indefinite and
uncertain.

The clerk of the trial court certifies "that the within and
foregoing transcript is compiled and bound under my direction as a true and correct transcript of the proceedings therein
contained, and that said transcript contains all the papers
specified in the *praecipe* filed with me, and further, that no
praecipe or order for reporter's transcript has been filed."
Whether the *praecipe* filed with the clerk enumerates all of
the proceedings had in the trial court, we are left to conjec-
ture.   From his certificate it would appear that it is not a
true and correct transcript of all of the proceedings, but is
made up of the papers specified in the *praecipe*.   Sess. Laws
1911, sec. 4818, p. 375, provides: "On an appeal from a final
judgment the appellant must furnish the court with a copy
of the notice of appeal, of the judgment-roll and of any bill
of exceptions or reporter's transcript. . . . . " The clerk's
certificate does not certify that the transcript contains a true
and correct copy of the judgment-roll.   It is easy to determine from the transcript what papers are included, which are
a part of the judgment-roll, but we are unable to determine
what papers are omitted that might properly be a part of
this judgment-roll.   The certificate of the clerk is insufficient.

We therefore conclude that there was a total failure to
comply with the statutes, or rules of this court, and that this
case comes within the rule announced in the case of the *First
Nat. Bank of American Falls, Idaho, v. Shaw,* 24 Ida. 134, 132
Pac. 802; *Strand v. Crooked River Min. & M. Co.,* 23 Ida.
577, 131 Pac. 5.   In the latter case it is held: "Where it appears from the record on appeal that the transcript was not
served upon the adverse party, and a motion is made in this
court to dismiss the appeal upon the ground that such transcript was not served, said motion will be sustained, as such

statute is mandatory and requires the transcript to be served."

Learned counsel for appellant earnestly contends that these objections have been waived under sec. 4809. That section has reference to the first and second grounds upon which counsel for respondent relies, but in our opinion has no application to the remaining three grounds, which, we think, are all well taken and fatal to this appeal.

If an appeal is to be considered by this court, counsel for appellant must exercise diligence in complying with the statutes and rules of this court governing such appeals. It is clearly the duty of counsel to diligently prosecute his appeal to a final determination in this court, and while, under the new practice act, as provided in Session Laws of 1911, pages 375–377, a great deal of the clerical work that was formerly required to be done by the attorney for appellant is now required of clerks of the district courts and court stenographers, counsel is not entirely relieved of responsibility. It is still his duty to procure from the district judge the necessary order directing the court reporter to prepare a transcript of the evidence, or specified portions thereof. It is also incumbent upon counsel to file with the clerk within the time allowed under the statute a *praecipe* for a transcript of the papers which he desires to be used on appeal, and should such *praecipe* fail to contain a request for all necessary papers or transcript and they are not found in the transcript on appeal, the responsibility will rest in the first instance with the counsel for appellant. It must also affirmatively appear that service upon counsel for respondent has been duly made of the transcript and brief within the time prescribed by the rules of this court; otherwise, upon motion, said appeal may be dismissed.

The appeal in this case is hereby dismissed. Costs are awarded to respondents.

Sullivan, C. J., and Morgan, J., concur.

(March 2, 1915.)

JOHN T. WOODLAND, Respondent, v. PORTNEUF-MARSH VALLEY IRRIGATION COMPANY, a Corporation, Appellant.

[146 Pac. 000.]

LIABILITY FOR DAMAGE CAUSED BY WASTE WATER—INDEPENDENT TORT-FEASORS—PROOF REQUIRED—MEASURE OF RECOVERY—INSTRUCTIONS.

1. Where one contributes as an independent tort-feasor toward causing an injury, he will be liable for the injury done by him, although his acts or negligence alone and without the contributing acts or negligence of others might not have caused the injury to occur.

2. Each one of several, acting independently, who wrongfully permits water to waste on to the land of another, is liable for his proportionate share of the injury caused thereby, even though the water allowed to run down by each would do no harm if not combined with that of the others, and the injury is actually caused by the combined flow wherein the waters from all sources are mixed and indistinguishable.

3. If injury follows as the combined result of the wrongful acts of several, acting independently, recovery may be had severally against each of such independent tort-feasors, in proportion to the contribution of each to the injury.

4. Exact and definite measurements of the respective quantities of water from different sources are not essential to sustain the verdict of a jury in determining what amount of damages a defendant corporation, as an independent tort-feasor, should pay as compensation for the injury caused by its part of such waters, although some evidence in that respect is essential.

5. *Held*, that the evidence in this case is sufficient to sustain the verdict in plaintiff's favor for the amount of damage caused by the defendant's waste water.

6. *Held*, that the court properly instructed the jury as to the measure of defendant's liability.

7. *Held*, that no reversible error appears in the trial court's rulings upon the admissibility of evidence.

APPEAL from the District Court of the Fifth Judicial District for Bannock County. Hon. J. M. Stevens, Presiding Judge.

Action for injury to hay crop by flooding land with waste water. Verdict and judgment for plaintiff. Defendant appeals. *Affirmed.*

Edwin Snow, for Appellant.

In actions at law, as distinguished from equity, independent tort-feasors, the act of each of whom alone would have caused some damage, are not liable jointly, but each is liable severally only for the proportion of the damage caused by him. (*Watson v. Colusa etc. Min. Co.*, 31 Mont. 513, 79 Pac. 14; *Equitable Powder Mfg. Co. v. Cleveland etc. R. Co.*, 155 Ill. App. 265, and affirmed in 246 Ill. 582, 92 N. E. 979; 2 Farnham on Waters, p. 1716; *Sun Company v. Wyatt*, 48 Tex. Civ. App. 349, 107 S. W. 934; *Willard v. Redbank Oil Co.*, 151 Ill. App. 433; *Pacific Livestock Co. v. Murray*, 45 Or. 103, 76 Pac. 1079.)

Budge & Barnard, for Respondent.

An irrigation company cannot collect natural drainage waters and pour them in one volume on lands of another so as to increase the damage above that which would have resulted from the usual and ordinary flow of such waters. (*Teeter v. Nampa etc. Irr. Dist.*, 19 Ida. 355, 114 Pac. 8.)

DAVIS, District Judge.—In this action the plaintiff, John T. Woodland, sought to recover damages in the sum of $1,500 for loss of his hay crop, alleged to have been caused by the flooding of his land with water from the canal system owned and operated by the Portneuf-Marsh Valley Irrigation Company, a corporation. The jury awarded plaintiff $700 damages, and defendant appeals from the judgment of the lower court in plaintiff's favor for this amount and costs.

It is established by the evidence and admitted by the company that some water from its canals contributed toward the flow that overflowed Woodland's land and injured his hay. In defense it is contended by the company that the evidence does not show that the water wrongfully discharged from the canals, or laterals of its irrigation system, was sufficient by itself to overflow the channel of the creek through Woodland's land or cause any of the injury to his crops. But this is not a good defense, even though true, because where one contributes as an independent tort-feasor toward causing an injury, he will be liable for the injury done by him, although his acts or negligence alone might not have caused any injury. In this case the evidence tends to prove that there were at least six sources from which the water came that injured Woodland's hay, and it is not contended by him that the company was responsible for more than one. And, while the evidence is very indefinite as to the relative and specific amount of water from each source, it is sufficient to show that considerable water from the company's canals wrongfully ran into the creek that overflowed its banks and flooded Woodland's property. And everyone who permits water to waste on to the land of others without right is liable for his proportionate share of the injury caused or the harm resulting therefrom, even though the water allowed to run down by each would do no harm if not combined with that of others, and the injury is caused by the combined flow wherein the waters of all are mixed and indistinguishable. If the injury follows as the combined result of the wrongful acts of several, acting independently, recovery may be had severally against each of such independent tort-feasors in proportion to the contribution of each to the injury. (Gould on Watercourses, par. 222; *Sloggy v. Dilworth*, 38 Minn. 179, 8 Am. St. 656, 36 N. W. 451; 21 Am. & Eng. Ency. of Law, 719.)

The evidence is sufficient to sustain a verdict in plaintiff's favor for the amount of damage caused by the company's waste water, where it appears by a preponderance of the evidence that the company wrongfully permitted waste water to mix with other waters and the combined flow spread over Woodland's land to his damage. Exact and definite measurements of such waters are not essential to sustain the verdict of a jury in determining what amount of damages a company should pay under such circumstances as compensation for the injury caused by its part of such waters, although some evidence in that respect is essential.

The evidence in this case appears to be sufficient to sustain the judgment, especially in view of the rule that this court will not disturb the verdict of a jury where there is a substantial conflict in the evidence on which the verdict is based.

The company requested an instruction as follows:

"If you find that the plaintiff was damaged by the waters of irrigation ditches of settlers or seepage water, combined with the water of the defendant, then the defendant would be liable only for the proportionate amount of damage actually caused by the waters from the defendant's own ditch."

The court gave in lieu thereof the following instruction:

"The defendant would not be responsible for damages caused to the plaintiff's crops by reason of rains, cloudbursts or any other natural causes, nor would it be responsible for any damage due to water being discharged upon the plaintiff's lands, if there was any discharged thereon, through the irrigation ditches or canals of individual settlers over which the defendant had no control. Nor would it be responsible for any damage caused by seepage water due to the irrigation by the settlers of their respective lands. The defendant is liable, if at all, only for such damage as you may find it actually caused to plaintiff's crops through negligently allowing waters of the Portneuf river, brought through its laterals for irrigation purposes, to escape upon plaintiff's lands."

The instruction given by the court correctly states the law, and was substantially the same in legal effect on the point wherein complained of as the instruction requested by the irrigation company which was refused and which refusal the company assigns as error.

There is no reversible error in the trial court's rulings upon the admissibility of evidence.

The judgment of the district court is therefore affirmed. Costs awarded to respondent.

Sullivan, C. J., and Morgan, J., concur.

(March 8, 1915.)

E. W. PEASE, Appellant, v. CITY OF PAYETTE, a Municipal Corporation, Respondent.

[146 Pac. 000.]

MUNICIPAL CORPORATION—PUBLIC IMPROVEMENTS CONTRACT—SPECIFICA-
TIONS—VALIDITY OF CONTRACT—IMPROVEMENT BONDS.

  1. The provisions in the specifications for street improvements to
the effect that the contractor shall be responsible for all defects,
damage to fences, sidewalks, water-pipes, sewers, etc., and other
specifications and requirements contained in subdivisions 8, 17, 27
and 32, do not make the contract invalid or void, as all of said
specifications require only what was necessary to be done in order
to construct and complete such improvements, and do not tend to
increase the cost of such improvements beyond what said contractor
should be required to do or pay under the laws of this state.

  2. The acceptance by the city of a private bond instead of a
surety company bond, as provided by subdivision 8 of the specifications, is not sufficient to invalidate the contract and could only be
taken advantage of by the city itself.

APPEAL from the District Court of the Seventh Judicial
District for Canyon County. Hon. Ed. L. Bryan, Judge.

Action to test the validity of a contract for the construction
of sidewalks and curbs in an Improvement District of the City
of Payette. Judgment for the defendant. *Affirmed.*

Alfred F. Stone, for Appellant.

The requirements of subdivisions 8, 17, 27 and 32 of the
specifications tend to increase the cost of construction, thereby
adding to the burden of the taxpayer, and for that reason
invalidate the contract in this case and the bonds to be issued
in payment for work done under such contract. (*Woollacott
v. Meekin,* 151 Cal. 701, 91 Pac. 612; *Blochman v. Spreckels,*
135 Cal. 662, 67 Pac. 1061, 57 L. R. A. 213.)

A contract was held void where similar provisions were embraced in the bond. (*Inge v. Board of Public Works,* 135 Ala.
187, 93 Am. St. 20, 33 So. 678.)

The provisions in a contract whereby the contractor is required to give bond "for keeping the streets so improved in thorough repair for the term of five years from the completion of the contract" not being authorized by statute invalidates the contract for the work and vitiates the assessment levied thereunder. (*Brown v. Jenks*, 98 Cal. 10, 32 Pac. 701; *Alameda Macadamizing Co. v. Pringle*, 130 Cal. 226, 80 Am. St. 124, 62 Pac. 394, 52 L. R. A. 264; *Portland v. Bituminous Paving Co.*, 33 Or. 307, 72 Am. St. 713, 52 Pac. 28, 44 L. R. A. 527.) This same principle would apply whether the guaranty were to cover a period of one week, a month or a year.

It is fair to presume that the acceptance by the city council of the private bond in this case was in fact a letting of the contract upon more favorable terms than were offered other bidders. This being the case, the contract is void. (*Wickwire v. City of Elkhart*, 144 Ind. 305, 43 N. E. 216.)

A. H. Bowen and Scatterday & Van Duyn, for Respondent.

The first division of sec. 8 of the specifications is evidently intended, made and created for the purpose of insuring that the contractor shall deliver to the city a good and complete sidewalk and curb and in accordance with the plans and specifications, and does not refer to what may happen to the sidewalk or curb after it is accepted by the city, but before. (*Schindler v. Young*, 13 Cal. App. 18, 108 Pac. 733.)

The second subdivision of sec. 8 is not objectionable, and the California courts, having *Blochman v. Spreckels*, 135 Cal. 662, 67 Pac. 1061, 57 L. R. A. 213, as their chief authority, have expressly so held. (*Lantz v. Fishburn*, 17 Cal. App. 583, 120 Pac. 1070.)

Municipal officers may modify a contract, provided such modification does not substantially change the character of the work. (28 Cyc. 1047 (b).) Moreover, the city has the power to waive strict compliance with the terms of a contract. (28 Cyc. 1054 (k).)

The guaranty is to make good, defects, and not to keep up streets which were not defective. (*Portland v. Bituminous*

Paving & Imp. Co., 33 Or. 307, 72 Am. St. 713, 52 Pac. 28, 44 L. R. A. 527.)

Contrary to the California decisions, the majority of cases hold that a contract to keep the pavement or street in repair, whether or not it is defective, is good, because it is simply a guaranty of good workmanship. (*Louisville v. Henderson*, 5 Bush (Ky.), 521; *Covington v. Dressman*, 6 Bush (Ky.), 210; *Barber Asphalt Paving Co. v. Ullman*, 137 Mo. 543, 38 S. W. 458; *Gosnell v. Louisville*, 14 Ky. Law, 719; *Cole v. People*, 161 Ill. 16, 43 N. E. 607; *Latham v. Wilmette*, 168 Ill. 153, 48 N. E. 311; *Wilson v. Trenton*, 60 N. J. L. 394, 38 Atl. 635; *Allen v. Davenport*, 107 Iowa, 90, 77 N. W. 532; *Osburn v. Lyon*, 104 Iowa, 160, 73 N. W. 650; *Schnectady v. Union College*, 66 Hun, 179, 21 N. Y. Supp. 147; *Barber Asphalt Pav. Co. v. City of Louisville*, 123 Ky. 687, 97 S. W. 31, 9 L. R. A., N. S., 154; *Allen v. Labsap*, 188 Mo. 692, 87 S. W. 926, 3 Ann. Cas. 306.)

The contractor should not furnish defective work, and if there is any defective work that occurs through his fault, it is but reasonable that the city should have the right to demand that this defective work should be remedied by the contractor. (*Dillingham v. Spartanburg*, 75 S. C. 549, 117 Am. St. 923, 56 S. E. 381, 9 Ann. Cas. 828, 8 L. R. A., N. S., 412.)

Norris & Norris, *Amici Curiae*.

The provisions of sec. 8 of the specifications render the said contract illegal and void. (*Blochman v. Spreckels*, 135 Cal. 662, 67 Pac. 1061, 57 L. R. A. 213; *Van Loenen v. Gillespie*, 152 Cal. 222, 96 Pac. 87; *Woollacott v. Meekin*, 151 Cal. 701, 91 Pac. 612; *Hatch v. Nevills*, 7 Cal. Unrep. 341, 95 Pac. 43; *Glassell v. O'Dea*, 7 Cal. App. 472, 95 Pac. 44; *Mulberry v. O'Dea*, 4 Cal. App. 385, 88 Pac. 367; *Stansbury v. Poindexter*, 154 Cal. 709, 129 Am. St. 190, 99 Pac. 182; *True v. Fox*, 155 Cal. 534, 102 Pac. 263; *Inge v. Board of Public Works*, 135 Ala. 187, 93 Am. St. 20, 33 So. 678.)

Well considered cases hold that where a city is authorized to contract for paving its streets, it has no authority to incorporate in the contract an agreement for future maintenance. (*City Council of Montgomery v. Barnett*, 149 Ala.

119, 43 So. 92; *Excelsior Paving Co. v. Pierce* (Cal.), 33 Pac.
727; *McAllister v. Tacoma,* 9 Wash. 272, 37 Pac. 447, 658;
Kansas City v. Hanson, 8 Kan. App. 290, 55 Pac. 513.)

The objection to such provisions is not removed by the testimony of the contractor that such requirements did not enhance
the amount of his bid, as others might have bid a less sum if
the contract had not contained such provisions. (*Brown v.
Jenks,* 98 Cal. 10, 32 Pac. 701; *Stansbury v. Poindexter,* 154
Cal. 709, 129 Am. St. 190, 99 Pac. 182; *Excelsior Paving Co.
v. Pierce* (Cal.), 33 Pac. 727; *Excelsior Paving Co. v. Leach*
(Cal.), 34 Pac. 116.)

SULLIVAN, C. J.—This action was brought against the
City of Payette upon an agreed statement of facts, to test the
validity of a certain contract entered into between the city and
Lathrop & McComsey, copartners, for the grading and constructing of curbs and sidewalks in Local Sidewalk, Curbing
& Improvement District No. 1, of said city, and to test the
validity of the bonds to be issued by the City of Payette for
the purpose of paying for the work done under such contract.

The City of Payette has created within its boundaries a local
improvement district known as Local Sidewalk & Curbing
Improvement District No. 1 of said city, and has made an
assessment against the property therein, apportioning thereto
the expense of the construction work contemplated. Said city
on or about January 5, 1914, by resolution of its council, required notice to be given to contractors for bids upon the contemplated construction of the work in such district, and in
pursuance thereof such notices were given.

The bids received thereunder were not opened on the day
set therefor by reason of the fact that W. A. Coughanour had
in the meantime obtained a temporary injunction against said
City of Payette, restraining the opening of said bids. Upon
the dissolution of said injunction a new notice was given, stating that bids would be received up to noon of April 10, 1914,
in response to which four bids were submitted. The bids were
not opened upon the day set therefor by reason of the fact
that said Coughanour took an appeal from the order dissolving
the injunction, which was by the supreme court of this state

affirmed on or about July 10, 1914 (*Coughanour v. City of Payette,* 26 Ida. 280, 142 Pac. 1076), and immediately thereafter the last bids received were opened and the contract for doing the work let to said Lathrop & McComsey. The bids for the construction of the work were made upon certain plans and specifications attached to the agreed statement of the case, which specifications contained among other subdivisions Nos. 8, 17, 26, 27 and 32.

The provisions of these subdivisions and the failure to comply with the provisions of subd. 26 plaintiff claims invalidated the contract and the bonds to be issued in payment of the work to be done thereunder. The provisions of said subd. 26 have not been complied with, in that the said Lathrop & McComsey gave a private bond and not a surety company bond as required by said subdivision, and gave such private bond for sixty per cent of the estimated cost of the work under the contract as let. Said private bond was approved and accepted by the council of the City of Payette. Upon the approval of said contract, said Lathrop & McComsey immediately proceeded to commence work under said contract and have performed about $7,000 worth of labor and will, unless restrained, complete such contract, and the City of Payette will, unless restrained, issue bonds of the aforementioned improvement district in payment of said contract, and will collect assessments from plaintiff and others similarly situated.

This matter was heard upon the agreed statement of facts by the seventh judicial district court in and for Canyon county, and judgment was entered in favor of the city, from which judgment this appeal is taken.

The questions presented on this appeal concern the proper construction of said subdivisions above mentioned of the specifications under which the contract was let, and whether the requirements thereof tend to increase the cost of the work and whether they would prevent contractors from bidding for said work.

Respondents in their brief divided their argument into two subdivisions, under the following heads:

1. Are subdivisions 8, 17, 26, 27 and 32 of the purported plans and specifications such as to render the contract invalid

if it be admitted that said subdivisions are a part of said contract?

2. Subdivisions 8 and 27 are no part of the plans and specifications of the contract.

Said subdivisions are as follows:

Subd. 8. Defects or Damages. "All settlements, defects or damages in any portion of the works, whether caused by the contractor, his agents or the public at large, or resulting from strikes, fires or any acts of nature shall be repaired and made at the contractor's expense. All damages to fences, trees, sidewalks, waterpipes, sewers or other public or private property along or near the line of the work, or in the vicinity thereof, must, wherever the engineer shall direct, be made good to the satisfaction of the owners of the same, at the entire expense of the contractor. No private property outside of the line of the right of way shall be entered by the contractor without his first obtaining the consent of the owner."

Subd. 17. Inspectors. "The city or the engineer may appoint inspectors and any such inspector shall always have the right to stop the work, if in his opinion, the contractor is not complying with these specifications, plans, instructions and orders; and if at any time the inspector shall stop the work, the contractor shall not proceed again with said work until the engineer shall have examined and passed upon the question in dispute and the engineer's decision shall be final. Any work done after the inspector has ordered it stopped, as well as all work found at variance with these specifications, shall be at once removed by the contractor."

Subd. 26. Bond for Completion of Work. "The successful bidder shall furnish a Surety Co. Bond satisfactory to the City Council within thirty (30) days after the acceptance of the proposal by the City, for the faithful performance and successful completion of the work, and said bond to amount to 40 per cent of the amount of the contract."

Subd. 27. Guarantee Bond. "On or before the completion of the work and before final payment is made, the contractor shall furnish a good and sufficient Surety Co. bond for $10,000.00, same to run for one year from final completion of works, guaranteeing that the works shall be free from all defects, either in construction or material, or both, and guaranteeing that the repairing of any such defects appearing in the work within one year from the completion of contract shall be paid for by the contractor, said repairs to be made under the direction of the engineer.''

Subd. 32. Engineering Expenses, etc. ''It is further understood and agreed that the contractor, in addition to furnishing material, labor and doing the work as hereinbefore mentioned at the unit prices herein named, shall pay to the City of Payette for the purpose of applying on the overhead expenses such as engineering, inspection, etc., the sum of One Thousand and no one-hundredths (1,000.00) Dollars, as follows, to wit: At the time of payment of each monthly estimate, the same percentage of $1,000.00 as shown by the estimate for that month of the percentage of the work completed in said month.''

Counsel for appellant contends that the requirements of said subdivisions 8, 17, 27 and 32 tend to increase the cost of the work and prevent contractors from bidding thereon; while counsel for respondent contends that said subdivisions of the specifications are no part of the contract, and even if they were considered as a part of the contract, they would not make the contract invalid or void.

There is nothing in the provisions of subd. 8 of said specifications that would tend to increase the cost of said work or prevent contractors from bidding thereon, and there is nothing contained in said provisions but what the city had the right to require the improvement district to become responsible or liable for and to pay the same.

The same may be said of subdivisions 17, 27 and 32 of said specifications. All of the provisions of said specifications require only what was necessary to be done in order to complete the improvements contemplated in the construction of said improvements. The giving of a guaranty bond of $10,000 to run for one year from the final completion of the works, guaranteeing that the work shall be free from all defects and guaranteeing that the repairing of all such defects that may appear in the work from one year from completion shall be paid for by the contractor, is only a reasonable provision in such contract. Experience shows that such work ought to last, if properly done and the proper material is used, for one year. If it proves within that year to be defective either in construction or material, or both, then the contractor must repair the same or make it good. This condition in the contract or specifications certainly would not deter the honest contractor from bidding for such work, and it is proper and right that the improvement district should pay for work of that kind that should last for at least a year under ordinary conditions.

Subd. 32 of said specifications provides that the contractor, in addition to furnishing material, labor and doing the work as specified, shall also pay to the City of Payette for the purpose of applying on the overhead expenses, such as engineering, inspection, etc., the sum of $1,000. This cost or expense was absolutely necessary in order to have the work properly done and is an expense that the district should pay. From the wording of that specification, the $1,000 is clearly not all that the work required of the engineer would cost the city, for the $1,000 provided for is as stated therein, "for the purpose of applying on the overhead expenses," etc., clearly indicating that said sum did not pay all of such expenses but perhaps the greater portion thereof, since a certain sum to be applied on the payment of an indebtedness does not contemplate that the application of such sum would pay the cost or expense in full.

Subd. 26 of said specifications requires the successful bidder to furnish a surety company bond, satisfactory to the city council etc., to the amount of 40% of the contract price, conditioned on the faithful performance and successful completion of said work.

Instead of requiring the successful bidder to furnish a surety company bond, the city council permitted them to furnish a private bond and approved such bond, and it is contended that that action on the part of the council was illegal and amounted to a discrimination against other bidders.

There is nothing in this contention, since the council had the right to accept a private bond instead of a surety company bond, if it so desired, of the successful bidder. No doubt all who bid for this work made their bids with the expectation of giving a surety bond, and the reason for the provision no doubt was that there are many bidders outside of the state who would not desire to give a private bond and maybe could not give one that the city council would approve. Nothing appears in the record but that the private bond was just as good and safe as a surety company bond. That breach of the provisions referred to is not sufficient to invalidate the contract and could only be taken advantage of by the city itself. If the work was done in a defective manner, or not in accordance with the specifications, the city might refuse to accept the same and would not be liable on *quantum meruit*. (See 28 Cyc. 1054 (i).) The city has authority to waive a strict compliance with the terms of the contract if it desires to do so. (28 Cyc. 1054 (k).)

Without analyzing or citing in this opinion the authorities referred to by counsel for respondent and appellant as well as those cited by counsel appearing *amici curiae*, we are satisfied from our examination of them that none of such authorities which this court is willing to follow would require a reversal of the judgment of the trial court, since said subdivisions of said specifications do not tend to increase the cost of such improvements beyond what the improvement district should be required to pay under the laws of this state.

We therefore hold that said contract is a valid contract and the bonds proposed to be issued in payment for said work are valid bonds.

Finding no reversible error in the record, the judgment is affirmed, with costs in favor of the respondent.

Budge and Morgan, JJ., concur.

INDEX—VOL. 26.

ACCOMPLICES.

Who are and Their Corroboration.

1. Under the provisions of sec. 7871, Rev. Codes, the corroborating evidence required to substantiate the testimony of an accomplice must be upon some material fact or circumstance which, standing alone and independent of the testimony of the accomplice, tends to connect the defendant with the commission of the offense. (*State v. Knudston*, 11 Ida. 524, 83 Pac. 226, approved.) (State v. Grant, 189.)

2. When the question, as to whether a witness is an accomplice, arises in a criminal case under sec. 7871, Rev. Codes, it is the duty of the trial court to instruct the jury on the law of accomplices, and leave the question as to whether or not any witness is an accomplice in the commission of the offense charged, for the decision of the jury as a matter of fact, unless it appear without substantial conflict in the testimony that such witness was an accomplice. (State v. Grant, 189.)

3. In order to make a person an accomplice in the commission of a crime, some aiding, abetting or actual encouragement, by such person must be shown. Mere presence at the plotting of a crime or silent acquiescence in its commission is not, in the absence of a legal duty to act, sufficient to constitute one an accomplice. (State v. Grant, 189.)

4. The failure to disclose known facts regarding the commission of a crime does not render one having such knowledge an accomplice of the person who committed the crime. (State v. Grant, 189.)

ACCOUNTS.
See Executors and Administrators, 8–11.

ADJOINING OWNERS.

Excavations and Notice Thereof.

1. Under the provisions of sec. 3092, Rev. Codes, it is made the duty of a coterminous owner of real estate to give previous reasonable notice to another coterminous owner of his intention to make excavations on his adjoining land. (Zilka v. Graham, 163.)

2. Excavation by an owner on his own land, causing damage to a building on an adjoining owner's land, without the knowledge of,

ADJOINING OWNERS (Continued).

or previous notice to, such adjoining owner, is evidence of want of care in doing the work. (Zilka v. Graham, 163.)

3. *Held*, that there is.substantial evidence to sustain the verdict of the jury. (Zilka v. Graham, 163.)

4. *Held*, that the court did not err in taxing the costs. (Zilka w. Graham, 163.)

ADMINISTRATORS.

See Executors and Administrators.

AGENCY.

See Principal and Agent.

ALIBI.

See Criminal Law, 10.

ALTERATION OF INSTRUMENTS.

See Bills and Notes.

AMENDMENT.

· See Pleading, 3.

APPEAL AND ERROR.

Notice of Appeal.

1. Under the provisions of sec. 4808, Rev. Codes, the notice of appeal must be served on the adverse party or his attorney. (Miller v. Wallace, 373.)

2. Under the provisions of said section, the notice of appeal must be served upon every party whose interests might be affected by the reversal of the order or judgment appealed from, irrespective of whether they are plaintiffs, defendants or intervenors. (Miller v. Wallace, 373.)

3. A party who is named as one of the defendants in a complaint and on whom it does not appear that summons has been served nor that he appeared in the action, on an appeal from a judgment entered in favor of his codefendant, is not an adverse party on whom the notice of appeal must be served, under the provisions of sec. 4808, Rev. Codes. (Kissler v. Moss, 516.)

Transcript and Record.

4. In all cases where an appeal is perfected, a transcript of the record must be served upon the adverse party and filed in this court within sixty days after the appeal is perfected, unless an extension

APPEAL AND ERROR (Continued).

of time be granted; otherwise the appeal will be dismissed. (Coon v. Sommercamp, 776.)

5. Where it appears from the record on appeal that the transcript was not served upon the adverse party and a motion is made in this court to dismiss the appeal for that reason, and where an affidavit by counsel for appellant, attempting to show service, but uncertain and indefinite in its terms, is filed subsequent to the hearing of the motion to dismiss the appeal, it will not be considered by the court as sufficient proof of service of the transcript and the motion to dismiss will be allowed. (Coon v. Sommercamp, 776.)

6. Upon an appeal from a judgment, the clerk is required to furnish the court with a copy of the notice of appeal, the judgment-roll and any bill of exceptions or reporter's transcript. Where the clerk certifies that the transcript of the proceedings in the trial court "contains all the papers specified in the *praecipe* filed with me," said certificate is insufficient. (Coon v. Sommercamp, 776.)

Undertaking and Costs.

7. A motion to dismiss an appeal upon the ground that no undertaking on appeal or deposit of money, in lieu thereof, was made or deposited with the clerk of the district court within five days after the service of the notice of appeal, will be denied and the appeal will be heard upon its merits when such an undertaking in due form and in the proper amount was, in fact, filed in time and transmitted to this court but omitted from the transcript through oversight on the part of the clerk. (Washington County Land & Development Co. v. Weiser Nat. Bank, 717.)

8. Whenever an action is brought by or against state, county or municipal officers, and such officers prosecute or defend in said action in their official capacity, acting for or defending the rights of the state, county or municipality, or any legal subdivision thereof, they are permitted to so act without furnishing costs or undertakings on appeal. (Sec. 4935, *supra.*) (Coon v. Sommercamp, 776.)

Review and Reversal.

9. Where there is a substantial conflict in the evidence, the verdict of the jury will not be disturbed on appeal. (Montgomery v. Gray, 585.)

10. Where counsel for respective parties agree that should the conclusion of the court be adverse to the contention of appellant upon one question, the remaining objections assigned become immaterial, and when it appears from the record that a consideration of said questions is not necessary to a final determination of the

APPEAL AND ERROR (Continued).

cause under consideration, the same will not be decided by the court. (Jennings v. Idaho Railway, Light & Power Co., 703.)

11. A judgment will not be reversed on account of alleged errors that have been consented to or invited, especially where it appears that appellant has not been prejudiced thereby. (Trask v. Boise King Placers Co., 290.)

12. Where a party is entitled to have a verdict directed in his favor at the close of the evidence and the case is reversed on his appeal, a new trial will not be ordered. The case will be remanded, with instructions that judgment be entered in his favor. (Exchange State Bank v. Taber, 723.)

12a. No judgment will be reversed upon appeal by reason of errors or defects in the proceedings below which do not affect the substantial rights of the parties. (Richardson v. Bohney, 35.)

Rehearing.

13. Granting a rehearing of a case does not *ipso facto* reverse a former decision, but it is suspended by the order of rehearing. (Cameron Lumber Co. v. Stack-Gibbs Lumber Co., 626.)

14. Where a rehearing is granted and the court fails to agree upon a decision in the case, it does not lose jurisdiction, and under section 3820, Rev. Codes, another hearing must be ordered. (Cameron Lumber Co. v. Stack-Gibbs Lumber Co., 626.)

15. Where there is a substantial conflict in the evidence, this court will not undertake to weigh the proof to ascertain which side has the preponderance, and where there is such conflict in the evidence, it will not disturb the findings of the trial court. (Cameron Lumber Co. v. Stack-Gibbs Lumber Co., 626.)

See Criminal Law, 1–9.

APPEARANCES.

In General.

1. A stipulation that the defendant have until a certain date to make settlement of the amount claimed by plaintiff and containing a promise on the part of the defendant that in the event the settlement is not made by that time, it will confess judgment in the action then pending between the parties, is not an appearance contemplated by sec. 4892, Rev. Codes. (Washington County Land & Development Co. v. Weiser National Bank, 717.)

2. A defendant appears in an action when he answers, demurs or gives the plaintiff written notice of his appearance or when an attorney gives notice of appearance for him. (Washington County Land & Development Co. v. Weiser National Bank, 717.)

APPEARANCES (Continued).

3. The filing of a petition and bond for a removal to the federal court is not an appearance in the state court, under the provisions of the Revised Codes of Idaho. (State v. American Surety Co., 652.)

ARSON.

Sentence.

1. *Held*, that under the provisions of sec. 1, chap. 200, of the laws of 1911 (Sess. Laws. 1911, p. 664), amending sec. 1 of the indeterminate sentence act of 1909, taken together with sec. 7008, Rev. Codes, fixing the penalty for the crime of arson in the first degree at a minimum sentence of two years and maximum for life, the defendant was legally sentenced to serve a maximum term of fifty years in the state penitentiary, with a minimum of twenty-five years. (State v. Grant, 189.)

ASSAULT TO COMMIT RAPE.

See Rape.

ATTORNEY FEES.

See Bills and Notes, 1; Mortgages, 5.

AUTOMOBILES.

See Motor Vehicle Act.

BANKRUPTCY.

Transfers and Assignments—Action by Trustee.

1. In an action by a trustee in bankruptcy to set aside a transfer, on the ground that it effects a preference, and also that it is voidable as a fraud upon other creditors, under subdivision "e" of sec. 67 of the present bankruptcy law; the question as to a preference is determined from the facts and circumstances, and unless these are such as to produce a reasonable cause of belief in the mind of the person receiving the transfer that its enforcement would effect a preference, the transaction must be held valid. On the question as to whether a certain transfer is void because it is a fraud upon other creditors, the question must be determined by the evidence in each case. (Cauthorn v. Burley State Bank, 532.)

2. *Held*, that title 12 of chapter 17, Rev. Codes, was suspended and superseded by the national bankruptcy law of 1898. (Capital Lumber Co. v. Saunders, 408.)

3. *Held*, that sec. 5932 is a necessary part of said title 12 and not now in force. (Capital Lumber Co. v. Saunders, 408.)

BANKRUPTCY (Continued).

4. *Held*, that assignments in conformity with the common-law rules relating to them are not void under sec. 3169. (Capital Lumber Co. v. Saunders, 408.)

5. *Held*, that under sec. 3171, Rev. Codes, the question of fraudulent intent as to transfers of property is one of fact. (Capital Lumber Co. v. Saunders, 408.)

6. In an action by a trustee of a bankrupt estate to set aside a transfer on the ground that a preference has, by such transfer, been created within the inhibition of the act of Congress, and the several acts amendatory thereof, to establish a uniform act of bankruptcy in the United States, said trustee must prove by sufficient evidence that the bankrupt (1) while insolvent, (2) within four months of the bankruptcy, (3) made the transfer in question, (4) that the creditor receiving the transfer will be thereby entitled to obtain a greater percentage of his debts than other creditors of the same class, and (5) that the creditor had reasonable cause to believe that the enforcement of such transfer would effect a preference. (Soule v. First National Bank, 66.)

7. In an action of this character an inquiry as to the intent of the bankrupt to effect a preference is not necessary. (Soule v. First National Bank, 66.)

8. The burden of proof that the creditor had reasonable cause to believe that the enforcement of a transfer would effect a preference is upon the trustee. (Soule v. First National Bank, 66.)

9. An instruction based upon a legislative enactment which had theretofore been repealed, and which was not then in force, is error. (Soule v. First National Bank, 66.)

10. Instruction based upon lack of denial, and admission thereby made, examined and found sufficient. (Soule v. First National Bank, 66.)

11. Instructions examined and found erroneous. (Soule v. First National Bank, 66.)

BANKS AND BANKING.

Bank Commissioners.

1. The legislature in enacting sec. 3001, Rev. Codes, making it the duty of the bank commissioner to make an examination of state banks, imposed such duty for the benefit and protection of the depositors as well as the public. (State v. American Surety Co., 652.)

2. A bank commissioner in the exercise of discretionary duties is not responsible to anyone receiving an injury through a breach of his official duty, unless he acts maliciously and wilfully wrong, or clearly abuses his discretion to the extent of acting unfaithfully and in bad faith. (State v. American Surety Co., 652.)

BANKS AND BANKING (Continued).

3. In an action by an injured party against the surety on the bond of the bank commissioner executed under sec. 191, Rev. Codes, for failure of said commissioner to faithfully perform his duty, it is not necessary to first proceed and have the damages of the injured party adjudged against the commissioner. (State v. American Surety Co., 652.)

4. Under a joint and several bond executed pursuant to sec. 191, Rev. Codes, it is not necessary to sue jointly the principal and surety, but suit may be maintained against either severally. (State v. American Surety Co., 652.)

5. *Held*, that the complaint herein states a cause of action. (State v. American Surety Co., 652.)

BILLS AND NOTES.

Alterations—Action on Note—Attorney Fees.

1. The order of trial in a civil case is provided by sec. 4383, Rev. Codes, and directs that the trial must proceed in the order there indicated, unless the judge, for special reasons, otherwise directs, and where an action is brought on promissory notes and the respondent admits the execution of such notes but makes special defenses thereto, it rests in the sound discretion of the trial court to direct the order of addressing the jury, and unless there is a clear abuse of discretion, this court will not disturb the verdict. (Exchange State Bank v. Taber, 723.)

2. Where a note appears to have been altered in a material respect, the *onus* is on the party seeking to enforce the payment to show that it is not void, but where the respondent in his answer and counterclaim, in express terms, admits the execution and delivery of the notes, which are set out in full in the complaint, and when introduced in evidence, are in the same condition as they appeared in the complaint, the respondent should not be permitted to introduce evidence tending to establish any alteration, nor should the court instruct the jury upon the law governing the alteration of written instruments. (Exchange State Bank v. Taber, 723.)

3. Where the notes are set out in the complaint and when introduced in evidence, are in the same condition as they appear in the complaint, and respondent admits in express terms the execution and delivery of the notes, it will be presumed that any alteration was made prior to the execution of the notes. (Exchange State Bank v. Taber, 723.)

4. Refusal to give certain instructions requested by appellant, *held* to be error. (Exchange State Bank v. Taber, 723.)

5. *Held*, that it was error to reject certain evidence offered by appellant. (Exchange State Bank v. Taber, 723.)

BILLS AND NOTES (Continued).

6. The admission of certain evidence over the objection of the appellant, *held* to be error. (Exchange State Bank v. Taber, 723.)

7. Evidence *held* sufficient to sustain the verdict of the jury and the judgment of the court awarding attorney's fees. (Pettingill v. MacWilliams, 344.)

8. *Held*, that the bank came into the possession of said promissory note in due course and before maturity. (Pettingill v. MacWilliams, 344.)

BONDS.

Estoppel to Question Validity.

1. A taxpayer may, by his conduct, be estopped from questioning the validity of municipal bonds because of alleged irregularities or infirmities in their issue. (Page v. Oneida Irrigation District, 108.)

See Appeal and Error, 7; Counties; Horticultural Act, 7; Municipal Corporations, 6, 7.

BOUNDARIES.

Disputes—Meander Lines.

1. Where the original government survey of a fractional section of land, abutting on a lake, left a tract of nearly 40 acres between the meander line of said section and the water line of the lake, which tract remained unsurveyed, and was not shown on the government plat, and thereafter a dispute arose between land owners and land claimants, as to whether such unplatted land belonged to the fractional section, such dispute involved a question of law which could not be determined by the parties without adjudication in the proper court. (Coolin v. Anderson, 47.)

See Mistake; Navigable Waters, 6–13.

BOUNTIES.

For Extermination of Predatory Animals.

1. Secs. 1197 and 1198, Rev. Codes, provide for the extermination of predatory animals through the employment by the livestock sanitary board of "experienced, competent and skilful hunters and trappers" at a *per diem* compensation. Such method having been specified by the statute, the board and the state veterinarian acting with it are precluded from resorting to other methods of extermination not authorized by law, such as the payment of bounties for the destruction of such animals by persons not in the employ of the sanitary board. (State v. Johnson, 203.)

2. *Held*, that the trial court properly advised the jury to acquit the defendants. (State v. Johnson, 203.)

BRIDGES.

Construction by Municipality.

1. *Held*, under the statutes of this state that the city council or village trustees of incorporated cities and villages have the exclusive control of the streets and highways within such corporate limits, and have full power to construct bridges and repair and maintain the same within such corporate limits. (City of Kellogg v. McRae, 73.)

2. *Held*, that the board of county commissioners have not the control of the roads and bridges within the corporate limits of a city or village, and that they are not required, under the law, to construct and maintain bridges exceeding sixty feet in length at the expense of the county, over streams crossing highways within such corporate limits. (City of Kellogg v. McRae, 73.)

BROKERS.

See Principal Agent.

BULK SALE ACT.

See Sales.

CAREY ACT LIEN.

See Irrigation, 16–21.

CHATTEL MORTGAGE.

In General.

1. Personal property described in a chattel mortgage as "1333 early spring lambs, branded O—" is a sufficient description as between the mortgagor and the mortgagee. (Hare v. Young, 691.)

2. A chattel mortgage, although not accompanied by an affidavit that it is executed in good faith and without any design to hinder, delay or defraud creditors, is valid as between the mortgagor and the mortgagee. (Hare v. Young, 691.)

2a. *Held*, a chattel mortgage on a stock of goods which provides that the mortgagors may retain possession of the goods, sell them in the usual course of business, and each week pay a certain per cent of the gross proceeds of sales on the mortgage debt, is not void *per se*, but the question of its validity must be determined by the good faith or lack of good faith of the parties to the transaction. (Cauthorn v. Burley State Bank, 532.)

3. Where the evidence shows that the mortgagor of personal property had, for many years, been in possession of the property, dealt with it as his own, sold and otherwise disposed of portions of it and mortgaged other portions of it without objection, although

CHATTEL MORTGAGE (Continued).

there is evidence tending to show that his interest was that of a lessee, the finding of the trial court that the mortgagor was the owner of the property at the time he gave the mortgage is sustained by the evidence. (Hare v. Young, 682.)

4. The facts in this case examined and found to justify the allowance of $750 as an attorney's fee to be awarded to plaintiffs under the terms of the note and mortgage. (Hare v. Young, 682.)

5. Allegations in an answer that a portion of the amount of money secured by a mortgage was a pre-existing debt, and that no levy was made on the property by the mortgagee, and that the mortgagee did not take nor attempt to take possession of it, *held*, to be immaterial, and that it was not error for the trial court to fail to make a finding of fact upon them. (Hare v. Young, 682.)

6. The evidence in this case examined and the conclusion reached that the trial court was justified in finding that the presumption of ownership created by the possession of the property, under the facts and circumstances in this case, is not overcome by the testimony introduced to rebut it. (Hare v. Young, 691.)

CHECKS.
See Larceny.

COMITY.
See Contracts.

COMMUNITY PROPERTY.
See Husband and Wife, 1–6.

COMPLAINT.
See Indictment and Information.

CONFLICT OF LAWS.
See Contracts.

CONTINUANCE.
In Criminal Case.

1. Where an affidavit for the postponement of the trial of a criminal action is based on the absence of a material witness and of a document in the possession of such witness, even though the testimony of such witness and the document itself are of impeaching character, and the affidavit shows that after being served with a subpoena in the case such witness has left the state to answer to a charge of felony in another state, refusing to surrender such docu-

CONTINUANCE (Continued).

ment because he deems it material in his own trial, but there is reasonable probability that he will return with the document and testify if the present trial is postponed as requested, for a period of ten days or two weeks, and it does not appear that either the court or the state will be incommoded by such postponement, it is an abuse of discretion on the part of the trial court to refuse such postponement. (State v. Cannon, 182.)

CONTRACTS.

Comity Between States.

1. In order to invoke the doctrine of comity between states with respect to contracts, it is incumbent upon the party claiming such a benefit to show that his is such a contract as is contemplated by the doctrine. He must produce proof that the contract in behalf of which he seeks to invoke this rule is a foreign contract contemplated by the rule. (Hare v. Young, 682.)

CORPORATIONS.

Foreign Companies.

1. Under sec. 2792, Rev. Codes, which provides "That foreign corporations complying with the provisions of this section shall have all the rights and privileges of like domestic corporations, including the right to exercise the right of eminent domain, and shall be subject to the laws of the state applicable to like domestic corporations," such corporation is not a citizen or resident of this state within the meaning of the foreign attachment laws, and is not exempt from attachment as a nonresident. (Jennings v. Idaho Railway, Light & Power Co., 703.)

2. A corporation organized under the laws of a foreign jurisdiction, although engaged in business in this state and having complied with the constitution and all the laws of this state affecting foreign corporations, is a nonresident and subject to attachment as such. (Jennings v. Idaho Railway, Light & Power Co., 703.)

3. Where a foreign corporation fails to comply with the laws of this state in filing its articles of incorporation and designating an agent upon whom service of process may be made with the Secretary of State and with the clerk of the district court of the county in which its principal place of business is located, it has no authority to do business in the state. (Dickens-West Mining Co. v. Crescent Mining & Milling Co., 153.)

4. Under the provisions of sec. 2792, Rev. Codes, a foreign corporation cannot take or hold title to any realty within this state prior to making the proper filings of its articles of incorporation and designation of agent, and any deed or conveyance of real prop-

CORPORATIONS (Continued).

erty to such corporation prior to such filings shall be absolutely void. (Dickens-West Mining Co. v. Crescent Mining & Milling Co., 153.)

COSTS.

See Appeal, 7; Eminent Domain, 5.

COUNTIES.

Fiscal Affairs—Bonds—Injunction.

1. Under the provisions of sec. 10 of an act of the legislature to create and organize the county of Gooding, and for other purposes (Sess. Laws 1913, p. 13), the county commissioners of Gooding county should make provision for the payment of the bonded indebtedness apportioned to it by levy and taxation at the times fixed by law for so doing, and in the same manner that the commissioners of Lincoln county could or should have done had Gooding county not been created. (Frazier v. Hastings, 623.)

2. Under the provisions of said section, the legislative intent was to give the same power and authority to the commissioners of Gooding county in dealing with said bonded indebtedness that the county commissioners of Lincoln county had prior to the creation of Gooding county. (Frazier v. Hastings, 623.)

3. Under the provisions of sec. 1960, Rev. Codes, the board of county commissioners of Lincoln county was authorized to issue negotiable coupon bonds of their county for the purpose of paying, redeeming, funding or refunding the outstanding indebtedness of the county, and after said Lincoln county debt had been apportioned to Gooding county, the board of commissioners had full authority to issue funding or refunding bonds in payment of said apportioned indebtedness. (Frazier v. Hastings, 623.)

4. *Held*, that the plaintiff is not entitled to a writ of injunction to restrain the county commissioners from issuing and selling such funding or refunding bonds. (Frazier v. Hastings, 623.)

5. Sec. 99 of chap. 58 of Sess. Laws 1913 was passed in obedience to the mandate of sec. 15 of art. 7 of the constitution. By said provision the legislature declared its purpose to place the counties of the state upon a cash basis. (Peavy v. McCombs, 143.)

6. By sec. 99 of chap. 58 of Sess. Laws 1913, the power of the board of county commissioners to issue bonds for the payment or redemption of outstanding county warrants is abrogated. This applies to warrants which were issued before said law went into effect, as well as to warrants which were issued after it went into effect. (Peavy v. McCombs, 143.)

COUNTIES (Continued).

7. Sec. 99 of chap. 58 of Sess. Laws 1913 repeals sec. 1960 of the Rev. Codes as amended by chap. 33 of the Laws of 1913, so far as said sec. 1960 empowers the county commissioners to issue county bonds to pay or redeem outstanding warrant indebtedness. (Peavy v. McCombs, 143.)

Fixing of Salaries—Mandamus.

8. Sec. 2118, Rev. Codes, as amended by Sess. Laws, 1911, chap. 103, p. 345, provides that, "It shall be the duty of the county commissioners to fix the annual salaries of all county officers at their regular session in April next preceding any general election, except the annual salary of county attorney." (Ward v. Holmes, 602.)

9. The adoption of sec. 6, art. 18 of the constitution, as amended (Ex. Sess. Laws 1912, p. 53), which provides, "That that sentence of sec. 6 of art. 18 of the constitution of the State of Idaho reading: 'The legislature by general and uniform laws shall provide for the election biennially in each of the several counties of the State, of county commissioners, a sheriff, a county treasurer, who is *ex-officio* public administrator, a probate judge, a county superintendent of public instruction, a county assessor, who is *ex-officio* tax collector, a coroner and a surveyor,' be amended by striking out the words 'who is *ex-officio* tax collector' after the words 'a county assessor' and inserting the words 'and also *ex-officio* tax collector' after the words 'public administrator,'" in no way affects the terms of such officers, the time of their election, or their compensation. (Ward v. Holmes, 602.)

10. County commissioners have no authority to increase or decrease the maximum or minimum compensation of county officers in anticipation of the adoption of a constitutional amendment. (Ward v. Holmes, 602.)

11. A writ of mandate should not be denied where a board of county commissioners exceed their authority in fixing the annual salaries of county officers below the minimum provided by law. (Ward v. Holmes, 602.)

See Bridges.

COURTS.

Supreme Court—Filling Vacancies.

1. An election to fill a vacancy in the office of justice of the supreme court is not authorized under the constitution of this state, and no attempt at a special election to fill such vacancy by writing in the name of the office to be filled and the person to be voted for would be legal and valid. (Budge v. Gifford, 521.)

COURTS (Continued).

2. Under the provisions of sec. 6, art. 4 of the state constitution, when a vacancy occurs in the office of justice of the supreme court, it becomes the duty of the governor to fill the same by appointment, and such appointee shall hold such office until the end of the term for which the original incumbent was elected. (Budge v. Gifford, 521.)

2a. Certain provisions of the constitution cited and commented on. (Budge v. Gifford, 521.)

3. All provisions of the state constitution relating to a given subject must be construed together, and where certain provisions are definite and explicit, they must be given precedence over expressions which are merely of a general character. (Budge v. Gifford, 521.)

4. Held, under the facts of this case the peremptory writ must issue. (Budge v. Gifford, 521.)

CREDITOR'S BILL.

In General.

Held, that a complaint on a judgment brought against a person alleged to have money of the judgment debtor in her possession, under the authority of the order provided for in sec. 4510, Rev. Codes, which substantially shows that the judgment was rendered by a court of competent jurisdiction, its date, amount and the parties thereto, and then alleges facts showing that proper proceedings under the provisions of chap. 2 of title 9, providing for proceedings supplementary to execution, had been taken, that the order provided for in said sec. 4510 had been duly obtained, and further alleges that the defendant has money belonging to the judgment creditor subject to execution in her possession, is sufficient when tested by a general demurrer. (Boise Butcher Co. v. Anixdale, 483.)

CRIMINAL LAW.

Appeal by State—Probate Court.

1. Where a defendant is tried in the probate court for selling intoxicating liquors without a license, under the provisions of sec. 1518, chap. 33, title 8, of the Rev. Codes, and is convicted and appeals to the district court, *held*, that the district court erred in dismissing said action on the motion of the defendant, on the ground that the probate court had no jurisdiction to try such case but should have held a preliminary examination. (State v. Stafford, 381.)

2. Held, that the misdemeanor for which the defendant was tried and convicted in the probate court was not the crime of sell-

CRIMINAL LAW (Continued).

ing liquor in a prohibition district, since the defendant was not charged in the complaint filed in said action with selling intoxicating liquors in a prohibition district, but was charged with selling liquor without first procuring the license required by law. (State v. Stafford, 381.)

3. Under the provisions of the first subdivision of sec. 8043, Rev. Codes, the state is authorized to take an appeal from a judgment for the defendant on demurrer to the indictment or information. (State v. Stafford, 381.)

4. Under the provisions of sec. 8325, Rev. Codes, when an appeal is taken from a justice's or probate court, the clerk of the district court must file the papers received and enter the action on the calendar in its order with other criminal cases, and such case must be tried anew in the district court at the next term thereof, unless for good cause the same is continued. (State v. Stafford, 381.)

5. When a criminal case is appealed from a probate court, the case stands on appeal the same as though it had been begun in the district court. It is there for a new trial on every point in question that could legally be raised therein. (State v. Stafford, 381.)

6–8. On an appeal from the probate court to the district court in a criminal case, the proceedings in the trial *de novo* is substantially the same as in a case before the district court on indictment or information. (State v. Stafford, 381.)

9. *Held*, under the provisions of the statute, the state has the authority to appeal in a case on appeal from the probate court in criminal cases, where the appeal is dismissed on the demurrer or motion of the defendant, on the ground that the probate court had no jurisdiction to try said case. (State v. Stafford, 381.)

Alibi.

10. If the defendant relies upon an *alibi* for the defense the burden of establishing such *alibi* is upon him. (*State v. Webb*, 6 Ida. 428, 55 Pac. 892, cited and approved. (State v. Bogris, 587.)

See Accomplices; Continuances.

DEDICATION.

See Highways.

DEEDS.

See Mortgages; Taxation, 11–16.

DEFAULT.

See Judgment, 1–5.

DISMISSAL AND NONSUIT.

Motion for Nonsuit.

1. Upon motion for nonsuit, as provided by sec. 4354, Rev. Codes, the defendant admits the existence of every fact which the evidence tends to prove or which could be gathered from any reasonable view of the evidence, and plaintiff is entitled to the benefit of all inferences in his favor which the jury would be justified in drawing from the testimony. (Southern Idaho Conference Assn. of Seventh Day Adventists v. Hartford Fire Ins. Co., 712.)

2. Evidence examined and *held* that upon close of plaintiff's case a nonsuit was properly granted. (Elder v. Idaho-Washington Northern Railroad, 209.)

DRUGGISTS.

See Intoxicating Liquors, 1–5.

EJECTMENT.

Ejectment—Location of City Lot—Sufficiency of Evidence.

1. *Held*, that the evidence is sufficient to support the finding of facts. (Fife v. Village of Glenns Ferry, 763.)

ELECTIONS.

Election Returns—Board of Canvassers—Mandamus.

1. Where the county board of canvassers rejects certain returns from certain precincts on account of informality, ambiguity or uncertainty, under the provisions of sec. 448, Rev. Codes, the returns rejected must be delivered by the board to the sheriff of the county, who must proceed at once to summon and call together the judges of election of such precinct and inform them that the return made by them has been rejected, and it is made the duty of such judges to meet publicly at the place where the election was held in such precinct and at once proceed to put said returns in due form and certify the same, and for the purpose of so doing they may have the ballot-box brought in and opened in their presence and the contents thereof inspected, and when such returns have been duly corrected, they must be delivered into the hands of the sheriff. (Davies v. Board of County Commissioners, 450.)

2. Sec. 442, Rev. Codes, provides what must be done by the judges of election after the canvass of the votes, and further provides that the poll-box and ballots must be kept with the seal unbroken for at least eight months, unless the same is required as evidence in a court of law in any case arising under the election laws of the state, and then only when the judge having the ballot-box in charge is served with a subpoena to produce the same. (Davies v. Board of County Commissioners, 450.)

ELECTIONS (Continued).

3. *Held,* that the provisions of said section are applicable when the returns are properly made and are not returned to the judges for correction. In that case the ballot-box must not be opened except as directed in said section; but where returns have been rejected, as provided by statute, and returned to the judges of election for correction, they may, under the provisions of sec. 448, open the ballot-box for the purpose of correcting the returns. (Davies v. Board of County Commissioners, 450.)

4. *Held,* that the provisions of secs. 442 and 448 must be construed together in order to ascertain and carry out the true intention of the legislature. (Davis v. Board of County Commissioners, 450.)

5. *Mandamus* will lie in a proper case to compel action on the part of a canvassing board, but it will not direct what the result of their action must be. (Davies v. Board of County Commissioners, 450.)

ELECTRICITY.

Liability of Company.

1. Where an electric light and power company made a contract for the painting of its transformer station, and an employee of the contractor, not familiar with the premises or the appliances, was injured by coming in contact with uninsulated and unprotected loose wires which were not obviously dangerous, and in regard to which he had received no warning, an action for damages may properly be prosecuted by the employee of the contractor against such corporation. (Gagnon v. St. Maries Light & Power Co., 87.)

2. Those who deal in electricity as a business are held to the highest degree of care with reference to all persons not themselves wrongdoers who in any capacity may accidentally or otherwise come in contact with their electrical appliances. (Gagnon v. St. Maries Light & Power Co., 87.)

EMINENT DOMAIN.

Valuation and Compensation.

1. *Held,* that it was error for the court to admit evidence showing the value to the appellant of the land to be condemned, since such valuation is not based on the market value of the land but on the necessities of appellant. (Rawson-Works Lumber Co. v. Richardson, 37.)

2. Compensation for the land taken in such cases must be reckoned from the standpoint of what the land owner loses by having his property taken and not from the benefit the property may be to the party desiring to take it, and it is error to admit evidence of the necessities of the condemnor and the value of the property to him for the purpose to which he intends to apply it. (Rawson-Works Lumber Co. v. Richardson, 37.)

EMINENT DOMAIN (Continued).

    3. *Held*, that the court erred in giving certain instructions. (Rawson-Works Lumber Co. v. Richardson, 37.)

    4. *Held*, that the court erred in refusing to give certain instructions requested by the plaintiff. (Rawson-Works Lumber Co. v. Richardson, 37.)

Costs in Condemnation Suit.

    5. In a suit in condemnation, under the constitution and statutes of this state, the costs of the proceeding and cost of appeal should be taxed against the condemnor where the appeal has been prosecuted by the party seeking condemnation. (Rawson-Works Lumber Co. v. Richardson, 45.)

EQUITY.

See Judgments, 6–9.

ESTATE OF DECEDENT.

See Executors and Administrators.

ESTOPPEL.

In General.

    1. Where a party by conduct has intimated that he consents to an act which has been done or will offer no opposition thereto, though it could not have been lawfully done without his consent, and he thereby induces others to do that from which they otherwise might have abstained, he cannot question the legality of the action to the prejudice of those who have acted on the fair inference to be drawn from his conduct. (Exchange State Bank v. Taber, 723.)

    2. *Held*, that to constitute estoppel *in pais*, there must have been either false representation as to material facts or wrongful, misleading silence. (Bigelow on Estoppel, p. 602.) (Bank of Orofino v. Wellman, 425.)

See Bonds.

EVIDENCE.

In General.

    1. The evidence *held* not sufficient to sustain the verdict. (McConnon & Co. v. Hodge, 376.)

    2. Evidence examined, and *held* that there is substantial evidence to support the verdict and findings of the jury. (Richardson v. Bohney, 35.)

    3. *Held*, that the evidence is sufficient to sustain the verdict. (Montgomery v. Gray, 583.)

    4. *Held*, that the evidence is sufficient to support the findings. (Campbell v. Bank & Trust Co., 201.)

EXCAVATIONS.
See Adjoining Owners.

EXECUTORS AND ADMINISTRATORS.
Appointment.

1. The order of priority in right of administration on the estate of a person dying intestate is fixed by the provisions of sec. 5351, Rev. Codes. (Wright v. Merrill, 8.)

2. Sec. 5365, Rev. Codes, which provides that administration may be granted to one or more competent persons although not otherwise entitled to the same, upon the written request of a person entitled, filed with the court, does not apply to nonresidents, since under the provisions of sec. 5355 a nonresident is not competent or entitled to appointment as an administrator. (Wright v. Merrill, 8.)

3. Under the provisions of sec. 5363, Rev. Codes, letters of administration must be granted upon proper application, although it appears that other persons have better rights to the administration, when such persons fail to appear and claim the issuance of such letters to themselves within a reasonable time after the death of the intestate. (Wright v. Merrill, 8.)

4. The provisions of this section require persons entitled or having better rights to administration to make application within a reasonable time for such appointment, and if they fail to make such application, letters should be granted to any qualified applicant who makes application therefor prior to the time that application is made by the one who may have had a better right. (Wright v. Merrill, 8.)

Jurisdiction of Probate Court—Setting Aside Judgment.

5. Under sec. 4229, Rev. Codes, a probate court has jurisdiction and power to relieve a party from a judgment, order or other proceeding taken against him through his mistake, inadvertence, surprise or excusable neglect. (Chandler v. Probate Court for Kootenai County, 173.)

6. Application for such relief must be made within a reasonable time, not later than six months from the rendering of the decree, or the making of the order, or the occurrence of the proceeding sought to be set aside. (Chandler v. Probate Court for Kootenai County, 173.)

7. Where certain property belonging to the deceased is not administered in probate proceedings, and the fact is not discovered until a final decree of distribution has been entered, the final decree should not for this reason be set aside on application of a creditor or party interested. The proper remedy is furnished by sec. 5650,

EXECUTORS AND ADMINISTRATORS (Continued).

Rev. Codes, which provides for the subsequent issuance of letters testamentary whenever other property of the deceased is discovered. (Chandler v. Probate Court for Kootenai County, 173.)

Account—Claims Against Estate.

8. It is not the duty of an administrator of the estate of a deceased person to file with the probate court claims against the estate which have been rejected by him. (Chandler v. Probate Court for Kootenai County, 173.)

9. Under sec. 5600, Rev. Codes, it is the duty as well as the right of anyone opposed to the final settlement of an administrator's account and final distribution of the estate, in a case where the proper statutory notice is given, to appear in the probate court, file his exceptions in writing, and contest the same. If an interested party neglects to do this, he is not entitled to have the order settling the account and the decree of final distribution set aside under sec. 4229, Rev. Codes. (Chandler v. Probate Court for Kootenai County, 173.)

10. If a creditor whose claim is rejected by the administrator of an estate neglects to file his exceptions to the final account of the administrator and the petition for final distribution and to contest the same, and the court, after giving the proper statutory notice, settles said account and renders a decree of final distribution, such creditor, upon later bringing his action against the estate, is not entitled to have said order and decree set aside under sec. 4229, Rev. Codes, on the ground that no money has been paid into the probate court to cover his claim. (Chandler v. Probate Court for Kootenai County, 173.)

11. Where promissory notes owned by a deceased resident of a California county and secured by mortgage on real estate in an Idaho county are duly administered in probate proceedings in the California county, and proceedings are later instituted in the probate court of an Idaho county to administer certain real estate situated in said county which the deceased owned at the time of his death, and the account of the Idaho administrator is settled and a final distribution of said real estate made by the Idaho court, the fact that the promissory notes were administered in the California court and were not included in the inventory or administered in the Idaho court is not ground for the Idaho court, upon petition of a creditor, to set aside the order settling the account and the final decree of distribution. (Chandler v. Probate Court of Kootenai County, 173.)

FOREIGN CORPORATIONS.

See Corporations.

FRAUDULENT TRANSFERS.
See Bankruptcy; Sales.

GUARDIAN AD LITEM.
See Parent and Child.

HAIGHT LIQUOR LAW.
See Intoxicating Liquors, 1–5.

HIGHWAYS.
Dedication, Obstruction and Vacation.

1. Where a strip of land is by parol agreement dedicated to the public for a highway, and the public by user accepts of such portion thereof as is in condition to be traveled but does not accept by user the part thereof over which travel is prevented by a steep bluff or hill; *held*, that the dedication only applies to the portion of said tract accepted and used by the public. (Thiessen v. City of Lewiston, 505.)

2. Where obstructions are placed wrongfully upon a part of a street or highway, they do not work a forfeiture of any rights of the public to the portion of such street or highway obstructed, however long continued. (Thiessen v. City of Lewiston, 505.)

3. Where a public highway has run diagonally across a 40-acre tract owned by plaintiff, and the proper authorities have established a new highway along the line of said 40-acre tract, at the instance and request of the owner, and vacated the "diagonal road," conditioned on the plaintiff's placing the newly established highway in a good and passable condition as a public highway, the public has a right to travel the "diagonal road" until such condition is complied with, and the vacation of such "diagonal road" does not take place until the new highway is placed in proper condition. (Rasmussen v. Silk, 341.)

See Bridges.

HOMESTEAD.
See Public Lands.

HORTICULTURAL ACT.
In General.

1. An act of the legislature, known as the Horticultural Act, approved February 27, 1903 (Sess. Laws 1903, p. 347), creates and defines the duties of the state board of horticultural inspection and provides for the appointment of a state horticultural inspector and deputies, provides money for their expenses, and provides

HORTICULTURAL ACT (Continued).

penalties for the failure to comply with the provisions of said act. (State v. Pioneer Nurseries Co., 332.)

2. Sec. 8 of said act provides, among other things, that no person, firm or corporation shall engage in or continue in the business of importing and selling within the state any fruit trees, etc., without first making application therefor to said board; and also provides that such application must be in writing and accompanied by a good and satisfactory bond in the sum of $1,000, conditioned on the faithful observance of all the provisions of said act and of the laws of the state of Idaho by such applicant or applicants, their agents and representatives. (State v. Pioneer Nurseries Co., 332.)

3. Sec. 10 of said act provides, among other things, penalties for the violation of said act. (State v. Pioneer Nurseries Co., 332.)

4. Sec. 13 provides that persons shipping fruit trees or trees of any kind, within the state, shall affix to each package, bundle or parcel a distinct mark, stamp or label showing the name of the shipper, the locality where grown and the variety of the tree or shrub. (State v. Pioneer Nurseries Co., 332.)

5. *Held*, that the title to said act is sufficient to cover every section and provision of said act. (State v. Pioneer Nurseries Co., 332.)

6. *Held*, that sec. 13 deals directly and primarily with horticultural matters, and comes within the purview of said title and is germane to the subject of horticulture. (State v. Pioneer Nurseries Co., 332.)

7. The bond required to be given under the provisions of said act requires the dealer to fully comply with all the provisions and laws in any wise relating to or concerning nursery stock. (State v. Pioneer Nurseries Co., 332.)

8. *Held*, that if a dealer violates the provisions of said act in regard to placing the proper name of the variety upon his trees, the sureties on said bond are liable for any damages that may be caused thereby to the amount of the bond. (State v. Pioneer Nurseries Co., 332.)

9. *Held*, that the provisions of said sec. 13 clearly come within the title to said act and are germane to the subject of horticulture. (State v. Pioneer Nurseries Co., 332.)

HUSBAND AND WIFE.

Community and Separate Property.

1. *Held*, that the finding of facts in this case to the effect that the property in controversy was the separate property of the wife was sustained by the evidence. (Bank of Orofino v. Wellman, 425.)

HUSBAND AND WIFE (Continued).

2. *Held*, under the facts of this case that the land involved is the separate property of the wife and not subject to the payment of the husband's indebtedness. (Wilkerson v. Aven, 559.)

3. *Held*, that a husband when free from debts and liabilities may make a gift to his wife from their community property, and that the same will then become her separate property and will not be liable for debts subsequently contracted by him. (Bank of Orofino v. Wellman, 425.)

4. A married woman bought a meat market which was personal property, placed her husband in possession of the shop, authorized him to manage and control the business, buy and sell meat, receive the money from sales and pay the bills incurred in the business and thereafter her husband, as manager of the business, went to a wholesale butcher company, represented himself as the proprietor of said meat market, bought meat there, and obtained credit from said company, which was given under the belief that he owned the shop and the business, and his wife never notified said company of her ownership of the property, and the company had no knowledge of it. *Held*, that under these circumstances she is estopped from asserting ownership to the property when it would result in the loss of a debt contracted by her husband. (Boise Butcher Co. v. Anixdale, 483.)

5. Evidence in this case examined, and *held* sufficient to support the finding and judgment that the property levied upon was the separate property of the wife and not the community property of the husband and wife. (Baldwin v. McFarland, 85.)

6. Evidence examined and *held* sufficient to support the judgment. (Baldwin v. McFarland, 85.)

INDEPENDENT CONTRACTOR.

In General.

1. The employee of an independent contractor doing work on the premises of another is an invitee by special agreement, and the proprietor of such premises is under obligation to see that he have a reasonably safe place to work and that he have reasonable protection against the consequences of hidden dangers known to the proprietor. (Gagnon v. St. Maries Light & Power Co., 87.)

INDICTMENT AND INFORMATION.

Complaint or Information.

1. Under the provisions of sec. 7509, Rev. Codes, a complaint or information is defined as an allegation in writing made to a magistrate that a person has been guilty of some designated offense. (State v. Stafford, 381.)

INDICTMENT AND INFORMATION (Continued).

2. The complaint or information is the name of the pleading by which a criminal action is instituted in a justice's or probate court, and the names "complaint" and "information" are used interchangeably and refer to the same kind of a pleading. (State v. Stafford, 381.)

INFANTS.

See Parent and Child.

INJUNCTION.

See Counties, 4.

INSOLVENCY.

See Bankruptcy.

INSURANCE.

In General.

1. Where a waiver of proof of loss is an issue in a case, all evidence tending to establish such waiver ought to be admitted. (Southern Idaho Conference Assn. of Seventh Day Adventists v. Hartford Fire Insurance Co., 712.)

2. The refusal of the court to admit certain evidence on the trial *held* reversible error. (Southern Idaho Conference Assn. of Seventh Day Adventists v. Hartford Fire Insurance Co., 712.)

INTERPRETERS.

See Witnesses.

INTOXICATING LIQUORS.

Druggist's Bond—Haight Liquor Law.

1. Under the provisions of sec. 4 of an act commonly known as the Haight Liquor Law (1913 Sess. Laws, pp. 121 and 415), a bond conditioned that the one giving it "shall use and dispense with such intoxicating liquors in accordance with the laws of the state of Idaho, then this obligation to be void; otherwise to remain in full force and effect," is a sufficient bond under the provisions of said act. (State v. Forch, 755.)

2. *Held,* that the provisions of said sec. 4 requiring a bond "conditioned that none of said liquors shall be used or disposed of for any purpose other than in compounding or preserving medicines, the sale of which would not subject him to the payment of the special tax required of liquor dealers, by the United States," is surplusage and contradictory to the legislative intent and purpose of said act, inasmuch as the purpose of said act was to permit

INTOXICATING LIQUORS (Continued).

druggists to sell intoxicating liquors in accordance with the provisions of such act. (State v. Forch, 755.)

3. Said condition of the bond is out of harmony and in conflict with the clear intent and purpose of said act. (State v. Forch, 755.)

4. *Held*, that the conditions of the bond given by the respondent make him and his sureties liable thereon if he violates any laws of the state of Idaho in the sale of intoxicating liquor. (State v. Forch, 755.)

5. Under the provisions of the Haight Liquor Law, a civil action may be maintained on the bond given in case of a violation of its conditions, and a criminal action may also be maintained for using or selling intoxicating liquors in violation of the provisions of said law. (State v. Forch, 755.)

Saloons—Dry and Wet Territory.

6. Where a new county is created from territory which was formerly comprised in "dry" counties and also territory that was formerly part of a "wet" county, and the legislature makes no provision as to whether the new county shall be a "wet" or "dry" county until a local option election is held in such county, *held*, that the whole of the new county so created becomes a "wet" county and subject to the license system until such time as the voters of the county shall vote the county "dry" under the provisions of the local option statute. (Village of American Falls v. West, 301.)

7. A saloon regularly licensed to sell intoxicating liquor within wet territory is thus expressly authorized by law to sell such liquor. And even though the results of such business be disastrous and deplorable, and are the direct cause of what would amount to a public nuisance had such license not been granted, the running of such saloon in the usual and regular manner authorized by law under such license cannot legally be abated as a nuisance, because sec. 3659, Rev. Codes, provides that "Nothing which is done or maintained under the express authority of a statute can be deemed a nuisance." (Village of American Falls v. West, 301.)

8. If the owner of a saloon takes an unfair advantage of his opportunity to handle liquor, and goes beyond his rights, granted under his license, to do things that amount to a public nuisance, such things should be abated, even though they are done in connection with a licensed saloon or are an effect thereof. The proper conduct of a lawful business cannot be enjoined, but its abuses and excesses may be prevented. (Village of American Falls v. West, 301.)

Prosecution for Unlawful Sales.

9. *Held*, that the misdemeanor for which the defendant was convicted in the probate court was one which the probate court

INTOXICATING LIQUORS (Continued).

had jurisdiction to try, to wit, that of selling liquor without a license, and was not a misdemeanor which required the probate court to hold a preliminary examination, and the defendant could not have been convicted of the misdemeanor of selling liquor in a prohibition district under the complaint filed in this case. (State v. Stafford, 381.)

See Nuisance.

IRRIGATION.

Promotion of Irrigation Project—Assignment—Mortgage.

1. Where a company is incorporated for the promotion of an irrigation scheme and to construct an irrigation system, consisting of reservoirs, dams and ditches, and such corporation enters into contracts with persons having land within such project to furnish them water at an agreed price per acre, divided into annual payments with interest on deferred payments, and agrees to complete such system within a certain time and furnish the purchasers of water rights with water, and agrees to turn such system over to such purchasers of water rights after its completion, and thereafter mortgages its interest in such system and water right and also assigns such water right contracts as security for borrowed money, which money is used in the construction of such system, *held,* that the person loaning the money only acquires such rights and interest as the irrigation company has in such project and such water right contracts, and cannot collect the payments that become due after the time has expired for the completion of such irrigation system and the delivery of water until the said system is completed and the water delivered in accordance with the terms of the water right contracts. (Childs v. Neitzel, 116.)

2. Under the provisions of said water right contracts, the Murphy Land & Irrigation Company agreed to complete said irrigation system and turn the same over to the purchasers of water rights within a specified time, and the Murphy company was not the trustee or agent of the water right purchasers for the construction of said system. (Childs v. Neitzel, 116.)

3. Neitzel, who loaned the money to said Murphy Land & Irrigation Company and took a mortgage and an assignment of said water contracts as security for the payment of the money so loaned, did not become an insurer for the Murphy company to the water right claimants that said system would be completed and the water furnished as provided by said contracts, but acquired no other right than that which the Murphy Irrigation Company had in the collection of deferred payments provided for by said contracts, and cannot enforce the collection of such payments and apply the same on his mortgage debt until said system has been completed and turned

IRRIGATION (Continued).

over to the water right purchasers as provided by such contracts. (Child v. Neitzel, 116.)

4. The fact that the purchasers of such water rights authorized the Murphy company to assign them does not estop them from setting up as a defense against the payment thereof that said system has not been completed as required by said contracts. (Childs v. Neitzel, 116.)

5. Mortgagees or assigns of irrigation project corporations can acquire no greater interest in such project or water right contracts connected therewith than such corporations have. (Childs v. Neitzel, 116.)

6. Sec. 15 of art. 11 of the state constitution prohibits the legislature from passing any law which would permit the leasing or alienation of any franchise so as to release or relieve such franchise or property held thereunder from any liabilities of the lessor or grantor or lessee or grantee, contracted or incurred in the operation, use or enjoyment of such franchise or any of its privileges. (Childs v. Neitzel, 116.)

7. Under the provisions of sec. 2 of art. 15 of the constitution, the right to collect rates or compensation for the use of water is a franchise and cannot be exercised except by authority of and in the manner prescribed by law. (Childs v. Neitzel, 116.)

8. Sec. 1 of art. 15 provides that the use of all water now appropriated or that may hereafter be appropriated for sale, rental or distribution is a public use, subject to the regulation and control of the state in the manner prescribed by law. (Childs v. Neitzel, 116.)

9. The Murphy Land & Irrigation Company is a public service corporation. (Childs v. Neitzel, 116.)

Deferred Payments—Payment of to Receiver.

10. *Held,* under the water right contracts involved in this case, the deferred payments for such water rights do not become due until water is made available for the reclamation and irrigation of the lands as provided by the terms of such contract; and when the water is made so available, the deferred payments become a lien on the land and the water right. (Childs v. Neitzel, 133.)

11. *Held,* that where a water contract holder pays any part or the whole of the deferred payments to the receiver, under the order of the court, he is entitled to a credit on such contract for the amount paid. (Childs v. Neitzel, 133.)

Right of Way for Irrigation Ditch—Parol License.

12. A parol license for a right of way for a ditch, if sought to be declared perpetual, would be an easement or interest in real

IRRIGATION (Continued).

property, which can only be created by operation of law, or a conveyance or other instrument in writing, subscribed by the party sought to be charged. (McReynolds v. Harrigfeld, 26.)

13. *Held*, that where the evidence fails to disclose that licensees have expended considerable money or made valuable improvements in reliance upon a parol license for a right of way for a ditch, and fails further to show that benefits or advantages have accrued to licensors thereunder, this court will not "by operation of law" declare such parol license an easement and not within the inhibition of sec. 6007, Rev. Codes. (McReynolds v. Harrigfeld, 26.)

14. If parties are placed in their original position and with their original rights, they are "*in statu quo.*" (McReynolds v. Harrigfeld, 26.)

Foreclosure of Carey Act Lien—Contracts Between State and Irrigation Company and Company and Settler.

15. In an action to foreclose a Carey Act lien under the provisions of sec. 1629, Rev. Codes, it is not necessary to allege in the complaint that the entire irrigation system has been completed, if it appears from the allegations of the complaint that an ample supply of water has been made permanently available for the tract of land upon which the lien is sought to be foreclosed, to the extent that the contract of the irrigation company to furnish such supply to the land in question has been fulfilled. (Idaho Irrigation Co. v. Pew, 272.)

16. Sec. 1629, Rev. Codes, conferring a lien on land and water for water furnished to land, and the amendment to the federal Carey Act (29 U. S. Stats. at L., p. 435), authorizing the state to create a lien on the land, must be construed together, and the lien cannot attach until the provisions of both acts have been complied with. (Idaho Irrigation Co. v. Pew, 272.)

17. The amendment to the federal Carey Act in fixing the amount of the lien upon the land to be created by the state at "the actual cost of reclamation and reasonable interest thereon from the date of reclamation until disposed of to actual settlers," contemplates the determination of such cost by the state, and that in a contract between the state and a corporation for the construction of irrigation works, such cost must be estimated or determined in advance as a basis for the contract between them. (Idaho Irrigation Co. v. Pew, 272.)

18. In a contract between a Carey Act irrigation company and a settler, in which, by reference, the terms and conditions of the contract between the state and the irrigation company are assented to, and the price of water rights is fixed upon the basis of the estimated cost of the works contained in the state contract, both

IRRIGATION (Continued).

the company and the settler are estopped from afterward raising the question as to whether such estimated cost is the actual cost of the works. (Idaho Irrigation Co. v. Pew, 272.)

19. In a suit to foreclose a Carey Act lien the cause of action arises under the state statute, and it is not necessary to allege in the complaint that a requirement of the federal statute, not contained in the state statute, has been complied with. (Idaho Irrigation Co. v. Pew, 272.)

20. Held, that the complaint in this case is not demurrable on the ground of being ambiguous, unintelligible or uncertain. (Idaho Irrigation Co. v. Pew, 272.)

Taxpayer Estopped—Irregularity in Bond Issue.

21. Where it is shown that a land owner within an irrigation district seeks to avoid the payment of assessments levied against his land by the district because of alleged irregularities or infirmities in the issue of bonds, and who, with full knowledge of such alleged defects or infirmities, has, by his silence, acquiesced in the expenditure of the fund derived from the sale of said bonds, and who has had knowledge that said bonds were passing into the hands of *bona fide* purchasers, *held*, that he will be estopped by his laches from being heard to object to the payment of such assessments. (Page v. Oneida Irrigation District, 108.)

See Public Lands.

ISLANDS.
See Navigable Waters.

JOINT TORT-FEASORS.
See Tort-feasors.

JOURNALS.
See Statutes.

JUDGMENT.
Default.

1. Where a defendant has been sued in a state court and summons has been served upon him, and, prior to the expiration of the term within which he is required to answer under the statute and without appearing or answering, he files a petition for a removal to the federal court, and an order denying the removal is made by the state court, and the record is thereafter transferred by the defendant to the federal court, when on motion in the latter court

JUDGMENT (Continued).

the cause is remanded to the state court for want of jurisdiction in the federal court, and the clerk of the district court enters the default of the defendant for failure to appear and answer; *held*, that the action of the clerk in entering the default of the defendant is regular and valid, and within the authority and direction of secs. 4140 and 4360, Rev. Codes, and that such default is not void for want of jurisdiction. (State v. American Surety Co., 652.)

2. Where the default has been entered by the clerk against the defendant, as was done in this case, the court has jurisdiction to hear the proofs submitted by the plaintiff and to enter judgment thereon. (State v. American Surety Co., 652.)

3. Under the above facts, where the defendant moves to have the default vacated on the ground of inadvertence, surprise or excusable neglect, *held*, that under the excuse presented and the facts of this case, as shown by the record, the trial court did not err in refusing to set aside said default. (State v. American Surety Co., 652.)

4. Sec. 4140, Rev. Codes, fixes the time within which a defendant shall appear and answer, and the fact that prior to the expiration of that time the defendant undertook to have the cause removed to the federal court and it was thereafter remanded, such action on the part of the defendant to change the forum will not serve to extend the time for answer in the state court and will not relieve the defendant from a default which it thus allows to be entered against it. (State v. American Surety Co., 652.)

4a. *Held*, under the facts of this case, that the default was not prematurely entered. (State v. American Surety Co., 652.)

4b. In case the defendant fails to appear, answer, demur or otherwise plead within the time prescribed by statute, the district judge has jurisdiction and power at chambers to enter a default and to hear testimony thereon and to enter judgment. (Washington County Land & Development Co. v. Weiser National Bank, 717.)

5. In case the defendant fails to answer, the trial court is without power to grant relief not demanded in the complaint, and if there be no prayer accompanying the complaint and no relief demanded, no judgment can be entered in favor of the plaintiff. (Washington County Land & Development Co. v. Weiser National Bank, 717.)

Setting Aside in Equity.

6. *Held*, under the law and evidence, that the court erred in setting aside the judgment sought to be set aside by this action. (Fales v. Weeter Lumber Co., 367.)

JUDGMENT (Continued).

7. One who seeks equity in a court of conscience must do equity before any relief will be granted. (Fales v. Weeter Lumber Co., 367.)

8. Where an equitable action is brought to vacate a judgment upon the ground that it was obtained without jurisdiction, it must appear that the judgment sought to be set aside is inequitable and unjust, and that plaintiff has a good defense thereto. (Fales v. Weeter Lumber Co., 367.)

9. If a judgment is regular on its face, it will never be opened up merely for the purpose of letting in the defense of the statute of limitations. (Fales v. Weeter Lumber Co., 367.)

LARCENY.

Of Checks.

1. Upon a prosecution for larceny of a check for a certain amount of money, no proof of actual value is required, according to the provisions of sec. 7053, Rev. Codes, as the law presumes that the face value of the check is the actual value. (State v. Bogris, 587.)

2. In a prosecution for the larceny of certain checks it is not incumbent upon the state, for the purpose of establishing the value of the checks stolen, to offer proof of their due execution by the payer, or to prove the fact that they were never indorsed by the payee. (State v. Bogris, 587.)

8. *Held,* that Exhibits "A" and "B," consisting of checks charged to have been stolen by the defendant in this case, and to have been indorsed by him with the name of the payee, were admitted in evidence in the first instance, not for the purpose of comparison of handwriting, but for the purpose of establishing the crime committed. (State v. Bogris, 587.)

7. The following instruction, "Where the state proved such a case as would sustain a verdict of guilty, and the defendant then offers evidence, the burden of proof is on said defendant to make out his defense, and when the proof is all introduced then the primary question is, in the light of all the evidence, is the defendant guilty beyond a reasonable doubt," is not prejudicial to the defendant, by merely making it incumbent upon him to offer sufficient proof to raise a reasonable doubt in the minds of the jury as to his guilt. (State v. Bogris, 587.)

9. In giving the following instruction, the trial court did not trespass upon the right of the jury to pass upon all questions of fact, in accordance with the provisions of subd. 6, sec. 7855, Rev. Codes:

"You are further instructed that if you believe from the evidence beyond a reasonable doubt that the property described in the information was stolen and that the defendant was found in the posses-

LARCENY (Continued).

sion of the property after it was stolen, then such possession is, in law, a strong, incriminating circumstance, tending to show the guilt of the defendant unless the evidence and the facts and circumstances thereunder show that he may have come honestly in possession of the same.

"In this connection I further instruct you that if you find from the evidence beyond a reasonable doubt that the property described in the information was found in the possession of the defendant, then in determining whether or not the defendant is guilty you should take into consideration all of the circumstances attending such possession." (State v. Bogris, 587.)

10. *Held*, that no error was committed by the trial court in the giving of instructions in this case or refusal to give certain instructions offered by the defendant. (State v. Bogris, 587.)

Possession or Receiving of Stolen Property.

11. The possession of recently stolen property is a circumstance from which, when unexplained, the guilt of the accused may be inferred. (*State v. Sanford*, 8 Ida. 187, 67 Pac. 492, cited and approved.) (State v. Bogris, 587.)

12. Where the information charges three persons with receiving stolen property, without stating whether the receiving of the same was joint or several, and one of the defendants asks for and receives a separate trial; *held*, that said defendant is not prejudiced by such defect in the information. (State v. Janks, 567.)

13. Any incriminating inference to be drawn from the possession of stolen property is not a presumption of law but is a deduction of fact to be considered by the jury. (State v. Janks, 567.)

14. Unless the fact is undisputed, the question whether stolen property found in the possession of a person has been "recently" stolen should be left to the jury to decide like any other material fact. It is error for the court to instruct the jury that possession of stolen property immediately after the theft is sufficient to warrant a conviction, and especially so where the evidence does not show that the defendant was in the possession of the property immediately after the theft. (State v. Janks, 567.)

LATERAL SUPPORT.

See Adjoining Owners.

LEASE.

Of Livestock—Recording.

1. Leases of more than ten head of livestock contracted in another state by citizens of another state, if said livestock is afterward brought by the lessee into Idaho, and thereafter and while

LEASE (Continued).

the property and the lessee are in Idaho, by agreement between the parties, the original lease is continued for a longer term than was originally agreed upon, the new agreement is such a contract as is required to be filed for record by section 1263 of the Political Code of Idaho. (Hare v. Young, 682.)

LEGISLATURE.

See Statutes.

LICENSE.

Parol License—Revocation.

1. Mere naked possession by the licensees of a right of way created by parol license is not sufficient to authorize such license to be declared irrevocable. (McReynolds v. Harrigfeld, 26.)

See Irrigation, 12.

LICENSE FEE.

See Motor Vehicle Act.

LIVESTOCK.

See Lease.

LOCAL OPTION.

• See Intoxicating Liquors, 6–8.

LOGGING.

See Navigable Waters.

MANDAMUS.

See Counties, 11; Elections, 5; Municipal Corporations, 13.

MASTER AND SERVANT.

Personal Injury to Employee.

1. Facts of this case examined, and *held* sufficient to support a verdict that the defendant was guilty of negligence and to warrant a verdict and judgment for damages. (Swanstrom v. Frost, 79.)

2. Where a log decker was injured by being knocked off the deck by a "gunning" log and sues his employer for damages and charges that the master was negligent in that he furnished a deaf teamster to drive the team that was doing the cross hauling, and that he did not furnish a reasonably safe place for the team, and that, on the contrary, the place where the team had to walk was so

MASTER AND SERVANT (Continued).

muddy, swampy and unsafe that it irritated and excited the team so that they could not be stopped upon signal, and that his injuries resulted from either a failure of the driver to hear the signal or the inability of the driver to stop the team upon receiving the signal, and there is some evidence in the record which would sustain either one or both of the contentions, the verdict and judgment in favor of the party injured will not be disturbed, even though the preponderance of the evidence is against his contention. (Swanstrom v. Frost, 79.)

MINES AND MINING.

Mining Excavations—Negligence.

1. It is lawful for the miner to sink holes, pits and shafts on mineral lands, and to do so is not of itself an act of negligence, and an excavation, pit or shaft made by a miner in the prosecution of his work is not of itself a nuisance. (Strong v. Brown, 1.)

2. The owner of a mining claim is not liable to the owner of livestock for damages resulting from livestock running at large falling into a pit, prospect hole or mining shaft left open by the miner, and the locator or owner of mining claims is not bound by law to fence or inclose the same in order to protect livestock running at large on the public domain from being injured by falling into the same. (Strong v. Brown, 1.)

Assessment Work.

3. *Held*, that the evidence fails to show that the annual assessment work was performed upon the mining claim, the title to which is involved in this action. (Dickens-West Mining Co. v. Crescent Mining & Milling Co., 153.)

MISTAKE.

By Grantor as to Boundaries—Relief.

1. The mistake of a purchaser, as to what was included within the bounds of a legal subdivision of land, cannot be the basis for equitable relief in his favor as against an action for the recovery of the purchase price, when it is not shown that any material misrepresentations were made by the vendor, and it appears that complainant himself was negligent. (Coolin v. Anderson, 47.)

2. *Held*, that the trial court committed no error in the admission or exclusion of evidence. (Coolin v. Anderson, 47.)

MORTGAGES.

1. S., an insolvent debtor, executed and delivered several warranty deeds in form to a corporation to which he was largely in-

MORTGAGES (Continued).

debted at the time to secure the debt, and certain attaching creditors of S. appeared in an action wherein said corporation prayed to have said deeds declared mortgages and foreclosed, and alleged the deeds to be fraudulent as to them, and asked that they be set aside; *held*, under the evidence that they were valid and in effect mortgages. (Capital Lumber Co. v. Saunders, 408.)

Foreclosure—Community Property—Unrecorded Deed.

2. Where M. J. G., daughter of J. H. G., made an entry of 160 acres of land under the homestead laws of the United States, with an understanding that her said father should assist her in improving said land and that she would thereafter convey to him one-half of said land, and after procuring patent from the government for such land she conveyed to her said father by deed in October, 1904, eighty acres of said land, and her said father withheld said deed from record until January 27, 1913, and procured a loan of over $4,000 from B. on the representation and as shown by the abstract of title to said land that the said daughter, M. J. G., was the owner of said land, and the said B. had no knowledge or information which would put her on inquiry as to whether said J. H. G. and his wife had any interest in said land, *held*, that the said mortgage is a valid and subsisting lien on said land and that the trial court did not err in granting the foreclosure thereof. (Blucher v. Shaw, 497.)

3. Under the provisions of sec. 3160, Rev. Codes, every conveyance of real property other than a lease for a term not exceeding one year is void as against any subsequent purchaser or mortgagee of the same property, or any part thereof, in good faith and for a valuable consideration, whose conveyance is first duly recorded. (Blucher v. Shaw, 497.)

4. The evidence *held* sufficient to show that neither B. nor her agent had any notice, constructive or otherwise, of the existence of said deed conveying one-half of said land from M. J. G., the daughter, to J. H. G., the father, prior to the execution of said mortgage, and that said mortgage was procured in good faith and for a valuable consideration. (Blucher v. Shaw, 497.)

Attorney Fee.

5. *Held*, that an attorney fee of $1,000, under the circumstances of this case, where the amount of $10,181.64 was recovered against defendant in a suit for foreclosure of a mortgage, defendant having gone to trial on an answer and cross-complaint, was properly allowed by the trial court. (Coolin v. Anderson, 47.)

See Irrigation, 5.

MOTOR VEHICLE ACT.

License or Registration Fee.

1. Chapter 179, Sess. Laws 1913, p. 558, is a law intended, among other things, to require those who operate motor vehicles upon the public highways to cause such vehicles to be registered and to pay therefor a license, or registration fee, which is in excess of the amount necessary to be raised for the purpose of policing such vehicles upon the public highways. (Application of Kessler, 764.)

2. The provisions of the constitution requiring all taxes to be uniform and to be levied and collected under general laws which shall prescribe such regulations as shall insure a just valuation of all property, refer to taxation according to the commonly accepted meaning of that term, and do not apply to license or registration fees. (Application of Kessler, 764.)

MUNICIPAL CORPORATIONS.

Improvement District—Ordinance of Intention—Description.

1. Under the provisions of sec. 2338, Rev. Codes, as amended by Sess. Laws 1911, p. 268, where the resolution or ordinance of intention describes the exterior boundaries of an improvement district proposed to be established, and also contains the number of the lots and blocks within such district that will be affected by such improvement, it is a sufficient compliance with the statute, since the streets and alleys can be readily ascertained and determined from said description. (Coughanour v. City of Payette, 280.)

2. The test as to whether the ordinance of intention complies with the law is whether it affords a proper opportunity to be heard by anyone who desires to protest against the establishment of an improvement district, and give reasonable notice of the intention of the city council to establish such district and make improvements therein. (Coughanour v. City of Payette, 280.)

3. Where the plaintiff as a property owner protests against the creation of a proposed improvement district, he thereby admits that he received notice of the intention to create said district. (Coughanour v. City of Payette, 280.)

4. *Held*, that Ordinance No. 246 substantially complies with the law in regard to what such an ordinance must contain. (Coughanour v. City of Payette, 280.)

5. *Held*, that the court did not err in dissolving the temporary injunction. (Coughanour v. City of Payette, 280.)

Public Improvements Contract—Specifications—Improvement Bonds.

6. The provisions in the specifications for street improvements to the effect that the contractor shall be responsible for all defects,

MUNICIPAL CORPORATIONS (Continued).

damage to fences, sidewalks, water-pipes, sewers, etc., and other specifications and requirements contained in subdivisions 8, 17, 27 and 32, do not make the contract invalid or void, as all of said specifications require only what was necessary to be done in order to construct and complete such improvements, and do not tend to increase the cost of such improvements beyond what said contractor should be required to do or pay under the laws of this state. (Pease v. City of Payette, 793.)

7. The acceptance by the city of a private bond instead of a surety company bond, as provided by subdivision 8 of the specifications, is not sufficient to invalidate the contract and could only be taken advantage of by the city itself. (Pease v. City of Payette, 793.)

Contracts, Expenditures and Indebtedness.

8. When a city enters into a contract by the terms of which it becomes liable for a large expenditure of money, exceeding in that year the income and revenue provided for it for said year, without fully complying with all the provisions of sec. 3, art. 8 of the constitution of Idaho relating to such expenditure, *held*, that said contract is void. (Boise Development Co. v. Boise City, 347.)

9. The word "liability," as used in said section, has its ordinary meaning, and signifies the state of being bound in law and justice to pay an indebtedness or discharge some obligation. (Boise Development Co. v. Boise City, 347.)

10. Where uncertain and contingent claims for alleged damages to the property of a corporation against a city are made a part of the consideration of a contract entered into between them, and said claims have never been liquidated, settled, or reduced to a definite fixed amount of indebtedness against said city, *before* the date of the contract, by a judgment or decree of court, arbitration, compromise, nor in any manner whatever, if these sums are liquidated, settled and fixed as a definite amount of indebtedness against the city for the first time by the contract itself, *held*, that this would constitute a *new debt*. (Boise Development Co. v. Boise City, 347.)

11. Where a contract is within the exercise of the powers and duties of a city council, and the city accepts the work done under such contract, it must pay for it. (Wycoff v. Strong, 502.)

Fiscal Year.

12. The fiscal year of certain municipalities under the law commences on the first Tuesday in May, and the enactment of a law allowing one-half of the taxes levied for city purposes to be paid · before the first Monday in January following and the other half

MUNICIPAL CORPORATIONS (Continued).

before the first Monday in July following, only changes the time
of the payment of the taxes and does not deprive the city of the
amount of taxes levied for the fiscal year, even though such taxes
were not collected during the fiscal year for which they were levied.
(Wycoff v. Strong, 502.)

Mandamus to Draw Warrant.

13. Where a city council allows a claim and directs the city clerk
to draw a warrant in payment thereof, and he refuses to do so, he
may be compelled to issue and countersign such warrant by writ of
mandate, as such duty is merely ministerial and requires no exercise
of discretion on the part of the clerk. (Wycoff v. Strong, 502.)

See Bonds; Bridges.

NAVIGABLE WATERS.

In General—Logging.

1. The navigable streams of this state are public highways,
over which every citizen has a right to carry commerce in such
manner and by such means as are best adapted to serve the purposes of the business in which he is engaged, but in doing this
he must have due consideration and reasonable care for the rights
of others to a like use of the waters of such stream. (Cameron Lumber Co. v. Stack-Gibbs Lumber Co., 626.)

2. Where booms and sorting works for logs placed in the river
do, to some extent, form a hindrance to the free navigation of
the river at times, such hindrance should be considered only an
incident to the reasonable use of the stream for floating and
securing logs. (Cameron Lumber Co. v. Stack-Gibbs Lumber Co.,
626.)

3. For such purpose and as incident to the reasonable use of
the river for running and securing logs, parties may use temporary
sheer or guide booms to direct the logs or lumber into proper places
into which to detain them for use. (Cameron Lumber Co. v. Stack-
Gibbs Lumber Co., 626.)

4. If an obstruction merely impairs or renders more difficult the
navigation of a stream without destroying it, an individual has no
right for cause of complaint, because he has no right to insist upon
the best possible accommodation. (Cameron Lumber Co. v. Stack-
Gibbs Lumber Co., 626.)

5. The Salmon river is a navigable stream, and is therefore a
public highway belonging to the state. (Callahan v. Price, 745.)

Title to Land—Boundaries—Islands.

6. A patent from the United States for land bordering on a
navigable lake or stream extends no farther than the natural high-
water line. (Callahan v. Price, 745.)

NAVIGABLE WATERS (Continued).

7. When lands border on a stream, the banks of which are both well-defined and where the stream separates at the head of an island into distinct channels constituting a well-defined stream on either side, the boundary line of the land granted extends only to the natural high-water mark. (Callahan v. Price, 745.)

8. Where there is no evidence offered at the trial, as in this case, which establishes or tends to establish the fact that the island in controversy was at any time attached to or a part of lots bounded by a stream, it was not error for the court to grant a nonsuit. (Callahan v. Price, 745.)

9. The United States, since the admission of Idaho to statehood, has the power to dispose of subdivisions or fractional subdivisions of public lands consisting of islands that existed in the territory of Idaho prior to its admission as a state. (Callahan v. Price, 745.)

10. Islands in existence when Idaho was admitted to the Union did not pass to the state or come within the disposing influences of its laws, but remained the property of the United States subject to disposal by it. (Callahan v. Price, 745.)

11. It is the settled law of this state that no title to islands, lakes or the beds of streams passes to the patentees of the United States by the sale of border lots; that the state holds the title to the beds of navigable lakes and streams below the natural high-water mark, for the use and benefit of the whole people, subject to the rights vested by the constitution in the United States. (Callahan v. Price, 745.)

12. Since statehood the state holds the title to the beds of all navigable lakes and streams, subject to the rights of the general government to regulate commerce, and the right by the public to the use of the same as public highways over which every citizen has a natural right to carry commerce, whether by ships, boats, the floating of logs or lumber, having due consideration and reasonable care for the rights of individuals as well as the public in the common use of such public highways. (Callahan v. Price, 745.)

13. The case of *Johnson v. Hurst*, 10 Ida. 308, 77 Pac. 785; *Lattig v. Scott*, 17 Ida. 506, 107 Pac. 47, *Johnson v. Johnson*, 14 Ida. 561, 95 Pac. 499, 24 L. R. A., N. S., 1240, and *Ulbright v. Baslington*, 20 Ida. 539, 119 Pac. 292, 294, are hereby overruled in so far as they conflict with this opinion. (Callahan v. Price, 745.)

NEGLIGENCE.

See Electricity.

NEGOTIABLE INSTRUMENTS.

See Bills and Notes; Master and Servant; Mines and Mining; Waters.

NEW TRIAL.

In General.

1. The action of the trial court refusing to strike from the files counter-affidavits submitted by the state on defendant's showing on motion for a new trial, on the ground that such counter-affidavits are immaterial and irrelevant, is not a ground for reversal of a judgment of conviction, where it does not appear that the defendant has been prejudiced by allowing such counter-affidavits to remain in the record. (State v. Grant, 189.)

2. The granting or denying of a new trial rests in the sound discretion of the trial court. (Montgomery v. Gray, 585.)

3. Where affidavits filed in support of a motion for a new trial contain a recital of such alleged facts as are merely cumulative, or it clearly appears that the facts contained in the affidavits might have been, by the exercise of ordinary diligence, procured at the trial, the trial court will be justified upon that ground, if upon no other, in denying the motion for a new trial. (Montgomery v. Gray, 585.)

4. Indefiniteness of a verdict is not a ground for granting a new -trial under the provisions of sec. 4439, Rev. Codes. (Trask v. Boise King Placers Co., 290.)

5. A wide discretion is vested in the trial court in determining the weight to be given to the statements contained in affidavits on motion for a new trial on the ground of newly discovered evidence, and the action of the trial court in denying such motion will not be disturbed where the discretion reposed is not shown to have been abused. (State v. Grant, 189.)

NONSUIT.

See Dismissal and Nonsuit.

NOTICE.

See Adjoining Owners 1; Appeal and Error, 1.

NUISANCE.

Abatement by Village.

1. A village is a proper party plaintiff to bring an action in the district court to obtain the abatement of a public nuisance causing special injury to the rights, morals or interests of such village, even though such nuisance be outside the village boundaries. (Village of American Falls v. West, 301.)

PARENT AND CHILD.

Actions—Guardian Ad Litem—Pleading—Judgment.

1. Where an action for injuries to a minor child was commenced by the mother on the theory that the mother, as the natural guardian

PARENT AND CHILD (Continued).

of such child, could recover for such injuries, both on her own behalf and on behalf of the minor, and the allegations of the complaint showed that to be plaintiff's theory of the case, and defendant answered on the same theory of the case, and evidence was introduced without objection sustaining the allegations of the complaint, and at the close of the introduction of evidence and by consent of counsel for defendant the complaint was amended by inserting in the title of the action the additional words, "For herself and on behalf of her minor son, W. E. Trask," and other amendments were allowed at the same time, additional instructions covering the amendments being given by the court to the jury, and such amendments did not involve the introduction of any further evidence or any new state of facts, and it appeared that defendant was in no way misled or prejudiced by the making of such amendments, the allowance thereof did not constitute a new cause of action, and was properly granted by the court under sec. 4229, Rev. Codes. (Trask v. Boise King Placers Co., 290.)

2. The appointment of a guardian *ad litem* after the trial of a case and on the hearing of a motion for new trial, by an order of the trial court *nunc pro tunc*, is not a jurisdictional defect, but at most an irregularity which does not of itself vitiate the proceedings. (Trask v. Boise King Placers Co., 290.)

3. Where the title of the cause as inserted in the verdict of the jury designates the plaintiff as "Mrs. Ina M. Trask," whereas in accordance with an amendment to the complaint previously made by consent the words "for herself and on behalf of her minor son W. E. Trask" should have been added, but were omitted through inadvertence, such informality will not vitiate or render uncertain the verdict, which is to be read with the aid of the pleadings and in the light of the instructions of the court. (Trask v. Boise King Placers Co., 290.)

4. Where, in an action to recover for injuries to a minor child, the jury rendered a verdict of $8,000 in favor of the mother and minor child, and on motion for new trial the court reduced the judgment to $5,000, and apportioned that sum, $1,000 to the mother and $4,000 to the minor child, on condition that the mother and the minor, through his guardian *ad litem*, should file disclaimers of any greater sums, and such disclaimers were filed with the court, both the mother and the minor are bound by the judgment, and the defendant cannot be heard to complain in the absence of any showing that it is prejudiced by the action of the court in so apportioning the judgment. (Trask v. Boise King Placers Co., 290.)

5. A minor is bound by a judgment in a case wherein he is a party and represented by a guardian *ad litem* regularly appointed,

PARENT AND CHILD (Continued).

when such guardian accepts the judgment of the court on behalf
of his ward. (Trask v. Boise King Placers Co., 290.)

6. *Held*, that it does not appear from the record in this case
that any substantial rights of appellant have been materially affected
by any error or defect that may have occurred during the trial or
proceedings. (Trask v. Boise King Placers Co., 290.)

PARTIES.

In General.

1. *Held*, that the court erred in holding that there was a defect
of parties plaintiff and that the Springston Lumber Company was
a necessary party plaintiff to the action. (Taylor v. Lytle, 97.)

2. Where an action is brought against M. and K. and it is
alleged in the complaint that K. acted as the agent and trustee of
the plaintiff in bringing an action and procuring a judgment against
M., and the prayer as to K. is that he be declared to be the agent
and trustee of the plaintiff in procuring such judgment, and that
the plaintiff is the owner thereof, and as to M. that the plaintiff
have a judgment against him for the identical debt included in the
other judgment in favor of K., and K. demurs to the complaint on
the ground that there is a misjoinder of parties defendant and
that the complaint does not state a cause of action as to him, *held*,
that the court did not err in sustaining said demurrer and entering a judgment of dismissal as to defendant M. (Kissler v. Moss,
516.)

3. Under the provisions of sec. 4178, Rev. Codes, failure on the
part of defendant to seasonably raise by demurrer questions involving lack of capacity on the part of the plaintiff to sue, or
defect or misjoinder of parties, must be deemed to be a waiver of
the right to thereafter raise such questions. (Trask v. Boise King
Placers Co., 290.)

PLEADING.

Negligence.

1. *Held*, that the complaint in this case states a cause of action.
(Gagnon v. St. Maries Light & Power Co., 87.)

2. Under the rule in force in this state requiring a liberal construction of pleadings, a demurrer to the complaint in a personal
injury case should not be sustained on the ground that it disclosed
contributory negligence on its face, when all the allegations of the
complaint taken together, and considered in the sense in which the
pleader has evidently used and employed the language therein contained, charge negligence of the defendant and care and diligence on
the part of plaintiff. (Gagnon v. St. Maries Light & Power Co., 87.)

PLEADING (Continued).

Amendment.

3. It is not an abuse of discretion upon the part of the trial court to refuse permission to amend a pleading where upon appeal a case has been remanded for a new trial, and where the amendments sought were directly contradictory to the original allegations, and where the amendments were sought for the apparent purpose of avoiding matters formerly alleged and proven in the case, and upon which issue had been joined, where no showing is made of excusable inadvertence or mistake, or of fraud upon the part of the other party contributing thereto. (Elder v. Idaho-Washington Northern R. R., 209.)

PLEDGES.

In General.

1. A pledgee must exercise ordinary and reasonable diligence to secure the fruits of the collateral, but he is held to no greater degree of diligence, and extraordinary care and efforts in the collection of the collaterals are not necessary. (Exchange State Bank v. Taber, 723.)

2. Where a person is jointly agreed upon by the pledgor and pledgee to make collection of collateral notes, he becomes the representative of both parties and neither can charge the other with negligence. (Exchange State Bank v. Taber, 723.)

POSSESSION.

As Evidence of Title.

1. Possession of personal property is *prima facie* evidence of ownership. (Hare v. Young, 691.)

PREDATORY ANIMALS.

See Bounties.

PRINCIPAL AND AGENT.

Sale by Agent not in Possession of Property—Lien for Commission.

1. Where an agent is employed to sell certain personal property but is not given possession thereof and has no authority to fix the price, determine the terms, close the sale of the same, or receive the purchase price, said agent does not have a lien upon the note and mortgage offered as a part of the purchase price of said personal property and delivered by the purchaser to the owner of said property in connection with the sale thereof, then by him placed in the hands of the agent simply and only to have him examine the same as to their value, see if the land mentioned in the mort-

PRINCIPAL AND AGENT (Continued).

gage is properly described therein, and determine from the abstract of title whether there were other liens or encumbrances upon it; the agent does not have a lien upon said note and mortgage for a commission for the sale of said personal property only. (Smith v. Bergstresser, 322.)

2. Under the provisions of sec. 3446, Rev. Codes, an agent who sells personal property of which he does not have possession and upon which he has rendered no service to the owner thereof, by labor, or skill, employed for the protection, improvement, safekeeping, or carriage thereof, has no lien for the purchase price, or any part thereof, which may come into his hands in connection with such sale. (Smith v. Bergstresser, 322.)

3. *Held*, that under the evidence in this case, respondent is not entitled to a lien upon the note and mortgage described in the complaint. (Smith v. Bergstresser, 322.)

PROBATE COURT.

See Criminal Law, 1–9.

PROBATE LAW.

See Executors and Administrators.

PUBLIC LANDS.

Reclamation Act—Homestead Entryman—Proof of Residence and Cultivation—Taxation.

1. Where a homestead entryman of land included within a government reclamation project presents proof to the proper government officer that he has complied with the law in relation to residence and cultivation of said land and secures a certificate from the United States that his proof has been accepted, further residence on the land is not required in order to obtain final certificate and patent, and patent will issue upon proof that at least one-half of the irrigable area in the entry as finally adjusted has been reclaimed and that all the charges and fees and commissions due on account thereof have been paid to the proper receiving officer of the government. (Cheney v. Minidoka County, 471.)

2. Where such entryman, in addition to establishing his residence on, and cultivation of, such land, has paid the United States five annual instalments on his water right amounting to $11 per acre, as provided by the reclamation act and the rulings of the Secretary of the Interior thereunder, and the entryman still owes the United States five annual instalments in payment of what is known as the construction charge for the irrigation canals and other works constructed by the United States for the purpose of furnish-

PUBLIC LANDS (Continued).

ing water to the land entered, he has an equitable interest in such land, which is "property" within the meaning of that word as used in the constitution and laws of this state, and the matter then rests wholly with the entryman whether he will make the deferred payments and the additional proof required by said reclamation act. (Cheney v. Minidoka County, 471.)

3. Under the provisions of secs. 2, 3 and 5, art. 7 of the state constitution, and sec. 1, Sess. Laws 1913, p. 173, all "property" within the state is liable to taxation, unless expressly exempted. (Cheney v. Minidoka County, 471.)

4. Under said reclamation act, where a person has so far complied with the provisions of said law as to residence and cultivation of the land for more than five years, he can complete his title at any time by making final proof and paying the deferred payments on his water right and the fees provided by law to be paid. Under said act the government simply retains title as security for the payment of the money owing on the purchase price of the water right for such land. (Cheney v. Minidoka County, 471.)

5. Held, under the facts of this case, that plaintiff's interest in said lands is "property," and subject to taxation. (Cheney v. Minidoka County, 471.)

6. The possessory right referred to in secs. 4554 et seq., Rev. Codes, is a squatter's right on public lands, and there is a clear distinction between such right and the right acquired by a formal homestead or other entry of public land under the laws of the United States. (Cheney v. Minidoka County, 471.)

7. When public land is surveyed by the government and filed upon by a qualified entryman it ceases to be public land, and if such entryman complies with the law and thereafter makes proper final proof and payments, he is entitled to a patent. (Cheney v. Minidoka County, 471.)

8. When such entryman makes his proof of residence and cultivation and there only remains the lien of the government for deferred payments on the water right for such land, the entryman's interest in such land is taxable. (Cheney v. Minidoka County, 471.)

9. The interest of the entryman in such land can be sold at delinquent tax sale and the lien of such sale foreclosed and the title thereto obtained, under the provisions of the present revenue law, chap. 58, Laws of 1913, p. 173. (Cheney v. Minidoka County, 471.)

10. Nothing that the taxing authorities have done or could do can or will affect the lien, rights or interests of the United States in such land for the deferred payments on the water right. (Cheney v. Minidoka County, 471.)

See Navigable Waters, 6–13.

PUBLIC UTILITIES ACT.

Construction of Statute—Powers of Commission—Review of Orders by Court.

1. The act known as the "Public Utilities Act" was passed at the twelfth session of the Idaho legislature, which session was adjourned on the 8th day of March, 1913, and said act was approved by the governor on March 13, 1913, and went into effect sixty days after the adjournment of said session of the legislature, to wit, on the 8th day of May, 1913. (Sess. Laws 1913, p. 247.) Said act provided for the organization of a public utilities commission and defined its powers and duties, and also the rights, remedies, powers and duties of public utilities, their officers, agents and employees, and the rights and remedies of patrons of public utilities. (Idaho Power & Light Co. v. Blomquist, 222.)

2. Under the provisions of sec. 10 of art. 4 of the constitution, every bill passed by the legislature becomes a law upon the approval and signing of the same by the governor. (Idaho Power & Light Co. v. Blomquist, 222.)

3. All property devoted to public use is held subject to the power of the state to regulate or control its use in order to secure the general safety, health and public welfare of the people, and when a corporation is clothed with rights, powers and franchises to serve the public, it becomes in law subject to governmental regulation and control. (Idaho Power & Light Co. v. Blomquist, 222.)

4. The legislature has plenary power in all matters of legislation except as limited by the constitution. (Idaho Power & Light Co. v. Blomquist, 222.)

5. There is nothing in the constitution that prohibits the legislature from enacting laws to regulate and control public utility corporations. (Idaho Power & Light Co. v. Blomquist, 222.)

6. The police power of the state is sufficiently broad and comprehensive to enable the legislature to regulate by law public utilities in order to promote the health, comfort, safety and welfare of the people, and thus regulate the manner in which public utility corporations shall construct their systems and carry on their business within the state. (Idaho Power & Light Co. v. Blomquist, 222.)

7. Under the state's police power, the legislature has authority to authorize said utility commission to determine whether a duplication of an electrical plant is required in a town or city for the convenience and necessity of the inhabitants. (Idaho Power & Light Co. v. Blomquist, 222.)

8. Under the provisions of said act, the commission has power absolutely to fix the rates, and it is unlawful for the utility to charge more or less than the rates so fixed. (Idaho Power & Light Co. v. Blomquist, 222.)

PUBLIC UTILITIES ACT (Continued).

9. Formerly competition was supposed to be the proper means of protecting the public and promoting the general welfare in respect to service of public utility corporations, but experience has demonstrated that public convenience and public needs do not require the construction and maintenance of numerous instrumentalities in the same locality, but, rather, the construction and maintenance only of those necessary to meet the public necessities, when such utilities are properly regulated by law. (Idaho Power & Light Co. v. Blomquist, 222.)

10. Said public utilities act provides that competition between public utility corporations of the classes specified shall be allowed only where public convenience and necessity demand or require it. (Idaho Power & Light Co. v. Blomquist, 222.)

11. Sec. 18, art. 11, of the state constitution prohibits combinations for the purpose of fixing prices or regulating production, and requires the legislature to pass appropriate laws to enforce the provisions of that section, and said public utilities act is justified by the provisions of said section, since its ultimate effect will be to prevent unreasonable rates and combinations by public utilities. (Idaho Power & Light Co. v. Blomquist, 222.)

12. Unregulated competition is the tool of unregulated monopoly. (Idaho Power & Light Co v. Blomquist, 222.)

13. Under the provisions of said act, unregulated competition is not needed to protect the public against unreasonable rates or unsatisfactory service; and there can now be no justification for unregulated competition or a duplication of utility plants under the pretense of preventing monopoly. (Idaho Power & Light Co. v. Blomquist, 222.)

14. Experience and history clearly show that public utility corporations cannot be safely intrusted to properly serve the public until they are regulated and placed under public control. (Idaho Power & Light Co. v. Blomquist, 222.)

15. The legislature has ample power to give the public utilities commission authority to refuse to give a certificate of convenience and necessity to a public utility where it seeks to duplicate a plant or system that is amply sufficient to serve properly the inhabitants of a community. (Idaho Power & Light Co. v. Blomquist, 222.)

16. The legislature may not delegate its purely legislative power to a commission, but having laid down by law the general rules of action under which a commission may proceed, it may require of that commission the application of such rules to particular situations and conditions and authorize an investigation of facts by the commission with a view to making orders in a particular

PUBLIC UTILITIES ACT (Continued).

matter within the rules laid down by such law. (Idaho Power & Light Co. v. Blomquist, 222.)

17. Power to regulate public utilities presupposes an intelligent regulation and necessarily carries with it the power to employ the means necessary and proper for such intelligent regulation. (Idaho Power & Light Co. v. Blomquist, 222.)

18. Under the law the standard by which rates, services, etc., must be fixed clearly contemplates reasonable rates, services, etc., which is a legislative matter and cannot be delegated; but the authority to determine what is a reasonable rate is purely administrative and can be delegated and was delegated to the commission in our public utilities act, and the several acts authorized to be performed by the commission may be reviewed by this court on a writ of *certiorari* or review, as provided by sec. 63a of said act, and under the provisions of that section all orders made by the commission may be reviewed by this court, and this court has the authority to determine whether such orders are unlawful. (Idaho Power & Light Co. v. Blomquist, 222.)

19. The contract right given to a public utility corporation by ordinance of a city does not come within the contract clause of the constitution of the United States, in that it can in no manner be affected by the police power of the state, and when a corporation acquires a franchise for the purpose of carrying on a corporate business within a city, it is accepted subject to the police power. (Idaho Power & Light Co. v. Blomquist, 222.)

20. It is provided by sec. 48a of said act that no electrical corporation shall "henceforth" begin the construction of an electrical plant, etc., without having first obtained a certificate of convenience and necessity from the commission; and a public utility corporation cannot slip in between the passage and approval of such act and its going into effect and procure an ordinance that would deprive the state of its right to regulate it in its operations under the police power of the state, especially where such corporation had not begun actual construction work and was not prosecuting such work in good faith and uninterruptedly and with reasonable diligence in proportion to the magnitude of the undertaking, as provided by sec. 48b of said act; for under the facts of this case the plaintiffs had not begun actual construction work on their system in either of said cities. (Idaho Power & Light Co. v. Blomquist, 222.)

21. The last proviso of sec. 48a provides that power companies may, without such certificate, increase the capacity of existing plants or develop new generating plants and market the product thereof. That proviso must not be so construed as to nullify the clear object and purpose of said act. If construed to give such

PUBLIC UTILITIES ACT (Continued).

corporations the power to establish new plants and lines and enter
into new fields for the sale of their products, then the main object
and purpose of said act would be nullified and defeated; and if
that proviso be construed in that way, it must be held as nugatory
and be disregarded. (Idaho Power & Light Co. v. Blomquist, 222.)

22. It was not the intention of the legislature under the provisions of sec. 48b to permit such corporations to extend their
lines into territory already occupied by a similar utility corporation, without first securing a certificate of convenience and necessity from said commission. (Idaho Power & Light Co. v. Blomquist,
222.)

23. *Held*, that the power of regulation as provided by said act
is not required to be specifically conferred by the provisions of
the state constitution, and that there is no inhibition in the constitution upon the legislature prohibiting the enactment of such law.
(Idaho Power & Light Co. v. Blomquist, 222.)

Compulsory Production of Books and Papers.

24. In a contest between a patron and a utility corporation in
regard to the establishment of reasonable rates, the Utilities Commission has power to require the corporation to produce any and all
records, contracts or papers bearing upon the questions in issue and
that would throw any light upon the question of reasonable rates;
and the commission has full power and authority to pass upon and
determine the relevancy or competency of all evidence offered to
prove or disprove the issues made by the pleadings, and this authority should be liberally exercised to enable parties to prepare properly
for trial. (Federal Mining & Smelting Co. v. Public Utilities Commission, 391.)

25. The business of the Washington Water Power Company, the
defendant in the original proceeding, is the manufacture and sale
of electricity to numerous customers, and the reasonable cost thereof
can only be determined by showing the actual value of the plant,
the actual cost to manufacture and deliver the electricity and all
necessary disbursements for that purpose, including taxes, also the
depreciation of the plant, plus a fair return on the money invested;
and to determine the questions that must be determined, it will
necessitate an examination of the plant and business of the corporation, and for that reason the plaintiff, in order to prepare itself
for trial, should have an inspection of all the books, papers and
documents of said utility corporation and all of its plants in so far
as the same will show, or tend to show, the reasonable value of
the plant and what it actually costs to manufacture and deliver
electricity and power. (Federal Mining & Smelting Co. v. Public
Utilities Commission, 391.)

PUBLIC UTILITIES ACT (Continued).

26. The Public Utilities Commission should, under suitable conditions, permit the Federal Mining Company to inspect the books, files and papers of said utility corporation in so far as they contain matter relating to, or in any way connected with, the fixing of the value of the plant and the reasonable rate to be charged for the product, and should give plaintiff ample time and opportunity for that purpose. (Federal Mining & Smelting Co. v. Public Utilities Commission, 391.)

27. Under the provisions of sec. 49 of said act, said commission is not bound by the technical rules of evidence, and by the provisions of sec. 29 of said act, said commission is authorized to do all things necessary to carry out the spirit and intent of said act. (Federal Mining & Smelting Co. v. Public Utilities Commission, 391.)

QUIETING TITLE.

In General.

1. *Held*, that the complaint states a cause of action, and that the allegations and denials contained in the amended answer and cross-complaint contain no defense to the action. (Rischar v. Shields, 616.)

2. Where S. and wife contract to purchase certain land from R. and to pay the purchase price in instalments at certain dates, and also agree to pay the taxes and assessments levied against said land and time is expressly made of the essence of the contract, and S. and wife fail to make the payments as provided by the contract, and R. serves notice of forfeiture after a default in the payments, it is no defense to an action to quiet title and to recover possession of the premises for the defendants to allege a defect in title and ask to have the money paid returned to them; and the vendor may rescind the contract for the failure to pay any of the instalments preceding the last without tender of the deed, since the payment of the last instalment and the delivery of the deed are mutual, concurrent and dependent obligations. (Rischar v. Shields, 616.)

3. *Held*, that the court did not err in entering judgment on the pleadings. (Rischar v. Shields, 616.)

4. The evidence *held* sufficient to sustain the findings of the court. (Kennedy v. Tuttle, 495.)

RAILROADS.

Right of Way—Construction of Crossing—Specific Performance.

1. Where a railroad company purchased a right of way across the lands of F. and paid certain cash consideration and entered into an agreement to construct a crossing over its right of way and track for the convenience, use and benefit of F., and for such con-

RAILROADS (Continued):

sideration and upon the execution of such a contract F. conveyed to the railroad company such right of way, and the company constructed its road thereon, it will not be sufficient excuse to constitute a defense to an action for specific performance of the contract that the roads by and over F.'s land have been changed and that the railroad track at the place where the crossing was to be constructed runs through a deep cut instead of on the surface, and that it will be necessary to build an overhead crossing instead of a grade crossing, and that the expense of constructing and maintaining the same will be heavier than was anticipated by the company at the time the contract was made. (Fox v. Spokane International Ry. Co., 60.)

2. Where the knowledge or means of knowledge of the future condition or changes that may take place are peculiarly within the possession of the railroad company which is about to construct a railroad and has agreed to maintain a crossing over its right of way and track, and it enters into a contract to maintain a crossing, it will not thereafter be heard to complain on the ground that the contract was unfair and became more onerous than was anticipated at the time the contract was entered into by reason of the track having to be laid through a cut instead of on the surface of the ground, and that other conditions have changed since the contract was entered into. (Fox v. Spokane International Railway Co., 60.)

3. Facts of this case examined and considered and *held* that it is a proper case for the specific performance of the contract and that no just defense is presented which would excuse or relieve the company from specific performance. (Fox v. Spokane International Railway Co., 60.)

RAPE.

In General.

1. The evidence in this case examined and found to be sufficient to justify the conviction of the defendant of the crime charged. (State v. Hopkins, 741.)

2. Where the evidence adduced by the state tends to show that a crime was committed during a two weeks' vacation in school at the Christmas holiday season and does not fix the date more definitely than that, and where the defendant relies upon an *alibi* and produces evidence tending to show his whereabouts from Dec. 24th to Jan. 1st, inclusive, and that he was not at the place where the evidence produced by the state tends to show the crime was committed, but produces no evidence tending to show his whereabouts during the remainder of the two weeks in question, the jury is justified in reaching the conclusion that the *alibi* relied on was not established. (State v. Hopkins, 741.)

RAPE (Continued).

3. Where there is a substantial conflict in the evidence and the evidence taken as a whole is sufficient to sustain the verdict, the verdict will not be disturbed. (State v. Hopkins, 741.)

4. *Held*, that the evidence is sufficient to support the verdict, and that the court did not err in refusing to give certain instructions. (State v. Driskill, 738.)

5. The defendant in a prosecution for the crime of assault with intent to commit rape was not deprived of a public trial as provided by art. 1, sec. 13, of the state constitution, and the statutes of the state, when the court in its discretion required all spectators and all persons except those necessarily in attendance to retire from the courtroom during the trial. (State v. Johnson, 609.)

6. *Held*, under the facts of this case that the court erred in not permitting the defendant to answer the following question: "How did you and your wife get along upon the ranch? Did you have any difficulty or quarrel?" (State v. Johnson, 609.)

7. *Held*, that the court did not err in giving certain instructions to the jury. (State v. Johnson, 609.)

8. *Held*, that the court erred in refusing to give the following requested instruction to the jury: "You are also instructed that in order to convict the defendant of the crime charged it will be necessary for you to find that he made an assault upon this young girl and actually intended to use whatever force was necessary to rape or carnally know her, and that he was prevented therefrom by the resistance of or force used by her, the said Anna Johnson, or by some other reason than that of his own inclination or determination to desist therefrom." (State v. Johnson, 609.)

9. The evidence *held* insufficient to support the verdict. (State v. Johnson, 609.)

RECEIVING STOLEN GOODS.
See Larceny, 11–14.

RECLAMATION ACT.
See Public Lands.

RECORD.
See Lease; Mortgages, 2.

REGENTS.
See University.

REHEARING.
See Appeal and Error, 13–15.

REMOVAL OF CAUSES.

In General.

1. When a defendant attempts to remove an action which he is not entitled to remove, and the state court refuses to surrender its jurisdiction, the state court may proceed with the cause and its subsequent proceedings are valid. (State v. American Surety Co., 652.)

SALES.

Bulk Sale Statute.

1. *Held,* that chap. 8 of title 10, Rev. Codes, which provides for "sales of goods in bulk," is a constitutional and valid law, that it does not constitute class legislation within the inhibition of the constitution, and that it is a proper and reasonable exercise of the state's police power. (Boise Assn. of Credit Men v. Ellis, 438.)

2. *Held,* that a stock of goods, wares and merchandise, when sold in bulk, does not by implication include the fixtures as a part of the sales. (Boise Assn. of Credit Men v. Ellis, 438.)

SCHOOLS AND SCHOOL DISTRICTS.

In General.

1. The duty of the county superintendent to apportion the indebtedness of an organized school district between a new district formed out of the old district and the remaining area thereof should be exercised only after the necessary legal steps leading to the creation of such new district have been taken, and such apportionment is not a necessary prerequisite or jurisdictional act in the formation of such district. (School District No. 15 v. Blaine County, 285.)

2. Where all proceedings for the purpose of dividing a school district and establishing a new district out of portions of an old one are regular and favorable to such creation up to and including the action of the county commissioners, the failure of the county superintendent thereafter to apportion the bonded indebtedness of the old district between the remaining portion thereof and the new district would not defeat or invalidate the creation of such new district, even though it were the duty of the county superintendent to take such action, which latter question is not decided. (School District No. 15 v. Blaine County, 285.)

3. Sec. 4935, Rev. Codes, which provides that "In any civil action or proceeding wherein the state or the people of the state, is a party plaintiff, or any state officer, in his official capacity, or on behalf of the state, or any county, or city, is a party plaintiff or defendant, no bond, written undertaking, or security can be required of the state, or the people thereof, or any officer thereof, or of any county, or city; but on complying with the other provisions of this code, the state, or the people thereof, or any state officer acting

SCHOOLS AND SCHOOL DISTRICTS (Continued).

in his official capacity, or any county or city, have the same rights, remedies and benefits as if the bond, undertaking or security were given and approved as required by this code," applies to county treasurers and *ex-officio* tax collectors in prosecuting an action for and on behalf of a rural high school district; said rural high school district being a political corporation of the state. (Coon v. Sommercamp, 776.)

SEPARATE PROPERTY.
See Husband and Wife, 1–6.

STATE UNIVERSITY.
See University.

STATUTES.

Passage and Enactment—Journals.

1. Under the provisions of sec. 15, art. 3, of the constitution, it is provided that no bill shall become a law unless the same shall have been read on three several days in each House previous to its final passage; provided, however, in case of urgency two thirds of the House where such bill may be pending may, upon a vote of the yeas and nays, dispense with that provision. (In re Drainage District No. 1 of Canyon Co., 311.)

2. Under the provisions of sec. 13, art. 3, each House is required to keep a journal of its proceedings, and the yeas and nays of the members of each House on any question may be, at the request of three members, entered on the journal. (In re Drainage District No. 1 of Canyon Co., 311.)

3. The journal entries made by either House may be resorted to as evidence to prove either the regularity or the irregularity of the passage of a law. (In re Drainage District No. 1 of Canyon Co., 311.)

4. It will not be presumed in any case from the mere silence of the journals that either House has exceeded its authority or disregarded a constitutional requirement in the passage of legislative acts, unless where the constitution has expressly required the journals to show the actions taken, as, for instance, where it requires the yeas and nays to be entered. (In re Drainage District No. 1 of Canyon Co., 311.)

5. Unless the journal shows affirmatively that the legislature has failed to comply with each step required to be taken in the passage of an act under the provisions of the constitution, the presumption is that the legislature did comply with all of such provisions. (In re Drainage District No. 1 of Canyon Co., 311.)

STATUTES (Continued).

6. The case of *Cohn v. Kingsley*, 5 Ida. 416, 49 Pac. 985, 38 L. R. A. 74, modified. (In re Drainage District No. 1 of Canyon Co., 311.)

Title of Act.

7. Under the provisions of sec. 16, art. 3, of the state constitution, every act should embrace but one subject and matters properly connected therewith, which subject must be expressed in the title. (State v. Pioneer Nurseries Co., 332.)

8. The purpose of said constitutional provision is to prevent fraud and deception in the enactment of laws, to avoid inconsistent and incongruous legislation and to reasonably notify legislators and the people of the legislative intent in enacting a law. (State v. Pioneer Nurseries Co., 332.)

Interpretation and Construction.

9. The title to an act may be resorted to as an aid in determining the intention of the legislature. (State v. Forch, 755.)

9a. When a statute contains a clause that is directly contrary to the legislative intent, as collected from the whole act, such clause will be treated as surplusage and be disregarded in the proper construction of such act. (State v. Forch, 755.)

10. If a statute is found by experience to be unwise or impracticable, relief must be sought through the legislature. Neither a state board in executing such statute, nor a court in construing it, has any authority to alter or amend it. (State v. Johnson, 203.)

11. The rule that statute *in pari materia* should be construed together applies with peculiar force to statutes passed at the same session of the legislature; they are to be construed together, and should be so construed, if possible, as to harmonize and give force and effect to the provisions of each. (Peavy v. McCombs, 143.)

12. Where two statutes passed at the same session of the legislature are necessarily inconsistent, that one which deals with the common subject matter in a more minute and particular way will prevail over one of a more general character. (Peavy v. McCombs, 143.)

13. Where two conflicting acts upon the same subject matter are passed at the same session of the legislature, and their conflict is such that they cannot be harmonized, and one of them contains an emergency clause and the other does not, and the one containing the emergency clause was passed by both Houses of the legislature and approved by the governor later than the other, *held*, under the circumstances, the act containing the emergency clause repeals the other to the extent of the inconsistency between them. (Peavy v. McCombs, 143.)

STATUTES (Continued).

Retroactive Interpretation.

14. No act of the legislature shall be construed to be retroactive or retrospective unless the intention on the part of the legislature is clearly expressed. The word "retroactive" need not be used in the statute, but the intent of the legislature may be gleaned from any language which appropriately expresses such purpose. (Peavy v. McCombs, 143.)

SUPPLEMENTARY PROCEEDINGS.
See Creditor's Bill.

SUPREME COURT.
See Courts.

TAXATION.

In General.

1. In matters of taxation the legislature possesses plenary power, except as such power may be limited or restricted by the constitution. It is not necessary that the constitution contain a grant of power to the legislature to deal with the question of taxation. (Application of Kessler, 764.)

2. The constitution of Idaho does not prohibit the state from raising revenue in the manner provided for in said chapter 179. (Application of Kessler, 764.)

Valuation and Assessment—Relief in Equity.

3. Where a railroad company is the owner of about 4,000 acres of land consisting of about one hundred 40-acre tracts distributed over a county and in many different sections, and it is alleged in the complaint that the assessor "by a systematic, intentional and illegal method of assessing said land placed thereon a valuation and assessment which after being equalized by the state board of equalization exceeded the full cash value of the property by 25 per cent," and that other and similar land of the same value in said county was assessed and valued at 75 per cent less than the appellant's lands, and that said valuation and assessment were placed on appellant's lands by the assessor without making any investigation whatever and in violation of law and of the rights of appellant, and said valuation and assessment were made with the design, systematic and illegal effort on the part of the assessor to unjustly and unlawfully discriminate against appellant and its property, *held*, that said allegations show an unlawful, illegal and fraudulent discrimination by the assessor in assessing said property. (Northern Pac. Ry. Co. v. County of Clearwater, 455.)

TAXATION (Continued).

4. In this class of cases courts of equity will not interfere to correct mere errors of judgment as to valuation of property, since value is a matter of opinion; but where the allegations of the complaint show that the officer refused to exercise his judgment and by an arbitrary and capricious exercise of official authority has fraudulently attempted to defeat the law instead of enforcing it, a court of equity will relieve against such illegal and fraudulent actions of an assessor. (Northern Pac. Ry. Co. v. County of Clearwater, 455.)

5. *Held*, that the facts alleged in the complaint, if proven, would establish fraud as a conclusion of law. (Northern Pac. Ry. Co. v. County of Clearwater, 455.)

6. *Held*, that where an assessor by a systematic, intentional and illegal method assessed property at more than double what he assessed other property of the same class and value, he perpetrates a fraud from which a court of equity, upon proper application, will relieve. (Northern Pac. Ry. Co. v. County of Clearwater, 455.)

7. In this case it is not a question of a mere difference of opinion as to the value of the property, but it is a question of no opinion or judgment at all as to the value, since it is admitted by the demurrer that the assessor did intentionally and illegally assess said property at more than double what other property of the same kind and value was assessed, and the law presumes that he intended the natural, inevitable effect of his acts in assessing said property. (Northern Pac. Ry. Co. v. County of Clearwater, 455.)

8. Equity will not relieve against an assessment merely because it happens to be at a higher rate than that of other property of the same class or kind, for the reason that absolute uniformity under an honest judgment may not be obtained; but where it is made to appear that honest judgment was not used and that an illegal and unlawful value was placed upon the property by the assessor, the injured party may obtain redress in a court of equity. (Northern Pac. Ry. Co. v. County of Clearwater, 455.)

9. In a case where the valuation is so unreasonable as to show that the assessor must have known that it was wrong and that he could not have been honest in fixing it, *held*, that such a valuation is clearly a fraud upon the owner. (Northern Pac. Ry. Co. v. County of Clearwater, 455.)

10. In a case of this kind, the trial court should require the plaintiff to pay the amount of taxes which the allegations of the complaint show are reasonable and just before issuing any restraining order against the collection of the portion of the tax alleged to have been illegally assessed. (Northern Pac. Ry. Co. v. County of Clearwater, 455.)

TAXATION (Continued).

Sales—Certificate and Deed—Redemption.

11. Under the provisions of sec. 1763, Rev. Codes, as amended at the special session of the legislature (Laws 1912, p. 43), no purchaser or assignee of such purchaser of any land at a tax sale shall be entitled to demand a tax deed therefor until the notice therein required shall be given. (Rice v. Rock, 552.)

12. Under the provisions of sec. 1649, Rev. Codes, the levy of a tax has the same effect as a judgment and becomes a lien upon the property, which lien can only be divested by the payment of the tax or the sale of the property. (Rice v. Rock, 552.)

13. Under the provisions of sec. 1762, Rev. Codes, on filing the certificate of tax sale with the *ex-officio* auditor and recorder, the lien vests in the purchaser and is only divested by the payment to the county treasurer, on certificate of the auditor, for the use of the purchaser, of the whole amount of money paid for such certificate, together with interest thereon. (Rice v. Rock, 552.)

14. At the time said certificates were issued, the law did not require the giving of any notice to the owner of the property, but the legislature has authority to change the remedy provided for the enforcement of certificate contracts provided they do not impair the obligation of the contract, so long as the obligation of performance remains in full force. (Rice v. Rock, 552.)

15. Provision of said sec. 1763 which requires said notice to be given at least three months and not more than five months before the expiration of the term of redemption is directory. (Rice v. Rock, 552.)

16. A period of time in which said notice is required to be given was made for the purpose of ending the period in which redemption could be made and not for the purpose of divesting the holder of his lien on the property described in his tax sale certificate. (Rice v. Rock, 552.)

17. *Held*, that after the expiration of the three-year period and up to the time the notice is given, the owner may redeem the property from tax sale. (Rice v. Rock, 552.)

18. Where a land owner owns two separate tracts of real estate in the same county aggregating 760 acres and resides in another county, and had been in the habit for more than twenty years of writing to the assessor for statement of the amount of taxes due for the year, and upon receiving the statement of the amount sending his check in payment therefor, and in the year 1907 wrote a similar letter to the tax collector inquiring the amount of his taxes, but failed to give a description of the land he owned in the county, and the assessor replied giving a statement of the amount due, and such statement omitted a tract of 320 acres, and the land owner paid

TAXATION (Continued).

the amount called for by the statement and received his receipt therefor, and failed and neglected to read the description contained in the receipt, and consequently failed to observe that he had not paid the taxes on all of his real estate in the county, but the amount so paid was approximately the same as he had paid the previous year upon his entire holdings in the county, and the 320 acres were thereafter advertised and sold for delinquent taxes, and the time for redemption expired and a tax deed was issued to the purchaser, and during the subsequent years the land owner had continued to pay the taxes on this tract of land as well as his other holdings in the county, and he had no notice of delinquency of taxes or sale of the property for 1907 until after the issuance of the deed, and he thereupon tendered the amount which had been paid together with interest and penalties, *held*, that the property owner upon payment of the taxes, together with interest, penalties and costs, will be entitled to a decree canceling and setting aside the tax deed and quieting his title to such property. (Fix v. Gray, 19.)

19. Where property was sold for taxes delinquent for the year 1907, and the red ink entry was entered upon the tax-roll as required by statute, and thereafter an entry was made opposite the description of the same land and on the same roll that the tax had been canceled by order of the board of commissioners, and the land owner never had any notice that there were any delinquent taxes held against the land nor that it had been sold for delinquent taxes, and paid his taxes from year to year thereafter on such land, and upon discovering that the land had been sold for delinquent taxes and immediately upon the issuance of a tax deed therefor tendered the amount of taxes so paid together with interest, penalties and costs to the purchaser, *held*, that the land owner was entitled to have the deed surrendered and canceled and that the tax sale was irregular and voidable. (Fix v. Gray, 19.)

See Public Lands, 9, 10.

TITLE OF ACT.

See Statutes, 7, 8.

TORT-FEASORS.

Joint and Several Liability.

1. Where two persons are sued as joint tort-feasors and the evidence clearly shows that only one of them is liable for the tort, judgment may be rendered against the one who is liable for the trespass. (Zilka v. Graham, 163.)

2. *Held*, that the court did not err in overruling the demurrer to the amended complaint. (Zilka v. Graham, 163.)

TORT-FEASORS (Continued).

3. *Held*, that the court did not err in the admission of certain evidence. (Zilka v. Graham, 163.)

4. *Held*, that the court did not err in giving a certain instruction to the jury. (Zilka v. Graham, 163.)

5. Where one contributes as an independent tort-feasor toward causing an injury, he will be liable for the injury done by him, although his acts or negligence alone and without the contributing acts or negligence of others might not have caused the injury to occur. (Woodland v. Portneuf-Marsh Valley Irr. Co., 789.)

6. If injury follows as the combined result of the wrongful acts of several, acting independently, recovery may be had severally against each of such independent tort-feasors, in proportion to the contribution of each to the injury. (Woodland v. Portneuf-Marsh Valley Irr. Co., 789.)

TRANSCRIPT.

See Appeal and Error, 4–6.

TRIAL.

In General.

1. A motion to set aside a verdict and judgment and for a judgment *non obstante veredicto* comes too late if made after judgment has been entered. Such motion must be made after the verdict and before the judgment is rendered. (Zilka v. Graham, 163.)

2. *Held*, that there is no evidence indicating that the verdict was rendered under the influence of passion and prejudice. (Montgomery v. Gray, 583.)

3. *Held*, that the court did not err in giving or refusing to give certain instructions. (Montgomery v. Gray, 583.)

UNIVERSITY.

Action Against Regents.

1. The district court has jurisdiction to try an action against the Board of Regents of the State University to recover a balance for money advanced and material furnished in the construction of a building to be used by the university. *Moscow Hardware Co. v. Regents*, 19 Ida. 420, 113 Pac. 731, and *First Nat. Bank v. Regents*, 19 Ida. 440, 113 Pac. 735, approved and followed. (First National Bank of Moscow v. Regents of the University of Idaho, 15.)

2. The act of March 6, 1913 (Sess. Laws 1913, p. 328), creating a State Board of Education, makes such board the successor to the old Board of Regents of the University of Idaho, and as such successor said State Board of Education has the power and authority to defend an action previously instituted against the old board

UNIVERSITY (Continued).

for a pre-existing obligation. (First National Bank of Moscow v. Regents of the University of Idaho, 15.)

3. *Held*, that the remedies sought by the plaintiff are not inconsistent remedies, and plaintiff could not be required to elect between them. (First National Bank of Moscow v. Regents of the University of Idaho, 15.)

4. *Held*, that the lower court committed no error prejudicial to the rights of appellant. (First National Bank of Moscow v. Regents of the University of Idaho, 15.)

UTILITIES COMMISSION.
See Public Utilities.

WARRANTS.
See Municipal Corporations, 13.

WATERS.
Waste of Water and Damages Therefrom.

1. Each one of several, acting independently, who wrongfully permits water to waste on to the land of another, is liable for his proportionate share of the injury caused thereby, even though the water allowed to run down by each would do no harm if not combined with that of the others, and the injury is actually caused by the combined flow wherein the waters from all sources are mixed and indistinguishable. (Woodland v. Portneuf-Marsh Valley Irr. Co., 789.)

2. Exact and definite measurements of the respective quantities of water from different sources are not essential to sustain the verdict of a jury in determining what amount of damages a defendant corporation, as an independent tort-feasor, should pay as compensation for the injury caused by its part of such waters, although some evidence in that respect is essential. (Woodland v. Portneuf-Marsh Valley Irr. Co., 789.)

3. *Held*, that the evidence in this case is sufficient to sustain the verdict in plaintiff's favor for the amount of damage caused by the defendant's waste water. (Woodland v. Portneuf-Marsh Valley Irr. Co., 789.)

4. *Held*, that the court properly instructed the jury as to the measure of defendant's liability. (Woodland v. Portneuf-Marsh Valley Irr. Co., 789.)

5. *Held*, that no reversible error appears in the trial court's rulings upon the admissibility of evidence. (Woodland v. Portneuf-Marsh Valley Irr. Co., 789.)

See Boundaries; Irrigation.

WILLS.

See Executors and Administrators.

WITNESSES.

In General.

1. Where a party to an action does not object to a question propounded to a witness, or having objected, expressly gives consent that the question may be answered, error cannot be predicated upon the action of the court in admitting the testimony nor upon the refusal of the court to strike out the answer if it is responsive to the question. (State v. Hopkins, 741.)

2. The state cannot be deprived of the right to cross-examine a witness by the mere statement that such witness does not speak the English language; and, if it is afterward established that such witness speaks and understands the English language, he is estopped from taking any advantage of his conduct in asserting his inability to speak and understand said language. (State v. Bogris, 587.)

3. Where the court instructs the jury to the effect that if any witness wilfully testified falsely as to any material fact, the jury were at liberty to disregard the entire testimony of such witness, except in case his testimony should be corroborated by other and reliable witnesses, the testimony of defendant having been impeached by the prosecution, but it appearing, so far as the record shows, that such instruction applied generally to all of the witnesses testifying in the case, the giving of such instruction was not error. (State v. Bogris, 587.)

Interpreters.

4. The question, whether or not a witness requires an interpreter, is a question for the court, and where counsel for defendant neglects to request the court to pass upon this question without the presence of the jury, he cannot afterward assign as error the action of the court in not excusing the jury while this matter was being considered. (State v. Bogris, 587.)

Lightning Source UK Ltd.
Milton Keynes UK
UKHW041203130219

337000UK00006BA/171/P